INTERPERSONAL DYNAMICS
Essays and readings on human interaction

THE DORSEY SERIES IN PSYCHOLOGY

EDITOR   HOWARD F. HUNT   *Columbia University*

INTERPERSONAL DYNAMICS

Essays and readings on human interaction

Edited by

WARREN G. BENNIS

President
University of Cincinnati

DAVID E. BERLEW

Development Research Associates
Newton Centre, Massachusetts

EDGAR H. SCHEIN

Professor of Organizational Psychology and Management
Massachusetts Institute of Technology

FRED I. STEELE

Development Research Associates
Newton Centre, Massachusetts

Third Edition · 1973

THE DORSEY PRESS   *Homewood, Illinois 60430*

IRWIN-DORSEY INTERNATIONAL   *London, England   WC2H 9NJ*

IRWIN-DORSEY LIMITED   *Georgetown, Ontario   L7G 4B3*

Third Edition

First Printing, May 1973

ISBN 0–256–01411–6
Library of Congress Catalog Card No. 72–98125
Printed in the United States of America

Foreword

I

As a graduate student many years ago, I remember musing over a comment by Gordon Allport that God had not seen fit to organize natural phenomena so that they would conform to man's neat and logical ordering of the scientific disciplines. Recently C. P. Snow has given other connotations to this point in his discussion of the "two worlds."

Perhaps nowhere is the abyss between formal logic and reality more evident than in man's attempt to order knowledge about his own behavior. There are today 24 divisions within the American Psychological Association, and these are presumably logically separable from each other as well as from the subdivisions of sociology, anthropology, political science, and psychiatry. In turn, none of these gives more than a nod of recognition to the insights of the playwright, the novelist, the poet, or the historian.

In the resultant confusion of tongues, it is refreshing to come upon a sophisticated attempt to bring systematic order to an important set of behavioral phenomena without regard to disciplinary jurisdiction. When my colleagues told me so in their Preface, I realized with a start that studies of these phenomena, although they form the very core of human existence, are scattered all over the map of the behavioral sciences and the humanities. The field of interpersonal relations is not even formally recognized as a scientific discipline in its own right!

Several things become apparent as a result of this endeavor. First, and most important, there is much useful knowledge scattered all through the behavioral science literature about the many different varieties of interpersonal relationships. The fact that it is so scattered has prevented us from discovering how much, in a sense, we know already.

It is unlikely to occur to us until such a systematic analysis is undertaken that there are *common* causal relationships affecting the behavior of lovers, friends, nurses and patients, prisoners and wardens, confidence men and their victims, teachers and students, consultants and clients, and mutual enemies. Since a sociologist interested in criminology has studied one of these relationships, and an educational psychologist has studied another, a psychoanalyst another, and an organization theorist another, and so on *ad infinitum*, the possibility of perceiving them as belonging to a *common* behavioral category is almost precluded.

A second "discovery" follows on the heels of the first: many of the profound insights of the novelist and the poet are remarkably consistent with the knowledge we have gained from systematic research. It would of course be surprising if this were not so, but it is only rarely that an attempt is made like the present one to bridge the "two worlds." Thus the careful, critical observations of behavior reflected in the work of a first class novelist are seen to be significantly related to the observation reflected in the report of a scientific research study. The methods are indeed different, but the slow process of accumulating useful knowledge about man's behavior is well served by both. It is time we gave more than lip service to this fact. The editors of this volume are to be commended for transcending (some will say violating) the existing norms concerning the distinctions between science and the humanities, too many of which are motivated merely by the desire to maintain status differences.

Third, the task undertaken here brings into focus some of the glaring gaps in our knowledge about these ubiquitous phenomena. The theoretical formulations presented in the essays by the editors are—as they are careful to point out—only first rough approximations. When one considers the different orientations of those who have studied bits and pieces of interpersonal relationships, it is a genuine, *tour de force* to produce even a tentative theoretical framework which ties the pieces together. Once this is done, the gaps and inconsistencies in the data become apparent. A careful perusal of these pages will suggest dozens of significant research studies—studies which need not stand alone, but which can contribute to the reformulation or the strengthening of this theory.

Any knowledgeable critic could "nit-pick" many details of the theory as it stands, but the breadth and depth of the formulation challenges him instead to undertake another task, namely to offer a better general theory. That challenge makes this an exciting book.

II

Since World War II and the Bomb, it has become increasingly difficult for the scientist in any field to disclaim responsibility for the uses to which knowledge is put. My colleagues have faced this issue squarely: ". . . we desire not only greater scientific attention to this field, but we *care* about improving the quality and nature of interpersonal relationships." They place themselves in the functional tradition by defining a good relationship in terms of the achievement of its primary goal, but they do not stop there. Their analysis of the "social conditions" and the "personal competencies" which appear to be essential to the achievement of the primary goals of interpersonal relationships is, for me at least, a noteworthy attempt to lay bare the assumptions and values underlying a given scientific endeavor.

Men everywhere are beginning to look toward the behavioral sciences as a source of helping in creating a better world. We who identify ourselves with these sciences do mankind a disservice unless we make transparently clear a fundamental "law" of human behavior: intellectual knowledge and emotional values and needs are inextricably interwoven in all but the most trivial human acts.

Scientific endeavor is not trivial; every step of the process from the initial choice of a "field" through the design of the research to the interpretation of results is profoundly influenced by personal and cultural values. The scientist can and must take precautions to minimize the effects of these subjective factors. Perhaps the most important precaution of all—at the same time the most difficult and the least recognized—is to perceive and understand and make explicit the values underlying his own work. (Fish discover water last!) Part V of this volume provides a model which deserves emulation.

The important point about such a model, by the way, is not whether the reader agrees with it, but whether he is explicit about why and how he disagrees. It is this dialogue—carried on in the public domain—which will ultimately make possible the use of scientific knowledge about human behavior to improve the welfare of all men. If the dialogue is continuous and public, the power yielded by scientific knowledge cannot for long be used by man to exploit his fellows. If it is not, fears like those expressed by Loren Baritz in his *The Servants of Power* will turn out to be well-founded.

The furtherance of this dialogue is a second challenge which makes this an exciting book.

DOUGLAS MCGREGOR

Preface

We can divide the problems Man faces into two classes, the *noninteractional* or man-in-relation-to nature, and the *interactional* or man-in-relation-to man. This latter class involves *human* interactions which make it necessary to take into account the activities, thoughts, and feelings of the other. We have made stunning progress with respect to the noninteractional class of problems, partly because they are "stable" problems. That is, they seem to "sit still" for the engineers or scientists who adapt or create an innovation, instrument, or idea which makes a "scientific breakthrough."

When it comes to the second class of problems, the human problems, we have been notoriously incompetent. One would think, judging from the report of history, that we simply cannot progress; that unlike knowledge about physical phenomena, human knowledge is not cumulative, that parents cannot teach their children nor learn from their own parents. On the very day we are writing this preface, Indians and U.S. marshalls are exchanging gunfire at Wounded Knee, S.D., civil strife continues in Northern Ireland, and a war rages on in Cambodia. Last year's newspapers would have carried almost identical news, with other place-names.

The trouble is that these national and international conflagrations have their counterparts at every level of human intercourse: in small groups, in marriages, in friendships, among lovers and siblings, between teachers and students, between worker and boss. Unless the protagonists are famous, the tensions go unnoticed, to be registered indirectly and anonymously in divorce rates, homicides, and gang wars or often in the more pedestrian way civilized people live with their human problems: poison pen letters, petty jealousies, unproductive relationships, prejudices, practical "jokes," destructive fantasies, unstable careers, ulcerative colitis, "frayed nerves," tranquilizers, and sleeping pills.

As human beings, we harbor moral outrage at these corrosive and destructive events. As social scientists, we consider it almost obligatory to explore and illuminate these problems. The unusual challenge lies in the fact that we do not practice as much as we know, and do not know as much as we could.

We cannot induce better practice through a book, but we can hope to enhance our understanding of those relationships that occur between small numbers of people, often only two. We believe that this understanding is crucial, not only to improve the nature and quality of interpersonal relationships, but also to make this area more central to the sciences of man. To rephrase Pope, the proper study of man is *man-in-relation-to man*.

Two related forces went into the creation of this book. One is an intellectual and academic concern with the loosely defined field of interpersonal relations. We hope to make it more central to the discipline of social psychology, to fill an important gap that exists between the study of groups and the study of personality. At the very least we think we have succeeded in sharpening up the boundaries of the territory.

Second, we *care* about improving our interpersonal relationships. "Life Is with People," reads the felicitous title of a book, and if our vision of the world is at all accurate we foresee greater and greater reliance on our fellow men, more and more interdependencies, and hence, a more vital need to understand those enormously complex human events we call *interpersonal dynamics*.

We have edited this book with an eye to the teacher and student of interpersonal relationship as well as to the intelligent laymen. In fact, the more of the latter who come into contact with these pages, the better. For we have tried to select articles and to write our original essays in good, clear English which can be understood by an interested reader. In preparing the second and this third edition, we have tried to weed out articles our students and colleagues have told us are too abstract, dense, turgid, or confusing, no matter how theoretically accurate they are. We have often replaced articles with others which say the same thing, only better.

Finally, we have tried to add articles which bear on current issues and problems. For this third edition, we have searched for articles about new forms of interpersonal relationships characteristic of the counterculture and the counter counterculture. We were disappointed by our inability to locate many such articles good enough to displace articles already included, and have been forced to conclude that either we do not read the right publications, or that really penetrating analyses follow the appearance of the phenomenon by several years. We found a few papers that we really liked, such as those by Silverstein, Friedlander, and Walton, and sincerely solicit suggestions from readers for future editions.

In the second edition, published in 1968, we added a total of 18 new articles, dropped 17, and retained 26 from the first edition published in 1964. In preparing this third edition, we have added 14 new articles, dropped 19 articles, and retained 29 articles from the second edition. Unfortunately, in order to add new and different material we have often been forced to drop what we consider outstanding papers; the Vogel and Bell paper on the emotionally disturbed child as the family scapegoat, Fromm-Reichmann's analysis of loneliness, and Becker's piece on the culture of dance musicians, none of which appear in this third edition, are cases in point.

Our basic theoretical framework has held up reasonably well, hence we have not reorganized the sections of the book. Several of our introductory essays were in part rewritten for the second edition; only minor editorial revisions were made for this edition.

We gratefully acknowledge the aid of Professor Walter Nord, Department of Psychology, Washington University, St. Louis, and Professor Donald O. Jewell, Department of Management, Georgia State University, whose discerning and helpful suggestions contributed significantly to our revision.

Since we prepared the first edition of this book as colleagues at the Sloan School of Management of M.I.T. in 1963–64, our career paths have varied and we no longer enjoy adjacent offices and daily interaction. Although by no means a substitute, our work together in preparing this third edition has helped to fill that void.

April 1973   W.G.B.
D.E.B.
E.H.S.
F.I.S.

Contents

Part IV

The instrumental relationship   373

Part V

Toward better interpersonal relationships   495

Introduction

*Well, what are you? What is it about you that you have always known as yourself? What are you conscious of in yourself: your kidneys, your liver, your blood vessels? No. However far back you go in your memory it is always some external manifestation of yourself where you come across your identity: in the work of your hands, in your family, in other people. And now, listen carefully. You in others—this is what you are, this is what your consciousness has breathed, and lived on, and enjoyed throughout your life, your soul, your immortality—*YOUR LIFE IN OTHERS.

BORIS PASTERNAK, *Dr. Zhivago*

This is our hope: to deepen and broaden the understanding of our life in others." We think it is of crucial importance, not only for its scientific yield, but for its potential to man's welfare. How we have attempted to realize our aim through this book is the purpose of this introductory essay.

PURPOSES OF THIS BOOK

Our main goal is to sketch out the conceptual territory and boundaries of the field of interpersonal relations more clearly, coherently, and integratively than has been done before. Our aim is to suggest a "focus of convenience" for the field.

If we are at least partly successful, then we believe that the study of interpersonal dynamics can play a major role in the behavioral sciences, rather than its present peripheral one. In other words, we hope that this volume will fill the gap which we see existing between the literature of rigorous experimental studies of groups (e.g. Cartwright and Zander[1]) and studies in general social psychology (e.g. Maccoby et al., *Readings in Social Psychology*.[2]) We want to move the scientific study of interpersonal relations from the periphery to the center of social psychology, making it a truly *social* psychology.

Our second aim is pragmatic. This means that we desire not only greater scientific attention, but we *care* about improving the quality and nature of interpersonal relationships. Undoubtedly, it is our passionate concern for *improvement* that fuels our intellectual energies. This passion is based upon more than the moral and ideological premises presented in Part V of this volume. It

---

[1] D. Cartwright and A. Zander (eds.), *Group Dynamics: Research and Theory* (2nd ed.; Evanston, Ill.: Row, Peterson & Co., 1960).

[2] E. E. Maccoby, T. M. Newcomb, and E. L. Hartley (eds.), *Readings in Social Psychology* (3d ed.; New York: Henry Holt & Co., 1958).

1

is also founded on the conviction that the quality of our interpersonal relations can affect not only important arenas of social conflict (such as racial and religious tensions, international conflicts, social disorganization, etc.) but also the quality of our productive and creative efforts.

Before going on to explain the organization of this book, let us take a detailed look at the academic status of the field of interpersonal dynamics.

THE CURRENT STATE OF THE FIELD AND OUR APPROACH TO IT

It might be useful to begin with a few words about the current academic state of interpersonal dynamics—as a field. As we do this we will be irresistibly drawn to our own views and biases. So what follows is the combination of description and viewpoint which determines our approach and orientation to the field of interpersonal dynamics.

It is a strange field: loosely organized, interdisciplinary and interstitial, i.e., tangent to or on the frontier of the behavioral sciences; it is a field without fixed boundaries or stable definitions. An analogy may help to bring it into better focus. We can compare it to a "foreign" territory, claimed by all because of its strategic importance, explored by only a few adventurers, and understood fully by none. It is not a "no-man's" land, however. It is everyman's land. And this means that long before the social scientist invaded this domain, the poets, troubadors, essayists, lyricists, and novelists were tilling its rich soil. In fact, the "humanists" have long claimed this territory for their own and have looked askance at the social scientist, referring to him as a poacher or *arriviste*, depending upon their mood and style.

The social scientist who does forage around in these uncharted lands not only receives abuse at the hands of the humanists, but also from his colleagues. Quite often, they will attack him harshly for losing his "scientific" bent; others, more subtly, say that he is "too dense" or that he creates a private language, bordering on neologisms. Even if his work is recognized, he is considered, at best, a soldier of fortune who should return to the fold, at worst, a fugitive.

Our analogy helps to bring into focus a number of points we can make about the current status of research and theory in the field of interpersonal dynamics.

1. There is as yet no single, comprehensive theory of interpersonal relations. Sociology, social psychology, and psychiatry have offered important insights to the understanding of its phenomena, but the area has resisted successful theoretical comprehension. "What single general proposition about human behavior have we established?" asked George Homans in 1950. His answer, alas, holds too much truth today: "And we shall find ourselves waiting for an answer."[3]

2. Because it is a new field as far as the social sciences are concerned and because of its complexity and subtlety, it tends to be treated in a discursive, exploratory, essayistic way, rather than a terse, positivistic, experimental way.

---

[3] George Homans, *The Human Group* (New York: Harcourt Brace, 1950), p. 115.

3. The third thing we can say about the field, implied in our analogy, is that despite its relevance to the behavioral sciences, it has been treated only tangentially in those fields. In social psychology, for example, we would expect it to play a fundamental role. This does not seem to be the case.[4] Social psychologists have been more interested in the group or in the individual than in interpersonal relationships. The field of psychiatry also has not yielded the expected results with respect to interpersonal theory. It has been dominated by a neuro-biophysiological philosophy of man, a reliance on the instincts and a silence regarding man's interactional behavior.[5] Anthropology and sociology fare no better, though a branch of sociology, known as the "symbolic interaction" school, has made crucial contributions to interpersonal theory. More about that later on. In summary, *the scientific study of interpersonal relations lags woefully behind the other areas of social research.*

4. Fourth, we can say that where disciplines *have* contributed to the understanding of interpersonal relations, where they have enriched its theoretical or research base, they have been "marginal" or *avant garde* groups or perhaps some sturdy iconoclasts. This is rather a blunt statement, one which undoubtedly requires qualification. Nevertheless, as we examined the main theoretical influences that shaped our own interests and when we thought to detect the theoretical origins of the papers selected for this volume it appeared to be true. But what about the lineage of the articles selected?

5. In the earlier edition of this volume, we relied on four major theoretical strands which, we wrote, "shaped our thinking, have dominated this book, and appear to provide the basic structure of the field of interpersonal relations." We summarized these influences as (1) symbolic interactionism, (2) interpersonal theory, (3) object relations, and (4) existentialism. The readings in this edition continue to reflect these influences but are augmented by still another, that of an *ecological,* character. Let us review briefly these five theoretical themes:

a) From sociology, the branch referred to earlier as *symbolic interactionism* has been crucial. The main premise of this school is that the data of interpersonal relations are symbols and these symbols constitute social reality. It is the language of drama, and hence the key concept for this approach is "social role." Cooley and Mead in the United States and Durkheim in Europe have been central in its development; in psychology, Baldwin, James, and Dewey have contributed to its heritage.

b) From psychiatry, we have been heavily influenced by the so-called "Washington School," the *Interpersonal Theory* of Harry Stack Sullivan and his associates. This branch of psychiatry has a good deal in common with the symbolic interactionists, for both view the processes of social communication as pivotal to their theories.

---

[4] F. Heider, *The Psychology of Interpersonal Relations* (New York: Wiley, 1958), p. 3.

[5] H. Guntrip, *Personality Structure and Human Interaction* (New York: International Universities Press, 1961), p. 17.

c) In addition to the Sullivanian influence, but less visible in this volume because of space limitations, is some of the work coming out of the English neo-Freudian school. Melanie Klein and W. R. D. Fairbairn have impressed us with their *object relations* point of view. Their influence can be felt only indirectly in this volume through the work of the English group theorist, W. R. Bion, whose theories are based on some of Melanie Klein's formulations. We have relied heavily on Bion in Part I, "Emotional Expressions in Interpersonal Relationships." The important thing to say about the "object relations" school is that it is an ego-psychology, i.e., it specifies an ego in relationship to its outside world, where impulses are seen as reactions of the ego to its relevant objects, and where the inner and outer worlds are seen as reciprocal in influence.[6]

d) Finally, those students of human behavior who cannot be grouped under any simple conceptual umbrella—except perhaps *existentialism*—but who are concerned with the *self* and its actualization have to be mentioned. We have in mind the work of men such as Carl Rogers, whose influence should be obvious from a quick glance at our Table of Contents; or the writings of Maslow, Jourard, and Wheelis, who share a tremendous concern with improving the quality of relationships.

e) This edition includes a paper by Philip Slater and a whole section on the "communication of feeling." For the most part, these selections can be grouped under an *ecological framework* of human interaction; that is, they tend to see man's interpersonal behavior governed by the constraints of spatial, and in fewer cases (but Slater's is a fine example), by temporal factors. For convenience, we are referring to this influence as an ecological orientation.[7]

These five sources—symbolic interactionism, Sullivanian theory, object-relations theory, existential psychology, and ecology—have fashioned the intellectual structure of this volume.[8] These choices, it should be remembered, were founded on their parent disciplines: social psychology and psychoanalytic theory. And when these five branches fuse with their parent streams, then we should have a viable scientific approach to interpersonal relations. The prospects are bright but realization is perhaps not too close.

6. What are the reasons why progress has been less rapid than one might expect in building a coherent skein of interpersonal theory? The reasons, we hazard, spring essentially from one source: the nominalistic bias of most behav-

---

[6] The interested reader should turn to the essay introducing Part I for not only a more complete statement but a more detailed exposition of the object-relations theory.

[7] E. T. Hall's book, *The Hidden Dimension* (New York: Doubleday, 1966), is a brilliant example of this approach, and we wish long sections of this book could be reproduced here, but our own publishing ecology (limited number of pages) was a major constraint upon our desires. In this edition, we have added a chapter from Hall's book. (See Part I.)

[8] Attributing theoretical influences is a risky business at best. The minute one ponders about the unconscious elements, then it becomes even more hazardous. And when one considers that there are *four* editors, the task becomes downright awkward. Obviously, our interests have been shaped by more than these five subfields; our backgrounds, training, and personalities must certainly be considered. These influences, however, cannot be so easily categorized and must remain silent but powerful.

ioral sciences which tends to focus exclusively on convenient boundary systems such as "the skin" or "the group." This bias tends to ignore the reality of the relationship in favor of its parts. In so doing, it preserves the individual-group dichotomy of popular culture, a duality which gets the student into as much trouble as it gets him out of. A fashionable horror of "organic theories of society" together with the very important need of all of us to see ourselves as individuals makes the individual-group dichotomy a tenuous one. Allport's remarks on personality theory bear this out:

> Virtually all the theories I have mentioned up to now conceive of personality as something integumented, as residing within the skin. There are theorists (Kurt Lewin, Martin Buber, Gardner Murphy, and others) who challenge this view, considering it too closed. Murphy says that we overstress the separation of man from the context of his living. Hebb has interpreted experiments on sensory deprivation as demonstrations of the constant dependence of inner stability on the flow of environmental stimulation. Why Western thought makes such a razor-sharp distinction between the person and all else is an interesting problem. Probably the personalistic emphasis in Judeo-Christian religion is an initial factor; and as Murphy has pointed out, the industrial and commercial revolutions further accentuated the role of individuality. Buddhist philosophy, by contrast, regards the individual, society, and nature as forming the tripod of human existence. The individual as such does not stick out like a raw digit. He blends with nature, and he blends with society. *It is only the merger that can be profitably studied.*[9]

But studying the merger—the relationship—has lagged behind because of our reliance on visible and operable, and not altogether profitable, boundary systems: the individual and the group.

This lag strikes us especially when we consider the language of interpersonal relationships,[10] or rather the lack of a precise and relevant language. The problem is only partly due to the complexity of the field, although when we read Sullivan's tortuous observations of A and A' communicating to B and B' within the purview of C and C' all interacting, distorting, and attending to multifarious cues generated by a concatenation of different As, Bs, and Cs, we tend to think that the complexity of interpersonal relationships creates insurmountable barriers to the construction of a valid language. The real problem has to do with the ubiquitous monadic myth of the individual. As Murray points out:

> Synthesism—or dyadic synthesism—first of all, calls for the elevation of the hardly utterable, shared values of participation in the creation and development of better forms and qualities of relationship (continuity of union, of mutual affection and respect, amid diversity of patterns of interaction) from a subordinate to a superordinate position, that is to say, the experience and fruits of affectional reciprocations, interpersonal and interna-

---

[9] Gordon Allport, "The Open System in Personality Theory," *Personality and Social Encounter* (Boston: Beacon Press, 1960), p. 47. Italics added.

[10] There is a discussion of the languages of interpersonal feelings in the essay introducing Part I. Here it is pointed out that two languages compete in the social sciences: the language of the *game* and the language of the *myth*. The former, according to Back is precise and formal; the latter is rich, meaningful, but ambiguous (K. W. Back, "The Game and the Myth," *Behavioral Science*, 8 [1963], pp. 66–71).

tional, would be more highly prized than personal and national superiority and aggrandizement. To appreciate the emotional revolution involved in this transposition of values, we have only to remind ourselves that all formerly venerated models of excellence or greatness have been glorifications of a single person, a single group or nation, a single theory of religion.[11]

In any case, the individual takes priority, and we find ourselves without shared referential tools for identifying and depicting an important dimension of life: unities, ensembles, and combinations of people in interaction.[12] Certainly a married couple must *present* a "social unit" as much as a person *presents* a "self"; certainly, there must be creative *relationships* as well as creative individuals; certainly, there must be *relationships* that are as permeable or closed, protean or placid, flexible or rigid, healthy or sick, as individuals. One is no more real or mystical than the other; both generate and receive human responses.

But our language as yet does not embrace these phenomena; and it will not—until the *merger* Allport talks about or the *synthesism* Murray suggests infiltrate the central domains of the behavioral sciences, rather than its interstitial crevices.

Let us summarize our orientation to the field of interpersonal relations. It is a new field, interdisciplinary and interstitial, but it is new only in the sense that it has stubbornly resisted rigorous scientific examination. There is, as yet, no single, comprehensive conceptual umbrella for the field. The five subfields of behavioral science disciplines from which we have drawn the most in this volume are: the symbolic interaction school of sociology, the interpersonal theories of Harry Stack Sullivan, the neo-Freudian object-relations school of psychiatry, the ecologists, and the existential psychologists and psychiatrists. None of these groups in themselves can be tightly compartmentalized or defined, but their slants or emphases show up in our own work. Finally, the main block toward developing a scientifically viable language of interpersonal relationships is partly due to the bias of Western thought that tends to focus on the individual or group. This book, *Interpersonal Dynamics,* takes the connection between the individual personality and the group—interpersonal relationships—as its pivotal concern.

ORGANIZATION OF THIS BOOK

This book consists of five parts. Each of the first four parts is oriented toward a basic aim—the *raison d'être*—of a relationship. We asked ourselves the question: why do people come together? Why do people engage in and involve others

---

[11] H. A. Murray, "Unprecedented Evolutions," *Daedalus,* 90 (1961), pp. 552–63.

[12] One exception to this is the crude and still inchoate attempt by Shepard and Bennis ("A Theory of Training by Group Methods," *Human Relations,* 9 [1956], pp. 403–14) to work out a language of interpersonal relationships. But their language, too, lacks an elegance and complexity still required. "Role" is a useful term, but, aside from its omnibus and ambiguous meanings, it is thought of as certain properties residing in an *incumbent,* rather than the cluster of expectational bonds exerted upon the role incumbent. The language of *sociometry* comes fairly close, as do the philosophical speculations of Buber and the Interaction Process Analysis of Bales. Still, the "I-Thou" concept and the "who-to-whom" matrix implies two units, not one. We still hold out for the merger!

in interpersonal relationships? This question was based on the thought that *all* interpersonal relationships are oriented toward some *primary goal,* some goal or function whose presence is necessary for the relationship to exist and whose absence would seriously undermine it. Obviously, a relationship exists for more than one purpose, but there is usually a salient reason for its formation.[13] The first four parts are organized around these primary goals.

Part I is entitled "Emotional Expressions in Interpersonal Relationships." It deals with the relationship that is formed for the purpose of fulfilling *itself,* such as love, marriage, or friendship. The main transaction in the relationship is "feelings." It deals with the expressive-emotional aspects of interaction, with love, hate, ambivalence, and alienation.

Part II is entitled "Some Interpersonal Aspects of Self-Confirmation." This part encompasses those relationships that are formed for establishing social realities of two types. One type exists to aid in personal development, such as attaining personal identity; the other type exists in order to comprehend external realities. In one case, evidence is required to define the person and the relationship; in the other, the relationship is used to adduce evidence concerning some external matter. "Who am I?" or "Who are we?" is the subject matter for the first type. "What is that?" or "How do we feel about that?" is the subject matter for the other. In either case, the basis for the relationship is *confirmation.*

Part III is entitled "Personal Change through Interpersonal Relationships." It deals with relationships that are formed for the purpose of *change* or *influence,* that is, relationships where one or both parties come together to create a change in each other or the relationship. The change may entail anything from acquiring new behaviors to personal growth; the change may be planned and institutionalized or spontaneous. This is a broad topic, encompassing many theoretical positions and many types of change. It covers, for example, such diverse matters as psychotherapy and "brainwashing," seduction and persuasion, indoctrination and socialization. The antecedents and consequences of interpersonal change and the processes which guide them are all topics treated in Part III.

Part IV is entitled "The Instrumental Relationship." It covers those relationships that are formed in order to produce or create some goal or task, outside of the relationship itself. A conductor and his violin section, a foreman and his workers, two collaborators on a research project: these are all examples of an instrumental relationship. How the nature and quality of the interpersonal relationship affect and relate to the task is the central concern of Part IV.

To express feelings, to establish social realities—to confirm, to change and influence, and to work and create: these are the main reasons for interpersonal relationships. These four primary tasks, then, make up the content and the organizing feature for the first four parts of this volume.

We have added a fifth part: "Towards Better Interpersonal Relationships." In this part we have tried to make explicit the values, ideals, and ethics of our choices throughout the volume. In addition we have attempted two other things.

---

[13] See the essay introducing Part V for a fuller discussion and rationale for this framework.

We propose, or rather *envisage*, an ideal interpersonal relationship based on some normative criteria. Given that ideal, we have suggested certain social and personal conditions and capacities necessary to realize that ideal state. In short, Part V is concerned with a vision of ideal human relations and the most effective ways to reach that state.

We have tried to show our practical concern in two ways. First, Part V deals exclusively with *improving* interpersonal relationships. In this section we have focused attention on the strategic variables that affect the quality and nature of interpersonal relationships. Second, we have attempted to include first-rate theoretical and research papers that employ clear English. We hope that these readings, through their analytic framework, can point the way toward more intelligent actions. This belief is based on Kurt Lewin's famous *dictum:* "There is nothing so practical as a good theory."

But action does now flow ineluctably from diagnosis. As Aristotle said over two thousand years ago: "In practical matters the end is not mere speculative knowledge of what is to be done, but rather the doing of it. It is not enough to know about Virtue, then, but we must endeavor to possess it, and to use it, or to take any other steps that may make us good."[14]

The knowledge available in this book may indeed sound like "eternal verities," too abstract, too remote from an experiential basis for either emotional resonance or guides to action. In any case, the practical steps that "make us good," to use Aristotle's words, are ultimately up to the reader and to us. We can only suggest some possible alternatives.

ESSAYS AND READINGS

It might be useful now to say a word or two about the format of the five parts. The parts are practically identical in arrangement in that each contains an introductory essay and a set of readings culled from the literature. In most cases the essays attempt to provide an overview of the particular subject matter as well as to introduce the readings that follow. In writing the essays we took some liberties which we hope will add to the book's value. We attempted to sketch out some personal ideas or to attempt a new theoretical wrinkle, a luxury not often permitted by our superegos or the ordinary journal article. Each of us was responsible for a part, though we attempted to influence and help each other without losing, we hope, the distinctive individual competencies our training and background allows. Bennis was responsible for Parts I and V as well as this Introduction; Berlew for Part II; Schein for Part III, and Steele, Part IV.

The readings represent, to our knowledge, some of the best writings in the area of interpersonal relations. They are a varied lot, going all the way from studies of rhesus monkeys to cab drivers, from fraternity houses to apocalyptic groups. The theories, research strategies, orientations, and scope are equally varied. We have included papers by one of our students and by the president

---

[14] Aristotle, *Aristotle's Psychology*, trans. W. A. Hammond (1902).

of the American Psychological Association; we have included fiction and short empirical studies; we have included papers by sociologists, psychologists, and psychiatrists of all stripes and persuasions. What they all have in common, what we strived to realize as our main criteria, are relevance, penetration, and clarification.

We did employ other criteria, however. We tried to ferret out the ignored classic; surely, this must be a dream of every anthologist. At the same time, we had to decide against the overpopular classic. We have had, too often, to sacrifice "precision" for "grasp"; and, given the state of this field, the reader will find the articles written more in the style of the essayist than the experimentalist, more in the language of the "myth" than the "game" to use Back's distinction.[15] We do have a number of rigorous, experimental studies included, to be sure. But the study that combines grasp and precision is rare, and, therefore, the majority of the selected readings are thoughtful, comprehensive, and essayistic. We are still working, to use Reichenbach's apt phrase, within the "context of discovery" rather than the "context of verification."

These are our criteria. Undoubtedly they were founded as well on some dubious notions about the vibrancy, energy, imagination, and creativity the authors bring to their work.

We have barely scratched the surface of this "strange territory" we call interpersonal dynamics. Just as one swallow does not make a summer, one book of essays and readings does not make a "field," or even the frontier of one.

To some extent, though, we hope we have succeeded in inching forward in our pursuit of the boundaries, strategic variables, and substance of *interpersonal dynamics*. Finally, we hope we have succeeded in illuminating and creating better understanding of *your life in others*.

---

[15] Back, "The Game and the Myth."

Part I

Emotional expressions in interpersonal relationships

> . . . I wish to show here an inward picture which does not become perceptible until I see it through the external. This external is perhaps quite unobtrusive but not until I look through it, do I discover that inner picture which I desire to show you, an inner picture too delicately drawn to be outwardly visible, woven as it is of the tenderest moods of the soul.
>
> SOREN KIERKEGAARD, *Either/Or*

This essay and the following readings in this section represent our attempt to search out the basic emotional transactions between people: the emotions that exist for no visible instrumental end. We wish to reckon with, following Kierkegaard, the "tenderest moods of the soul"; so we will be speaking of feelings that bind and estrange, feelings that contort into angry knots of discord and those that grow into natural affection, feelings that flow directly into action and those that are transformed and disguised into devious paths, feelings that overwhelm and inspire and those that depress and disgust. This section, then, holds up an imperfect mirror to phenomena that can be only indirectly observed and crudely measured—the raw, almost incomprehensible experiences, at the edge of verbal awareness, we call *interpersonal feelings*.

There are four sections to this essay. Section I, which follows immediately, discusses the perspective we bring to and the problems we see in the study of the emotional expressions in interpersonal dynamics. Section II samples a number of schemes and frameworks for ascertaining the existence and strength of interpersonal feelings. Sections III and IV represent the core material of this essay. In Section III, we present our own typology of the emotional modalities expressed in interpersonal relationships; Section IV, in addition to introducing the readings of this part, examines three basic interpersonal expressions of feelings: "going toward" (love), "going against" (hate), and "going away" (alienation and withdrawal).

1. SOME PRELIMINARY CONSIDERATIONS

1. Scope and definition of interpersonal feelings

We regard an interpersonal relationship as an irreducible element of reality. Just as we cannot have a line without the presence of two dots, we cannot have an expression of an interpersonal feeling without the existence of two people. We hope to avoid the "myth of isolation" and to stress the "connectedness" of human encounters.

Second, we will focus only on those interactional dimensions which have an emotional base, that is, the interdependencies and transactions that involve the expression of feelings by the participants. Thus *this essay and the subsequent readings will be concerned with that class of human interactions where feelings are basic and pivotal in the interpersonal exchange.*

Third, we regard interpersonal feelings—the emotional or affective transactions—as the basic, raw data of interpersonal relationships. We do not need to argue about whether these feelings can be reduced to more genotypic categories, such as instincts or impulses; or do we need or desire to assert that certain feelings are "better" or "deeper," or are derivatives or causes of each other. Questions about the causal pairings of interpersonal feelings, of whether one is the obverse or precipitate of another or whether they are instinctive, acquired, or learned need not concern us here. For our part, love is as *basic* as hate and as *real* as loneliness. What we do assert is that the expression of interpersonal feelings is basic to the existence of the relationship, that interpersonal feelings can be ascertained and measured, that they are causal elements in how people will behave, that they have real effects, and that they can be studied without recourse to a physiological or instinctual theory.[1]

These emphases—the irreducibility of the relationship, the primacy of feelings and their "reality"—characterize this essay. One further thought should be added before going on. Arthur Lovejoy, the historian of ideas, coined the term "metaphysical pathos" to describe the subtle and imperceptible, even unconscious, attitudes that guide one's theoretical predilections. Nowhere is this temperamental disposition so visible as it is in the study of personality and interpersonal relations. There is only a thin line between what one is and what one wants, between descriptive realities and normative desires. It is not only true, for example, that Hobbes and Freud developed theories different from Gordon Allport or Carl Rogers; they also brought to their theories a completely different world view. Our metaphysical pathos, too, tinctures this essay as well as the rest of the volume. Wherever we can, we try to make it explicit; indeed, Part V is devoted solely to some normative issues surrounding interpersonal dynamics. Our hope here is to penetrate "reality" wherever it leads us.

---

[1] This is a far more complicated problem than we make it out to be. We cannot, however, be more than arbitrary at this juncture. Our oversimplified assumptions will permit us to deal with more complex issues later on.

2. The present state of theory

There is as yet no single, comprehensive theory of interpersonal relations. Sociology, social psychology, and psychiatry have offered important insights to the understanding of interpersonal phenomena, but the area escapes superarrogation by one discipline.[2]

As we shall see later on in this essay, when we review the main theoretical influences feeding into the study of interpersonal feelings, we have had to draw on a wide range of disciplines and concepts. The plethora of terms used to describe interpersonal feelings testifies to the range of theories and disciplines. We find ourselves using terms such as: assumptions, needs, interpersonal response traits, orientation, impulses, and feelings. They are all used to circumscribe the class of behavioral events we are calling "interpersonal feeling."

In this section of readings, dealing with human interaction with an *affective* base, we have found the work of Harry Stack Sullivan (the so-called "Washington School of Psychiatry") and other neo-Freudian theory particularly helpful. On the other hand, in other parts of our volume, particularly Parts III and IV where we cover topics such as creativity, work, and change, the theories of the "symbolic-interactionists" (represented by the writings of Becker, Strauss, Goffman) seem more appropriate.

3. The languages of interpersonal theory, scientific and humanistic

It might be useful at this point to say a few words about the problem of discussing interpersonal feelings in a quasiscientific way. This presents something of a dilemma, for interpersonal feelings have to do with man's private experiences; his visceral reactions, experiences of pain and pleasure, delight or disgust, love, fear, boredom, are all intensely private and only partially communicable. These matters have long been considered to be the domain of the humanities. Science, on the other hand, may be thought of as a device for investigating, ordering and, communicating the more public of human experiences such as sense experiences and the intellectual experiences of logical thought.[3] Loosely speaking, then, the cultural elite, the humanists, have constructed a language which roughly expresses the existential situation of the individual in his world while the scientist creates a precise language which deals with objects which are independent of human beings.

Any language, though, is a process of symbolization. This is as true for poetry as it is for mathematics. What makes matters more difficult for the language of feelings is the fact that feelings are reflexive by nature; that is, the object of analysis, the person, does his *own* abstraction and symbolization. (The physical sciences can avoid this difficulty as they avoid the study of people.) Because of

---

[2] See the introductory essay for a more detailed statement on the "state of theory."

[3] Aldous Huxley, "The Only Way to Write a Modern Poem about a Nightingale," *Harper's Magazine*, Vol. 227, No. 1359 (1963), pp. 62–66.

this "reflexive dilemma," the language of interpersonal feelings has stubbornly defied logical analysis or even adequate description.

Today in the social sciences, two languages compete for primacy: the language of the "game" and the language of the "myth."[4] Game languages follow the model of the physical sciences by defining all terms operationally and in formal terms. ". . . Analysis of social interaction is made in terms of moves and countermoves. . . . In all these fields the trend toward miniature systems is indicative of the model of a tight situation, rigidly defined, where individuals can be assumed to conform to a set of rules which can be completely specified."[5]

The language of the game seems most appropriate for the class of problems we referred to earlier as interactional problems devoid of affect, where the rules are explicit, where formal models can simulate a "tight situation, rigidly defined."

But what of the problems which hold the most interest for us, interactional situations *with* affect? How would the language of the game treat the following passage from a book of fiction?

Her back seemed mysteriously taut and hard; the body of a strange woman retains more of its mineral content, not being transmuted, through familiarity, into pure emotion. In a sheltered corner of the room we stopped dancing altogether and talked, and what I distinctly remember is how her hands, beneath steady and opaque appraisal of her eyes, in nervous slurred agitation blindly sought mine and seized and softly gripped, with infantile instinct, my thumbs. Just my thumbs she held, and as we talked she moved them this way and that as if she were steering me. When I closed my eyes, the red darkness inside my lids was trembling, and when I rejoined my wife, and held her to dance, she asked, "Why are you panting?"[6]

The language of the game could not easily untangle or encompass the range of interpersonal feelings and interactions described. Yet the excerpt is altogether unextraordinary in good fiction. This type of human experience requires a more complicated and subtle expression than the language of the game.

Back suggests as an alternate language the "language of the myth." It is a language adapted to the human capacity to grasp the complexity and nuance of vital human problems, which game languages might sacrifice to increasing precision.

The language of the myth becomes the means of expressing those theories of social science which try to encompass an unlimited field of applicability, which appear to contain some truth but seem fated to be subject to unending controversies over interpretation. They frequently revert to the use of accepted mythology to make a point clear. Freud's theories, for example, fit closely the definition of a theory couched in the language of the myth. The concepts which he uses, such as ego, id, superego, have no precise denotable referent. The meaning derives from the experiences of the listener, and it is clear to him

---

[4] K. W. Back, "The Game and the Myth," *Behavioral Science*, Vol. 8 (1963), pp. 66–71.

[5] *Ibid.*, p. 68.

[6] John Updike, *Pigeon Feathers* (New York: Crest Books, 1953), p. 176.

that something beyond the simple concepts, which are practically personifications, is meant.[7]

We cannot endorse completely Back's analysis of the two languages of social science. It is somewhat oversimplified, and he tends to exaggerate the differences through polarization. At the same time, there is no denying that the language we presently use to denote the expression of interpersonal feelings falls short both of the precision of the game and the beauty of the myth.

With these three preliminary considerations spelled out, we are now in a better position to come closer to the core material of this essay. In the following section, we will sample a wide array of approaches which encompass different aspects of interpersonal feelings.

II. A BRIEF SURVEY OF APPROACHES TO ASCERTAINING INTERPERSONAL FEELINGS

We said earlier that there is no single, comprehensive theory of interpersonal feelings. There are, though, a number of researchers and theoreticians who have attempted to ascertain and conceptualize the properties of interpersonal feelings through a variety of techniques. We think it would be useful at this point to sample a variety of these approaches in order to grasp the main dimensions of the field.

It will be convenient for us to organize this section in terms of the two principle ways of ascertaining interpersonal feelings. In this way we can accomplish two things at once: to acquaint the reader with these methods, but also, more basically, to examine the way theorists have conceptualized the domain of interpersonal feelings.

The two principle ways of ascertaining interpersonal feelings are some form of *self-description* and some *observation* system, whereby an observer scores interpersonal interactions, usually act-by-act.

1. Self-rating methods

Our main example of the use of a self-description inventory to identify and measure interpersonal feelings is FIRO, deriving its name from the "*F*undamental *I*nterpersonal *R*elations Orientation." The FIRO is a questionnaire developed by W. C. Schutz[8] which consists of a check list of 54 statements designed to measure an individual's propensities along three interpersonal dimensions. These three dimensions were derived partly from a factor analysis done by

---

[7] Back, "The Game and the Myth," p. 69.

[8] W. C. Schutz, *FIRO: A Three-Dimensional Theory of Interpersonal Behavior* (New York: Holt, Rinehart & Winston, 1958); and "Interpersonal Underworld," *The Planning of Change*, by W. G. Bennis, K. D. Benne, and R. Chin (eds.) (New York: Holt, Rinehart & Winston, 1961).

Schutz[9] and partly from a theoretical disposition favoring the group theories of Bion.[10]

Schutz's work starts from the assumption that each individual has different intensities of needs and different mechanisms for handling them but that all people have three basic interpersonal needs in common:

The need for *inclusion.* This is the need to maintain a satisfactory relation between the self and other people with respect to interaction or belongingness.

The need for *control.* This is the need to maintain a satisfactory relation between oneself and other people with respect to power and influence.

The need for *affection.* This is the need to maintain a satisfactory relation between the self and other people with regard to love and affection.

FIGURE 1
Extreme types on the three interpersonal dimensions

Expressed behavior		Dimension	Wanted behavior	
Extreme high	*Extreme low*	*Dimension*	*Extreme high*	*Extreme low*
Oversocial	Undersocial	*Inclusion*	Social-compliant	Countersocial
Autocrat	Abdicrat	*Control*	Submissive	Rebellious
Overpersonal	Underpersonal	*Affection*	Personal-compliant	Counterpersonal

From W. C. Schutz, "Interpersonal Underworld," in *The Planning of Change*, by W. G. Bennis, K. D. Benne, and R. Chin (eds.) (New York: Holt, Rinehart & Winston, 1961), p. 298.

Thus, *inclusion* has to do with the degree of commitment, belongingness, and participation an individual requires in human interaction; *control* has to do with the degree of influence and power an individual requires; and *affection* has to do with the degree of closeness, intimacy, an individual desires.

One additional factor has to be mentioned in order to present Schutz's theory in more or less complete form. For each dimension we can imagine that an individual *expresses* a need toward other people and that he *wants* a need fulfilled for him by another person. For example, on the inclusion dimension, we can see how one person may have a strong need to include others, to bring them into his groups easily and quickly. This same person, though, may have a low need to *want* inclusion; that is, he may not care if others include him. Thus, one aspect is what we *do* with relation to other people; this is called *expressed behavior.* The second is what we *want* from other people; this is called *wanted behavior.* Figure 1 shows the extreme types along the three dimensions.

---

[9] *Ibid.,* 1968.

[10] W. R. Bion, *Experiences in Groups and Other Papers* (New York: Basic Books, 1959). The work of D. Stock and H. Thelen, *Emotional Dynamics and Group Culture* (New York: New York University, 1958), is also associated with the FIRO dimensions.

A second example of the kinds of dimensions of interpersonal feeling which can be ascertained from self-descriptions is shown in Figure 2. This list, summarized by Krech, Crutchfield, and Ballachey[11] in their recent textbook, presents twelve primary response traits (equivalent to Schutz's needs and what we are

FIGURE 2
Some primary interpersonal response traits

Role Dispositions
    Ascendance (opposite: social timidity). Defends his rights, does not mind being conspicuous; not self-reticent; self-assured; forcefully puts self forward.
    Dominance (opposite: submissiveness). Assertive; self-confident; power-oriented; tough, strong-willed; order-giving; directive leader.
    Social initiative (opposite: social passivity). Organizes groups; does not stay in background; makes suggestions at meetings; takes over leadership.
    Independence (opposite: dependence). Prefers to do own planning, to work things out in own way; does not seek support or advice; emotionally self-sufficient.

Sociometric Dispositions
    Accepting of others (opposite: rejecting). Nonjudgmental in attitude toward others, permissive; believing and trustful; overlooks weaknesses and sees best in others.
    Socioability (opposite: unsociability). Participates in social affairs; likes to be with people; outgoing.
    Friendliness (opposite: unfriendliness). Genial, warm, open and approachable; approaches other persons easily; forms many social relationships.
    Sympathetic (opposite: unsympathetic). Concerned with the feelings of others; displays kindly generous behavior; defends underdog.

Expressive Dispositions
    Competitiveness (opposite: noncompetitiveness). Sees every relationship as a contest—others are rivals to be defeated; self-aggrandizing; noncooperative.
    Aggressiveness (opposite: nonaggressiveness). Attacks others directly or indirectly; shows defiant resentment of authority; quarrelsome; negativistic.
    Self-consciousness (opposite: social poise). Embarrassed when entering a room after others are seated; suffers excessively from stage fright; hesitates to volunteer in group discussions; bothered by people watching him at work; feels uncomfortable if different from others.
    Exhibitionistic (opposite: self-effacing). Is given to excess and ostentation in behavior and dress; seeks recognition and applause; shows off and behaves queerly to attract attention.

D. Krech, R. S. Crutchfield, and E. L. Ballachey, *Individual in Society* (New York: McGraw-Hill, 1962), 106.

calling feelings) derived from self-descriptions. These were classified into three arbitrary categories and purportedly are representative of the salient interpersonal dimensions.

---

[11] D. Krech, R. S. Crutchfield, and E. L. Ballachey, *Individual in Society* (New York: McGraw-Hill Book Co., Inc., 1962).

2. Observation: Act-by-act analysis

One deficiency of self-rating forms is the absence of validating data. Individuals frequently do not see themselves accurately and it is obvious that our interpersonal relations contain important areas of ignorance due to inadequate information, systematic distortions, and selective inattentions. Recently, for example, Bennis and Peabody[12] showed that self-ratings on FIRO were not significantly correlated with observers' ratings. It will be profitable to examine this discrepancy between self and observer's ratings in some deatil.

Sullivan[13] explores this idea in his analysis of interpersonal communication. It is his contention that we systematically *experience* feelings which we do not admit to ourselves and which would therefore not appear as salient on any self-rating inventory. Feelings such as hostility or aggressiveness, for example, are part of the total person and are occasionally experienced. But to all intents and purposes, as the individual construes it, they are not part of the experienced self; hence, they make up the "not-self" or "denied-self."[14]

Sullivan[15] tells of a hypothetical couple, Mr. and Mrs. A. Mrs. A, according to an observer, makes a derogatory remark to her husband, Mr. A, after which Mr. A becomes quite tired. Mr. A is not aware of being offended; he is only aware of being weary. He becomes more withdrawn and preoccupied with his weariness. Under cover, according to Sullivan, Mr. A retaliates in a dominantly hostile, noncollaborative way: "A and Mrs. A are not collaborating in an exchange of hostility. She has acted against him, perhaps with full awareness of her motivation; but he "suffers weariness" while unwittingly acting against her, in his weariness ceasing to be aware of her relevance in his motivation. . . ."[16]

Mr. A, in fact, experienced, lived through, and underwent the hostile action of his wife; he reacted to it and then suffered what at first glance seemed like an irrelevant state: weariness. But if we studied Mr. A more closely we would see that this is not the whole story. Sullivan points out that if we had a slow-motion camera and some rather special equipment we could observe that Mr. A experienced something connected with Mrs. A's remarks. For example, we would be able to detect postural tensions in some parts of his face and increased tensions in various parts of the skeletal structure.

Now if also in our apparatus for augmenting our observational abilities, we had included a device for phonographically recording the speech and adventitious vocal phenomena produced by Mr. A, we would have found interesting data in the field of his peculiarly

---

[12] W. G. Bennis and D. Peabody, "The Conceptualization of Two Personality Orientations and Sociometric Choice," *The Journal of Social Psychology*, Vol. 57 (1962), pp. 203–15.

[13] H. S. Sullivan, "Psychiatry: Introduction to the Study of Interpersonal Relations," *A Study of Interpersonal Relations, New Contributions to Psychiatry*, P. Mullahy (ed.) (New York: Hermitage Press, 1949), pp. 98–121.

[14] W. G. Bennis, "Interpersonal Communication," in *The Planning of Change*, by W. G. Bennis, K. D. Benne, and R. Chin (eds.) (New York: Holt, Rinehart & Winston, 1961).

[15] Sullivan, "Psychiatry."

[16] Sullivan, "Psychiatry." p. 106.

expressive behavior. There would appear a series of phenomena, beginning, perhaps, with an abrupt subvocal change in the flow of breath. There might appear a rudimentary sort of gasp. A rapid inhalation may be coincident with the shift in postural tension that we observed in the skeletal muscles. There may then have been a respiratory pause. When Mr. A speaks, we find that his voice has changed its characteristics considerably, and we may secure, in the record of his first sentence, phonographic evidence of a continuing shift of vocal apparatus, first towards an "angry voice" and then to one somewhat expressive of a state of weary resignation. In brief, *with refinements of observational technique* applied to the performances of Mr. A as an organism, we find that we can no longer doubt that he experienced, even if he did not perceive, the personal significance of Mrs. A's hostile remark.[17]

This discussion points to a dilemma frequently encountered by students of interpersonal behavior: the discrepancy between self-reports and expressed behavior observed by others. Both methods are obviously "valid"; self-ratings ascertain self-image and observer reports detect how others perceive the self. Carl Rogers and others make a good deal of the discrepancy between self and others' perceptions (see Part II of this volume). Our concern here, however, is not the idea of "congruence"; rather we are concerned with the range and complexity in the expression of interpersonal feelings and the need for behavioral measurements to augment the self-rating method.

A number of reliable systems for observing microscopically the act-by-act interactions between people have been developed. Perhaps the best known of these is the Interaction Process Anslysis devised by Bales.[18] Figure 3 shows the system of categories used as well as a key to their meaning. Of the twelve categories, notice that only six of them deal with the social-emotional sphere of human interaction; categories 1–3 and 10–12 deal with positive and negative emotional acts, respectively. The remaining six categories, 4–9, deal with instrumental problem-solving processes; numbers 4–6 signify initiating acts and 7–9 signify receiving acts. According to Bales, both instrumental and social-emotional acts are necessary for effective problem solving. Our main interests in this section are the socio-emotional categories.

There are other systems more specifically geared for observing and recording interpersonal *feelings*. Leary[19] has developed a measurement system of sixteen interpersonal variables based on the theories of Harry Stack Sullivan. All expressed emotional behavior can be categorized in terms of two orthogonal dimensions: hostility-affiliation and dominance-submission. Mills[20] has developed a Sign Process Analysis based on sign theory and sociological theory which categorizes *objects* discussed (such as group member, "boss," etc.) and what *valuation*

---

[17] Sullivan, "Psychiatry," p. 108. Italics added.

[18] R. F. Bales, *Interaction Process Analysis* (Cambridge, Mass.: Addison-Wesley, 1950).

[19] T. Leary, "The Theory and Measurement Methodology of Interpersonal Communication," *Psychiatry*, Vol. 18 (1955), pp. 147–61.

[20] T. M. Mills, *Group Transformation: An Analysis of a Training Group* (Englewood Cliffs, N.J.: Prentice-Hall, 1964).

FIGURE 3
Interaction process analysis

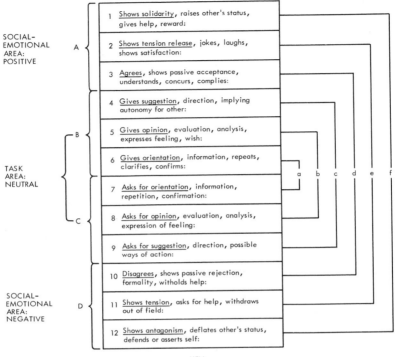

KEY:

A. Positive Reactions
B. Attempted Answers
C. Questions
D. Negative Reactions

a. Problems of Communication
b. Problems of Evaluation
c. Problems of Control
d. Problems of Decision
e. Problems of Tension Reduction
f. Problems of Reintegration

R. F. Bales, *Interaction Process Analysis* (Cambridge, Mass.: Addison-Wesley, 1950).

is expressed toward the object, positive or negative. More recently, Mann[21] has developed an observation scheme which is designed to assess and record the implications of each act initiated by a group member for the state of his feelings toward the leader of the group. Mann's scheme consists of three main areas: (1) *Impulse Area*, which includes hostility, resisting, withdrawing, guilt-inducing; making reparation, identifying, accepting, moving toward; (2) *Authority Relations Area*, which includes showing dependence, independence, counterdepen-

---

[21] R. D. Mann, *Interpersonal Styles and Group Development* (New York: John Wiley and Sons, Co., 1967).

dence; and (3) *Ego State Area,* which includes expressing anxiety, denying anxiety, showing self-esteem, expressing depression, and denying depression.

It is possible that Mann's interaction scheme, while focusing exclusively on expressed feelings in member-leader relations, may be applicable to member-member relations. If so, this may be the first comprehensive system which enables one to describe in molecular detail emotional responses heretofore inferred. Ego states and impulse areas, most particularly, govern an important segment of interpersonal behavior. It is possible now to record these phenomena as they are expressed.

Of course, act-by-act observational schemes have their drawbacks, too. The problem of *inference* is perplexing. How does the observer gauge the intent of the remark? Does he even try to or does he look only at the effect of the remark? Does he reckon with the unconscious as well as conscious purpose? How does he score multiple meanings? How does he deal with displacement? What about such puzzling phenomena as silences? How unambiguous can a statement be? How does an observer determine what a unit is? Could it be that adding atomistic and molecular units of behavior will miss the possibly greater impact of *one* remark? All these are questions which the act-by-act observation schemes have to cope with in one manner or another.

It was not our intention to delve deeply into the methodological problems or to describe in microscopic detail the self-description and observation scoring systems for ascertaining interpersonal feelings.[22] Rather our major goal was to present an array of approaches or orientations to the area. The reader has undoubtedly noticed, and may have been bothered by, the proliferation of terms coined to describe what we are calling interpersonal feelings: needs, assumptions, orientations, "who-to-whom" interactions, emotional states, impulses, interpersonal response traits, etc. Although the operational referents may vary, the terms are concerned with the same class of phenomena: emotional expression in interpersonal relationships.

Before going on to Section III of this essay, one final point should be made concerning the kinds of measurement employed to ascertain interpersonal feelings. We have argued that both the self-rating inventories and the observational systems have their advantages and limitations. We would like to demonstrate this more clearly through the use of Sullivan's interpersonal theory.[23]

We can assume, first of all, that people vary with respect to levels of awareness. We saw in the example by Harry Stack Sullivan that Mr. A was simply not aware of the feeling he experienced. But we saw how an observer could have identified the feeling Mr. A was experiencing, leading to the discrepancies between self-rating and observer ratings we commented on earlier. To complicate matters even more, it is possible that Mr. A was *concealing* something from the observer or

---

[22] The interested reader should consult the original sources to gain more detailed information with respect to these scoring schemes. We merely wanted to display, not demonstrate, these schemes.

[23] Sullivan, "Psychiatry."

his wife which neither could detect. After all, patients can "fool" their analysts and we have all learned to dissemble—or simply to conceal aspects of our self to others. So we not only have unconscious distortions, but also conscious *concealing.*

In order to portray this problem more graphically, the reader should turn to Figure 4.[24] Quadrant I is the area of greatest congruence, the sector of behavior where there should be no significant difference between self-rating and observer ratings. Quadrant II is the "blind area," a result of not being able to see things in ourselves which others can detect. This case is similar to the one Sullivan describes, and it is this phenomenon which accounts for the discrepancy between self and other ratings. In Quadrant III is the "concealed" area, that domain of behavior that represents things *we* know but do not reveal to others. Finally, Quadrant IV is the "unknown" area, a deeply buried unconscious area that can be revealed only through depth analysis.

FIGURE 4

	Known to self	Not known to self
Known to others	I. *High congruence* "Announced self"	II. *Blind area* "Denied self"
Not known to others	III. *Concealed area* "Concealed self"	IV. *Unknown* "Unknown self"

What derivations can we make now about the ascertaining of interpersonal feelings? First, an important variable is the *"congruence" or integrity of the individual.* If he is "out of communication" with himself—i.e., Quadrant II—the self-rating inventory will not be a valid indicator of his interpersonal behavior. In fact, there should be a discrepancy between what an observer detects and what the person observes in himself. A second variable is the degree of *trust* or *psychological* safety in the situation. Lack of trust leads to the case of Quadrant III, where the individual knows something he does not reveal. In this case, a self-rating inventory would be more valid than the observer scoring—or, certainly, the scores should be discrepant. Finally, we can say that the validity of the instrument *depends on the interpersonal area to be ascertained.* A deep, unconscious motive may not be visible to the ordinary instruments used. In other words a feeling can be ascertained only if there is some social expression of it.

In conclusion, we can say that a self-rating inventory and observer scores may be equally valid in Quadrant I; observer scores would be superior in Quadrant II; self-ratings would be more valid in Quadrant III[25]; for Quadrant IV, only depth interviews or projective tests could detect these feelings.

---

[24] This analysis and Figure 4 are adapted from the work of J. Luft, "The Johari Window," *Human Relations Training News,* Vol. 5 (1961), pp. 6–7.

[25] This, of course, depends on who is going to "see" the self-rating forms. If the person trusts the tester or if the tester is an unknown, but safe, person, then the self-rating inventory may be

III. THREE THEORETICAL APPROACHES TO INTERPERSONAL EMOTIONS

Early in this essay, in our preliminary considerations, we stated that there was no single, comprehensive theory of interpersonal relations. We also noted that our main influences have come from psychoanalytic theory, interpersonal theory, and existential theory. At this point we would like to go beyond this preliminary statement to see if we can order and organize these three streams of influence. Our hope is to identify their basic elements so that the substructure of interpersonal feelings can be more fully understood.

FIGURE 5
Three approaches to interpersonal feelings

Theory	Source of conflict	Source of anxiety	Goal
Instinct theory	Man/Nature	Lack of impulse control	Adaptation, pleasure
Interpersonal theory	Man/Man	Lack of consensual validation	Valid communication
Existential theory	Man/Self	Lack of meaning and/or integrity	Identity

We have found it convenient to divide the theoretical structure of interpersonal feelings into three branches: *instinct theory* or psychoanalytic theories associated with Freud; *interpersonal theory* or the theories associated with Harry Stack Sullivan and some neo-Freudians; and *existentialist theory* associated with May et al.[26] As shown in Figure 5 we can organize these theories around three features: source of conflict, source of anxiety, and goal.

1. Source of conflict

All the above approaches imply that emotional states are aroused in order to cope with a *conflict* situation. In the case of *instinct theory*, the conflict is between man and his basic biological nature, the physical aspects of the organism. As tempting as it is to "psychologize" these biological conditions—and even ortho-

---

accurate. More complicated—but more interesting—are the games we play with ourselves, quite apart from Quadrant II where we deny seeing certain things in ourselves or Quadrant III where we conceal things from others. We are referring to that class of "self-dissembling" where we choose certain responses on a personality test, for example, knowing full well it isn't "us" we're describing, but a pleasant version of ourself. It's a bit like cheating at solitaire. This case can't be explained by any of the four Quadrants in Figure 4. It is not concealing or denying *or* public. We are playing a game—not vis-à-vis others—but with ourselves, our conscious ego-ideals.

[26] R. May, *Existential Psychology* (New York: Random House, 1961).

dox Freudians are guilty of this—there should be no question about the basic biological nature of instinct theory.

Interpersonal theory focuses on the man-man tensions; essentially, interpersonal theory is a theory of human relations. In contrast to the instinct theory, impulses, drives, striving toward goals are considered by the interpersonal theorists as useless abstractions necessitated by the narrow bioneurological vision of psychoanalytical theory. As Sullivan said: "So if a person really thinks that his thoughts about nerves and synapses and the rest have a higher order of merit than his thoughts about signs and symbols, all I can say is, Heaven help him."[27] Interpersonal theory, then, is the study of the processes that result from man-man tensions.

Finally, *existential theory* concerns itself primarily with man in tension with his "self." Ludwig Binswanger, leader of the European existential psychiatry movement, held that the main weakness in psychoanalytic theory—a weakness he considered profound enough to prevent him from becoming a "Freudian" —was its omission of man in relation to himself.[28] But the self, as the existentialists know it, is a very complicated mechanism:

> My "being"—which by definition must have unity if it is to survive as a being—has three aspects, which we may term "self," "person," and "ego." The "self" I use as the subjective center, the experiencing of the fact that I am the one who behaves in thus and thus ways; the "person" we may take as the aspect in which I am accepted by others, the "person" of Jung, the social roles of William James; and the "ego" we may take as Freud originally enunciated it, the specific organ of perception by which the self sees and relates to the outside world . . . the point I do wish to make strongly is that *being* must be presupposed in discussions of ego and identity, and that the *centered self* must be basic to such discussions.[29]

The self is the center of existential theory, and the major conflict is the self in tension with the ego and the person.

2. When the conflict situation is not satisfactorily resolved, anxiety ensues

The key concept here is *anxiety,* and each approach to interpersonal feelings employs it in a crucial way. For *instinct theory,* anxiety occurs when biological impulses, the instincts, overwhelm the ego. In its most primitive form, we can observe this in Freud's writings when he asserts that: ". . . the aim of the death instinct is to undo connections and so to destroy things.[30]

In *interpersonal theory,* the presence of anxiety indicates the lack of "em-

---

[27] H. Guntrip, *Personality Structure and Human Interaction* (New York: International Universities Press, 1961), p. 176.

[28] May, "Existential Psychology," p. 32.

[29] May, "Existential Psychology," p. 48.

[30] Sigmund Freud, *An Outline of Psychoanalysis* (New York: Norton, 1949), p. 20.

pathy," or at a more primitive level a "not-understood state." For Sullivan, effective human relations can occur only when individuals develop "consensual validation," a state where the primary, referential tools of communication are shared. Not to be understood is to not exist, to be destroyed. Anxiety for the *existentialist* is the threat to *being* caused by a lack of *meaning* for the self. It is that state where the self is not coterminous with the ego or the person and where the lack of integrity leads to despair and state of meaninglessness.

3. How is anxiety reduced?

The organism, in *instinct theory*, avoids anxiety by reaching some desired state or goal, by seeking some adaptation or pleasure which, in turn, lessens the conflict. In other words, the ego must be able to maintain some balance between its biological impulses and the outside reality.

For the *interpersonal theorist*, anxiety is reduced when the interpersonal unit has reached a state of "valid communication." That is, when participants in an interpersonal encounter have reached the stage where they have developed methods for achieving and testing consensus, they have successfully reached the goal.

For *existentialism*, "identity" is the desired anxiety-free state. In the famous quote from Sartre, "We are out choices," he is implying that existentialism means centering on the existing—i.e., deciding—person. There is no such thing as truth or reality in existential thought aside from the human being participating and experiencing his identity.

What derivations can we make with this typology? First of all, we can say that interpersonal theory is the only one of the three approaches that makes interpersonal feelings per se pivotal to the theory. Instinct theory and existential theory encompass interpersonal feelings, to be sure, but only as derivatives of "deeper" motives. *Others* are important in existential theory, but only as agents in *self-actualization; others* are important in instinct theory, but only as they lead to more effective impulse control.[31]

Our classification scheme also allows us to sort out a number of different approaches to interpersonal feelings and organize them. It should be apparent, for example, that the FIRO theory of Schutz[32] and the Sullivanian scheme of Leary[33] belong in the interpersonal theory sphere. The group theory of W. R. Bion,[34] the interaction scheme of Bales,[35] and the philosophical speculations of Martin Buber[36] must also be located there. While there are differences among

---

[31] This statement, as it now stands, is too blunt and unqualified. But the *emphasis* should be clear. The important work of the ego-psychologists (Hartmann, Kris, Erikson) and the English psychoanalysts M. Klein and W.R.D. Fairbairn stands out as an exception to this emphasis.

[32] Schutz, *FIRO* (1958).

[33] Leary, Theory and Measurement."

[34] Bion, *Experience in Groups.*

[35] Bales, *Interaction Process Analysis.*

[36] M. Buber, *I and Thou* (Edinburgh: T. & T. Clark, 1957).

these various theories, some trivial and some important, they all place primary emphasis on the relationship of man to man.

Existential theory, as we have mentioned, stresses concepts focusing on the "self." Existential psychologists such as Rogers, Maslow, and May tend to use concepts such as a "self-actualization," "existential loneliness," and "identity." It is interesting to note that when existentialists discuss loneliness, they often regard it as an affectively positive state[37]; interpersonal theorists, on the other hand, tend to treat it as a morbid, even psychotic, state.[38]

Finally, it should be stated that approaches like Mann's[39] fall into the instinct theory sector because of their reliance on the expression of impulses.

There are some difficulties with the typology which should be mentioned. Most significant for us is the fact that some interpersonal and personality theorists cannot be so easily categorized. Erik Erikson, for example, falls into the "ego-psychology" school of instinct theory; on the other hand, his governing theoretical concern has been "identity." To make matters even more complicated, he is considered by some as an interpersonal theorist, his entire theory of development resting on interpersonal dimensions. We find the same problem in the work of the English branch of the neo-Freudians, M. Klein[40] and Fairbairn,[41] who have developed an "object relations" psychology. Where do they belong? They cannot be omitted from the interpersonal sphere. This is particularly true of Fairbairn, who places primary emphasis on object relations and contends that libido is not primarily pleasure seeking but *object* seeking.[42]

Despite these qualifications, our classification system will help guide us in our next and final section of this essay.[43]

STYLES OF INTERPERSONAL FEELINGS

Our readings which follow are organized in terms of a classification system of interpersonal styles developed by Karen Horney.[44] It consists of three styles or modalities of how people relate to each other: (*a*) characteristically relating

---

[37] C. E. Moustakas, *Loneliness* (Englewood Cliffs, N.J.: Prentice-Hall, Inc., 1961).

[38] F. Fromm-Reichmann, "Loneliness," *Psychiatry*, Vol. 22 (1959), pp. 1–15.

[39] Mann, *Interpersonal Styles.*

[40] M. Klein, *Contributions of Psychoanalysis, 1921–1945* (London: Hogarth Press, 1950).

[41] W. R. D. Fairbairn, *Psychoanalytic Studies of the Personality* (New York: Basic Books, 1952).

[42] Guntrip, *Personality Structure*, p. 253.

[43] We cannot resist a speculation on a possible future direction of a creative synthesis in the theory of interpersonal feelings. It can be foreshadowed, we believe, in the work of Erikson, Klein, Fairbairn, Sullivan, and the ego-psychologists. All these theorists emphasize, to a greater or lesser degree, the autonomy and integration of the ego, the reality and significance of relationships and environment in personal development, and the significance of adaptation. An integration of these theories holds genuine promise for the theoretician. Since this essay was written, a brilliant beginning along these lines was made by J. D. Sutherland ("Object-Relations Theory and the Conceptual Model of Psychoanalysis," *British Journal of Medical Psychology*, Vol. 36, No. 109 [1963], pp. 109–24), who attempted to integrate ego-psychology and "object-relations theory."

[44] K. Horney, *Our Inner Conflicts* (New York: Norton, 1945).

to others by moving *toward* them; (*b*) characteristically relating to others by moving *against* them; and (*c*) characteristically relating to others by moving *away* from them. These styles have to do with love, hate, and aloneness or alienation, and we have arranged our readings to correspond to these polarities of interpersonal expression. Let us begin by examining the interpersonal aspects of moving toward: love.

1. Going toward: Love and interpersonal intimacy

In a recent book on "love," the advertising blurb reads: "Love—a short word that means so many different things. Everybody wants it; far from everybody can give it. Yet we all think we know what it means. Is it something natural that we don't need to think about or is it art? . . . To practice the art of loving is more difficult than ever under today's pressure . . ."[45] This statement "on love" represents a more-or-less average attitude toward the topic: puzzlement and confusion, chagrin and awe, yet fascination with its "curative" and harmful effects. And yet with all the cosmic and religious overtones, the concept of love, complicated and elusive as it is, must serve as one of the basic dimensions of interpersonal feelings. It *is* a complicated topic, primarily because of its rich heritage in spiritual, physical, and psychological thought. To a zoologist, like Kinsey, love can be defined in terms of orgiastic potency; to a theologian, it can be explained or understood only in terms of man's relation to God; and to a psychologist it is often either an embarrassment or a source of an argument about operational referents.

In any case, its primacy and importance in the sphere of interpersonal feelings are assured. We are preoccupied with love because of its instinctual, human, and philosophical nature. Terms which are derivative of or synonymous with love pervade psychological literature: *libido, eros,* and object-relations from psychoanalytic theory; "intimacy" from the first phase of adulthood in Erikson's theory[46] and the second step in "group maturity" according to Bennis and Shepard.[47] Bion speaks of "pairing,"[48] Schutz of "affection,"[49] Sorokin of "altruistic love,"[50] Murray of "synthesism,"[51] Wolff of "surrender,"[52] Harlow of "heterosexual affectional systems,"[53] Fromm of "overcoming of human separate-

[45] Erich Fromm, *The Art of Loving* (London: Unwin, 1962), frontispiece.

[46] E. H. Erikson, *Childhood and Society* (New York: W. W. Norton, 1960).

[47] W. G. Bennis and H. A. Shepard, "A Theory of Group Development," *Human Relations,* Vol. 9 (1956), pp. 415–37.

[48] Bion, *Experiences in Groups.*

[49] Schutz, *FIRO.*

[50] P. Sorokin, *Explorations in Altruistic Love and Behavior* (Boston: Beacon Press, 1950).

[51] H. A. Murray, "Synthesism," *Daedalus,* Vol. 90 (1961), pp. 552–63.

[52] K. Wolff, "Surrender and Religion," *Journal for the Scientific Study of Religion,* Vol. 2, (1962), pp. 36–50.

[53] H. Harlow, "The Heterosexual Affectional System in Monkeys," *American Psychologist,* Vol. 17, No. 1 (1962): See pages 36–51 of this volume.

ness."[54] We could multiply these examples but the point hardly requires more evidence.

It is tempting, though perhaps foolhardy, to make some tentative statement about "what love is." We invite our readers to examine the work of Allport,[55] Frankl,[56] and Fromm[57] in this respect.

Those authors, alas, as thoughtful and penetrating as they are, leave us wistful, imbued still further with a Faustian restlessness. The fact is that modern psychology has failed to come to terms with love.[58] It tends to be treated in a number of ways: like a "hot potato," or starched into crisp abstractions, or elevated beyond human comprehension or capacity. But one shouldn't blame modern psychology for this "flight from tenderness" any more than the mortals who participate in the exodus.

In the essay introducing Part V of this volume we attempt to "come to terms" with love in a particularly *normative* way. For the moment, forecasting what is ahead, let us go this far: Love is a relationship between two people which allows a full and spontaneous impact. "Full and spontaneous" means: *All. Here. Now.* Love is a kind of fusion with the essence of the other person, but where the two people concerned clearly see their boundary conditions; they know where one begins and the other stops; there is no confusion about "who's who." Love is where two people can care for, show responsibility and respect for, and understand each other.[59] Love is where there is an active concern for the growth and development of the other. In addition, love is adapted to an external reality: to work, to developing a family, to relating to some external social institution.[60]

So we view love as satisfying what the psychoanalyst calls an "object relationship," what Sullivan and others would refer to as "valid communication," and what the existential theorist would term "existential union." But none of these phrases gets close to the basic, deep, potent experience which can make us competent and helpless, savage and tender, jealous and possessive, rational or insane, productive or slothful, lewd or prim, hopeful or cynical. In fact, what other human experience can account for the presence of such complex and polar emotions?[61]

At this point, it might be useful to introduce the readings that fall in this classification of "going toward." Harry Harlow's paper is a delightful study on sexual and loving behavior among monkeys. Paradoxically, while it employs rigor-

---

[54] Fromm, *Art of Loving.*

[55] G. W. Allport, *Personality and Social Encounter* (Boston: Beacon Press, 1960).

[56] V. E. Frankl, *The Doctor and the Soul* (New York: Knopf, 1962), chap. 4.

[57] Fromm, *Art of Loving.*

[58] Allport, *Personality and Social Encounter,* p. 199.

[59] Fromm, *Art of Loving,* p. 25.

[60] See P. Slater "On Social Regression," *American Sociological Review* (June, 1963), pp. 339–64.

[61] We cannot avoid the "metaphysical pathos" we spoke of earlier with respect to normative wishes tincturing accurate description. The very idea of "love" is a normative concept, almost by definition. Hostility or hatred seems less so; perhaps we are more confident of its presence. Or perhaps we believe that the scientific study of hatred is more "manly" than discovering the riddle of love.

ous scientific methods and rhesus monkeys, its findings hold the most interest for psychoanalytic theory. Lewin and Mayer in their papers develop the concept of "friendship" as a special, very important aspect of positive relationships and one that our first edition almost ignored (as does the entire field of social psychology). Both Lewin and Mayer discuss the "distancing" involved in friendship —Lewin, from the point of view of cultural differences, and Mayer, from the point of view of how friends use "openness" or "closeness" of communication to modulate tension.

2. Going against: Hate and fantasy

Moving against people has to do with anger, irritation, hostility, competitiveness, exploitativeness, hate. Its biological counterpart to sex is death and its ubiquitousness is profound. In fact, hate has much in common with love: it is active; it is direct contact; it is an encounter. In fact, it is as difficult to untwine them in life as it is in science: where love is, hate is.

Its centrality to the study of interpersonal feelings is no less than love. *Thanatos* and aggression play an important part in Freud's theories; counterpersonalness is featured in Schutz's work and fight and counterpairing in the group theory of Bion. But we do not need to turn to theory or concepts to corroborate the existence of the aggressive emotion; we have only to observe our everyday experience. A section from Saul Bellow's novel, *The Victim,* brings this point out well:

People met you once or twice and they hated you. What was the reason; what inspired it? . . . You had only to be yourself to provoke them. Why? A sigh of helplessness escaped Leventhal. If they still believed it would work, they would make little dolls of wax and stick pins in them. And why do they pick out this, that, or the other person to hate—Tom, Dick or Harry? No one can say. They hate your smile or the way you blow your nose or use a napkin. Anything will do for an excuse. And meanwhile this Harry, the object of it, doesn't even suspect. How should he know someone is carrying around an image of him (just as a woman may paste a lover's picture on the mirror of her vanity case or a man his wife's snapshot in his wallet) carrying it around to look at and hate? It doesn't even have to be a reproduction of poor Harry. It might as well be the king of diamonds. . . . It doesn't make a bit of difference. Leventhal had to confess that he himself had occasionally sinned in this respect, and he was not obviously a malicious person. But certain people did call out this feeling. He saw Cohen, let us say, once or twice, and then, when his name was mentioned in company, let fall an uncomplimentary remark about him. Not that this Cohen had ever offended him. But what were all the codes and rules, Leventhal reflected, except an answer to our own nature? Would we have to be told "Love!" if we loved as we breathed? No, obviously. Which was not to say that we didn't love but we have to be assisted whenever the motor started missing. . . .[62]

The fictional character quoted, "the victim," communicates a desperate, fruitless complexity about the nature of hostility. He knows hostility is real, that it appears inevitable and impulsive, and that the targets of hostility, the victims,

---

[62] Saul Bellow, *The Victim* (New York: Viking Press, Compass Books, 1958), pp. 80–81.

are selected without reason. We can say all this about love, too. We seem to be left with some of the same ambiguities and complexities when we try to become analytical about hate as we do about love, and perhaps for the same reasons.

There are things we do know about hostility; we know that hostility is related to "frustration," or to some tension the individual is undergoing. However, this explains both too much and too little; individuals vary tremendously in their tolerance of frustration as well as what they perceive to be frustrating. In addition, frustration is only one kind of stimulus which may lead to aggression. So the "frustration-leads-to-aggression" hypothesis is useful, though a bit too restrictive for our analytic purposes.

We prefer the broader perspective of identifying the *threatening conditions* that lead to aggression. Some of these threatening conditions are known to be related to hostility: competition, jealousy, envy, deprivation, status-anxiety, forms of social degradation, thwarted aspirations, to name only a few. We can see more clearly now that "frustration" in the usual sense it is employed is only one form of threat, "that motivational and emotional state which results from persistent blockage of goal-directed behavior."[63] We can also see that threats can emanate from without or from within. An example of the former is a feared boss or a hated rival who spitefully jeopardizes the career of a highly motivated subordinate. An example of the latter is the flood of emotion experienced by an individual during an anxiety attack. In either case the threat imperils—or is perceived to be imperilling—the ego. Thus, our formulation regarding the expression of hostility would be:

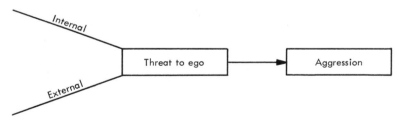

This formulation advances us a little, but we still have to know more about the elements of a threatening situation and how different types of individuals react to these stimuli. We also need to know far more than we now do regarding the people "chosen" as victims. If we can gain more understanding of the interpersonal exchanges between aggressor and victim, we will be on our way toward a theory of interpersonal relationships. This means adumbrating the complexity of the unconscious collusion between the oppressed and the aggressor and the peculiar meaning of the exchange for both.

Some light can be thrown on this issue if we examine the special case of

---

[63] Krech, Crutchfield, and Ballachey, *Individual in Society*, p. 134.

"prejudice."[64] James Baldwin[65] points out that the reason the white man hates the Negro is because the Negro reminds him of those conflictual areas in his personality which the white man struggles to repress: sexuality, rampant impulses, id forces the white man does not "own up to." The same argument was made about anti-Semitism in Hitler's Germany. In both cases we can see that hostility was expressed to certain targets in order to alleviate inner conflict. By identifying these impulses in others and then projecting them outward, the individual is able to reduce his own anxiety. Note two factors in this process: (1) that hostility is a defensive maneuver entered into in order to avoid anxiety; (2) that the targets selected are not random, that they relate to conflicts the aggressor has and cannot consciously face.

This formulation permits us to understand more fully the role of hostility in *interpersonal* relationships. What we can detect is an interesting parallel between the origin of hostility in an individual when he selects a particular target to discharge his anger, and the origin of hostility in a pair or group when it selects a certain target. In both cases we can identify the basis of conflict *via* understanding the victim and the peculiar meaning of the victim for the aggressors. Vogel and Bell in their research on the role of scapegoating in family settings show that the targets of hostility are not accidental, that the person selected is intimately related to the source of tension: "If the parents' most serious unresolved problems were with male figures, the child chosen to represent the family conflict was usually a male child. Similarly, sibling order could be a strong factor. If one or both parents had difficulties with older brothers, an older boy in ghe family might become the scapegoat."[66] Some victims of hostility are "satisfactory" and others are not. Victims are satisfactory only if they enable the attackers to alleviate some important conflict within the aggressive pair.

Another example of this unconscious maneuvering was shown by Bennis,[67] who analyzed a case of severe aggression toward a group member who emerged as an informal leader of the group while the formal leader was absent. When the formal leader returned, the substitute leader was excessively attacked for no apparent reason. We should point out that this particular person was selected as the informal leader because of his perceived resemblance to the formal leader. It was inferred that the critical rage vented toward the substitute was due to the feelings of revenge which could not be expressed openly toward the "deserting"

---

[64] We are talking here and throughout this section on "going against" of excessive or defensive hostility. We do not have in mind *appropriate* hatred or rage as that, for example, which might be directed toward a destructive person. Prejudice, by definition, implies a type of hostility which is excessive, off-target, and caused by reasons quite often unconscious to the aggressor; there is *always* some distortion of reality in prejudice. Realistic or appropriate hostility, as we define it, is based on some legal constraints and ethical codes; it is willful, directed to the appropriate source of threat, and conscious.

[65] James Baldwin, *The Fire Next Time* (New York: Dial Press, 1963).

[66] E. Vogal and N. Bell, "The Emotionally Disturbed Child as the Family Scapegoat," *The Family*, N. W. Bell and E. F. Vogal (eds.) (Glencoe, Ill.: The Free Press, 1960), pp. 382–97.

[67] Bennis, "Defenses against 'Depressive-Anxiety' in Groups: The Case of the Absent Leader," *Merrill-Palmer Quarterly*, Vol. 7 (1961), pp. 3–30.

leader. Thus the substitute leader was the victim of hostility which was felt, but unexpressed, toward the formal leader. This enabled the group to avoid, for the time being, their negative impulses toward the formal authority, a more anxiety-producing and threatening object for them than their peer.

From these examples we can detect the complicated vicissitudes of hostility. It serves a number of purposes simultaneously. First, it avoids anxiety in the organism whether a pair, a group, or a person. Second, it identifies the source of the anxiety and projects it outward, thereby doing two things at once: discharging hostility and destroying what one can't face internally. Third, the victims frequently unconsciously collude with the aggressors in becoming the target of the aggressors' rage.[68] Fourth, and most centrally, *hostility preserves distance and precludes a full and spontaneous relationship between the oppressed and the attacker.* This is equally true for the "cooperating oppressors" (the husband and wife who scapegoat a child) as it is between couple and child. Continued scapegoating causes a lack of communication, which in turn prevents discovery of the sources of their conflicts. But as long as the conflict is not discovered and "worked through," the scapegoating continues.

And now we can return to Saul Bellow's victim and his profound questions: "People met you once or twice and they hated you. What was the reason; what inspired it?" We are still unable to formulate a satisfactory answer for him. What may be put into clearer focus, though, is the idea that in a relationship of hate, neither the victim nor the aggressor can influence or change the nature of their emotional exchange until their own relationship is more fully understood. There is an essential helplessness for the victim; he cannot "do anything" when he is used and exploited as a target for "projective identification";[69] the aggressor is equally helpless for he dimly perceives that the anxiety he is attempting to ward off may have only peripheral relevance to the victim.

So far we have discussed hostility as an altogether undesirable state, as a defense against anxiety and as a "distancing" factor in interpersonal relationships. There are, of course, positive and productive aspects of hostility. Freud[70] believed that civilization springs from instinctual renunciation; repressed aggression leads to work under many conditions and sublimation and substitution are often channeled into the service of "good works." More recently, Semrad and Arsenian[71] have contended that hostility may lead to increased productivity in group set-

---

[68] This is highly speculative as well as complicated. In the study by Bennis ("Absent Leader," *Merrill-Palmer Quarterly*, 1961) referred to earlier, it was found that the two individuals who drew the most hostility during the formal leader's absence were attacked because they persisted in reminding the group of his absence. In both cases the fathers of these two men died during their childhood. Thus, it seemed possible that they were evoking hostility as a way of draining off guilt associated with an earlier loss, a loss for which they feel in some degree responsible.

[69] The concept of "projective identification" developed by Melanie Klein appears to fit all the cases under the heading of "prejudice." M. Klein, "On Identification," in *New Directions in Psychoanalysis* (New York: Basic Books, 1956), chap. 13.

[70] Sigmund Freud, *Civilization and Its Discontents* (London: Hogarth, 1930).

[71] E. Semrad and J. Arsenian, "On the Concept of Billets" (Boston: Massachusetts Mental Health Center, 1958), unpublished manuscript.

tings. Mills[72] shows, in an ingenious experiment, that certain forms of hostility— toward the person in authority—may be extremely functional for work in interpersonal settings.

Let us review the papers that are included in this edition under the "going against" section. First, the experiment by Milgram (see page 60) reveals some perplexing findings about "destructive obedience."[73] It raises some issues—including the ethics of science (summarized in Baumrind's letter included in this edition)—which leave the editors aroused and uncertain. In fact, we struggled for some time (before printing this in the first edition) among ourselves but finally decided that the results of this experiment, extraordinary and cruel as they are, throw light on a very important issue. Published after the first edition went to press, Diana Baumrind explores some of the ethical questions which confronted us when the first edition was published in 1963. From E. T. Hall's classic, *The Hidden Dimension,* we have included a brilliant illustration of what we have termed an "ecological approach to interpersonal relationships." Almost any chapter of the book would suffice, but we thought that a culturally induced "going against" (or, equally appropriate for the other two modalities, for that matter) would be welcome to our readers.

Both love and hate, as we said earlier, share some common properties. They both mobilize affect and involvements; they represent the basic currency in interpersonal changes. Let us go on to the third modality now, "moving away."

3. Going away: Isolation and withdrawal

In his essay "On Narcissism," Freud[74] pointed to the "introversion of the libido": the fact, often observed in the clinic, that people seemed to have withdrawn their attention and feelings from the external world to themselves. Horney describes this type of interpersonal style in the following manner:

> The underlying principle . . . is never to become so attached to anybody or anything that he or it becomes indispensable. Another pronounced need is for privacy. The person is like the person in a hotel room who rarely removes the "Do Not Disturb" sign from his door. His independence, like the whole phenomenon of detachment of which it is a part, has a negative orientation; it is aimed at not being influenced, coerced, tied, obligated.[75]

Loneliness, withdrawal, isolation, estrangement, alienation are all words that seem descriptive of this interpersonal style; catatonic stupor, depression, and psychosis are all clinical correlates of what we have in mind by "going away." Let us be clear about what we do *not* mean by "isolation and withdrawal."

---

[72] Mills, *Group Transformation.*

[73] S. Milgram, "Behavioral Study of Obedience," *Journal of Abnormal and Social Psychology,* Vol. 67, No. 4 (1963), pp. 371–78. See pp. 60–72 of this volume.

[74] Sigmund Freud, "On Narcissism: An Introduction," *Collected Papers, IV* (London: Hogarth, 1953).

[75] Horney, *Inner Conflicts.*

We do not mean that condition of life where a person broadens and deepens his humanity through an experience of "loneliness." Moustakas,[76] for example, tells us movingly about his "gripping, painful, exhilarating, and beautiful experience of being utterly alone and separated from others." We do not mean isolation or withdrawal caused by "reality factors," such as moving into a strange city or the self-imposed withdrawal due to "role imprisonment." Woodrow Wilson wrote to friends about his own loneliness caused by holding public office which brought him only "irreparable loss and desperate suffering."[77] We do not mean by withdrawal those temporary aberations sometimes noticed as a pathological reaction to stress and referred to by Greenson[78] and Strassman, Thaler, and Schein,[79] as "apathy." We do not have in mind, when we talk of isolation and withdrawal, those individuals who think of themselves as "mavericks" or "independent thinkers" who refuse to conform or those individuals who view themselves as vigilantes of dissent.

When we talk of "going away" what we have in mind is a characteristic orientation toward the outside world and interpersonal relationships which can be summarized by Sartre's: "Hell is other people." We have in mind a *chronic* withdrawal from involvement with the environment, a loss of contact with external reality. The kind of loneliness and isolation we have in mind is similar to Fromm-Reichmann's notion of loneliness: it is nonconstructive and disintegrative. So we are not discussing here "independence" or "autonomy" or "self-actualization" or any of those "peak experiences" an individual reports when he is "at one" with himself. We are referring to that state of human affairs, possibly as unbiquitous as love and hate, which realizes its aims through reduced contact with external reality.

It is something of a contradiction to talk of isolation and withdrawal as an *interpersonal* style. The "moving against and moving toward" styles are in contact with their environments, while the "moving away" style is detached and dead insofar as other people are concerned. There are, however, at least three types of "going away" which evolve in an interpersonal context with resulting unique interactions.

1. First we can mention *narcissistic withdrawal,* or what Slater refers to as "the withdrawal in strength." The narcissist doesn't "need" people in the conventional sense; he appears autonomous and ingenious, a man with power, fascination, and charisma.[80] The paradox is that the narcissist—the most inward of

---

[76] Moustakas, *Loneliness.*

[77] *Ibid,* p. 82.

[78] R. R. Greenson *Psychoanalytic Quarterly,* Vol. 18 (1949).

[79] H. D. Strassman, M. B. Thaler, and E. H. Schein, "A Prisoner of War Syndrome: Apathy as a Reaction to Severe Stress," *American Journal of Psychiatry,* Vol. 112 (1956).

[80] We should point out that this is true only when the ego strength of the narcissist is strong and adaptive. See Philip Slater's, "On Social Regression," *American Sociological Review* (June 1963) pp. 334–64.

men—seems to have a certain seductive fascination for most people and it is upon him that other men lean;[81] he is the one that others seek to follow and emulate.[82] The narcissist does not lean on others; so the relationship which ensues is a "tilted" one, one without reciprocation, but interpersonal nevertheless. The interesting thing here is that most people simply will not leave the narcissist "alone," a point Slater makes with brilliant insistence.

2. The main point of Slater's essay has to do with *social regression,* a form of interpersonal withdrawal which draws the social anxiety of the group because of its violations—real and fantasied—of group and societal norms. It is a form of libidinal contraction, a withdrawal in concert with someone else, which denies the existence of others and imperils the integrity of social institutions. An example of social regression might be a violation of the incest taboo where a brother and sister engage in sexual relations; or where a man and woman "live in sin." What is important for us to note is the social and interpersonal aspects of this withdrawal and how the libidinal contraction tends to intensify the expression of interpersonal feelings of the withdrawing unit.[83]

3. The last form of withdrawal we will mention here was covered in the first edition of *Interpersonal Dynamics* by Bateson et al. in their brilliant analysis of communication difficulties.[84] Their theoretical framework identifies the kinds of communication patterns set up in families (although painfully noticeable in other social patterning, such as authority relations in organizations) which can lead to various forms of psychoses. We can refer to this type of withdrawal as the "double-bind," withdrawal caused by a complete inability to understand the mixed signals induced by ambivalence. So when the mother tells her child to "go to bed," the child can interpret this message in various ways—such as "get the hell out of my sight!" or "Darling, you'd better get the proper amount of sleep." Or when the boss asks his subordinate if he's too autocratic, the subordinate may not understand whether he should respond with submission or rebellion. And so on.

The readings in the "going away" section reflect our interest in the interpersonal aspect of withdrawal and isolation. (The Bateson et al. and Slater readings, which appeared in the first edition, are also good examples of social forms of withdrawal.) In this edition, we have included a reading by Slater on nonpermanent relations (typically induced by a terrifying rate of social mobility) and a new paper by Robert Weiss on certain deficiencies in social relations, illustrated by parents without partners. In addition, we have reprinted the delightful, bitter-

---

[81] Freud, 1953.

[82] J. Adelson, "The Teacher as a Model," *American Scholar,* Vol. 30 No. 3 (1961), pp. 383–406. See p. 335 this volume.

[83] In the Thomas Mann story, "The Blood of the Walsungs" (*Stories of Three Decades* [New York: Knopf, 1936], pp. 279–319), note that the dyadic withdrawal of the twins ended in sexual intercourse.

[84] Gregory Bateson, Don D. Jackson, Jay Haley, and John Weakland, "Toward a Theory of Schizophrenia," *Behavioral Science* (October 1956), pp. 251–64.

sweet fable (reminiscent of Thurber's best writing) by Allen Wheelis, the psycho-analyst turned writer.

Our knowledge is still meager; we know very little. Fromm-Reichmann says:

> . . . loneliness is one of the least satisfactory conceptualized psychological phenomena, not even mentioned in most psychiatric textbooks. Very little is known among scientists about its genetics and psychodynamics, and various different experiences which are descriptively and dynamically as different from one another as culturally determined loneliness, self-imposed aloneness, compulsory solitude, isolation, and real loneliness are all thrown into the one terminological basket called "loneliness."[85]

These words of Fromm-Reichmann could be applied to all three interpersonal styles examined in this essay: love, hate, *and* isolation. We are also left, alas, with a distinct feeling that our analysis of aggression was more convincing than our discussion of love. Who can say why? What we are left with now, at the close of this essay, is an awesome feeling that we have barely scratched the surface of our topic and that we must again turn for help outward to the poet and inward to ourselves.

The heterosexual affectional system in monkeys[*][1]

Harry F. Harlow

The inspiration for this address came from observational data obtained from seven guinea pigs—two males and three females in a colony and two females brought in temporarily. Observations were provided by my ten-year-old daughter Pamela. These observations were made with love and endearment, and the behavior observed was endearment and love. Furthermore, these observations were made at a level of objectivity difficult for an adult to attain in this field.

Male and female guinea pigs are very fond of each other. They stare blissfully into the limpid pink or ruby or midnight-blue pools of each other's eyes. They nuzzle and they cuddle and the end production is not characterized by rush or

[85] Fromm-Reichmann, "Loneliness."

[*] "The Heterosexual Affectional System in Monkeys," Harry F. Harlow. Reprinted from the *American Psychologist* (January 1962). Used by permission.

[1] This research was supported by funds received from the Graduate School of the University of Wisconsin, from the Ford Foundation, and from Grant M-4528, National Institutes of Health.

rape. After all, one does not have to hurry if there is no hurry to be had. This, Pamela has witnessed several times. A caged, virgin adult female was brought by a friend for mating. Twirp, Pamela's large, black, gentle male, was put into the cage with the new female. He purred, nuzzled her, brushed up against her, smelled and licked her, and gradually conquered the frightened animal. A half-hour later they were snuggled up next to each other, peaceful and content, and they lived in bliss for several weeks until another friend brought in her female and Twirp repeated his patient, gentle approach. Twirp has convinced me that some male guinea pigs, at least, are endowed with an innate sense of decency, and I am happy to say that this is the way most male monkeys behave. I presume that there are some men who have as deep a depth of dignity as guinea pigs.

The guest stands, unfortunately, ended peaceful coexistence in the colony. For many months the five adult guinea pigs had lived amiably in one large cage, with Twirp in command and the second male playing second fiddle. While Twirp was host to the visiting females, White Patch commanded the permanent harem. When Twirp was reintroduced to the colony cage, it took but ten seconds to discover that he would not be tolerated. White Patch bared his teeth and lunged at Twirp, and to save the males, a new cage was acquired.

This led to various divisions of the females and led Pamela to discover particular male guinea pigs like particular female guinea pigs, and they squeal piteously when separated, even when the female is so bulging with babies that she can offer the male nothing in terms of drive reduction. Particular female guinea pigs like particular male guinea pigs. Tastes seem fairly stable, for even after weeks of peaceful residence with the unfavored male, the female will still attempt to get to her favorite male, and after weeks of quiet residence with unfavored females, the male will still try to get to his favorite female.

The females, like the males, defend their rights. In the happy one-cage days two females were separated from the group to care for their litters. White Thrush, in an advanced stage of pregnancy, lived alone with the males. When Chirp was returned to the colony cage after three weeks of maternal chores, both males approached enthusiastically, making friendly gestures. But Hell hath no fury like a female guinea pig spurned, and White Thrush would not tolerate infidelity. She hissed at Chirp, and lunged, and as Chirp fled from the cage, White Thrush pursued, teeth bared. The males also pursued, clucking and purring in anticipation. The males won, and White Thrush sulked the rest of the day. Guinea pigs apparently have a well-developed heterosexual affectional system.

Sex behavior in the guinea pig has been intensively investigated, and there are exhaustive studies on what has been called the sex drive, but I know of no previous mention of or allusion to the guinea pig's heterosexual affectional system. No doubt this stems from the paradigm which has been established for research in this area.

In a typical experiment a male guinea pig and a female guinea pig in estrus are taken from their individual cages, dropped into a barren chamber, and observed for 15 minutes. In such a situation there is a high probability that something is going to happen and that it will happen rapidly and repeatedly. The thing that happens will be reliable and valid, and all that one needs to do to score it is to count. It is my suggestion that from this time onward it be known as the "flesh count." Sometimes I wonder how men and women would behave if they were dropped naked into a barren chamber with full realization that they had only fifteen minutes to take advantage of the opportunities offered them. No doubt there would be individual differences, but we would obtain little information on the human heterosexual affectional system from such an experiment.

FIGURE 1
Initial response to female sexual-present posture. The male subsequently accepted the invitation.

Sex is not an adventitious act. It is not here today and gone tomorrow. It starts with the cradle, and as a part of the human tragedy it wanes before the grave. We have traced and are tracing the development of the heterosexual affectional system in monkeys.

We believe that the heterosexual affection system in the rhesus monkey, like all the other affectional systems, goes through a series of developmental stages —an infantile heterosexual stage, a preadolescent stage, and an adolescent and mature heterosexual stage. Although these stages are in considerable part overlapping and cannot be sharply differentiated in time, we would think of the infantile stage as lasting throughout the first year and being characterized by inadequate and often inappropriate sexual play and posturing. The preadolescent stage, beginning in the second year and ending in the third year in the female and the fourth year in the male, is characterized by adequate and appropriate sexual play and posturing, but incompleteness. The adolescent and adult stage is characterized by behaviors which are similar in form but give rise to productive outcomes which are also reproductive.

Since in this paper sex is an unavoidable issue, we present illustrations of normal adult macaque monkey sex behavior. Sexual invitation may be initiated by the female, as in Figure 1, by a present pattern with buttocks oriented toward the male, tail elevated, and the female looking backward with a fear-grimace (not threat) pattern involving flattened ears and lip smacking. As you can see, this pattern need not involve rape nor even rush on the part of the male. The male may also solicit, as in the case of the animal in the foreground of Figure 2; this animal has assumed a posture soliciting either grooming or more intimate favors. These patterns seldom elicit violent, uncontrolled, reflex behaviors. Normal male

FIGURE 2
Initial response to male sexual-present posture. The female (No. 48) subsequently approached and groomed the male.

and female overt sex behavior is shown in Figure 3, the male having assumed the complex sex posture involving ankle clasp, dorsoventral mounting, and clasp of the female's buttocks. The partner demonstrates the complete female sexual pattern of elevating the buttocks, lowering the head, and looking backward. There have been millions of rhesus monkeys for millions of years, and there will be more in the future.

We have traced the development of the infantile heterosexual stage during the first year of life in two test situations using observational techniques. One is our playroom, illustrated in Figure 4, which consists of a room 8 feet high with 36 feet of floor space. In this room are a platform, ladder, revolving wheel, and flying rings to encourage the infants' adaptation to a three-dimensional world, and there is an assortment of puzzles and toys for quieter activities. Two groups of four infants each, half of each group male and half female, have been observed

FIGURE 3
Normal male and female sexual positioning

FIGURE 4
Playroom test situation

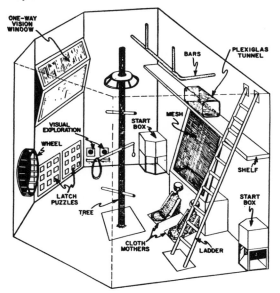

in the playroom daily over many months. The second apparatus is shown in Figure 5. This is the playpen situation, and it consists of four large living cages and adjoining pens. Each living cage houses a mother and infant, and a three-inch by five-inch opening in the wall between cage and playpen units enables the infants to leave the home cage at any time but restrains the mothers. The playpen units are separated by wiremesh panels which are removed one or two hours a day to allow the infants to interact in pairs during the first 180 days and both in pairs and in groups of four during the next half-year of life. Again, we are referring to data gathered from two playpen setups, each housing four infants and their real or surrogate mothers. Insofar as the infantile heterosexual stage is concerned, it makes little or no difference from which situation we take our data.

FIGURE 5
Playpen test situation

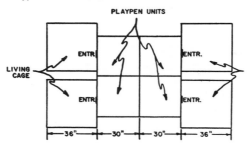

The outstanding finding in both the playroom and playpen is that male and female infants show differences in sex behavior from the second month of life onward. The males show earlier and more frequent sex behavior than do females, and there are differences in the patterns displayed by the sexes. The males almost never assume the female sex-posture patterns, even in the earliest months. The females, on the other hand, sometimes display the male pattern of sex posturing, but this is infrequent after ten months of age. Predominantly, females show the female pattern, and exceptional instances are to other females, not males. Frequency of sex behavior for both males and females increases progressively with age. There is no latency period—except when the monkeys are very tired.

The early infantile sexual behaviors are fragmentary, transient, and involve little more than passivity by the female and disoriented grasping and thrusting by the male. Thus, the male may thrust at the companion's head in a completely disoriented manner or laterally across the midline of the body, as in Figure 6. However, it is our opinion that these behaviors are more polymorphous than perverse.

Thus, as soon as the sexual responses can be observed and measured, male and female sexual behaviors differ in form. Furthermore, there are many other

FIGURE 6
Immature male and female sexual posturing, playroom observation

behaviors which differ between males and females as soon as they can be observed and measured. Figure 7 shows the development of threat responses by males and females in the playroom, and these differences are not only statistically significant, but they also have face validity. Analysis of this behavior shows that males threaten other males and females but that females are innately blessed with better manners; in particular, little girl monkeys do not threaten little boy monkeys.

The withdrawal pattern—retreat when confronted by another monkey—is graphed for the playroom in Figure 8, and the significance is obvious. Females evince a much higher incidence of passive responses, which are characterized by immobility with buttocks oriented toward the male and head averted, and a similar pattern, rigidity, in which the body is stiffened and fixed.

In all probability the withdrawal and passivity behavior of the female and the forceful behavior of the male gradually lead to the development of normal sex

FIGURE 7
Frequency of threat responses by males and females in the playroom

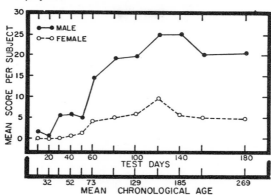

FIGURE 8

Frequency of withdrawal responses by males and females in the playroom

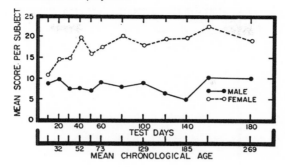

behaviors. The tendency for the female to orient away from the male and for the male to clasp and tussle at the female's buttocks predisposes the consorts to assume the proper positions. The development of the dorsally oriented male sex-behavior pattern as observed in the playroom situation is shown in Figure 9 and may be described as a composite yearning and learning curve.

Infant male and female monkeys show clear-cut differences in behavior of far greater social significance than neonatal and infantile sex responses. Grooming patterns, which are basic to macaque socialization, show late maturation, but as is seen in Figure 10, when they appear, they sharply differentiate the two sexes. Caressing is both a property and prerogative of the females. Basic to normal macaque socialization is the infant-infant or peer-peer affectional system, and this arises out of and is dependent upon the play patterns which we have described

FIGURE 9

Percentage of all male mounts (immature and mature) in the playroom that shows dorsal orientation (mature pattern)

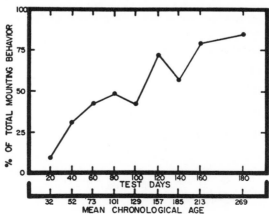

FIGURE 10

Frequency of grooming responses made by males and females in the playroom

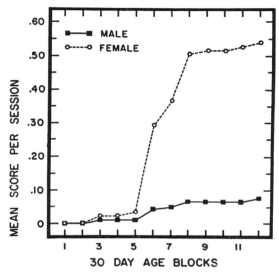

elsewhere and only mention here. As is shown in the solid lines of Figure 11, play behavior in the playroom is typically initiated by males, seldom by females. However, let us not belittle the female, for they also serve who only stand and wait. Contact play is far more frequent among the males than the females and is almost invariably initated by the males. Playpen data graphed in Figure 12 show that real rough-and-tumble play is strictly for the boys.

I am convinced that these data have almost total generality to man. Several

FIGURE 11

Frequency of play-initiations by males and females to monkeys of the same (male-male, female-female) and other sex (male-female, female-male). Observations are from the playroom.

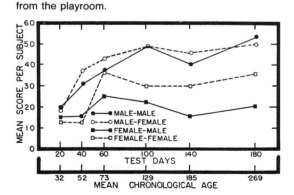

months ago I was present at a school picnic attended by 25 second-graders and their parents. While the parents sat and the girls stood around or skipped about hand in hand, 13 boys tackled and wrestled, chased and retreated. No little girl chased any little boy, but some little boys chased some little girls. Human beings have been here for two million years, and they'll probably be here two million more.

These secondary sex-behavior differences probably exist throughout the primate order, and, moreover, they are innately determined biological differences

FIGURE 12
Frequency of occurrence of "rough-and-tumble" play for two males and two females in the playroom through the first year of life

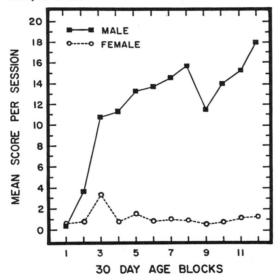

regardless of any cultural overlap. Because of their nature they tend automatically to produce sexual segregation during middle and later childhood, but fortunately this separation is neither complete nor permanent. Behavioral differences may very well make it easy through cultural means to impose a sexual latency period in the human being from childhood to puberty. We emphasize the fact that the latency period is not a biological stage in which primary sex behavior is suppressed, but a cultural stage built upon secondary behavioral differences.

We believe that our data offer convincing evidence that sex behaviors differ in large part because of genetic factors. However, we claim no originality for the discovery of intersex behavioral differences. In 1759 Laurence Sterne in his book *Tristram Shandy* described male and female differences at the most critical period in Tristram Shandy's development; indeed, it would not be possible to conceive of a more critical period.

"*Pray, my dear,* quoth my mother, *have you not forgot to wind up the*

*clock?___Good G____! cried my father, making an exclamation, but taking care
to moderate his voice at the same time___Did ever woman, since the creation
of the world, interrupt a man with such a silly question?"*[2]

Men and women have differed in the past and they will differ in the future.

It is possible that the listener has been dismayed by the frequent reference
to sex and the relatively infrequent reference to affection. Out of these infantile
behavior patterns, both sexual and nonsexual, develop the affectional bonds and
the social ordering that appear to be important or even essential to the full
development of the heterosexual affectional system of macaques. Traumatic
affectional errors, both transient and prolonged, may have devastating effects
upon subsequent social and sexual behaviors.

For some years we have been attempting to establish experimental neuroses
in infant monkeys by having them live on unfriendly and inconsistent mother
surrogates. One preparation was a rejecting mother that on schedule or demand
separated her baby when a wire frame embedded in her spun-nylon covering was
displaced violently upward and backward. The baby was disturbed, but as soon
as the frame was returned to its resting position, the baby returned to cling to
its surrogate mother as tightly as ever. Next we developed an air-blast mother
with a series of nozzles down the entire center of her body which released
compressed air under high pressure—an extremely noxious stimulus to monkeys.
The blasted baby never even left the mother, but in its moments of agony and
duress, clung more and more tightly to the unworthy mother. Where else can
a baby get protection? Apparently our infant had never read Neal Miller's theory
that avoidance gradients are precipitous and approach gradients gradual and
tenuous, for love conquered all.

We next devised a shaking mother, which on schedule or demand shook her
infant with unconscionable violence until its teeth chattered. The infant endured
its tribulations by clinging more and more tightly. At the present time we believe
we may be on the threshold of success through Jay Mawbray's creation of the
porcupine mother, which extrudes brass spikes all over its ventral surface. Preliminary studies on two infants suggest that they are emotionally disturbed. Whether
or not we eventually succeed, the fact remains that babies are reluctant to develop
experimental neuroses, and at one time we even wondered if this were possible.

During the time that we were producing these evil mothers, we observed the
monkeys which we had separated from their mothers at birth and raised under
various mothered and nonmothered conditions. The first 47 baby monkeys were
raised during the first year of life in wire cages so arranged that the infants could
see and hear and call to other infants but not contact them. Now they are five
to seven years old and sexually mature. As month after month and year after year
have passed, these monkeys have appeared to be less and less normal. We have
seen them sitting in their cages strangely mute, staring fixedly into space, rela-

---

[2] Sterne, Laurence. *The Life and Opinions of Tristram Shandy, Gentleman,* J. A. Work (ed.),
(New York: Odyssey Press, 1940), p. 5.

tively indifferent to people and other monkeys. Some clutch their heads in both hands and rock back and forth—the autistic behavior pattern that we have seen in babies raised on wire surrogates. Others, when approached or even left alone, go into violent frenzies of rage, grasping and tearing at their legs with such fury that they sometimes require medical care.

Eventually we realized that we had a laboratory full of neurotic monkeys. We had failed to produce neurotic monkeys by thoughtful planning and creative research, but we had succeeded in producing neurotic monkeys through misadventure. To err is human.

Because of housing pressures some of these monkeys and many of our surrogate-raised monkeys lived in pairs for several years while growing to sexual maturity, but we have seldom seen normal sex behavior, and we certainly have not had the validating criterion of newborn baby monkeys. Instead, these monkeys treat each other like brother and sister, proving that two can live in complete propinquity with perfect propriety as long as no one cares.

Their reason for being, as we saw it, was to produce babies for our researches, and so at this point we deliberately initiated a breeding program which was frighteningly unsuccessful. When the older, wire-cage-raised males were paired with the females at the peak of estrus, the introduction led only to fighting, so violent and vicious that separation was essential to survival. In no case was there any indication of normal sex behavior. Frequently the females were the aggressors; even the normal praying mantis waits until the sex act is completed.

Pairing such cloth-surrogate-raised monkeys as were sexually mature gave little better end results. Violent aggression was not the rule, and there was attempted sex behavior, but it was unreproductive since both the male and female behaviors were of the infantile type we have already described.

At this point we took the 17 oldest of our cage-raised animals, females showing consistent estrous cycles and males obviously mature, and engaged in an intensive re-education program, pairing the females with our most experienced, patient, and gentle males, and the males with our most eager, amiable, and successful breeding females. When the laboratory-bred females were smaller than the sophisticated males, the girls would back away and sit down facing the males, looking appealingly at these would-be consorts. Their hearts were in the right place, but nothing else was. When the females were larger than the males, we can only hope that they misunderstood the males' intentions, for after a brief period of courtship, they would attack and maul the ill-fated male. Females show no respect for a male they can dominate.

The training program for the males was equally unsatisfactory. They approached the females with a blind enthusiasm, but it was a misdirected enthusiasm. Frequently the males would grasp the females by the side of the body and thrust laterally, leaving them working at cross purposes with reality. Even the most persistent attempts by these females to set the boys straight came to naught. Finally, these females either stared at the males with complete contempt or attacked them in utter frustration. It became obvious that they, like their human counterparts, prefer maturer men. We realized then that we had established, not a program of breeding, but a program of brooding.

We had in fact been warned. Our first seven laboratory-born babies were raised in individual cages while being trained on a learning test battery. William Mason planned to test their social behaviors subsequently, and great care had been taken to keep the babies socially isolated and to prevent any physical contacts. Neonatal baby monkeys required 24-hour-a-day care, and infant monkeys need ministrations beyond a 40-hour week. We had assigned the evening care to Kathy, a maternal bit of fluff who had worked for several years as a monkeytester while studying to become an elementary school teacher.

Checking on his wards one night near 10 P.M., Mason found Kathy sitting on the floor surrounded by seven baby monkeys, all eight of the primates playing happily together. Before the horrified scientist could express his outrage, Kathy had risen to her full height of five feet two. Already anticipating the carping criticisms which he was formulating, she shook her finger in his face and spoke with conviction: "Dr. Mason, I'm an education student and I know that it is improper and immoral to blight the social development of little children. I am right and you are wrong!"

Although we were angry with Kathy, we did think there was a certain humor in the situation and we did not worry about our monkeys. We simply transferred Kathy to an office job. Alas, she could not have been more right and we could not have been more wrong! We have already described the social-sexual life of these 7 monkeys and the next 40 to come.

Two years later we had more than theoretical reasons to be disturbed because Mason tested a group of these isolation-raised monkeys, then between 2.5 and 3.5 years of age, and found evidence of severe social abnormalities, which might be described as a sociopathic syndrome. He matched the laboratory-raised monkeys on the basis of weight and dentition patterns with monkeys that had been born and raised in the wild for the first 12 to 18 months, then captured and subjected to various kinds of housing and caging treatments for the next year or two. In the test situations the laboratory-raised monkeys, as compared with feral monkeys, showed infantile sexual behavior, absence of grooming, exaggerated aggression, and absence of affectional interaction as measured by cooperation.

We are now quite certain that this sociopathic syndrome does not stem from the fact that the baby monkeys were raised in the laboratory but from *how* they were raised in the laboratory. Our infants raised in the laboratory by real monkey mothers and permitted opportunity for the development of normal infant-infant affection demonstrate normal male and female sexual behavior when they enter the second year of life. Furthermore, our playroom and playpen studies show that infant monkeys raised on cloth mothers but given the opportunity to form normal infant-infant affectional patterns also develop normal sexual responses.

In a desperate attempt to assist a group of 18 three- to four-year-old cloth-surrogate-raised monkeys, half of them males and half females, we engaged in

FIGURE 13
Group of cloth-surrogate-raised monkeys on the monkey island in the Madison Zoo

a group-psychotherapy program, placing these animals for two months on the monkey island in the Madison Zoo, as shown in Figure 13. Their summer vacation on the enchanted island was not without avail, and social grooming responses rapidly developed and were frequent in occurrence. After a few days of misunderstanding, patterns of social ordering developed, and a number of males and females developed friendship patterns. Unfortunately, sexual behavior was infrequent and the behavior that was observed was completely inadequate —at least from our point of view. In desperation we finally introduced our most experienced, most patient, and most kindly breeding male, Smiley (the male in Figures 1 and 2), and he rapidly established himself as king of the island and prepared to take full advantage of the wealth of opportunity which surrounded him. Fortunately, the traumatic experiences he encountered with unreceptive females have left no apparent permanent emotional scars, and now that he has been returned to our laboratory breeding colony, he is again making an important contribution to our research program. If normal sexual behavior occurred, no member of our observational team ever saw it, and had a female become pregnant, we would have believed in parthenogenesis.

But let us return to the monkeys that we left on the island and the older ones that we left in their cages. A year has passed, and the frustrations that both we and our monkeys experienced are in some small part nothing but a memory. We constructed larger and more comfortable breeding cages, and we designed a very large experimental breeding room 8 feet by 8 feet by 8 feet in size with appropriate platforms and a six-foot tree. Apparently, we designed successful seraglios for I can report that not all love's labors have been lost. It does appear that the males are completely expendable unless they can be used in a program of artificial insemination. Certainly we can find no evidence that there is a destiny that shapes their ends unless some Skinnerite can help us with the shaping process. We have, however, had better success with some of the females, particularly the females raised on cloth surrogates.

FIGURE 14
Typical behavior of unmothered mother toward her infant. Mother is looking upward while crushing her baby against the cage floor.

Even so, one of the wire-caged-raised females is a mother and another is pregnant. Three cloth-surrogate females are mothers and four or five are expectant. We give all the credit to three breeding males. One, Smiley, does not take "no" for an answer. Smiley has a way with females. Patient, gentle, and persuasive, he has overcome more than one planned program of passive resistance. One female did not become pregnant until the fifth successive month of training. Month after month she has changed, and now she is mad about the boy. Male No. 342 behaves very much like Smiley. Even when females threaten him, he does not harm them. Given time, he has been able to overcome more than one reluctant dragon, and he is a master of the power of positive suggestion.

Breeding male No. 496 has helped us greatly, particularly with the younger, cloth-surrogate-raised females. His approach differs from that of Smiley and No. 342. His technique transcends seduction, and in contact bridge terms it may be described as an approach-forcing system.

Combining our human and male-monkey talents, we are winning the good fight and imparting to naive and even resistant female monkeys the priceless gift of motherhood. Possibly it is a Pyrrhic victory. As every scientist knows, the solution of one scientific problem inevitably leads to another, and this is our fate (Figure 14). Month after month female monkeys that never knew a real mother themselves become mothers—helpless, hopeless, heartless mothers devoid, or almost devoid, of any maternal feeling.

Resolving social conflicts[*]

Kurt Lewin

THE SOCIAL DISTANCE BETWEEN INDIVIDUALS IN THE UNITED STATES AND IN GERMANY

Considering the structure of the individual as a social being, there seem to be the following differences between the typical American and typical German. The average *"social distance"* (the term used as in sociology) *between different individuals seems to be smaller in the United States so far as the surface regions,* or, as one may say, the *"peripheral regions,"of the personality are concerned.* That means the American is more willing to be open to other individuals and to share certain situations with other individuals than the German.

Quite commonly strangers on the street may greet one another with a smile, a behavior unusual in Germany. People waiting for the bus may start to discuss the weather, and in the train, conversation between strangers starts more easily than in Germany. (There is certainly a difference between the people of a large and a small town, both in the United States and Germany. The Englishman,

* *Resolving Social Conflicts*, pp. 18–22, 23–25, by Kurt Lewin. Copyright 1948 by Harper & Row, Publishers, Incorporated. Reprinted by permission of the publishers.

at least outside of England, may be even more reserved in such situations than a German.) The American seems more friendly and more ready to help a stranger. It is more customary in the United States to invite a visitor, who is not a personal friend, to lunch or to one's home, than in Germany under similar circumstances. Nearly every German coming to the United States admires the natural ease and the efficiency with which the American generally takes care of all the minor difficulties a newcomer has to face.

In boarding houses one finds people sitting in their rooms with the door wide open, so that anyone might step in. The American seems to have decidedly less need for privacy in certain regions of life. It is possible to find the office door of even a president of a college open all day; so everybody can see with whom he is conversing and in what manner he is acting. Such behavior would be unthinkable in Germany even for an unimportant official, one of whose techniques in getting respect and showing his importance is to let people wait a long time in front of his closed door. In the United States it would be bad taste to let other persons wait, however great the difference in the social status of the persons involved may be. This difference between the United States and Germany is very striking, and is an expression of the democratic attitude toward the equal rights of everybody and of the greater general accessibility of the American.

The average American talks less loudly than the German, both in a private conversation, and in public. It may well be that this is due to the fact that the peripheral regions of the U-type are more accessible. Besides the G-type tends, as we will see, to a more emotional and aggressive behavior.[1]

Nevertheless, the average "social distance" between persons in the United States seems not to be smaller in every respect, but only in regard to more peripheral layers of the person. The more intimate "central" regions of personality seem to be at least as separated between different persons, and at least as difficult to get access to as among Germans. For instance, relations between boys and girls might progress in the United States more easily up to a certain point, whereas the step leading to an intimate relationship seems to be more clearly marked than in Germany. In Germany, there is a more gradual transition in social relationships from the very peripheral to the very intimate. Germans entering the United States notice usually that the degree of friendly and close relation, which one may achieve as a newcomer within a few weeks, is much higher than under similar circumstances in Germany. Compared with Germans, Americans seem to make quicker progress towards friendly relations in the beginning, and with many more persons. Yet this development often stops at a certain point; and the quickly acquired friends will, after years of relatively close relations, say good-by as easily as after a few weeks of acquaintance.

---

[1] The "layering" of personality structure in terms of accessibility of social distance is graphically shown in Figure 1. Essentially, Lewin is saying that the outer boundaries (peripheral) are easier to penetrate in the American (U-type) and relatively inaccessible at the deeper levels of personality. The German (G-type) shows the opposite boundary system: low accessibility at the peripheral areas and more possibilities for reaching the core areas of personality. [Eds.]

AN OPERATIONAL DEFINITION OF SOCIAL DISTANCE

If one wants to express these facts with topological and dynamic concepts, one has to ask what "social distance" between persons means from an operational point of view.

Two groups of facts seem to be possible for an operational definition of social distances:

1. One can start with the difference between the more "peripheral" and the more "central" regions of the person, taking the operational definition from the many kinds of experiments in which the relation of an activity to these different layers have proved to be of primary importance (experiments on psychological satiation, emotions, quasi-needs). The more central regions are defined as the more intimate, personal regions. In these regions, the individual usually is more sensitive than in the peripheral.

2. The second definition could make use of the way social distances generally are proved in sociology: The person A is asked whether he would share certain situations (like traveling in the same car, playing games together, dancing together, marrying) with a certain person B. The differences in social distance can be defined as different degrees of intimacy of the situation which the person is willing to share with the other.

A certain distance, therefore, means, dynamically speaking, the accessibility of certain situations or activities of the person B for the person A, and the nonaccessibility for more intimate situations. This accessibility to certain situations or activities is equivalent (or very closely related) to the possibility of B to communicate with certain, but not with the more central, layers of A.

So far as the state of the person A is concerned, a smaller social distance to B than to C means that more central regions of A are open to B than to C. The statement about the typical American compared with the typical German would mean that, *ceteris paribus*, the peripheral layers of the American show less resistance against communication from another person.

One can represent the greater "openness" by coordinating to the peripheral layers themselves or to their boundaries less resistance against communicative actions from outside. Figure 1 represents the state of the typical American (U-type, Figure 1a) compared with the German (G-type, Figure 1b).

In the diagram, the degree of resistance aagainst communication from outside is represented by stronger boundaries (heavier lines) around the layer in question. I distinguish arbitrarily the same number of layers within the person.

Using such means, one would have to symbolize the U-type, let us say, by four peripheral regions with easily permeable boundaries. Only the very central (fifth) region is insulated from communication to a high degree. In the G-type only the most peripheral region (first) is easily accessible. The more central are relatively difficult of approach. A major boundary lies already between the regions 1 and 2 (Figure 1b).

The facts available seem not to permit a statement about the relative permea-

FIGURE 1

Personality structure. The thickness of the boundary lines between the personality layers represents the difference in accessibility. The hatched area corresponds to the "private" region of the person.

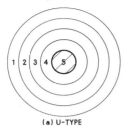
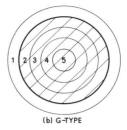

(a) U-TYPE   (b) G-TYPE

bility of every region. But they do seem to permit statements about position of the first main resistance against *invasion* from outside.

EMOTION, FRIENDSHIP, AND FRICTION

A second fact could be mentioned which is somewhat related to the same structural differences. The American is much less likely to respond with anger, or at least with open anger, to the hundred small misfortunes of everyday life. Several facts seems to converge to this effect. The American reacts generally to such accidents more from the point of view of action (he considers what has to be done next in order to remedy the situation), the German more from a moral point of view (he considers whose fault it was). Furthermore, such incidents are less likely to touch central regions of the person. In other words, the range of events which correspond to the peripheral, nonprivate regions, seems to be comparatively greater for the American. This is entirely in line with our basic statement. As the private field includes more layers for the G-type, he is likely to act more emotionally.

This fact is of especial importance for the interrelationship between several

FIGURE 2

Two persons (A and B) in communication

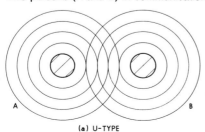
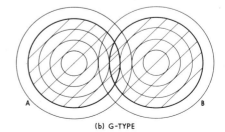

(a) U-TYPE   (b) G-TYPE

persons. One can ask how many layers of two persons (A and B, Figure 2) can come in contact with each other without touching the "private" regions. Communication between regions can be represented by overlapping, or by a common boundary of the regions in question. From our basic assumption, it follows that more regions can overlap in the U-type than in the G-type before private regions are touched. For instance, the overlapping of the three outer layers does not involve a communication between the private regions of the U-type (Figure 2a), whereas such overlapping would involve private regions of the G-type (Figure 2b).

This should have two results: It should make possible *relatively close relations between persons of the U-type without a deep personal friendship*. On the other hand, these persons should be *less in danger of personal friction*. Such friction occurs more easily if personal regions are touched. The facts mentioned seem to be well in line with both conclusions.

ACTIONS AND IDEALS

The fact that there are more regions which are not considered "private" by the American does not mean that these peripheral regions are considered of less importance by him. On the contrary, if one considers the structure of the person as a whole, our basic assumption implies that the relative weight of the nonprivate regions is greater for a person of the U-type than for the G-type. The facts mentioned above point already in this direction.

A second fact can be mentioned here. The peripheral layers of personality include what one can call the "motoric" or "executive" region of a person. This region is the outer layer of the person, the one closest to the environment. It corresponds to the appearance and action of the person. That the relative weight of the appearance seems to be greater for the U-type was mentioned above. The *actions* are relatively emphasized in the U-type. The American, as compared with the German, emphasizes achievement more than ideology or status. In science he emphasizes practice more than theory. The U-type prefers to make extensive "empirical" collection of facts. The greater relative weight which the central regions, and therefore the ideals and other "irreal" facts have for the German, is of fundamental importance for so-called German idealism as against American pragmatism. A similar difference in attitude between Germans and Americans is striking in the fields of politics and religion.

The self-restraint of friends*

John E. Mayer

In the spring of 1954 a group of 88 college women, mostly juniors and seniors, who were attending a large metropolitan college were asked to place themselves in a number of imaginary situations and to indicate how they would react. One of the situations, upon which the following analysis is based, was as follows:

> Suppose that a good friend of yours *has just met* a boy whom she seems to be quite interested in. For one reason or another you have an unfavorable opinion of him.
>
> What do you think you would do in such a situation? That is, would you tell your friend how you felt? If yes, why? If not, why not?

Fifteen percent said they would discuss their feelings with their friend; 20 percent said they would not; while 65 percent qualified their answers, indicating that under certain conditions they would act one way but under other conditions they would act otherwise. Before considering some of these conditions, what are some of the main reasons given by respondents for either expressing or withholding their opinions?

REASONS FOR EXPRESSING OPINION

Those who say they would discuss the matter with the friend, under some or all conditions, reveal that the relationship between them and their friend overshadows that between the friend and the suitor. In more formal terms, X, the friend in question, simultaneously occupies the role of a good friend and a person in a courtship relationship; the question of which role shall receive priority is solved by this group of respondents in favor of the former.

This emphasis is indicated in a number of ways. Some point out that the unrestricted sharing of feelings is one of the prerogatives of a friendship relationship. A few go further and believe that such sharing is obligatory.

* From "The Self-Restraint of Friends: A Mechanism in Family Transition," *Social Forces*, Vol. 35 (1957), pp. 230–38. Abridged and reprinted by permission of the author and *Social Forces*.

It so happens that recently a friend of mine started going steady with a boy I do not like. I think it my duty, as a good friend, to freely express my opinions. As a friend, she knows I am only interested in her welfare, and to keep from her my true feelings is more the actions of an enemy.

Others are more inclined to stress what may be the unhappy consequences of remaining silent.

If a good friend of mine met a boy that I disapproved of for one reason or another, I would definitely tell her. This is true especially if she did not see the faults herself. . . . My reasons for telling her my opinions are that I would not like to see her make a mistake or be unhappy.

REASONS FOR WITHHOLDING OPINION

It is equally apparent that those who place restraints upon the expression of their feelings are responding primarily to X's other role—that of someone in a courtship relationship.

In accounting for their own reticence, their responses are peppered with moral directives: "It's none of my business"; "I have no right to interfere." Sometimes reference is made as to how the girl friend should conduct herself in this situation. "It's up to her to discover the boy's assets and liabilities." "One has the right to pick and choose one's boy friends." Such sentiments clearly reflect the norms that regulate the relationship between those who are courting and those in the immediate social environment, e.g., friends, relatives. When it comes to choosing a marriage partner, it is accepted that others will minimize their influence, while at the same time it is incumbent upon those involved to reach their own decision and to take full responsibility for their choice.

While some of the respondents appeal directly to what they feel are intrinsically "right" and "wrong" ways of acting, others are more concerned with the possible consequences of violating the norms. A danger is that their friends might resent hearing their opinion and, even worse, that the friendship might be seriously jeopardized.

If I spoke my mind, she might resent it and feel that I am attempting to domineer and influence her.

I would not tell my friend how I felt because the quickest way to lose a good friend and make an enemy is to say something about the fellow she likes.

Foremost considerations in reaching a decision

The large majority of respondents—and the majority would have probably been even larger if the students had been questioned further—did not give undisputed precedence to one alternative while completely subordinating the other. In varying degrees they were sensitive to the demands of both relationships and were, consequently, pulled in opposing directions at the same time. They resolved their dilemma, at least on paper, by examining more closely various aspects of the situation described and then specifying the conditions under which they would take one course rather that the other. In the following are some of the considerations they felt would be the most relevant in helping them to decide whether to voice an opinion or to maintain silence.

1. How involved are the couple? The closer the attachment, the more cautious are friends apt to become in publicizing their low estimate of the boy. When the two people are quite absorbed in each other, to speak one's mind without careful forethought is viewed as "interfering," "inflicting one's opinion," and "sticking one's nose into other people's business."[1]

2. How close are the friends? In general, the closer the association, the smaller are the barriers to communication.

If it were an honest and close friendship I would tell her my opinions. . . .

Yes, I would tell her if she was a very good friend of mine and if we discussed things openly together in the past.

3. Who brings up the subject? Respondents feel considerably less restraint when they are asked for their views.

I would not volunteer information. However, my friend would probably ask me and then I would answer *tactfully.*

But even though one's opinion is solicited, this is no guarantee that it will be truthfully given.

If she were to ask me my opinion about him I would simply say, "I don't know him well enough to say whether or not I like him; but I think he's nice."

4. What is the basis of one's dislike? A primary question concerns the reliability of one's unfavorable impression of the boy.

If I felt that my opinion was well-grounded I would express my thoughts very objectively to the girl. If I just had a feeling about the fellow, I would give him time to prove or disprove my opinion of him.

Even though early impressions are repeatedly confirmed, there still remains the question of whether the basis of one's dislike is serious enough to warrant bringing it out into the open.

Sometimes you meet people, and for no particular reason they "strike you the wrong way." In such a case I would not express my opinion concerning the boy. If on the other hand, there are outstanding characteristics, such as nastiness, stinginess, assuming a dominant air, etc., which make the boy dislikable and a bad companion than I would express my opinion.

---

[1] The tendency of friends to curb their influence, which continues throughout the courtship period, reaches its climax after the couple are married. It is expected that above all, marriage should be a private relationship between husband and wife and that many of its internal aspects should not be revealed to others. However much the spouses may work toward this end, the withdrawal action of friends—their long practiced self-restraint—is instrrumental in making it a private relationship.

In actuality, respondents are faced with more than simply reaching a yes or no decision as to whether or not they should give voice to their sentiments. If it is decided that conditions warrant speaking up, there still remains the question as to how much of one's opinion should be expressed. Opinion, like color, runs through many gradations, and to convey a negative opinion is not necessarily to impart its full strength.

As might be expected, there is a marked tendency to convey a less damaging impression than is actually felt, and for this purpose a variety of techniques is used. Some respondents would simply understate the intensity of their negative estimate of the boy, while others would respond frankly but cushion the blow with an enthusiastic account of his assets. Another technique, designed to minimize the impact of one's opinion, is to cast serious doubts upon its reliability; e.g., "It is only my opinion and I certainly could be wrong."

In sum, communication between friends tends to be curtailed in varying degrees under the following conditions: when the couple are engrossed in each other, when the friendship between the girls is only a casual one, when the friend's opinion is not solicited, and when the friend feels her low regard for the boy may lack substance. Since such conditions as these occur with some regularity in the social life of individuals, their net effect in silencing adverse opinion may well be considerable.

The self-restraint of friends

Focusing upon the pattern of self-restraint identified above, it is of interest how early in the relationship of the couple this pattern tends to become invoked. When a romance is well advanced, with the partners heading toward marriage, not to interfere is a well-recognized obligation. However, it will be recalled that, in the situation presented to the respondents, the couple had only recently met, and presumably the romance was still in its initial stages. Yet, even at this point, there was a marked tendency to withhold negative comment.

The strength of this tendency is suggested by the fact that upon occasion it competes successfully with the interaction patterns obtaining between good friends. It is between friends that the flow of opinion and sentiment, both favorable and unfavorable, tends to be less censored and restricted than in most other types of associations. Such patterns of communication, often of long duration, are apt to be well established and not easily swept aside; for them to be interrupted suggests the existence of a counterbalancing force of considerable magnitude.

Finally, the tentative nature of the preceding remarks should be kept in mind. For one thing, the answers of a group of respondents to a hypothetical situation are not necessarily infallible indicators of their behavior in the actual situation. Furthermore, there is the question of the extent to which the same patterns would appear within other sectors of the population. In particular, to what extent would the tendency toward self-restraint manifest itself within other groups, e.g., males, different age groups, different social levels?[2]

Behavioral study of obedience[*]

Stanley Milgram

Obedience is as basic an element in the structure of social life as one can point to. Some system of authority is a requirement of all communal living, and it is only the man dwelling inisolation who is not forced to respond, through defiance or submission, to the commands of others. Obedience, as a determinant of behavior, is of particular relevance to our time. It has been reliably established that from 1933–45 millions of innocent persons were systematically slaughtered on command. Gas chambers were built, death camps were guarded, daily quotas of corpses were produced with the same efficiency as the manufacture of appliances. These inhumane policies may have originated in the mind of a single person, but they could only be carried out on a massive scale if a very large number of persons obeyed orders.

Obedience is the psychological mechanism that links individual action to political purpose. It is the dispositional cement that binds men to systems of authority. Facts of recent history and observation in daily life suggest that for many persons obedience may be a deeply ingrained behavior tendency, indeed, a prepotent impulse overriding training in ethics, sympathy, and moral conduct. C. P. Snow points to its importance when he writes:

When you think of the long and gloomy history of man, you will find more hideous crimes have been committed in the name of obedience than have ever been committed

---

[2] Because of the tradition of greater male independence and self-reliance, males will presumably be even more restrained from influencing their friends. If true, this suggests a number of interesting implications. Because males who are seeking mates may be subject to a lesser degree of control, it is possible that they will depart more from the standards of their friends. As a result, the latter may be less favorably disposed toward their friends' wives than females will be toward their friends' husbands. Accordingly, one would expect that after the marriage there would be a greater likelihood of strain arising between male as compared to female friends, and that more of the male friendships would be discontinued as a result. From the standpoint of the married couple, their joint friendship circle would possibly include, for the same reason, a smaller proportion of the husband's than of the wife's pre-marital friends.

[*] From *Journal of Abnormal and Social Psychology*, Vol. 67, No. 4 (1963), 371–78. Used by permission.

in the name of rebellion. If you doubt that, read William Shirer's "Rise and Fall of the Third Reich." The German Officer Corps were brought up in the most rigorous code of obedience . . . in the name of obedience they were party to, and assisted in, the most wicked large scale actions in the history of the world.[1]

While the particular form of obedience dealt with in the present study has its antecedents in these episodes, it must not be thought all obedience entails acts of aggression against others. Obedience serves numerous productive functions. Indeed, the very life of society is predicated on its existence. Obedience may be ennobling and educative and refer to acts of charity and kindness, as well as to destruction.

GENERAL PROCEDURE

A procedure was devised which seems useful as a tool for studying obedience.[2] It consists of ordering a naive subject to administer electric shock to a victim. A simulated shock generator is used, with 30 clearly marked voltage levels that range from 15 to 450 volts. The instrument bears verbal designations that range from Slight Shock to Danger: Severe Shock. The responses of the victim, who is a trained confederate of the experimenter, are standardized. The orders to adminster shocks are given to the naive subject in the context of a "learning experiment" ostensibly set up to study the effects of punishment on memory. As the experiment proceeds the naive subject is commanded to administer increasingly more intense shocks to the victim, even to the point of reaching the level marked Danger: Severe Shock. Internal resistances become stronger, and at a certain point the subject refuses to go on with the experiment. Behavior prior to this rupture is considered "obedience," in that the subject complies with the commands of the experimenter. The point of rupture is the act of disobedience. A quantitative value is assigned to the subject's performance based on the maximum intensity shock he is willing to administer before he refuses to participate further. Thus for any particular subject and for any particular experimental condition the degree of obedience may be specified with a numerical value. The crux of the study is to systematically vary the factors believed to alter the degree of obedience to the experimental commands.

The technique allows important variables to be manipulated at several points in the experiment. One may vary aspects of the source of command, content and form of command, instrumentalities for its execution, target object, general social setting, etc. The problem, therefore, is not one of designing increasingly more numerous experimental conditions, but of selecting those that best illuminate the *process* of obedience from the sociopsychological standpoint.

---

[1] C. P. Snow, "Either/Or," *Progressive*, Feb., 1961, p. 24.

[2] S. Milgram, "Dynamics of Obedience" (Washington, D.C.: National Science Foundation, January 25, 1961), mimeo.

RELATED STUDIES

The inquiry bears an important relation to philosophic analyses of obedience and authority (Arendt,[3] Friedrich,[4] Weber[5]), an early experimental study of obedience by Frank,[6] studies in "authoritarianism" (Adorno, Frenkel-Brunswik, Levinson, and Sanford,[7] Rokeach[8]), and a recent series of analytic and empirical studies in social power (Cartwright[9]). It owes much to the long concern with *suggestion* in social psychology, both in its normal forms (e.g., Binet[10]) and in its clinical manifestations (Charcot[11]). But it derives, in the first instance, from direct observation of a social fact; the individual who is commanded by a legitimate authority ordinarily obeys. Obedience comes easily and often. It is a ubiquitous and indispensable feature of social life.

METHOD

Subjects

The subjects were 40 males between the ages of 20 and 50, drawn from New Haven and the surrounding communities. Subjects were obtained by a newspaper advertisement and direct mail solicitation. Those who responded to the appeal

TABLE 1
Distribution of age and occupational types in the experiment

Occupations	20–29 years n	30–39 years n	40–50 years n	Percentage of total (occupations)
Workers, skilled and unskilled.............	4	5	6	37.5
Sales, business, and white-collar...........	3	6	7	40.0
Professional.........................	1	5	3	22.5
Percentage of total (age).................	20	40	40	

Note: Total *n* = 40.

[3] H. Arendt, "What Was Authority?" in *Authority*, C. J. Friedrich (ed.) (Cambridge: Harvard Univ. Press, 1958), pp. 81–112.

[4] C. J. Friedrich (ed.), *Authority* (Cambridge: Harvard Univ. Press, 1958).

[5] M. Weber, *The Theory of Social and Economic Organization* (Oxford: Oxford Univ. Press, 1947).

[6] J. D. Frank, "Experimental Studies of Personal Pressure and Resistance," *J. Gen. Psychol.*, Vol. 30 (1944), pp. 23–64.

[7] T. Adorno, Else Frenkel-Brunswik, D. J. Levinson, and R. N. Sanford, *The Authoritarian Personality* (New York: Harper, 1950).

[8] M. Rokeach, "Authority, Authoritarianism, and Conformity," in *Conformity and Deviation*, I. A. Berg and B. M. Bass (eds.) (New York: Harper, 1961), pp. 230–57.

[9] D. Cartwright (ed.), *Studies in Social Power* (Ann Arbor: Univ. of Michigan Institute for Social Research, 1959).

[10] A. Binet, *La Suggestibilité* (Paris: Schleicher, 1900).

[11] J. M. Charcot, *Oeuvres Complètes* (Paris: Bureaux du Progrès Médical, 1881).

believed they were to participate in a study of memory and learning at Yale University. A wide range of occupations is represented in the sample. Typical subjects were postal clerks, high school teachers, salesmen, engineers, and laborers. Subjects ranged in educational level from one who had not finished elementary school, to those who had doctorate and other professional degrees. They were paid $4.50 for their participation in the experiment. However, subjects were told that payment was simply for coming to the laboratory, and that the money was theirs no matter what happened after they arrived. Table 1 shows the proportion of age and occupational types assigned to the experimental condition.

Personnel and locale

The experiment was conducted on the grounds of Yale University in the elegant interaction laboratory. (This detail is relevant to the perceived legitimacy of the experiment. In further variations, the experiment was dissociated from the university, with consequences for performance.) The role of experimenter was played by a 31-year-old high school teacher of biology. His manner was impassive, and his appearance somewhat stern throughout the experiment. He was dressed in a gray technician's coat. The victim was played by a 47-year-old accountant, trained for the role; he was of Irish-American stock, whom most observers found mild-mannered and likable.

Procedure

One naive subject and one victim (an accomplice) performed in each experiment. A pretext had to be devised that would justify the administration of electric shock by the naive subject. This was effectively accomplished by the cover story. After a general introduction on the presumed relation between punishment and learning, subjects were told:

But actually, we know *very little* about the effect of punishment on learning, because almost no truly scientific studies have been made of it in human beings.

For instance, we don't know how *much* punishment is best for learning—and we don't know how much difference it makes as to who is giving the punishment, whether an adult learns best from a younger or an older person than himself—or many things of that sort.

So in this study we are bringing together a number of adults of different occupations and ages. And we're asking some of them to be teachers and some of them to be learners.

We want to find out just what effect different people have on each other as teachers and learners, and also what effect *punishment* will have on learning in this situation.

Therefore, I'm going to ask one of you to be the teacher here tonight and the other one to be the learner.

Does either of you have a preference?

Subjects then drew slips of paper from a hat to determine who would be the teacher and who would be the learner in the experiment. The drawing was rigged so that the naive subject was always the teacher and the accomplice always the learner. (Both slips contained the word "Teacher.") Immediately after the drawing, the teacher and learner were taken to an adjacent room and the learner was strapped into an "electric chair" apparatus.

The experimenter explained that the straps were to prevent excessive movement while the learner was being shocked. The effect was to make it impossible for him to escape from the situation. An electrode was attached to the learner's wrist, and electrode paste was applied "to avoid blisters and burns." Subjects were told that the electrode was attached to the shock generator in the adjoining room.

In order to improve credibility the experimenter declared, in response to a question by the learner: "Although the shocks can be extremely painful, they cause no permanent tissue damage."

Learning task. The lesson administered by the subject was a paired-associate learning task. The subject read a series of word pairs to the learner, and then read the first word of the pair along with four terms. The learner was to indicate which of the four terms had originally been paired with the first word. He communicated his answer by pressing one of four switches in front of him, which in turn lit up one of four numbered quadrants in an answer-box located atop the shock generator.

Shock generator. The instrument panel consists of 30 lever switches set in a horizontal line. Each switch is clearly labeled with a voltage designation that ranges from 15 to 450 volts. There is a 15-volt increment from one switch to the next going from left to right. In addition, the following verbal designations are clearly indicated for groups of four switches going from left to right: Slight Shock, Moderate Shock, Strong Shock, Very Strong Shock, Intense Shock, Extreme Intensity Shock, Danger: Severe Shock. (Two switches after this last designation are simply marked XXX.)

Upon depressing a switch; a pilot light corresponding to each switch is illuminated in bright red; an electric buzzing is heard; an electric blue light, labeled "voltage energizer," flashes; the dial on the voltage meter swings to the right; various relay clicks are sounded.

The upper left-hand corner of the generator is labeled Shock Generator, Type ZLB, Dyson Instrument Company, Waltham, Mass. Output 15 Volts–450 Volts.

Details of the instrument were carefully handled to insure an appearance of authenticity. The panel was engraved by precision industrial engravers, and all components were of high quality. No subject in the experiment suspected that the instrument was merely a simulated shock generator.

Sample shock. Each naive subject is given a sample shock on the shock generator, prior to beginning his run as teacher. This shock is always 45 volts, and is applied by pressing the third switch of the generator. The shock is applied to the wrist of the naive subject, and has its source in a 45-volt battery wired into the generator. This further convinces the subject of the authenticity of the generator.

Shock instructions. The subject is told to administer a shock to the learner each time he gives a wrong response. Moreover—and this is the key command—the subject is instructed to "move one level higher on the shock generator each time the learner flashes a wrong answer." He is also instructed to announce the voltage level before administering a shock. This serves to continually remind subjects of the increasing intensity of shocks administered to the learner.

Preliminary and regular run. Pretests revealed that the procedure of reading words and administering shocks requires some practice before it can be handled smoothly. Therefore, immediately preceding the regular run, the teacher is given a preliminary series of 10 words to read to the learner. There are 3 neutral words in the practice series (i.e., words that the learner answers correctly), so that shocks are administered for 7 of the words, with the maximum shock at 105 volts (moderate shock). Almost all subjects master the procedure by the time the preliminary run is over.

Subjects are then presented with a second list, and are told that the procedure is is the same as for the first list; the experimenter adds, however: "When you get to the bottom of the list, repeat it over again, and continue giving shocks, until the learner has learned all the pairs correctly." The experimenter instructs the subject to, "start from 15 volts and increase the shock level one step each time the learner gives a wrong answer."

Feedback from the victim. In all conditions the learner gives a predetermined set of responses to the word pair test, based on a schedule of approximately three wrong answers to one correct answer. In the present experimental condition no vocal response or other sign of protest is heard from the learner until Shock Level 300 is reached. When the 300-volt shock is administered, the learner pounds on the wall of the room in which he is bound to the electric chair. The pounding can be heard by the subject. From this point on, the learner's answers no longer appear on the four-way panel.

At this juncture, subjects ordinarily turn to the experimenter for guidance. The experimenter instructs the subject to treat the absence of a response as wrong answer, and to shock the subject according to the usual schedule. He advises the subjects to allow 5–10 seconds before considering no response as a wrong answer, and to increase the shock level one step each time the learner fails to respond correctly. The learner's pounding is repeated after the 315-volt shock is administered; afterwards he is not heard from, nor do his answers reappear on the four-way signal box.

Experimenter feedback. At various points in the experiment the subject may turn to the experimenter for advice on whether he should continue to administer shocks. Or he may indicate that he does not wish to go on. It was important to standardize the experimenter's responses to these inquiries and reactions.

If the subject indicated his unwillingness to go on, the experimenter responded with a sequence of "prods," using as many as necessary to bring the subject into line.

Prod 1: Please continue, *or* Please go on.
Prod 2: The experiment requires that you continue.
Prod 3: It is absolutely essential that you continue.
Prod 4: You have no other choice, you *must* go on.

The prods were always made in sequence: Only if Prod 1 had been unsuccessful could Prod 2 be used. If the subject refused to obey the experimenter after Prod 4, the experiment was terminated. The experimenter's tone of voice was at all times firm, but not impolite. The sequence was begun anew on each occasion that the subject balked or showed reluctance to follow orders.

Special prods. If the subject asked if the learner was liable to suffer permanent physical injury, the experimenter said: "Although the shocks may be painful, there is no permanent tissue damage, so please go on." [Followed by Prods 2, 3, and 4 if necessary.]

If the subject said that the learner did not want to go on, the experimenter replied: "Whether the learner likes it or not, you must go on until he has learned all the word pairs correctly. So please go on." [Followed by Prods 2, 3, and 4 if necessary.]

Dependent measures

The primary dependent measure for any subject is the maximum shock he administers before he refuses to go any further. In principle this may vary from 0 (for a subject who refuses to administer even the first shock) to 30 (for a subject who administers the highest shock on the generator). A subject who breaks off the experiment at any point prior to administering the thirtieth shock level is termed a *defiant* subject. One who complies with experimental commands fully, and proceeds to administer all shock levels commanded, is termed an *obedient* subject.

Further records. With few exceptions, experimental sessions were recorded on magnetic tape. Occasional photographs were taken through one-way mirrors. Notes were kept on any unusual behavior occurring during the course of the experiments. On occasion, additional observers were directed to write objective descriptions of the subjects' behavior. The latency and duration of shocks were measured by accurate timing devices.

Interview and dehoax. Following the experiment, subjects were interviewed; open-ended questions, projective measures, and attitude scales were employed. After the interview, procedures were undertaken to assure that the subject would leave the laboratory in a state of well being. A friendly reconciliation was arranged between the subject and the victim, and an effort was made to reduce any tensions that arose as a result of the experiment.

RESULTS

Preliminary notions

Before giving an account of the experimental results, it is instructive to consider how persons predict others will perform when commanded to administer powerful shocks to another person. Fourteen Yale seniors, all psychology majors, were provided with a detailed description of the experimental situation. They were asked to reflect carefully on it, and to predict the behavior of 100 hypothetical subjects. More specifically, they were instructed to plot the distribution of obedience of "100 Americans of diverse occupations, and ranging in age from 20 to 50 years," who were placed in the experimental situation.

There was considerable agreement among the respondents on the expected behavior of hypothetical subjects. All respondents predicted that only an insignificant minority would go through to the end of the shock series. (The estimates ranged from 0 to 3 percent; i.e., the most "pessimistic" member of the class predicted that of 100 persons, 3 would continue through to the most potent shock available on the shock generator—450 volts.) The class mean was 1.2 percent. The question was also posed informally to colleagues of the author, and the most general feeling was that few if any subjects would go beyond the designation Very Strong Shock.

Result of experiment I

Subjects accept situation. With few exceptions subjects were convinced of the reality of the experimental situation, that they were administering shocks to another person, and the most potent shocks were extremely painful. In the postexperimental interview subjects were asked: "How painful to the learner were the last few shocks that you administered to him?" Subjects were instructed to indicate their answers on a printed 14-point scale ranging from "Not at all painful" to "Extremely painful." The modal response was 14 (Extremely painful) with the mean at 13.42.

Signs of extreme tension. Many subjects showed signs of nervousness in the experimental situation, and especially upon administering the more powerful shocks. In a large number of cases the degree of tension reached extremes that are rarely seen in sociopsychological laboratory studies. Subjects were observed to sweat, tremble, stutter, bite their lips, groan, and dig their fingernails into their flesh. These were characteristic rather than exceptional reponses to the experiment.

One sign of tension was the regular occurrence of nervous laughing fits. Fourteen of the 40 subjects showed definite signs of nervous laughter and smiling. The laughter seemed entirely out of place, even bizarre. Full-blown, uncontrollable seizures were observed for 3 subjects. On one occasion we observed a seizure so violently convulsive that it was necessary to call a halt to the experiment. The subject, a 46-year-old encyclopedia salesman, was seriously embarrassed by his untoward and uncontrollable behavior. In the postexperimental interviews subjects took pains to point out that they were not sadistic types, and that the laughter did not mean they enjoyed shocking the victim.

Distribution of scores. It had been conjectured that persons would not, in general, agree to administer shocks beyond the level designated as Very Strong Shock. The distribution of maximum shocks for this experiment is shown in Table 2. The obtained distribution of scores deviates radically from the prediction.

Upon command of the experimenter, each of the 40 subjects went beyond

TABLE 2
Distribution of breakoff points

Verbal designation and voltage indication	*Number of subjects for whom this was maximum shock*
Slight Shock:	
15	0
30	0
45	0
60	0
Moderate Shock:	
75	0
90	0
105	0
120	0
Strong Shock:	
135	0
150	0
165	0
180	0
Very Strong Shock:	
195	0
210	0
225	0
240	0
Intense Shock:	
255	0
270	0
285	0
300	5
Extreme Intensity Shock:	
315	4
330	2
345	1
360	1
Danger: Severe Shock:	
375	1
390	0
405	0
420	0
XXX	
435	0
450	26

the expected breakoff point. No subject stopped prior to administering Shock Level 20. (At this level—300 volts—the victim kicks on the wall and no longer provides answers to the teacher's multiple-choice questions.)

Of the 40 subjects, 5 refused to obey the experimental commands beyond the 300-volt level. Four more subjects administered one further shock, and then refused to go on. Two broke off at the 330-volt level, and 1 each at 345, 360, and 375 volts. Thus a total of 14 subjects defied the experimenter. It is instructive to reprint their remarks at the point of defiance, as transcribed from the tape recordings:

[0124] I think he's trying to communicate, he's knocking. . . . Well it's not fair to shock the guy . . . these are terrific volts. I don't think this is very humane. . . . Oh, I can't go on with this; no, this isn't right. It's a hell of an experiment. The guy is suffering in there. No, I don't want to go on. This is crazy. [Subject refused to administer more shocks.]

[0123] He's banging in there. I'm gonna chicken out. I'd like to continue, but I can't do that to a man. . . . I'm sorry I can't do that to a man. I'll hurt his heart. You take your check. . . . No really, I couldn't do it.

These subjects were frequently in a highly agitated and even angered state. Sometimes, verbal protest was at a minimum, and the subject simply got up from his chair in front of the shock generator, and indicated that he wished to leave the laboratory.

Of the 40 subjects, 26 obeyed the orders of the experimenter to the end, proceeding to punish the victim until they reached the most potent shock available on the shock generator. At that point, the experimenter called a halt to the session. (The maximum shock is labeled 450 volts, and is two steps beyond the designation: Danger: Severe Shock.) Although obedient subjects continued to administer shocks, they often did so under extreme stress. Some expressed reluctance to administer shocks beyond the 300-volt level, and displayed fears similar to those who defied the experimenter; yet they obeyed.

After the maximum shocks had been delivered, and the experimenter called to a halt to the proceedings, many obedient subjects heaved sighs of relief, mopped their brows, rubbed their fingers over their eyes, or nervously fumbled cigarettes. Some shook their heads, apparently in regret. Some subjects had remained calm throughout the experiment, and displayed only minimal signs of tension from beginning to end.

DISCUSSION

The experiment yielded two findings that were surprising. The first finding concerns the sheer strength of obedient tendencies manifested in this situation. Subjects have learned from childhood that it is a fundamental breach of moral conduct to hurt another person against his will. Yet, 26 subjects abandon this tenet in following the instructions of an authority who has no special powers to enforce his commands. To disobey would bring no material loss to the subject;

no punishment would ensue. It is clear from the remarks and outward behavior of many participants that in punishing the victim they are often acting against their own values. Subjects often expressed deep disapproval of shocking a man in the face of his objections, and others denounced it as stupid and senseless. Yet the majority complied with the experimental commands. This outcome was surprising from two perspectives: first, from the standpoint of predictions made in the questionnaire described earlier. (Here, however, it is possible that the remoteness of the respondents from the actual situation, and the difficulty of conveying to them the concrete details of the experiment, could account for the serious underestimation of obedience.)

But the results were also unexpected to persons who observed the experiment in progress, through one-way mirrors. Observers often uttered expressions of disbelief upon seeing a subject administer more powerful shocks to the victim. These persons had a full acquaintance with the details of the situation, and yet systematically underestimated the amount of obedience that subjects would display.

The second unanticipated effect was the extraordinary tension generated by the procedures. One might suppose that a subject would simply break off or continue as his conscience dictated. Yet, this is very far from what happened. There were striking reactions of tension and emotional strain. One observer related:

I observed a mature and initially poised businessman enter the laboratory smiling and confident. Within 20 minutes he was reduced to a twitching, stuttering wreck, who was rapidly approaching a point of nervous collapse. He constantly pulled on his earlobe, and twisted his hands. At one point he pushed his fist into his forehead and muttered: "Oh God, let's stop it." And yet he continued to respond to every word of the experimenter, and obeyed to the end.

Any understanding of the phenomenon of obedience must rest on an analysis of the particular conditions in which it occurs. The following features of the experiment go some distance in explaining the high amount of obedience observed in the situation.

1. The experiment is sponsored by and takes place on the grounds of an institution of unimpeachable reputation, Yale University. It may be reasonably presumed that the personnel are competent and reputable. The importance of this background authority is now being studied by conducting a series of experiments outside of New Haven, and without any visible ties to the university.

2. The experiment is, on the face of it, designed to attain a worthy purpose—advancement of knowledge about learning and memory. Obedience occurs not as an end in itself, but as an instrumental element in a situation that the subject construes as significant, and meaningful. He may not be able to see its full significance, but he may properly assume that the experimenter does.

3. The subject perceives that the victim has voluntarily submitted to the authority system of the experimenter. He is not (at first) an unwilling captive impressed for involuntary service. He has taken the trouble to come to the

laboratory presumably to aid the experimental research. That he later becomes an involuntary subject does not alter the fact that, initially, he consented to participate without qualification. Thus he has in some degree incurred an obligation toward the experimenter.

4. The subject, too, has entered the experiment voluntarily, and perceives himself under obligation to aid the experimenter. He has made a commitment, and to disrupt the experiment is a repudiation of this initial promise of aid.

5. Certain features of the procedure strengthen the subject's sense of obligation to the experimenter. For one, he has been paid for coming to the laboratory. In part this is canceled out by the experimenter's statement that: "Of course, as in all experiments, the money is yours simply for coming to the laboratory. From this point on, no matter what happens, the money is yours."[12]

6. From the subject's standpoint, the fact that he is the teacher and the other man the learner is purely a chance consequence (it is determined by drawing lots) and he, the subject, ran the same risk as the other man in being assigned the role of learner. Since the assignment of positions in the experiment was achieved by fair means, the learner is deprived of any basis of complaint on this count. (A similar situation obtains in Army units, in which—in the absence of volunteers—a particularly dangerous mission may be assigned by drawing lots, and the unlucky soldier is expected to bear his misfortune with sportsmanship.)

7. There is, at best, ambiguity with regard to the prerogatives of a psychologist and the corresponding rights of his subject. There is a vagueness of expectation concerning what a psychologist may require of his subject, and when he is overstepping acceptable limits. Moreover, the experiment occurs in a closed setting, and thus provides no opportunity for the subject to remove these ambiguities by discussion with others. There are few standards that seem directly applicable to the situation, which is a novel one for most subjects.

8. The subjects are assured that the shocks administered to the subject are "painful but not dangerous." Thus they assume that the discomfort caused the victim is momentary, while the scientific gains resulting from the experiment are enduring.

9. Through Shock Level 20 the victim continues to provide answers on the signal box. The subject may construe this as a sign that the victim is still willing to "play the game." It is only after Shock Level 20 that the victim repudiates the rules completely, refusing to answer further.

These features help to explain the high amount of obedience obtained in this experiment. Many of the arguments raised need not remain matters of speculation, but can be reduced to testable propositions to be confirmed or disproved by further experiments.[13]

---

[12] Forty-three subjects, undergraduates at Yale University, were run in the experiment without payment. The results are very similar to those obtained with paid subjects.

[13] A series of recently completed experiments employing the obedience paradigm is reported in S. Milgram "Some Conditions of Obedience and Disobedience to Authority," *Human Relations*, 1964.

The following features of the experiment concern the nature of the conflict which the subject faces.

10. The subject is placed in a position in which he must respond to the competing demands of two persons: the experimenter and the victim. The conflict must be resolved by meeting the demands of one or the other; satisfaction of the victim and the experimenter are mutually exclusive. Moreover, the resolution must take the form of a highly visible action, that of continuing to shock the victim or breaking off the experiment. Thus the subject is forced into a public conflict that does not permit any completely satisfactory solution.

11. While the demands of the experimenter carry the weight of scientific authority, the demands of the victim spring from his personal experience of pain and suffering. The two claims need not be regarded as equally pressing and legitimate. The experimenter seeks an abstract scientific datum; the victim cries out for relief from physical suffering caused by the subject's actions.

12. The experiment gives the subject little time for reflection. The conflict comes on rapidly. It is only minutes after the subject has been seated before the shock generator that the victim begins his protests. Moreover, the subject perceives that he has gone through but two-thirds of the shock levels at the time the subject's first protests are heard. Thus he understands that the conflict will have a persistent aspect to it, and may well become more intense as increasingly more powerful shocks are required. The rapidity with which the conflict descends on the subject and his realization that it is predictably recurrent may well be sources of tension to him.

13. At a more general level, the conflict stems from the opposition of two ddeply ingrained behavior dispositions: first, the disposition not to harm other people, and second, the tendency to obey those whom we perceive to be legitimate authorities.

Some thoughts on ethics of research: After reading Milgram's "behavioral study of obedience"*

Diana Baumrind

Certain problems in psychological research require the experimenter to balance his career and scientific interests against the interests of his prospective subjects. When such occasions arise the experimenter's stated objective frequently is to do the best possible job with the least possible harm to his subjects. The experimenter seldom perceives in more positive terms an indebtedness to the subject for his services, perhaps because the detachment which his functions require prevents appreciation of the subject as an individual.

Yet a debt does exist, even when the subject's reason for volunteering includes course credit or monetary gain. Often a subject participates unwillingly in order to satisfy a course requirement. These requirements are of questionable merit ethically, and do not alter the experimenter's responsibility to the subject.

Most experimental conditions do not cause the subjects pain or indignity, and are sufficiently interesting or challenging to present no problem of an ethical nature to the experimenter. But where the experimental conditions expose the subject to loss of dignity, or offer him nothing of value, then the experimenter is obliged to consider the reasons why the subject volunteered and to reward him accordingly.

The subject's public motives for volunteering include having an enjoyable or stimulating experience, acquiring knowledge, doing the experimenter a favor which may some day be reciprocated, and making a contribution to science. These motives can be taken into account rather easily by the experimenter who is willing to spend a few minutes with the subject afterwards to thank him for

* Reprinted from the *American Psychologist*, Vol. 19 (1964), pp. 421–23.

his participation, answer his questions, reassure him that he did well, and chat with him a bit. Most volunteers also have less manifest, but equally legitimate, motives. A subject may be seeking an opportunity to have contact with, be noticed by, and perhaps confide in a person with psychological training. The dependent attitude of most subjects toward the experimenter is an artifact of the experimental situation as well as an expression of some subjects' personal need systems at the time they volunteer.

The dependent, obedient attitude assumed by most subjects in the experimental setting is appropriate to that situation. The "game" is defined by the experimenter and he makes the rules. By volunteering, the subject agrees implicitly to assume a posture of trust and obedience. While the experimental conditions leave him exposed, the subject has the right to assume that his security and self-esteem will be protected.

There are other professional situations in which one member—the patient or client—expects help and protection from the other—the physician or psychologist. But the interpersonal relationship between experimenter and subject additionally has unique features which are likely to provoke initial anxiety in the subject. The laboratory is unfamiliar as a setting and the rules of behavior ambiguous compared to a clinician's office. Because of the anxiety and passivity generated by the setting, the subject is more prone to behave in an obedient, suggestible manner in the laboratory than elsewhere. Therefore, the laboratory is not the place to study degree of obedience or suggestibility, as a function of a particular experimental condition, since the base line for these phenomena as found in the laboratory is probably much higher than in most other settings. Thus experiments in which the relationship to the experimenter as an authority is used as an independent condition are imperfectly designed for the same reason that they are prone to injure the subjects involved. They disregard the special quality of trust and obedience with which the subject appropriately regards the experimenter.

Other phenomena which present ethical decisions, unlike those mentioned above, *can* be reproduced successfully in the laboratory. Failure experience, conformity to peer judgment, and isolation are among such phenomena. In these cases we can expect the experimenter to take whatever measures are necessary to prevent the subject from leaving the laboratory more humiliated, insecure, alienated, or hostile than when he arrived. To guarantee that an especially sensitive subject leaves a stressful experimental experience in the proper state sometimes requires special clinical training. But usually an attitude of compassion, respect, gratitude, and common sense will suffice, and no amount of clinical training will substitute. The subject has the right to expect that the psychologiest with whom he is interacting has some concern for his welfare, and the personal attributes and professional skill to express his good will effectively.

Unfortunately, the subject is not always treated with the respect he deserves. It has become more commonplace in sociopsychological laboratory studies to manipulate, embarrass, and discomfort subjects. At times the insult to the subject's sensibilities extends to the journal reader when the results are reported. Milgram's (1963) study in a case in point. The following is Milgram's abstract of his experiment:

This article describes a procedure for the study of destructive obedience in the laboratory. It consists of ordering a naive S to administer increasingly more severe punishment to a victim in the context of a learning experiment. Punishment is administered by means of a shock generator with 30 graded switches ranging from Slight Shock to Danger: Severe Shock. The victim is a confederate of E. The primary dependent variable is the maximum shock the S is willing to administer before he refuses to continue further. 26 S's obeyed the experimental commands fully, and administered the highest shock on the generator. 14 S's broke off the experiment at some point after the victim protested and refused to provide further answers. The procedure created extreme levels of nervous tension in some S's. Profuse sweating, trembling, and stuttering were typical expressions of this emotional disturbance. One unexpected sign of tension—yet to be explained—was the regular occurrence of nervous laughter, which in some S's developed into uncontrollable seizures. The variety of interesting behavioral dynamics observed in the experiment, the reality of the situation for the S, and the possibility of parametric variation within the framework of the procedure, point to the fruitfulness of further study [p. 371].

The detached, objective manner in which Milgram reports the emotional disturbance suffered by his subject contrasts sharply with his graphic account of that disturbance. Following are two other quotes describing the effects on his subjects of the experimental conditions:

I observed a mature and initially poised businessman enter the laboratory smiling and confident. Within 20 minutes he was reduced to a twitching, stuttering wreck, who was rapidly approaching a point of nervous collapse. He constantly pulled on his earlobe, and twisted his hands. At one point he pushed his fist into his forehead and muttered: "Oh God, let's stop it." And yet he continued to respond to every word of the experimenter, and obeyed to the end [p. 377].

In a large number of cases the degree of tension reached extremes that are rarely seen in sociopsychological laboratory studies. Subjects were observed to sweat, tremble, stutter, bite their lips, and dig their fingernails into their flesh. These were characteristic rather than exceptional responses to the experiment.

One sign of tension was the regular occurrence of nervous laughing fits. Fourteen of the 40 subjects showed definite signs of nervous laughter and smiling. The laughter seemed entirely out of place, even bizarre. Full-blown, uncontrollable seizures were observed for 3 subjects. On one occasion we observed a seizure so violently convulsive that it was necessary to call a halt to the experiment . . . [p. 375].

Milgram does state that,

After the interview, procedures were undertaken to assure that the subject would leave the laboratory in a state of well-being. A friendly reconciliation was arranged between the subject and the victim, and an effort was made to reduce any tensions that arose as a result of the experiment [p. 374].

It would be interesting to know what sort of procedures could dissipate the type of emotional disturbance just described. In view of the effects on subjects, traumatic to a degree which Milgram himself considers nearly unprecedented in sociopsychological experiments, his casual assurance that these tensions were dissipated before the subject left the laboratory is unconvincing.

What could be the rational basis for such a posture of indifference? Perhaps Milgram supplies the answer himself when he partially explains the subject's destructive obedience as follows, "Thus they assume that the discomfort caused the victim is momentary, while the scientific gains resulting from the experiment are enduring [p. 378]." Indeed such a rationale might suffice to justify the means used to achieve his end if that end were of inestimable value to humanity or were not itself transformed by the means by which it was attained.

The behavioral psychologist is not in as good a position to objectify his faith in the significance of his work as medical colleagues at points of breakthrough. His experimental situations are not sufficiently accurate models of real-life experience; his sampling techniques are seldom of a scope which would justify the meaning with which he would like to endow his results; and these results are hard to reproduce by colleagues with opposing theoretical views. Unlike the Sabin vaccine, for example, the concrete benefit to humanity of his particular piece of work, no matter how competently handled, cannot justify the risk that real harm will be done to the subject. I am not speaking of physical discomfort, inconvenience, or experimental deception per se, but of permanent harm, however slight. I do regard the emotional disturbance described by Milgram as potentially harmful because it could easily effect an alteration in the subject's self-image or ability to trust adult authorities in the future. It is potentially harmful to a subject to commit, in the course of an experiment, acts which he himself considers unworthy, particularly when he has been entrapped into committing such acts by an individual he has reason to trust. The subject's personal responsibility for his actions is not erased because the experimenter reveals to him the means which he used to stimulate these actions. The subject realizes that he would have hurt the victim if the current were on. The realization that he also made a fool of himself by accepting the experimental set results in additional loss of self-esteem. Moreover, the subject finds it difficult to express his anger outwardly after the experimenter in a self-acceptant but friendly manner reveals the hoax.

A fairly intense corrective interpersonal experience is indicated wherein the subject admits and accepts his responsibility for his own actions, and at the same time gives vent to his hurt and anger at being fooled. Perhaps an experience as distressing as the one described by Milgram can be integrated by the subject, provided that careful thought is given to the matter. The propriety of such experimentation is still in question even if such a reparational experience were forthcoming. Without it I would expect a naive, sensitive subject to remain deeply hurt and anxious for some time, and a sophisticated, cynical subject to become even more alienated and distrustful.

In addition the experimental procedure used by Milgram does not appear suited to the objectives of the study because it does not take into account the special quality of the set which the subject has in the experimental situation. Milgram is concerned with a very important problem, namely, the social consequences of destructive obedience. He says,

Gas chambers were built, death camps were guarded, daily quotas of corpses were produced with the same efficiency as the manufacture of appliances. These inhumane policies may have originated in the mind of a single person, but they could only be carried out on a massive scale if a very large number of persons obeyed orders [p. 371].

But the parallel between authority-subordinate relationships in Hitler's Germany and in Milgram's laboratory is unclear. In the former situation the SS man or member of the German Officer Corps, when obeying orders to slaughter, had no reason to think of his superior officer as benignly disposed towards himself or their victims. The victims were perceived as subhuman and not worthy of consideration. The subordinate officer was an agent in a great cause. He did not need to feel guilt or conflict because within his frame of reference he was acting rightly.

It is obvious from Milgram's own descriptions that most of his subjects were concerned about their victims and did trust the experimenter, and that their distressful conflict was generated in part by the consequences of these two disparate but appropriate attitudes. Their distress may have resulted from shock at what the experimenter was doing to them as well as from what they thought they were doing to their victims. In any case there is not a convincing parallel between the phenomena studied by Milgram and destructive obedience as that concept would apply to the subordinate-authority relationship demonstrated in Hitler Germany. If the experiments were conducted "outside of New Haven and without any visible ties to the university," I would still question their validity on similar although not identical grounds. In addition, I would question the representativeness of a sample of subjects who would voluntarily participate within a noninstitutional setting.

In summary, the experimental objectives of the psychologist are seldom incompatible with the subject's ongoing state of well-being, provided that the experimenter is willing to take the subject's motives and interests into consideration when planning his methods and correctives. Section 4b in *Ethical Standards of Psychologists* (APA, undated) reads in part:

Only when a problem is significant and can be investigated in no other way is the psychologist justified in exposing human subjects to emotional stress or other possible harm. In conducting such research, the psychologist must seriously consider the possibility of harmful aftereffects, and should be prepared to remove them as soon as permitted by the design of the experiment. Where the danger of serious aftereffects exists, research should be conducted only when the subjects or their responsible agents are fully informed of this possibility and volunteer nevertheless [p. 12].

From the subject's point of view procedures which involve loss of dignity, self-esteem, and trust in rational authority are probably most harmful in the long run and require the most thoughtfully planned reparations, if engaged in at all. The public image of psychology as a profession is highly related to our own actions, and some of these actions are changeworthy. It is important that as research psychologists we protect our ethical sensibilities rather than adapt our personal standards to include as appropriate the kind of indignities to which Milgram's subjects were exposed. I would not like to see experiments such as Milgram's proceed unless the subjects were fully informed of the dangers of serious aftereffects and his correctives were clearly shown to be effective in restoring their state of well being.

REFERENCES

American Psychological Association. *Ethical Standards of Psychologists: A Summary of Ethical Principles.* Washington, D.C.: APA, undated.

Milgram, S. "Behavioral Study of Obedience," *Journal of Abnormal Social Psychol.,* Vol. 67 (1963), pp. 37–78.

Proxemics[1] in a cross-cultural context: Germans, English, and French*

Edward T. Hall

The Germans, the English, the Americans, and the French share significant portions of each other's cultures, but at many points their cultures clash. Consequently, the misunderstandings that arise are all the more serious because sophisticated Americans and Europeans take pride in correctly interpreting each other's behavior. Cultural differences which are out of awareness are, as a consequence, usually chalked up to ineptness, boorishness, or lack of interest on the part of the other person.

THE GERMANS

Whenever people from different countries come into repeated contact they begin to generalize about each other's behavior. The Germans and the German

[1] Proxemics can be defined as the relationship between space and ecology and their effect on human interaction.

Swiss are no exception. Most of the intellectual and professional people I have talked to from these two countries eventually get around to commenting on American use of time and space. Both the Germans and the German Swiss have made consistent observations about how Americans structure time very tightly and are sticklers for schedules. They also note that Americans don't leave any free time for themselves (a point which has been made by Sebastian de Grazia in *Of Time, Work, and Leisure*).

Since neither the Germans nor the Swiss (particularly the German Swiss) could be regarded as completely casual about time, I have made it a point to question them further about their view of the American approach to time. They will say that Europeans will schedule fewer events in the same time than Americans do and they usually add that Europeans feel less "pressed" for time than Americans. Certainly, Europeans allow more time for virtually everything involving important human relationships. Many of my European subjects observed that in Europe human relationships are important whereas in the United States the schedule is important. Several of my subjects then took the next logical step and connected the handling of time with attitudes toward space, which Americans treat with incredible casualness. According to European standards, Americans use space in a wasteful way and seldom plan adequately for public needs. In fact, it would seem that Americans feel that people have no needs associated with space at all. By overemphasizing the schedule Americans tend to underemphasize individual space needs. I should mention at this point that all Europeans are not this perceptive. Many of them go no further than to say that in the United States they themselves feel pressured by time and they often complain that our cities lack variety. Nevertheless, given these observations made by Europeans one would expect that the Germans would be more upset by violations of spatial mores than the Americans.

Germans and intrusions

I shall never forget my first experience with German proxemic patterns, which occurred when I was an undergraduate. My manners, my status, and my ego were attacked and crushed by a German in an instance where thirty years' residence in this country and an excellent command of English had not attenuated German definitions of what constitutes and intrusion. In order to understand the various issues that were at stake, it is necessary to refer back to two basic American patterns that are taken for granted in this country and which Americans therefore tend to treat as universal.

First, in the United States there is a commonly accepted, invisible boundary around any two or three people in conversation which separates them from others. Distance alone serves to isolate any such group and to endow it with a protective wall of privacy. Normally, voices are kept low to avoid intruding on others and if voices are heard, people will act as though they had not heard. In this way, privacy is granted whether it is actually present or not. The second pattern is somewhat more subtle and has to do with the exact point at which a person is experienced as actually having crossed a boundary and entered a room. Talking through a screen door while standing outside a house is not considered by most Americans as being inside the house or room in any sense of the word. If one is standing on the threshold holding the door open and talking to someone inside, it is still defined informally and experienced as being *outside*. If one is in an office building and just "pokes his head in the door" of an office he's still outside the office. Just holding on to the door-jamb when one's body is inside the room still means a person has one foot "on base" as it were so that he is not quite inside the other fellow's territory. None of these American spatial definitions is valid in northern Germany. In every instance where the American would consider himself *outside* he has already entered the German's territory and by definition would become involved with him. The following experience brought the conflict between these two patterns into focus.

It was a warm spring day of the type one finds only in the high, clean, clear air of Colorado, the kind of day that makes you glad you are alive. I was standing on the doorstep of a converted carriage house talking to a young woman who lived in an apartment upstairs. The first floor had been made into an artist's studio. The arrangement, however, was peculiar because the same entrance served both tenants. The occupants of the apartment used a small entryway and walked along one wall of the studio to reach the stairs to the apartment. You might say that they had an "easement" through the artist's territory. As I stood talking on the doorstep, I glanced to the left and noticed that some fifty to sixty feet away, inside the studio, the Prussian artist and two of his friends were also in conversation. He was facing so that if he glanced to one side he could just see me. I had noted his presence, but not wanting to appear presumptuous or to interrupt his conversation, I unconsciously applied the American rule and assumed that the two activities—my quiet conversation and his conversation— were not involved with each other. As I was soon to learn, this was a mistake, because in less time than it takes to tell, the artist had detached himself from his friends, crossed the intervening space, pushed my friend aside, and with eyes flashing, started shouting at me. By what right had I entered his studio without greeting him? Who had given me permission?

I felt bullied and humiliated, and even after almost thirty years, I can still feel my anger. Later study has give me greater understanding of the German pattern and I have learned that in the German's eyes I really had been intolerably rude. I was already "inside" the building and I intruded when I could *see* inside. For the German, there is no such thing as being inside the room without being inside the zone of intrusion, particularly if one looks at the other party, no matter how far away.

Recently, I obtained an independent check on how Germans feel about visual intrusion while investigating what people look at when they are in intimate, personal, social, and public situations. In the course of my research, I instructed subjects to photograph separately both a man and a woman in each of the above contexts. One of my assistants, who also happened to be German, photographed his subjects out of focus at public distance because, as he said, "You are not really supposed to look at other people at public distances *because it's intruding.*" This may explain the informal custom behind the German laws against photographing strangers in public without their permission.

The "private sphere"

Germans sense their own space as an extension of the ego. One sees a clue to this feeling in the term "Lebensraum," which is impossible to translate because it summarizes so much. Hitler used it as an effective psychological lever to move the Germans to conquest.

In contrast to the Arab, as we shall see later, the German's ego is extraordinarily exposed, and he will go to almost any length to preserve his "private sphere." This was observed during World War II when American soldiers were offered opportunities to observe German prisoners under a variety of circumstances. In one instance in the Midwest, German P.W.s were housed four to a small hut. As soon as materials were available, each prisoner built a partition so that he could have *his own space.* In a less favorable setting in Germany when the *Wehrmacht* was collapsing, it was necessary to use open stockades because German prisoners were arriving faster than they could be accommodated. In this situation each soldier who could find the materials built his own tiny dwelling unit, sometimes no larger than a foxhole. It puzzled the Americans that the Germans did not pool their efforts and their scarce materials to create a larger, more efficient space, particularly in view of the very cold spring nights. Since that time I have observed frequent instances of the use of architectural extensions of this need to screen the ego. German houses with balconies are arranged so that there is visual privacy. Yards tend to be well fenced; but fenced or not, they are sacred.

The American view that space should be shared is particularly troublesome to the German. I cannot document the account of the early days of World War II occupation when Berlin was in ruins but the following situation was reported by an observer and it has the nightmarish quality that is often associated with inadvertent cross-cultural blunders. In Berlin at that time the housing shortage was indescribably acute. To provide relief, occupation authorities in the American zone ordered those Berliners who still had kitchens and baths intact to share them with their neighbors. The order finally had to be rescinded when the already overstressed Germans started killing each other over the shared facilities.

Public and private buildings in Germany often have double doors for sound-proofing, as do many hotel rooms. In addition, the door is taken very seriously by Germans. Those Germans who come to America feel that our doors are flimsy and light. The meanings of the open door and the closed door are quite different in the two countries. In offices, Americans keep doors open; Germans keep doors closed. In Germany, the closed door does not mean that the man behind it wants to be alone or undisturbed, or that he is doing something he doesn't want someone else to see. It's simply that Germans think that open doors are sloppy and disorderly. To close the door preserves the integrity of the room and provides a protective boundary between people. Otherwise, they get too involved with each other. One of my German subjects commented, "If our family hadn't had doors, we would have had to change our way of life. Without doors we would have had many, many more fights. . . . When you can't talk, you retreat behind a door. . . . If there hadn't been doors, I would always have been within reach of my mother."

Whenever a German warms up to the subject of American enclosed space, he can be counted on to comment on the noise that is transmitted through walls and doors. To many Germans, our doors epitomize American life. They are thin and cheap; they seldom fit; and they lack the substantial quality of German doors. When they close they don't sound and feel solid. The click of the lock is indistinct, it rattles and indeed it may even be absent.

The open-door policy of American business and the closed-door patterns of German business culture cause clashes in the branches and subsidiaries of American firms in Germany. The point seems to be quite simple, yet failure to grasp it has caused considerable friction and misunderstanding between American and German managers overseas. I was once called in to advise a firm that has operations all over the world. One of the first questions asked was, "How do you get the Germans to keep their doors open?" In this company the open doors were making the Germans feel exposed and gave the whole operation an unusually relaxed and unbusinesslike air. Closed doors, on the other hand, gave the Americans the feeling that there was a conspiratorial air about the place and that they were being left out. The point is that whether the door is open or shut, it is not going to mean the same thing in the two countries.

Order in space

The orderliness and hierarchical quality of German culture are communicated in their handling of space. Germans want to know where they stand and object strenuously to people crashing queues or people who "get out of line" or who do not obey signs such as "Keep out," "Authorized personnel only," and the like. Some of the German attitudes toward ourselves are traceable to our informal attitudes toward boundaries and to authority in general.

However, German anxiety due to American violations of order is nothing compared to that engendered in Germans by the Poles, who see no harm in a little disorder. To them lines and queues stand for regimentation and blind authority. I once saw a Pole crash a cafeteria line just "to stir up those sheep."

Germans get very technical about intrusion distance, as I mentioned earlier. When I once asked my students to describe the distance at which a third party would intrude on two people who were talking, there were no answers from the Americans. Each student knew that he could tell when he was being intruded on but he couldn't define intrusion or tell how he knew when it had occurred. However, a German and an Italian who had worked in Germany were both members of my class and they answered without any hesitation. Both stated that a third party would intrude on two people if he came within seven feet!

Many Americans feel that Germans are overly rigid in their behavior, unbending and formal. Some of this impression is created by differences in the handling of chairs while seated. The American doesn't seem to mind if people hitch their chairs up to adjust the distance to the situation—those that do mind would not think of saying anything, for to comment on the manners of others would be impolite. In Germany, however, it is a violation of the mores to change the position of your chair. An added deterrent for those who don't know better is the weight of most German furniture. Even the great architect Mies van der Rohe, who often rebelled against German tradition in his buildings, made his handsome chairs so heavy that anyone but a strong man would have difficulty in adjusting his seating position. To a German, light furniture is anathema, not only because it seems flimsy but because people move it and thereby destroy the order of things, including intrusions on the "private sphere." In one instance reported to me, a German newspaper editor who had moved to the United States had his visitor's chair bolted to the floor "at the proper distance" because he couldn't tolerate the American habit of adjusting the chair to the situation.

THE ENGLISH

It has been said that the English and the Americans are two great people separated by one language. The differences for which language gets blamed may not be due so much to words as to communications on other levels beginning with English intonation (which sounds affected to many Americans) and continuing to ego-linked ways of handling time, space, and materials. If there ever were two cultures in which differences of the proxemic details are marked it is in the educated (public school) English and the middle-class Americans. One of the basic reasons for this wide disparity is that in the United States we use space as a way of classifying people and activities, whereas in England it is the social system that determines who you are. In the United States, your address is an important cue to status (this applies not only to one's home but to the business address as well). The Joneses from Brooklyn and Miami are not as "in" as the Joneses from Newport and Palm Beach. Greenwich and Cape Cod are worlds apart from Newark and Miami. Businesses located on Madison and Park avenues have more tone than those on Seventh and Eighth avenues. A corner office is more prestigious than one next to the elevator or at the end of a long hall. The Englishman, however, is born and brought up in a social system. He is still Lord—no matter where you find him, even if it is behind the counter in a fishmonger's stall. In addition to class distinctions, there are differences between the English and ourselves in how space is allotted.

The middle-class American growing up in the United States feels he has a right to have his own room, or at least part of a room. My American subjects, when asked to draw an ideal room or office, invariably drew it for themselves and no one else. When asked to draw their present room or office, they drew only their own part of a shared room and then drew a line down the middle. Both male and female subjects identified the kitchen and the master bedroom as belonging to the mother or the wife, whereas Father's territory was a study or a den, if one was available; otherwise, it was "the shop," "the basement," or sometimes only a workbench or the garage. American women who want to be alone can go to the bedroom and close the door. The closed door is the sign meaning "Do not disturb" or "I'm angry." An American is available if his door is open at home or at his office. He is expected not to shut himself off but to maintain himself in a state of constant readiness to answer the demands of others. Closed doors are for conferences, private conversations, and business, work that requires concentration, study, resting, sleeping, dressing, and sex.

The middle- and upper-class Englishman, on the other hand, is brought up in a nursery shared with brothers and sisters. The oldest occupies a room by himself which he vacates when he leaves for boarding school, possibly even at the age of nine or ten. The difference between a room of one's own and early conditioning to shared space, while seeming inconsequential, has an important effect on the Englishman's attitude toward his own space. He may never have a permanent "room of his own" and seldom expects one or feels he is entitled to one. Even Members of Parliament have no offices and often conduct their business on the terrace overlooking the Thames. As a consequence, the English are puzzled by the American need for a secure place in which to work, an office. Americans working in England may become annoyed if they are not provided with what they consider appropriate enclosed work space. In regard to the need for walls as a screen for the ego, this places the Americans somewhere between the Germans and the English.

The contrasting English and American patterns have some remarkable implications, particularly if we assume that man, like other animals, has a built-in need to shut himself off from others from time to time. An English student in one of my seminars typified what happens when hidden patterns clash. He was quite obviously experiencing strain in his relationships with Americans. Nothing seemed to go right and it was quite clear from his remarks that we did not know how to behave. An analysis of his complaints showed that a major source of irritation was that no American seemed to be able to pick up the subtle clues that there were times when he didn't want his thoughts intruded on. As he stated it, "I'm walking around the apartment and it seems that whenever I want to be alone my roommate starts talking to me. Pretty soon he's asking 'What's the matter?' and wants to know if I'm angry. By then I am angry and say something."

It took some time but finally we were able to identify most of the contrasting features of the American and British problems that were in conflict in this case. When the American wants to be alone he goes into a room and shuts the door—he depends on architectural features for screening. For an American to refuse to talk to someone else present in the same room, to give them the "silent treatment," is the ultimate form of rejection and a sure sign of great displeasure. The English, on the other hand, lacking rooms of their own since childhood, never developed the practice of using space as a refuge from others. They have in effect internalized a set of barriers, which they erect and which others are supposed to recognize. Therefore, the more the Englishman shuts himself off when he is with an American the more likely the American is to break in to assure himself that all is well. Tension lasts until the two get to know each other. The important point is that the spatial and architectural needs of each are not the same at all.

Using the telephone

English internalized privacy mechanisms and the American privacy screen result in very different customs regarding the telephone. There is no wall or door against the telephone. Since it is impossible to tell from the ring who is on the other end of the line, or how urgent his business is, people feel compelled to answer the phone. As one would anticipate, the English when they feel the need to be with their thoughts treat the phone as an intrusion by someone who doesn't know any better. Since it is impossible to tell how preoccupied the other party will be they hesitate to use the phone; instead, they write notes. To phone is to be "pushy" and rude. A letter or telegram may be slower, but it is much less disrupting. Phones are for actual business and emergencies.

I used this system myself for several years when I lived in Santa Fe, New Mexico, during the depression. I dispensed with a phone because it cost money. Besides, I cherished the quiet of my tiny mountainside retreat and didn't want to be disturbed. This idiosyncrasy on my part produced a shocked reaction in others. People really didn't know what to do with me. You could see the consternation on their faces when, in answer to the question, "How do I get in touch with you?" I would reply, "Write me a post card. I come to the post office every day."

Having provided most of our middle-class citizens with private rooms and escape from the city to the suburbs, we have then proceeded to penetrate their most private spaces in their home with a most public device, the telephone. Anyone can reach us at any time. We are, in fact, so available that elaborate devices have to be devised so that busy people can function. The greatest skill and tact must be exercised in the message-screening process so that others will not be offended. So far our technology has not kept up with the needs of people to be alone with either their families or their thoughts. The problem stems from the fact that it is impossible to tell from the phone's ring who is calling and how urgent his business is. Some people have unlisted phones but then that makes it hard on friends who come to town who want to get in touch with them. The government solution is to have special phones for important people (traditionally red). The red line bypasses secretaries, coffee breaks, busy signals, and teen-agers, and is connected to White House, State Department, and Pentagon switch-boards.

Neighbors

Americans living in England are remarkably consistent in their reactions to the English. Most of them are hurt and puzzled because they were brought up on American neighboring patterns and don't interpret the English ones correctly. In England propinquity means nothing. The fact that you live next door to a family does not entitle you to visit, borrow from, or socialize with them, or your children to play with theirs. Accurate figures on the number of Americans who adjust well to the English are difficult to obtain. The basic attitude of the English toward the Americans is tinged by our ex-colonial status. This attitude is much more in awareness and therefore more likely to be expressed than the unspoken right of the Englishman to maintain his privacy against the world. To the best of my knowledge, those who have tried to relate to the English purely on the basis of propinquity seldom if ever succeed. They may get to know and even like their neighbors, but it won't be because they live next door, because English relationships are patterned not according to space but according to social status.

Whose room is the bedroom?

In upper middle-class English homes, it is the man, not the woman, who has the privacy of the bedroom, presumably as protection from children who haven't yet internalized the English patterns of privacy. The man, not the woman, has a dressing room; the man also has a study which affords privacy. The Englishman is fastidious about his clothes and expects to spend a great deal of time and attention in their purchase. In contrast, English women approach the buying of clothes in a manner reminiscent of the American male.

Talking loud and soft

Proper spacing between people is maintained in many ways. Loudness of the voice is one of the mechanisms which also varies from culture to culture. In England and in Europe generally, Americans are continually accused of loud talking, which is a function of two forms of vocal control: (a) loudness, and (b) modulation for direction. Americans increase the volume as a function of distance, using several levels (whisper, normal voice, loud shout, etc.). In many situations, the more gregarious Americans do not care if they can be overheard. In fact, it is part of their openness showing that we have nothing to hide. The English do care, for to get along without private offices and not intrude they have developed skills in beaming the voice toward the person they are talking to, carefully adjusting it so that it just barely overrides the background noise and distance. For the English to be overheard is to intrude on others, a failure in manners and a sign of socially inferior behavior. However, because of the way they modulate their voices the English in an American setting may sound and look conspiratorial to Americans, which can result in their being branded as troublemakers.

Eye behavior

A study of eye behavior reveals some interesting contrasts between the two cultures. Englishmen in this country have trouble not only when they want to be alone and shut themselves off but also when they want to interact. They never know for sure whether an American is listening. We, on the other hand, are equally unsure as to whether the English have understood us. Many of these ambiguities in communication center on differences in the use of the eyes. The Englishman is taught to pay strict attention, to listen carefully, which he must do if he is polite and there are not protective walls to screen out sound. He doesn't bob his head or grunt to let you know he understands. He blinks his eyes to let you know that he has heard you. Americans, on the other hand, are taught not to stare. We look the other person straight in the eye without wavering only when we want to be particularly certain that we are getting through to him.

The gaze of the American directed toward his conversational partner often wanders from one eye to the other and even leaves the face for long periods. Proper English listening behavior includes immobilization of the eyes at social distance, so that whichever eye one looks at gives the appearance of looking straight at you. In order to accomplish this feat, the Englishman must be eight or more feet away. He is too close when the 12-degree horizontal span of the macula won't permit a steady gaze. At less then eight feet, one *must* look at either one eye or the other.

THE FRENCH

The French who live south and east of Paris belong generally to that complex of cultures which border the Mediterranean. Members of this group pack together more closely than do northern Europeans, English, and Americans. Mediterranean use of space can be seen in the crowded trains, buses, automobiles, sidewalk cafés, and in the homes of the people. The exceptions are, of course, in the châteaus and villas of the rich. Crowded living normally means high sensory involvement. Evidence of French emphasis on the senses appears not only in the way the French eat, entertain, talk, write, crowd together in cafés, but can even be seen in the way they make their maps. These maps are extraordinarily well thought out and so designed that the traveler can find the most detailed information. One can tell from using these maps that the French employ all their senses. These maps make it possible for you to get around and they also tell you where you can enjoy a view; where you'll find picturesque drives, and, in some instances, places to rest, refresh yourself, take a walk, and even eat a pleasant meal. They inform the traveler which senses he can expect to use and at what points in his journey.

Home and family

One possible reason why the French love the outdoors is the rather crowded conditions under which many of them live. The French entertain at restaurants and cafés. The home is for the family and the outdoors for recreation and socializing. Yet all the homes I have visited, as well as everything I have been able to learn about French homes, indicate that they are often quite crowded. The working class and the petite bourgeoisie are particularly crowded, which means that the French are sensually much involved with each other. The layout of their offices, homes, towns, cities, and countryside is such as to keep them involved.

In interpersonal encounters this involvement runs high; when a Frenchman talks to you, he really looks at you and there is no mistaking this fact. On the streets of Paris he looks at the woman he sees very directly. American women returning to their own country after living in France often go through a period of sensory deprivation. Several have told me that because they have grown accustomed to being looked at, the American habit of *not* looking makes them feel as if they didn't exist.

Not only are the French sensually involved with each other, they have become accustomed to what are to us greatly stepped-up sensory inputs. The French automobile is designed in response to French needs. Its small size used to be attributed to a lower standard of living and higher costs of materials; and while there can be no doubt but that cost is a factor, it would be naïve to assume that it was the major factor. The automobile is just as much an expression of the culture as is the language and, therefore, has its characteristic niche in the cultural biotope. Changes in the car will reflect and be reflected in changes elsewhere. If the French drove American cars, they would be forced to give up many ways of dealing with space which they hold quite dear. The traffic along the Champs-Elysées and around the Arc de Triomphe is a cross between the New Jersey Turnpike on a sunny Sunday afternoon and the Indianapolis Speedway. With American-size autos, it would be mass suicide. Even the occasional "compact" American cars in the stream of Parisian traffic look like sharks among minnows. In the United States, the same cars look normal because everything else is in scale. In the foreign setting where they stand out, Detroit iron can be seen for what it is. The American behemoths give bulk to the ego and prevent overlapping of personal spheres inside the car so that each passenger is only marginally involved with the others. I do not mean by this that all Americans are alike and have been forced into the Detroit mold. But since Detroit won't produce what is wanted, many Americans prefer the smaller, more maneuverable European cars which fit their personalities and needs more closely. Nevertheless, if one simply looks at the styles of the French cars, one sees greater emphasis on individuality than in the United States. Compare the Peugeot, the Citroen, the Renault and the Dauphine and the little 2 C.V. shoebox. It would take years and years of style changes to produce such differences in the United States.

French use of open spaces

Because total space needs must be maintained in balance, the urban French have learned to make the most of the parks and the outdoors. To them, the city is something from which to derive satisfaction and so are the people in it. Reasonably clean air, sidewalks up to seventy feet wide, automobiles that will not dwarf humans as they pass on the boulevards make it possible to have outdoor cafés and open areas where people congregate and enjoy each other. Since the French savor and participate in the city itself—its varied sights, sounds, and smells; its wide sidewalks and avenues and parks—the need for insulating space in the automobile may be somewhat less than it is in the United States where humans are dwarfed by skyscrapers and the products of Detroit, visually assaulted by filth and rubbish, and poisoned by smog and carbon dioxide.

The star and the grid

There are two major European systems for patterning space. One of these, "the radiating star" which occurs in France and Spain, is sociopetal. The other, the "grid," originated in Asia Minor, adopted by the Romans and carried to England at the time of Caesar, is sociofugal. The French-Spanish system connects all points and functions. In the French subway system, different lines repeatedly come together at places of interest like the Place de la Concorde, the Opéra, and the Madeleine. The grid system separates activities by stringing them out. Both systems have advantages, but a person familiar with one has difficulty using the other.

For example, a mistake in direction in the radiating center-point system becomes more serious the farther one travels. Any error, therefore, is roughly equivalent to taking off in the wrong direction. In the grid system, baseline errors are of the 90-degree or the 180-degree variety and are usually obvious enough to make themselves felt even by those with a poor sense of direction. If you are traveling in the right direction, even though you are one or two blocks off your course, the error is easily rectified at any time. Nevertheless, there are certain inherent advantages in the center-point system. Once one learns to use it, it is easier for example to locate objects or events in space by naming a point on a line. Thus it is possible, even in strange territory, to tell someone to meet you at the 50 KM mark on National Route 20 south of Paris; that is all the information he needs. In contrast, the grid system of co-ordinates involves at least two lines and a point to locate something in space (often many more lines and points, depending on how many turns one has to make). In the star system, it is also possible to integrate a number of different activities in centers in less space than with the grid system. Thus, residential, shopping, marketing, commercial, and recreation areas can both meet and be reached from central points.

It is incredible how many facets of French life the radiating star pattern touches. It is almost as though the whole culture were set up on a model in which power, influence, and control flowed in and out from a series of interlocking centers. There are sixteen major highways running into Paris, twelve into Caen (near Omaha Beach), twelve into Amiens, eleven for Le Mans, and ten for Rennes. Even the figures don't begin to convey the picture of what this arrangement really means, for France is a series of radiating networks that build up into larger and larger centers. Each small center has its own channel, as it were, to the next higher level. As a general rule, the roads between centers do not go through other towns, because each town is connected to others by its own roads. This is in contrast to the American pattern of stringing small towns out like beads on a necklace along the routes that connect principal centers.

In *The Silent Language* I have described how the man in charge of a French office can often be found in the middle—with his minions placed like satellites on strings radiating outward from him. I once had occasion to deal with such a "central figure" when the French member of a team of scientists under my direction wanted a raise because his desk was in the middle! Even De Gaulle bases his international policy on France's central location. There are those, of course, who will say that the fact that the French school system also follows a highly centralized pattern couldn't possibly have any relationship to the layout of offices, subway systems, road networks, and, in fact, the entire nation, but I could not agree with them. Long experience with different patterns of culture has taught me that the basic threads tend to be woven throughout the entire fabric of a society.

The reason for the review of the three European cultures to which the middle class of the United States is most closely linked (historically and culturally) is as much as anything else a means of providing contrast to highlight some of our own implicit patterns. In this review it was shown that different use of the senses leads to very different needs regarding space no matter on what level one cares to consider it. Everything from an office to a town or city will reflect the sense modalities of its builders and occupants. In considering solutions to problems such as urban renewal and city sinks it is essential to know how the populations involved perceive space and how they use their senses.

Some social consequences of temporary systems*

Philip E. Slater

Social change brings pain and costs as well as relief and benefits. What will life be like in a society based on temporary systems? How will people relate to one another? To what extent will such an organizational pattern simply accentuate conditions already present in our society?

One obvious effect of the widespread extension of temporary systems would be a sharp increase in geographic mobility. If task forces are to be organized on a temporary basis around specific problems there is no particular reason why their formation should be locally restricted. Individuals will be brought together on the basis of talent and availability, and geographic location will be less important as an impediment than prior commitments. We will then become a nation of itinerants, moving continually on an irregular and perhaps even nonrecurrent circuit of jobs. What is mildly characteristic of the academic world today will become accelerated and general throughout the economy. While work may become more meaningful, will not the reverse be true of "private life"?

We know something about the effects of mobility, for we live in what is undoubtedly the most mobile society that has ever existed anywhere in the world. It is true that there have been many societies that continually moved from place to place. But these nomadic tribes moved as a group, and usually over a fixed route. They carried their possessions, their relationships, their entire way of life along with them, unchanged. In most cases, even the land did not really change since every part of the route was reencountered at predictable intervals, save in times of climatic or military cataclysm (which although they make history, are grossly unrepresentative). They were just as rooted to the land as a peasant farmer, but to a corridor instead of a region.

Mobility in modern society is quite another matter. Here individuals or family units are plucked out of their social context and transplanted. They may never live in the same place twice. While they may stay within the same society (although these boundaries may also weaken in the future), they must form new relationships, adapt to a new physical environment, new norms, and so on. Those who remain behind must repair the social fissure that the transients have created.

The consequences of mobility for our culture are profound. George Pierson has argued with great force that most of what is distinctively American can be traced to it (1964, pp. 119 ff.). Optimism, conservatism, other-directedness, individualism, equalitarianism, superficiality, identity-diffusion, gregariousness, alienation, homogeneity, money-mindedness, loneliness, nostalgia, anxiety, conformity, activity, achievement-orientation, pragmatism, love of novelty, materialism, youth worship—all of these real or imagined qualities bear some relationship to this tendency of modern Americars to uproot themselves at relatively frequent intervals.

But we must distinguish between those characteristics which spring directly from the effects of mobility itself, and those which derive from mechanisms designed to soften these effects. Thus moving about frequently tends to detach the individual from enduring and significant relationships—this is a primary effect. But the difficulty of continually forming new bonds and breaking old ones might be mitigated by developing ways of accelerating the process of acquaintance: an informality, and easy friendliness, a capacity for ready, if superficial, relationship. This would be a secondary effect—one which need not automatically occur, but which might evolve as a compensatory mechanism.

PRIMARY CONSEQUENCES OF TEMPORARY SYSTEMS

We can hypothesize two primary and three secondary consequences of increased mobility and temporary systems, all of them little more than extrapolation from existing conditions. First, the process of individuation, of the separation of the individual from those permanent groups which provide him with ready-made values and traits, and from which he derives his identity, will accelerate. His ability to say "I am a——" prior to the completion of his education or training will disappear utterly. His experience will become more unique, his knowledge and work more narrowly specialized, his social existence more atomized.

The second effect will be a concomitant feeling—acute and pervasive—of alienation, of anomie, of meaninglessness. These feelings will, as usual, be misconstrued as a function of everyone having become alike, although the striving toward uniformity is actually a secondary phenomenon, an attempt to *counteract* the feelings of alienation and anomie. On the contrary, these feelings arise when the individual is deprived of a permanent, contextual group toward whom he feels a bond of likeness, heightened by one or two points of specialization which define his role in that group.

Human beings are all equipped with the same emotional repertoire, the same basic needs, the same basic defenses. Out of these they evolve more idiosyncratic structures which we call personality or, when they are based on shared definitions of meaning, culture. These differences help maintain boundaries between individuals and between groups but at the cost of some violence to the emotional life of the individual. His body may tell him, as a human being, to respond in a given way to a punch in the nose, or a sexual stimulus, or a loss, or a rejection, but he may have learned, as a member of a specific culture, or as one playing a special role within that culture, not to react in this human way, but rather in some way which defines him more uniquely.

To be more unique, in other words, is to be less human, more of a social artifact. One man learns to lose the capacity to respond to a given situation with love, another with anger, another with jealousy, another with tears, and so on. This process of emotional crippling we call personality development. Its positive side is a hypertrophy of other responses which permit a kind of emotional specialization within the group. In a permanent group the individual can sense his likeness with others, while the self-alienation that arises from his specialized response system is mitigated by his close and constant contact with other specialists, who express his needs and feelings for him as he does for them. In a culture in which a man cannot weep, his women may weep for him. If he is a group jester and not supposed to feel gloomy, there will be some dour compatriot to do this for him, and so on. And where the group as a whole warps human feeling in a given direction, defining its differentness from other groups, his similarity with those around him palliates his sense of alienation from his feelings.

When an individual loses a more or less permanent role in a permanent group, his specialization becomes pointless and somewhat burdensome. He becomes a part in search of a whole, feeling neither enough like others to avoid a sense of being alone and lost, nor sufficiently included in a stable pattern of differentiation to have a sense of himself as a distinguishable entity embedded in a pattern of other such entities. In a society which places a value on individualism this inability to experience oneself leads paradoxically to a cry for *more* uniqueness, more eccentricity, more individuation, thus exacerbating the system.

The only conceivable solution to this problem is, to put it bluntly, the obliteration of differences: the maximization of uniformity, of homogeneity, of sameness among people. This is based, however, on two assumptions. The first assumption is that we accept mobility as a given. It might be felt that the price paid for mobility, for flexibility, for democracy in fact, is too high—that we should try and find ways to bring the entire movement of our time to a sudden and grinding halt before everything of value in human life is lost. I do not regard this as possible, nor am I certain it is desirable. Before settling for the manifold ills that mankind has borne throughout history we owe ourselves the resolution at least to peer into the unknown and imagine what it might hold, and what might be made of it.

The second assumption is the more crucial, since if it does not obtain, few people would wish to accept the first. Homogenization could only be tolerated if people are uniformly transformed into full human beings, rather than remaining specialized semipersons as we are now constituted. Fantasies of uniformity have always made the negative assumption that such uniformity would be a similarity of limitedness—that all humans will become robots, or assume the specialized posture of a gregarious suburbanite, or that of a submissive peasant, or whatever. In other words, we imagine with horror that all humans will be forced to accept some specialized stance now voluntarily adopted by a few. But such a homogenization would not be viable, since (*a*) it would retain the same constraints under which we now suffer without providing the compensatory mechanisms of vicarious expression, the sense of separate-although-embedded identity, (*b*) the advantages of a social division of labor would be lost, and the society as a whole would suffer from the loss of variety, the lack of human resources. This does not mean that such a system cannot be essayed—we can see attempts to evolve this kind of uniformity in segments of our own society—it only means that a society so structured will fail. A viable society must somehow avail itself of a great variety of contradictory human responses. If members of that society are to be limited in the ways they can respond, then it is necessary that they be limited in different ways—otherwise generalized shortages will (and do) arise. Conversely, if a society is to function with similar participants, each one must be complex and unrestricted in available response patterns. They must have the capacity to be introverted *and* extroverted, controlled *and* spontaneous, independent *and* dependent, gregarious *and* seclusive, loving *and* hostile, strong *and* weak, and so on.

This is, of course, utopian. Human beings will never achieve this degree of humanness; nor will complete uniformity ever be achieved, happily. We are merely saying that insofar as uniformity is sought, incompleteness must be eschewed. Less variety from person to person requires more variety within each person. The individual will be more changeable, less predictable from moment to moment, from situation to situation, less able to play the same tune all his life long. Wardrobes may, taken as a whole, be more similar, but each one far more varied, and the variety of dress in any given social situation much greater than today.

SECONDARY CONSEQUENCES OF TEMPORARY SYSTEMS

I. Interchangeability

The first secondary consequence has already been dealt with indirectly. If one must make and break relationships rapidly then it becomes increasingly important that people be as interchangeable as possible, and this is most simply achieved through uniformity. It is, of course, a basic principle of mass production and has extended itself in a variety of ways throughout our culture, leading to complaints of dullness and monotony. One revealing expression of the principle is the motel. An American today can travel almost anywhere in the country and stop at a motel to find himself in an entirely familiar environment. He would indeed be hard put to distinguish one from another. As relationships become increasingly temporary the need to establish such instant familiarity will correspondingly increase.

But people are not motels, for the most part, and we have already pointed out the necessity for an enrichment of the individual before interchangeability will be viable. No such problem exists for the motel: the human need for variety in physical surroundings is extremely limited, even trivial, and we may expect the monotony of our physical environment to maintain its accelerative rate of growth, only slightly damped by self-conscious remedial measures.

Interchangeability is a threatening concept. It violates every principle of association known to man and conjures up an image of social chaos. Yet it is only a logical extension of the evolution of associational principles up to this moment.

The most primitive and elemental principle of association is territoriality, which simply states that the greater the physical distance between A and B, the less important they are to each other. It exists in pure form almost nowhere at the human level, and almost everywhere at the animal level (cf. Hall, 1966, pp. 7–37; Lorenz, 1966; Scott, 1958, pp. 206 ff.). Although alloyed with other principles it is still of vital importance in human society today. If we make the necessary modification, for moving units, of substituting propinquity of *pathways* for static propinquity, it is still the most powerful single factor in human relationships, from marital choice (Koller, 1962) to interfamilial relationships (Festinger et al., 1950; Whyte, 1956, pp. 365–86). It lingers as an important bond even when the propinquity is made artificial by temporal separation (Mead, 1964, pp. 131–41).

The limitations of territoriality are obvious: it is impossible to construct any large-scale organization on this principle alone since there is no way to achieve centralization. Village A can relate to village C only through intermediate village B, and if A and C are equidistant from B, there is no basis for assigning greater weight to one or the other.

But all existing human societies, however primitive, share at least one other associational principle which redresses this deficiency. This principle is kinship, which states that the greater consanguineal distance (always to some extent arbitrarily defined by the culture) between A and B, the less important they are to each other. This principle is modeled after the territorial one but is liberated from dependence upon the physical environment. When it is combined with exogamous marriage rules it cuts across the territorial principle, permitting multiple loyalties and the coalescence of larger social units.

Both of these principles are universal today, but in modern urban societies they have been severely intruded upon by a third, as Simmel observed some time ago in his analysis of "social circles" (Simmel, 1964, pp. 127 ff.). This principle, which is capable of infinite subdivision, but which we might crudely label the principle of common interest, states that the fewer the interests shared by A and B the less important they are to each other. (The interests may, but need not, be utilitarian.) This principle goes further than kinship in detaching association from fixed external conditions. While the kinship principle is based in part on cultural definitions, the common interest principle is entirely so based, and hence is totally manipulable in cultural terms. It not only permits still larger and more complex social systems, but also adds an element of flexibility; territories and kin relationships cannot change, but interests can and do.

The growth of temporary systems will tend further to limit the spheres of territoriality and kinship. But it also challenges the common interest principle in its traditional form. The concept of interchangeability inaugurates a fourth principle, which we might call the principle of temporary relevance. It is not really new, but merely an extension of the common interest principle. It eliminates *any fixed basis* for human relationships, although the temporary bases derive from common interest. Thus any permanence in human association will depend upon the survival of the earlier principles.

Now it can be seen from this progression that each principle frees human relationships more and more from dependence upon external constraints, permitting more freedom of choice and a wider range of possible encounters. What is threatening about interchangeability is (*a*) the introduction of transitoriness as a necessary rather than accidental feature of social life, and (*b*) the apparent violation of our popular belief that people choose to relate to one another on the basis of the intrinsic qualities of the other person. The first threat is a real one which we will discuss later on in detail. The second is in large part illusory, based on a sentimental misconception of social relationships.

Obviously the principles of territoriality and kinship ignore the intrinsic qualities of the individual altogether. This is expressed in a number of adages and homilies to the effect that one can choose one's friends but not one's relatives or neighbors (although the latter is only partially true today). Choice is thus offered as a sop to compensate for the loss of stability, security, and permanence. The choice is not really an individual one, however, and is in that sense an illusion. We are conditioned by our culture and by our early socialization experiences to make certain kinds of choices with fair predictability. Our interest patterns bring us into contact with similar individuals whom we then "choose." The principle of temporary relevance faces up to this reality with rather brutal honesty.

But it must be remembered that total interchangeability will never be achieved. If it could be, temporary systems would not be necessary, for they assume at least a technical specialization. But such temporary working groups will have little else reliably in common besides their task—again, by definition. They cannot serve as a social circle, nor will it be easy to enter and leave other circles on so rapid a basis, at least as they are now constituted. It will be increasingly necessary to take people as one finds them—to relate immediately, intensely, and without the basis of traditional social props, rituals, and distancing mechanisms. Distance will be provided by transience, and the old patterns of gamesmanship, of extended, gradual and incomplete unmasking will become appropriate. By the time the individual reaches his "here-is-the-real-me" flourish he will find himself alone again. It seems clear that one of the unintended functions of "sensitivity training" or "basic encounter" groups is an anticipatory socialization mechanism for a world of temporary systems, since they emphasize openness, "feedback," immediacy, communication at a "feeling" level, the "here-and-now," more awareness of and ability to express "deeper" feelings, and so on. Group members often express surprise and chagrin at their capacity to respond with warmth and intensity to individuals they would in other situations have regarded with indifference, fear, or contempt. After the initial shock has worn off the inevitability of preference hierarchies is rediscovered, but a sense of the degree to which opportunities for significant relationships are wasted by casual stereotyping is usually retained. Such an awareness would be a precondition of a society of temporary systems.

II. Other-directedness

Another secondary consequence of temporary systems would be the development of more flexible normative mechanisms. This again represents the intensification of an existing trend rather than a new departure. Mobility and change rule out the efficacy of any permanent system of social control. *External controls* depend upon the permanent embeddedness of the individual in the same social unit—a condition which has largely vanished from the civilized world. *Internalized controls of a fixed kind* rapidly become irrelevant to a changing social environment. Our society has long required, and obtained, a system of internalized controls which incorporates moral relativism—what Riesman has called "other-direction." The individual must at one and the same time be capable of self-restraint while recognizing that groups vary in what they consider desirable and undesirable social behavior (Riesman et al., 1955, pp. 37–38). He must be acutely sensitive and responsive to group norms while recognizing the essential arbitrariness, particularity, and limited relevance of all moral imperatives.

This idea is offensive to many and has generated a whole tradition of angry nostalgia among postwar critics of American society. Riesman himself, while not in the least responsible for the gross distortions of his basic argument, shares in this nostalgia to a certain degree. His use of the term "gyroscope" to describe the conformity mechanism of the inner-directed man (Riesman et al., 1955, pp. 31 ff.) betrays this sentiment (A less flattering metaphor would be a wind-up toy.). For the inner-directed individual is programmed at birth to display a limited range of responses in all situations, regardless of environmental variation, and while this may well be considered heroic, it is, like all heroic manifestations, excessively simple-minded. Even computers have achieved a higher degree of sophistication.

A society organized around temporary systems promises even greater virtuosity in flexible self-controls and further reduction in the shrinking store of half-heartedly embraced moral absolutes. It is important to recognize, however, that we are not heralding the disappearance of the "superego" (or whatever one wishes to label human normative responses). Anyone who interprets contemporary trends in terms of a "loosening" of social restraints on impulse is reading the signals with one eye closed. The simple (and largely ineffectual) "no" of the Puritan divine made far fewer inroads on instinctual expression and created far fewer moral dilemmas than the "fun morality" Wolfenstein discusses (1963, pp. 168–75). More play in work also means more work in play, until all acts become both playful and instrumental, public and private, and no sphere of human expression is altogether uncontaminated.

III. Intensification and dedifferentiation of the marital relationship

One of the more tiresome cliches of family sociology is that the modern family has somehow declined in significance, having been stripped of so many of its earlier functions. To this calamity is then attributed a host of social problems, notably divorce.

It is a mistake only a sociologist could make. For if we concentrate our attention on the marital bond it becomes immediately apparent that the hazards to which the bond is currently subject flow from a surfeit rather than a loss of functions. These functions, however, are primarily emotional. Two married persons in a stable and permanent social context need little from each other. Psychological and interpersonal needs can be satisfied in a variety of other relationships—kin, neighborhood, friendship. In many societies and subcultures deeply entrenched patterns of sex segregation make intimate communication between the sexes difficult or impossible—men and women literally live in different worlds. Wherever this stability begins to break down, husband and wife tend to increase their emotional demands upon each other. Elizabeth Bott was probably the first to point out this effect, observing that couples in "close-knit" relational networks maintained a rigid division of labor, were deeply involved in external bonds, and placed little emphasis on shared interests, joint recreation, or a satisfying sexual relationship. Couples in "loose-knit" networks, on the other hand, showed little division of labor, emphasized marital "togetherness," and were highly self-conscious about childrearing techniques (Bott, 1957, p. 198). The transition from working-class to middle-class status and from "urban villager" to suburban environments tends to bring about a loosening of relational networks and is therefore usually associated with an increase in the intensity and intimacy of the marital bond, and a decrease in marital and parental role differentiation (Komarovsky, 1964; Slater, 1961; Litwak, 1966, p. 14).

Although sociologists have generally argued, with good reason, that higher income, education, and other attributes of middle-class standing are stabilizing forces for marriage (but cf. Hillman, 1962), one would anticipate that the greater burden placed on the marital bond by the reduction of alternative intimate and enduring relationships would augment the rate of marital dissolution. In a non-mobile society one expects of marriage only a degree of compatibility. Spouses are not asked to be lovers, friends, and mutual therapists. But it is increasingly true of our own society that the marital bond is the closest, deepest, most important, and putatively most enduring relationship of one's life. Paradoxically, therefore, it is increasingly likely to fall short of the demands placed upon it and be dissolved. As emotional alternatives are removed, its limitations become less and less tolerable. The social ties of modern Americans are becoming so ephemeral that a permanent point of reference seems essential, and this perhaps accounts for the heroic effort made in our society—through marriage manuals, counselors, psychotherapists, magazine articles, and so on—to find ways of enabling the marriage relationship to bear the enormous emotional burdens placed on it.

The future of marriage in a society of temporary systems remains ambiguous. There is no inherent reason why families could not remain permanent in such a society—moving as a unit when moves occur. Yet there are several strains which such family mobility creates, and which tend to pull it apart in the absence of compensatory mechanisms. The family as a whole cannot be as easily included in the temporary system framework as the single individual. Many large corporations with mobile executives have recognized this problem, but their attempts to remedy it have been rather ambivalent. By trying to include the wife and family in organization thinking they have acted alternately to stabilize and to rupture the marital bond: the former through including the family in corporation activities, providing therapeutic facilities, and so on; the latter by demanding that the husband's organizational commitment always come first, and by penalizing the husband for the wife's personality and behavior. As Whyte observes, in his discussion of these practices, "divorce rarely disqualifies a man," since the wife may have been "outgrown" by her rising executive husband (Whyte, 1962, pp. 118 ff.).

The most obvious strain in a society based on temporary systems would be produced by the wife having a career of her own. This would mean that at any moment competing job requirements or opportunities might threaten to separate them geographically. This is an increasing problem in the academic world, where more and more professional couples are appearing. Unless the wife is willing to assume a consistently ancillary status it is often difficult for the couple both to find desirable positions in the same community. It is perhaps for this reason that there has been a decrease in the entry of educated women into the profession. Yet the dedifferentiation of marital roles accompanying mobility constitutes a powerful force for feminine parity, and a mobile society must either accept the pull of competing careers or the push of feminine discontent. Our society has tended, with some ambivalence, toward the latter, and the result has been (in addition to much outcry, argument, and public discussion) an exaggerated investment of feminine achievement motivation into the childrearing process. While the social costs of either solution are high, it is difficult to envision a more serious risk than that which results from children having to validate their mothers' competence through their own successes, "creativity," and mental health.

Even if this problem could somehow be eliminated, pressures on the marital bond through time would remain. It is not merely a question of the executive "outgrowing" the wife. The male who participates intensively in a series of temporary systems would be changed by each, and each would make a different set of emotional demands upon him. Different aspects of his personal repertory would be exaggerated or muted in each new system, and his wife would somehow be forced to adapt to these in the context of maintaining the one stable and permanent adult relationship in both their lives.

As noted earlier, contemporary transformations in social relationships largely take the form of converting spatial effects into temporal ones. The idea of temporary systems itself assumes such a conversion, for as routine tasks become automated, those requiring human participation will increasingly relate to the boundaries of current experience—to invention, ambiguity, unusual synthesis, catastrophic changes, and so on. This means that the skills required will include larger quantities of creativity, imagination, social perception, and personal insight, and will hence draw upon all layers of the personality with maximum involvement and commitment. Such involvement will tend to drive other social affiliations out—temporary systems will inherently be what Coser calls "greedy organizations" (Coser, 1967). But only temporarily so, by definition. Instead of partial commitment to a relatively large number of groups over a relatively long period of time, we will see relatively total commitment to a single group over a short time period—the organizational equivalent of "serial monogamy" replacing a kind of permanent polygamy.

The metaphor reminds us that some sociologists have imagined the marital relationship to be undergoing a similar alteration—decreasing its temporal span as it increases its intensity. Time imposes a limit previously maintained by other important relationships (kin, neighborhood, friendship). Is this the pattern which will become characteristic of the future? Will the serial monogamy of adolescent "going steady" relationships become a model for the entire society? Will marriage itself become a temporary system, situationally specific, tied to a particular locality and task?

The principal barrier to this solution is the childrearing process. It is in fact difficult to imagine ways of integrating the raising of children with temporary systems. Not only the constant separations and changes of parents, but even the geographical moves themselves would have damaging consequences. For our society is one which depends upon the autonomy of the childhood peer-group as a way of "quarantining" cohorts. If this were not so, a child moving from place to place with his family would not suffer the social impairment that we know he does in the United States. Peer-group relations are simply too important, and the child who must continually make and break them is operating with an enormous handicap.

But this is assuming a transitional state in which some individuals are operating under the new system and some are not. What if *everyone* were geared to temporary systems and interchangeability? Then every boy in the neighborhood would be the "new boy," or would very recently have been, and every child would have rotating parents. Could children adjust to such a general state of affairs, or would it produce shallow, superficial, unreliable, "psychopathic" adults (cf. Slater, 1964, pp. 20 ff.)? Would the society then become transformed into something totally different? Would such individuals care about the kinds of issues we are concerned with here? Would it matter if they did not? We must be careful not to define as intrinsically pathogenic the conditions which generate deviant behavior in our own society—not to impose upon the limitless opportunities of the future those treasured axioms which are the product of the social pathology of our own era. Could a world of "superficial," fickle, unscrupulous, but nonaggressive individuals make the world any more dangerous than it is? Threaten the demise of culture any more? All we can say with any confidence about the assumptions under which we normally operate is that they have enabled us to manipulate the environment a good deal and to make the earth almost uninhabitable. An objective comparison between the joys and dangers of primitive as against civilized life invariably ends in a toss-up.

We can reasonably assume that: (1) the more the infant child is initially dependent upon a small number of nurturing agents the more disturbing will be their loss; (2) loss of the mother between six months and a year would probably interfere with the development of personality characteristics necessary for adequate functioning in a mobile society (Caplan, 1955, pp. 123–55); (3) any attempt to meet the problem of multiple parents (one assumes the child would normally remain with the mother) by de-emphasizing paternal participation in the socialization process would generate serious difficulties for male personality development (Burton and Whiting, 1961). If these difficulties can be met, the viability of a matching familial form of temporary system is simply an open question.

One must remember, however, that social mechanisms do not emerge full-blown, but arise out of other such mechanisms. One could object to any hypothetical social arrangement on the grounds that the transition to it would be intolerable, leading to attempts to thwart and counteract the direction of change. This seems highly likely in the case of the kinds of trends we have been discussing. It is hard to conceive of any mixture of the family structures juxtaposed here that would not be considerably more disturbing than a pure type of either. This will help to generate unusual modifications and syntheses that we can not possibly envision now.

We may also anticipate an increase in the opposition to those basic assumptions which precipitate technological change in our society. There will be more questioning of the utilitarian axioms of our lives as the traditional ideas of progress continue to tarnish, and as some underdeveloped countries, operating with different assumptions, leapfrog into a less cultured and more satisfying modernity. There will be even more emphasis on hedonistic, experience-oriented approaches to life, with or without drugs. There will be more nostalgia, more revivals, more clinging to real and imagined pasts. There will be more world-rejecting fantasies of static, loving, bucolic utopian communities, many of which will be carried into action.

We cannot begin to weight these factors properly and imagine into what combinations they will be molded. What I have tried to do in this chapter is to suggest some of the forces at work in generating change, some of the strains which they must inevitably create, and some hypothetical "solutions" to what are fundamentally insoluble dilemmas of social life.

REFERENCES

Bott, Elizabeth. *Family and Social Network*. London: Tavistock, 1957.

Burton, R. V. and Whiting, J. W. M. "The Absent Father and Cross-Sex Identity." *Merrill-Palmer Quarterly*, Vol. 7, 1961, pp. 85–95.

Caplan, G. *Mental Health Aspects of Social Work in Public Health*. Berkeley: University of California School of Social Welfare, 1955.

Coser, Lewis A. *Continuities in the Study of Social Conflict*. New York: Free Press, 1967.

Festinger, L., Schacter, S. and Back, K. *Social Pressures in Informal Groups*. New York: Harper, 1950.

Hall, E. T. *The Hidden Dimension*. New York: Garden City: Doubleday, 1966.

Hillman, Karen G. "Marital Instability and Its Relation to Education, Income, and Occupation: An Analysis Based on Census Data," in *Selected Studies in Marriage and the Family* (eds. R. F. Winch, R. McGinnis, and H. R. Barsinger), pp. 111–26. New York: Holt, Rinehart & Winston, 1962.

Koller, M. R. "Residential and Occupational Propinquity," in *Selected Studies in Marriage and the Family* (eds. R. F. Winch, R. McGinnis, and H. R. Barsinger), pp. 472–77. New York: Holt, Rinehart & Winston, 1962.

Komarovsky, Mirra. *Blue Collar Marriage*. New York: Random House, 1964.

Litwak, E. "Technological Innovation and Ideal Forms of Family Structure in an Industrial Democratic Society." Unpublished manuscript, University of Michigan School of Social Work, February 1966.

Lorenz, K. *On Aggression*. New York: Harcourt, Brace, 1966.

Mead, Margaret. "We Are All Third Generation," in *The Character of Americans* (ed. M. McGiffert), pp. 131–41. Homewood, Ill.: Dorsey, 1964.

Pierson, G. W. "The M-Factor in American History," in *The Character of Americans* (ed. M. McGiffert), pp. 118–30, Homewood, Ill.: Dorsey, 1964.

Riesman, D., Glazer, N., and Denny, R. *The Lonely Crowd*. Garden City, N.Y.: Doubleday, 1955.

Scott, J. P. *Animal Behavior*. Chicago: University of Chicago Press, 1958.

Simmel, G. *Conflict and the Web of Group-Affiliations*. New York: The Free Press, 1964.

Slater, P. E. "Prolegomena to a Psychoanalytic Study of Aging and Death," in *New Thoughts on Old Age* (ed. R. Kastenbaum), pp. 19–40. New York: Springer, 1964.

Slater, P. E. "Parental Role Differentiation." *American Journal of Sociology,* Vol. 67 (1961), pp. 296–308.

Whyte, W. H., Jr. *The Organization Man,* pp. 365–86. New York: Garden City, Doubleday, 1956.

Whyte, W. H., Jr. "The Wife Problem," in *Selected Studies in Marriage and the Family* (eds. R. F. Winch, R. McGinnis, and H. R. Barsinger). New York: Holt, Rinehart & Winston, 1962.

Wolfenstein, Martha. "Fun morality: An Analysis of Recent American Child-Training Literature," in *Childhood in Contemporary Cultures* (eds. M. Mead and M. Wolfenstein), pp. 168–78. Chicago: University of Chicago Press, 1963.

Materials for a theory of social relationships[*]

Robert S. Weiss

A number of theories of the socioemotional functions of social ties are explicit, or seem implicit, in current work. The problem is, of course, central in study of human experience. It is that of what we gain through relationships. It may be of value to review two of the theories, since in combination they served as initial orientations for the work reported here.[1]

The first theory proposes that individuals possess a "fund of sociability," a readiness and need to interact with others, which may be distributed in various ways, but is in any event of constant amount.[2] In this view individuals might

[*] This paper is based on work on the functions of social ties supported by a grant from NIMH, number MH409214-02, and from the Social Security and Welfare Administration of the Department of Health, Education, and Welfare, Grant Number 294. The paper appeared as a section of "Social Relationships and the Aged Individual," *Daedalus* (Winter 1967). Read at conference of Harvard Program on Technology and Science, 1967.

[1] Other approaches, distinct from those discussed here, include: Peter Blau's emphasis on the goal-directed nature of relationships, also a theme in the work of George Homans; instinct theories, which perhaps should not be included in a listing of current work; the division of relationships or components of relationships into those which are security seeking and those which are satisfaction seeking, which occurs in the work of both Karen Horney and Harry Stack Sullivan; a variety of sociologically functionalist views, new versions of which are constantly appearing; and the views of Freud, which seem to see behavior as an expression of biological energy which may be directed or diffused through a variety of devices.

[2] The fund-of-sociability idea has been put forward most recently by Joel I. Nelson in "Clique Contacts and Family Orientations," *American Sociological Review,* Vol. 31, No. 5 (October 1966), pp. 663–72. He points out that a similar statement is contained in the work of Elizabeth Bott, *Family and Social Network* (Tavistock, 1957). The theory was considered but rejected by Theodore Caplow

with equal satisfaction engage in a great deal of intense contact with a few others, or in a more limited amount of less intense contact with a great many others. Difficulty would be encountered only if the demands on the fund were too great or the opportunities for expenditure from the fund too limited or, possibly, if the channels available for expenditure were for some reason uncongenial.

The second theory might be characterized as the theory of the mediating primary group. This theory distinguishes between primary relationships, which are close, frequent, face-to-face, and accompanied by warmth and commitment, and secondary relationships, which are essentially instrumental. (Examples of the latter would include relationships, required by work—with the exception of some relationships with colleagues of long standing; memberships in formal organizations; and emotionally unimportant relationships with acquaintances, individuals who provide services, and the like.) The theory proposes that our beliefs, attitudes, and understandings are formed in good part through interaction with other members of the primary groups to which we belong. It holds that without any primary group affiliations we would drift into a state of normlessness or anomie. Participation in other sectors of the society expresses the goals and values established in primary group interaction, but an individual might withdraw from secondary contacts and yet not find himself in difficulty so long as he continued to be an active participant in one or more primary groups.[3]

The first empirical materials I want to present come from a study of the Parents Without Partners organization.[4] This is a national association of fairly autonomous local chapters, each providing a variety of programs for parents who are for any reason alone. For about a year a colleague and I attended meetings of the Boston chapter, participated in programs, and interviewed current and former members. Two research questions concerned us: first, what loss had these individuals sustained with the dissolution of their marriage; and second, in what way did membership make up for the loss?

Our initial hypothesis, on beginning the study, was based on an underlying view which combined elements of the two theories just described. We assumed

and Robert Forman in their "Neighborhood Interaction in a Homogenous Community," *American Sociological Review*, Vol. 15, No. 2 (June 1950), pp. 357–66. A theory which, though not identical, resembles that of a fund-of-sociability is contained in Philip Slater's "On Social Regression," *American Sociological Review*, Vol. 28, No. 3 (June 1963), pp. 339–64. This paper discusses alternative deployments of what is assumed to be a constant amount of libidinal energy.

[3] The ideas referred to here have a long history in both German and American sociology. A valuable review is given by Edward Shils in "The Study of the Primary Group," Daniel Lerner and Harold Lasswell (eds.), *The Policy Sciences* (Stanford, Calif.: Stanford University Press, 1951), pp. 44–69. See also Elihu Katz and Paul Lazarsfeld, "The Rediscovery of the Primary Group; Case Histories of the Intervening Variable," *Personal Influence* (Glencoe, Ill.: Free Press, 1955), pp. 34–42. A recent example of the tendency to see all close relationships as of a kind is Nicholas Babchunk and Alan P. Bates, "The Primary Relations of Middle-Class Couples; A Study in Male Dominance," *American Sociological Review* (June 1963), pp. 377–84.

[4] My associate in this work was Father Carroll Bourg, S.J., now at the Society for Christ in Baltimore, Maryland. We would like to acknowledge the help of Professor Donald Klein of the Institute for Applied Behavioral Sciences, National Training Laboratories, in Washington, D.C., and of the research committee of the Boston chapter of Parents Without Partners, Inc.

that individuals require a certain amount of "primary" contact—which we interpreted as contact in which emotions might be expressed—and this amount may be obtained either through a great deal of interaction within a single relationship or through less intense interaction within a number of relationships. We therefore anticipated that members of the organization would report that they had been lonely and restless after the dissolution of their marriage, but that the interchange with other members which accompanied immersion in organizational activity had made up some part of the loss.

We found that although Parents Without Partners offered single parents assistance with a host of difficulties they were likely to encounter in their social life and in their roles as parents, most members seemed to have joined simply because they were lonely. Loneliness seemed to have been experienced by the great majority of members who talked about the matter. In addition, it seemed clear that loneliness was a direct consequence of the loss of the marital relationship, rather than a secondary consequence of the change in social role or increase in financial strain which might have accompanied the dissolution of the marriage. A qualification of this assertion is that this seemed not to have been true, or to have been true to a lesser extent, when the marriage had not been the only source of emotional interchange in the individual's life; an example would be a woman who had been extremely close before the dissolution of her marriage to her sister, girl friend, or mother.[5]

Another problem which might be associated with the absence of a marital tie, in addition to loneliness, was a tendency to overrespond to a perceived setback or slight, sometimes with depression, sometimes with anger. Members of the organization often considered themselves and each other to be unusually touchy, and indeed we were on more than one occasion led to agree with them. We were led to speculate about the existence of a syndrome of emotional isolation, whose symptoms would include both loneliness and oversensitivity.

For some individuals, membership in PWP was of great help. For others it seemed to be of little value, or whatever value it had was outweighed by dissatisfactions. Among those who were helped by the organization, many reported that the chief contribution of the organization to their well-being was that it provided a means for them to meet others in the same situation as themselves, with whom they could exchange experiences and, in some cases, become friends. Men and women differed a good deal here. Men were apt to put more stress on service to the organization or on dating and less emphasis on friendships. But if we consider only female members, then the sponsorship of friendships or friendship-like relationships might be seen as the chief contribution the organization made to their well-being.[6]

---

[5] There are a number of descriptions in the literature of marriages in which both husband and wife maintain close relationships with same-sex peers or in which the wife remains close to her mother. See, for example, Mirra Komarovsky, *Blue-Collar Marriage* (New York: Random House, 1964).

[6] The difference in friendship-like relationships formed by men and by women may perhaps be communicated by saying that where women developed commitments to each other, men developed commitments to the Parents Without Partners organization. Women would call each other fre-

The interesting question was whether these friendships, or the combination of friendships and participation in organizational activities, would compensate for the absence of marriage, at least in relation to loneliness. On this point our findings were unequivocal: they did not. Members remained lonely; friends and activities, perhaps particularly discussion groups, helped in that they made the loneliness easier to manage, but they did not end it, or even appreciably diminish it.[7] One woman described the uses and limitations of friendship in these words: "Sometimes I have the girls over, and we talk about how hard it is. Misery loves company, you know."

Our work to this point made it clear that friendships, however valuable they may be in other ways, do not supply the functions once supplied by marriage. Therefore, either the functions of friendship are qualitatively different from those of marriage, or if they are qualitatively the same, they are supplied in distinctly lesser quantity.

To decide between these alternatives we required a situation where individuals maintained effective marriages but were without friends. Our expectation was that if marriage and friendship provide different functions, then we should find individuals whose lives lacked friendships to be experiencing distress, despite the existence of a marriage. If on the other hand marriage provided the same functions as friendship, but more intensely, we should find these individuals getting along almost as well as anyone else, with perhaps some marginal distress due to the absence of quantitatively less important friendships.

For the last two years we have been slowly gathering data about the experiences of newcomer couples, beginning with a pilot study of half a dozen couples who had moved to the Boston suburbs from at least two states away, and continuing with a more intensive study of two additional newcomer families.[8] These newcomers to the Boston area provided us with a group of individuals who were temporarily without friends.

We found in all but two of our newcomer couples that after a period of time without friends the wife experienced severe distress, while the primary difficulty

---

quently, sometimes daily, to chat, would exchange visits, and would spend evenings in a group, just because they liked being with each other. Men rarely called or visited each other except on organizational business, but organizational business could become extensive enough to cause a man to spend a good part of his evenings and weekends participating with other men and with the more active women in the management of the community. The amount of organizationally sponsored sociability engaged in by active men and by active women seemed to be about the same, but the definitions of the relationships they formed were somewhat different. In this connection it is significant that women outnumbered men among members by a ratio of about four to one.

[7] For both men and women loneliness could be allayed, though perhaps only temporarily, by dating. Our data here are not as dense as we would wish, but there is much evidence that dating did seem to be substitutive, for a time at least, for the particular function of the marital tie whose absence is signalled by loneliness. The remarkable capacity of a new dating relationship to combat loneliness, despite the apparent absence of a basis for effective emotional integration, may depend on the development of an illusion of sympathetic understanding, to which both participants contribute energetically but on continued acquaintance is dispelled.

[8] My associate in this work is Elizabeth Hartwell.

for the working husband seemed to have been an inability to understand what was happening to his wife. The housebound wife's distress was different in quality, but comparable in intensity, to the distress reported as having followed the dissolution of a marriage. One way of describing the qualitative difference is that the dissolution of a marriage seems to result in a sense of emotional isolation, while the absence of friends, for the woman who stays at home, seems to result in a sense of social isolation. The absence of anyone who shares the woman's problems, interests, and concerns—who cares about the same things she cares about—seems to lead to a loss of engagement with the homemaking tasks which would otherwise be the focus of her energies. Despite the warmth which may exist in her marriage, she is likely to become painfully bored, as the subjective concomitant of a loss of investment in her activities. One newcomer wife who had in her former home been extremely active and had considered herself reasonably happy found herself drinking a great deal, possibly compulsively; another, even more at a loss, proposed that the family return to the area of her parents' home, whatever the damage this would do to her husband's career. The other newcomer wives who had similarly severe initial difficulties did manage to establish friendships after a time, and then the initial period seemed to them to have been simply an unhappy phase, about which they perhaps made too much fuss.

The husbands escaped the newcomer blues because they found men at work with whom they could talk about the things that concerned them: the job, news events, sports, driving patterns and other customs of the new area, and so on. Their jobs prevented social isolation. Two of the men with whom we worked, an Army sergeant and a production supervisor, listed for us the people with whom they chatted during the day, and the number was impressive. Of the exceptional wives, one was married to a man who had moved his family into a neighborhood just being developed, where everyone was a newcomer, and it was easy for his wife to form friendships with other wives in exactly her situation. He did this because in a previous move he had bought a house in an old neighborhood, where friendship circles were already formed, and had found that his wife became so bored that she began a schedule of night school courses which forced him to stay home alone with the children much of the week. The other exceptional wife had no children and was therefore able to solve the problem of social isolation neatly by going to work.

Taking all our cases into account we may generalize that in the absence of social ties in which central life concerns are shared, individuals will experience a sense of social isolation. We may conclude that just as friends do not make up for a lost marriage, so marriage does not make up for lost friends.[9]

---

[9] In none of the couples we have thus far studied have we found that husbands and wives share enough so that the shop talk of the one matters greatly to the other. An exception to this generalization may be couples in which both husband and wife are trained in the same profession. A colleague's wife, herself a Ph.D., reports that although she and her husband have moved several times, she has never experienced "newcomer blues," since she is able to participate with her husband in his work.

These findings are incompatible with the idea that relationships are relatively undifferentiated in function, since it is clear that friendship and marriage provide distinct functions. The findings also are not compatible with the idea that the essential distinction among relationships is between those which are primary and those which are secondary, since marriage and friendship seem each to fit in the primary category, and yet their functions are different. We are led to another theory of the nature of social ties which proposes that individuals require that a number of distinct functions be supplied by the relationships they integrate with others, and that failure in any regard will result in distress. It also seems the case that relationships tend to specialize in the function they fulfill, in the sense that emotional integration but not social integration is provided by marriage, while the converse is true for friendship. In addition, just as relationships specialize by function, so they seem to specialize in their assumptions; and, in fact, it may well be the specialization of assumptions which leads to specialization of function. In a relationship of multiple functions—an office romance would be an example of such a relationship—the participants relate to each other at different times in terms of different sets of assumptions. They ordinarily will choose assumptions appropriate to whatever setting they are in, but they also develop a signal system involving vocabulary, voice tone, and gesture, which, along with its other functions, communicates the set of assumptions operative at any given time. When we find such multifunction relationships, it may be analytically justifiable to speak of a plurality of relationships involving the same two individuals.

The specialization of relationships is probably always incomplete. Undoubtedly there is a certain level of emotional integration in every friendship, though ordinarily not a great deal. At times, however, either or both participants in a friendship may respond to a need for emotional exchange, and the friendship assumptions may be flooded out temporarily; one likely consequence of such sudden redefinition is apt to be uneasiness between the participants when they attempt to reinstate the former assumptions. In general, in our observation to date, marriage tends to provide more than one function, but few other relationships do to any great extent. In addition, the resistance to redefinition of relational assumptions are ordinarily strong enough that an individual can only temporarily redefine the assumptions of one or more of his remaining relationships to serve as replacements for a lost relationship.

To this point I have described just two forms of functional relationship. On the basis of our work with Parents Without Partners, we believe we can identify five interactional systems, all of which are necessary for individual well-being, and which differ in assumptions, content, and functions. We may find in time that this category system must be modified in some way, but so far it has seemed adequate. We have named the five types of social ties by what seems to be the function each provides the individual who maintains it: emotional integration, social integration, opportunity for nurturance, reassurance of worth, and provision of assistance.

1. *Emotional integration* is provided by relationships in which emotions are expressed and reacted to in a way which is stabilizing for the participants. Maintenance of such a relationship seems to require both frequency and regularity of interaction, as well as acceptance that emotional expression is appropriate to the relationship. This function is provided by marriage; by dating relationships at least for a time; among some women by relationships with a close friend, a sister, or mother; and among some men in certain situations between "buddies."[10]

2. *Social integration* is provided by relationships in which participants share concerns, because of similar situations or because they are striving for the achievement of similar objectives. Such relationships permit the development of a shared interpretation of experience, as well as the exchange of information and ideas. Within these relationships one finds companionship and an opportunity for an exchange of services, especially in the area of mutual interest. This function is provided both by friendships and by by relationships among colleagues; among women, more frequently the first, while among men, more frequently the second.[11]

3. *Opportunity for nurturance* is provided by relationships in which the adult takes responsibility for the well-being of a child, and so can develop a sense of being needed. Responsibility for children seems to add to the value of the goals of a wide variety of activities in an individual's life.[12]

4. *Reassurance of worth* is provided by relationships which attest to an individual's competence in some role. Colleague relationships function in this way for some men, particularly men whose work is difficult or highly valued. Relationships within the family may function in this way for other men, for whom competence depends not on particular skills, but rather on the ability to support a family, and for whom respect depends on recognition of competence as a breadwinner. For women who work this function may be provided by relationships with colleagues; for women who stay home, relationships with husbands,

---

[10] For a discussion of this function of marriage see Robert O. Blood, Jr. and Donald Wolfe, *Husbands and Wives* (Free Press, 1960), particularly their chapter 7, "Understanding and Emotional Well-Being." That is not intrinsic to marriage is one conclusion of Mirra Komorovsky's *Blue-Collar Marriage*. A different relationship which may provide the same function is described in "Buddy relations and combat performance," by Rodger Little, *The New Military*, edited by Morris Janowitz (Russell Sage, 1964.) Mr. Little writes, "A buddy had to 'understand' in a deeply personal sense. Buddies became therapists to one another. . . ."

[11] Studies of retired men suggest that they experience a boredom and restlessness very similar to the condition we have found among newcomer wives. See Eugene A. Friedmann and Robert J. Havighurst, *The Meaning of Work and Retirement* (Chicago, 1954.) Nicholas Babchuck and Alan Bates have some interesting comments on the content of friendships between middle-class couples, "The Primary Relations."

[12] In a somewhat cursory search of the sociological literature, I have found only a very few discussions of the motivations of parents in having children. One suggestion has been that children are a consumption item, like a second car or a swimming pool, which may represent one way of disposing of surplus funds. There seems very little recognition in the general literature, however, that having children may contribute to the well-being of the parents. The literature on adoption may be richer, but to this point I have not been able to find corroboration for the assessments made on the basis of our work with Parents Without Partners.

children, and acquaintances who recognize their homemaking skill may provide this function.[13]

5. *Assistance* is provided by a wide variety of relationships when there is urgent need, but primarily by neighbors and by close kin otherwise. Only within close kin ties, especially lineal ties, may one expect assistance which is not severely limited in time and extent.[14]

Although our on-going research has thus far produced only limited evidence which bears on this, it is our conjecture that the absence of any one of the functions necessary to well-being is signaled by a distinct form of distress, different in kind but not in degree, from the symptoms which accompany other deficits.

We conjecture that deficits and symptoms are associated in this way: the absence of emotional integration results in loneliness; of social integration in boredom; of opportunity for nurturance in a sense of emptiness or pointlessness; of reassurance of worth in a sense of worthlessness; and of assistance in a sense of vulnerability or of having been abandoned. This schedule of causes and conditions is an attempt to represent in a compact, if overly pat, way what seem to be differences in the quality of the distress reported as accompanying different deficits. It is difficult to say, at least at this point, that some deficits are more disorganizing than others; that absence of emotional integration, for example, is more disorganizing than absence of opportunity for nurturance. One can cite, in this connection, childless couples who were as downcast by difficulty in arranging for an adoption as any lonely person might be by difficulty in finding love. Any deficit seems to create a condition of dissatisfaction marked by restlessness and occasional bouts of acute distress.

In continuing work we are attempting to give more substance to this discussion of the assumptions, content, and functions of relationships, and the deficits associated with their absence. We have already encountered as a complicating feature the coexistence of relationships which lead, for example, to pressure on marriages from commitments to kin. We assume that in still other ways we will find the framework sketched here to need elaboration.

---

[13] In at least one discussion virtually all motivation for work is reduced to a need for "ego-recognition"; see Rensis Likert, *New Patterns of Management* (New York: McGraw-Hill, 1961.) See also, for data regarding the analogous valuings of housework, Robert S. Weiss and Nancy M. Samuelson, "Feelings of Worth among American Women," *Marriage and Family Living* (November 1957).

[14] The importance of help in the relationships of parents and grown children is attested to by, among others, Marvin Sussman, "The Help Pattern in the Middle-Class Family," in Sussman (ed.), *Source Book in Marriage and the Family,* (New York: Houghton Mifflin, 1962.) See also, for the subjective experience of being symbolically without kin, "Christmas in an Apartment Hotel," Mark Benney, Robert Weiss, Rolf Meyersohn, and David Riesman, *American Journal of Sociology,* (November 1959).

The illusionless man and the visionary maid*

Allen B. Wheelis

Once upon a time there was a man who had no illusions about anything. While still in the crib he had learned that his mother was not always kind; at two he had given up fairies; witches and hobgoblins disappeared from his world at three; at four he knew that rabbits at Easter lay no eggs; and at five on a cold night in December, with a bitter little smile, he said goodbye to Santa Claus. At six when he started school, illusions flew from his life like feathers in a windstorm: he discovered that his father was not always brave or even honest, that Presidents are little men, that the Queen of England goes to the bathroom like everybody else, and that his first grade teacher, a pretty round-faced young woman with dimples, did not know everything, as he had thought, but thought only of men and did not know much of anything. At eight he could read, and the printed word was a sorcerer at exorcising illusions—only he knew there were no sorcerers. The abyss of hell disappeared into the even larger abyss into which a clear vision was sweeping his beliefs. Happiness was of course a myth; love a fleeting attachment, a dream of enduring selflessness glued onto the instinct of a rabbit. At twelve he dispatched into the night sky his last unheard prayer. As a young man he realized that the most generous act is self-serving, the most disinterested inquiry serves interest; that lies are told by printed words, even by words carved in stone; that art begins with a small "a" like everything else, and that he could not escape the ruin of value by orchestrating a cry of despair into a song of lasting beauty; for beauty passes and deathless art is quite mortal. Of all those people who lose illusions he lost more than anyone else, taboo and prescription alike; and as everything became permitted nothing was left worthwhile.

He became a carpenter, but could see a house begin to decay in the course of building—perfect pyramid of white sand spreading out irretrievably in the grass, bricks chipping, doors sticking, the first tone of gray appearing on white

* "The Illusionless Man and the Visionary Maid," from *The Illusionless Man* by Allen Wheelis. Harper & Row paperback edition, 1971. Reprinted by permission of author.

111

lumber, the first film of rust on bright nails, the first leaf falling in the shining gutter. He became then a termite inspector, spent his days crawling in darkness under old houses, lived in a basement room and never raised the blinds, ate canned beans and frozen television dinners, let his hair grow and his beard. On Sundays he walked in the park, threw bread to the ducks—dry French bread, stone-hard, would stamp on it with his feet, gather up the pieces, and walk along the pond, throwing it out to the avid ducks paddling after him, thinking glumly that they would be just as hungry again tomorrow. His name was Henry.

One day in the park he met a girl who believed in everything. In the forest she still glimpsed fairies, heard them whisper; bunnies hopped for her at Easter, laid brilliant eggs; at Christmas hoofbeats shook the roof. She was disillusioned at times and would flounder, gasp desperately, like a fish in sand, but not for long; would quickly, sometimes instantly, find something new, and actually never gave up any illusion, but would lay it aside when necessary, forget it, and whenever it was needed, back it would come. Her name was Lorabelle, and when she saw a bearded young man in the park, alone among couples, stamping on the hard bread, tossing it irritably to the quacking ducks, she exploded into illusions about him like a Roman candle over a desert.

"You are a great and good man," she said.

"I'm petty and self-absorbed," he said.

"You're terribly unhappy."

"I'm morose . . . probably like it that way."

"You have suffered a great deal," she said. "I see it in your face."

"I've been diligent only in self-pity," he said, "have turned away from everything difficult, and what you see are the scars of old acne shining through my beard; I could never give up chocolate and nuts."

"You're very wise," she said.

"No, but intelligent."

They talked about love, beauty, feeling, value, life, work, death—and always she came back to love. They argued about everything, differed on everything, agreed on nothing, and so she fell in love with him. "This partakes of the infinite," she said.

But he, being an illusionless man, was only fond of her. "It partaketh mainly," he said, "of body chemistry," and passed his hand over her roundest curve.

"We have a unique affinity," she said. "You're the only man in the world for me." "We fit quite nicely," he said. "You are one of no more than five or six girls in the county for me." "It's a miracle we met," she said. "I just happened to be feeding the ducks." "No, not chance; I couldn't feel this way about anybody else."

"If you'd come down the other side of the hill," he said, "you'd be feeling this way right now about somebody else. And if I had fed squirrels instead of ducks I'd be playing with somebody else's curves."

"You're my dearest darling squirrel," she said, "and most of all you're my silly fuzzy duck, and I don't know why I bother to love you—why are you such a fool?

Who dropped you on your head?—come to bed!" On such a note of logic, always, their arguments ended.

She wanted a wedding in church with a dress of white Alençon lace over cream satin, bridesmaids in pink, organ music, and lots of people to weep and be happy and throw rice. "You'll be so handsome in a morning coat," she said, brushing cobwebs off his shoulders, "oh and stripped pants, too, and a gray silk cravat, and a white carnation. You'll be divine." "I'd look a proper fool," he said, "and I'm damned if I'll do it." "Oh please! It's only once." "Once a fool, voluntarily, is too often." "It's a sacrament." "It's a barbarism." "Symbols are important." "Then let's stand by the Washington Monument," he said, "and be honest about it."

"You make fun," she said, "but it's a holy ceremony, a solemn exchange of vows before man and God."

"God won't be there, honey; the women will be weeping for their own lost youth and innocence, the men wanting to have you in bed; and the priest standing slightly above us will be looking down your cleavage as his mouth goes dry; and the whole thing will be a primitive and preposterous attempt to invest copulation with dignity and permanence, to enforce responsibility for children by the authority of a myth no longer credible even to a child."

So . . . they were married in church: his hands were wet and his knees shook, he frowned and quaked; but looked divine, she said, in morning coat and striped pants; and she was serene and beautiful in Alençon lace; the organ pealed, weeping women watched with joy, vows were said, rice thrown, and then they were alone on the back seat of a taxi, her lips seeking his, murmuring, "I'm so happy, darling, so terribly happy. Now we'll be together always."

"In our community," he said, "and for our age and economic bracket, we have a 47.3 per cent chance of staying together for twenty years."

She found for them a white house on a hill in a field of red poppies and white daisies, with three tall maple trees. There they lived in sunlight and wind, and she began to fill their life with fragile feminine deceptions, worked tirelessly at them, and always there was something new. She concealed the monotony of eating by variety, never two meals the same, one morning French toast in the shape of their house, the next a boiled egg with smiling painted face and a tiny straw hat; cut flowers on the table, color and sweetness blooming from a Dutch vase, as if unrelated to manure; Italian posters on the wall as if they had traveled; starched white curtains at the windows, as if made of a brocade too rich and heavy to bend; morning glories covering the outhouse with royal purple. When he came home at night she would brush the cobwebs from his hair, make him bathe and shave and dress—to appear as if he had not worked in dirt. She made wonderful sauces, could cook anything to taste like something else, created a sense of purity by the whiteness of tablecloth, of delicacy by the thinness of crystal, would surround a steak with parsley as if it were not flesh but the bloom of a garden, supported her illusions with candlelight and fine wine, and smiled at him across the table with lips redder than real. In the bedroom candlelight again, and yet another nightgown to suggest a mysterious woman of unknown delights, and a heavy perfume, as if not sweat but sweetness came from her pores.

Being an illusionless man, he admitted that he liked these elegant mirages, found them pleasant, that it was good to sleep with her fine curves under his hand, her sweet smells in his nose, that he slept better now than when he lived alone. He became less gloomy, but not much.

One Sunday afternoon, walking hand in hand in sunshine through the poppies and daisies, he noticed her lips moving. "What are you saying?" he said. "Do you love me?" "I'm fond of you," he said; "love is an illusion." "Is there anybody else? I'm terribly jealous." "Jealousy is the illusion of complete possession." "Do other women attract you?" "Yes." "Some men are not like that." "Some men are liars." he said.

She became pregnant, bought baby clothes, tried out names, was always singing. "Please be happy," she said. "By 1980 the world population will . . ." "Oh be quiet!" he said.

She prepared a room for the baby, hung curtains, bought a crib, read books, became apprehensive. "Will he be all right? What do you think? Will he be a good baby? He doesn't have to be pretty, you know, that's not important, but I'd like him to be intelligent. And will he have two eyes and the right number of fingers and toes? I want him to have everything he needs and nothing too much. What do you think?" "Some minor congenital aberrations are inevitable," he said; "the major malformations are less. . . ." "Don't say such things," she said. "Why do you scare me?" "I was just. . . . "Oh . . . and will I know what to do?" she said, ". . . how to take care of him? What do you think? Will I be any good at it?"

One night he felt her lips moving in his hair. "Praying?" he said. "Yes." "What did you ask?" "That someday you will say you love me."

She felt weak, became sick; in bed she looked pale and scared. "Will the baby be all right?" she said. "Don't ever leave me. What are you thinking? Tell me." She began to bleed, was terrified, lay very still, but lost the baby anyway.

She was depressed then, her face motionless and dark. "I lost it because you don't love me," she said.

"There is no established correlation," he said, "between the alleged state of love, or lack of it, and the incidence of miscarriage."

"I'm not wanting statistics," she screamed.

"What then?"

"Nothing. Everything. It's not enough . . . just being 'fond.' I hate fondness. What's the matter with you? It wouldn't have happened . . . I want to be loved!"

"You're being hysterical," he said, "and you're not finishing your sentences."

Suddenly, all at once, she looked at him with a level detached gaze and did not like what she saw. "You were right," she said; "you *are* petty and self-absorbed. What's worse, you have a legal mind and there's no poetry in you. You don't give me anything, don't even love me, you're *dull.* You were stuck in a hole in the ground when I found you, and if I hadn't pulled you out you'd be there still. There's no life in you. I give you everything and it's not enough, doesn't make any difference. You can't wait to die, want to bury yourself now and me with you. Well I'm not ready yet and I'm not going to put up with it any longer, and now I'm through with you and I want a divorce."

"You've lost your illusions about me," he said, "but not the having of illusions. . . ."

"While you," she said, "have lost your illusions about everything, and can't get over being sore about it."

". . . they'll focus now on someone else. . . ."

"Oh I hope so!" she said; "I can hardly wait."

". . . you waste experience."

"And you waste *life!*"

He wouldn't give her a divorce, but that didn't matter; for she couldn't bear the thought of his moving back to that basement, and anyway, she told herself, he had to have someone to look after him; so they lived together still and she cooked for him when she was home and mended his clothes and darned his socks, and when he asked why, she said, with sweet revenge, "Because I'm fond of you, that's all. Just fond."

She got a job with a theater, typed scripts and programs, worked nights in the box office, let her hair grow into a long silken curtain curled up at the bottom below her shoulders, wore lose chiffon blouses with clown sleeves, trailed filmy scarves from her neck, and fell in love with an actor named Cyrus Anthony de Maronodeck. Her a's broadened and she affected a way of turning her head with so sudden a movement that it could not go unnoticed; no longer did she walk in or out of a room, she strode.

"Cyrus is so *interesting!*" she said, "makes everything an adventure, concentrates energy and passion into a moment until it glows!" She struck a pose: "'When I die,' he says, 'I may be dead for a long time, but while I'm here I'll live it to the hilt.'" "A philosopher, too," Henry said.

One Sunday night Cyrus borrowed a thousand dollars from Lorabelle for his sick mother; and the following day transpired that he had borrowed also the weekend receipts from the box office and had taken his leave of the company. For several days Lorabelle wouldn't believe it, waited for word from him, bit her fingernails—until he was apprehended in Loredo crossing the border with a blonde.

She worked next in a brokerage house operating an enormous and very intelligent machine which tapped and hummed and whirred and rotated, sent its carriage hopping up and down and side to side, performed seventeen mathematical calculations without ever a mistake, took pictures of everything and had illusions about nothing—but Lorabelle did, and presently fell in love with her boss, Mr. Alexander Orwell Mittelby, a sixty-year-old man who loved her with a great passion, she told Henry, but who was married and unfortunately could not get a divorce because his wife was a schizophrenic, had a private nurse in constant attendance; the shock of divorce, Mr. Mittelby had said, would kill her.

"Alex is unique," Lorabelle told Henry, "simply not like the rest of us . . . not at all. He has no interest in himself, has grown beyond that. I've never met a man so mature, so genuinely wise. 'All my personal goals lie in the past,' he told me; 'the only thing left is to seek the common good.' He has no patience with personal problems, complexes . . . that sort of thing . . . sees the romantic protest for what it is: adolescent complaining. Oh Henry, I wish you could know him. He faces life with so much courage—such a gallant careless courage. 'Despair is a luxury,' he says, 'and I can't afford it.' "

Lorabelle wore short tight skirts, high needle-like heels, jeweled glasses, and her hair bouffant; she read the *Wall Street Journal* and *Barron's Weekly*, studied the new tax legislation, spoke out for laissez faire in discussion groups, and at an Anti-World-Federalist dinner chanced to meet Mrs. Mittelby, who was not a schizophrenic at all, but a plain shrewd woman with a wrinkled face, gray hair, and a very sharp tongue. Lorabelle stared at her with deepening shock. "My husband's secretaries," Mrs. Mittelby said, "always seem stunned by my sanity . . . then seek other employment."

In her depression Lorabelle turned away from people, rented a cabin on an island, left Henry to look after himself, came home only on weekends, spent her days walking on deserted beaches, her nights alone writing an autobiographical novel by lamplight. "It's really a kind of self-analysis," she said, "but I want so much to make it beautiful."

After a few months she fell in love with a fisherman. "His name is Jim," she said to Henry. "That's all, just Jim. And he's like his name, exactly: simple, strong, uncomplicated. I wish you could know each other."

"Bring him to dinner!" Henry shouted. "Let him live here! Give him my clothes, my bed!"

"Don't be angry. You'd like him; you couldn't help it. He's so kind, so gentle, so much a part of the elements: in his eyes the wind and the ocean—you can see them!—in his hand the strength, the toughness . . . the grip on the helm in a storm, in his bearing the straightness of the tall pointed firs, in his character the solid rock of the coast."

"If he had a foundation," Henry said, "he'd be a house with a swimming pool."

Lorabelle cut her hair short, wore boots and a sou'wester, scanned the sky for weather signs, studied navigation charts, hung a tide table on the wall. "I want a divorce," she said. "No." "Why? You don't love me." "To protect you from your own bad judgment. You'd be married six times before you were forty if you were free." "Then I'll run away with him," she said.

And she would have, but the sheriff got there first, arrested Jim for bigamy: plain Jim had three last names and a wife with each, and while he sat in jail the three of them squabbled for the fishing boat, which was all he owned.

Lorabelle gave up the cabin, burned her manuscript, and moved back home; wept and wailed and could not be consoled. "There's something wrong with *my* sanity," she said. "I can't do it myself. I'd better see a psychoanalyst." "You'll get a whopping transference," Henry said.

She went to a Dr. Milton Tugwell, took to analysis with great facility, worked quickly through her depression, went four times a week and wished it were more. "I'm so terribly lucky," she said to Henry. "There are so many analysts, you know—good, bad, indifferent—I had no way of knowing . . . and he turns out to be the *one* analyst for me. No one else would be right."

"It really *is* a kind of miracle, isn't it?" Henry said.

"No, really! I mean it. There's a special affinity between us, I felt it the very first session. We speak the same language; sometimes he knows what I'm thinking before I say it—sometimes even before I know I'm thinking it. It's amazing. And he has the most astonishing memory, remembers *everything*. And the way—Oh Henry! if you could only know him, hear him talk!—the way he fits these things together! things you'd never realize were connected. . . ."

Dr. Tugwell made many excellent interpretations: Lorabelle learned about her orality, anality, penis envy, oedipus complex, and, as a kind of bonus, had many insights also into Henry and shared them with him, surprised at his lack of responsiveness.

One night at the theater she saw Dr. Tugwell in the company of a tall gray-haired woman with a hard face. His wife, Lorabelle thought, and something clicked for her, an insight all on her own: *Dr. Tugwell was unhappy with this woman.* So this was the source of that sad note in his voice. He deserved better. She wanted to make him happy, as a woman; and she could, she knew she could. She looked narrowly at Mrs. Tugwell. Then it occurred to her (the analysis must be taking effect, she thought; this was her second insight in an hour) that Dr. Tugwell might have some special feeling of this sort for her, and the more she thought about it the more obvious it became.

When in her next hour she talked of these matters, Dr. Tugwell said nothing except, "What comes to mind about that?" and she was disappointed, but then realized that he could not speak, that he was the prisoner of a professional commitment which required him to stifle his feeling for her. She walked in the meadow on the hill in sunshine, and knew in her heart what must be hidden in his; and someday, she thought, when the analysis was over maybe he would get a divorce and Henry would give her a divorce, and she and Dr. Tugwell would meet on a different basis. She picked a daisy, pulled the petals, and it came out right. Softly she tried his name on her lips, "Milton, darling," and blushed, "sweetest Milt . . . honey," felt him walk beside her, his hand slip around her waist, heard his deep beloved voice begin, "Lorabelle, there is something I must tell you. . . ."

The analysis lasted longer than any of her affairs, perhaps because, paying for her sessions, she valued them more than meetings with lovers, or perhaps because her illusions did not encounter anything hard enough in Dr. Tugwell's silence to cause breakage; but after five years Henry came to the end of his resources and tolerance, said he would pay for no more sessions. This proved him cruel and unfeeling, Lorabelle thought, and reported it triumphantly to Dr. Tugwell who, strangely, regarded it as reasonable.

Lorabelle wept through the last hour, tears making lakes in her ears, overflowing on the pillow, dripping from her chin as she stood up, shaking, to face him, her voice quavering as she thanked him for the changes in her, breaking as she said goodbye. Yet at that very moment she had the comfort of a secret vision: now that she was no longer his patient he was free to become her lover. But days passed and he didn't call; weeks and the vision was shaken; a month and she was desolate. She went back to see him; and this time, sitting in a chair before him, feeling oddly dislocated, really did see him. There along was the green couch on which she had lain for so many hours, from which she had looked up at the blank ceiling, had raved, rambled, complained, and wept; and there—shrinking back slightly from the violence of her disappointment—was the man of her dreams who had listened, out of sight, behind the couch: dark suit of expensive cloth and cut, perfectly pressed, dark tie, silk shirt with white-on-white design, high cordovan sheen on calf-skin loafers, shell-rimmed glasses flashing a nervous glare. There was strain in his voice, she thought; he used jargon, was more detached than he need have been: a continuing transference problem, he said . . . not infrequent . . . might require further analysis . . . unresolved father attachment . . . he had committed her hours . . . could do nothing now . . . sorry . . . perhaps later . . . call him in three months.

For weeks Lorabelle stayed home in deep silent gloom, wouldn't eat, wouldn't dress; but bounced back finally, as she always did, got a job selling tickets at a carousel, and there met Adelbert Bassew, big game hunter—"What a man!" she exclaimed to Henry; "six feet six, all fire and brawn. Imagine!"—who asked her on a safari. And so it continued through the days and weeks of their lives, year after year: Catholic Church, Christian Science, yoga; Al, Bob, and Peter; Paris, Rome, and Nairobi; technocracy, mysticism, hypnotism; short hair, long hair, wig; and whenever she would say, in that rapturous tone of hers, "I realize now . . .," Henry would know she had abandoned one illusion and was already firmly entrapped by the next. They became poor on her pursuits, lived in a basement; her illusions became sillier, shabbier, until finally she was sending in box-tops from cereal packages. Crow's feet appeared around her eyes, white hair among the gold; her skin became dry and papery. But as she got older something about her stayed young: the springing up of hope, the intoxicating energy, the creation of a new dream from the ruin of the old. From the despair of disillusion always she would find her way back: to a bell-like laughter with the rising note of an unfinished story, to a lilt of voice like the leap of water before rapids, to a wild dancing grace of legs and hips like a horse before a jump, to the happy eyes so easily wet with sympathy or love.

But these same years made Henry older than his actual age, more withdrawn, bitter, morose; his face haggard, lined; his hair gray. Every day he got up and went to work, but did nothing else—would not read a book or walk in the park or listen to music. In the evenings he would drink; but gin nourished no illusion, brought no pleasure, only numbness and finally sleep. Lorabelle felt anger and pity and contempt, all at the same time, and would rail at him. "Just look at yourself: drunk, dirty, head hanging like a sick cat . . . How can you stand yourself? What are you trying to do? made me feel guilty? . . . Well I don't. Playing the martyr? Is that it? What's the matter with you? Why don't you find someone else if you're so unhappy with me?"

Henry would shrug, thinking there are no happy marriages and it would be no different with anyone else; but sometimes, far at the back of his unhappy mind, he would come upon the truth: he stayed with her because, with all her witless pursuit of illusions, she nevertheless stirred him—like the wren, trapped under a house, that had flown in his face: he had caught it in his hand, felt the terrified struggle, the concentration of heat, the tremolo of heartbeat too faint and fast to count. Lorabelle brought him no comfort; but, holding her, he felt life, and would not give it up. And sometimes in the midst of her railings Lorabelle would know that she stayed with Henry—not simply, as she said, because he wouldn't give her a divorce—but because he was a rock and she leaned on him.

But even rocks may crumble, and one Monday morning did not move when the alarm went off; he lay still, eyes open, looking at the empty face of the clock, thinking numbly of millions of termits burrowing in wood who would suffer no further interference from him.

He stayed in bed most of the day, ate little, drank much, said nothing. The next day was the same, and the next, and so all week; and on Friday it occurred to Lorabelle that—Henry having apparently retired from business—she must earn the living. After her morning coffee, therefore, she sat down at her desk to compose the fourth line of a jingle about soap flakes; first prize would bring a thousand dollars. Next she invented a hatpin that could neither fall out of a hat nor prick a finger; drew a careful sketch of the device, and addressed it to the U.S. Patent Office; this might make a fortune, she thought. Then she collected all her green stamps: not many, she mused, but enough for a present for Henry. She prepared his lunch on a tray, found him lying in bed staring at the ceiling; he would say nothing and would not eat. She put on her best dress, arranged flowers by his bed, and kissed him on the nose. "I'll be back soon," she said.

It was a beautiful day, the sun shining, wind moving here and there among the trees like playful strokes of a great invisible brush. "I know he will be all right," she said to herself, and posted her jingle and her invention, saying a little prayer for each. She went then to a fortune-teller, an old West Indian woman, who told her that someone dear to her was ill and would die. Lorabelle was shocked and left immediately, brought three sweepstakes tickets in Henry's name to fight the prediction, said another prayer, went on to the supply house and got a pipe and slippers for her green stamps. For a dollar she bought jonquils—

because they were pretty and would make him happy—then counted her money. With the two dollars that were left she bought a steak to tempt his appetite.

At home she found him in pyjamas sitting at the table drinking gin. "Oh sweetheart!" she said, "you break my heart . . . I won't have it, I just won't have it . . . you understand? Cheer up now. I've got presents for you." She put the pipe in his hand, brought tobacco, put the slippers on his bare feet—"There! You see? Aren't they nice? And so warm. A perfect fit! You like them?"—but he said nothing. She began to sing, trying not to cry, then broke off: "Oh, and I have something else . . . another wonderful surprise, you'll see. Now don't come in the kitchen," she added, unnecessarily. She broiled the steak, put it on a heated plate, garnished it with water cress, put jonquils on the tray, a chef's cap on her head, lighted candles, and brought it in singing the Triumphal March from *Aida*, placed it before him with a flourish and sweeping low bow. He turned away. "Oh please, do eat it," she cried; "I got it just for you. It's delicious, you'll see! Try it . . . it would be so good for you."

"Where's the gin?" he said.

"Don't drink any more; you'll get sick. I'm so worried. Eat now. You'll feel better, I know you will, really . . . I just know it. Here, let me feed you."

She cut a bit of steak, waved it under his nose, held it to his mouth, touched his lips; he knocked it away, the fork clattering to the floor, the morsel skittering into a corner. She picked them up, took away the tray. In the kitchen she threw the fork at the calendar, kicked the garbage can, wept; then she composed herself and went back, humming, to the living room; Henry had not moved. Lorabelle put up a card table, took newspaper clippings from her purse, spread out maps of the city: she was working on a treasure hunt. Only three clues had been published, and already she had an idea where the treasure might be. The first prize was five thousand dollars; tomorrow she would take a shovel and go digging.

"Where's the gin?" Henry said.

"There isn't any more, sweetheart. And a good thing because you've had too much . . . you're drunk, you're ruining your health."

"Give me some money," he said tonelessly.

"We haven't any."

He got up, walked unsteadily to the table where she was sitting, opened her purse and took out her wallet. A few coins fell to the table, rolled on the floor; there were no bills. He turned her handbag upside down; an astrology chart tumbled out, then a Christian Science booklet, a handbill from the Watchtower Society, *Palmistry in Six Easy Lessons,* dozens of old sweepstakes tickets and the three new ones, *Love and the Mystic Union,* fortunes from Chinese cookies (one of which, saying "He loves you," she snatched away from him), a silver rosary, a daily discipline from the Rosicrucians, the announcement of a book titled *Secret Power from the Unconscious through Hypnosis*—but no money. He shook the bag furiously and threw it in a corner, surveyed the litter before him with unblinking bloodshot eyes, his face expressionless. "Stupid fool!" he said thickly. "Purse full of illusions . . . suitcase full of illusions . . . whole god-damned lousy life full of illusions . . ." He turned away, stumbled back to the table, put the empty gin bottle to his mouth, turned it over his head, broke it on the hearth.

"Oh my dear," Lorabelle cried, her eyes wet, "you keep waiting for the real thing, but this is all there is." He turned ponderously, facing her, eyes like marble; she came to him. "These are the days . . . and nights . . . of our years and they're passing—look at us! We're getting old—and what else is there?"

"Bitch!"

She faltered, raising her arm, but recovered and went on to touch the side of his head where the hair was gray. "Do please come back to life; I don't want you to die; I'd be so lonely. I'd forget all the bad times and remember all the wonderful things . . . where have they gone? . . . you feeding the ducks, stamping on the bread—so sweet you were!"

"Get out."

The gray stonelike face above her did not move, not even the eyes. A death mask, she thought; the fortune-teller was right. "Oh my dear! I feel so sad." She cried, lowered her head; with a convulsive movement she caught his hand, pressed it to her heart. "It hurts so," she said. "For years you've been cutting yourself off . . . more and more. I'm the only one still holding you, and now you're drifting away. Don't die, sweetheart, let me help you, hold on to me!"

He freed his hand and hit her in the face, sent her crashing into the wall, started after her, thinking, "Where's that broken bottle?" realized with a sense of numb strangeness that he wanted to kill her . . . paused. She stood looking at him, tears running down her face, then left the room. He turned back to the table, sat heavily, observed the hand that had hit her; the fingers felt numb. Before him on the table was the hatpin she had worked with that morning: long sharp pin, black plastic ball at one end, at the other an odd device of safety pins and scotch tape. "Illusion!" he said, grabbing it up in clenched fist and driving it deep into the table; the plastic ball broke, the base of the pin went through his hand, stuck out three inches on top. There was no blood. His hand hung there in mid-air, quivering slightly, like an insect pinned to a card. He moved his fingers: a white crab without a shell, he thought, impaled on a boy's stick. Blood appeared around the pin; the feeling of numbness crept up his arm; he wanted a drink, didn't want to die yet, wasn't ready. Numbness came now to the other arm. He began tugging at the pin, ten cold crab legs fumbling around a spike.

The next morning he shaved, got dressed, and ate breakfast; felt restless, wanted to do something but didn't know what. "Will you go for a walk with me?" he said. Lorabelle was tired, her eyes red, hadn't slept, but was never altogether without hope. "Yes," she said.

They walked by rivers, over bridges, through forests, sat in dry grass and watched a tiny squirrel at the tip of a branch in a fir tree; walked through meadows, by cliffs, over dunes, along the beach, saw two sea stars in a tide pool waving their arms at each other; walked on streets between high buildings, through crowds, watched a little girl feeding pigeons by a fountain. Lorabelle was silent and dejected, her hair scraggly, her shoulders stooped. Something was moving inside Henry, pressing him; he wanted to say something but didn't know what.

That evening as they sat together in their basement room, silent and unhappy, the phone rang. Henry, having known since childhood that a telephone ring means requests, burdens, and obligations, did not move; and for the first time Lorabelle—to whom the same sound meant love, opportunity, adventure—did not answer. Henry looked up, saw that she was exhausted: "Let it ring," he said. She nodded, but couldn't bear the sense of someone calling unheeded, began to hope as she walked, walked faster as she hoped, was soon running lest she be too late, and a few moments later was exclaiming in astonishment and joy: "What? . . . No! . . . Really? . . . Yes! yes! oh yes . . . he's right here . . . No, I have it . . . So much! That's wonderful! . . . Marvelous!" then flung herself in Henry's arms, weeping, laughing, "You've won the Irish Sweepstakes! $137,000! Can you imagine! My God . . . !"

Henry was pleased, but confused and vaguely disturbed; said it was hers not his, since she had bought the ticket. "No, no," she said, "I bought it in your name, and it's yours, and I'm so happy I could cry. . . ." She wiped her tears. ". . . you need it, darling, more than I . . . because I've always known about miracles but you haven't known, but now maybe you will, a little, and I'm so glad it happened for you. Isn't it marvelous?"

"It won't be much after taxes."

"Oh but still a lot," she said, "a very great deal. Just think . . . ! We'll go to Paris and live in the Ritz, and you'll have a dark blue suit and a gray silk tie and cufflinks of lapis and maybe a black stick with a little silver. You'll stand very straight and swing the stick lightly, back and forth, as we stroll on the *Boulevard St. Germain* and the *Rue St. Honoré*, and I'll be so proud." She sat on his lap, eyes glistening, hugged him, kissed the gray hair by his ear. "Then we'll get a Citroën and drive down the Loire, and come finally to beautiful sand and water. Oh, and Monte Carlo! We'll stand around the casino watching the Texas oilmen and the pretty girls and the diamond bracelets; we'll hold hands and look on at roulette and moisten our lips and be like poor cautious tourists, and nobody will know we're rich. Then you'll toss out a ten thousand dollar bill: 'Red,' you'll say. That's all, just that: 'Red,' in a quiet voice, and people will fall silent and stare, and the croupier's hand will tremble, and the wheel will spin and oh! . . . it won't matter whether it's red or black because it's just money either way, not love, and we'll go to Rome and rent a villa, and when. . . ."

"We're broke," he said, "long before Rome. In Genoa we couldn't pay the hotel bill. Remember? Had to sell your jewels . . . and my walking stick."

"Oh no!" she said, "there you go, already sad. . . . Then we remembered the *other* bank account—how could you forget?—found we had plenty of money . . . We go on to Rome, rent a villa and in the evening sit on the terrace holding hands, flowers blooming all around us, and to the west on the crest of a hill seven cypress trees in a row, an orange sun sinking between the black trunks, the whole sky a brilliant golden drum; and you'll feel a throbbing of your heart and a kind of singing rapture, and you'll press my hand and say, 'I love you.' "

Henry was touched by her fantasy and felt some lightness of heart: it would be nice to have some money, he thought—how incredible!—and maybe they really would enjoy a trip. That night they slept in each other's arms and the next day the windfall was gone: it had been a mistake; the officials were terribly sorry; it was another man with the same name and almost the same telephone number, who owned a candy store and had five children, weighed three hundred pounds, and was pictured in the newspaper with his family, seven round beaming faces. Lorabelle was in despair, but Henry was tranquil, still felt that lightness of heart. He comforted Lorabelle and stroked her finally to sleep in the evening, her wet face on his shoulder. It was an illusion, he thought, and for a while I believed it, and yet—curious thing—it has left some sweetness. Throughout the night he marveled about this—could it be he had won something after all?—and the next day, crawling under the rotting mansion of a long-dead actor, he looked a termite in the eye and decided to build a house.

He bought land by the sea and built on a cliff by a great madrona tree which grew out horizontally from the rock, a shimmering cloud of red and green; built with massive A-frames, bolted together, stressed, braced, anchored in concrete to withstand five-hundred-mile winds, a house—in the best illusory style, he thought wryly—to last forever. But the cliff crumbled one night in a storm during a twenty-four foot tide; Lorabelle and Henry stood by hand in hand in the rain and lightning, deafened by crashing surf and thunder, as the house fell slowly into the sea while the great madrona remained, anchored in nothing but dreams. They went then to live in an apartment, and Henry worked as a carpenter, built houses for other people, began planning another house of his own.

One evening after dinner Henry was sitting at the table, smoking a pipe, working on blueprints; across the room Lorabelle, at her desk, bent over a "Who Am I?" contest. ("We might win $3,500," she had said; "just think of it! Wouldn't that be marvelous? Oh the things we will do . . .!") She was humming now, a waltz from *Die Fledermaus*. Henry looked up, observed the happy face bent to the illusory task, the golden hair streaked with gray falling across her cheek, the wrinkles of laughter now indelible around her eyes, the putting of pencil to mouth like a child, puzzled . . . laid down his pipe. "I love you, Lorabelle," he said. She looked up, startled: "What . . . did you say?" "I love you," he said. She blushed, started to rise, the pencil falling from her hand: "But . . . but . . . you said it was an illusion." It is, he thought, because love claims the future and can't hold it; but claims also the present, and we have that. Not wanting to confuse her or start an argument, he said only, "I love you anyway." She ran to him, weeping with joy, "Oh Henry, I'm so happy, so terribly happy! This is all we lacked . . . all we'll ever need." He took her and the moment in his arms, kissed her, and said nothing.

He built a house on a plateau in a sheltered valley, protected from wind and water; blasted a gigantic hole in solid granite, floated the house on a bubble of pure mercury for earthquakes, built walls of reinforced concrete seven feet thick, doors and cabinets of stainless steel, pipes and lightning rods of copper, roof of inch-thick slate. "Oh, Henry, I'm so proud!" Lorabelle said. "I'd like to see what could happen to this house." "You'll see," he said darkly. It cost a fortune and they couldn't meet the payments; the bank took it over, sold it to a university as a seismographic station; Henry and Lorabelle moved to an attic in the city.

One afternoon Lorabelle came home in a rapturous mood. "Oh, Henry, I've met the most wonderful man! A graduate student of Far Eastern studies and . . . you know, sort of a mystic himself . . . such a spiritual quality . . . name is Sermelrad Apfelbaum . . . gives seminars on Buddhism." "Sounds like the real thing all right," Henry said bitterly. After dinner Lorabelle put on a diaphanous dress of black chiffon with a flowing lavender scarf, a gold chain around her neck, a sapphire on her finger, perfume in her hair. "Where are you going?" Henry said. "To meet Semelrad," she said; "he's so wonderfully kind, and so generous . . . is going to tutor me privately till I catch up with the class." "You're not going anywhere," Henry said. "I'm not a child, Henry," Lorabelle said with dignity. "But you *are*—precisely," Henry said. Lorabelle reminded him that theirs was a relationship of equality, with the same rights, that she must live her own life, make her own decisions, her own mistakes if need be; and when this failed to convince him she tossed back her head, affected great hauteur, and marched out of the room. Henry caught her at the door, turned her over his knee, applied the flat of his hand to the bottom of his delight; and it was perhaps that same night—for she did not go out—that Lorabelle got pregnant, and this time didn't lose it: the baby was born on Christmas, blue eyes and golden hair, and they named her Noel.

Henry built a house of solid brick in a meadow of sage and thyme, and there Noel played with flowers and crickets and butterflies and field mice. Most of the time she was a joy to her parents, and some of the time—when she was sick or unkind—she was a sorrow. Lorabelle loved the brick house, painted walls, hung pictures, and polished floors; on hands and knees with a bonnet on her head she dug in the earth and planted flowers, looked up at Henry through a wisp of hair with a happy smile; "We'll never move again," she said. But one day the state sent them away and took over their house to build a freeway. The steel ball crashed through the brick walls, bulldozers sheared away the flower beds, the great shovels swung in, and the house was gone. Henry and Lorabelle and Noel moved back to the city, lived in a tiny flat under a water tank that dripped continuously on the roof and sounded like rain.

Henry and Lorabelle loved each other most of the time, tried to love each other all the time, to create a pure bond, but could not. It was marred by the viciousness, shocking to them, with which they hurt each other. Out of nothing they would create fights, would yell at each other, hate, withdraw finally in bitter silent armistice; then, after a few hours, or sometimes a few days, would come together again, with some final slashes and skirmishes, and try to work things out—to explain, protest, forgive, understand, forget, and above all to compromise. It was a terribly painful and always uncertain process; and even while it was under way Henry would think bleakly, "It won't last, will never last; we'll get through this one maybe, probably, then all will be well for a while—a few hours, days, weeks if we're lucky—then another fight over something—what?—not possible to know or predict, and certainly not to prevent . . . and then all this to go through again; and beyond that still another fight looming in the midst ahead, coming closer . . . and so on without end." But even while thinking these things he still would try to work through the current trouble because, as he would say, "There isn't anything else." And sometimes there occurred to him, uneasily, beyond all this gloomy reflection, an even more sinister thought: that their fights were not only unavoidable but also, perhaps, necessary; for their passages of greatest tenderness followed hard upon their times of greatest bitterness, as if love could be renewed only by gusts of destruction.

Nor could Henry ever build a house that would last forever, no more than anyone else; but he built one finally that lasted quite a while, a white house on a hill with lilac and laurel and three tall trees, a maple, a cedar, and a hemlock. It was an ordinary house of ordinary wood and the termites caused some trouble and always it needed painting or a new roof or a faucet dripped or something else needed fixing, and he grew old and gray and finally quite stooped doing these things but that was all right, he knew, because there wasn't anything else.

Noel grew up in this house—a dreamy, soft-spoken girl, becoming more and more beautiful—wore her long hair in pigtails, practiced the piano, sang in a high true voice, played in the meadow, caught butterflies among the lilac. At nineteen she fell in love with Falbuck Wheeling who wore a tattered brown leather jacket and roared in on a heavy motorcycle dispelling peace and birds and butterflies, bringing noise and fumes and a misery Henry felt but could not define. Falbuck had a hard bitter face, said little, would sit at the kitchen table sullen and uncomfortable, and Henry could never get him into conversation because whatever the subject—literature, government, justice—Falbuck would sit staring at him, silent and disbelieving, until finally with a few labored and nasty words he would assert some rottenness behind the facade; then, as if exhausted by this excursion into communication, he would get up, taking Noel as if he owned her, and roar away. Noel spent her days with him, and soon her nights, wore jeans and an old army shirt with the tails hanging out, let her hair hang loose and tangled, smoked cigarettes in a long black holder. Henry and Lorabelle talked earnestly to this wild, changed girl, now hardly recognizable as their daughter, advised caution and delay, but to no avail: she married Falbuck and went to live with him in a tiny room over a motorcycle shop. Henry and Lorabelle were left alone in the house on the hill, in peace now, with butterflies and the sound of wind in the three trees, and wished she were back.

Every morning Henry took his tools and went to his work of building houses—saw the pyramid of white sand spreading out in the grass, the bricks chipping, the doors beginning to stick, the first tone of gray appearing on white lumber, the first leaf falling in the bright gutter—but kept on hammering and kept on sawing, joining boards and raising rafters; on weekends he swept the driveway and mowed the grass, in the evenings fixed the leaking faucets, tried to straighten out the disagreements with Lorabelle; and in all that he did he could see himself striving toward a condition of beauty or truth or goodness or love that did not exist, but whereas earlier in his life he had always said, "It's an illusion," and turned away, now he said, "There isn't anything else," and stayed with it; and though it cannot be said that they lived happily, exactly, and certainly not ever after, they did live. They lived—for a while—with ups and downs, good days and bad, and when it came time to die Lorabelle said, "Now we'll never be parted," and Henry smiled and kissed her and said to himself, "There isn't anything else," and they died.

Part II

Some interpersonal aspects of self-confirmation

INTRODUCTION

American psychology has only recently acknowledged the important role played by human relationships in man's search for a sense of personal identity and personal worth. Perhaps Harry Stack Sullivan and Carl Rogers more than any other writers have been responsible for this humanizing trend in our psychological tradition. One of the most important contributions of this trend has been the emphasis it has placed on the individual's potential for personal development and growth. This essay will examine some of the interpersonal processes relevant to such personal development.

In this essay we shall discuss what we believe to be two major components or subprocesses of self-confirmation. We shall call the first of these the process of *self-evaluation*. All of us have beliefs about our relative and our ultimate worth. We feel superior to some persons but inferior to others. We may or may not feel "worthy." Most of us expend considerable energy trying to maintain or change our beliefs about how good we are. It is this continual process of self-evaluation and re-evaluation that determines an individual's level of self-esteem or sense of personal worth.

We shall refer to the second major component of self-confirmation as the process of *self-definition*. Just as we have beliefs about our worth, so we also have beliefs about who we are and what we are. Some persons, particularly adolescents, seem to be engaged in a desperate struggle to define themselves. Others appear to be concerned primarily with maintaining or preserving beliefs about themselves. Still other persons seem to know what they are now, but are intent on discovering what they might become. In every case, however, attempts to define the self result in certain beliefs about the self, or what we shall refer to as a "self-image" or "identity."[1]

---

[1] "Identity," "self-concept," and "self-image" are used interchangeably in this essay.

127

The first section of this essay will examine some of the interpersonal aspects of *self-evaluation.* Our primary focus will be on *re-evaluation* of self, or the possibility of change in level of self-esteem after adolescence. However, the section begins with a discussion of the initial development of self-esteem, and an examination of some critical elements of parent-child interaction. After a description of several possible outcomes of early relationships, we turn to a consideration of strategies for maintaining self-esteem. The first section closes with a consideration of self-exposure as a strategy for testing possibly invalid assumptions about self-worth, and an examination of some problems involved in obtaining useful "evaluative" feedback.

The second section of the essay examines the relevance of interpersonal relationships to the process of *self-definition.* The section begins with a brief examination of some ways an identity is formed, and then takes up problems of maintaining an identity or self-image. The second section closes with consideration of the possibility of enlarging or extending one's personal identity. The concept of "selflessness" and the role of "descriptive" feedback from other persons are discussed in this context.

SELF-EVALUATION

A. The development of self-esteem

The basic unit of interaction that concerns us is a very simple one. One person acts and in doing so intentionally or unintentionally exposes a part of his self —something of what he is, or thinks he is, or hopes he is. A second person responds to the first person's act and to his exposed self. Very frequently his reactions convey approval or disapproval, acceptance or rejection. In this simple unit of social interaction lies one of the keys to the process of self-evaluation.

The process of learning about ourselves begins very early in life. Clearly not all of it involves social interaction. The infant explores his body and experiences recurrent organic sensations which lead to the evolution of a sense of bodily self. He interacts with his physical environment and learns the distinction between what is himself and what is not himself. But the infant also learns very quickly that some of his actions elicit responses of approval, attention, love. Others seem to go unnoticed. Still others are responded to with withdrawal, coldness, or irritation. As he progresses from infancy to young childhood, he discovers more and more evaluative elements in the responses of others to his behavior or to his self.

The result of these different responses to his acts soon becomes quite apparent. Acts that elicit responses of attention or approval or affection tend to occur more and more frequently. Behavior that elicits withdrawal or coldness or rejection occurs less and less frequently.[2] Gradually the overt personality of the child, as

---

[2] There are, of course, exceptions to this general tendency, such as when a child resists or aggresses against his parents, or tests their love by being "bad," or more pathological cases where the child

manifested in his behavior, is shaped by the people with whom he interacts.

However, because of the human capacity for self-consciousness, the process of personality formation is not entirely a matter of simple reinforcement. The child's patterns of behavior arouse responses *within himself* leading to a set of perceptions of himself which become stable. Once a self as a stabilizing concept begins to emerge, the child associates certain of his acts with this self, even if others ignore or punish them. In this case the acts may become a covert part of the child's self, and others' responses to those acts become judgments of parts of the child's self. T. A. Harris, in his book *I'm OK—You're OK*, has written with great insight regarding the impact of infant and early childhood experiences on both our self-esteem and identity as adults. Chapter 2 of his book, entitled "Parent, Adult and Child," is included as a reading in Part II of this volume.

Most of us who are parents set an impossible task for ourselves: we want our children to believe that our love for them is unconditional but we also want them to behave in a reasonably acceptable manner. To accomplish the latter we must respond differentially to their behaviors, to the different parts of their selves that are manifested in their behavior. We must communicate approval in response to some, disapproval in response to others. A child must inevitably experience our disapproval as a withholding or withdrawal of love, *and therefore our love as conditional,* regardless of our intentions and real feelings.

It may be helpful to think rather crudely of the evolution of a "good self" and a "bad self." We behave, and in doing so we always manifest or expose a part of our self. In some cases our behavior elicits a response from others that we perceive as accepting, approving, loving. Thus we learn that certain parts of our selves are acceptable and lovable. Subjectively, we experience these parts of our self as our "good self." In other instances, our acts elicit reactions we perceive as disapproving, rejecting, unloving. When this happens we learn that certain parts of our self are not acceptable or lovable to others. These we experience as our "bad self."[3]

What we have described is congruent with Freud's notions about self-esteem or self-love as outlined in his paper, "On Narcissism: An Introduction."[4] Freud argued that the infant cathects his ego, or loves himself as he is. Thus he is completely acceptable to himself and his self-love or self-esteem is maximal. However, as the infant becomes a child he learns the difference between what he is and what his parents (and society) want him to be. He learns that certain parts of himself are no longer acceptable and lovable to his parents. Two things then happen. First, his libido deserts his ego and cathects an idealized image of his self that he feels would be completely accepted and loved by his parents, i.e.,

---

acts in order to obtain a response—any response—in order to establish an *existence*, regardless of the evaluation of these elicitative acts.

[3] Those parts of the "bad self" which we selectively *inattend-to* would comprise what Sullivan calls the "not self."

[4] S. Freud, "On Narcissism: An Introduction," in *Collected Papers*, Vol. IV, Joan Riviere (trans.) (London: Hogarth Press, 1956).

his ego ideal. He no longer loves and accepts himself for what he is, but rather loves and accepts himself only to the extent that he approximates his ego ideal. Effectively, then, the acceptance or rejection of others determines his acceptability to himself, or his self-esteem. Second, he tends to repress or suppress those parts of his self that are not consonant with his ego ideal. They become his "bad" self, unacceptable and unlovable to others and thus to himself.

Types of outcomes of parental strategies. Generally speaking, we can conceive of three types of outcomes of early experiences with acceptance and rejection.

1. A person may learn that no matter how he behaves or tries to "be," he cannot be assured of the love and esteem of other people. He becomes convinced of his own worthlessness, or at the very least, has serious doubts about his lovability. Maternally deprived and rejected children will often fall in this category.

There are several behavior patterns we might expect from the individual with very low self-esteem. He may simply give up. This might take the form of deep depression and suicidal tendencies, or of acting out good and bad impulses alike without regard for the reactions of other people or of society generally. Such a person might exhibit his "bad self," either to confirm his feelings of worthlessness or to receive the punishment he feels he deserves.

The person who has not given up, who has accepted himself as a person with some worth, will behave quite differently. He may expose to other people as little of his self as possible to avoid the feedback that will confirm his fears. Or he may behave narcissistically by exposing only the best things about his self, or things that are not really his self at all, and demand the approval and love of others. But as long as there is a glimmer of hope, exposing much of his real self is a terrible risk because one bit of negative feedback, real or perceived, may serve to extinguish that glimmer.

2. A second outcome of early experience, at the opposite extreme from the first, is to learn that love is unconditional, that whatever one does or feels—or *is*—he is loved and is therefore worthy of love. In our society, given the socialization practices we employ, this outcome is rarely observed. A person with such high self-esteem will be capable of responding naturally and spontaneously, as a whole person, in any situation. The possibility that relationships after childhood can lead to such an outcome will be discussed later in this essay.

3. It is with the third outcome, somewhere between the first and second, that most of us must live. We have learned that we are loved and are worthy of love at certain times but not at other times. Whether we are loved or not depends on how we are behaving, what parts of ourselves we are exposing. As we pass childhood this becomes translated into a feeling that certain things about us are acceptable and lovable, whereas other things are not. This outcome tends to be associated with several behavioral strategies designed to maintain or preserve self-esteem.

B. Maintaining self-esteem

The feeling or expectancy that if someone knew everything about us they could not accept or love us has profound implications for behavior. There appear to be three primary effects. First, it leads to a tendency to *hide* those parts of our self which we feel are less than totally acceptable. We relate to others as part persons rather than whole persons.

Second, the feeling that parts of our self are unlovable often results in a tendency to *pretend* we are something we are not, to wear masks, to erect facades.[5] Pretending has a number of advantages over hiding. For one thing it includes hiding; we can play a part that does not include "bad" parts of our self. We can even act out or expose our "bad self," but as part of the role we are playing, not as part of us.[6] If we are rejected while playing a part we are comforted by our belief that it is not our real self that has been found wanting.[7]

Third, doubts concerning self-worth encourage *cautious and ritualized behavior*. To respond spontaneously and naturally involves the risk of unintentional exposure of "bad" parts of the self and the possibility that fears of unacceptability will be confirmed. Thus there is a tendency not to be spontaneous or natural but to be guarded and deliberate in any new situation that may arise. Often persons who are reserved or aloof are in fact exercising caution.

All three of the effects described above are essentially strategies designed to avoid the rejection anticipated if more of the self were visible to others. Fear of rejection in this case stems not so much from the possible frustration of affiliative needs as from possible confirmation of the person's fears of being unacceptable to others. Maintaining self-esteem is a life-long concern for most of us, and for many of us the possibility of even a single instance of rejection by another presents a terrible threat and one to be carefully guarded against.

C. Re-evaluation of self

1. *Self-exposure.* The same strategies or behavior tendencies that serve to maintain self-esteem also prevent any real self-growth. There can be no basic change in self-esteem without testing the assumption that if others knew certain things about us we would be unloved. That assumption cannot be tested except

---

[5] Carl Rogers in *On Becoming a Person* (Boston: Houghton Mifflin, 1961), chap. 18, subsumes both hiding and pretending under the more general heading of "incongruence." People are incongruent, according to Rogers, when there is a lack of correspondence or match between (1) what they are experiencing and their awareness of it, or (2) their awareness and what they communicate about their awareness to other persons. In the first instance, they are hiding from or deluding themselves; in the second they are hiding from or deluding others.

[6] Erving Goffman focuses on impression making and pretense in his book, *The Presentation of Self in Everyday Life* (Garden City, N.Y.: Doubleday Anchor, 1959). In his brilliant paper, "On Face-Work: An Analysis of Ritual Elements in Social Interaction," (page 175, this volume) he analyzes social rituals that facilitate both "hiding" and "pretending."

[7] Michael Silverstein, in his paper "The Development of Identity: Power and Sex Roles in Academia" which follows this essay, describes with great insight the function of "pretending" in self-protection.

by exposing all of the self to others and observing their reaction. We may discover that others accept and love us even after we have exposed our "bad self" to them. If so, relearning or re-evaluation of self can occur, leading to a greater sense of personal worth. Of course, we may also have our fear that we are unworthy of love confirmed by others and thus experience a loss of self-esteem.

2. *Validity of assumptions about self-worth.* What chance is there that a person's doubts about his self-worth are realistic? If his doubts are unwarranted, testing through self-exposure should logically lead to their dissipation or extinction. But if they are realistic fears, greater exposure of self may lead only to their reinforcement and a further loss of self-esteem.

There are several reasons for expecting doubts about self-worth to be unrealistic, mostly stemming from the fact that the most serious of these doubts originate in infancy and early childhood. First, some of the most persistent assumptions about the acceptability or unacceptability of parts of the self are formed before the child's faculties for making fine discriminations have fully developed, resulting in a tendency for him to overgeneralize.[8] For example, a child who feels threatened with loss of love for hitting other children may "learn" to believe that any of the aggressive impulses he feels make him unworthy of love.

Second, a child cannot be objective about his parent's love for him and may see the threat of loss of love where in fact it does not exist. His perceptions may be distorted or autistic due to immature notions of causality, a vague conception of time, intense affect, or a simple lack of experience and the perspective it provides. This can lead to invalid assumptions, as when a child assumes that something he did caused his mother to desert him, when in fact she had to go to the hospital.

A third reason we can expect many assumptions about self-worth to be invalid is that they are frequently based on the reactions of just one or two persons, usually the parents. Parents may find something about their child unacceptable because they are intolerant and not capable of loving any other human unconditionally, or because the child has become involved in his parent's neurosis.[9] In other cases, changing standards of behavior make it impossible for parents to accept their children, and for their children to accept themselves. Because of changed attitudes toward sex in our society, for example, strictly brought up young people often experience guilt and loss of self-esteem for behaving in ways that are unacceptable to their parents but perfectly acceptable among their peers.

Finally, the simple fact that what may be quite unacceptable in a child may be acceptable or even desirable in an adolescent or adult may lead to incorrect assumptions about self-worth. A child may feel threatened by loss of love if he

---

[8] For an illuminating and thorough discussion of the characteristics of learning that occurs during infancy and early childhood, see D. C. McClelland, *Personality* (New York: Holt, Rinehart and Winston, 1951), pp. 441–58.

[9] For an enlightening discussion of neurotic interaction between parent and child, see E. Vogel and N. Bell, "The Emotionally Disturbed Child as the Family Scapegoat," in *The Family* (Glencoe, Ill.: Free Press, 1960).

is willful or overly independent as a child. However, this same independence in the male adult may lead to acceptance and success.

To summarize, the probability that an individual's doubts about his self-worth are based on adequate evidence of his unacceptability to a number of relatively unconflicted persons who know him well is very low.

3. *Evaluative feedback.* By "evaluative feedback" we mean social cues or "reflected self-appraisals" useful for evaluation or re-evaluation of the self. Not all persons are concerned with self-improvement. Persons with low self-esteem, for example, are primarily concerned with *reassurance.* They tend to search others' responses to them only for clues of approval or disapproval, acceptance or rejection. Narcissists seek the compliments, admiration, and applause of other persons in a desperate and continuous effort to dispel doubts about their ultimate worth as human beings. There is little concern among such people for realistic self-appraisal or self-improvement.

For most persons, however, evaluative feedback serves a potentially useful function. Through self-exposure and feedback persons can test assumptions about their acceptability or lovability and thereby develop greater self-esteem. Evaluative feedback makes it possible to develop and maintain a realistic conception of one's competencies and liabilities, strengths and weaknesses. Finally, evaluative feedback serves as a basis for self-improvement; unless we become aware of our weaknesses and shortcomings, we cannot set about overcoming them.

There are two general classes of social responses that people tend to use as feedback for purposes of evaluating self-worth. When people interact, however formally or impersonally, they frequently give off very subtle cues regarding their feelings about the other person. We can all this *indirect feedback.* The second class, which we will call *direct feedback,* consists of verbal statements explicitly describing one person's perceptions of or reactions to another.

There are several points of interest concerning the nature and use of indirect feedback. It is often ambiguous. A smile may be a polite social habit, but it may also convey warmth and approval. Aloofness may indicate disapproval, but it may also indicate an individual's fear of intimacy. The problem of ambiguous feedback is magnified by the fact that people tend to see what they expect to see, to be particularly sensitive to those cues in their environment which confirm their expectancies. Thus, if a person expects others to find him unacceptable, he will tend to see smiles as polite only and aloofness as rejection.

Indirect feedback tends to be overgeneralized. The feeling that we are being rejected, if the cues are subtle, may develop gradually. If so, it is difficult to associate someone's rejection of us with a specific act, or one small part of our self that we exposed. Rather, we tend to experience the incident as a rejection of our whole self, or all those parts of our self about which we have doubts.

Indirect feedback does not allow for justification or explanation. It frequently happens that we find something about another person unacceptable until we understand why he is that way, until he has a chance to explain his self to us. Just as frequently the feedback may reveal more about the giver than the receiver. If inaccurate feedback is communicated indirectly, there is little chance it will be questioned or corrected by others. If the reason for another's reaction to us cannot be openly explored, there is no way to determine whether or not the feedback was justified.

It should be clear that indirect feedback is not very useful, and can be harmful, for purposes of self-evaluation. The person receiving the feedback must draw inferences from subtle, often ambiguous, cues without the opportunity to explore the exact meaning of or reasons for the feedback.

Direct feedback is potentially more useful for evaluating self-worth. However, even direct feedback can be useless if it does not reflect frank appraisals or reactions.

One major reason for lack of frankness is our cultural taboo on criticizing another person, particularly to his face. We tend to admire people who claim, "There is some good in everyone, and I look for that," or, "If I do not have something good to say about someone, I do not say anything at all."[10] These are high-sounding sentiments, but they also convey the message that it is wrong to look critically at another person and even worse to communicate criticism. Maslow has noted that even our definitions of love do not ordinarily include the obligation to feedback or criticize.[11]

One result of our tendency to say only positive things to each other is that we cannot really trust others to be honest with us. If people suppress their criticism and look for something polite or tactful to say, even positive feedback becomes suspect and, therefore, of little benefit. It is little wonder that we often are not comforted by others' reassurances that they accept and love us despite what we have exposed of our self.

Because of the taboo we place on face-to-face criticism, negative feedback tends to be accompanied by strong emotions on the part of both giver and receiver. Many persons will level criticism only if they first become angry. As a result we learn to react defensively or strike back, responding to the threat we have learned to associate with criticism. Because of our emotional response we tend to experience the criticism as a rejection of our whole self and thus something to be warded off or discredited at all costs.

We cannot blame the scarcity of direct evaluative feedback entirely on social

---

[10] A parallel to this is the anti-intellectual component: "What I don't know won't hurt me"; "Let sleeping dogs lie," etc.

[11] A. H. Maslow, "Summer Notes on Social Psychology of Industry and Management at Non-Linear System, Inc., Del Mar, California," unpublished manuscript (1962).

Maslow goes on to point out the irony of our willingness to let someone go on making the same mistake over and over, ostensibly out of kindness, but really because we are afraid of hurting him and being struck back. As contrast, he cites the Bruderhof where one aspect of Christian love is to be honest with others, even when it hurts. If a faculty member is a bad teacher because he mumbles on and on it is considered to be a brotherly duty, and an expression of caring, to tell him so (*ibid.*, pp. 5–6.).

Retaliation is one main factor that inhibits feedback. Another is the danger that if one exposes a perception or feeling about another, he *may* have to change it. Or even more: he may have to get *closer* to the target of criticism. (In the essay introducing Part I, we pointed to the "distancing" function of the stereotype—or untested perception.)

custom. Frequently people ask others to evaluate them, but at the same time give off subtle cues that they do not really want to hear anything other than reassurance. On the other hand, we sometimes withhold feedback because we do not want another person to change. We get used to others being the way they are, our relationships with them stabilize and become comfortable, and we may even obtain satisfaction from their weaknesses and imperfections. In fact it is likely that we use other people, particularly hated or scapegoat targets, in a defensive way to keep our own anxiety at a minimum. Evaluative feedback, even though it might be helpful to the other person, would only upset a satisfying relationship. Finally, people are frequently *afraid* to offer even helpful criticism. They are afraid that they might hurt the other person and/or might be hurt themselves by an act of retaliation on his part.

4. *Facilitating relationships.* The prototype of a relationship that facilitates positive self-reevaluation or increased self-esteem is one in which unconditional love is combined with direct feedback.

Some relationships between adults come to approximate this state. A relationship of this sort begins when people trust each other enough to start exposing more and more of themselves to each other. Each person exposes his self in small increments, tentatively, waiting for a response. If the response is disapproval or rejection, the relationship freezes at that point, is terminated, or the testing begins anew. If each exposure is met with acceptance, there is a continual build-up of trust, a growing confidence that they will not hurt each other intentionally. The process is mutually reinforcing, since when one person trusts enough to make himself vulnerable by exposing himself, trust is generated in the other person.

A successful relationship from the standpoint of an increase in self-esteem is one where the individuals are committed to openness and trust in their human transactions, and find themselves accepted or loved. There is concrete evidence of each individual's acceptability, with a corresponding increase in self-esteem.

Let us briefly summarize what we have said about the process of self-evaluation. Experiences with acceptance and rejection during infancy and childhood are basic to the development of our self-esteem as adults. However, re-evaluation of self with a consequent increase in self-esteem can occur after childhood, usually as a result of testing assumptions about self-worth through exposing the self to others and obtaining feedback. Relearning of this type depends primarily on direct feedback that is both honest and unambiguous. Thus, while exposure of self can be an effective strategy for confirming self-worth, it must occur in the context of a relationship that can tolerate honest expression of feelings.

SELF-DEFINITION

In this section we are concerned with a second major component of self-confirmation—the process of self-definition. Every person has certain beliefs about who or what he is; taken together, these beliefs are a person's self-image, or identity.

Here we shall focus on interpersonal processes that bear on how such beliefs are formed, how they are maintained, and how they change.

A. Identity formation

Erik Erikson has defined identity formation in the following manner: ". . . identity formation . . . is a lifelong development largely unconscious to the individual and to his society. Its roots go back all the way to the first self-recognition: in the baby's earliest exchange of smiles there is something of a self-realization coupled with a mutual recognition."[12]

With respect to identity formation, it may be useful to examine some ideas of G. H. Mead, who perhaps more than any other theorist before or since views the self as predominantly a social product; Mead[13] emphasized the importance of face-to-face interaction with others: from the time we are very young children, we constantly act toward others and they respond to us. One result of the continuous exchange between ego and alter is that we learn about our selves; each act directed toward us contains cues about how others see and experience us as individuals. Thus our beliefs about our self, our self-image, are in large measure a reflection of others' perceptions of us. The phrases "looking glass self" coined by Cooley and "reflected self-appraisal" by Sullivan are graphic statements of this process.

Not all beliefs about self are formed as a result of face-to-face interaction. Festinger[14] has used the term "social comparison process" to describe another way people appraise and evaluate different aspects of their selves. In some cases it may be more efficient, or less risky, to compare our self to another person whose social stimulus value is known to us. In this way, we may develop certain beliefs about our selves without benefit of direct feedback fron other persons. It seems probably that as we pass from childhood into adolescence and adulthood, more and more of our beliefs about our self are formed indirectly, through some form of social comparison process.

B. Maintaining an identity

Festinger[15] has distinguished between what he calls *physical* and *social* reality. Beliefs and opinions about physical reality can be validated by physical measurement: we can test our belief that glass is fragile by striking it with a hammer. Social reality cannot be tested by physical means. There is no physical measure-

[12] E. Erickson, "The Problem of Ego Identity," in *Identity and Anxiety*, Stein, Vidich, and White (eds.) (Glencoe, Ill.: Free Press 1960), p. 47.

[13] G. H. Mead, *Mind, Self, and Society* (Chicago: Univ. of Chicago Press, 1934).

[14] L. Festinger, "A Theory of Social Comparison Processes," *Human Relations*, Vol. 7 (1954), pp. 117–40.

[15] L. Festinger, "Informal Social Communication," *Psychological Review*, Vol. 57 (1950), pp. 271–82.

ment, for example, that can tell us decisively whether Republicans or Democrats are more adept at handling problems of foreign policy. Festinger goes on to assert that beliefs, attitudes, or opinions about social reality are correct, valid, or proper only to the extent they are anchored in a group of people with similar beliefs.

Many beliefs about self fall into the category of social reality. There are no physical means of determining whether we are in fact a leader of men, good-looking, or exceptionally tactful. Therefore, validation or confirmation of many beliefs about who or what we are must ultimately depend upon social consensus.

There are at least two varieties of beliefs that must be socially validated and confirmed if an individual's self-image or identity is to remain secure: (1) beliefs about the self, about who and what we are, and (2) beliefs about the nature of social reality.

1. *Beliefs about self.* An individual's self-image is confirmed when other persons' responses to him indicate that their beliefs about who and what he is correspond with his own. There is a mutual recognition of his self, and the validity of his self-image is confirmed. Under conditions that provide consistent social confirmation of all aspects of the self, a strong and integrated identity or self-image will develop and be sustained. As a result there is less need to search for responses that confirm the self, or to shield one's self from disconfirming responses. There is greater freedom to respond spontaneously to a situation, to *be*, without a binding concern for the consistency or recognizability of the self-image that is presented. Operating from such a position of strength, a person can dare to *hear* feedback about who he is and what he is, and thus can continually test the validity of his beliefs about his self.

The psychological importance of maintaining a consistent self-image is evident from the existence of elaborate social rituals that function primarily to reduce the probability of disconfirmation, particularly in casual social contacts. "Being tactful," for example, consists essentially of responding to other people in a way that does not challenge the validity of the self they are publicly presenting. The two papers by Erving Goffman included in this volume are excellent analyses of such rituals.

The "identity diffusion" and uncertainty that results when the self is not confirmed by others, or when it is disconfirmed, has been described by a number of authors. In his moving essay, "The Therapeutic Despair,"[16] Leslie Farber writes of his *despair* when a patient refuses to confirm him in his role as therapist or healer by getting well. Erik Erikson has suggested that *identity crises* result when other people, or society, are willing to recognize a person only as something he cannot or does not want to be. He points out that social confirmation of *some* identity, even a negative one, is often preferable to a lack of confirmation and the uncertainty and confusion that results: ". . . many a late adolescent, if faced with continuing diffusion, would rather be nobody or somebody bad, or indeed, dead—and this totally, and by free choice—than be not-quite-somebody."[17]

---

[16] L. Farber, "The Therapeutic Despair," *Psychiatry*, Vol. 1 (1958), pp. 7–20.
[17] Erikson, "The Problem of Ego Identity," p. 62.

Finally, in his perceptive and fascinating tale[18] about a young British Colonial officer, George Orwell graphically illustrates the relationship between identity diffusion and *susceptibility to influence.* Unhappy with his role but desperate ". . . to avoid looking a fool," the young officer acts out the oft-quoted wisdom that "people become what you expect them to be."[19]

2. *Beliefs about reality.*[20]   It is important to most people to believe that they are rational and objective, that their world view is "realistic" and accurate. This element of self-image is confirmed through validation of various beliefs or assumptions about the world. When these beliefs and assumptions involve social reality, their validation depends upon interaction with other persons who share a common image of the nature of reality.

Confidence in one's self as someone who has valid beliefs about the nature of reality is prerequisite for discovery, for daring to see the world in new ways. We depend on people with such confidence to lead in defining and redefining social reality, to raise questions even about beliefs supported by social consensus. Persons who lack confidence in the validity of their perceptions and beliefs will feel pressures to conform, to accept the beliefs of others as more valid than their own. However, in a heterogeneous society no man can be a complete conformist; the validity of many of our beliefs is challenged by the different beliefs of other people, other groups. Nevertheless, the effort we expend to make sure we have some social support for our views is evidence of our dependence on shared perceptions and beliefs for confirmation of a core part of the self.

One of the most common ways we confirm our views that are not universally held is by associating with people who *do* share and thus confirm our perceptions, attitudes, opinions, and beliefs. Persons who have lived for an extended period in an alien culture often speak of their relief at having their world view confirmed upon their return home. Festinger, Riecken, and Schachter[21] and Hardyck and Braden[22] have provided penetrating descriptions of the reactions of apocalyptic groups to disconfirmations of some important beliefs and expectations. In the case of members of the "Lake City" group described by Festinger *et al.,* the reaction to disconfirmation was to proselytize and attract new members to the group in order to restore the individual's confidence in his beliefs and thus prevent identity-diffusion, if not disintegration. In contrast, the highly cohesive "True Word" group discussed by Hardyck and Braden apparently provided the social confirmation required for individual members to maintain their beliefs in the face of physical disconfirmation without proselytizing. In both cases, how-

---

[18] Included in this volume (see pp. 190–95).

[19] See the essay introducing Part III for a more complete discussion of the relationship between self-confirmation and susceptibility to influence or personal change.

[20] In this part we are focusing on social processes relevant to definition of self. See the description of a "Type B" relationship in the essay introducing Part V for a discussion of interpersonal processes which lead to both self-definition and definition of external reality.

[21] L. Festinger, H. W. Riecken, Jr., and S. Schachter, *When Prophecy Fails* (Minneapolis: Univ. of Minnesota, 1956).

[22] Page 213 this volume.

ever, one clear implication is that lack of confirmation of important beliefs about the environment threatens certain beliefs about the self and leads to defensive rather than reality-testing strategies.

People also respond to a lack of social support or confirmation of their perceptions and beliefs by changing them to conform to those of their most salient reference group.[23] The paper by Friedlander which follows in Part II describes changes in perceptions and beliefs of a young black researcher with several such reference groups.

C. Identity extension

In this section we are concerned with identity change, specifically the growth or extension of identity or self-image.

1. *Self-realization.* The verb "to realize" has more than one meaning. Among other things, it implies both *knowing* and *making concrete or real*, suggesting two ways that a self-image might be extended. Self-realization, as we conceive of it, involves both becoming consciously aware of the self as it presently exists, and extending the self to include latent potentialities. The discussion of self-esteem in an earlier section of the essay is directly relevant to the first aspect of self-realization: self-awareness. There we suggested that doubts about self-worth can lead to repression as well as suppression of certain parts of the self; hiding, pretending, and caution are strategies for self-delusion as well as for deluding others. Here we are more concerned with self-realization in the sense of discovering what the self *can* be.

2. *Self-realization through "selflessness."* For us, the key to self-realization, to discovering what the self *can* be is selflessness: we become our self only as we can forget our self. Fingarette has described selflessness in the following terms:

. . . "selflessness" is a characteristic mystic concept associated with the "enlightened" state . . . It does not mean the absence of a self in the psychoanalytic sense of that term, nor does it refer to the absence of the ego or of the "self-representations," or to the loss of ability to distinguish "inner" and "outer" as in hallucination or estrangement . . . "Selflessness," being a term in a "subjective" language, expresses the lack of conscious awareness of self. But this is true in a sense which cannot be made unambiguous in ordinary language. We can point to the unawareness in question by referring to its psychological conditions: it is that "normal" unselfconsciousness characteristic of experience which is primarily nonanxious and motivated by neutralized drives functioning within the non-conflictful portions of the ego. It is an unselfconsciousness akin to the normal unawareness of our breathing.[24]

A person capable of selflessness must be sure enough of his worth as an individual, self-accepting enough, that he does not need to hide, or pretend, or be cautious; instead he can respond openly, spontaneously, and naturally to new

---

[23] See the essay introducing Part III.

[24] H. Fingarette, "The Ego and Mystic Selflessness," in *Identity and Anxiety*, Stein, Vidich, and White (eds.) (Glencoe Ill.: Free Press, 1960), pp. 580–81.

situations and new people. Only by temporarily suspending the conscious desire for consistency, the need to be what we know we can be successfully and safely, can we find out what *else* we might be. Only by responding *unselfconsciously,* momentarily freed from too great dependence on what we have been, can we discover what variety there is within us.

It should be emphasized that while selflessness connotes a lack of conscious awareness of self in action, it is a *suspension* of awareness, not the incapacity to be aware. It is this distinction that differentiates the person capable of selflessness from the schizophrenic. Although the term "selflessness" often has been used to describe only the rather esoteric states of the religious mystic or drug addict, it is probable that most persons with some "nonconflictful portions of the ego" can behave selflessly, or unselfconsciously, in some situations.

Selflessness also implies the capacity to observe one's self in a detached and objective fashion. A person's first impulse in the face of critical feedback from the environment is to defend the self, to preserve the status quo, to look out for his self-interests. Under these conditions it is difficult, if not impossible, to evaluate feedback objectively and use it constructively. Selflessness, on the other hand, suggests the capacity to become temporarily detached from one's self, to stand back and look at the self as another person might. If the ability to behave unselfconsciously is the first step toward identity extension, then the capacity to view our behavior objectively is certainly the second.

3. *Facilitating relationships.* Selflessness and self-realization can occur to the degree that a person feels worthy in a relationship. The parties to the relationship will feel that they are accepted, that the other has made a positive decision concerning their value of them. There will be a feeling that this decision is final and will stand in the face of any new aspects of the self that might emerge.

Furthermore, the persons involved will feel they are accepted for what they are; their images of each other will neither be too grandiose nor too modest. Expectations of each other will be realistic.

Finally, there will be an implicit assumption that one person will not deliberately hurt the other to satisfy his own needs, a quality of a relationship often called *trust.*

It appears, therefore, that self-definition and self-evaluation interact with each other. The person has to be something in order to be evaluated, and the person has to be positively evaluated in order to be something new.

In a paper which follows this essay, Carl Rogers describes with considerable insight and wisdom some characteristics of interpersonal relationships that further selflessness and self-growth.

4. *Descriptive feedback.* Learning about our self from the responses of others to us does not stop with the end of childhood and the initial development of a sense of identity. During our discussion of self-evaluation, we suggested that low self-esteem is associated with a tendency to perceive only the evaluative elements in the responses of others to us—the approval or disapproval, acceptance or rejection. The need to maintain a certain level of self-esteem seems to take precedence over all else, and doubt about self-worth stimulates "selfishness" or "selfconsciousness," rather than selflessness. Most people, however, at least in some areas can become temporarily self-detached to observe the reactions of others to their self. They can go beyond the evaluative feedback to the descriptive cues that can help them discover *what* they are rather than just how acceptable they are. In his paper on the development of identity (p. 159, this volume), Michael Silverstein provides a highly personal account of his progression from preoccupation with the evaluations of others to a fuller discovery of his self.

The distinction between indirect and direct feedback, made in connection with evaluative feedback, is also relevant here. However, whereas indirect feedback is of little use and may even be harmful, for purposes of self-evaluation, it plays an extremely important role in self-definition. The responses of others to our behavior, often nonverbal, may contain information they might not be able to express more directly. Nevertheless, it frequently is not enough. Persons who attend human relations training laboratories such as those sponsored by the National Training Laboratories[25] almost invariably express a desire to be told point blank how other people perceive them. This is particularly true of persons with a relatively strong sense of personal worth who are not worried about, or even particularly interested in, others' *evaluations* of them.

The shortage of useful descriptive feedback stems partly from difficulty in predicting whether the person who receives the descriptive feedback will respond to it as just that, or whether he will scan it only for its evaluative content. Psychologists face this problem when they try to feed back the results of psychological tests; teachers face a similar dilemma when they discuss a student's work with him, or counsel a student on possible careers. All too often persons who want and can make good use of descriptive feedback are denied it because the person who might help them has had a bad experience with someone who could hear only the evaluative elements in the feedback he was given.

SUMMARY

This essay represents an attempt to point up some of the interpersonal aspects of self-confirmation. We have focused on self-evaluation and self-definition as two processes critical to self-confirmation and having important interpersonal ramifications. Rather than try to draw conclusions, it seems more appropriate to close with an illustration that dramatizes many of the points we have made.

As part of a research project, forty-five young managers in a large utility company were interviewed extensively about their career problems. Nearly all of the men had been hired right out of college as management trainees, and had been working for this particular organization for six years. As one might expect, a variety of complaints and problems were unearthed, but one in particular stood out because of the intense frustration associated with it.

[25] E. H. Schein and W. G. Bennis, *Personal and Organizational Change Through Group Methods* (New York: Wiley, 1964).

Several of the young managers had been quite successful up to the time they began their business careers, and as a result they had no reason to believe they would not continue to be successful. Each had, at the beginning of his career, rather high expectations of what he would accomplish. The image each had of himself was that of a highly competent person who would rise to the top among a group of his peers.

Before long, however, their experiences in the company began to challenge their self-images. They did not move ahead particularly fast, only keeping pace with or falling behind the majority of their peers. This experience was quite at odds with the expectations they had. The environment offered several possible rationalizations for failure. Because of the period of business regression, promotions were frozen. The company was automating various functions, cutting back on the total number of employees and thus the number of management positions. The company was consolidating small work units into larger ones, giving more responsibility to individual managers, but eliminating managerial positions in the process.

The basic dilemma these men expressed was whether or not in the face of feedback from their environment they should reevaluate themselves and readjust their self-images to be more consistent with the cues they were receiving. Many of their colleagues were quick to perceive and accept the evaluative cues contained in the company's response to them and to reevaluate themselves accordingly. Others, less confident of their worth as individuals, sought only reassurance, rationalizing or denying their predicament. These men could do neither, at least not on the basis of the impersonal and frequently ambiguous feedback available to them. They did express a desperate need for respected superiors to give them absolutely objective, point-blank feedback on their potential as managers. With honest, direct feedback they could trust, they felt they could decide whether to modify their self-image appropriately, or to try to confirm their self-image in another company. However, they were unable to persuade their superiors to be absolutely honest and open with them; the superiors apparently either felt they would be hurting rather than helping their subordinate by leveling with him, or they had been taught it was poor management. In any case, the organization failed to recognize the capacity these men had to use direct feedback constructively, with the result that the men in question were unable to resolve their dilemma.

Clearly there are no simple solutions to the dilemmas the young managers are confronting. Self-esteem and self-image are the hardcore of personality, but we have little control over their development, and lack the knowledge and techniques to influence or alter them reliably. Recently, however, there has been an increasing awareness of the importance of interpersonal processes, and a growing concern with "creative human relationships," or relationships that facilitate personal growth. This section, indeed this entire book, is a reflection of that concern.

Parent, adult, and child*

Thomas A. Harris

> *The passion for truth is silenced by answers which have the weight of undisputed authority.*
>
> PAUL TILLICH

Early in his work in the development of Transactional Analysis, Berne observed that as you watch and listen to people you can see them change before your eyes. It is a total kind of change. There are simultaneous changes in facial expression, vocabulary, gestures, posture, and body functions, which may cause the face to flush, the heart to pound, or the breathing to become rapid.

We can observe these abrupt changes in everyone: the little boy who bursts into tears when he can't make a toy work, the teen-age girl whose woeful face floods with excitement when the phone finally rings, the man who grows pale and trembles when he gets the news of a business failure, the father whose face "turns to stone" when his son disagrees with him. The individual who changes in these ways is still the same person in terms of bone structure, skin, and clothes. So what changes inside him? He changes *from* what *to* what?

This was the question which fascinated Berne in the early development of Transactional Analysis. A thirty-five-year-old lawyer, whom he was treating, said, "I'm not really a lawyer, I'm just a little boy." Away from the psychiatrist's office he was, in fact, a successful lawyer, but in treatment he felt and acted like a little boy. Sometimes during the hour he would ask, "Are you talking to the lawyer or to the little boy?" Both Berne and his patient became intrigued at the existence and appearance of these two real people, or states of being, and began talking about them as "the adult" and "the child." Treatment centered around separating the two. Later another state began to become apparent as a state distinct from "adult" and "child." This was "the parent" and was identified by behavior which was a reproduction of what the patient saw and heard his parents do when he was a little boy.

FIGURE 1
The personality

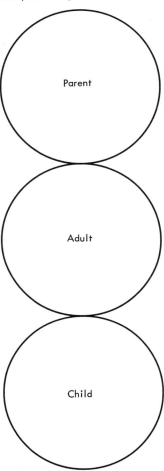

Changes from one state to another are apparent in manner, appearance, words, and gestures. A thirty-four-year-old woman came to me for help with a problem of sleeplessness, constant worry over "what I am doing to my children," and increasing nervousness. In the course of the first hour she suddenly began to weep and said, "You make me feel like I'm three years old." Her voice and manner were that of a small child. I asked her, "What happened to make you feel like a child?" "I don't know," she responded, and then added, "I suddenly felt like a failure." I said, "Well, let's talk about children, about the family. Maybe we can discover something inside of you that produces these feelings of failure and despair." At another point in the hour her voice and manner again changed suddenly. She became critical and dogmatic: "After all, parents have rights, too. Children need to be shown their place." During one hour this mother changed to three different and distinct personalities: one of a small child dominated by feelings, one of a self-righteous parent, and one of a reasoning, logical, grown-up woman and mother of three children.

Continual observation has supported the assumption that these three states exist in all people. It is as if in each person there is the same little person he was when he was three years old. There are also within him his own parents. These are recordings in the brain of actual experiences of internal and external events, the most significant of which happened during the first five years of life. There is a third state, different from these two. The first two are called Parent and Child, and the third, Adult. (See Figure 1.)

These states of being are not roles but psychological realities. Berne says that "Parent, Adult, and Child are not concepts like Superego, Ego, and Id . . . but phenomenological realities."[1] The state is produced by the playback of recorded data of events in the past, involving real people, real times, real places, real decisions, and real feelings.

THE PARENT

The Parent is a huge collection of recordings in the brain of unquestioned or imposed external events perceived by a person in his early years, a period which we have designated roughly as the first five years of life. This is the period before the social birth of the individual, before he leaves home in response to the demands of society and enters school. (See Figure 2.) The name Parent is most descriptive of this data inasmuch as the most significant "tapes" are those provided by the example and pronouncements of his own real parents or parent substitutes. Everything the child saw his parents do and everything he heard them say is recorded in the Parent. Everyone has a Parent in that everyone experienced external stimuli in the first five years of life. Parent is specific for every person, being the recording of that set of early experiences unique to him.

The data in the Parent was taken in and recorded "straight" without editing. The situation of the little child, his dependency, and his inability to construct meanings with words made it impossible for him to modify, correct, or explain. Therefore, if the parents were hostile and constantly battling each other, a fight was recorded with the terror produced by seeing the two persons on whom the child depended for survival about to destroy each other. There was no way of including in this recording the fact that the father was inebriated because his business had just gone down the drain or that the mother was at her wits' end because she had just found she was pregnant again.

In the Parent are recorded all the admonitions and rules and laws that the child heard from his parents and saw in their living. They range all the way from the earliest parental communications, interpreted nonverbally through tone of

---

[1] E. Berne, *Transactional Analysis in Psychotherapy* (New York: Grove Press, 1961), p. 24.

FIGURE 2
The Parent

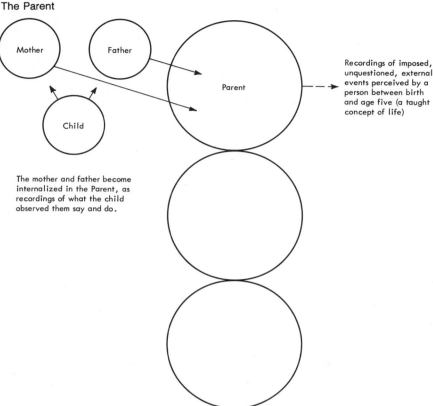

Recordings of imposed, unquestioned, external events perceived by a person between birth and age five (a taught concept of life)

The mother and father become internalized in the Parent, as recordings of what the child observed them say and do.

voice, facial expression, cuddling, or noncuddling, to the more elaborate verbal rules and regulations espoused by the parents as the little person became able to understand words. In this set of recordings are the thousands of "no's" directed at the toddler, the repeated "don'ts" that bombarded him, the looks of pain and horror in mother's face when his clumsiness brought shame on the family in the form of Aunt Ethel's broken antique vase.

Likewise are recorded the coos of pleasure of a happy mother and the looks of delight of a proud father. When we consider that the recorder is on all the time we begin to comprehend the immense amount of data in the Parent. Later come the more complicated pronouncements: Remember, Son, wherever you go in the world you will always find the best people are Methodists; never tell a lie; pay your bills; you are judged by the company you keep; you are a good boy if you clean your plate; waste is the original sin; you can never trust a man; you can never trust a woman; you're damned if you do and damned if you don't; you can never trust a cop; busy hands are happy hands; don't walk under ladders; do unto others as you would have them do unto you; do others in that they don't do you in.

The significant point is that whether these rules are good or bad in the light of a reasonable ethic, they are recorded as *truth* from the source of all security, the people who are "six feet tall" at a time when it is important to the two-foot-tall child that he please and obey them. It is a permanent recording. A person cannot erase it. It is available for replay throughout life.

This replay is a powerful influence throughout life. These examples—coercing, forcing, sometimes permissive but more often restrictive—are rigidly internalized as a voluminous set of data essential to the individual's survival in the setting of a group, beginning with the family and extending throughout life in a succession of groups necessary to life. Without a physical parent the child would die. The internal Parent also is lifesaving, guarding against many dangers which, perceived experientially, could cause death. In the Parent is the recording, "Don't touch that knife!" It is a thunderous directive. The threat to the little person, as he sees it, is that his mother will spank him or otherwise show disapproval. The greater threat is that he can cut himself and bleed to death. He cannot perceive this. He does not have adequate data. The recording of parental dictates, then, is an indispensable aid to survival, in both the physical and the social sense.

Another characteristic of the Parent is the fidelity of the recordings of inconsistency. Parents say one thing and do another. Parents say, "Don't lie," but tell lies. They tell children that smoking is bad for their health but smoke themselves. They proclaim adherence to a religious ethic but do not live by it. It is not safe for the little child to question this inconsistency, and so he is confused. Because this data causes confusion and fear, he defends himself by turning off the recording.

We think of the Parent predominantly as the recordings of the transactions between the child's two parents. It may be helpful to consider the recordings of Parent data as somewhat like the recording of stereophonic sound. There are two sound tracks that, if harmonious, produce a beautiful effect when played together. If they are not harmonious, the effect is unpleasant and the recording is put aside and played very little, if at all. This is what happens when the Parent contains discordant material. The Parent is repressed or, in the extreme, blocked out altogether. Mother may have been a "good" mother and father may have been "bad," or vice versa. There is much useful data which is stored as a result of the transmission of good material from one parent; but since the Parent does contain material from the other parent that is contradictory and productive of anxiety, the Parent as a whole is weakened or fragmented. Parent data that is discordant is not allowed to come on "audibly" as a strong influence in the person's life.

Another way to describe this phenomenon is to compare it with the algebraic equation: a plus times a minus equals a minus. It does not matter how big the plus was, or how little the minus was. The result is always a minus—a weakened, disintegrated Parent. The effect in later life may be ambivalence, discord, and despair—for the person, that is, who is not free to examine the Parent.

Much Parent data appears in current living in the "how-to" category: how to hit a nail, how to make a bed, how to eat soup, how to blow your nose, how to thank the hostess, how to shake hands, how to pretend no one's at home, how to fold the bath towels, or how to dress the Christmas tree. The *how* to comprises a vast body of data acquired by watching the parents. It is largely useful data which makes it possible for the little person to learn to get along by himself. Later (as his Adult becomes more skillful and free to examine Parent data) these early ways of doing things may be updated and replaced by better ways that are more suited to a changed reality. A person whose early instructions were accompanied by stern intensity may find it more difficult to examine the old ways and may hang onto them long after they are useful, having developed a compulsion to do it "this way and no other."

The mother of a teen-ager related the following parental edict, which had long governed her housekeeping procedures. Her mother had told her, "You *never* put a hat on a table or a coat on a bed." So she went through life never putting a hat on a table or a coat on a bed. Should she occasionally forget, or should one of her youngsters break this old rule, there was an overreaction that seemed inappropriate to the mere violation of the rules of simple neatness. Finally, after several decades of living with this unexamined law, mother asked grandmother (by then in her eighties), "Mother, *why* do you never put a hat on a table or a coat on a bed?"

Grandmother replied that when she was little there had been some neighbor children who were "infested," and her mother had warned her that it was important they never put the neighbor children's hats on the table or their coats on the bed. Reasonable enough. The urgency of the early admonition was understandable. In terms of Penfield's findings it was also understandable why the recording came on with the original urgency. Many of the rules we live by are like this.

Some influences are more subtle. One modern housewife with every up-to-date convenience in her home found she simply did not have any interest in buying a garbage-disposal unit. Her husband encouraged her to get one, pointing out all the reasons this would simplify her kitchen procedures. She recognized this but found one excuse after another to postpone going to the appliance store to select one. Her husband finally confronted her with his belief that she was *deliberately* not getting a garbage disposal. He insisted she tell him why.

A bit of reflection caused her to recognize an early impression she had about garbage. Her childhood years were the Depression years of the 1930's. In her home, garbage was carefully saved and fed to the pig, which was butchered at Christmas and provided an important source of food. The dishes were even washed without soap so that the dishwater, with its meager offering of nutrients, could be included in the slops. As a little girl she perceived that garbage was important, and as a grown woman she found it difficult to rush headlong into purchasing a new-fangled gadget to dispose of it. (She bought the disposal unit and lived happily ever after.)

When we realize that thousands of these simple rules of living are recorded in the brain of every person, we begin to appreciate what a comprehensive, vast store of data the Parent includes. Many of these edicts are fortified with such additional imperatives as "never" and "always" and "never forget that" and, we may assume, pre-empt certain primary neurone pathways that supply ready data for today's transactions. These rules are the origins of compulsions and quirks and eccentricities that appear in later behavior. Whether Parent data is a burden or a boon depends on how appropriate to the present, on whether or not it has been updated by the Adult, the function of which we shall discuss in this chapter.

There are sources of Parent data other than the physical parents. A three-year-old who sits before a television set many hours a day is recording what he sees. The programs he watches are a "taught" concept of life. If he watches programs of violence, I believe he records violence in his Parent. That's how it is. That is life! This conclusion is certain if his parents do not express opposition by switching the channel. If they enjoy violent programs the youngster gets a double sanction—the set and the folks—and he assumes permission to be violent provided he collects the required amount of injustices. The little person collects his own reasons to shoot up the place, just as the sheriff does; three nights of cattle rustlers, a stage holdup, and a stranger foolin' with Miss Kitty can be easily matched in the life of the little person. Much of what is experienced at the hands of older siblings or other authority figures also is recorded in the Parent. Any external situation in which the little person feels himself to be dependent to the extent that he is not free to question or to explore produces data which is stored in the Parent. (There is another type of external experience of the very small child which is not recorded in the Parent, and which we shall examine when we describe the Adult.)

THE CHILD

While external events are being recorded as that body of data we call the Parent, there is another recording being made simultaneously. This is the recording of *internal* events, the responses of the little person to what he sees and hears. (Figure 3.) In this connection it is important to recall Penfield's observation that "the subject feels again the emotion which the situation originally produced in him, and he is aware of the same interpretations, true or false, which he himself gave to the experience in the first place. Thus, evoked recollection is not the exact photographic or phonographic reproduction of past scenes or events. It is reproduction of what the patient *saw and heard and felt and understood.*"[2] [Italics added.]

[2] W. Penfield, "Memory Mechanisms," *A.M.A. Archives of Neurology and Psychiatry,* 67 (1952) : 178–198, with discussion by L. S. Kubie et al.

FIGURE 3
The Child

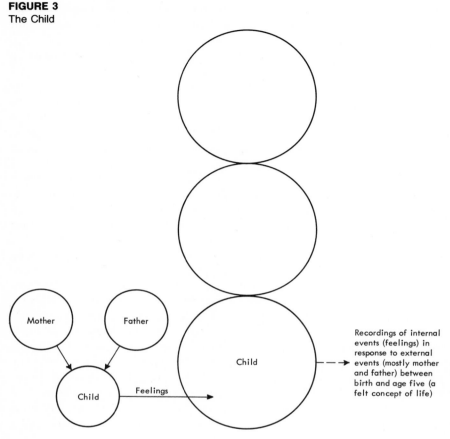

It is this "seeing and hearing and feeling and understanding" body of data which we define as the Child. Since the little person has no vocabulary during the most critical of his early experiences, most of his reactions are *feelings.* We must keep in mind his situation in these early years. He is small, he is dependent, he is inept, he is clumsy, he has no words with which to construct meanings. Emerson said we "must know how to estimate a sour look." The child does not know how to do this. A sour look turned in his direction can only produce feelings that add to his reservoir of negative data about himself. *It's my fault. Again. Always is. Ever will be. World without end.*

During this time of helplessness there are an infinite number of total and uncompromising demands on the child. On the one hand, he has the urges (genetic recordings) to empty his bowels ad lib., to explore, to know, to crush and to bang, to express feelings, and to experience all of the pleasant sensations associated with movement and discovery. On the other hand, there is the constant demand from the environment, essentially the parents, that he give up these basic satisfactions for the reward of parental approval. This approval, which can disappear as fast as it appears, is an unfathomable mystery to the child, who has not yet made any certain connection between cause and effect.

The predominant by-product of the frustrating, civilizing process is negative feelings. On the basis of these feelings the little person early concludes, "I'm not OK." We call this comprehensive self-estimate the NOT OK, or the NOT OK Child. This conclusion and the continual experiencing of the unhappy feelings which led to it and confirm it are recorded permanently in the brain and cannot be erased. This permanent recording is the residue of having been a child. Any child. Even the child of kind, loving, well-meaning parents. It is the *situation of childhood* and *not* the intention of the parents which produces the problem. An example of the dilemma of childhood was a statement made by my seven-year-old daughter, Heidi, who one morning at breakfast said, "Daddy, when I have an OK Daddy and an OK Mama, how come *I'm* not OK?"

When the children of "good" parents carry the NOT OK burden, one can begin to appreciate the load carried by children whose parents are guilty of gross neglect, abuse, and cruelty.

As in the case of the Parent, the Child is a state into which a person may be transferred at almost any time in his current transactions. There are many things that can happen to us today which recreate the situation of childhood and bring on the same feelings we felt then. Frequently we may find ourselves in situations where we are faced with impossible alternatives, where we find ourselves in a corner, either actually, or in the way we see it. These "hook the Child," as we say, and cause a replay of the original feelings of frustration, rejection, or abandonment, and we relive a latter-day version of the small child's primary depression. Therefore, when a person is in the grip of feelings, we say his Child has taken over. When his anger dominates his reason, we say his Child is in command.

There is a bright side, too! In the Child is also a vast store of positive data. In the Child reside creativity, curiosity, the desire to explore and know, the urges to touch and feel and experience, and the recordings of the glorious, pristine feelings of first discoveries. In the Child are recorded the countless, grand *a-ha* experiences, the firsts in the life of the small person, the first drinking from the garden hose, the first stroking of the soft kitten, the first sure hold on mother's nipple, the first time the lights go on in response to his flicking the switch, the first submarine chase of the bar of soap, the repetitious going back to do these glorious things again and again. The feelings of these delights are recorded, too. With all the NOT OK recordings, there is a counterpoint, the rhythmic OK of mother's rocking, the sentient softness of the favorite blanket, a continuing good response to favorable external events (if this is indeed a favored child), which also is available for replay in today's transactions. This is the flip side, the happy child, the carefree, butterfly-chasing little boy, the little girl with chocolate on her face. This comes on in today's transactions, too. However, our observations both of small children and of ourselves as grownups convince us that the NOT OK feelings far outweigh the good. This is why we believe it is a fair estimate to say that everyone has a NOT OK Child.

Frequently I am asked, When do the Parent and Child stop recording? Do the Parent and Child contain only experiences in the first five years of life? I believe that by the time the child leaves the home for his first independent social experience—school—he has been exposed to nearly every possible attitude and admonition of his parents, and thenceforth further parental communications are essentially a reinforcement of what has already been recorded. The fact that he now begins to "use his Parent" on others also has a reinforcing quality in line with the Aristotelian idea that that which is expressed is impressed. As to further recordings in the Child, it is hard to imagine that any emotion exists which has not already been felt in its most intense form by the time the youngster is five years old. This is consistent with most psychoanalytic theory, and, in my own observation, is true.

If, then, we emerge from childhood with a set of experiences which are recorded in an inerasable Parent and Child, what is our hope for change? How can we get off the hook of the past?

THE ADULT

At about ten months of age a remarkable thing begins to happen to the child. Until that time his life has consisted mainly of helpless or unthinking responses to the demands and stimulations by those around him. He has a Parent and a Child. What he has not had is the ability either to choose his responses or to manipulate his surroundings. He has had no self-direction, no ability to move out to meet life. He has simply taken what has come his way.

At ten months, however, he begins to experience the power of locomotion. He can manipulate objects and begins to move out, freeing himself from the prison of immobility. It is true that earlier, as at eight months, the infant may frequently cry and need help in getting out of some awkward position, but he is unable to get out of it by himself. At ten months he concentrates on inspection and exploitation of toys. According to the studies conducted by Gesell and Ilg, the ten-month-old child

. . . enjoys playing with a cup and pretends to drink. He brings objects to his mouth and chews them. He enjoys gross motor activity: sitting and playing after he has been set up, leaning far forward, and re-erecting himself. He secures a toy, kicks, goes from sitting to creeping, pulls himself up, and may lower himself. He is beginning to cruise. Social activities which he enjoys are peek-a-boo and lip play, walking with both hands held, being put prone on the floor, or being placed in a rocking toy. Girls show their first signs of coyness by putting their heads to one side as they smile.[3]

---

[3] Arnold Gesell and Frances L. Ilg, *Infant and Child in the Culture of Today* (New York: Harper, 1943), pp. 116–22.

FIGURE 4
Gradual emergence of the Adult beginning at ten months

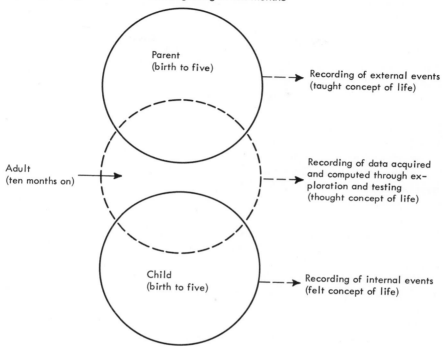

The ten-month-old has found he is able to do something which grows from his own awareness and original thought. This self-actualization is the beginning of the Adult. (Figure 4.) Adult data accumulates as a result of the child's ability to find out for himself what is different about life from the "taught concept" of life in his Parent and the "felt concept" of life in his Child. The Adult develops a "thought concept" of life based on data gathering and data processing.

The motility which gives birth to the Adult becomes reassuring in later life when a person is in distress. He goes for a walk to "clear his mind." Pacing is seen similarly as a relief from anxiety. There is a recording that movement is good, that it has a separating quality, that it helps him see more clearly what his problem is.

The Adult, during these early years, is fragile and tentative. It is easily "knocked out" by commands from the Parent and fear in the Child. Mother says about the crystal goblet, "No, no! Don't touch that!" The child may pull back and cry, but at the first opportunity he will touch it anyway to see what it is all about. In most persons the Adult, despite all the obstacles thrown in its way, survives and continues to function more and more effectively as the maturation process goes on.

The Adult is "principally concerned with transforming stimuli into pieces of information, and processing and filing that information on the basis of previous experience."[4] It is different from the Parent, which is "judgmental in an imitative way and seeks to enforce sets of borrowed standards, and from the Child, which tends to react more abruptly on the basis of prelogical thinking and poorly differentiated or distorted perceptions." Through the Adult the little person can begin to tell the difference between life as it was taught and demonstrated to him (Parent), life as he felt it or wished it or fantasied it (Child), and life as he figures it out by himself (Adult).

The Adult is a data-processing computer, which grinds out decisions after computing the information from three sources: the Parent, the Child, and the data which the Adult has gathered and is gathering (Figure 5). One of the important functions of the Adult is to examine the data in the Parent, to see whether or not it is true and still applicable today, and then to accept it or reject it; and to examine the Child to see whether or not the feelings there are appropriate to the present or are archaic and in response to archaic Parent data. The goal is not to do away with the Parent and Child but to be free to examine these bodies of data. The Adult, in the words of Emerson, "must not be hindered by the name of goodness, but must examine if it be goodness"; or badness, for that matter, as in the early decision, "I'm not OK."

The Adult testing of Parent data may begin at an early age. A secure youngster is one who finds that most Parent data is reliable: "They told me the truth!"

"It really *is* true that cars in the street are dangerous," concludes the little boy who has seen his pet dog hurt by a car in the street. "It really *is* true that things go better when I share my toys with Bobby," thinks the little boy who has been given a prized possession by Bobby. "It really *does* feel better when my pants aren't wet," concludes the little girl who has learned to go to the bathroom by herself. If parental directives are grounded in reality, the child, through his own Adult, will come to realize integrity, or a sense of wholeness. What he tests holds up under testing. The data which he collects in his experimentation and examination begin to constitute some "constants" that he can trust. His findings are supported by what he was taught in the first place.

It is important to emphasize that the verification of Parent data does not erase the NOT OK recordings in the Child, which were produced by the early imposition of this data. Mother believes that the only way to keep three-year-old Johnny out of the street is to spank him. He does not understand the danger. His response is fear, anger, and frustration with no appreciation of the fact that his mother loves him and is protecting his life. The fear, anger, and frustration are recorded. These feelings are not erased by the later understanding that she was right to do what she did, but the understanding of how the original situation of childhood produced so many NOT OK recordings of this type can free us of their continual

---

[4] Berne, *Transactional Analysis in Psychotherapy.*

FIGURE 5
The Adult gets data from three sources

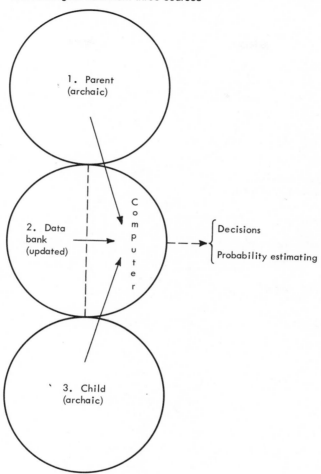

replay in the present. *We cannot erase the recording, but we can choose to turn it off!*

In the same way that the Adult updates Parent data to determine what is valid and what is not, it updates Child data to determine which feelings may be expressed safely. In our society it is considered appropriate for a woman to cry at a wedding, but it is not considered appropriate for that woman to scream at her husband afterward at the reception. Yet both crying and screaming are emotions in the Child. The Adult keeps emotional expression appropriate. The Adult's function in updating the Parent and Child is diagramed in Figure 6. The

FIGURE 6
The updating function of the Adult through reality testing

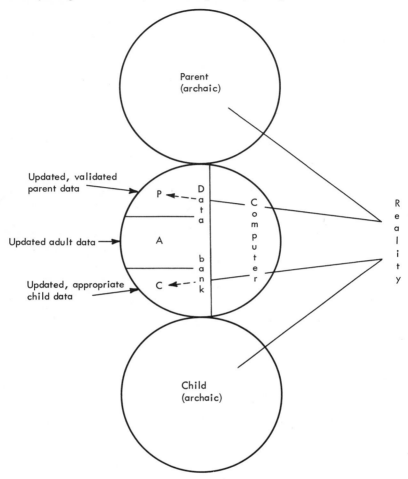

Adult within the Adult in this figure refers to updated reality data. (The evidence once told me space travel was only fantasy; now I know it is reality.)

Another of the Adult's functions is *probability estimating.* This function is slow in developing in the small child and, apparently, for most of us, has a hard time catching up throughout life. The little person is constantly confronted with unpleasant alternatives (either you eat your spinach or you go without ice cream), offering little incentive for examining probabilities. Unexamined probabilities can underlie many of our transactional failures, and unexpected danger signals can cause more Adult "decay," or delay, than expected ones. There are similarities here to the stock ticker in investment concerns, which may run many hours behind on very active trading days. We sometimes refer to this delay as "computer lag," a remedy for which is the old, familiar practice of "counting to ten."

The capacity for probability estimating can be increased by conscious effort. Like a muscle in the body, the Adult grows and increases in efficiency through training and use. If the Adult is alert to the possibility of trouble, through probability estimating, it can also devise solutions to meet the trouble if and when it comes.

Under sufficient stress, however, the Adult can be impaired to the point where emotions take over inappropriately. The boundaries between Parent, Adult, and Child are fragile, sometimes indistinct, and vulnerable to those incoming signals which tend to recreate situations we experienced in the helpless, dependent days of childhood. The Adult sometimes is flooded by signals of the "bad news" variety so overwhelming that the Adult is reduced to an "onlooker" in the transaction. An individual in this situation might say, "I knew what I was doing was wrong, but I couldn't help myself."

Unrealistic, irrational, non-Adult responses are seen in a condition referred to as traumatic neurosis. The danger, or "bad news" signal, hits the Parent and the Child at the same time it hits the Adult. The Child responds in the way it originally did, with a feeling of NOT OK. This may produce all kinds of regressive phenomena. The individual may again feel himself to be a tiny, helpless, dependent child. One of the most primitive of these phenomena is thought blocking. One place this can be seen is in psychiatric hospitals that have a locked-door policy. When the door is locked on a new patient, his retreat is rapid and pronounced. This is why I am opposed to treating patients in a setting where the emphasis is on parental care. Catering to the helpless Child in the individual delays the reconstructive process of restoring the Adult to the executive function.

An ideal hospital would be a comfortable motel with "play area" for the Child, surrounding a clinic building devoted to activities designed for achieving autonomy of the Adult. The nurses would not wear uniforms or serve as parents to the patients. Instead, nurses in street clothing would apply their skills and training to help each individual learn the identity of his Parent, Adult, and Child.

In our treatment groups we use certain colloquial catch phrases such as, "Why don't you stay in your Adult?" when a member finds his feelings are taking over. Another of these is, "What was the original transaction?" This is asked as a means of "turning on the Adult" to analyze the similarity between the present incoming signal producing the present distress and the original transaction, in which the small child experienced distress.

The ongoing work of the Adult consists, then, of checking out old data, validating or invalidating it, and refiling it for future use. If this business goes on smoothly and there is a relative absence of conflict between what has been taught and what is real, the computer is free for important new business, *creativity*. Creativity is born from curiosity in the Child, as is the Adult. The Child provides the "want to" and the Adult provides the "how to." The essential requirement for creativity is computer time. If the computer is cluttered with old business there is little time for new business. Once checked out, many Parent directives become automatic and thus free the computer for creativity. Many of our decisions in day-to-day transactions are automatic. For instance, when we see an arrow pointing down a one-way street, we automatically refrain from going the opposite way. We do not involve our computer in lengthy data processing about highway engineering, the traffic death toll, or how signs are painted. Were we to start from scratch in every decision or operate entirely without the data that was supplied by our parents, our computer would rarely have time for the creative process.

Some people contend that the undisciplined child, unhampered by limits, is more creative than the child whose parents set limits. I do not believe this is true. A youngster has more time to be creative—to explore, invent, take apart, and put together—if he is not wasting time in futile decision making for which he has inadequate data. A little boy has more time to build a snowman if he is not allowed to engage Mother in a long hassle about whether or not to wear overshoes. If a child is allowed to be creative by painting the front room walls with shoe polish, he is unprepared for the painful consequences when he does so at the neighbor's house. Painful outcomes do not produce ok feelings. There are other consequences that take time, such as mending in the hospital after a trial-and-error encounter with a car in the street. There is just so much computer time. Conflict uses a great deal. An extremely time-consuming conflict is produced when what parents say is true does not seem to be true to the Adult. The most creative individual is the one who discovers that a large part of the content of the Parent squares with reality. He can then file away this validated information in the Adult, trust it, forget about it, and get on with other things—like how to make a kite fly, how to build a sand castle, or how to do differential calculus.

However, many youngsters are preoccupied much of the time with the conflict between Parent data and what they see as reality. Their most troubling problem is that they do not understand why the Parent has such a hold on them. When Truth comes to knock at the Parent's door, the Parent says, "Come, let us reason together." The little child whose father is in jail and whose mother steals to support him may have a loud recording in his Parent, "You never trust a cop!" So he meets a friendly one. His Adult computes all the data about this nice guy, how he gets the ball game started in the sand lot, how he treats the gang to popcorn, how he is friendly, and how he speaks in a quiet voice. For this youngster there is conflict. What he sees as reality different from what he has been taught. The Parent tells him one thing and the Adult another. During the period of his actual dependency upon his parents for security, however tenuous this security may be, it is likely he will accept the parents' verdict that cops are bad. This is how prejudice is transmitted. *For a little child, it may be safer to believe a lie than to believe his own eyes and ears.* The Parent so threatens the Child (in a continuing internal dialogue) that the Adult gives up and stops trying to inquire into areas of conflict. Therefore, "cops are bad" comes through as truth. This is called *contamination* of the Adult.

The development of identity: Power and sex roles in academia[*]

Michael Silverstein[1]

In the time since this article was written I have become increasingly aware of the sexism implicit in it. The major part of this sexism rests in the unspoken but underlying assumption that it is addressed to all readers, when in fact it deals exclusively with male experience. Thus for female readers it perpetuates the definition of social reality as an essentially masculine pattern of relationships. I wrote of my experience as a man, relating almost exclusively to men, within the context of male-dominated institutions. The "persons" I speak of in the article are almost invariably male. Therefore it is essential that I make it clear that I do not pretend to speak to the experience of women.

I.   The usefulness of a history is to show the operation of process. In this case, the process is the development of an identity. By using my experiences as an example. I hope to show the experiential reality of the one-dimensionality of this society in determining an individual's identity. This is done through the key institution of sex roles. What I must grow up to be, what it must mean to me to be a male human being, was presented to me as inevitable and unquestionable. Masculinity was defined for me by the social world I was part of as a set of personal characteristics that must become a part of my identity. I, like all male children, was taught that my value as a person depended on my power over others. I was taught that I must compete for personal power, and that to be successful I must conceal feelings of weakness, tenderness, and dependence, and present myself to other men as self-sufficient and insensitive.

In spite of the all-pervasiveness of this lesson, I finally found myself in full rebellion against "manhood." The source of this rebellion was something that seemed entirely external to the reality of the world I was taught about—the fact of my Gayness. To those of us who identify with the Gay Liberation movement,

---

[*] Reprinted from the *Journal of Applied Behavioral Science*, vol. 8, no. 5, 1972. Abridged and used by permission of the publisher and author.

[1] The author is a member of The Gay Men's Collective of the Berkeley Community Clinic.

Gayness has come to mean far more than the original fact of our homosexuality. The description of how I came to reject the definition of myself as a Man is also a description of how I came to understand the concept of Gayness, by coming to an understanding of the political reality of the psychological characteristics of "manliness."

Our lives are lived in the context of social institutions. In my case, these processes worked themselves out in the context of academia. This was not accidental. I found myself in academia because it had been presented to me as a less masculine milieu than most social institutions. Yet it turned out that success in this sphere is as much dependent on those personality traits defined as male as it is in any other part of the society. Thus in describing my academic career, I believe I can show how the social needs men are taught to act upon are essential to the functioning of even the less masculine-appearing social institutions.

Ultimately, this assertion leads to the generalization that the masculine personality, man's learned drive for interpersonal dominance, is the psychic engine required for capitalist society to function. Those with real power, ruling-class white males, in order to perpetuate the existing social structure and thus ensure their continued control, use their control of the educational, communication, entertainment, and religious institutions to create men who seek a positive self-image in their power over others. Thus they have at their disposal middle-class men motivated to operate the organizational machinery of capitalism by a desire to achieve power, and working-class men who can be reconciled to their real powerlessness by personal power over their women and the possibility of successful competition for personal power with rivals of their own class. In addition, white working-class men are given at least a vicarious power over third world peoples. Similarly, those in power also require women to learn to evaluate their self-worth by their success in emotionally and materially supporting a man in his struggle for power, rather than acting as competitors themselves. The present paper illustrates how the masculine drive for power is the essential motivating force in the functioning of academic institutions.

But these abstractions can only define the argument, they can never advance it. My experiences aren't abstractions to me, my life depends on them. "Manhood" now appears to me not as a sociological concept, but as a Procrustean bed the society would force me into; my struggle against it is a struggle to keep from being mutilated out of all human shape. My academic career was a life-and-death struggle I just barely survived. It is the reality of this struggle I want to communicate. It was well under way by the time I was ten years old.

II.   By the time I was ten, the central fact of my life was the demand that I become a man. By then the most important relationships by which I was taught to define myself were those I had with other boys. I already knew that I must see every encounter with another boy as a contest in which I must win or at least hold my own. School was the major arena of this contest, especially the playground and physical education. The same lesson continued everywhere, after school, even in Sunday school. My parents, relatives, teachers, the books I read, movies I saw, all taught me that my self-worth depended on my manliness, my willingness to stand up to the other boys. This usually didn't mean a physical fight, though the willingness to stand up and "fight like a man" always remained a final test. But the relationship between us usually had the character of an armed truce. Girls weren't part of this social world at all yet, just because they weren't part of this contest. They didn't have to be bluffed, no credit was gained by cowing them, so they were more or less ignored. Sometimes when there were no grown-ups around we would let each other know we liked each other, but most of the time we did as we were taught.

So I knew what I had to do to be a man. One could only succeed at establishing his manliness or be a failure, a sissy, someone who couldn't stand up and fight. One didn't choose to be a sissy, a loser—one lost. Since manliness was, of course, what everyone would want, the unmanly must be those who were too weak to make it as a man.

By the time I was in junior high, I defined myself and was defined by the other boys as a loser, as the class sissy. Largely this meant that I saw myself as a failed man. Yet (I now realize) the beginning of my Gayness was the beginning of my attempt to choose to be what I was. I began to redefine myself positively, to redefine what it meant *not* to be a successful Man. In so doing, I was moving outside of the social reality I had been born to.

My first attempt at self-affirmation was to insist to myself that I didn't really want to be a Man anyway. Much of this was sour grapes, of course, and I knew it. But there really was a part of me that, in opposition to everything I had been taught, really didn't want to be a man. I didn't know anything about homosexuality then, I didn't even know about sex. But from the time I was five years old, I had wanted to touch and hold the bodies of other boys, and when I had done so I had felt warm and comfortable, and affectionate toward them. By the time I was eight or nine I had learned how bad and dirty, how unmanly, this was, and I was so scared of being caught at it that I stopped. But the desire remained, a gigantic thing always there. It was totally outside the reality of what it was to be a man. Yet it was so real, so undeniably a part of me, that it forced me to see myself as outside the world of all the other boys I knew. It was not just that I couldn't be a man, it was also that I knew about this part of me that could never be satisfied by manhood, because it wanted something that no man would ever want. For the reward of success as a man is power over other men—and I understood that this need I had could never be satisfied by power. I wasn't exactly sure what I wanted, what I actually wanted to do with another boy. But I knew that whatever it was, it required that we both want it, that it was only itself if given freely. All sorts of fantasies were going on in my head, completely dominating my consciousness. They were all rather vague, but they all involved relating to other boys in very unmanly ways, ways that had nothing to do with power.

So although I tried to be Man, I could never entirely put my heart into the contest when the reward for success seemed incompatible with what I really wanted. This may seem rather abstract for a 13-year old, but I believe I understood the reality of the world far better at thirteen than I did for a long time thereafter. It was at this time that I set out to find an alternative to manhood, something else that I could grow up to be. (Ultimately, this would lead to the goal of Gayness, the rejection of the whole dimension of masculinity-feminity as a scale on which people find their proper status, and the attempt to create a new concept of peoplehood. But that came later.)

I didn't feel ready yet to take on the world in junior high, so I started looking around in the world as it had been presented to me to find a place for myself. One choice I could have made was to decide that since I wouldn't be a man I would be like a woman instead. Many young Gay males make that choice. I thought I saw another alternative, something else I could be, which was a recognized part of the world I knew, yet wasn't a man. In fact, this alternative turned out to be a twenty-year-long detour into a blind alley, the blind alley of an academic career. But at the time I thought I saw an escape route: I would grow up to be a Brain.

Brains were a little weird group of people I had heard about for a long time, in comic books, on television shows, and from my family. I remembered "the Absent-Minded Professors" in the comic books. They wore caps and gowns and were barefoot. While other men were the heroes of the story—did the fighting—they did all sorts of funny unreal things, like asking how the world worked, which didn't really matter because such interests didn't lead to any power. Looking around for something I could be other than a man, I seized on them as the most unmanly males visible. So I set out to be a Brain.

In the next few years, I learned more about what being a Brain means. About this time dating started replacing sports as the most important medium of competition among men. Instead of fighting with our own bodies, we were now supposed to fight over the bodies of women. It was the guys who were already established as toughest and strongest who won the most girls, of course, and since I had already decided I wasn't going to be like them, I wouldn't fight here either. It never occurred to me that this had anything at all to do with the physical need I felt. (There isn't any word available to let me describe what seems to me to be such a simple and basic feeling: to mutually and physically show affection with another person. It's simpler, less dramatic, than "making love", nothing climactic or special, just comfortable, mundane, one of the best parts of the day-to-day living of a life.) Anyhow, it never occurred to me that this need had anything to do with the way big guys used girls. What I wanted was something you did with your friends, and the real winners, the real men, made it clear they didn't even regard women as people. But being a Brain got me out of this too, because by now I had learned something more about Brains. They are sexless. In fact, they are all but bodiless. As a Brain I had an excuse for not chasing girls. (By now I needed an excuse very badly: I was terrified they'd think I was a queer.) I didn't chase girls because I never did anything with my body at all. So rather,

I started pretending my body wasn't there. I was fat, dirty, and sloppy, and wore "out-of-it" clothes.

By high school I was firmly established as The Brain, good in the classroom, lousy on the sports field, and sexless. And I was perfecting my role on a more sophisticated level: I was an Intellectual. This meant making plans for what I wanted to do when I grew up. My family taught me that the least manly of all Brains are college professors. Their reasons were quite convincing. To my family, an adult shows his manliness by his success in supporting his wife and children. Professors go to college as long as doctors and lawyers, but they don't support their families nearly as well, and knowing this they waste all that time in school anyway. No real man would act like that, my family said. That decided me. Brains don't fight like men; they don't fuck like men; they don't even work like men. If I wanted to grow up into something other than a man, the best way I could do it was by being a Brain, a college professor.

Entering college, my act was pretty well down. My self-image and sense of self-worth were based on my conception of myself as an intellectual, an ascetic, and an aesthete. Art, literature, "things of the mind," these were both my major source of pleasure and the basis of a sense of myself as superior—more sensitive, more moral—to real men. Of course, the pleasure was largely a consolation for loneliness, and the self-worth contained much self-hate as well, especially of my body. But I saw no alternative. I never planned to have any sex or let anyone know I wanted to. The only physical pleasure I allowed myself was food. People seemed to buy the act, and I found I could relate to them in a friendly enough way as long as we kept our distance. I continued as always, great in the class room, lousy on the playing field. But now something strange started to happen. The playing field started to fade out and what replaced it was so unexpected that it took me years to understand what was happening.

Intellectual abilities and attainments had always been presented to me as essentially unmasculine, something a real man wouldn't take seriously, because they weren't practical (that is, they didn't lead to power). They were an escape from masculinity into asceticism, the source of the only positive self-image I could imagine. I had hoped that by graduate school, with the Big Men On Campus off to the professional and graduate business schools, I might find myself among other people like myself, and that as unmanly intellectuals, we might find some new way to relate to each other.

Instead, now that all the Big Men were gone, it seemed that all the other Brains wanted to play at being Men. Only now they'd play their way. But their way was my way. My sanctuary from male competitiveness had become another one of its arenas. And the weapons being used, words, were something I was accomplished in the use of. For the first time in my life I could be a Big Man, a winner. Moreover, I started doing this without even knowing it. I just went on as I always had. Suddenly, I started finding myself being proclaimed a winner in a contest I never knew I had entered.

My perception of myself had changed, but I wasn't aware of having deliberately changed myself. Rather, it seemed as if the world had changed around me, so that by remaining as I had always been, I now found myself in a very new position relative to the social milieu.

The graduate Sociology Department at UCLA was as masculine as any locker room. The female graduate students were self-effacing, weren't taken seriously in the competition, and didn't seem to take themselves seriously. (Of the three exceptions I can remember, two are now radical feminists, and the third killed herself.) But I didn't recognize the games being played, because the main way I had recognized them in the past was from the perspective of a loser. Suddenly finding myself in the middle of the game as a winner, I didn't know where I was for quite a while. But I knew that I was one of the bright young men of the department. I was awarded a Special Research Training Fellowship of the National Institute of General Medical Sciences. I talked more than anybody else in all the seminars and could keep the other men from getting in a word edgewise. And I found myself enjoying the hell out of doing it.

For the first time in my life I had some taste of power over others. While I still appeared to my teachers as rather naive and erratic, nonetheless, I was finally treated like a Man. Even my family decided that college professors did pretty well after all. For the first (and last) time in my life, my family regarded me as a success. I just about forgot about being the sissy of my junior high, and I started believing that I was just a late bloomer, that now I was coming into my manhood at last.

Except that I knew that none of it was real. I knew I was just pretending to be a Man, because by this time I had come to know what it meant that I was a homosexual, that the most I would ever be capable of was a facade of manliness. I realized that to go beyond the facade would be more than I would ever be willing or able to do.

Even in academic circles, being a successful man means more than just success as an academician. The successful man doesn't just succeed in his career; he uses that success to win all the rewards common to a successful man. This requires that he achieve recognition as a prominent member of his community. And part of this is being a householder, the head of a family. Even an academician has to get himself at least one woman and a child or two. I was still an outsider to this world. I felt neither the desire nor the ability to become the head of a household. Thus although I had access to masculine power for the first time, I still didn't want what this power must be used to purchase if it is to be actualized in this society. And I was sure that as soon as this became apparent, people would realize that I wasn't a Man after all.

Thus the power I started to attain in the academic world never meant the same thing to me as it would have to a heterosexual man. I believe this power was typical of that wielded by "successful" homosexuals, in that I experienced it as essentially defensive. It was not a weapon to win for myself the masculine prize I still didn't want, but a shield to hide my failure from public view. No matter now powerful I might appear to others, the most I could ever hope from this power was security, safety—never gratification. If this is true of apparently powerful homosexual men, then no matter how much they appear a part of and committed to the society, their attachment is based on fear and defensiveness; their only hope of gratification lies in abandoning their power and abandoning their commitment to the society in which it is the greatest possible gratification.

(None of this is to deny the objective reality of the power actually wielded by middle-class, white, male, educated homosexuals, such as myself. From the perspective of the students I would teach, of third world people, of women, I had the power to act as their oppressor. I would have this power by virtue of my academic position, my credentials, and the "expert" skills I had been taught. All of these are rooted in class and male privilege. I am only saying that the benefits I got from such power were not meaningful to me.

But this does not mean my exercise of power would be any less real or oppressive to my subordinates, and implies no obligation on their part to accept the legitimacy of my power. The tendency of powerful men to ask oppressed peoples to feel sympathy for their feelings of inauthenticity and powerlessness seems essentially hypocritical to me. What I expect from those I have power over is nothing but the demand that I relinquish such power. Similarly when more powerful men tell me that their power is of no benefit to them, my only response is to point out that this should make them more willing to relinquish it.

This brings me back to my point. I believe that homosexual men such as myself can give up class and sex privileges more easily than straight men, because the benefits we gain from them are not as real. Only then can we assert any solidarity with other oppressed peoples).

At this time in my life, I wasn't willing to give up my privileges, because I saw no alternative way I could live. So I set out to be a success after all. Academia might just be another masculine cage, but at least it was one where I found myself on one of the higher perches. Just to be confident I could pass for a man, especially with my family, was something to be grateful for. I had even picked out a specialty: I hoped to make it as the Big Man in alienation theory.

But now, just when I was ready to play at being a man and strive for success, the game changed again. As I reached the end of graduate school and started looking for a job, the most important arena of competition moved from the polemics of the classroom to the use of entrepreneurial and managerial skills within the bureaucracies of academic departments. Success was now determined by the sale of your products and future products: writings and research projects. These were to be sold to academic departments, publishers, and agencies that funded research grants. While the polemical skills that let me argue successfully for the correctness of my analysis of things were relevant to this kind of competition, other skills were more important, such as the ability to write long, formal, highly-structured, and bureaucratically sound research proposals. I first ran into this new set of required skills in applying for fellowships. Then came applying for a job. I was already getting scared by the prospect that a successful career would require a concentration on these things. I could do them if I had to, but they didn't bring even the spurious gratification of power in the classroom. They didn't seem to be any fun—only drudgery, alienated labor. They were the means to a successful career, but the end never seemed worth it.

Again the world seemed to have changed around me. Without any self-conscious change on my part, the gratification I could draw from my environment began to lessen. By this time I had gone to my first sociology convention, and any hope I had left that I might find some other non-men around was smashed by the sight of all the bustling young executive-types, drinks in hand, button-holing each other to sound out prospects. Seeing this, I realized why my family had decided that it would be all right for me to be a college professor.

Nevertheless, I got a job at C.C.N.Y. Arriving in New York in the fall of 1967, I had a whole new personality ready for presentation, down to a bushy beard. By now I knew that as long as I kept things on an abstract and intellectual level—and we Men kept them there—I could be articulate to the point of glibness, and self-confident to the point of smugness. I was distantly friendly and impersonally cheerful to everyone. I was pretty sure I could pass as a man now.

But I still knew that passing wouldn't help. And thus the dirty, ugly, angry city of New York pounded into me every day I spent in it—I was too lonely to give a damn about making it, too lonely to take anything as meaningless as a successful academic career seriously. I'm still grateful to New York for this. When I got there and felt what it was like, I needed people so badly I wanted to die most of the time. This forced me to get down to the real business of living and start finding out how to get in touch with other people, and with myself.

So, once in New York, my most urgent need was other people. Looking around me, I saw two groups of them: my colleagues and the students. Since my colleagues were the group from which I was supposed to draw my friends, I turned to them first. What I found should not have been surprising: they were not as different from me as I had thought. But somehow the differences were such that they made the similarities between us barriers.

A lot of my colleagues looked as if they had been pretty lousy at sports as kids, and had had a hard time hustling up a date. And I wasn't the only one who had read about the "Absent-Minded Professor." Plenty of them had ended up in the academy for reasons similar to mine, but they were still very different from me, most importantly because as adults they had finally found that they could make it as Men, if they worked at it, and they certainly were working at it. The rewards of manliness were real goals for them.

But a more obvious difference was also more paradoxical. Many of them seemed less "Manly" than I. They hadn't done nearly as well as I had in the word games of graduate seminars. They had finally found their arena of successful competition, the one I hadn't yet mastered. They were the entrepreneurs, the letter writers, the applicants for grants, the hard-working time-servers on committees. Their scholarly writing was based on the ability to do the endless, tedious drudgery of devising complicated and highly structured formulae, which they could then follow precisely in defining, collecting, analyzing, and interpeting data; all this is the central activity of American sociology. The same skills served for structuring a text, a series of classroom lectures, or the agenda of a committee meeting. And, as they and I both knew, these are the skills that lead to as much success and masculine power as are available to the academician. But even though the interpersonal skills of polemic discussion are objectively less valuable, they are still seen as an immediate expression of manly power. On a personal level, such academicians are still intimidated by men who talk better than they can. Most of my colleagues were personally withdrawn and somewhat shy. They were virtually all married, and generally related closely only to their wives.

In spite of these personal characteristics, they were very much Men in their fascination with power. They were awed by those with more power than they had, and were extremely jealous of their own power, though it was often trivial or fictitious. This became obvious as I got involved in faculty politics. The chairmen of about half the departments (the liberals) and some "junior faculty" were meeting every week to work out an elaborate scheme to emasculate the President by appointing one of their own as Provost under him. The plot failed amidst infighting and bumbling. Later in the Faculty Senate (where I was a junior senator) incredibly elaborate debates were held between the same liberal faction and the administration supporters over the exact working of complicated resolutions recommending how the college should deal with its adversaries, the students. All the resolutions were as meaningless as the earlier plot had been. The whole phantom of faculty power was like the court intrigue of a central European government in exile: It meant nothing at all. All the real power had always rested with a Board of Higher Education appointed by city politicians. The college administration was answerable above, not below, and the only access to real power the faculty had was by promotion from above into the administration, in return for services rendered. The professors were powerless after all. The real men with real power just didn't have to take them seriously.

There weren't many women on the faculty, and, aside from a few exceptional women, they were mainly junior partners to husbands who were higher ranking academics or other professionals. The only independent, professionally minded unmarried woman in our department was widely rumored to be a "bull-dyke." Whether the rumor was true or not is irrelevant; it effectively served to isolate her. I was certainly afraid to associate with anyone so characterized.

Not all the professors fitted into this pattern, of course. Some of them, especially the younger, "hipper," radical professors were also quite good at talking, and like me had established their manliness in the polemics of the intellectual arena. I could enjoy talking to them: we shared a similar political perspective, and felt closer to, and less intimidated, by students than other faculty did. The friends I made among the faculty came from this group.

But here too there were real barriers. Both categories of faculty defined themselves as Men. The academy could offer them more of a real reward than it could ever offer to me. For them, a "successful academic career" would enable them to buy all the accessories of what passes for a successful life—a wife, children, a place as an influential member of the community. I never entirely trusted the men who could be a part of the system if they chose to.

In some ways I found the young, hip, radical faculty even less trustworthy than their more conventional senior colleagues. They were the Big Men on Campus now, if not in terms of real power, at least in terms of interpersonal relationships. And they knew it and showed it, from being the ones most likely to be playing around with "the girls," to making no secret of their opinion of the administration and its faculty allies as a bunch of "cocksuckers." In fact in personal encounter these young studs weren't at all above bullying the old "queers," whether on an intellectual level—making them feel like inarticulate ignoramuses, or just by overwhelming them with the masculinity of their come-ons. Knowing that I was accepted by the radicals as more or less one of the Men out to get the bunch of "faggots" running the place wasn't particularly reassuring.

But I understood that after all they believed Men are entitled to power over non-men (women) and failed men (faggots). They called themselves radicals and socialists, and called for an end of the oppression of the third world and of the white poor. But in their own lives, in their behavior toward women and other men, they showed that they still believed in the right of the strong to rule the weak. They still used their power to control people, and they still judged themselves and others by the criterion of relative power. They wanted to redistribute power, but were committed to it as the measurement of personal worth.

In some ways I learned from them. I learned that there was some power I did want, the power to rule my own life. I decided that I must have the power to free myself from those with power over me. So I stopped thinking of myself as an anarchist pacifist, and started thinking of myself as a radical Marxist. I will not trust as an ally any man who rests his sense of self-worth on the extent of his personal power. I trusted the hip, radical faculty men then, no more than I trust the big men of the movement now.

What about other Gay teachers? They were in hiding, of course. Only as I was leaving did I find out who some of them were. Generally, they were the most invisible, innocuous people on the faculty. They had been around long enough to learn that the first law of survival for a Gay person is never to call attention to oneself. It is not for me—and certainly not for straight people—to judge their behavior. They were doing what they had been taught they had to do to survive.

My colleagues could not meet my needs for friendship. So I turned to the students. My first encounter with them had been the first morning of the semester. At 8 A.M. I found the first of three groups of 80 people staring at me. As a promising graduate student, I had been continually groomed to do research, and to define myself as a researcher. Teaching was a minor chore I'd pick up on the side. Consequently, I had never been in front of a class before in my life, and I was very scared. I stammered through the first day, but made it somehow. By the end of the week it was much easier, though there were occasional flashes of panic. By the second week I was starting to get into it, and by the end of a month, I was home. The endless, effortless flow of words that had made me the terror of the graduate seminar would still turn the trick. In a class of thirty graduate students, I had kept the other men from getting a word in edgewise; with undergraduates, inexperienced and already accepting my right to speak as much as I wanted, it was all my show. This was just opposite to the pattern of most of my colleagues. Since they tended to shy away from verbal encounter and argument, from masculine competition on that level, they were generally intimidated by any direct contest with students. Their ability to compete was exerted at a distance, by paper proxies; their victories were in endurance contests in the production of paperwork evaluated by weight. They were particularly afraid of young people, who represented an enigmatic and possibly hostile force to them. They knew young people so little that they feared they were on the edge of revolution.

I didn't need to use my formal authority to have power over my students. First of all, I didn't find them particularly intimidating. As a vicarious hippie and a vicarious radical for years, I understood the youth culture as only an envious outsider could. (Neither hippies nor radicals have much use for queers.) Most importantly, I didn't see students as an outside threat to an establishment of which I was a part—I saw myself as far more outside it than they were.

In fact, my real power over students lay just in my ability to give up formal authority. By abdicating my sole right to define the situation I seduced the students into speaking up, presenting their own ideas, disagreeing with me. Then I'd smash them. I put on quite a show. But I was intimidated by students, too (male students at least—I was just starting to see women as people); I was intimidated by them as men, usually men who were bigger, stronger, better-looking than I was. But in class they were on my home ground. I was more than eager to give up all external power, professional authority, and fight on a man-to-man basis. I was finally getting back at the kind of man who had always beat the shit out of me. This was far better than just making them study hard for tests.

And on top of all this I was loved. For I could afford to be generous. I didn't actually humiliate students. I just wanted a general acknowledgement that I was smarter than they were. The atmosphere was one of easy informality, with an undertone of benevolent paternalism, typical of the classroom of the "radical" teacher. Since this is about the freest atmosphere any student is likely to find in a classroom, I was appreciated. Within a few months I had a reputation as one of the grooviest of the hip, young, radical teachers. By the second year, I could depend on all the Big Radical Men of the school being in my classes, considering me an ally, or even something of a guru.

Soon, most of my close friends were students, former students, and other people I met through them. They were generally younger than I was, poorer than I was, and didn't have their lines down nearly as well as I did. I was guru, father-figure, and host. My apartment was a meeting place for young, hip radicals. Usually a few of them were crashing there. In my office or the cafeteria, I usually had an entourage of half a dozen students or so.

(Some of this was real. Sometimes I did manage to establish real human contact. There are people—students and colleagues—whom I love, and who love me, whom I met while I was teaching.)

But with so much game playing, so many power trips, I came close to being a Man after all. Finally, though, with all the gratification, victory, power, and recognition, it still wasn't real; I still couldn't believe in it. For what I got from people still depended on the power I had over them—that was all society would ever offer to me as a professional success, and it wasn't enough. I could make it as a teacher, guru, advisor, but I never believed I was any of these things; they were never real enough to satisfy me. Outside of these roles, my friends who were straight men would never give me what I really wanted from them. Sex was part of it, of course. In fact, at the time I believe I experienced it as the major part, since I lived in a seemingly eternal state of sexual tension and frustration. The whole atmosphere of the milieu I'd built up for myself reeked of sublimated sexuality. But looking back on it (from the perspective of having had a lot of sex, and finding out that didn't help much either), the real reason I couldn't settle for the kind of life and relationships I had was less direct. My friends were the most important people in the world to me. My relationships with them were the most important part of my life. But for them, no matter how much they liked me, no matter how much they looked up to me, even, their relationships with me were of secondary importance. Their most important relationships were with women—wives or girlfriends. Our time together was when they didn't have dates, or when their wives had something else to do. Or I was a guest of the family, or was dragged along on a date.

This wasn't due to any personal failure either on my part or theirs. They were part of a society in which a man's real intimacy and commitment can be expressed only toward a woman. That is, he can reveal himself and make himself emotionally dependent only on someone who is not a potential rival, but who, on the contrary, has been trained to be emotionally supportive of men rather than competitive with them, and to expect a position of dependency. Before another man, a rival, a display of emotional commitment is an indication of weakness. Masculine solidarity, male bonding, is a real phenomenon in this society among straight men. But it is a coalition of equals against inferiors for the maintenance of power. The personal relationships within such coalitions are a grown-up version of the armed truce that has existed among men since boyhood. Such relationships are satisfying to straight men who are interested in maintaining power and can turn to subservient women for emotional support, but they were not satisfying to me at all. And these were the only kinds of relationships with other men that my straight male friends were really comfortable with. I needed close emotional relationships with other men; my straight friends did not. Such relationships are threatening to the masculine facade of self-sufficiency; this threat is behind much of the straight man's revulsion with Gayness. Even the best-intentioned, most liberal straight male friend is not going to place the same value on a friendship with a Gay man that the Gay man places on it.

So as I got over being grateful for what I had, I started to panic at the thought that this was the best I could ever expect if I continued to live my life in the only way that seemed open to me. The best I could look forward to within the straight world was to be a friend of the family, to depend for my emotional needs on people to whom I was a pleasant, but superfluous, relationship.

My life didn't change at this time, but the level of desperation I felt began to build up. Later, when the possibility of change did appear to me, this desperation would be the motivating force that would push me ahead.

But even with all my desperation, I still couldn't see any space for change, any place to go. Until then, everything I had been taught about Gay men had made it totally unthinkable for me to accept myself openly as one of them. Ever since their existence had been admitted to me, I had been taught increasingly sophisticated reasons why they were not to be taken seriously as people. For years the only knowledge I had of the category of people in which I was included came through dirty jokes. Later I learned that Gay people were to be pitied as cases of arrested development. The message that came across was that they were pitiful, crippled, tormented creatures, always good for a laugh. But in any case, Gay people could not be taken seriously. Since it was tremendously important for me that I take myself seriously, I was completely unwilling to see myself as part of a group depicted as vain, frivolous, child-like, foolish—or as a tormented, mutilated metaphor for human loneliness.

My fear of this image was so great that it prevented me from having any real contact with Gay people, which might have shattered the image. The only way I saw open to me to avoid self-hate was telling myself I must be different from the rest of those fairies. Thus the image of the homosexual presented in this society not only teaches all men to be afraid of, to hide their own Gayness, it teaches those of us who cannot hide our Gayness from ourselves to avoid and be contemptuous of other Gay people. Even when our sexual needs bring us together, there is often a mutual distrust and contempt based on our early internalization of the society's stereotypes, and this works against any real solidarity among us. Then the isolation of Gay people from each other can be pointed to by the society that creates it as evidence of the neurotic inability of homosexuals to relate to one another.

This describes my life up to my twenty-eighth year. But I was desperate enough now so that very little was necessary to break me out of the pattern I was in. Gay Liberation did it. The Gay Liberation movement is a very complicated thing; it requires extensive analysis. But for me, in 1969, there was nothing complicated about it at all. I went to the November Peace March in Washington, and I saw five Gay men with a Gay Liberation banner. I don't think I can ever communicate how important a thing that was for me. Nothing would ever be the same again. I saw five people with a Gay Liberation banner. People.

They didn't look ridiculous, silly, or grotesque. They were talking to each other like friends; they didn't seem tormented, lonely, miserable. They were people, like me, at a peace march, and proud of being Gay. They looked like people I could talk to, about serious things, about my life.

As before, the change seemed not so much in myself as in the world around me. This time a new part of the world seemed to open up to me, a new space, the space to be Gay without conforming to the stereotypes that I had rejected. The motivation to move into such a space was provided by the desperation that had been inside me for a long time.

Nothing happened right away. But all sorts of things were going on in me. For a while I was extremely depressed. Some time around the middle of December I reached the decision that I wanted to be Gay. In the middle of January, I went to my first meeting of the Gay Liberation Front. I started becoming a different person, and the world started appearing to me as a different kind of place. Before, my homosexuality had made me an outsider, alienated from society. But the social reality I had been taught still gave me the terms in which I defined myself. I had seen myself from the perspective of the dominant society as a tiny isolated satellite revolving around an immense social universe. Now I had contacted other people out there, and suddenly it appeared that what I had been taught about such people wasn't true. There were people like me, and I didn't have to be isolated. I didn't understand at first why I had been lied to. But now that I could talk to others like myself, it gradually dawned on us that the lie was essential for the ruling class to keep America running. Men have to believe that anyone who chooses not to be a Man is a failure or a fool, if they are to be driven to function by a need to prove their masculine power. As we understood this, all the self-hate of our isolation started to turn outward in a growing torrent of rage. I had never really hated anything before—except part of myself. Now I began to hate this society, and I began wanting to destroy all of it.

Meanwhile, my academic career was quietly dying of neglect. My emotional life was the focus of all my energies. Teaching was very much a part of it; the rest of the package wasn't. I applied for no grants, set up no research projects, and served on no committees in more than a perfunctory way. The only thing that still meant anything to me aside from teaching was writing. But as my conception of sociology became more subjective and problem-oriented, it became harder and harder to write about something that didn't touch on my personal experience as an extremely alienated closet Gay, and I wasn't ready for that yet.

More and more, I felt detached from the motivational system that was supposed to keep me functioning in the academic context. An academic career had never seemed to me to be more than a "faute de mieux" excuse for a life. With the possibilities that Gay Liberation offered, I didn't feel any need for settling for academic life any more.

Now I was up for tenure, and the alternative to tenure was dismissal. The sociology department faculty committee, much to my surprise, recommended me for tenure. Perhaps it was because they wanted one "experimental teacher" around, who had rapport with students. Also I believe they liked me, since I was the least manly of the radical teachers. I didn't try to bully them personally, and I wasn't trying to take over power in the department. I was seen as radical, but not as personally threatening. They, like the radicals, perhaps sensed they didn't have to take me seriously as a Man. However, the real Big Man of the department voted against me, higher authority supported him, and I was fired. The reasons, as tradition dictates, were kept as obscure as possible, but one official suggested to the student newspaper that my behavior was "unprofessional." Quite a number of radical faculty were fired that year, eight in the sociology department alone. I got to be one of the Sociology 8, and a building was taken in our honor and held for several hours. In any case, I was out.

IV.   My academic career was now drawing to a close. I had finally stopped being a Brain and had become a Gay person working at being a teacher. I was out of the closet and working actively in the The Gay Liberation Front. The whole academic world was becoming increasingly peripheral to my social reality, as I struggled to redefine myself within a new Gay community we were and are struggling to create.

But being a "good teacher" still seemed meaningful, and was still an important source of gratification for me. And I still felt too isolated, too cut off from the support of a community, to live without a job. So I looked around for another place to teach. Several senior colleagues who liked me helped me. I wanted to stay in New York, to continue working with the Gay Liberation Front, but I could not work it out.

So in the fall of 1970, I found myself starting the second and last job of my academic career, at California State College, Hayward. It was essentially an epilogue. Teaching there was never the central part of my life that teaching at C.C.N.Y. had been. My life was in adjacent Berkeley, and in the Gay community there. A whole new set of struggles had begun for me, including my first real attempts to define and explore my sexuality. But that is another story, outside my academic career.

In any case my experience at Hayward was brief, a smaller-scale replay of events at C.C.N.Y. I found it more than ever impossible to associate with my colleagues without getting quite depressed. There was an almost metaphysical air to the unreality with which they viewed the world. They were equally out of touch with the social and historical events proceeding around them, and with their own emotions, desires, and weaknesses as human beings. To be in the same space with them was to be sealed in a crystalline little world, out of time, out of space, where all of the world, for all eternity, was precisely determined by clearly specified guidelines, set down by the appropriately designated authorities. They drew about them a world without creativity, without passion, without morality.

In such an atmosphere, far more bureaucratic and technocratic, far less intellectual than C.C.N.Y., I nonetheless felt more free to teach and act as I felt I should, since I now had so much less commitment to survival in such a world. Consequently, this time I was fired at the end of one year. The suggested reason was that I had failed to develop a professional self-image and tended to identify with students. That was the end of my academic career.

V. Well, where does that leave me now? Coming out of the blind alley of academia I had been led into by my failure to see that Brains turn into Men after all, trying to get back to where I was when I was ten. Back then I had decided I didn't want to be a Man. I never entirely gave up that decision. Defensiveness, a desire for security, and the surprising fact of my "masculine" competence in an academic setting—all of this led me into being a male impersonator for far too long, and I got so used to it that it was very hard to stop. But I am not now, nor have I ever been a Man.

Right now my life is learning what it means to be Gay. At the moment I'm living in a big old house with five other Gay Men. We've been living together for a year now, supporting ourselves with savings and various odd jobs, and trying to learn to relate to each other. We are breaking up soon. We didn't make it. We were still too frozen in the old patterns, still too much Men. But we learned something in the process. Two of us are working at setting up a new collective, and we'll try again. There's no turning back; there's only a void behind us. And what's ahead of us only begins to exist as we create it.

I also have to decide what to do with all the knowledge and skills I've learned in my life in the straight world—with the resources and power these give me access to. Now that I don't define myself as an intellectual, I have come to terms with intellectualism. When I was a Brain, things of the mind were the source of my sense of self-worth and a consolation for loneliness. Now I have other, less alienated sources of self-worth, but it will be a long time (if ever) before I can live without such consolation. As an academician, I learned to use ideas as weapons to establish my power over others. Now I reject a self-concept based on power. Yet I am involved more than ever in a struggle against all the power of this society; in this struggle, it is only through the use of ideas that I can feel I am fighting back against my oppressors. Thus this paper.

Finally I have no answers. I don't know where I am going, only the direction in which I must proceed. I often feel alone and isolated in this journey, but that is changing. Slowly, with many false starts, we are coming together. We are frightened because we are leaving all of the world we knew behind us, with whatever security it provided. It is still very hard to trust each other with our lives. But there is no going back, and we are building the future as we go. We must create a new world, if we are to be able to go on living. We are determined to live, so the future is ours.

On face-work: An analysis of ritual elements in social interaction[*]

Erving Goffman

Every person lives in a world of social encounters, involving him either in face-to-face or mediated contact with other participants. In each of these contacts, he tends to act out what is sometimes called a *line*—that is, a pattern of verbal and nonverbal acts by which he expresses his view of the situation and through this his evaluation of the participants, expecially himself. Regardless of whether a person intends to take a line, he will find that he has done so in effect. The other participants will assume that he has more or less willfully taken a stand, so that if he is to deal with their response to him he must take into consideration the impression they have possibly formed of him.

The term *face* may be defined as the positive social value a person effectively claims for himself by the line others assume he has taken during a particular contact. Face is an image of self delineated in terms of approved social attributes —albeit an image that others may share, as when a person makes a good showing for his profession or religion by making a good showing for himself.

A person tends to experience an immediate emotional response to the face which a contact with others allows him; he cathects his face; his "feelings" become attached to it. If the encounter sustains an image of him that he has long taken for granted, he probably will have few feelings about the matter. If events establish a face for him that is better than he might have expected, he is likely to "feel good"; if his ordinary expectations are not fulfilled, one expects that he will "feel bad" or "feel hurt." In general, a person's attachment to a

* Excerpted from Erving Goffman, "On Face-Work: An analysis of Ritual Elements in Social Interaction." Reprinted by special permission of The William Alanson White Psychiatric Foundation, Inc., *Psychiatry,* Vol. 18, No. 3 (Aug. 1955), pp. 213–31. Footnotes renumbered. Copyright 1955 by The William Alanson White Psychiatric Foundation Inc.

particular face, coupled with the ease with which disconfirming information can be conveyed by himself and others, provides one reason why he finds that participation in any contact with others is a commitment. A person will also have feelings about the face sustained for the other participants, and while these feelings may differ in quantity and direction from those he has for his own face, they constitute an involvement in the face of others that is as immediate and spontaneous as the involvement he has in his own face. One's own face and the face of others are constructs of the same order; it is the rules of the group and the definition of the situation which determine how much feeling one is to have for face and how this feeling is to be distributed among the faces involved.

A person may be said to *have*, or *be in*, or *maintain* face when the line he effectively takes presents an image of him that is internally consistent, that is supported by judgments and evidence conveyed by other participants, and that is confirmed by evidence conveyed through impersonal agencies in the situation. At such times the person's face clearly is something that is not lodged in or on his body, but rather something that is diffusely located in the flow of events in the encounter and becomes manifest only when these events are read and interpreted for the appraisals expressed in them.

A person may be said to *be in wrong face* when information is brought forth in some way about his social worth which cannot be integrated, even with effort, into the line that is being sustained for him. A person may be said to *be out of face* when he participates in a contact with others without having ready a line of the kind participants in such situations are expected to take. The intent of many pranks is to lead a person into showing a wrong face or no face, but there will also be serious occasions, of course, when he will find himself expressively out of touch with the situation.

When a person senses that he is in face, he typically responds with feelings of confidence and assurance. Firm in the line he is taking, he feels that he can hold his head up and openly present himself to others. He feels some security and some relief—as he also can when the others feel he is in wrong face but successfully hide these feelings from him.

When a person is in wrong face or out of face, expressive events are being contributed to the encounter which cannot be readily woven into the expressive fabric of the occasion. Should he sense that he is in wrong face or out of face, he is likely to feel ashamed and inferior because of what has happened to the activity on his account and because of what may happen to his reputation as a participant. Further, he may feel bad because he had relied upon the encounter to support an image of self to which he has become emotionally attached and which he now finds threatened. Felt lack of judgmental support from the encounter may take him aback, confuse him, and momentarily incapacitate him as an interactant. His manner and bearing may falter, collapse, and crumble. He may become embarrassed and chagrined; he may become shamefaced. The feeling, whether warranted or not, that he is perceived in a flustered state by others, and that he is presenting no usable line, may add further injuries to his feelings, just as his change from being in wrong face or out of face to being shamefaced can add further disorder to the expressive organization of the situation. Following common usage, I shall employ the term *poise* to refer to the capacity to suppress and conceal any tendency to become shame-faced during encounters with others.

In our Anglo-American society, as in some others, the phrase "to lose face" seems to mean to be in wrong face, to be out of face, or to be shamefaced. The phrase "to save one's face" appears to refer to the process by which the person sustains an impression for others that he has not lost face. Following Chinese usage, one can say that "to give face" is to arrange for another to take a better line than he might otherwise have been able to take, the other thereby gets face given him, this being one way in which he can gain face.

As an aspect of the social code of any social circle, one may expect to find an understanding as to how far a person should go to save his face. Once he takes on a self-image expressed through face he will expected to live up to it. In different ways in different societies he will be required to show self-respect, abjuring certain actions because they are above or beneath him, while forcing himself to perform others even though they cost him dearly. By entering a situation in which he is given a face to maintain, a person takes on the responsibility of standing guard over the flow of events as they pass before him. He must ensure that a particular *expressive order* is sustained—an order which regulates the flow of events, large or small, so that anything that appears to be expressed by them will be consistent with his face. When a person manifests these compunctions primarily from duty to himself, one speaks in our society of pride; when he does so because of duty to wider social units, and receives support from these units in doing so, one speaks of honor. When these compunctions have to do with postural things, with expressive events derived from the way in which the person handles his body, his emotions, and the things with which he has physical contact, one speaks of dignity, this being an aspect of expressive control that is always praised and never studied. In any case, while his social face can be his most personal possession and the center of his security and pleasure, it is only on loan to him from society; it will be withdrawn unless he conducts himself in a way that is worthy of it. Approved attributes and their relation to face make of every man his own jailer; this is a fundamental social constraint even though each man may like his cell.

Just as the member of any group is expected to have self-respect, so also he is expected to sustain a standard of considerateness; he is expected to go to certain lengths to save the feelings and the face of others present, and he is expected to do this willingly and spontaneously because of emotional identification with the others and with their feelings. In consequence, he is disinclined to witness the defacement of others.[1] The person who can witness another's humiliation and unfeelingly retain a cool countenance himself is said in our society to be

---

[1] Salesmen, especially street "stemmers," know that if they take a line that will be discredited unless the reluctant customer buys, the customer may be trapped by considerateness and buy in order to save the face of the salesman and prevent what would ordinarily result in a scene.

"heartless," just as he who can unfeelingly participate in his own defacement is thought to be "shameless."

The combined effect of the rule of self-respect and the rule of considerateness is that the person tends to conduct himself during an encounter so as to maintain both his own face and the face of the other participants. This means that the line taken by each participant is usually allowed to prevail, and each participant is allowed to carry off the role he appears to have chosen for himself. A state where everyone temporarily accepts everyone else's line is established. This kind of mutual acceptance seems to be a basic structural feature of interaction, especially the interaction of face-to-face talk. It is typically a "working" acceptance, not a "real" one, since it tends to be based not on agreement of candidly expressed heartfelt evaluations, but upon a willingness to give temporary lip service to judgments with which the participants do not really agree.

The mutual acceptance of lines has an important conservative effect upon encounters. Once the person initially presents a line, he and the others tend to build their later responses upon it, and in a sense become stuck with it. Should the person radically alter his line, or should it become discredited, then confusion results, for the participants will have prepared and committed themselves for actions that are now unsuitable.

Ordinarily, maintenance of face is a condition of interaction, not its objective. Usual objectives, such as gaining face for oneself, giving free expression to one's true beliefs, introducing depreciating information about the others, or solving problems and performing tasks, are typically pursued in such a way as to be consistent with the maintenance of face. To study face-saving is to study the traffic rules of social interaction; one learns about the code the person adheres to in his movement across the paths and designs of others, but not where he is going, or why he wants to get there. One does not even learn why he is ready to follow the code, for a large number of different motives can equally lead him to do so. He may want to save his own face because of his emotional attachment to the image of self which it expresses, because of his pride or honor, because of the power his presumed status allows him to exert over the other participants, and so on. He may want to save the others' face because of his emotional attachment to an image of them, or because he feels that his coparticipants have a moral right to this protection, or because he wants to avoid the hostility that may be directed toward him if they lose their face. He may feel that an assumption has been made that he is the sort of person who shows compassion and sympathy toward others, so that to retain his own face, he may feel obliged to be considerate of the line taken by the other participants.

By *face-work* I mean to designate the actions taken by a person to make whatever he is doing consistent with face. Face-work serves to counteract "incidents"—that is, events whose effective symbolic implications threaten face. Thus poise is one important type of face-work, for through poise the person controls his embarrassment and hence the embarrassment that he and others might have over his embarrassment. Whether or not the full consequences of face-saving actions are known to the person who employs them, they often become habitual and standardized practices; they are like traditional plays in a game or traditional steps in a dance. Each person, subculture, and society seems to have its own characteristic repertoire of face-saving practices. It is to this repertoire that people partly refer when they ask what a person or culture is "really" like. And yet the particular set of practices stressed by particular persons or groups seems to be drawn from a single logically coherent framework of possible practices. It is as if face, by its very nature, can be saved only in a certain number of ways, and as if each social grouping must make its selections from this single matrix of possibilities.

The members of every social circle may be expected to have some knowledge of face-work and some experience in its use. In our society, this kind of capacity is sometimes called tact, *savoir-faire*, diplomacy, or social skill. Variation in social skill pertains more to the efficacy of face-work than to the frequency of its application, for almost all acts involving others are modified, prescriptively or proscriptively, by considerations of face.

I have already said that the person will have two points of view—a defensive orientation toward saving his own face and a protective orientation toward saving the others' face. Some practices will be primarily defense and others primarily protective, although in general one may expect these two perspectives to be taken at the same time. In trying to save the face of others, the person must choose a tack that will not lead to loss of his own; in trying to save his own face, he must consider the loss of face that his action may entail for others.

In many societies there is a tendency to distinguish three levels of responsibility which a person may have for a threat to face that his actions have created. First, he may appear to have acted innocently; his offense seems to be unintended and unwitting, and those who perceive his act can feel that he would have attempted to avoid it had he foreseen its offensive consequences. In our society one calls such threats to face *faux pas*, *gaffes*, boners, or bricks. Second, the offending person may appear to have acted maliciously and spitefully, with the intention of causing open insult. Third, there are incidental offenses; these arise as an unplanned but sometimes anticipated by-product of action—action which the offender performs in spite of its offensive consequences, although not out of spite. From the point of view of a particular participant, these three types of threat can be introduced by the participant himself against his own face, by himself against the face of others, by the others against their own face, or by the others against himself. Thus the person may find himself in many different relations to a threat to face. If he is to handle himself and others well in all contingencies, he will have to have a repertoire of face-saving practices for each of these possible relations to threat.

THE BASIC KINDS OF FACE-WORK

The avoidance process.   The surest way for a person to prevent threats to his face is to avoid contacts in which these threats are likely to occur. In all societies one can observe this in the avoidance relationship[2] and in the tendency for certain delicate transactions to be conducted by go-betweens.[3] Similarly, in many societies, members know the value of voluntarily making a gracious withdrawal before an anticipated threat to face has had a chance to occur.[4]

Once the person does chance an encounter, other kinds of avoidance practices come into play. As defensive measures, he keeps off topics and away from activities which would lead to the expression of information that is inconsistent with the line he is maintaining. At opportune moments he will change the topic of conversation or the direction of activity. He will often present initially a front of diffidence and composure, suppressing any show of feeling until he has found out what kind of line the others will be ready to support for him. Any claims regarding self may be made with belittling modesty, with strong qualifications, or with a note of unseriousness; by hedging in these ways he will have prepared a self for himself that will not be discredited by exposure, personal failure, or the unanticipated acts of others. And if he does not hedge his claims about self, he will at least attempt to be realistic about them, knowing that otherwise events may discredit him and make him lose face.

Certain protective maneuvers are as common as these defensive ones. The person shows respect and politeness, making sure to extend to others any ceremonial treatment which might be their due. He employs discretion; he leaves unstated facts which might implicitly or explicitly contradict and embarrass the positive claims made by others. He employs circumlocutions and deceptions, phrasing his replies with careful ambiguity so that the others' face is preserved even if their welfare is not.[5] He employs courtesies, making slight modifications of his demands on or appraisals of the others so that they will be able to define the situation as one in which their self-respect is not threatened. In making a

---

[2] In our own society an illustration of avoidance is found in the middle- and upper-class Negro who avoids certain face-to-face contacts with whites in order to protect the self-evaluation projected by his clothes and manner. See, for example, Charles Johnson, *Patterns of Negro Segregation;* New York, Harper, 1943; ch. 13. The function of avoidance in maintaining the kinship system in small preliterate societies might be taken as a particular illustration of the same general theme.

[3] An illustration is given by Kenneth S. Latourette, *The Chinese: Their History and Culture* (New York, Macmillan, 1942): "A neighbor or a group of neighbors may tender their good offices in adjusting a quarrel in which each antagonist would be sacrificing his face by taking the first step in approaching the other. The wise intermediary can effect the reconciliation while preserving the dignity of both" (Vol. 2: p. 211).

[4] In an unpublished paper Harold Garfinkel has suggested that when the person finds that he has lost face in a conversational encounter, he may feel a desire to disappear or "drop through the floor," and that this may involve a wish not only to conceal loss of face but also to return magically to a point in time when it would have been possible to save face by avoiding the encounter.

[5] The Western traveler used to complain that the Chinese could never be trusted to say what they meant but always said what they felt their Western listener wanted to hear. The Chinese used to complain that the Westerner was brusque, boorish, and unmannered. In terms of Chinese standards, presumably, the conduct of a Westerner is so gauche that he creates an emergency, forcing the Asian to forgo any kind of direct reply in order to rush in with a remark that might rescue the Westerner from the compromising position in which he had placed himself. (Smith, *Chinese Characteristics* [New York: Revell, 1894], ch. 8, "The Talent for Indirection.") This is an instance of the important group of misunderstandings which arise during interaction between persons who come from groups with different ritual standards.

belittling demand upon the others, or in imputing uncomplimentary attributes to them, he may employ a joking manner, allowing them to take the line that they are good sports, able to relax from their ordinary standards of pride and honor. And before engaging in a potentially offensive act, he may provide explanations as to why the others ought not to be affronted by it. For example, if he knows that it will be necessary to withdraw from the encounter before it has terminated, he may tell the others in advance that it is necessary for him to leave, so that they will have faces that are prepared for it. But neutralizing the potentially offensive act need not be done verbally; he may wait for a propitious moment or natural break—for example, in conversation, a momentary lull when no one speaker can be affronted—and then leave, in this way using the context instead of his words as a guarantee of inoffensiveness.

When a person fails to prevent an incident, he can still attempt to maintain the fiction that no threat to face has occurred. The most blatant example of this is found where the person acts as if an event which contains a threatening expression has not occurred at all. He may apply this studied nonobservance to his own acts—as when he does not by any outward sign admit that his stomach is rumbling—or to the acts of others, as when he does not "see" that another has stumbled.[6] Social life in mental hospitals owes much to this process; patients employ it in regard to their own pecularities, and visitors employ it, often with tenuous desperation, in regard to patients. In general, tactful blindness of this kind is applied only to events which, if perceived at all, could be preceived and interpreted only as threats to face.

A more important, less spectacular kind of tactful overlooking is practiced when a person openly acknowledges an incident as an event that has occurred, but not as an event that contains a threatening expression. If he is not the one who is responsible for the incident, then his blindness will have to be supported by his forbearance; if he is the doer of the threatening deed, then his blindness will have to be supported by his willingness to seek a way of dealing with the matter which leaves him dangerously dependent upon the cooperative forbearance of the others.

Another kind of avoidance occurs when a person loses control of his expressions during an encounter. At such times he may try not so much to overlook the incident as to hide or conceal his activity in some way, thus making it possible for the others to avoid some of the difficulties created by a participant who has not maintained face. Correspondingly, when a person is caught out of face because he had not expected to be thrust into interaction, or because strong feelings have disrupted his expressive mask, the others may protectively turn away from him or his activity for a moment, to give him time to assemble himself.

The corrective process.   When the participants in an undertaking or encounter fail to prevent the occurrence of an event that is expressively incompatible with the judgments of social worth that are being maintained, and when the

---

[6] A pretty example of this is found in parade-ground etiquette which may oblige those in a parade to treat anyone who faints as if he were not present at all.

event is of the kind that is difficult to overlook, then the participants are likely to give it accredited status as an incident—to ratify it as a threat that deserves direct official attention—and to proceed to try to correct for its effects. At this point one or more participants find themselves in an established state of ritual disequilibrium or disgrace, and an attempt must be made to re-establish a satisfactory ritual state for them. I use the term *ritual* because I am dealing with acts through whose symbolic component the actor shows how worthy he is of respect or how worthy he feels others are of it. The imagery of equilibrium is apt here because the length and intensity of the corrective effort is nicely adapted to the persistence and intensity of the threat.[7] One's face, then, is a sacred thing, and the expressive order required to sustain it is therefore a ritual one.

The sequence of acts set in motion by an acknowledged threat to face, and terminating in the re-establishment of ritual equilibrium, I shall call an *interchange*. Defining a message or move as everything conveyed by an actor during a turn at taking action, one can say that an interchange will involve two or more moves and two or more participants. Obvious examples in our society may be found in the sequence of "Excuse me" and "Certainly," and in the exchange of presents or visits. The interchange seems to be a basic concrete unit of social activity and provides one natural empirical way to study interaction of all kinds.

MAKING POINTS—THE AGGRESSIVE USE OF FACE-WORK

Every face-saving practice which is allowed to neutralize a particular threat opens up the possibility that the threat will be willfully introduced for what can be safely gained by it. If a person knows that his modesty will be answered by others' praise of him, he can fish for compliments. If his own appraisal of self will be checked against incidental events, then he can arrange for favorable incidental events to appear. If others are prepared to overlook an affront to them and act forbearantly, or to accept apologies, then he can rely on this as a basis for safely offending them. He can attempt by sudden withdrawal to force the others into a ritually unsatisfactory state, leaving them to flounder in an interchange that cannot readily be completed. Finally, at some expense to himself, he can arrange for the others to hurt his feelings, thus forcing them to feel guilt, remorse, and sustained ritual disequilibrium.[8]

When a person treats face-work not as something he need be prepared to perform, but rather as something that others can be counted on to perform or

---

[7] This kind of imagery is one that social anthropologists seem to find naturally fitting. Note, for example, the implications of the following statement by Margaret Mead in her "Kinship in the Admiralty Islands" (*Anthropological Papers of the American Museum of Natural History*, 34 : 183–358): "If a husband beats his wife, custom demands that she leave him and go to her brother, real or officiating, and remain a length of time commensurate with the degree of her offended dignity" (p. 274).

[8] The strategy of maneuvering another into a position where he cannot right the harm he has done is very commonly employed but nowhere with such devotion to the ritual model of conduct as in revengeful suicide. See, for example, M. D. W. Jeffreys, "Samsonic Suicide, or Suicide of Revenge Among Africans," *African Studies* (1952) 11 : 118–22.

to accept, then an encounter or an undertaking becomes less a scene of mutual considerateness than an arena in which a contest or match is held. The purpose of the game is to preserve everyone's line from an inexcusable contradiction, while scoring as many points as possible against one's adversaries and making as many gains as possible for oneself. An audience to the struggle is almost a necessity. The general method is for the person to introduce favorable facts about himself and unfavorable facts about the others in such a way that the only reply the others will be able to think up will be one that terminates the interchange in a grumble, a meager excuse, a face-saving I-can-take-a-joke laugh, or an empty stereotyped comeback of the "Oh yeah?" or "That's what you think" variety. The losers in such cases will have to cut their losses, tacitly grant the loss of a point, and attempt to do better in the next interchange. Points made by allusion to social class status are sometimes called snubs; those made by allusions to moral respectability are sometimes called digs; in either case one deals with a capacity at what is sometimes called "bitchiness."

In aggressive interchange the winner not only succeeds in introducing information favorable to himself and unfavorable to the others, but also demonstrates that as interactant he can handle himself better than his adversaries. Evidence of this capacity is often more important than all the other information the person conveys in the interchange, so that the introduction of a "crack" in verbal interaction tends to imply that the initiator is better at footwork than those who must suffer his remarks. However, if they succeed in making a successful parry of the thrust and then a successful riposte, the instigator of the play must not only face the disparagement with which the others have answered him but also accept the fact that his assumption of superiority in footwork has proven false. He is made to look foolish; he loses face. Hence it is always a gamble to "make a remark." The tables can be turned and the aggressor can lose more than he could have gained had his move won the point. Successful ripostes or comebacks in our society are sometimes called squelches or toppers; theoretically it would be possible for a squelch to be squelched, a topper to be topped, and a riposte to be parried with a counterriposte, but except in staged interchanges this third level of successful action seems rare.[9]

THE CHOICE OF APPROPRIATE FACE-WORK

When an incident occurs, the person whose face is threatened may attempt to reinstate the ritual order by means of one kind of strategy, while the other participants may desire or expect a practice of a different type to be employed. When, for example, a minor mishap occurs, momentarily revealing a person in

---

[9] In board and card games the player regularly takes into consideration the possible responses of his adversaries to a play that he is about to make, and even considers the possibility that his adversaries will know that he is taking such precautions. Conversational play is by comparison surprisingly impulsive; people regularly make remarks about others present without carefully designing their remarks to prevent a successful comeback. Similarly, while feinting and sandbagging are theoretical possibilities during talk, they seem to be little exploited.

wrong face or out of face, the others are often more willing and able to get blind to the discrepancy than is the threatened person himself himself. Often they would prefer him to exercise poise,[10] while he feels that he cannot afford to overlook what has happened to his face and so becomes apologetic and shame-faced, if he is the creator of the incident, or destructively assertive, if the others are responsible for it.[11] Yet on the other hand, a person may manifest poise when the others feel that he ought to have broken down into embarrassed apology—that he is taking undue advantage of their helpfulness by his attempts to brazen it out. Sometimes a person may himself be undecided as to which practice to employ, leaving the others in the embarrassing position of not knowing which tack they are going to have to follow. Thus when a person makes a slight *gaffe*, he and the others may become embarrassed not because of inability to handle such difficulties, but because for a moment no one knows whether the offender is going to act blind to the incident, or give it joking recognition, or employ some other face-saving practice.

COOPERATION IN FACE-WORK

When a face has been threatened, face-work must be done, but whether this is initiated and primarily carried through by the person whose face is threatened, or by the offender, or by a mere witness,[12] is often of secondary importance. Lack of effort on the part of one person induces compensatory effort from others; a contribution by one person relieves the others of the task. In fact, there are many minor incidents in which the offender and the offended simultaneously attempt to initiate an apology.[13] Resolution of the situation to everyone's apparent satis-

---

[10] Folklore imputes a great deal of poise to the upper classes. If there is truth in this belief it may lie in the fact that the upper-class person tends to find himself in encounters in which he outranks the other participants in ways additional to class. The ranking participant is often somewhat in-dependent of the good opinion of the others and finds it practical to be arrogant, sticking to a face regardless of whether the encounter supports it. On the other hand, those who are in the power of a fellow-participant tend to be very much concerned with the valuation he makes of them or witnesses being made of them, and so find it difficult to maintain a slightly wrong face without becoming embarrassed and apologetic. It may be added that people who lack awareness of the symbolism in minor events may keep cool in difficult situations, showing poise that they do not really possess.

[11] Thus, in our society, when a person feels that others expect him to measure up to approved standards of cleanliness, tidiness, fairness, hospitality, generosity, affluence, and so on, or when he sees himself as someone who ought to maintain such standards, he may burden an encounter with extended apologies for his failings, while all along the other participants do not care about the standard, or do not believe the person is really lacking in it, or are convinced that he is lacking in it and see the apology itself as a vain effort at self-elevation.

[12] Thus one function of seconds in actual duels, as well as in figurative ones, is to provide an excuse for not fighting that both contestants can afford to accept.

[13] See, for instance, Jackson Toby, "Some Variables in Role Conflict Analysis" [*Social Forces* (1952) 30 : 323–37]: "With adults there is less likelihood for essentially trivial issues to produce conflict. The automatic apology of two strangers who accidentally collide on a busy street illustrates the integrative function of etiquette. In effect, each of the parties to the collision says, 'I don't know whether I am responsible for this situation, but *if* I am, you have a right to be angry with me, a right that I pray you will not exercise.' By defining the situation as one in which both parties must

faction is the first requirement; correct apportionment of blame is typically a secondary consideration. Hence terms such as tact and *savoir-faire* fail to distinguish whether it is the person's own face that his diplomacy saves or the face of the others. Similarly, terms such as *gaffe* and *faux pas* fail to specify whether it is the actor's own face he has threatened or the face of other participants. And it is understandable that if one person finds he is powerless to save his own face, the others seem especially bound to protect him. For example, in polite society, a handshake that perhaps should not have been extended becomes one that cannot be declined. Thus one accounts for the *noblesse oblige* through which those of high status are expected to curb their power of embarrassing their lessers,[14] as well as the fact that the handicapped often accept courtesies that they can manage better without.

Since each participant in an undertaking is concerned, albeit for differing reasons, with saving his own face and the face of the others, then tacit cooperation will naturally arise so that the participants together can attain their shared but differently motivated objectives.

One common type of tacit cooperation in face-saving is the tact exerted in regarded to face-work itself. The person not only defends his own face and protects the face of the others, but also acts so as to make it possible and even easy for the others to employ face-work for themselves and him. He helps them to help themselves and him. Social etiquette, for example, warns men against asking for New Year's Eve dates too early in the season, lest the girl find it difficult to provide a gentle excuse for refusing. This second-order tact can be further illustrated by the widespread practice of negative-attribute etiquette. The person who has an unapparent negatively valued attribute often finds it expedient to begin an encounter with an unobtrusive admission of his failing, especially with

---

abase themselves, society enables each to keep his self-respect. Each may feel in his heart of hearts, 'Why can't that stupid ass watch where he's going?' But overtly *each plays the role of the guilty party* whether he feels he has been miscast or not" (p. 325).

[14] Regardless of the person's relative social position, in one sense he has power over the other participants and they must rely upon his considerateness. When the others act toward him in some way, they presume upon a social relationship to him, since one of the things expressed by interaction is the relationship of the interactants. Thus they compromise themselves, for they place him in a position to discredit the claims they express as to his attitude toward them. Hence in response to claimed social relationships every person, of high estate or low, will be expected to exercise *noblesse oblige* and refrain from exploiting the compromised position of the others.

Since social relationships are defined partly in terms of voluntary mutual aid, refusal of a request for assistance becomes a delicate matter, potentially destructive of the asker's face. Chester Holcombe, *The Real Chinaman* (New York, Dodd, Mead, 1895) provides a Chinese instance: "Much of the falsehood to which the Chinese as a nation are said to be addicted is a result of the demands of etiquette. A plain, frank 'no' is the height of discourtesy. Refusal or denial of any sort must be softened and toned down into an expression of regretted inability. Unwillingness to grant a favor is never shown. In place of it there is seen a chastened feeling of sorrow that unavoidable but quite imaginary circumstances render it wholly impossible. Centuries of practice in this form of evasion have made the Chinese matchlessly fertile in the invention and development of excuses. It is rare, indeed, that one is caught at a loss for a bit of artfully embroidered fiction with which to hide an unwelcome truth" (pp. 274–75).

persons who are uninformed about him. The others are thus warned in advance against making disparaging remarks about his kind of person and are saved from the contradiction of acting in a friendly fashion to a person toward whom they are unwittingly being hostile. This strategy also prevents the others from automatically making assumptions about him which place him in a false position and saves him from painful forebearance or embarrassing remonstrances.

Tact in regard to face-work often relies for its operation on a tacit agreement to do business through the language of hint—the language of innuendo, ambiguities, well-placed pauses, carefully worded jokes, and so on. The rule regarding this unofficial kind of communication is that the sender ought not to act as if he had officially conveyed the message he has hinted at, while the recipients have the right and the obligation to act as if they have not officially received the message contained in the hint. Hinted communication, then, is deniable communication; it need not be faced up to. It provides a means by which the person can be warned that his current line or the current situation is leading to loss of face, without this warning itself becoming an incident.

Another form of tacit cooperation, and one that seems to be much used in many societies, is reciprocal self-denial. Often the person does not have a clear idea of what would be a just or acceptable apportionment of judgments during the occasion, and so he voluntarily deprives or depreciates himself while indulging and complimenting the others, in both cases carrying the judgments safely past what is likely to be just. The favorable judgments about himself he allows to come from the others; the unfavorable judgments of himself are his own contributions. This "after you, Alphonse" technique works, of course, because in depriving himself he can reliably anticipate that the others will compliment or indulge him. Whatever allocation of favors is eventually established, all participants are first given a chance to show that they are not bound or constrained by their own desires and expectations, and that they have a properly modest view of themselves, and that they can be counted upon to support the ritual code. Negative bargaining, through which each participant tries to make the terms of trade more favorable to the other side, is another instance; as a form of exchange perhaps it is more widespread than the economist's kind.

A person's performance of face-work, extended by his tacit agreement to help others perform theirs, represents his willingness to abide by the ground rules of social interaction. Here is the hallmark of his socialization as an interactant. If he and the others were not socialized in this way, interaction in most societies and most situations would be a much more hazardous thing for feelings and faces. The person would find it impractical to be oriented to symbolically conveyed appraisals of social worth, or to be possessed of feelings—that is, it would be impractical for him to be a ritually delicate object. And as I shall suggest, if the person were not a ritually delicate object, occasions of talk could not be organized in the way they usually are. It is no wonder that trouble is caused by a person who cannot be relied upon to play the face-saving game.

FACE AND SOCIAL RELATIONSHIPS

When a person begins a mediated or immediate encounter, he already stands in some kind of social relationship to the others concerned, and expects to stand in a given relationship to them after the particular encounter ends. This, of course, is one of the ways in which social contacts are geared into the wider society. Much of the activity occurring during an encounter can be understood as an effort on everyone's part to get through the occasion and all the unanticipated and unintentional events that can cast participants in an undesirable light, without disrupting the relationships of the participants. And if relationships are in the process of change, the object will be to bring the encounter to a satisfactory close without altering the expected course of development. This perspective nicely accounts, for example, for the little ceremonies of greeting and farewell which occur when people begin a conversational encounter or depart from one. Greetings provide a way of showing that a relationship is still what it was at the termination of the previous coparticipation, and, typically, that this relationship involves sufficient suppression of hostility for the participants temporarily to drop their guards and talk. Farewells sum up the effect of the encounter upon the relationship and show what the participants may expect of one another when they next meet. The enthusiasm of greetings compensates for the weakening of the relationship caused by the absence just terminated, while the enthusiasm of farewells compensates the relationship for the harm that it is about to be done to it by separation.[15]

It seems to be a characteristic obligation of many social relationships that each of the members guarantees to support a given face for the other members in given situations. To prevent disruption of these relationships, it is therefore necessary for each member to avoid destroying the others' face. At the same time, it is often the person's social relationship with others that leads him to participate in certain encounters with them, where incidentally he will be dependent upon them for supporting his face. Furthermore, in many relationships, the members come to share a face, so that in the presence of third parties an improper act on the part of one member becomes a source of acute embarrassment to the other members. A social relationship, then, can be seen as a way in which the person is more than ordinarily forced to trust his self-image and face to the tact and good conduct of others.

---

[15] Greetings, of course, serve to clarify and fix the roles that the participants will take during the occasion of talk and to commit participants to these roles, while farewells provide a way of unambiguously terminating the encounter. Greetings and farewells may also be used to state, and apologize for, extenuating circumstances—in the case of greetings for circumstances that have kept the participants from interacting until now, and in the case of farewells for circumstances that prevent the participants from continuing their display of solidarity. These apologies allow the impression to be maintained that the participants are more warmly related socially than may be the case. This positive stress, in turn, assures that they will act more readily to enter into contacts than they perhaps really feel inclined to do, thus guaranteeing that diffuse channels for potential communication will be kept open in the society.

THE NATURE OF THE RITUAL ORDER

The ritual order seems to be organized basically on accommodative lines, so that the imagery used in thinking about other types of social order is not quite suitable for it. For the other types of social order a kind of schoolboy model seems to be employed: if a person wishes to sustain a particular image of himself and trust his feelings to it, he must work hard for the credits that will buy this self-enhancement for him; should he try to obtain ends by improper means, by cheating or theft, he will be punished, disqualified from the race, or at least made to start all over again from the beginning. This is the imagery of a hard, dull game. In fact, society and the individual join in one that is easier on both of them, yet one that has dangers of its own.

Whatever his position in society, the person insulates himself by blindness, half-truths, illusions, and rationalizations. He makes an "adjustment" by convincing himself, with the tactful support of his intimate circle, that he is what he wants to be and that he would not do to gain his ends what the others have done to gain theirs. And as for society, if the person is willing to be subject to informal social control—if he is willing to find out from hints and glances and tactful cues what his place is, and keep it—then there will be no objection to his furnishing this place at his own discretion, with all the comfort, elegance, and nobility that his wit can muster for him. To protect this shelter he does not have to work hard, or join a group, or compete with anybody; he need only be careful about the expressed judgments he places himself in a position to witness. Some situations and acts and persons will have to be avoided; others, less threatening, must not be pressed too far. Social life is an uncluttered, orderly thing because the person voluntarily stays away from the places and topics and times where he is not wanted and where he might be disparaged for going. He cooperates to save his face, finding that there is much to be gained from venturing nothing.

Facts are of the schoolboy's world—they can be altered by diligent effort but they cannot be avoided. But what the person protects and defends and invests his feelings in is an idea about himself, and ideas are vulnerable not to facts and things but to communications. Communications belong to a less punitive scheme than do facts, for communications can be by-passed, withdrawn from, disbelieved, conveniently misunderstood, and tactfully conveyed. And even should the person misbehave and break the truce he has made with society, punishment need not be the consequence. If the offense is one that the offended persons can let go by without losing too much face, then they are likely to act forbearantly, telling themselves that they will get even with the offender in another way at another time, even though such an occasion may never arise and might not be exploited if it did. If the offense is great, the offended persons may withdraw from the encounter, or from future similar ones, allowing their withdrawal to be reinforced by the awe they may feel toward someone who breaks the ritual code. Or they may have the offender withdrawn, so that no further communication can occur. But since the offender can salvage a good deal of face from such operations, withdrawal is often not so much an informal punishment for an offense as it is merely a means of terminating it. Perhaps the main principle of the ritual order is not justice but face, and what any offender receives is not what he deserves but what will sustain for the moment the line to which he has committed himself, and through this the line to which he has committed the interaction.

Throughout this paper it has been implied that underneath their differences in culture, people everywhere are the same. If persons have a universal human nature, they themselves are not to be looked to for an explanation of it. One must look rather to the fact that societies everywhere, if they are to be societies, must mobilize their members as self-regulating participants in social encounters. One way of mobilizing the individual for this purpose is through ritual; he is taught to be perceptive, to have feelings attached to self and a self expressed through face, to have pride, honor, and dignity, to have considerateness, to have tact and a certain amount of poise. These are some of the elements of behavior which must be built into a person if practical use is to be made of him as an interactant, and it is these elements that are referred to in part when one speaks of universal human nature.

Universal human nature is not a very human thing. By acquiring it, the person becomes a kind of construct, built up not from inner psychic propensities but from moral rules that are impressed upon him from without. These rules, when followed, determine the evaluation he will make of himself and of his fellow-participants in the encounter, the distribution of his feelings, and the kinds of practices he will employ to maintain a specified and obligatory kind of ritual equilibrium. The general capacity to be bound by moral rules may well belong to the individual, but the particular set of rules which transforms him into a human being derives from requirements established in the ritual organization of social encounters. And if a particular person or group or society seems to have a unique character all its own, it is because its standard set of human-nature elements is pitched and combined in a particular way. Instead of much pride, there may be little. Instead of abiding by the rules, there may be much effort to break them safely. But if an encounter or undertaking is to be sustained as a viable system of interaction organized on ritual principles, then these variations must be held within certain bounds and nicely counterbalanced by corresponding modifications in some of the other rules and understandings. Similarly, the human nature of a particular set of persons may be specially designed for the special kind of undertakings in which they participate, but still each of these persons must have within him something of the balance of characteristics required of a usable participant in any ritually organized system of social activity.

Shooting an elephant[*]

George Orwell

In Moulmein, in Lower Burma, I was hated by large numbers of people—the only time in my life that I have been important enough for this to happen to me. I was subdivisional police officer of the town, and in an aimless, petty kind of way anti-European feeling was very bitter. No one had the guts to raise a riot, but if a European woman went through the bazaars alone somebody would probably spit betel juice over her dress. As a police officer I was an obvious target and was baited whenever it seemed safe to do so. When a nimble Burman tripped me up on the football field and the referee (another Burman) looked the other way, the crowd yelled with hideous laughter. This happened more than once. In the end the sneering yellow faces of young men that met me everywhere, the insults hooted after me when I was at a safe distance, got badly on my nerves. The young Buddhist priests were the worst of all. There were several thousands of them in the town and none of them seemed to have anything to do except stand on street corners and jeer at Europeans.

All this was perplexing and upsetting. For at that time I had already made up my mind that imperialism was an evil thing and the sooner I chucked up my job and got out of it the better. Theoretically—and secretly, of course—I was all for the Burmese and all against their oppressors, the British. As for the job I was doing, I hated it more bitterly than I can perhaps make clear. In a job like that you see the dirty work of Empire at close quarters. The wretched prisoners huddling in the stinking cages of the lock-ups, the grey, cowed faces of the long-term convicts, the scarred buttocks of the men who had been flogged with bamboos—all these oppressed me with an intolerable sense of guilt. But I could get nothing into perspective. I was young and ill-educated and I had had to think out my problems in the utter silence that is imposed on every Englishman in the East. I did not even know that the British Empire is dying, still less did I know that it is a great deal better than the younger empires that are going to supplant it. All I knew was that I was stuck between my hatred of the empire I served and my rage against the evil-spirited little beasts who tried to make my job impossible. With one part of my mind I thought of the British Raj as an unbreakable tyranny, as something clamped down, in *saecula saeculorum*, upon the will of prostrate peoples; with another part I thought that the greatest joy in the world would be to drive a bayonet into a Buddhist priest's guts. Feelings like these are the normal by-products of imperialism; ask any Anglo-Indian official, if you can catch him off duty.

One day something happened which in a roundabout way was enlightening. It was a tiny incident in itself, but it gave me a better glimpse than I had had before of the real nature of imperialism—the real motives for which despotic governments act. Early one morning the sub-inspector at a police station the other end of the town rang me up on the 'phone and said that an elephant was ravaging the bazaar. Would I please come and do something about it? I did not known what I could do, but I wanted to see what was happening and I got on to a pony and started out. I took my rifle, an old .44 Winchester and much too small to kill an elephant, but I thought the noise might be used in *terrorem.* Various Burmans stopped me on the way and told me about the elephant's doings. It was not, of course, a wild elephant, but a tame one which had gone "must." It had been chained up, as tame elephants always are when their attack of "must" is due, but on the previous night it had broken its chain and escaped. Its mahout, the only person who could manage it when it was in that state, had set out in pursuit, but had taken the wrong direction and was now twelve hours' journey away, and in the morning the elephant had suddenly reappeared in the town. The Burmese population had no weapons and were quite helpless against it. It had already destroyed somebody's bamboo hut, killed a cow and raided some fruit-stalls and devoured the stock; also it had met the municipal rubbish van and, when the driver jumped out and took to his heels, had turned the van over and inflicted violences upon it.

The Burmese sub-inspector and some Indian constables were waiting for me in the quarter where the elephant had been seen. It was a very poor quarter, a labyrinth of squalid bamboo huts, thatched with palm-leaf, winding all over a steep hillside. I remember that it was a cloudy, stuffy morning at the beginning of the rains. We began questioning the people as to where the elephant had gone and, as usual, failed to get any definite information. That is invariably the case in the East; a story always sounds clear enough at a distance, but the nearer you get to the scene of events the vaguer it becomes. Some of the people said the elephant had gone in one direction, some said that he had gone in another, some professed not even to have heard of any elephant. I had almost made up my mind that the whole story was a pack of lies, when we heard yells a little distance away. There was a loud, scandalized cry of "Go away, child! Go away this instant!" and an old woman with a switch in her hand came round the corner of a hut, violently shooing away a crowd of naked children. Some more women followed, clicking their tongues and exclaiming; evidently there was something that the children ought not to have seen. I rounded the hut and saw a man's dead body sprawling in the mud. He was an Indian, a black Dravidian coolie, almost naked, and he could not have been dead many minutes. The people said that the elephant had come suddenly upon him round the corner of the hut, caught him with its trunk, put its foot on his back, and ground him into the earth. This was the rainy season and the ground was soft, and his face had scored a trench a foot deep and a couple of yards long. He was lying on his belly with arms crucified and head sharply twisted to one side. His face was coated with mud, the eyes wide open, the teeth bared and grinning with an expression of unendurable agony. (Never tell me, by the way, that the dead look peaceful. Most of the corpses I have seen looked devilish.) The friction of the great beast's foot had stripped the skin from his back as neatly as one skins a rabbit. As soon as I saw the dead man I sent an orderly to a friend's house nearby to borrow an elephant rifle. I had already sent back the pony, not wanting it to go mad with fright and throw me if it smelt the elephant.

The orderly came back in a few minutes with a rifle and five cartridges, and meanwhile some Burmans had arrived and told us that the elephant was in the paddy fields below, only a few hundred yards away. As I started forward practically the whole population of the quarter flocked out of the houses and followed me. They had seen the rifle and were all shouting excitedly that I was going to shoot the elephant. They had not shown much interest in the elephant when he was merely ravaging their homes, but it was different now that he was going to be shot. It was a bit of fun to them, as it would be to an English crowd; besides they wanted the meat. It made me vaguely uneasy. I had no intention of shooting the elephant—I had merely sent for the rifle to defend myself if necessary—and it is always unnerving to have a crowd following you. I marched down the hill, looking and feeling a fool, with the rifle over my shoulder and an ever-growing army of people jostling at my heels. At the bottom, when you got away from the huts, there was a metalled road and beyond that a miry waste of paddy fields a thousand yards across, not yet ploughed but soggy from the first rains and dotted with coarse grass. The elephant was standing eight yards from the road, his left side towards us. He took not the slightest notice of the crowd's approach. He was tearing up bunches of grass, beating them against his knees to clean them and stuffing them into his mouth.

I had halted on the road. As soon as I saw the elephant I knew with perfect certainty that I ought not to shoot him. It is a serious matter to shoot a working elephant—it is comparable to destroying a huge and costly piece of machinery —and obviously one ought not to do it if it can possibly be avoided. And at that distance, peacefully eating, the elephant looked no more dangerous than a cow. I thought then and I think now that his attack of "must" was already passing off; in which case he would merely wander harmlessly about until the mahout came back and caught him. Moreover, I did not in the least want to shoot him. I decided that I would watch him for a little while to make sure that he did not turn savage again, and then go home.

But at that moment I galanced round at the crowd that had followed me. It was an immense crowd, two thousand at the least and growing every minute. It blocked the road for a long distance on either side. I looked at the sea of yellow faces above the garish clothes—faces all happy and excited over this bit of fun, all certain that the elephant was going to be shot. They were watching me as they would watch a conjurer about to perform a trick. They did not like me, but with the magical rifle in my hands I was momentarily worth watching. And suddenly I realized that I should have to shoot the elephant after all. The people expected it of me and I had got to do it; I could feel their two thousand wills pressing me forward, irresistibly. And it was at this moment, as I stood there with the rifle in my hands, that I first grasped the hollowness, the futility of the white man's dominion in the East. Here was I, the white man with his gun, standing in front of the unarmed native crowd—seemingly the leading actor of the piece; but in reality I was only an absurd puppet pushed to and fro by the will of those yellow faces behind. I perceived in this moment that when the white man turns tyrant it is his own freedom that he destroys. He becomes a sort of hollow, posing dummy, the conventionalized figure of a sahib. For it is the condition of his rule that he shall spend his life in trying to impress the "natives," and so in every crisis he has got to do what the "natives" expect of him. He wears a mask, and his face grows to fit it. I had got to shoot the elephant. I had committed myself to doing it when I sent for the rifle. A sahib has got to act like a sahib; he has got to appear resolute, to know his own mind and do definite things. To come all that way, rifle in hand, with two thousand people marching at my heels, and then to trail feebly away, having done nothing—no, that was impossible. The crowd would laugh at me. And my whole life, every white man's life in the East, was one long struggle not to be laughed at.

But I did not want to shoot the elephant. I watched him beating his bunch of grass against his knees, with that preoccupied grandmotherly air that elephants have. It seemed to me that it would be murder to shoot him. At that age I was not squeamish about killing animals, but I had never shot an elephant and never wanted to. (Somehow it always seems worse to kill a *large* animal.) Besides, there was the beast's owner to be considered. Alive, the elephant was worth at least a hundred pounds; dead, he would only be worth the value of his tusks, five pounds, possibly. But I had got to act quickly. I turned to some experienced-looking Burmans who had been there when we arrived, and asked them how the elephant had been behaving. They all said the same thing: he took no notice of you if you left him alone, but he might charge if you went too close to him.

It was perfectly clear to me what I ought to do. I ought to walk up to within, say, twenty-five yards of the elephant and test his behavior. If he charged, I could shoot; if he took no notice of me, it would be safe to leave him until the mahout came back. But also I knew that I was going to do no such thing. I was a poor shot with a rifle and the ground was soft mud into which one would sink at every step. If the elephant charged and I missed him, I should have about as much chance as a toad under a steam-roller. But even then I was not thinking particularly of my own skin, only of the watchful yellow faces behind. For at that moment, with the crowd watching me, I was not afraid in the ordinary sense, as I would have been if I had been alone. A white man mustn't be frightened in front of "natives"; and so, in general, he isn't frightened. The sole thought in my mind was that if anything went wrong those two thousand Burmans would see me pursued, caught, trampled on and reduced to a grinning corpse like that Indian up the hill. And if that happened it was quite probable that some of them would laugh. That would never do. There was only one alternative. I shoved the cartridges into the magazine and lay down on the road to get a better aim.

The crowd grew very still, and a deep, low, happy sigh, as of people who see the theatre curtain go up at last, breathed from innumerable throats. They were going to have their bit of fun after all. The rifle was a beautiful German thing with cross-hair sights. I did not then know that in shooting an elephant one would shoot to cut an imaginary bar running from ear-hole to ear-hole. I ought, therefore, as the elephant was sideways on, to have aimed straight at his ear-hole; actually I aimed several inches in front of this, thinking the brain would be further forward.

When I pulled the trigger I did not hear the bang or feel the kick—one never does when a shot goes home—but I heard the devilish roar of glee that went up from the crowd. In that instant, in too short a time, one would have thought, even for the bullet to get there, a mysterious, terrible change had come over the elephant. He neither stirred nor fell, but every line of his body had altered. He looked suddenly stricken, shrunken, immensely old, as though the frightful impact of the bullet had paralysed him without knocking him down. At last, after what seemed a long time—it might have been five seconds, I dare say—he sagged flabbily to his knees. His mouth slobbered. An enormous senility seemed to have settled upon him. One could have imagined him thousands of years old. I fired again into the same spot. At the second shot he did not collapse but climbed with desperate slowness to his feet and stood weakly upright, with legs sagging and head drooping. I fired a third time. That was the shot that did for him. You could see the agony of it jolt his whole body and knock the last remnant of strength from his legs. But in falling he seemed for a moment to rise, for as his hind legs collapsed beneath him he seemed to tower upward like a huge rock toppling, his trunk reaching skywards like a tree. He trumpeted, for the first and only time. And then down he came, his belly towards me, with a crash that seemed to shake the ground even where I lay.

I got up. The Burmans were already racing past me across the mud. It was obvious that the elephant would never rise again, but he was not dead. He was breathing very rhythmically with long rattling gasps, his great mound of a side painfully rising and falling. His mouth was wide open—I could see far down into caverns of pale pink throat. I waited a long time for him to die, but his breathing did not weaken. Finally I fired my two remaining shots into the spot where I though his heart must be. The thick blood welled out of him like red velvet, but still he did not die. His body did not even jerk when the shots hit him, the tortured breathing continued without a pause. He was dying, very slowly and in great agony, but in some world remote from me where not even a bullet could damage him further. I felt that I had got to put an end to that dreadful noise. It seemed dreadful to see the great beast lying there, powerless to move and yet powerless to die, and not even to be able to finish him. I sent back for my small rifle and poured shot after shot into his heart and down his throat. They seemed to make no impression. The tortured gasps continued as steadily as the ticking of a clock.

In the end I could not stand it any longer and went away. I heard later that it took him half an hour to die. Burmans were bringing dahs and baskets even before I left, and I was told they had stripped his body almost to the bones by the afternoon.

Afterwards, of course, there were endless discussions about the shooting of the elephant. The owner was furious, but he was only an Indian and could do nothing. Besides, legally I had done the right thing, for a mad elephant has to be killed, like a mad dog, if its owner fails to control it. Among the Europeans opinion was divided. The older men said I was right, the younger men said it was a damn shame to shoot an elephant for killing a coolie, because an elephant was worth more than any damn Coringhee coolie. And afterwards I was very glad that the coolie had been killed; it put me legally in the right and it gave me a sufficient pretext for shooting the elephant. I often wondered whether any of the others grasped that I had done it solely to avoid looking a fool.

Emerging blackness in a white research world*

Frank Friedlander

The Research methodology of behavioral science is, in part, a reflection of the social forces of our time. It is therefore not surprising that the methodological literature increasingly contains reactions against and challenges to research studies of social irrelevance,[1] research methods which treat human beings imperson-

---

* Reproduced by the permission of the Society for Applied Anthropology from *Human Organization*, Vol. 29, No. 4, Yr. 70.

[1] See, for example, George W. Fairweather, *Methods for Experimental Social Innovation*, New York: John Wiley, 1957; Herbert C. Kelman, *A Time to Speak on Human Values and Social Research*, San Francisco: Jossey-Bass, 1968.

ally and mechanistically,[2] and research findings which are impotent in terms of improving or changing the *status quo.*[3] These pressures toward increased relevance, humanism, and action are also major themes underlying some of the emerging values of contemporary society.[4] The focus of the present study is precisely upon this sort of changing and developing research methodology which is embedded in an intricate network of personal, group, and organizational transactions. The quality and force of these transactions, in turn, is affected by major emerging social issues, and by institutions which themselves are undergoing rapid change.

One of the issues is the reaction against a research emphasis upon external rigor, control and standardization that includes rather questionable assumptions.[5] It assumes, first, that rigorousness is an ideal state which can be more closely approximated as the researcher is able to define his problem and the relevant variables unambiguously. The more easily the variables can be observed and measured, the greater the reliability, future public verifiability and general rigor of the research. Finally, the more control the researcher has over his variables, the more scientifically rigorous his study will be. At the same time,

Our penchant for "control" of variables in our research enterprise is the façade for our penchant for mastery . . . in the larger sense of control of the behavior of others. In the interests of control in research, we select such sets of alternatives which promise the greatest degree of control of the behavior of those whom we study.[6]

Disenchantment with such scientific rigor has produced a growing receptivity to more phenomenological processes. There has been a movement away from research which stereotypes the roles of researcher and subject and maintains the distance between them toward researcher/subject collaboration within a humanistic framework. The movement is away from research in which the primary purpose is to describe and analyze man's basic nature to an increased emphasis on action-research strategies which will identify the steps leading to the improvement of mankind through behavioral, social, and organizational change.[7]

[2] For example, David Bakan, *On Method: Toward a Reconstruction of Psychological Investigation,* San Francisco: Jossey-Bass, 1967; Frank Friedlander, "Behavioral Research as a Transactional Process," *Human Organization,* Vol. 27, 1968, pp. 369–79; Sidney M. Jourard, *Disclosing Man to Himself,* Princeton, New Jersey: Van Nostrand, 1968.

[3] For example, Barney G. Glaser and Anselm L. Strauss, *The Discovery of Grounded Theory: Strategies for Qualitative Research,* Chicago: Aldine, 1967; Fairweather, *Methods;* Bakan, *On Method.*

[4] For example, Rensis Likert, *The Human Organization: Its Management and Value,* New York: McGraw-Hill, 1967; James F. T. Bugental, *Challenges of Humanistic Psychology,* New York: McGraw-Hill, 1967; R. D. Laing, *The Politics of Experience,* New York: Pantheon Books, 1967.

[5] Some of the questionable assumptions are specified by C. Argyris, "Some Unintended Consequences of Rigorous Research," *Psychological Bulletin,* Vol. 70, 1968, pp. 185–97. See also D. Bakan, "The Mystery Master Complex in Contemporary Psychology," *American Psychologist,* Vol. 20, 1965, 186–201.

[6] Bakan, *ibid.,* p. 188.

[7] See, for example, Warren G. Bennis, Kenneth D. Benne, and Robert Chin, *The Planning of Change,* New York: Holt, Rinehart and Winston, 1962.

A second issue concerns the system of values which underlies bureaucracies and which is being seriously challenged in terms of its ability to cope with the demands of changing tasks and human values. The shift here is from formal bureaucratic structures to more participative or organic structures.[8] This, too, is related to traditional research methodologies with their emphasis on rigor and control as these are applied by the researcher and utilized by the bureaucratic executive. "Rigorousness is to a researcher what efficiency is to an executive: an ideal state that is always aspired to, never reached, and continually revered."[9]

A third issue derives from the emerging identity and potency of the black race, with its recent transition from a focus upon integration to that of the formation of a separate cultural identity. The issue is confounded by age and by socioeconomic distinctions in which there is some tendency for the younger and less affluent groups to favor a separate black identity; but it is nevertheless an issue which affects the entire black/white community.[10]

All three of these issues are today arenas of struggle and confusion with respect to maintaining traditional ways, trying to sift out those parts of the traditional which still have merit, and experimenting with and learning new ways. The study described here is a microcosm of those struggles. The principal actors are three units (institutions): (1) a 140-man organization funded by the Government to place 2,000 hard-core unemployed people in stable employment; (2) the "hardcore" who were recruited, trained, and placed in jobs; and (3) a small university research team which designed and conducted an extensive study of attitude changes in the program participants. Each had a distinct set of cultural values which provided its members with a design for living and a ready-made set of solutions for human problems—thus serving a significant adaptive function; and these cultures affected the research methodology.

The first unit was the organization which initiated and conducted the training and placement program—here given the fictitious name RETAP (Recruiting, Training, and Placement). It was established, organized and maintained for the purpose of providing services and jobs for participants in the program. Although it had separate funding, it received some money from the same agency as the research team; but RETAP was located in the central downtown area of the city whereas the research team was based about five miles away in the same city. The second unit was the amorphous group of RETAP participants—a largely unorganized collection of young and mainly (84 percent) Negro men who had, on the average, been unemployed for fifteen weeks prior to job placement through the program. The third unit was an eight-member research team associated with

---

[8] See, for example, Warren G. Bennis, "The Decline of Bureaucracy and Organization of the Future," and "Democracy is Inevitable," in *Changing Organizations*, New York: McGraw-Hill, 1966, pp. 3–33.

[9] Argyris, *op. cit.*, p. 185.

[10] The terms "black" and "Negro" are not synonymous as used in this article. Black implies a strong Afro-American identity in terms of values, behavior, and appearance, and strong pride in these. The term Negro refers to those whose prime reference group is middle-class white Americans.

a large university and funded by a Government agency to do a one-year study of the training and placement program.

It is the interactions between the research team and RETAP participants, and between the research team and the RETAP organization, which is the primary analytical focus of this paper. Only occasional reference will be made to relationships between the RETAP organization and potential or actual trainees since my interest is the research process itself. What happened to the research can be understood in the light of: (1) value differences between traditional and action-oriented research; (2) structural differences between bureaucratic and informal organizations; and (3) cultural differences among the several parties involved in the research. The data for this "research on the research process" (*how* we learned *what* to learn) were gathered primarily through informal participant observation during the course of the more formal research on the RETAP program, and from intensive interviews of members of the three actor units. Where these interviews indicated disagreement among the relevant parties, I have tried to incorporate the divergent views into the following report.

RESEARCH, RUMBLINGS AND REVISION

The research method, as initially proposed, was designed to measure the impact of the training program and job placement on fourteen separate attitudes of the RETAP participants toward work and life.[11] The instruments for doing this were to be administered at three points in time: the day the participant was recruited into the program: the last day of his training; and after he had been placed and was working on a job. In this, our methods during the first few months of the project reflected white middle-class, academically oriented values as to what was important and relevant in research. The methods also stressed rigor, objectivity, standardization, and control in accordance with the team's scientific ideals. As a result the primary mode of communication between RETAP participants and the research team was a rather lengthy questionnaire administed to groups of about ten participants by a white graduate student who personified the culture which had produced the questionnaire.

Observations and informal discussions with participants indicated that they were responding to the questionnaire and the administrator with varying degrees of cooperation, apathy, suspicion, and hostility. Not only did the questionnaire reflect white middle-class concepts and phrases; it also required a vocabulary level which embarrassed and frightened the respondents. Even when the entire questionnaire was read aloud, many participants did not comprehend the meaning of the questions. And for participants who could read well, having the questionnaire read to them was both disturbing and insulting. Their resentment led some

---

[11] This was only one of three major components of the total research effort; but the other parts—impact of the Program upon changes in the companies employing RETAP participants and studies of the effectiveness of the staff organization of the RETAP Program—did not so directly involve relations between researchers and trainees.

to refuse to take the questionnaire, while others initiated disruptions in their groups. Some, too, deliberately falsified responses. Apathetic participants, on the other hand, answered randomly rather than investing the energy necessary for conscientious response. Some participants, however, were cooperative or obedient;[12] they tried to complete the questionnaire and succeeded or failed, depending upon their verbal skills.

The research situation of a white man asking standardized questions about personal attitudes toward work and life reminded participants of similar prior experiences such as being tested in school and in job applications which, as often as not, had resulted in humiliation and failure. Some also had been tested by juvenile court psychologists and reacted negatively to these parts of the questionnaire which resembled psychological tests. Furthermore, a large number of the items in the questionnaire looked as it they were related to job placement in the RETAP Program. So despite our assurances, there was a tendency to give "right" answers just in case we were lying. At a more pervasive level, participants saw no payoff for themselves in the situation. They obviously did not value abstract notions such as "research data," "scientific knowledge," and the like. Much of the questionnaire was therefore completely irrelevant to their here-and-now lives and concerns.[13]

The general response of the research team to these problems was twofold. First, they thought the participants did not understand or appreciate the purposes of the research—a problem that could not readily be solved. On the other hand, they thought the questionnaire was perhaps a bit difficult considering the educational level of the participants. Some revisions were therefore introduced mainly in the form of shortening by removing duplicate or similar items. Wording changes were also made to bring the questionnaire closer to the group's level of understanding; and some response options were changed or reduced—for example, a conventional semantic differential format was replaced by a new experimental pictorial form. The intent was to make the questionnaire more palatable and less tedious, but the revisions did not change the basic method or climate of the transaction between the research team and the participants. The questionnaire remained an impersonally administered white instrument designed to extract information of relevance to the researcher as quickly and efficiently as possible.

At this point, the research team decided that a Negro research assistant was a necessary addition to the team in order to establish better rapport with participants. The team felt that it needed a person who could relate effectively to the

---

[12] See, for example, S. Milgram, "Behavioral Study of Obedience," *Journal of Abnormal and Social Psychology*, Vol. 67, 1963, pp. 371–78; M. T. Orne, "On the Social Psychology of the Psychological Experiment: With Particular Reference to Demand Characteristics and Their Implications," *American Psychologist*, Vol. 17, 1962, pp. 776–83; R. Rosenthal, "Experimenter Outcome-Orientation and the Results of the Psychological Experiment," *Psychological Bulletin*, Vol. 61, 1964, pp. 405–12.

[13] More severe objections to a research method or goal are particularly likely to be voiced by research subjects who also serve as clients in the same system. The client role may lead them to question not only the training program, but especially the research conditions. See, for example, Stewart E. Perry, *The Human Nature of Science*, New York: The Free Press, 1966.

white academic community as represented by the research team; to the levels of the black community represented by the hard-core unemployed and militant RETAP participants; and to middle-class employees of the RETAP organization which was about 90 percent Negro. The team talked of the creative impact such a person might have on the research process and on the RETAP system, including the black participants.

Chuck, a Negro, was therefore hired as Research Assistant. He was a high school graduate who had held a variety of jobs in the past and had spent the previous year in Europe. Impressed by the opportunity to help and attracted by the possibility of university association, he accepted the job offer despite some ambivalence. He felt that working with underprivileged elements of his own race would help him get a better grip on what it meant to be black, independent of white criteria and standards. At the same time, he was concerned about his competence in a university research group, and had a vague uneasiness about being misused as a black infiltrator among his own people. In retrospect, he states that his primary position was that of a "Negro," which he defined (again retrospectively) as a "secondhand middle-class person who feels one up on his brothers in the ghetto on the basis of his contacts in both white and black worlds; he prefers to live in the middle-class Negro community or an integrated community." At the time of his appointment, however, he did not communicate this ambivalence to the research team which put a "man for all seasons" identity on him on the basis of their perceptions of his flexibility and their vague and limited notions of what should be done to make the research instrument acceptable to RETAP participants.

For the next month or two, both the research team and the RETAP organization were relatively satisfied with the progress of the research project. The research team felt that Chuck was implementing the concepts and methods they were dedicated to. The staff of the RETAP organization felt that whatever research was needed was being done, although in general they perceived research as superfluous to the organization's existence and growth since its sole purpose was to recruit, train and place in jobs some 2,000 previously unemployed (and unemployable) persons in the first year of operation. Its four departments—Recruitment, Training, Placement, Job Coaching—were highly bureaucratized, thus favoring impersonal and formal movement of the participants through the organization to be ultimately registered quantitatively as so many job placements.

Actually, both the research team and the RETAP organization were acting as bureaucratic mechanisms with a job to do. For the research team, this meant administering an increasing number of questionnaires and processing them through keypunch and computer sequences. Using sheer numbers as a criterion of success, and designing ways to maximize these numbers, is a disease of convenience in modern society which both the research team and RETAP organization suffered from—the former by viewing large numbers of completed questionnaires as an indication of success, the latter by using the large numbers of participants processed through its pogram as dramatic evidence to cite to all agencies or persons concerned with the program. For the researchers at this period, it was a matter of proceeding along well-planned, highly structured and efficient ways of asking their previously posed questions. There was some concern with improving procedures and methods in the interests of accuracy and reliability, but little concern with obtaining any feedback from respondents on the basic meaning and relevance of what was being done.

During this same period, Chuck began to experience certain internal dissonance around the task itself, largely as a result of feedback from participants depicting their (continued) suspicion, hostility, and apathy toward the questionnaire but also, in part, because of his own reactions to the questionnaire and the testing milieu. This was reflected in a view of himself as being used by white people to act instrumentally upon his own people. He stated that the entire RETAP research was contaminated by its whiteness—white assumptions and methodology; white language in the research instrument; white rigidity and standardization of the form; white administrative notions such as expectations about processing certain numbers of participants per day; white in its failure to realize that participants experience the world in gross terms, not the subtle ones asked for on the questionnaire; and white in terms of using a questionnaire administered at three points in time so as to measure change. Concerning the black concept of time, for example, Chuck pointed out:

Time means nothing to a black—he doesn't do anything with his time—that's where he is. To a guy who stands on a corner for six months, an appointment at ten o'clock means nothing—his life is on that corner—like nothing happens in terms of time—nothing happens in the ghetto in terms of time—you don't plan ahead.

These temporal conceptualizations are drastically different from the "structure geometry" (as Chuck referred to it) of the research design and of the whites on the research team.

While Chuck, as Research Assistant, understood the procedural mechanisms of the research process, he felt somewhat overwhelmed by his inability to understand the underlying research concepts, language, and methods, and by his inability to express himself in response to these feelings. This, however, did not cause him to play a passive role in terms of either being used as an instrument or administering an instrument. As RETAP participants increasingly confronted him with their suspicion, hostility, and apathy toward the questionnaire, and as he sensed the irrelevance of the questionnaire, Chuck's feelings of being manipulated by the research team intensifed.

Why should I have to give this white, irrelevant, uncomprehendable questionnaire to those guys down there? It doesn't mean anything to them, and the way they're filling it out, it can't really mean anything to the research team.

He therefore pressed for changes; specifically, he claimed the questionnaire was too long and repetitive, was composed of white middle-class jargon, and was too impersonal when administered to large groups of twelve participants. He proposed creating a more natural interview setting in which he would ask the participants in small groups of two or three, and in his (and their) own language, the items in the questionnaire, and then discuss responses with them.

The research team resisted. Such alterations posed the threat of introducing unknown sources of variance into the final research results. The Principal Researcher, for example, claimed:

> These suggested changes will lower the reliability of the instruments. We just won't know whether changes indicated by the questionnaire responses in work attitudes are the result of modifications in the questionnaire, in the method of administration, or in the actual attitudes of participants. And besides—the two-man interview session will be more time consuming and is bound to reduce our sample size. And yet . . . I realize that that our current method is a very impersonal, mechanistic one, and creates a relationship between Chuck and participants which provides mechanistic impersonal data . . . data with questionable validity.

Thus, while the research team resisted changes in the research processes, it also realized the inadequacies in the current processes. The forces causing its resistance stemmed from identification with what is viewed as respectable behavioral science—rigor, control, standardization, and consistency of data gathering methods and variables. The energy toward change, on the other hand, derived from the team's fresh realizations that the current method was alien to the Research Assistant, the RETAP participants, and to the relationship between these two parties. The data produced from this relationship were likely to be not only irrelevant but invalid. The central issue for the research team seemed to be whether it would act on its new learning about the irrelevance of the current research process or whether it would prolong the current methodology so as to proclaim greater assurance of its findings at the end of the project. The latter assurance would come from a larger sample size, and more consistent instrumentation and administration.

The team's decision was to change from a formal group-administered questionnaire (with up to twelve participants) to a smaller, structured interview setting. Here two participants were brought together informally to respond to the questionnaire. The Research Assistant read the items directly from the questionnaire, but also had an opportunity to explain their meaning. He was able to talk with participants, and their questions or comments were encouraged.

The research team provided itself with a scientific rationale for this decision. It set up a comparative methodological substudy in which the results from the prior method of formal group-administered questionnaire were compared to those of the new informal structured-interview method.

NEGRO AND BLACK IN A BUREAUCRATIC CONTEXT

During the first few months, the upper echelons of the RETAP organization perceived Chuck as a "token test administrator" only. Chuck himself used the word "token" in the sense that his job was to give questionnaires in accordance with middle-class bureaucratic (mass production) concepts of processing certain numbers of people in certain amounts of time. The message he was hearing from both the research team and the RETAP administration was, "You don't have time to do anything except administer questionnaires. You're the Research Assistant and this is another thing over here. This is big business." More specifically, he heard members of the research team saying that he was to relate to blacks— but his job was only to administer a certain number of questionnaires to a certain number of people each day. This role stereotype was soon picked up by the RETAP administration. This fit well with its intended role for him, since the organization did not want him as an active agent in feeding back information about the program to the participants, to the RETAP administration, or to the research team. Thus, the various pressures on the Assistant as he interacted with all three parties facilitated a dual role. On one hand, he was to perform a job—the administration of a certain quantity of questionnaires per time period. On the other hand, he was to establish rapport with participants, but not let these ties and relationships deter him from his officially designated task assignment. He states that the intensity of his internal dissonance increased during this time as a result of his relating to the research team as a Negro, to the participants increasingly as a black brother, and to the RETAP Negro staff as a "troublemaker on the side of the participants."

The first consistent negative reactions to the Assistant were from elements in the RETAP organization. According to Chuck, elements in the organization felt that the ideal participant was a conservatively dressed, clean looking Negro. In his selection of participants for questionnaire administration, he would go from class to class, picking "down-and-outers"—which included not only economically and educationally disadvantaged participants, but also those in African dress whom the RETAP administration was attempting to influence toward more acceptable dress. Chuck claimed:

Members of the RETAP bureaucracy criticized me for picking the participants I picked, ignoring the others I picked. The power structure at RETAP was Negro and they wanted research participants in that same image.

The reaction of both the RETAP administration and the research team to the "down-and-outer" selection method was to enforce a more random method. The Assistant was instructed to select participants by using their roster number. This method fulfilled the needs of both the research team and the RETAP administration, but for different reasons. For the research team, randomization was essential to prevent biased results, and was thus in accord with the scientific culture. For the RETAP administration, randomization meant that unbalanced attention and relationships would not be established with a subculture that was contrary to the norms it hoped to establish.

Chuck's identification with black participants and his resentment of the Negro RETAP bureaucracy were both increasing in intensity. He resented the bureaucratic way that the participants were being handled. He relates, for example, the following incident:

Participants are coming up to me and saying, "I'm getting a raw deal." For example, they say they wanted to go to barber school because that's what they wanted to do, and they would go over to the vocational opportunity section, but the guy there would tell them that's all you guys want to do—go to barber school. Well, you know that's very offensive to me personally. Almost secondarily, I was considering what was happening to the participant. So I would say to him, "Go back to the guy, or I will go over there with you and ask him what he said to you." And I'd just go with him, because I couldn't believe this could actually happen. Then I'd go to an administrator or whoever was on top of the situation, and tell him, "Do you know what this guy just said to this participant?" And he'd say, "Well, you know . . . but that doesn't concern you. . . ." He just kind of passed it off. And I take it back to the research team and talk about it there and it would get passed off there, too. And I'd really get annoyed. Why should I do what they're asking me to do when much more important things are taking place—much more important data is being produced?

Chuck's identification with black participants and increasing alienation from both the research team and the RETAP administration were intricately related to his changing appearance during the first few months of the program. During the first few weeks on the job, he had dressed in typical white collar, tie, and suit jacket. The next step was to don wire-rimmed glasses and grow a beard. Chuck relates the sequence of events as follows:

They responded to my beard and wire-rim glasses, symbols of the new generation, the new people, "in" and ahead of what's happening. Then one of the fellows in the program, a Muslim, gave me a skull cap from Africa, and it was just kind of a cool thing to wear—and I wore it. And the response from the RETAP administration was just overwhelmingly negative. That's when they started to tack Black Nationalist and Muslim labels on me. And that's when I realized that if that was happening to me, that's what's happening to the participants who are Black Nationalists or Muslim as well as the ones who are just not very well-dressed people. And that's when I started to take a very strong identification— "I'm with this guy over here—and you're wrong—and you can't criticize me because I'm part of the research team." There was some power I was feeling, and at that point I was starting to use it. And I started to wear a dashiki[14]—and I felt that if that put RETAP administrators uptight, it's okay for them to be uptight 'cause I'm not going to get fired. I knew the research team would support me—they had said that my rapport with participants was an important part of my job. Wearing the costume was not pseudo for me either. It was where I was 'cause I'd been put uptight by both sides now [the research team as well as the RETAP administrators].

There were differences of opinion concerning the impact of Chuck's African garb upon the various levels within the RETAP organization. He himself perceived the upper echelons of the RETAP administration as becoming increasingly distressed. The staff could not openly challenge his African dress, and therefore felt awkward in challenging participants who dressed similarly. But he saw the younger staff beginning to share with him more of their disappointment with the program, particularly as it related to the way the bureaucracy was treating participants. While upper-levels were reacting negatively to his dress and

---

[14] A dashiki is a shirt-like African garment now worn by many American blacks.

to his militant role, lower-levels were reacting positively to these same characteristics and to his pertinent questions and attempts to assist the organization in being more helpful to the participants.

RETAP administrators, meanwhile, viewed Chuck's dress as causing curiosity and interest, but not as establishing rapport with the lower-levels in the organization. According to upper-level administrators, much of the organization staff saw his dress as inappropriate, particularly since the organization was attempting to prepare participants for greater acceptance within the white industrial community. As one administrator mentioned:

Chuck's dress was contrary to what we were trying to do. We were trying not to force the differences in our participants upon potential employers, but to blend them as much as possible. It's much harder to get a job with a dashiki—to buck those social norms. Many would wear African garb if we let them, but it certainly wouldn't help in getting them jobs. Chuck's African dress is an artificial way of establishing a relationship with participants. It doesn't help any.

Chuck's increasing resentment toward the system in which he was operating caused him to ask deeper questions of the participants and of persons in the lower echelons of the RETAP staff:

For example, I challenged a grooming instructor who criticized a black whose hair had been straightened and who wore an Oleg Casini sweater and forty-dollar shoes. The participant was told he wasn't clean and sharp. What was really meant is that the man would make a bad impression in white society.

Many such comments by Chuck were fed back to the RETAP administration. He reports that he was getting an increasing reputation as a Black Nationalist because "I'm taking a blacker—stronger, more questioning, more solid with my own kind—position than middle-class Negroes in the RETAP power structure who identified with both black and white camps."

As perceived by Chuck, his image was an increasing threat to the RETAP bureaucracy. It was in sharp contrast to their initial role stereotype of him as a questionnaire administrator. Asking questions of participants was relatively harmless, particularly since answers were fed back primarily to the research team. But asking questions of the RETAP lower echelons about the quality of services offered might result in a negative image of the organization and lowered morale for its members. On the other hand, the upper echelons saw Chuck's interactions with the lower echelons as having less impact. They tended to deny Chuck's confrontations concerning his own relevance to the organization.

At this point, Chuck was enjoying the potency and individuality of this new-found role:

I'm putting on a costume and I'm starting to really like who I am—and who I'm rejecting. And I know it's alienating a large part of the organization. But that's okay with me because I'm no longer identifying with that. That was the transition between the suit and the dashiki. What right do I have to wear a suit? I'm becoming more accepted when I come into that classroom. And I'm still from the University.

Chuck felt strength was derived from being heard—from pointing out the weakness and irrelevance of the research project and the RETAP Program. When he confronted these issues, he felt potent—and black. And, reaffirming his affiliation with the University research team to participants gained for him additional social acceptability.

RESEARCH NEEDS: BLACK REVISION AND WHITE STABILITY

While maintaining his label as a member of the research team in order to legitimize his presence in the RETAP program, Chuck continued to try to change the kind of research being performed. He reported to the research team that the content, conceptual framework, and language of the instruments were still foreign and irrelevant to the black culture which, he hoped, would be the beneficiary of the research. He stressed the complete impotency of the instrument and the research for effecting any change in the RETAP program in order to make it more useful and relevant to his black brothers:

Here I started to realize that I was low man on the research team. As I fed back my reactions about how we were not collecting relevant data and how participants really felt about going through the program . . . from good to terrible . . . and how our research design and questionnaire ignored all of this, I realized that the research team wasn't paying any meaningful attention to me. They talked about doing later studies but at the same time I saw this study missing a lot that would be valuable to the participants and their lives today. One member of the research team in particular would try to understand and empathize but would repeatedly insist that we had a bigger commitment to the original design and to produce a systematic and consistent analysis of the changes in participant's attitudes.

While the passage of time increased Chuck's awareness of the need for changes in the research method, it increased equally the resistance of the research team to modification of its method. In the words of the Principal Researcher:

With nearly two-thirds of the research project completed, it would be silly for us to change anything in the questionnaire. It would be almost like starting a new study. We really need to standardize our instrument and procedures as much as possible. . . . We need to strive for greater consistency, and not change our procedures every time we find something new. We need to build up our sample size so as to build up a solid groundwork of knowledge about these people and their problems. If we keep changing our design, we'll wind up with nothing.

It is clear that what was "nothing" for the Principal Researcher was a very important "something" for the Research Assistant, and what was meaningful to the Principal Researcher was seen as irrelevant to the Research Assistant. The contrasting values of what was an important, valid, and relevant research process suggested very different research strategies and action steps.

At one point, realizing his futility in trying to change the research design, Chuck suggested that a new questionnaire administrator be hired, since this was a simple and mechanical job. This, in his mind, would release him to perform the more valuable functions of counseling and guiding participants at the RETAP center. The response from another member of the research team to this suggestion was:

While it makes a lot of sense, it would decrease the validity of the research instrument since a new questionnaire administrator would obviously conduct himself in different ways . . . and cause variance in responses due more to questionnaire administrators than changes in participants' attitudes.

Again, the scientific upbringing and culture in which the research team existed dictated a sense of responsiblity for maintaining a relatively rigorous and consistent research format. These demands for consistency not only confined Chuck to his previously established role, but prohibited him from moving out of that role (except by resigning from the research team).

Scientific considerations were not the sole basis for the research team's increasing resistance to the Research Assistant and his suggestions. During the first few months of the program, a gradual distrust of his intentions had been growing among members of the research team. Many of his suggestions and criticisms of the research design were seen as simply efforts to avoid his assigned functions or to enable him to live a more casual and free life at the RETAP center. As the program progressed, team members began to distrust reports by Chuck of the number of participants he had interviewed, or whether he had even come to work on certain occasions. When he met with research team members, the latter became increasingly wary of his intentions, requests, and reported findings. There were growing but unexpressed feelings that he might be taking advantage of potential guilt feelings of white team members to gain leeway in his job behavior in the RETAP program. The research team gradually began to feel used by the Research Assistant just as the Assistant had earlier felt used by the research team.

In order to make his role more acceptable to the RETAP organization, Chuck was instructed not to report information directly to the RETAP administrators. This made him anxious and impatient with the research team. He took it as a personal rejection and was hurt that the research team would not pass on his "actual research" results to the organization in a powerful way, or pass on his informal results in a way that would be heard, since he himself had tried to pass them on and had been criticized for the effort. His reaction is typified by the following comments:

The research team starts giving me this "this is what you're supposed to be doing" stuff: . . . you can't say officially to a RETAP staff man what is really on your mind or even ask him what's on his. You did this last week and someone squealed and now we're on the spot. Basically, don't talk to administrators and staff. Just give the questionnaire and talk only to participants.

Chuck now saw himself rejected by both RETAP and the research team. He saw only one channel for his commitment and identification—the participants themselves. He thus developed greater intimacy with several participants and came to be respected and sought after by them for informal counseling and advice on the workings of the system, including the best places to complain and seek redress. These activities occupied up to half of his time, thus leaving the other half for his more legitimate research duties. This caused a good deal of resentment on the part of the research team. As one member commented:

He was the key . . . the key link between the team and the participants. We depended upon him heavily, and when he spent half of his time on his research functions, we really felt he was letting us down. That's when we started applying some bureaucratic pressures on him to perform adequately.

The Research Assistant looks back on this division of time with some guilt, but not nearly enough to compensate for the strong feelings of potency and benefit he felt he was having on the RETAP program and the participants. His feelings of loyalty and commitment to the research team and to the research were drastically reduced. In retrospect, he reports this reduced commitment to the research as follows:

I felt no ownership of the data—why should I feel I'm doing something important when I saw no way that it was helping the blacks? It's whitey taking another look at us again—without helping.

He felt sufficiently used—and embarrassed and resentful about being used—that he occasionally specified to participants the only rules of the game he saw as equitable to both parties. For example, when giving the third administration of the questionnaire (for which participants were paid five dollars), he would say, "Look man, it's honkey money . . . just play the game and you'll get your five dollars."

At this point, the Assistant developed what he considered his own private research design which he communicated to no one. He recollects that he was no longer interested in the "faulty instrument and the worthless results it was producing." He would not administer the instrument and focused instead on the feelings and reactions of the participants alone. There was, however, nothing he could do with the information he had collected since his communications channels to the RETAP organization and the research team were sealed, from his point of view. He compensated as best he could by directing the participants to others in the system who might be able to help. He states:

I could see that it was wrong to administer the questionnaires at all so I stopped doing it. The whites have no right to ask a black person to do this kind of work because it really isn't helping the participants. It has nothing to do with the job-getting process which is of vital concern to the participants. It was only to measure the effectiveness of the RETAP and it did this imperfectly because of the white instrument and the impossibility of feedback that would be heard. I still went downtown to the RETAP center but only did the things that were important to me with the participants. I knew guys would come up and talk to me. I didn't even have to ask them.

In retrospect, he feels that his action role was greatly enhanced by the prior experience and identification with the research team.

The fact that I was part of a research team gave me a research identity and I started behaving like a researcher would behave . . . like not being biased against data which are contradictory to my own thinking . . . to be able to conceptualize what's happening . . . to move with the data. So it's not like I came in just like an advisor or action man, but I was aware of the kind of thing we call science: something open and unbiased to whatever is being said rather than straight advocacy of something. The science approach means I can be clearer on the kinds of data I collect. Because I know what research is, I can use it for action purposes. It's like I'm a free musician . . . my music grows out of my emotion and whatever I'm playing. So I forget the rules . . . I don't use the rules . . . but the rules invariably come out because the first thing I got in touch with are the rudimentary things about the music.

SUMMARY AND CONCLUSION

It should now be clear that the research process in this study was the result of a complex set of interacting, and often conflicting, values. These values coincided, in large part, with the three institutional units in the study. The first was a respect for science and what it presents as a rigorous means of acquiring knowledge—at the expense of action, particularly action which involves change in design. This set of values pervaded the research team, which saw its function as one of designing a thorough and rigorous research instrument to carry forward and possibly refine throughout the term of the project. The results from this instrument would then be subjected to a complex statistical analysis which would contribute to a body of knowledge about job attitudes and changes in these. Intermingled with the values of science were white middle-class concepts of work, life-style, time, and ethics which were strongly reflected both in the research questionnaire and in the manner in which the data were collected. Although the research team was a relatively small group (never more than eight people), it found itself increasingly utilizing bureaucratic mechanisms in order to control the quantity and quality of its product.

The second set of values were those found within the RETAP administration which saw itself as a mechanism for turning out large numbers of people oriented toward and ready for employment within a white middle-class society with white middle-class concepts of dress, work, and life style. Just as the research concepts and methods emanated from a white middle-class society, so also did the RETAP program despite the fact that it was administered by Negroes. One of its expressed purposes was to prepare unemployed blacks for white society and for greater acceptability by white employers. Training programs of this type involve efforts to subvert cultural characteristics which are defensive reactions to white society and alien to that society. David Wellman describes a similar program as follows:

The desire for work was not the problem. The real problem was what the program demanded of the young men. It asked that they change their manner of speech and dress, that they ignore their lack of skills and society's lack of jobs, and that they act as if their arrest records were of no consequence in obtaining a job. It asked most important, that they pretend *they*, and not society, bore the responsibility for their being unemployed. TIDE (the Program) didn't demand much of the men: Only that they become white.[15]

In order to cope with the diversity of backgrounds and education of people coming in to their program and to produce large quantities (about 2,000) of "oriented," job-ready people, the RETAP administration set up a "production line" in which the individual idiosyncrasies and special needs of some participants became impediments to the goals of training and placing large numbers of people. Bureaucratic mechanisms were established to maintain uniformity and quantity on this production line. Research on this operation, and specifically on the quantity of its output in terms of participant's changed attitudes, was considered by RETAP as superfluous as best and at worst as a potential threat should its inadequacy be exposed.

The third set of values were those held by the large mass of RETAP participants. Since this was an unorganized group, it is difficult to pinpoint its value system. From the fact that they were predominately black, of a relatively low education level, and obviously unemployed, we can infer that their values centered largely on their needs for a job and financial stability, and for recognition and acceptance of the integrity of their life-style.

The research team, realizing the inadequacy of its relationship with the participants, hired a Negro on the somewhat vague and ill-founded expectation that he would identify with the black participants sufficiently to establish rapport but at the same time play the more science-oriented role of questionnaire administrator. This Negro research assistant could, theoretically, have identified with and acted according to the values of either the research team or the RETAP organization. As it turned out, he identified with neither. Instead, he identified strongly with the black participants and found a potent role in acting in their behalf. He found both white science and the Negro RETAP organization irrelevant to the plight of the participants and unresponsive to his own needs and values as a potent black individual.

The action role of the Research Assistant was never legitimized by either the RETAP administration or the research team; and both put continual pressure on him—the research team to be instrumental in gathering data, and the RETAP organization not to raise issues around either its inadequacies in mass-producing job placements or the value differences between Negro staff and black participants. Yet if the Assistant had stopped pushing and confronting issues, less learning would have occurred in both the research team and the RETAP organization. It was the Assistant's sense of potency and conviction (despite an initial feeling of the "scariness" in the face of white research) that enabled some

_____
[15] David Wellman, "The Wrong Way to Find Jobs for Negroes," *Trans-action*, Vol. 5, No. 5, 1968, p. 10.

members of both the research team and the RETAP organization to become aware of what was happening and what was not happening. And it was the awareness of the separate "Negro" and "black" elements within himself that allowed the Research Assistant to act or not to act in terms of these two parts. In his own words:

The Negro is not a pusher, and part of me is Negro . . . and this part was telling me to shut up and play it cool. The Negro in me accepts the white *status quo*. It was the black in me that was pushing for changes in both the RETAP program and the research. And it takes a lot of "blackness" to research a black program.

One of the paramount issues raised by the processes discussed in this paper is the meaning and spirit of research. I assume that research is a process whereby one learns systematically about a set of events or people in order to provide a better framework for understanding and action. But perhaps of even greater importance, this research project has indicated an additional dimension; namely that *research is also a process of learning* how *and* what *to learn*. It shows us what is relevant to learn and to understand, how to acquire this learning and under-standing, and how to act upon this learning and understanding in order to learn about what to learn next. This contrasts sharply with the more traditional concept of research as a prestructured, well-thought-out design and methodology for acquiring and building a body of knowledge from a preestablished set of questions or hypotheses.[16]

Most traditional research makes the assumption that the researcher already knows what should be learned. For him, therefore, learning what to learn is not a function of the research process. In fact, such learning upsets his initial plans, and he resists it. But in so resisting, he cuts off those who *are* learning what to learn, learning what to act on, and acting on what they have learned. For example, at one point the Research Assistant commented "I always thought research was looking around and finding out what was happening. When I heard, 'we can't do this and we can't do that,' I thought . . . well we're doing research, why can't we do it?"

Learning how to learn and how to act upon this learning becomes a discovery process, and a highly turbulent one since it is unpredictable. If the researcher's learning results from his observations of the participants' learning, questions arise about how much the researcher should act upon this new learning. Traditional behavioral science tells us that if a researcher is to study changes in another person, the researcher must stay constant—or change in a known way—in order to draw accurate inferences about the direction and magnitude of change in what he is measuring. Yet if the research is successful in inducing change, it produces new knowledge which it would seem naive for the researcher not to act upon.

---

[16] For some similar conclusions about the nature of the research process, see Glaser and Strauss, *Discovery*, pp. 229–232; Bakan, "The Mystery Master Complex," p. xiii; and Sidney M. Jourard, "To Be or Not to Be . . . Transparent," in Sidney M. Jourard (ed.) *To Be or Not to Be . . . Existential-Psychological Perspectives on the Self*, University of Florida Monographs, Social Sciences No. 34, University of Florida Press, Gainesville, 1967, pp. 27–36.

Thus, a successful program creates changes in participants, thereby teaching the researcher something new. If he acts upon this learning, and changes either the set of variables being studied or the methodology being used, he changes also the complete set of parameters which guide the research.

It seems obvious from our own research experience that we were studying and trying to understand changes in ourselves as researchers as well as changes in the RETAP participants. In fact, because we learned, revised, and changed, we could view both the research process and the participants from each of our newly revised perspectives. We learned about the insignificance and irrelevance of both what we were trying to learn and the way we were trying to learn it. As this happened, our concern grew about the data we were not collecting. "Knowing" was learning about what we were not learning. The more we became aware of our own learning process, the more we become aware that we were not learning much from our own research results. But members of the research team also found that persistent parts within themselves represented the more traditional research methodologies, and these values prevented us from making any drastic changes. We therefore found ourselves learning more and more about what to learn, but clinging tenaciously to our preestablished research designs and "scientific" values.

EMERGING WHITENESS: AN EPILOGUE

I have presented many of the research issues in this paper in the context of a Negro/black identity crisis in Chuck. I might have equally well described these same issues in terms of the white identity crisis in each of the rest of us in the white research team. While Chuck was the symbol of activity, relevance, freedom and exploration in his research, and while he represented a closeness and concern for those whom he studied, many of these same values and characteristics were in each of us as white researchers. But these parts were timid, unspoken, unreleased—shrouded by other parts which sought the continuity, control, certainty, and distance of our research tradition. The struggle between these two parts within each of us resulted in shades of gray rather than stark white researchers.

By differentiating these separate parts within us, by becoming sensitive to the feelings that each arouses within us, we can arrive at a more constructive integration of these parts. We can respond primarily from a part of us that represents the traditional researcher or from a part that represents the active, free, relevant explorer: a part that wants to increase the distance between the other and us in order to understand him, and a part that wants to learn through collaboration and intimacy with him—a part which treats the other as the subject of our study, and a part that treats us as the principal subject of our own experimental intervention—a part that is concerned only with our hypotheses about the other, and a part that is concerned with the other's hypotheses about us—a part that wants to preserve continuity, and a part that wants to facilitate and enact change—a part that strives to maximize the certainty and parsimony of our explanations, and a part that strives to enrich the fertility of our experience—a part that wants to build impregnability into our findings, and a part that wants to build sensitivity into our learning processes—a part that wants to nail something down once and for all, and a part that wants to be on the lookout for fresh perspectives and alternative constructions of man—a part that wants to seek everlasting truth, and a part that wants to let transient truths pattern our search—a part that wants to prove the realities of the inevitable, and a part that wants to explore and implement the impossible dream.

Thus, the issue in this paper is not merely an emerging blackness in a white research world, but an emerging whiteness in a kaleidoscopic world; not only an identity crisis for the Negro and black, but one also for the white researcher; not merely compromise with the rigor of traditional scientific norms, but also compromise with the human qualities of knowledge and the knowledge of human qualities; not just the fear of becoming less rigorous in the research process, but also the fear of becoming more human, more free, more spontaneous, more open, more active, and more relevant. These are the major issues which the researcher faces. Their resolution becomes increasingly imperative as the researcher finds himself more peripheral to contemporary social forces and more incidental to contemporary human relationships. If the researcher can integrate his humanness and his science, his human experimentation and his scientific experimentation, then research can become a vital part of the on-going human enterprise.

Prophecy fails again: A report of a failure to replicate[*]

Jane Allyn Hardyck and Marcia Braden[1]

On July 4 of a recent year, a group of 135 men, women, and children vanished from their homes in a small southwestern town. Their homes were sealed; the

[*] Reprinted in its entirety from Jane Allyn Hardyck and Marcia Braden, "Prophecy Fails Again: A Report of a Failure to Replicate." *J. Abn. Soc. Psychol.*, Vol. 65, No. 2 (1962), pp. 136–41. Footnotes renumbered. Used by permission.

[1] This investigation was carried out during the tenure of a Predoctral Research Fellowship from the National Science Foundation to the first author and a Predoctoral Research Fellowship from the National Institute of Mental Health, United States Public Health Service, to the second author. The collection of data was undertaken in cooperation with the Studies in International Conflict and Integration, Stanford University, directed by Robert North. The authors would like to thank Larry Robertson, who helped in collecting the data, and Leon Festinger, who helped by his criticisms of many drafts of this paper.

windows were covered with newspapers; the cluster of houses was deserted. The only message they had left was a sign on the door of their church, reading "Gone for two weeks, camp meeting."

The neighbors of the group and the town officials soon discovered where the members of the Church of the True Word[2] had gone. In response to prophecies of a forthcoming nuclear disaster, the group had for many months been building and stocking underground fallout shelters, with as much secrecy as possible. On July 4, one of their prophets received a message, "The Egyptians are coming; get ye to the safe places," and they immediately obeyed what they believed to be a command from God. They were huddled in their shelters, awaiting the nuclear catastrophe. For 42 days and nights they remained there, in expectation of imminent disaster. While they stubbornly sat underground, the authors walked around the hot, dusty desert town piecing together the history of the group from interviews with townspeople and the few group members who, disillusioned, left the shelters.

The Church of the True Word is an evangelical Christian church associated with the Pentecostal movement. Its members believe in the Bible as the literal word of God and accept as operating today the gifts of the Holy Spirit delineated in First Corinthians of the New Testament, Chapters 12 and 14. These gifts include speaking and interpreting tongues, personal prophecy, and healing by faith. The titular head of the group, a Mrs. Shepard, is their minister and chief prophet, although important decisions are made only after she has consulted with two of the group members, Peter Jameson and David Blake, both of whom are also ordained ministers.

The "colony," as they call themselves, springs from two main sources. Mrs. Shepard established a following about 5 years ago in the small southwestern town, and soon began work on the present church building. In this, she had the help of Jameson and Blake, who at the time were missionaries to Central America from two congregations in the Middle West. The second source of members of the Church of the True Word was these midwestern churches.

Even in the early days of her ministry, Mrs. Shepard was preaching preparedness for nuclear attack, and almost 4 years ago a prophecy was received in the Midwest to the effect that "in fewer years than I have fingers on my right hand" there would be nuclear devastation. The more recent history of the Church of the True Word began with another prophecy. On November 23, 8 months before the group finally went underground, a prophet in the Midwest received word that "you have 6 months to prepare." On receiving this message, Blake, Jameson, and various others packed up and moved to the Southwest and about February began to build fallout shelters and homes.

The shelters were built "through the inspiration of God," according to the specifications of Civil Defense, which is, for these people, "the Noah's Ark of today." They were not designed as bomb shelters, since the group believed that

---

[2] This is a fictitious name which, we believe, captures the flavor of the actual name of the group. All other names and places used in this paper have been similarly disguised.

their town would receive only fallout from a direct hit on Desert City, which lay 50 miles to the west. There were probably five large shelters under houses and four smaller ones dug in an open field nearby. The larger ones were quite livable, although far from luxurious, as they lacked modern plumbing and were rather badly ventilated. The shelters were stocked with canned and dehydrated food, large cans of water, and other necessities, and were provided with generators for use when public power failed.

For the group to make such careful and extensive preparations, they must have had a rather clear and specific idea of what was to happen. Indeed they did. From a particular interpretation of portions of the Book of Revelation, they believed that about one-third of the population of the earth would be wiped out by nuclear warfare and that injuries and sickness would be widespread among the survivors. The members of the Church of the True Word also expected that after the disaster they would receive special powers from God so that they might perform miracles of healing beyond what they were already able to do, and might be enabled to spread the gospel to all nations within the short space of about a year. It was the necessity of saving themselves for this purpose that dictated that they must keep their preparations secret. They feared that if the location and nature of their shelters were generally known, they would be unable to prevent others from breaking in at the time of the attack, thus creating a situation in which no one could survive.

From February until the "deadline" of May 23, many more families from the midwest congregations arrived to join in the preparations. There were also, of course, several families from the local community who were members of the church and who helped in the work. The shelters were not finished by May 23, and much apprehension arose among the members of the group. In an anxious flurry of preparations they waited until July 4, when they received the message, we believe through Mrs. Shepard, "The Egyptians are coming; get ye to the safe places." They then entered the shelters—29 families, about 135 men, women, and children.

HYPOTHESES TO BE TESTED

Our interest in the True Word group arose because of their apparent similarity to the "doomsday groups" discussed by Festinger, Riecken, and Schachter in *When Prophecy Fails*.[3] The historical accounts of such groups as well as an empirical study of a more recent group, the Lake City Group, suggest that the failure of the members to confirm their pessimistic predictions led them to increase in fervor of belief and in proselyting. Festinger et al. state five conditions that they feel must be met for this to occur:

---

[3] L. Festinger, H. Riecken, and S. Schachter, *When Prophecy Fails* (Minneapolis: Univ. of Minnesota Press, 1956).

1. A belief must be held with deep conviction and it must have some relevance to action, that is, to what the believer does or how he behaves.
2. The person holding the belief must have committed himself to it; that is, for the sake of his belief, he must have taken some important action that is difficult to undo. In general, the more important such actions are, and the more difficult they are to undo, the greater is the individual's commitment to the belief.
3. The belief must be sufficiently specific and sufficiently concerned with the real world so that events may unequivocally refute the belief.
4. Such undeniable disconfirmatory evidence must occur and must be recognized by the individual holding the belief.

   The first two of these conditions specify the circumstances that will make the belief resistant to change. The third and fourth conditions together, on the other hand, point to factors that would exert powerful pressure on a believer to discard his belief.
5. The individual believer must have social support. It is unlikely that one isolated believer could withstand the kind of disconfirming evidence we have specified. If, however, the believer is a member of a group of convinced persons who can support one another, we would expect the belief to be maintained and the believers to attempt to proselyte or to persuade nonmembers that the belief is correct.[4]

These five conditions define a situation in which the believer has two sets of cognitions that clearly do not fit together. That is, he is experiencing a great deal of dissonance between the cognitions corresponding to his belief and the cognitions concerning the failure of the predicted event to occur. This situation, however, is one in which it is almost impossible for the individual to reduce his dissonance. He cannot give up his strongly held beliefs, and he cannot deny that the predicted event has failed to occur. He is also unable either to reduce the importance of his commitment to his beliefs or to make the disconfirmation irrelevant to them. Therefore, the believer who holds to his belief under these conditions has but one recourse if he is to reduce the dissonance; he must seek new information consonant with his beliefs. One of the best sources of new consonant cognitions is the knowledge that others' beliefs are the same. The authors suggest, then, that the need for new supporting cognitions will lead the believer to try to convince others of the validity of his beliefs.

SUITABILITY OF THE TRUE WORD GROUP FOR A TEST OF THE HYPOTHESIS

Our purpose in learning about the history and beliefs of the True Word group was to determine whether the group met the conditions enumerated in *When Prophecy Fails* and thus would provide a test of the hypothesis under consideration. The first condition is that the group members must hold their belief with deep conviction and that the belief have some relevance to action. It is quite clear that the members held their general religious belief system with deep

---

[4] *Ibid.*, p. 4.

conviction. Many were originally ministers or missionaries actively engaged in Christian work, and most of the members to whom we spoke would refer to "gifts" they themselves or members of their families possessed. Also, as far as we were able to discover, Mrs. Shepard was respected by all of the congregation as a truly exceptional prophet. Thus, since the prophecy probably came from her and was loosely tied to their belief system, it seems clear that it would be very strongly believed by the majority of the congregation. The obvious fact that the group had acted on their belief by building and entering the shelters is the strongest evidence for their belief in the prophecy and also, of course, proof that the belief had relevance for action.

The second condition is that the person holding the belief must have committed himself to it by some action difficult to undo. For the Midwest contingent, the commitment was extreme. They had given up their jobs, had picked up and moved over a thousand miles, and had invested a great deal of time, effort, and money in the building and stocking of homes and shelters. Those from the local area had perhaps given up less, but in several cases they also had lost jobs and had invested considerable sums of money. The things that they have done they cannot undo; the money is spent and the jobs are lost. Most important, none of them can deny or take back the fact that he spent 42 days in hot, humid, crowded shelters and he did this because of his belief.

The third condition, that the belief must be sufficiently specific and sufficiently concerned with the real world so that events may unequivocally refute it, is also quite easy to document. At the time that the group went into the shelters, they believed that a nuclear attack was imminent, and that they would not come out of the shelters until that attack had occurred. That is, they expected to return to a world that had been devastated.

The fourth point, that "undeniable disconfirmatory evidence must occur and must be recognized by the individual holding the belief," is also clearly met. No nuclear attack occurred while the group was in the shelters, and they did not return to a devastated world. Thus, we must conclude that the True Word group suffered the unequivocal disconfirmation of a specific prediction.

The last condition that must be met in order that the True Word group may provide an adequate test of the hypothesis is that the individual believer have social support. This was so clearly the case that it hardly needs documentation. The members of the group had been living together as a separate, rather isolated community for several months prior to July 4. Indeed, some of the members had known each other for years and many were related by blood or marriage. During the time of the disconfirmation, social support was not only present, it was unavoidable. There were as many as 35 people in each shelter, and the shelters provided absolutely no privacy. Furthermore, the shelters were organized in such a way that each contained at least one very strongly convinced member who could hold his group together, and all of the shelters were connected by an intercom system so that the leaders could be consulted in case any members should begin to weaken.

It can be concluded, then, that the five conditions enumerated by Festinger et al. are met by the True Word group. Therefore, if the theory as specified is valid, we should expect to observe an increase in fervor of belief, a greater openness to publicity, and strong attempts to proselyte upon their emergence from their shelters. This, of course, follows from the postulated need for the group members to reduce their dissonance and their inability to do this by any means other than by gaining new cognitions consonant with their belief.

BEHAVIOR OF THE GROUP FOLLOWING THE DISCONFIRMATION

In the very early morning of August 16, the 103 "faithful" who had remained in the shelters for the full 42 days received the word to come out. At about 9 A.M. they held a joyous reunion in the church, led by their pastor, in which they asked, "Did you have victory?" In unison came the reply, "Yes, praise the Lord!!!" Mrs. Shepard spoke of how their faith had not been shaken, "The Lord has brought the people closer to Him, there is not division, there's fellowship here and we are the holiness people." Many other church members gave testimonies as to how their stay in the shelters had both strengthened their Christian fellowship and increased their belief.

The information concerning the first meeting was obtained from reporters who had been present. During the following week, the authors were able to speak with almost all of the members of the group, to attend their frequent church services, and to interview many of the members, including the leaders, Jameson, Blake, and Mrs. Shepard, quite intensively.

It is clear from our observations that the beliefs of the group remained intact. The group members did have a reinterpretation of the purpose of their stay in the shelters that served as an explanation for the failure of the prediction. They had discovered by looking back over all of their messages that it had never been stated that an attack was imminent; they had simply misinterpreted God's purposes. Really, God had just been using them to warn a world that was asleep, while at the same time He was testing their faith. They passed the test and thus proved themselves even more worthy to be among God's elect. We further discovered that they all continued to believe that an attack would come soon. Thus, the group members should be suffering from dissonance; the reinterpretation may have lessened it somewhat, by giving them some reason for having sat so long in the shelters. But their prediction had been shown to be wrong, and they still believed; they should, then, seek publicity and attempt to proselyte.

This did not occur; one must look very hard to uncover even the slightest indication that the members of the Church of the True Word wished to find new converts to their beliefs. The prayer meeting on the morning of August 16 was a golden opportunity if the group wanted to seek new believers. The press was there en masse, including several reporters, cameramen, and TV representatives. One newsman, who had kept in close touch with the group from the beginning of their stay in the shelters, did report that the group was a little more friendly to the press than formerly. Blake asked the press to print certain passages from the scriptures in their reports, and these passages, which speak of wide-spread destruction, are clearly intended as a warning to the world. Also, Mrs. Shepard, at this time and later, spoke favorably of all the free publicity they had gained for the Lord by the worldwide coverage of their activities. However, the group members were relatively indifferent to the attempts of Civil Defense officials to contact them and turned away curious tourists who asked to see their shelters. Furthermore, they made no immediate attempts to interest the towns-people in their church services. There is no indication from the behavior of the group when they first emerged or from our observations of them during the following week that they had any intentions of going out to seek new believers on a large scale.

DISCUSSION

The True Word group meets all of the criteria for a test of the theory as set forth in *When Prophecy Fails*, and yet their behavior following the disconfirmation does not conform to the expectations derived from that theory. Clearly, either the theory is wrong,[5] or it is incomplete in the sense that it specifies insufficiently the variables determining the predicted proselyting. We have two suggestions to make concerning differences between the True Word group and those previously studied that might have affected the differences in behavior that were observed.

The first difference that we wish to consider is that of the amount of social support present within the group. It is stated in *When Prophecy Fails* that one of the conditions necessary for proselyting to occur is the presence of social support for the believers. That is, a certain minimum amount of support is needed so that the individual believer may maintain his beliefs against the disconfirma-tion. But what might be the effect of additional amounts of social support? We would like to suggest that the more social support an individual receives above the minimum he needs to maintain his belief, the less need he will have to proselyte.

For this suggestion to be acceptable, it must be assumed, first, that there is some limit to the amount of support that is useful to an individual in his attempts to reduce his dissonance. For example, if only a few of your friends agree with a cherished belief of yours, you may be tempted to seek support by convincing others that you are right. On the other hand, if everyone with whom you associate agrees with you, you will feel very little need to go out and attempt to influence others in order to gain more support for your belief. Second, it must be assumed that a person will choose that means of reducing dissonance that is least likely to introduce new dissonance and most likely to reduce that which already exists. In the situation faced by the True Word group, and by other such groups, talking

---

[5] Leon Festinger, personal communication.

to other already convinced group members could not introduce new dissonance. In fact, interacting with others who had survived the same disconfirmation and who had emerged with their beliefs unshaken would be the best sort of support an individual could have. On the other hand, talking to the skeptical would be very likely to introduce new dissonance, since the person approached would probably reject one's attempts at influence and counter with arguments of his own. Thus, one would expect that, if at all possible, a person would choose to interact with those who agree with him rather than with the unbelievers.

In a group such as the True Word group with strong social support and a strongly shared belief system, the believer can turn to any other member for confirmation of his beliefs. Following our two assumptions, then, a member of such a group would first choose to talk to other members in his attempts to reduce his dissonance. If in this way he is able to garner new cognitions consonant with his belief up to the limit that he can use, he will then feel no need to seek further support by proselyting. On the other hand, a believer who is a member of a group such as the Lake City group, in which there is less support and more disagreement with regard to the belief system, would be much less likely to encounter sufficient support from his fellows. Thus, he may well have to resort to the otherwise less preferred means of gaining new consonant cognitions, that of proselyting.

It is easy to document the fact that the Lake City group did not provide social support to a degree that even approached that provided by the True Word group. First of all, the Lake City group was not well under way until about 5 months prior to the predicted date of the catastrophe; on the other hand, many members of the True Word group had worked together for several years. Further, the Lake City group had never lived as a community separated from the rest of the world as did the True Word group. This close association present in the True Word group should, one would think, foster a degree of trust in and understanding of the other members that far exceeded that which developed in the Lake City group.

With regard to shared beliefs, there was often disagreement among the members of the Lake City group. For example, the messages received by the two primary leaders of the group often contradicted each other. In contrast, the members of the True Word group were unanimous in their support of Mrs. Shepard, as far as we were able to observe. There was one leader, and one coherent set of beliefs shared by all of the group members. In conclusion, the Lake City group seems to have been characterized by only a minimal degree of social support, and we are suggesting that this degree of support was far from sufficient to reduce the dissonance suffered by the members as a result of the disconfirmation. As a result, the members, in search of further support, felt the need to proselyte. In contrast, the True Word group was very close and had a strongly shared belief system. Thus, they may well have had as much support within the group as they could utilize to reduce their dissonance and consequently felt no need to proselyte.

An interesting, although almost anecdotal, further piece of support for this suggestion comes from a very short article written by a Dutch psychologist, Van Peype,[6] in a Dutch newspaper. He briefly visited a group called the "Communita," who had gathered together near the top of Mont Blanc in expectation of a flood that would destroy the world on July 14. They had existed as a group for over 4 years, and many of the members had lived in the lodge on Mont Blanc for several months, separated from the other people living in the area. They had one prophet, one coherent body of beliefs, and, as far as Van Peype reports, a feeling of community and fellowship. When their prediction was disconfirmed, the leader announced to the waiting reporters, "You should be happy that we made that error. Our faith does not waver . . . Amen."[7] He said no more to the assembled crowd and was reluctant to talk to Van Peype. The members had, then, not given up their belief and yet they showed no indications of a desire to proselyte. In the apparent degree of social support that was present, this group resembles the True Word group much more than it does the Lake City group, and their behavior following disconfirmation was essentially the same.

A second difference between the True Word group and the Lake City group that may have affected the amount of proselyting we observed lies in the amount of ridicule the groups received from the outside world. It would seem reasonable that if a group is receiving considerable ridicule from nonmembers, one way of reducing dissonance that would be apparent to them would be to convince these "unbelievers" that the group is right. If, however, the group is not receiving this sort of treatment from outsiders, this means of reducing dissonance would tend to be a great deal less salient to them. Furthermore, ridicule from others adds more dissonance to that which the group suffers from the disconfirmation. Thus, a very direct way of actually reducing part of the dissonance would be to eliminate the source of ridicule by converting the scoffers.

As far as we were able to determine, the True Word group received very little ridicule from townspeople and the press, considering the unusual step they had taken. The greatest amount of censure the group received seemed to come from other evangelical churches rather than from people in general. In talking to the local townspeople we often encountered statements such as "Yes, we knew they were building bomb shelters. We believe in doing that, too." The Civil Defense officials in the area even presented the group with an award for "the service which they have performed for the public." After the group had left the shelters, the Mayor of the town was quoted in the newspaper as saying, "I sincerely hope no one ridicules them for their beliefs." Newspaper accounts of the group were in general factual and did not make fun of the group.

The treatment the Lake City group received was very different.[8] Again, the news stories were generally factual and straightforward. But the headlines were cruel. In response to the announcement of the prediction, one paper headlined,

---

[6] W. F. Van Peype, Nu de Wereld op 14 Juli niet is vergaan, *Vrij Ned.*, July 30, 1960, p. 3.

[7] *Ibid.*

[8] Festinger *et al, op cit.*, p. 137.

"Tuesday—That Sinking Feeling," and another reported, "World Won't End, but Boy It Sure Will Shake." Columnists and editorial writers were equally unkind. Thus, since the Lake City group suffered more ridicule than did the True Word group, it might be supposed that it was easier for the Lake City group to see proselyting as an effective way of reducing the dissonance they had after the disconfirmation.

Evidence from the Mont Blanc group[9] gives somewhat equivocal support for this second suggestion. Van Peype reported that the Communita was very well thought of by the people in the town near their lodge, and was never ridiculed by them. However, they did receive some ridicule at the hands of reporters.

In conclusion, the True Word group, who had suffered a major disconfirmation of an important prediction, held to their beliefs and yet did not proselyte for them. This fact is in clear contradiction to expectation derived from the theory set forth in *When Prophecy Fails*. However, since dissonance theory has received considerable support in laboratory situations, it seems unlikely that it is completely wrong. Thus, we have assumed that the specification of the conditions that must obtain in the disconfirmation situation, in order that the predicted proselyting might occur, was insufficient. The two suggestions we have made for further conditions are that the group provide only minimal social support for its members and that the group receive ridicule from the outside world. It is, of course, impossible to know from the study of one group whether either of these has any relevance to proselyting. We can only say that there were clear differences on both these factors between the Lake City and True Word groups. We would like to suggest, then, that these two factors be considered and kept in mind by those investigating similar "doomsday groups" in the future.

SUMMARY

On July 4, 1960, a group of 135 men, women and children began a 42-day stay in underground shelters in response to a prophecy of widespread nuclear disaster. Since their situation bore marked similarities to that of the group studied in *When Prophecy Fails*, their reactions to the disconfirmation of their prediction were observed in order to test the theory set forth in that book. Although the group members clung to their belief in the face of disconfirmation, and even seemed to increase in fervor, they did not attempt to proselyte for their belief. This result is contrary to expectations derived from the observations and the theory presented by Festinger et al.[10] Two variables, the degree of social support available within the group and the amount of ridicule the group received, are suggested as possibly having effected this difference in behavior.

---

[9] W. F. Van Peype, personal communication.
[10] *When Prophecy Fails.*

The characteristics of a
helping relationship*

Carl R. Rogers

I have long had the strong conviction—some might say it was an obsession—that the therapeutic relationship is only a special instance of interpersonal relationships in general, and that the same lawfulness governs all such relationships. This was the theme I chose to work out for myself when I was asked to give an address to the convention of the American Personnel and Guidance Association at St. Louis, in 1958.

Evident in this paper is the dichotomy between the objective and the subjective which has been such an important part of my experience during recent years. I find it very difficult to give a paper which is either wholly objective or wholly subjective. I like to bring the two worlds into close juxtaposition, even if I cannot fully reconcile them.

My interest in psychotherapy has brought about in me an interest in every kind of helping relationship. By this term I mean a relationship in which at least one of the parties has the intent of promoting the growth, development, maturity, improved functioning, improved coping with life of the other. The other, in this sense, may be one individual or a group. To put it in another way, a helping relationship might be defined as one in which one of the participants intends that there should come about, in one or both parties, more appreciation of, more expression of, more functional use of the latent inner resources of the individual.

Now it is obvious that such a definition covers a wide range of relationships which usually are intended to facilitate growth. It would certainly include the relationship between mother and child, father and child. It would include the relationship between the physician and his patient. The relationship between teacher and pupil would often come under this definition, though some teachers would not have the promotion of growth as their intent. It includes almost all counselor-client relationships, whether we are speaking of educational counseling, vocational counseling, or personal counseling. In this last-mentioned area it would include the wide range of relationships between the psychotherapist and the

* Excerpted from Carl R. Rogers, *On Becoming A Person* (Boston: Houghton Mifflin, 1961), chap. 3, pp. 39–58, "The Characteristics of a Helping Relationship," Used by permission.

hospitalized psychotic, the therapist and the troubled or neurotic individual, and the relationship between the therapist and the increasing number of so-called "normal" individuals who enter therapy to improve their own functioning or accelerate their personal growth.

These are largely one-to-one relationships. But we should also think of the large number of individual-group interactions which are intended as helping relationships. Some administrators intend that their relationship to their staff groups shall be of the sort which promotes growth, though other administrators would not have this purpose. The interaction between the group therapy leader and his group belongs here. So does the relationship of the community consultant to a community group. Increasingly the interaction between the industrial consultant and a management group is intended as a helping relationship. Perhaps this listing will point up the fact that a great many of the relationships in which we and others are involved fall within this category of interactions in which there is the purpose of promoting development and more mature and adequate functioning.

THE QUESTION

But what are the characteristics of those relationships which *do* help, which do facilitate growth? And at the other end of the scale is it possible to discern those characteristics which make a relationship unhelpful, even though it was the sincere intent to promote growth and development? It is to these questions, particularly the first, that I would like to take you with me over some of the paths I have explored, and to tell you where I am, as of now, in my thinking on these issues.

THE ANSWERS GIVEN BY RESEARCH

It is natural to ask first of all which there is any empirical research which would give us an objective answer to these questions. There has not been a large amount of research in this area as yet, but what there is is stimulating and suggestive. I cannot report all of it but I would like to make a somewhat extensive sampling of the studies which have been done and state very briefly some of the findings. In so doing, oversimplification is necessary, and I am quite aware that I am not doing full justice to the researches I am mentioning, but it may give you the feeling that factual advances are being made and pique your curiosity enough to examine the studies themselves, if you have not already done so.

Studies of attitudes

Most of the studies throw light on the attitudes on the part of the helping person which make a relationship growth-promoting or growth-inhibiting. Let us look at some of these.

A careful study of parent-child relationships made some years ago by Baldwin[1] and others at the Fels Institute contains interesting evidence. Of the various clusters of parental attitudes toward children, the "acceptant-democratic" seemed most growth-facilitating. Children of these parents with their warm and equalitarian attitudes showed an accelerated intellectual development (an increasing I.Q.), more originality, more emotional security and control, less excitability than children from other types of homes. Though somewhat slow initially in social development, they were, by the time they reached school age, popular, friendly, nonaggressive leaders.

Where parents' attitudes are classed as "actively rejectant" the children show a slightly decelerated intellectual development, relatively poor use of the abilities they do possess, and some lack of originality. They are emotionally unstable, rebellious, aggressive, and quarrelsome. The children of parents with other attitude syndromes tend in various respects to fall in between these extremes.

I am sure that these findings do not surprise us as related to child development. I would like to suggest that they probably apply to other relationships as well, and that the counselor or physician or administrator who is warmly emotional and expressive, respectful of the individuality of himself and of the other, and who exhibits a nonpossessive caring, probably facilitates self-realization much as does a parent with these attitudes.

Let me turn to another careful study in a very different area. Whitehorn and Betz[2] investigated the degree of success achieved by young resident physicians in working with schizophrenic patients on a psychiatric ward. They chose for special study the seven who had been outstandingly helpful, and seven whose patients had shown the least degree of improvement. Each group had treated about fifty patients. The investigators examined all the available evidence to discover in what ways the A group (the successful group) differed from the B group. Several significant differences were found. The physicians in the A group tended to see the schizophrenic in terms of the personal meaning which various behaviors had to the patient, rather than seeing him as a case history or a descriptive diagnosis. They also tended to work toward goals which were oriented to the personality of the patient, rather than such goals as reducing the symptoms or curing the disease. It was found that the helpful physicians, in their day by day interaction, primarily made use of active personal participation—a person-to-person relationship. They made less use of procedures which could be classed as "passive permissive." They were even less likely to use such procedures as interpretation, instruction or advice, or emphasis upon the practical care of the patient. Finally, they were much more likely than the B group to develop a

---

[1] A. L. Baldwin, J. Kalhorn, and F. H. Breese, "Patterns of Parent Behavior," *Psychol. Monogr.*, Vol. 58, No. 268 (1945), pp. 1–75.

[2] B. J. Betz, and J. C. Whitehorn, "The Relationship of the Therapist to the Outcome of Therapy in Schizophrenia," *Psychiat. Research Reports # 5. Research Techniques in Schizophrenia.* (Washington, D.C., American Psychiatric Association, 1956), pp. 89–117; also "A Study of Psychotherapeutic Relationships between Physicians and Schizophrenic Patients, *Amer. J. Psychiat.*, Vol. III (1954), pp. 321–31.

relationship in which the patient felt trust and confidence in the physician.

Although the authors cautiously emphasize that these findings relate only to the treatment of schizophrenics, I am inclined to disagree. I suspect that similar facts would be found in a research study of almost any class of helping relationship.

Another interesting study focuses upon the way in which the person being helped perceives the relationship. Heine[3] studied individuals who had gone for psychotherapeutic help to psychoanalytic, client-centered, and Adlerian therapists. Regardless of the type of therapy, these clients report similar changes in themselves. But it is their perception of the relationship which is of particular interest to us here. When asked what accounted for the changes which had occurred, they expressed some differing explanations, depending on the orientation of the therapist. But their agreement on the major elements they had found helpful was even more significant. They indicated that these attitudinal elements in the relationship accounted for the changes which had taken place in themselves: the trust they had felt in the therapist; being understood by the therapist; the feeling of independence they had had in making choices and decisions. The therapist procedure which they had found most helpful was that the therapist clarified and openly stated feelings which the client had been approaching hazily and hesitantly.

There was also a high degree of agreement among these clients, regardless of the orientation of their therapists, as to what elements had been unhelpful in the relationship. Such therapist attitudes as lack of interest, remoteness or distance, and an over-degree of sympathy, were perceived as unhelpful. As to procedures, they had found it unhelpful when therapists had given direct specific advice regarding decisions or had emphasized past history rather than present problems. Guiding suggestions mildly given were perceived in an intermediate range—neither clearly helpful nor unhelpful.

Fiedler, in a much quoted study,[4] found that expert therapists of differing orientations formed similar relationships with their clients. Less well known are the elements which characterized these relationships, differentiating them from the relationships formed by less expert therapists. These elements are an ability to understand the client's meanings and feelings, a sensitivity to the client's attitudes, and a warm interest without any emotional overinvolvement.

A study by Quinn[5] throws light on what is involved in understanding the client's meanings and feelings. His study is surprising in that it shows that "understanding" of the client's meanings is essentially an attitude of *desiring* to

---

[3] R. W. Heine, "A Comparison of Patients' Reports on Psychotherapeutic Experience with Psychoanalytic, nondirective, and Adlerian Therapists," unpublished doctoral dissertation, University of Chicago, 1950.

[4] F. E. Fiedler, "Quantitative Studies on the role of Therapists Feelings toward Their Patients," in O. H. Mowrer (ed.), *Psychotherapy: Theory and Research* (New York: Ronald Press, 1953), chap. 12.

[5] R. D. Quinn, "Psychotherapists' Expressions as an Index to the Quality of Early Therapeutic Relationships," unpublished doctoral dissertation, University of Chicago, 1950.

understand. Quinn presented his judges only with recorded therapist statements taken from interviews. The raters had no knowledge of what the therapist was responding to or how the client reacted to his response. Yet it was found that the degree of understanding could be judged about as well from his material as from listening to the response in context. This seems rather conclusive evidence that it is an attitude of wanting to understand which is communicated.

As to the emotional quality of the relationship, Seeman[6] found that success in psychotherapy is closely associated with a strong and growing mutual liking and respect between client and therapist.

An interesting study by Dittes[7] indicates how delicate this relationship is. Using a physiological measure, the psychogalvanic reflex, to measure the anxious or threatened or alerted reactions of the client, Dittes correlated the deviations on this measure with judges' ratings of the degree of warm acceptance and permissiveness on the part of the therapist. It was found that whenever the therapist's attitudes changed even slightly in the direction of a lesser degree of acceptance, the number of abrupt GSR deviations significantly increased. Evidently when the relationship is experienced as less acceptant the organism organizes against threat, even at the physiological level.

Without trying fully to integrate the findings from these various studies, it can at least be noted that a few things stand out. One is the fact that it is the attitudes and feelings of the therapist, rather than his theoretical orientation, which is important. His procedures and techniques are less important than his attitudes. It is also worth noting that it is the way in which his attitudes and procedures are *perceived* which makes a difference to the client, and that it is this perception which is crucial.

"Manufactured" relationships

Let me turn to research of a very different sort, some of which you may find rather abhorrent, but which nevertheless has a bearing upon the nature of a facilitating relationship. These studies have to do with what we might think of as manufactured relationships.

Verplanck,[8] Greenspoon[9] and others have shown that operant conditioning of verbal behavior is possible in a relationship. Very briefly, if the experimenter says "M'hm," or "Good," or nods his head after certain types of words or statements, those classes of words tend to increase because of being reinforced.

---

6 J. Seeman, "Counselor Judgments of Therapeutic Process and Outcome," in C. R. Rogers, and R. F. Dymond (eds.), *Psychotherapy and Personality Change* (University of Chicago Press, 1954), chap. 7.

7 J. E. Dittes, "Galvanic Skin Response as a Measure of Patient's Reaction to Therapist's Permissiveness," *J. Abnorm. & Soc. Psychol.*, Vol. 55 (1957), pp. 295–303.

8 W. S. Verplanck, "The Control of the Content of Conversation: Reinforcement of Statements of Opinion," *J. Abnorm. & Soc. Psychol.*, Vol. 51 (1955), pp. 668–76.

9 J. Greenspoon, "The Reinforcing Effect of Two Spoken Sounds on the Frequency of Two Responses," *Amer. J. Psychol.*, Vol. 68 (1955), pp. 409–16.

It has been shown that using such procedures one can bring about increases in such diverse verbal categories as plural nouns, hostile words, statements of opinion. The person is completely unaware that he is being influenced in any way by these reinforcers. The implication is that by such selective reinforcement we could bring it about that the other person in the relationship would be using whatever kinds of words and making whatever kinds of statements we had decided to reinforce.

Following still further the principles of operant conditioning as developed by Skinner and his group, Lindsley[10] has shown that a chronic schizophrenic can be placed in a "helping relationship" with a machine. The machine, somewhat like a vending machine, can be set to reward a variety of types of behaviors. Initially it simply rewards—with candy, a cigarette, or the display of a picture— the lever-pressing behavior of the patient. But it is possible to set it so that many pulls on the lever may supply a hungry kitten—visible in a separate enclosure— with a drop of milk. In this case the satisfaction is an altruistic one. Plans are being developed to reward similar social or altruistic behavior directed toward another patient, placed in the next room. The only limit to the kinds of behavior which might be rewarded lies in the degree of mechanical ingenuity of the experimenter.

Lindsley reports that in some patients there has been marked clinical improvement. Personally I cannot help but be impressed by the description of one patient who had gone from a deteriorated chronic state to being given free grounds privileges, this change being quite clearly associated with his interaction with the the machine. Then the experimenter decided to study experimental extinction, which, put in more personal terms, means that no matter how many thousands of times the lever was pressed, no reward of any kind was forthcoming. The patient gradually regressed, grew untidy, uncommunicative, and his grounds privilege had to be revoked. This (to me) pathetic incident would seem to indicate that even in a relationship to a machine, trustworthiness is important if the relationship is to be helpful.

Still another interesting study of a manufactured relationship is being carried on by Harlow and his associates,[11] this time with monkeys. Infant monkeys, removed from their mothers almost immediately after birth, are, in one phase of the experiment, presented with two objects. One might be termed the "hard mother," a sloping cylinder of wire netting with a nipple from which the baby may feed. The other is a "soft mother," a similar cylinder made of foam rubber and terry cloth. Even when an infant gets all his food from the "hard mother" he clearly and increasingly prefers the "soft mother." Motion pictures show that he definitely "relates" to this object, playing with it, enjoying it, finding security in clinging to it when strange objects are near, and using that security as a home

---

[10] O. R. Lindsley, "Operant Conditioning Methods Applied to Research in Chronic Schizophrenia," *Psychiat. Research Reports # 5. Research Techniques in Schizophrenia* (Washington, D.C.: American Psychiatric Association, 1956) pp. 118–53.

[11] H. F. Harlow, "The Nature of Love," *Amer. Psychol.*, Vol. 13 (1958), pp. 673–85.

base for venturing into the frightening world. Of the many interesting and challenging implications of this study, one seems reasonably clear. It is that no amount of direct food reward can take the place of certain perceived qualities which the infant appears to need and desire.

Two recent studies

Let me close this wide-ranging—and perhaps perplexing—sampling of research studies with an account of two very recent investigations. The first is an experiment conducted by Ends and Page.[12] Working with hardened chronic hospitalized alcoholics who had been committed to a state hospital for sixty days, they tried three different methods of group psychotherapy. The method which they believed would be most effective was therapy based on a two-factor theory of learning; a client-centered approach was expected to be second; a psychoanalytically oriented approach was expected to be least efficient. Their results showed that the therapy based upon a learning theory approach was not only not helpful, but was somewhat deleterious. The outcomes were worse than those in the control group which had no therapy. The analytically oriented therapy produced some positive gain, and the client-centered group therapy was associated with the greatest amount of positive change. Follow-up data, extending over one and one-half years, confirmed the in-hospital findings, with the lasting improvement being greatest in the client-centered approach, next in the analytic, next the control group, and least in those handled by a learning theory approach.

As I have puzzled over this study, unusual in that the approach to which the authors were committed proved *least* effective, I find a clue, I believe, in the description of the therapy based on learning theory.[13] Essentially it consisted (a) of pointing out and labeling the behaviors which had proved unsatisfying, (b) of exploring objectively with the client the reasons behind these behaviors, and (c) of establishing through reeducation more effective problem-solving habits. But in all of this interaction the aim, as they formulated it, was to be impersonal. The therapist "permits as little of his own personality to intrude as is humanly possible." The "therapist stresses personal anonymity in his activities, i.e., he must studiously avoid impressing the patient with his own (therapist's) individual personality characteristics." To me this seems the most likely clue to the failure of this approach, as I try to interpret the facts in the light of the other research studies. To withhold one's self as a person and to deal with the other person as an object does not have a high probability of being helpful.

The final study I wish to report is one just being completed by Halkides.[14]

[12] E. J. Ends, and C. W. Page. "A Study of Three Types of Group Psychotherapy with Hospitalized Male Inebriates," *Quar. J. Stud. Alcohol,* Vol. 18 (1957) pp. 263–77.

[13] C. W. Page, and E. J. Ends, "A Review and Synthesis of the Literature Suggesting a Psychotherapeutic Technique Based on Two-Factor Learning Theory," unpublished manuscript, loaned to the writer.

[14] G. Halkides, "An Experimental Study of Four Conditions Necessary for Therapeutic Change," unpublished doctoral dissertation, University of Chicago, 1958.

She started from a theoretical formulation of mine regarding the necessary and sufficient conditions for therapeutic change.[15] She hypothesized that there would be a significant relationship between the extent of constructive personality change in the client and four counselor variables: (*a*) the degree of empathic understanding of the client manifested by the counselor; (*b*) the degree of positive affective attitude (unconditional positive regard) manifested by the counselor toward the client; (*c*) the extent to which the counselor is genuine, his words matching his own internal feeling; and (*d*) the extent to which the counselor's response matches the client's expression in the intensity of affective expression.

To investigate these hypotheses she first selected, by multiple objective criteria, a group of ten cases which could be classed as "most successful" and a group of ten "least successful" cases. She then took an early and late recorded interview from each of these cases. On a random basis she picked nine client-counselor interaction units—a client statement and a counselor response—from each of these interviews. She thus had nine early interactions and nine later interactions from each case. This gave her several hundred units which were now placed in random order. The units from an early interview of an unsuccessful case might be followed by the units from a late interview of a successful case, etc.

Three judges, who did not know the cases or their degree of success, or the source of any given unit, now listened to this material four different times. They rated each unit on a seven point scale, first as to the degree of empathy, second as to the counselor's positive attitude toward the client, third as to the counselor's congruence or genuineness, and fourth as to the degree to which the counselor's response matched the emotional intensity of the client's expression.

I think all of us who knew of the study regarded it as a very bold venture. Could judges listening to single units of interaction possibly make any reliable rating of such subtle qualities as I have mentioned? And even if suitable realibility could be obtained, could eighteen counselor-client interchanges from each case—a minute sampling of the hundreds or thousands of such interchanges which occurred in each case—possibly bear any relationship to the therapeutic outcome? The chance seemed slim.

The findings are surprising. It proved possible to achieve high reliability between the judges, most of the inter-judge correlations being in the 0.80's or 0.90's, except on the last variable. It was found that a high degree of empathic understanding was significantly associated, at a .001 level, with the more successful cases. A high degree of unconditional positive regard was likewise associated with the more successful cases, at the .001 level. Even the rating of the counselor's genuineness or congruence—the extent to which his words matched his feelings—was associated with the successful outcome of the case, and again at the .001 level of significance. Only in the investigation of the matching intensity of affective expression were the results equivocal.

---

[15] C. R. Rogers, "The Necessary and Sufficient Conditions of Psycho-Therapeutic Personality Change," *J. Consult. Psychol.*, Vol. 21 (1957), pp. 95–103.

It is of interest too that high ratings of these variables were not associated more significantly with units from later interviews than with units from early interviews. This means that the counselor's attitudes were quite constant throughout the interviews. If he was highly empathic, he tended to be so from first to last. If he was lacking in genuineness, this tended to be true of both early and late interviews.

As with any study, this investigation has its limitations. It is concerned with a certain type of helping relationship, psychotherapy. It investigated only four variables thought to be significant. Perhaps there are many others. Nevertheless it represents a significant advance in the study of helping relationships. Let me try to state the findings in the simplest possible fashion. It seems to indicate that the quality of the counselor's interaction with a client can be satisfactorily judged on the basis of a very small sampling of his behavior. It also means that if the counselor is congruent or transparent, so that his words are in line with his feelings rather than the two being discrepant; if the counselor likes the client, unconditionally; and if the counselor understands the essential feelings of the client as they seem to the client—then there is a strong probability that this will be an effective helping relationship.

Some comments

These then are some of the studies which throw at least a measure of light on the nature of the helping relationship. They have investigated different facets of the problem. They have approached it from very different theoretical contexts. They have used different methods. They are not directly comparable. Yet they seem to me to point to several statements which may be made with some assurance. It seems clear that relationships which are helpful have different characteristics from relationships which are unhelpful. These differential characteristics have to do primarily with the attitudes of the helping person on the one hand and with the perception of the relationship by the "helpee" on the other. It is equally clear that the studies thus far made do not give us any final answers as to what is a helping relationship nor how it is to be formed.

How can I create a helping relationship?

I believe each of us working in the field of human relationships has a similar problem in knowing how to use such research knowledge. We cannot slavishly follow such findings in a mechanical way or we destroy the personal qualities which these very studies show to be valuable. It seems to me that we have to use these studies, testing them against our own experience and forming new and further personal hypotheses to use and test in our own further personal relationships.

So rather than try to tell you how you should use the findings I have presented I should like to tell you the kind of questions which these studies and my own clinical experience raise for me, and some of the tentative and changing hypotheses which guide my behavior as I enter into what I hope may be helping relationships, whether with students, staff, family, or clients. Let me list a number of these questions and considerations.

1. Can I *be* in some way which will be perceived by the other person as trustworthy, as dependable or consistent in some deep sense? Both research and experience indicate that this is very important, and over the years I have found what I believe are deeper and better ways of answering this question. I used to feel that if I fulfilled all the outer conditions of trustworthiness—keeping appointments, respecting the confidential nature of the interviews, etc.—and if I acted consistently the same during the interviews, then this condition would be fulfilled. But experience drove home the fact that to act consistently acceptant, for example, if in fact I was feeling annoyed or skeptical or some other nonacceptant feeling, was certain in the long run to be perceived as inconsistent or untrustworthy. I have come to recognize that being trustworthy does not demand that I be rigidly consistent but that I be dependably real. The term "congruent" is one I have used to describe the way I would like to be. By this I mean that whatever feeling or attitude I am experiencing would be matched by my awareness of that attitude. When this is true, then I am a unified or integrated person in that moment, and hence I can *be* whatever I deeply *am*. This is a reality which I find others experience as dependable.

2. A very closely related question is this: Can I be expressive enough as a person that what I am will be communicated unambiguously? I believe that most of my failures to achieve a helping relationship can be traced to unsatisfactory answers to these two questions. When I am experiencing an attitude of annoyance toward another person but am unaware of it, then my communication contains contradictory messages. My words are giving one message, but I am also in subtle ways communicating the annoyance I feel and this confuses the other person and makes him distrustful, though he too may be unaware of what is causing the difficulty. When as a parent or a therapist or a teacher or an administrator I fail to listen to what is going on in me, fail because of my own defensiveness to sense my own feelings, then this kind of failure seems to result. It has made it seem to me that the most basic learning for anyone who hopes to establish any kind of helping relationship is that it is safe to be transparently real. If in a given relationship I am reasonably congruent, if no feelings relevant to the relationship are hidden either to me or the other person, then I can be almost sure that the relationship will be a helpful one.

One way of putting this which may seem strange to you is that if I can form a helping relationship to myself—if I can be sensitively aware of and acceptant toward my own feelings—then the likelihood is great that I can form a helping relationship toward another.

Now, acceptantly to be what I am, in this sense, and to permit this to show through to the other person, is the most difficult task I know and one I never fully achieve. But to realize that this *is* my task has been most rewarding because it has helped me to find what has gone wrong with interpersonal relationships which have become snarled and to put them on a constructive track again. It has meant that if I am to facilitate the personal growth of others in relation to me, then I must grow, and while this is often painful it is also enriching.

3. A third question is: Can I let myself experience positive attitudes toward this other person—attitudes of warmth, caring, liking, interest, respect? It is not easy, I find in myself, and feel that I often see in others, a certain amount of fear of these feelings. We are afraid that if we let ourselves freely experience these positive feelings toward another we may be trapped by them. They may lead to demands on us or we may be disappointed in our trust, and these outcomes we fear. So as a reaction we tend to build up distance between ourselves and others—aloofness, a "professional" attitude, an impersonal relationship.

I feel quite strongly that one of the important reasons for the professionalization of every field is that it helps to keep this distance. In the clinical areas we develop elaborate diagnostic formulations, seeing the person as an object. In teaching and in administration we develop all kinds of evaluative procedures, so that again the person is perceived as an object. In these ways, I believe, we can keep ourselves from experiencing the caring which would exist if we recognized the relationship as one between two persons. It is a real achievement when we can learn, even in certain relationships or at certain times in those relationships, that it is safe to care, that it is safe to relate to the other as a person for whom we have positive feelings.

4. Another question the importance of which I have learned in my own experience is: Can I be strong enough as a person to be separate from the other? Can I be a sturdy respecter of my own feelings, my own needs, as well as his? Can I own and, if need be, express my own feelings as something belonging to me and separate from his feelings? Am I strong enough in my own separateness that I will not be downcast by his depression, frightened by his fear, or engulfed by his dependency? Is my inner self hardy enough to realize that I am not destroyed by his anger, taken over by his need for dependence, nor enslaved by his love, but that I exist separate from him with feelings and rights of my own? When I can freely feel this strength of being a separate person, then I find that I can let myself go much more deeply in understanding and accepting him because I am not fearful of losing myself.

5. The next question is closely related. Am I secure enough within myself to permit him his separateness? Can I permit him to be what he is—honest or deceitful, infantile or adult, despairing or overconfident? Can I give him the freedom to be? Or do I feel that he should follow my advice, or remain somewhat dependent on me, or mold himself after me? In this connection I think of the interesting small study by Farson[16] which found that the less well adjusted and less competent counselor tends to induce conformity to himself, to have clients who model themselves after him. On the other hand, the better adjusted and

---

[16] R. E. Farson, "Introjection in the Psychotherapeutic Relationship," unpublished doctoral dissertation, University of Chicago, 1955.

more competent counselor can interact with a client through many interviews without interfering with the freedom of the client to develop a personality quite separate from that of his therapist. I should prefer to be in this latter class, whether as parent or supervisor or counselor.

6. Another question I ask myself is: Can I let myself enter fully into the world of his feelings and personal meanings and see these as he does? Can I step into his private world so completely that I lose all desire to evaluate or judge it? Can I enter it so sensitively that I can move about in it freely, without trampling on meanings which are precious to him? Can I sense it so accurately that I can catch not only the meanings of his experience which are obvious to him, but those meanings which are only implicit, which he sees only dimly or as confusion? Can I extend this understanding without limit? I think of the client who said, "Whenever I find someone who understands a *part* of me at the time, then it never fails that a point is reached where I know they're *not* understanding me again . . . What I've looked for so hard is for someone to understand."

For myself I find it easier to feel this kind of understanding, and to communicate it, to individual clients than to students in a class or staff members in a group in which I am involved. There is a strong temptation to set students "straight," or to point out to a staff member the errors in his thinking. Yet when I can permit myself to understand in these situations, it is mutually rewarding. And with clients in therapy, I am often impressed with the fact that even a minimal amount of empathic understanding—a bumbling and faulty attempt to catch the confused complexity of the client's meaning—is helpful, though there is no doubt that it is most helpful when I can see and formulate clearly the meanings in his experiencing which for him have been unclear and tangled.

7. Still another issue is whether I can be acceptant of each facet of this other person which he presents to me. Can I receive him as he is? Can I communicate this attitude? Or can I only receive him conditionally, acceptant of some aspects of his feelings and silently or openly disapproving of other aspects? It has been my experience that when my attitude is conditional, then he cannot change or grow in those respects in which I cannot fully receive him. And when—afterward and sometimes too late—I try to discover why I have been unable to accept him in every respect, I usually discover that it is because I have been frightened or threatened in myself by some aspect of his feeling. If I am to be more helpful, then I must myself grow and accept myself in these respects.

8. A very practical issue is raised by the question: Can I act with sufficient sensitivity in the relationship that my behavior will not be perceived as a threat? The work we are beginning to do in studying the physiological concomitants of psychotherapy confirms the research by Dittes in indicating how easily individuals are threatened at a physiological level. The psychogalvanic reflex—the measure of skin conductance—takes a sharp dip when the therapist responds with some word which is just a little stronger than the client's feeling. And to a phrase such as, "My you *do* look upset," the needle swings almost off the paper. My desire to avoid even such minor threats is not due to a hypersensitivity about

my client. It is simply due to the conviction based on experience that if I can free him as completely as possible from external threat, then he can begin to experience and to deal with the internal feelings and conflicts which he finds threatening within himself.

9. A specific aspect of the preceding question but an important one is: Can I free him from the threat of external evaluation? In almost every phase of our lives—at home, at school, at work—we find ourselves under the rewards and punishments of external judgments. "That's good"; "that's naughty." "That's worth an A"; "that's a failure." "That's good counseling"; "that's poor counseling." Such judgments are a part of our lives from infancy to old age. I believe they have a certain social usefulness to institutions and organizations such as schools and professions. Like everyone else I find myself all too often making such evaluations. But, in my experience, they do not make for personal growth and hence I do not believe that they are a part of a helping relationship. Curiously enough a positive evaluation is as threatening in the long run as a negative one, since to inform someone that he is good implies that you also have the right to tell him he is bad. So I have come to feel that the more I can keep a relationship free of judgment and evaluation, the more this will permit the other person to reach the point where he recognizes that the locus of evaluation, the center of responsibility, lies within himself. The meaning and value of his experience is in the last analysis something which is up to him, and no amount of external judgment can alter this. So I should like to work toward a relationship in which I am not, even in my own feelings, evaluating him. This I believe can set him free to be a self-responsible person.

10. One last question: Can I meet this other individual as a person who is in process of *becoming*, or will I be bound by his past and by my past? If, in my encounter with him, I am dealing with him as an immature child, an ignorant student, a neurotic personality, or a psychopath, each of these concepts of mine limits what he can be in the relationship. Martin Buber, the existentialist philosopher of the University of Jerusalem, has a phrase, "confirming the other," which has had meaning for me. He says "Confirming means . . . accepting the whole potentiality of the other. . . . I can recognize in him, know in him, the person he has been . . . *created* to become. . . . I confirm him in myself, and then in him, a relation to this potentiality that . . . can now be developed, can evolve."[17] If I accept the other person as something fixed, already diagnosed and classified, already shaped by his past, then I am doing my part to confirm this limited hypothesis. If I accept him as a process of becoming, then I am doing what I can to confirm or make real his potentialities.

It is at this point that I see Verplanck, Lindsley, and Skinner, working in operant conditioning, coming together with Buber, the philosopher or mystic. At least they come together in principle, in an odd way. If I see a relationship

---

[17] M. Buber, and C. Rogers, "Transcription of Dialogue Held April 18, 1957, Ann Arbor, Mich., unpublished manuscript.

as only an opportunity to reinforce certain types of words or opinions in the other, then I tend to confirm him as an object—a basically mechanical, manipulable object. And if I see this as his potentiality, he tends to act in ways which support this hypothesis. If, on the other hand, I see a relationship as an opportunity to "reinforce" *all* that he is, the person that he is with all his existent potentialities, then he tends to act in ways which support *this* hypothesis. I have then—to use Buber's term—confirmed him as a living person, capable of creative inner development. Personally I prefer this second type of hypothesis.

Conclusion

In the early portion of this paper I reviewed some of the contributions which research is making to our knowledge *about* relationships. Endeavoring to keep that knowledge in mind I then took up the kind of questions which arise from an inner and subjective point of view as I enter, as a person, into relationships. If I could, in myself, answer all the questions I have raised in the affirmative, then I believe that any relationships in which I was involved would be helping relationships, would involve growth. But I cannot give a positive answer to most of these questions. I can only work in the direction of the positive answer.

This has raised in my mind the strong suspicion that the optimal helping relationship is the kind of relationship created by a person who is psychologically mature. Or to put it in another way, the degree to which I can create relationships which facilitate the growth of others as separate persons is a measure of the growth I have achieved in myself. In some respects this is a disturbing thought, but it is also a promising or challenging one. It would indicate that if I am interested in creating helping relationships I have a fascinating lifetime job ahead of me, stretching and developing my potentialities in the direction of growth.

Part III

Personal change through interpersonal relationships

A. ORGANIZATION OF THIS ESSAY

In our previous two essays we have considered interpersonal emotions and the process of identity formation and reality testing. Interpersonal relationships also serve the function of inducing or facilitating change in one or both parties through a process of influence. The interpersonal events which occur in socialization, education, role training, persuasion, seduction, consultation, therapy, and the like will be our focus in the present essay.

Almost any change in behavior, beliefs, attitudes, and values is mediated by interpersonal relationships of one kind or another. The child learns the mores and values of his society from parents and parent-surrogates; pupils learn from teachers; patients learn from therapists; salesmen influence their customers' buying behavior and product attitudes; friends and lovers induce subtle changes in each other; seductive persons influence the behavior and self-image of those prone to seduction. Some of the changes which result from interpersonal relationships are considered desirable by both parties and sanctioned by society; some are desirable but not sanctioned; some are desirable to only one party; and some are not desired by either the participants in the relationship or by society.

As we confront the bewildering array of types of change which result from interpersonal relationships, we face a number of issues which must be clarified and which will serve as the major foci for the organization of this essay. The questions we will try to deal with are:

1. Can the *types* of change processes be classified into some meaningful framework?
2. Can the *process* of change be conceptualized in terms of a model which will have meaning for the different types of change identified?
3. Can one begin to develop a theory of interpersonal influence by identifying some *mechanisms* which occur within the broader process of change?

We will attempt to develop tentative answers to these questions in terms of the following general scheme. For the first question we have used a frame of reference which starts not with the individual but with society. Thus, from a societal point of view, there are two basic dimensions which prove useful in identifying different types of change or influence: (1) the degree to which the process is *planned* by the individual or social group; and (2) the degree to which the process is *institutionalized*. By institutionalized influence we mean influence which results from *stable recognized patterns of interaction sanctioned by society* rather than accidental or unstable encounters. The four types of change or influence which result are shown in Figure 1 at the beginning of the next section.

For question *two*, the problem of the process of change, we have used a frame of reference which is anchored in a time dimension. Change is a process which occurs over time and must, therefore, be conceptualized in terms of *phases* or *stages*. We have found Lewin's conceptualization of the change process—a stage of *unfreezing*, a stage of *changing*, and a stage of *refreezing*—a convenient starting point, and have elaborated some mechanisms within these stages.

For question *three*, we have used a heterogeneous, eclectic point of view which reflects several theoretical strands. The symbolic interactionist point of view highlights the kinds of interpersonal forces which make people stable. Unless such forces are altered, no personal change can occur. The process assumes that man's stability derives from the confirmations he receives from his network of *significant others*. In analyzing the mechanisms by which *changes* occur, we will rely more heavily on psychoanalytic and cognitive models of learning. In analyzing the stage of *refreezing*, we find ourselves once again leaning on the symbolic interactionist point of view.

The problem of terminology

A central issue which we must confront is the problem of what kinds of terms to choose when discussing interpersonal change processes. In using the words *change* or *influence* rather than *growth* or *learning*, we have attempted to buttress our desire to be morally neutral about the process by choosing terms which are as nonevaluative as possible. Though they are awkward, we will adopt the terms *change agent* and *change target* when referring to the parties in the relationships. When referring to what is changed or influenced, we will use primarily two terms—*behavior* and *attitudes*. *Behavior* refers to *overt* acts which may or may not reflect covert mental processes or feelings. *Attitudes* blanket the whole range of *covert* responses from beliefs and values on one extreme, to feelings, impulses, and motives at the other extreme.

Two other issues

The first issue concerns the question of whether to include in our conceptual scheme problems of influence through the mass media of communication as in propaganda, advertising, or educational television. Because such influence is clearly a one-way process flowing from an impersonal source to a passive audience, we have chosen not to treat it here. The mass media do not involve *inter*personal dynamics as central mechanisms of change.

A second issue concerns the problem of the level of abstraction or generality to seek in any preliminary theoretical structuring of an area of human interaction. Do we seek the abstract generality of a social learning theory like Miller and Dollard's,[1] or do we settle for the descriptive uniqueness of a novel like Hulme's *The Nun's Story?*[2] Both deal with the problem of how people change in response to or in concert with other people. But, where Miller and Dollard seek generality through aggregating many processes under one very abstract mechanism, the principle of reinforcement, Hulme seeks understanding by fully describing the nuances of each instance of influence which she could identify in the process of becoming a nun. Our position would approximate Merton's[3] in seeking the interim solution of a "theory of the middle level," recognizing that in this quest, we risk losing both generality and intuitive understanding.

B. BASIC TYPES OF CHANGE PROCESSES

Figure 1 shows our classification of types of change processes in terms of whether the process is planned or unplanned, and in terms of whether it occurs through an institutionalized mechanism or not.

1. *Planned institutionalized* influence is exemplified in the socialization of the child, education, institutionalized rehabilitation and therapy, formal role training

FIGURE 1
Classification of types of change process

	Institutionalized	*Not institutionalized*
Planned.................	Formal socialization Education Formal role training Institutional therapy Rehabilitation Brainwashing	Persuasion Selling Seduction Therapy Coaching Consultation Human relations training
Unplanned................	Unintended consequence of the above process	Emergent change

---

[1] N. E. Miller and John Dollard, *Social Learning and Imitation* (New Haven: Yale Univ. Press, 1941).

[2] K. Hulme, *The Nun's Story* (Boston: Little, Brown & Co., 1956).

[3] R. Merton, *Social Theory and Social Structure* (Glencoe, Ill.: Free Press, 1949).

in organizations or professional training institutions like academies or medical schools, and brainwashing or other attempts to reeducate through formal institutional mechanisms. Society designates certain official positions, the occupants of which perform change agent roles—parents, teachers, therapists, indoctrinators. The targets of influence—children, students, criminals, or patients—are also designated through official procedures or institutions.

The content or area in which influence is supposed to occur is circumscribed: children have to learn the basic culture and values of the society in which they live; students have to learn a designated curriculum; criminals have to learn certain social values and approved behavior patterns; and patients have to learn the behavior patterns, motives, attitudes, and values, defined as "normal" or "healthy" in the society in which they live. The nature of the change in the target person is generally defined as *basic* and is expected to be stable; it concerns the fundamental beliefs and values of the society. The influence is generally expected to flow in one direction only—from agent to target.[4]

2. *Unplanned institutionalized* influence is change which results through formal institutional mechanisms of influence but which is unintended and often undesired. In a way, each of the institutionalized forms of influence have their planned and unplanned outcomes. Thus, in the process of socialization, the child learns not only the parents' overt values and attitudes but also often acquires their conflicts and antisocial impulses. Parents sometimes communicate their fears and repressed impulses in the very attempt to teach their child not to have those same fears and impulses. In the same way, teachers, therapists, and bosses communicate attitudes which they seek to hide, through behavior inconsistent with their official position. Some of the more tragic aspects of socialization and role training result when the change agent discovers that he has been more successful in imparting undesired behavior and attitudes than those desired ones which his official position required him to impart.

The disintegrative forces within any society, organization, or group are exposed in the unintended consequences of socialization or role training. Lack of integration manifests itself when change agents disagree among themselves on what is to be taught or when they carry within themselves the personal counterpart of the cultural conflict. Perhaps it is the necessity to minimize such conflict which causes institutions to put so much emphasis on the proper selection of change agents. Change agents such as priests, teachers, and therapists must be minimally conflicted and highly congruent with the values of that institution. They must minimize unplanned uninstitutionalized outcomes.[5]

---

[4] Those occasional cases in which children, criminals, or patients influence parents, teachers, or therapists provide the kind of dramatic exceptions which highlight the degree to which we tend to take the unidirectional flow of influence for granted in the settings of home, school, prison, or hospital.

[5] The fact that society has relatively less control over who becomes a parent introduces some interesting problems. Adolescent delinquency or schizophrenia can both be viewed as unintended features of the socialization process because of lack of certain qualifications in the parents. On the other hand, Israeli experiments with the kibbutz illustrate an attempt by society to control socialization more closely.

3. *Planned uninstitutionalized* influence occurs when one participant in an interpersonal relationship decides (for whatever reason) to influence another participant or to induce some change in him. Examples of this kind of process fall into two general categories:

a) Those where the change target is assumed to have some initial, conscious resistance to the change, as in persuasion, selling, or seduction; and

b) Those where the change target is considered to be a willing accomplice to the change, as in informal role training, coaching, or consultation.[6]

In either of the above cases, the change agent usually assumes his role voluntarily. He may or may not operate with formal, official sanctions to influence others. The status of change target is also accepted voluntarily; in the former case, as a result of being put into that position by the activities of the change agent; in the latter case, as a result of his own initiative.

The nature of the change may or may not be as basic as that defined by planned institutionalized influence processes, but, generally, we associate this type of influence with the more surface and less permanent aspects of the change target's personality. The agent of change in this type of process has fewer formal rewards and punishments available with which to control the target. Hence, the agent is more vulnerable to counterinfluence from the target if the latter chooses to define the situation as one in which he will change only if the agent also changes (through not necessarily in the same area). This type of influence is therefore more likely to be reciprocal than is institutionalized influence.[7]

4. *Unplanned uninstitutionalized* influence or *emergent change* is a spontaneous outcome of the relationship and may involve one or both parties in the relationship. It is often associated with relationships formed primarily for reasons *other* than influence, i.e., influence is not a pivotal function of the relationship. Thus, lovers and friends induce a variety of changes in each other; the members of a work or athletic team influence each other in areas unrelated to their immediate work or play situations; and fleeting contacts between people in spontaneous situations often produce marked changes in one or both of them.

The statuses of change agent and change target are difficult, if not impossible, to identify because a mutual influence often occurs with the result that both people simultaneously occupy both statuses. The change may involve anything from relatively trivial behavior accommodations to major reorientations of values.

---

[6] The change target is, of course, often *unconsciously* resistant to the change induction.

[7] Certain cases, like the practice of private psychotherapy, are difficult to categorize in terms of our scheme. Society has institutionalized the role of the doctor and has created for the psychiatrist the mandate to change people who are defined as patients. But, this very process of definition is highly fluid and unplanned. Similarly, there are a variety of change agents who have social sanction but who operate outside institutional structures without detailed planning either on their part or on the part of the change target. In our society, uncles, big brothers, advisers, leaders, and charismatic personalities fall into this borderland between uninstitutionalized and institutionalized change.

C. THE PROCESS AND MECHANISMS OF CHANGE OR INFLUENCE

The conceptual scheme shown in Figure 2 was developed to encompass the kinds of changes in beliefs, attitudes, and values which we regard as fairly "central" or "deep"; changes which occur during socialization, therapy, and other processes involving the person's self or identity. The scheme also draws attention to a much neglected problem, that of having to unlearn something before something new can be learned. Most of the kinds of changes we are concerned with involve attitudes or behaviors which are integrated around the self, where change implies the giving up of something to which the person has previously become committed and which he values.

FIGURE 2
The process of influence and the mechanisms underlying each stage

Stage 1. *Unfreezing:* creating motivation to change
Mechanisms: *a)* Lack of confirmation or disconfirmation
b) Induction of guilt-anxiety
c) Creation of psychological safety by reduction of threat or removal of barriers

Stage 2. *Changing:* developing new responses based on new information
Mechanisms: *a)* Cognitive redefinition through
(1) Identification: information from a single source
(2) Scanning: information from multiple sources

Stage 3. *Refreezing:* stabilizing and integrating the changes
Mechanisms: *a)* Integrating new responses into personality
b) Integrating new responses into significant ongoing relationships through reconfirmation

Any change in behavior or attitudes of this sort tends to be emotionally resisted because even the possibility of change implies that previous behavior and attitudes were somehow wrong or inadequate, a conclusion which the change target would be motivated to reject. If change is to occur, therefore, it must be preceded by an alteration of the present stable equilibrium which supports the present behavior and attitudes. It is this step, difficult to pin down precisely, which we believe Lewin correctly saw as akin to "unfreezing"—making something solid into a fluid state. Any viable conceptual scheme of the influence process must begin with the process of unfreezing and thereby take account of the inherent threat which change represents. For any change to occur, the defenses which tend to be aroused in the change target must be made less operative, circumvented, or used directly as change levers.

Once the change target's present equilibrium has been upset, once he has become motivated to change, he will seek information relevant to his dilemma.

That is, he will seek cues as to the kind of changes to make in his behavior or attitudes which will reestablish a comfortable equilibrium for him. Such information may come from personal or impersonal sources, from a single other person or an array of others, from a single communication or a prolonged search. It is this process, the seeking out, processing, and utilization of information for the purpose of achieving new perceptions, attitudes, and behaviors, which we have called "changing."

There remains the problem of whether the new behavior and attitudes fit well with the person's other behavior and attitudes, and whether they will be acceptable to his significant others. The process of integrating new responses into the ongoing personality and into key emotional relationships leads ultimately to changes which may be considered to be stable. If the new responses do not fit or are unacceptable to important others, a new process of unfreezing is initiated and a new cycle of influence is thereby set up. *Stable* change thus implies a reintegration or a stage of "refreezing," to continue with Lewin's terminology. Just as unfreezing is necessary for change to begin, refreezing is necessary for change to endure.

Let us next examine some of the key mechanisms which can be identified in each stage of the influence process.

1. Mechanisms of unfreezing

Lack of confirmation or disconfirmation. The assumption which underlies a conceptual scheme such as the one proposed is that the change target's significant behavior, beliefs, attitudes, and values are organized around and supported by his self-image. It is further assumed that the person presents himself differently in different social situations. Therefore, it is his "operating self-image" which is relevant in any given situation.[8] This operating self-image does not exist in isolation but is usually integrated with the person's definition of the situation and his image of the other people in the situation. For example, when a young man enters a classroom and adopts the appropriate self-image of "student," this image is integrated with his view of the larger situation as a school in which certain kinds of learning are supposed to take place, and with his image of others who are defined as teachers and fellow students.

Because of the interdependence of self-image, definition of the situation, and image of others in the situation, the process of unfreezing can begin by a failure of confirmation or actual disconfirmation in any one of the three aspects of the total situation.[9] The change target can be confronted with the information: (1) that his self-image is out of line with what others and the situation will grant

---

[8] The readings by Goffman, pages 175–89 and pages 273–84 are excellent analyses of the process of constructing "operating self-images."

[9] In the fairly common situation where information conflicts, where both confirming and disconfirming cues are available, the person probably tends to pay attention only to the confirming cues. As long as any confirmation occurs, therefore, there are no real unfreezing forces present.

him or be able to sustain; (2) that his definition of the situation is out of line with "reality" as defined by others in the situation; (3) that his image of the others is out of line with their image of themselves or of each other; and (4) one or more of the above in combination.

For example, the student entering the classroom may have seen himself as a passive listener only to discover suddenly that the teacher has called upon him; he may have defined the classroom as primarily a place to relax and meet girls, but discover that the course is, in fact, "hard" and that the instructor defines the classroom as a place for active participation by students; he may have perceived the instructor as a *laissez-faire* type of "good fellow," only to discover that the instructor sees himself as a tough taskmaster determined to make his classroom into a real learning environment. Each of these types of information can be thought of as *disconfirmatory* of some assumption which the student had made about himself, the situation, and/or the others in the situation.

By contrast, *lack of confirmation* occurs when relevant information is lacking. Thus, if the student placed high value on himself as a ladies' man and defined classrooms as places to meet coeds, he would experience lack of confirmation if he discovered that there were no girls among his fellow students. Another example might be the case of two students who initially reinforce in each other a self-image of indifference to learning and engage in horseplay during class meetings. If the teachers asks them to sit far apart, and if little opportunity to interact outside of class exists, one could say that these aspects of their self-image would subsequently be lacking in confirmation. In a situation where aspects of the self fail to be confirmed, one may predict that a *gradual* atrophy or unlearning of those aspects will occur.[10] In a situation where aspects of the self are actually disconfirmed, the person confronts a more immediate disequilibrium which requires some immediate change or new learning.

The induction of guilt anxiety.   The induction of guilt-anxiety refers to the process wherein the person reacts to lack of confirmation or disconfirmation, not by rejecting the information or its source, but by feeling some sense of inadequacy or failure in himself. The sense of inadequacy may (1) be felt in reference to a failure in living up to some ideal self-image; (2) result from a feeling of disappointing others whose reactions are valued; or (3) result from a failure to honor some obligation that has been assumed. Such feelings may be summarized by the concept of "guilt-anxiety." Change will occur in the attempt to reduce or, more commonly, to *avoid* guilt anxiety.[11]

---

[10] The best examples of lack of confirmation occurred in Communist controlled POW camps in which prisoners were systematically segregated from each other and their social structure undermined to such a degree that mutual mistrust led to virtually no meaningful communication. See E. H. Schein, "The Chinese Indoctrination Program for Prisoners of War," *Psychiatry*, Vol. 19 (1959), pp. 149–72, and the paper by Schein in this section (pages 284–300). For a more extensive discussion of Communist indoctrination methods, see E. H. Schein with I. Schneier and C. H. Barker, *Coercive Persuasion* (New York: W. W. Norton, 1961), and R. J. Lifton, " 'Thought Reform' of Western Civilians in Chinese Communist Prisons," *Psychiatry*, Vol. 19 (1956), pp. 173–95.

[11] See Schein, Schneier, and Barker in this part for a further discussion of guilt.

Creation of psychological safety by reduction of threat or removal of barri-ers. Unfreezing can also occur through the reduction of threat or the removal of barriers to change. In these instances, one must assume that the change target already has some motive or desire to change but experiences a conflict which prevents the actual change from occurring. Either the change is inherently anxiety provoking because it brings with it the unknown, or else it is perceived by the person to have consequences which he is unwilling or unable to bear. The change agent may in these instances (1) try to reassure the change target; (2) try to help him bear the anxiety attendant upon change; or (3) attempt to show the target that the outcome is more palatable than he may have assumed.

Looking at the three unfreezing mechanisms together, we can say that a change or influence process can only be started when there is some *optimum balance* of disconfirmation, guilt anxiety, and psychological safety. It is the achievement of this balance which makes the job of change agent so difficult and, at the same time, so creative.

If disconfirmation and/or guilt anxiety are too high, the change target will either leave the situation or, if this is not possible, will become defensive and more rigidly cling to his present equilibrium. He will deny the validity of, or fail to perceive, disconfirming cues, and will repress feelings of guilt anxiety. If psychological safety is also high, the target might risk being less defensive, but it is difficult to create conditions where disconfirmation and safety are both very high.

If psychological safety is low, even minimal disconfirmations will appear as threats, thus reducing the likelihood that the person will pay attention to them. On the other hand, if psychological safety is high, conditions may be set up where either small disconfirmations in the present situation start a change process, or where *remembered disconfirmation from past experiences* serves to start the process of change. Thus, when a person enters a very supportive therapeutic relationship, he may find that he can begin to explore disconfirmatory experiences which happened long ago but which for the first time he can allow himself to plumb the real meaning of. In other words, it is not always necessary for the disconfirmation to occur in the psychological present. All of us have accumulated a history of disconfirmations which, however, never led to change because there was insufficient psychological safety to permit us to really pay attention to the cues. Once we are in a supportive safe relationship, these early cues can lead to significant change.[12]

Examples of the unfreezing process

To illustrate these ideas, let us consider some examples from each of the basic types of change cited above.

---

[12] As Harris points out in his excellent discussion of transactional analysis, every person comes through childhood with many feelings of being "NOT OK" because of the multiple disconfirmations experienced. All of these experiences are recorded in the person and must, in adulthood, be worked through in order for the person to achieve a sense of "I'm OK." See T. A. Harris, *I'm OK—You're OK* (New York: Harper & Row, 1967).

1. *Institutionalized* influence, both planned and unplanned, typically operates through routinized, often institutionalized, methods of *disconfirmation*. The child, the criminal, and the sick person are systematically punished for responses out of line with expected cultural norms. Deviant behavior is pointed out and sanctions are brought to bear if it continues.

Institutions devoted to producing a change in self-image such as rehabilitation centers, schools, military academies, and mental hospitals usually begin their influence process by dramatic disconfirmations which Goffman has called "mortifications of the self."[13] Thus, the entrant may be deprived of his clothes, his name, his personal possessions, his hair, and his status, all of which communicates to him, in as clear a fashion as possible, that his old identity will be minimally valued in the new setting. Even the *voluntary* entrant into the institution may find that the change demanded of him is more than he bargained for, thus requiring him to unfreeze further before successful influence can occur. Stories of officer training procedures in a tough academy or in an Officers Candidate School and descriptions of the religious novitiate abound with examples of this type of unfreezing.[14]

Guilt anxiety is induced when (1) the change target perceives himself as having failed to live up to the image which society expects of him as conveyed either implicitly or explicitly by his parents, teachers, and significant others or (2) when he feels he has disappointed change agents who have invested time and effort in changing him. The unfulfilled obligation theme is reflected in the parental message that children *owe* certain kinds of behavior to their parents because of the heavy investment the parents have made in the children. Other kinds of change agents, such as therapists, also use this process. By investing a great deal of time, effort, and emotional energy in their change targets, they may succeed in arousing a need to change in the target who sees this as a form of repayment for the efforts invested in him.

The best examples of *threat or barrier reduction* may be found in the educational efforts which view certain kinds of limited performance in children not as instances of limited capacity, but as instances of learning blocks. Only when such blocks are removed is the child able to operate at full capacity. Many forms of rehabilitation and therapy operate on the assumption that one cannot *induce* motives toward change, but can attempt to locate and unblock such motives in patients and delinquents. It is our own assumption that both kinds of influence operate—that which takes advantage of motives already present in the person, and that which initiates the process by inducing motives through lack of confirmation or through actual disconfirmation.

2. In *planned uninstitutionalized* forms of influence, we find the process of disconfirmation somewhat less organized but no less potent. Goffman in his essay

---

[13] E. Goffman, "On the Characteristics of Total Institutions," *Proceedings of the Symposium on Preventive and Social Psychiatry* (Washington, D.C.: Walter Reed Army Institute of Research, 1957).

[14] For an excellent example see Hulme, *The Nun's Story.*

"On Cooling the Mark Out" (pages 273–84), provides an excellent example. A person invests in a get-rich-quick scheme, thinking of himself as a sharp operator, only to discover that not only has he failed to become rich but also has been defrauded by confidence men. The sudden discovery that what we claim to be and have committed ourself to is thoroughly discredited by others and external events serves to operate as a powerful force toward some new self-definition.

The major difference between the institutionalized and uninstitutionalized processes lies in the degree to which the potential change target can evade the situation in which unfreezing and changing is likely to occur. In most institutionalized change situations, both agent and target accept the fact that some change in the target is expected. In uninstitutionalized situations, by contrast, the influence agent may initially confront a potential target who will resist the role of target and refuse to define the situation as one in which influence is legitimate.

The salesman must first convince the person to see himself as a *potential* customer. Only then can he try to sell the particular product. The consultant often finds himself in a situation where the person most in need of change is the one least likely to recognize this need. The consultation process may then involve a long period of unfreezing in which the major goal is to help the client define the situation as one in which he can accept help for himself. Only then does the question shift to *what kind* of change is relevant for the client. But, even then, the potential customer or client can terminate the relationship at any time and thus evade any further influence attempts.[15]

The agent of uninstitutionalized influence can not make use of coercive power or some of the more basic rewards and punishments which are available to parents, teachers, and doctors. As a result, he must rely more heavily on the manipulation of guilt anxiety or on unblocking already present motives to change by showing the potential target that he is not living up to some ideal which he himself has stated or that his ideals have some flaw in them. Both processes presuppose that the influence agent has somehow captured the attention of the target and is able to present himself in a believable and convincing manner (see pages 259–60 and Adelson's paper, pages 335–44 for a further discussion of this point).

Having captured the potential customer's attention, the salesman can (1) try to show him how buying a certain product is essential to the upholding of a self-image which the salesman presumes or knows that the customer holds; (2) try to build an ideal self-image for him which can be achieved primarily through purchase of the product; or (3) try to reduce whatever anxiety or barrier the customer is assumed to have about the purchase (e.g., "You can buy it on the installment plan," or "It will only cost you pennies a week"). Dramatic instances of failure to influence may result when the change agent incorrectly diagnoses the nature of the target's anxieties or barriers.

The consultant similarly tries to influence his client by (1) pointing the way

---

[15] For a full discussion of this process see E. H. Schein, *Process Consultation* (Reading, Massachusetts: Addison-Wesley, 1969).

toward a desired state; (2) demonstrating that this state can only be achieved through certain changes which the consultant advocates; and (3) helping the client to overcome barriers to these changes. The coach uses the trainee's desire for some ideal performance as a lever for influence, though sometimes he also functions as the person who defines what the ideal should be. An excellent analysis of this process is given in Strauss's essay on coaching a person to prepare him for promotion or some other change in status (see pages 267–73). The ability of a coach to be reassuring and to deal with barriers, without compromising performance standards, may be one of the important characteristics which differentiates the good from the poor coach.

A strategy which the change agent may employ to unfreeze the target is to elicit, either by persuasion, seduction, or outright trickery, some behavior which is inconsistent with the image the person is trying to uphold or achieve. This type of disconfirmation produces immediate embarrassment and guilt, and thus serves to initiate the influence process. In the sales situation, this process would be exemplified by the seduction of the steadfast "noncustomer" into trying out some product. Once he has agreed to a trial, he has implicitly given up his self-image as a "noncustomer." He has opened the door to further sales efforts as well as to guilt feelings which may be based either on his sense of failure to live up to his "noncustomer" image or on his reluctance to disappoint the salesman who has now invested more heavily in him.

The consultant often does not have to elicit behavior inconsistent with the client's self-image. Such behavior may already be present, but outside of the client's awareness. The consultant's problem then becomes one of how to point out the inconsistency so as to produce sufficient guilt to induce change without producing so much anxiety as to create defensiveness and thus block change.

3. In the case of *emergent change*, the influence process also begins by lack of confirmation, disconfirmation, the induction of guilt anxiety, and the reduction of threat. However, the interpersonal messages which initiate the process are more spontaneous and may not be sent with the explicit aim of influencing the other party. Friends or lovers, in their desire to maximize mutual gratification in their relationship, will tend to be highly sensitive to disconfirmatory messages or lack of confirmation. Such sensitivity may result from the fact that mutual confirmation is the basis for defining the closeness of the relationship in the first place. That is, the growth of intimacy can be conceived of as a series of successive experiments by the parties to the relationship. As each private area of the self is tentatively exposed, the response of the other party is carefully calibrated so as to determine the amount of acceptance or confirmation it implies. As given areas are confirmed, i.e., as the person feels more and more "accepted," he may be motivated to experiment with ever more private areas.

However, in any relationship, certain areas will, in fact, not be acceptable to the other party, thus necessitating either some change in one or both parties, or an agreement to avoid that area in the relationship. The relationship of friends or lovers is therefore characterized by a constant tension between the process of mutual influence and mutual acceptance. Depending on the actual personalities which the partners bring with them, there will be some areas in which mutual acceptance is high. No change will be required in either party because of an initial harmony of personalities and roles. There will be some areas where the presented self of one partner (A) is more central to him than whatever disconfirmatory feelings or reactions are aroused in the other partner (B). In this case, B will change. He will withhold his reactions and gradually try to unlearn them. Finally, there will be some areas where the centrality of the disconfirmatory reactions in B is greater than the centrality of A's presented part of himself. In this case, A will attempt to change that part of himself so as not to arouse the painful reaction in B on future occasions.

Much of the emotional work of a close relationship is the complex dialogue which this difficult calculus of feelings make necessary. Each partner must obtain valid information about the relative cost of changes in himself and changes in the other in order to make those changes which seem mutually desirable by properly balancing disconfirmation, reassurance, and help.

From the point of view of the psychologist, a further complexity derives from the fact that many factors influence how a given person will react to information about himself, and how he will decide how central some part of himself is relative to some part of his partner. The person who feels more strongly about something and who is able to present himself as totally sincere may induce change in another person even if his own behavior is "sick," "antisocial," and ultimately destructive to the change target. The successful persuader may well be the person who can convince others that it would cost him more to change than it would cost them to accommodate.

4. In summary, we have argued that any interpersonal change or influence presupposes a process of unfreezing which in turn consists of several other processes which occur singly or in combination. These are: (1) a process of *disconfirmation* or *lack of confirmation* of some part of the change target's self; (2) the *induction of guilt anxiety;* and/or (3) the creation of psychological safety by *reduction of threat or removal of barriers to change* if some change motive is already present in the target person.

The process of unfreezing has been discussed in considerable detail because it is this stage of the influence process which is usually given least attention. Indeed, in the traditional social psychological literature on attitude change, the process is hardly considered at all. The present theoretical formulation makes unfreezing a critical and necessary step in any change process. Without unfreezing, no change will occur, no matter how much effort is put into selling, persuading, coercing, rewarding, or punishing. Or to put it another way, the reason why so many change efforts run into resistance or outright failure is usually directly traceable to their not providing for an effective unfreezing process before attempting a change induction.

2. Mechanisms of changing

Cognitive redefinition. The problem of learning a *new* response or changing an attitude can be thought of as a problem of seeking out *reliable* and *valid* information from a plethora of sources which may or may not be credible to the target. In making this assertion, we are limiting the learning or change situation to those situations which are governed by *social reality* as contrasted with *physical reality;*[16] that is, we are only considering situations in which validity is *consensually* judged in terms of the beliefs and attitudes of others.

How does the change target choose and make up his mind from the welter of sources available? In the typical, stable social situation, the person pays attention to those sources of information (other people) who confirm his present behavior and attitudes. If others fail to provide confirmation or actually disconfirm present attitudes, yet the person must continue to interact with them (e.g., because the job demands it), we have a typical unfreezing situation with respect to those attitudes. The person knows something is wrong and that some kind of change is demanded of him, but he does not automatically know what is wrong and how to correct the situation.

In order to determine what is wrong or how to change, the person must first re-examine certain assumptions or beliefs he has about himself, others, and his definition of the situation. He must then decide if these assumptions are unwarranted or inconsistent with feelings and evaluations which the others in the situation hold about themselves, him, and the situation. *The first step in the change process, then, is to develop alternate assumptions and beliefs through a process of cognitive redefinition of the situation.*

This process involves (1) *new definitions* of 'terms in the semantic sense, (2) a *broadening of perceptions* or expanded consciousness which changes the frame of reference from which objects are judged, and/or (3) *new standards of evaluation and judgment.* The new attitudes and behavior which are the eventual outcome of the influence process result from this intermediate step of cognitive redefinition.

From this perspective, the process of unfreezing can be viewed as *becoming open* to certain kinds of information which are actually or potentially available in the environment. The process of changing is the *actual assimilation* of new information resulting in cognitive redefinition and new personal constructs.[17] These, in turn form the basis for new attitudes and new behavior.

---

[16] L. Festinger, "Informal Social Communication," *Psychological Review* Vol. 57 (1950), pp. 271–82.

[17] We are using constructs here in the sense that G. A. Kelly, *The Psychology of Personal Constructs* [New York: Norton, 1955], defined them as the beliefs, assumptions, and evaluations a person has about some object in his social world.

The best examples of this process were provided to us by the Chinese Communists (see Schein's analysis in this part, pp. 284–300). The prisoner changed his attitudes only after a prolonged process of unfreezing, the end result of which was a readiness to pay attention to the cues which cell mates were providing all along. Once he was paying attention to this category of information, the prisoner discovered that his meanings for words such as "crime" were different from theirs, and his standards

In making cognitive redefinition pivotal to the change process, we have clearly allied ourselves with Gestalt theories of learning and have rejected reinforcement theories of learning. We would like to point out, however, that the reinforcement principle is very much relevant to the process of unfreezing and refreezing. The process of influence *begins* with the failure to obtain certain social reinforcements (lack of confirmation or disconfirmation); the process of influence *ends* with the reinforcement (confirmation) of new attitudes and behavior. The reinforcement principle cannot conveniently explain the actual mechanisms by which new assumptions, beliefs, or constructs develop in turn lead to new attitudes and behaviors. We reject the notion of blind trial and error learning in the realm of social reality, favoring instead a position which makes the assimilation of information from the social environment the central process. The person does experiment in the process of change, but each experiment is based on some new definition of himself, others, and the situation and has, therefore, already been preceded by some cognitive redefinition.

The question arises whether this mechanism of change is always conscious or not. The answer is clearly negative. We have dramatic examples of cognitive redefinition in the realm of physical perceptions which occur entirely without awareness. There is no reason to doubt the existence of a similar process in the realm of social reality. The best examples come from psychophysical studies of judgments of weight or brightness. The entire frame of reference and pattern of judgments of the same stimuli can be altered simply by introducing an anchoring stimulus at either extreme of the scale.[18] The subject does not realize that his judgments have changed, yet clearly, cognitive redefinition has taken place. In the realm of social perception and rumor transmission, we have similar effects. Once certain key stimuli are introduced as anchors (e.g., identifying a certain person in the story as a Negro), the scale of judgment of other stimuli shifts though the person may be completely unaware of the process.[19]

Let us turn now to the next problem, that of the *source of information* which the person utilizes in redefining his cognitions about himself, others, and his situation. At one extreme, we have the acquisition of new information through a single source via some process of *identification*. The cues to which the person responds are those that come from a model to whom the person has chosen to relate himself emotionally. At the other extreme, we have the acquisition of new information through *scanning* a multiple array of sources, which may vary in salience and credibility but which do not elicit the kind of emotional focusing implied by identification. The sources are usually other people, but they need

---

of judgment based on his frame of reference were different from their standards because of their different frame of reference. Once he had redefined his own semantics and attempted to view the world from the cell-mates' frame of reference by applying their standards, he could accept himself as a guilty criminal and make a sincere profession.

[18] H. Helson, "Adaptation-Level as a Basis for a Quantitative Theory of Frames of Reference," *Psychological Review*, Vol. 55 (1948), pp. 297–313.

[19] G. W. Allport and L. Postman, *The Psychology of Rumor* (New York: Holt, 1947).

to be physically present to exert an influence. Their information may have just as much potency in written or broadcasted form.

We have labeled these two extreme forms of information acquisition by the terms *identification* and *scanning*, recognizing that there are many forms, like imitation, which fall in between. Let us now examine each of these processes in greater detail.[20]

Cognitive redefinition through identification. We can distinguish two basically different kinds of identification which have major consequences for the kind of influence or change produced in a change target. We have labeled these as *Type I* or *defensive* identification and *Type II* or *positive* identification. The conditions for, psychological process of, and outcomes of these two types are shown in Figure 3.[21]

Looking first at the *conditions* for identification, we note that *defensive identification* tends to occur in settings which the target has entered involuntarily and from which he cannot escape. He usually experiences a sense of helplessness, relative impotence, fear, and threat. The relationship to the change agent is an imbalanced one in that the agent has most of the power. The agent usually occupies a formal position supported by institutionalized sanctions. The target's role is to change or learn and not to ask too many questions. The prototype of this relation is the child vis-à-vis the powerful parent or the concentration camp prisoner vis-à-vis his captor.

Positive identification, by contrast, tends to occur in situations which the target has entered voluntarily and from which he feels free to leave. He experiences a sense of autonomy and feels he can make choices. Instead of fear and threat vis-à-vis the change agent, he experiences trust and faith. The power relationship is less tilted and is generally not supported by formal positions or institutional sanctions, though they may be present, as in the case of the psychotherapist. The prototype of this relationship is the mutual identification of husband and wife or close friends.

In terms of the *psychological processes* involved in the two types of identification, *defensive identification* generally implies a relationship in which the change agent operates as the primary source of unfreezing (i.e., he provides the bulk of the disconfirming cues). The target responds to this situation by becoming preoccupied with the change agent's position or status which is perceived to be the primary source of the change agent's power. The preoccupation with the

---

[20] This analysis has been influenced by Kelman's excellent work on mechanisms of attitude change (H. C. Kelman, "Compliance, Identification, and Internalization: Three Processes of Attitude Change" *Conflict Resolution*, Vol. 2 [1958], pp. 51–60). We have not used his concepts of *compliance, identification,* and *internalization* because of our emphasis on deeper levels of change than those he deals with in his experiments. Kelman's concepts have greatly aided, however, in achieving some conceptual clarity in this area.

[21] The analysis of identification follows closely Slater's analysis of personal and positional identification. Our analysis, however, deals more with adult processes whereas his focuses on childhood socialization. For an excellent analysis see P. E. Slater, "Toward a Dualistic Theory of Identification" *Merrill-Palmer Quarterly*, Behavior and Development, Vol. 7, No. 2 (1961), pp. 113–26.

FIGURE 3
Analysis of two types of identification

	Type I *Defensive identification*	*Type II* *Positive identification*
Conditions for the process	Target is captive in the change situation Target role nonvoluntarily acquired Agent in formal change agent position Target feels helpless, impotent, fearful, and threatened Target must change	Target is free to leave situation Target takes role voluntarily Agent does not necessarily occupy formal role Target experiences autonomy, sense of power, and choice Target experiences trust and faith in agent Target can terminate change process
Psychological processes involved	Agent is primary source of unfreezing Target becomes position oriented to acquire the agent's perceived power Target has limited and distorted view of agent, and lacks empathy for agent Target tends to imitate limited portions of agent's behavior	Agent is usually not the source of unfreezing Target becomes person oriented because agent's power is seen to reside in his personality, not his position Agent will be chosen on the basis of trust, clarity, and potency Target sees richness and complexity of agent as a person Target tends to assimilate what he learns from the model
Outcomes	New behavior in target is stilted, ritualized, restrictive, and narrowing New behavior is more likely to be acceptable to the influencing institution	New behavior in target is enlarging, differentiated, spontaneous, and enabling of further growth New behavior is personally more meaningful but may be less acceptable to influencing institution

position, in turn, implies a limited and often distorted view of the identification model. The change target tends to pay attention only to the power-relevant cues, tends to have little or no empathy for the person actually occupying the position, and tends to imitate blindly and often unconsciously only certain limited portions of the model's behavior. Or, to put it another way, if existing attitudes and parts of the target's self are chronically and consistently disconfirmed in a coercive way, one solution for the target is to abandon them completely and to substitute those attitudes and values perceived to a property of the powerful disconfirmer.

Positive identification, by contrast, tends to be *person*—rather than *position* —oriented. The potential model is rarely the source of unfreezing and hence is less threatening. The model's power or salience is perceived to lie in some personal attributes rather than in some formal position. Because the change target feels free to leave the situation, he will use the criteria of trust and clarity to choose a model which, in turn, will lead to a fuller richer view of the personality of the model. He will tend to have empathy for the model and genuinely to assimilate the new information obtained from seeing the world through the model's eyes rather than directly imitating his behavior. Thus the target's new behavior and attitudes may not actually resemble the model's too closely. The whole process of identification will be more spontaneous, differentiated, and will enable further growth, rather than be compulsive and limiting.

Looking now at the *outcome,* we see that *defensive identification* leads to a more restricted, ritualized, and stilted set of responses and attitudes. On the other hand, *positive identification* leads to an enlarged, more differentiated, and fluid set of responses and attitudes. There is a greater likelihood of the latter process leading to psychological growth. However, the likelihood that the changes will be acceptable to the institution which has initiated the change process may be greater if defensive identification has taken place.

In both types of identification, the basic mechanism of change is the utilization of interpersonal cues which come from a change agent with whom the target identifies himself. These cues serve as the basis for redefining the cognitions the target holds about himself, others, and the situations in which he finds himself. But, it is obvious that a great deal of change occurs through processes other than these two types of identification. Even in the most coercive institutions, defensive identification may account for only a small portion of the total change in the target. To gain a more balanced picture of change mechanisms, we must look at the other end of the information acquisition scale, to the process we have called *scanning.*

Cognitive redefinition through scanning. The process of *scanning* can best be differentiated from the process of *identification* by the degree to which the change target or learner focuses on multiple models as contrasted with a single model in his social environment. Scanning thus involves a "cafeteria" approach to the utilization of the interpersonal information, and the absence of strong emotional relationships between the change target and his sources of relevant information. At the extreme, *scanning* implies attention to the *content* of the message regardless of the person, whereas *identification* implies attention to the *person* regardless of the content. In both cases, other people tend to be the primary source of information, but in scanning, others become salient only in terms of their perceived relevance or expertness in solving the particular problem which is bothering the change target.

The contrast between *scanning* and *identification* can best be exemplified in a group engaged in group therapy or in human relations training. Let us assume that each member of the group is unfrozen with respect to some areas of himself and is seeking information which will permit him to redefine his situation so as to reach a more comfortable equilibrium. An example of *defensive identification* would be the case of the group member who, because of his great fear of the authority of the therapist or staff member in the group, attempts to change by mimicking and imitating what he perceives to be the staff member's behavior and attitudes. An example of *positive identification* would be the case of the group member who establishes a close emotional relationship with another group member or the staff member, and attempts to view his own problems from the perspective of this other person. An example of *scanning* would be the case of the group member who looks to any source in the group for reactions which bear upon the particular problem he perceives, and attempts to integrate *all* the reactions he obtains. To reiterate, when a person scans, he relates himself primarily to the *information* he receives, *not* to the particular *source* from which the information comes.[22]

How does scanning compare with identification in the change outcome? In the case of scanning, the target may have a more difficult time locating reliable and useful information, but the solution he eventually finds is likely to fit better into his personality because of his power to accept or reject information voluntarily. If the change goal is personal growth, the change agent should attempt to produce a setting conducive to scanning or positive identification, and avoid a setting conducive to defensive identification. If the change goal is the acceptance of a particular set of behaviors and attitudes, the change agent should attempt to produce a setting conducive to positive identification and provide the target with a good representative of the point of view to be learned. To achieve the latter change goal, defensive identification would be next best and scanning would appear to be least likely to succeed.

A digression: Attributes of potential positive identification models

It is our assumption that scanning is the primary process by which people change, and that it would always occur in the absence of certain salient, threatening, or seductive people in the social environment. Once certain people become salient, identification becomes more probable. We would further assume that role relationships which are institutionalized, thus making certain people salient through their position, tend to elicit primarily a defensive type of identification. Parents, teachers, and bosses are good examples of such roles. An intriguing question is, in the absence of such preordained role relationships, what factors make people salient as potential identification models, particularly for positive

---

[22] Scanning could involve noninteractive processes such as reading, observing the reactions of others, conscious attempts at self-analysis and reorganization of own thoughts, listening to advice, and other similar processes. What limits such noninteractive processes as a basis for attitude and behavior change, however, is that the information obtained often turns out to be irrelevant or useless to the problems the target is working on. More useful information is likely to come from the individuals with whom the target is interacting in that he can at least infer their reactions and their way of looking at things.

identification? The following discussion outlines two typologies which appear to be relevant to this problem. They concern the kinds of attributes which make people more or less likely to be chosen as positive identification models.

Typology A: Attributes which recreate family relationships. In any given interpersonal situation, the relative age, status, experience, and formal position of the potential model *vis-à-vis* the change target will determine whether the relationship will tend to be structured in terms of a parent-child, older sibling-child, or peer group relationship. Potential models can therefore be thought of as surrogates of parents, older sibling, or peers and their attributes can be analyzed in terms of the likelihood that they will represent one or another of such types for the change target. For purposes of this discussion, we will label such potential models as:

1. *Father* figures
2. *Big brother* figures
3. *Peer* figures
4. *Transitional* types, i.e., from peer to big brother and big brother to father.

The likelihood that a given person in the change target's environment will be perceived and treated as a father, big brother, peer, or person in transition will depend on that person's actual formal status relative to the target, his degree of perceived similarity to such figures from the target's earlier life, and his own presentation of himself (conscious or unconscious) as a father, big brother, or peer.

The type of emotional relationship which is recreated has implications for the *trustworthiness, clarity,* and actual *content* of what can be transmitted to the change target. Specifically, we would hypothesize that, other things being equal, peer figures are more likely to be trusted than fathers. We would also hypothesize that peer figures are more understandable and clearer than big brothers, who are, in turn, more understandable and clearer than father figures. Therefore, the likelihood of positive identification is greatest with peer figures and least with father figures.

These hypotheses are based on two underlying theoretical assumptions. One is that the more powerful we perceive a potential model to be and the more dependent we are upon him, the less likely we are to trust him, in the sense of perceiving his goals and motives to be similar to our own. The second assumption is that the more similarity we perceive between a potential model's experiences and our own, the more likely we are to be able to understand him and trust him. In the paradigm of child-parent relationships, the child is less likely to trust and understand his father than his brother because the father is perceived to be powerful, independent, and impossible to influence. The child sees the father as living in a different world and as having had experiences which are perceived to be so dissimilar to his own that he cannot help but question whether the father can understand him and therefore whether he can be trusted.

In stating these hypotheses we are speaking probabilistically. There are, of course, many situations where father figures do elicit trust and do serve as clear models. There are equally as many situations where the competition between brothers or peers destroys trust, however clear the brother model may be. Consequently, big brothers and peers may elicit *defensive* identification, but generally speaking fathers would tend to do so more often. It is likewise true that fathers may elicit *positive* identification, but big brothers and peers would tend to do so more often.

The kinds of influences which can be and generally are exerted by peers and big brothers often lead to behavior, attitudes, and values in the change target which run counter to those desired by the formal change institutions such as the family or school. Thus, while peer culture is a powerful instrument of influence, its values often run counter to those of the society in which the peer culture exists, setting the "parental" and peer culture into conflict with each other. *If* positive identification with parent figures can be achieved, the change target can learn the key norms, values, and behavior patterns of the society or organization to which he belongs. The dilemma of socialization, therefore, is how to balance the greater power of potentially countercultural change agents against the more functional learning to be obtained from change agents who have less chance of becoming influential.

Some applications of typology A. The relevance of this typology to the process of *socialization* is obvious. Somewhat less obvious is the fact that we tend to *recreate* these kinds of relationships in *adult* change or influence situations. An understanding of the change outcomes of such situations may then depend upon our ability to understand correctly the nature of the relationship which exists between change agent and target. For example, we rarely analyze the ubiquitous superior-subordinate relationship of modern organizational life in terms of whether the superior functions essentially as a father, big brother, or peer. Yet, we may not be able to understand why some superiors are able to influence the values of their subordinates more than others unless we stop to consider the role of such relationships.

Many business organizations, for example, have found that apprenticing a new member to an older, senior, high-ranking individual in the firm results in relatively little constructive learning in the new man. On the other hand, a productive and influential relationship results when the new man is assigned to a person only slightly older and one or two levels higher. Similarly, it is probably not accidental that so many induction programs, whether in military or civilian organizations, build in a "buddy" or "big brother" system. The function of these systems is to communicate the *informal* culture of the organization to the inductee, a task which would be difficult for the immediate superior to fulfill because of the likelihood that he would be viewed as a father figure and, therefore, as a symbol of only *formal* organizational values and norms.

The role of peer group influence can be seen clearly in prisons and certain mental hospitals where the inmates or patients band together to form a culture of their own in order to resist the formal authority of the institution. As new members join the organization, they learn the peer culture far more rapidly than the official value system. In industry, the counterpart of this phenomenon is "restriction of output," where such restriction is based on peer group norms of a "fair day's work for a fair day's pay." Once such norms have become established, incentive systems based on individual performance are relatively powerless to combat peer group pressures. Because the peer group relationship is such a powerful one, it has great potential for the transmission of organizational norms and values. The problem, from the point of view of the change agent, is how to insure the *congruence between peer group norms and organizational values.* Induction programs, such as those conducted by the Marines or by certain corporations which involve the peer group in "around the clock" organizational activities and which function primarily in terms of *group* incentives, appear to be able to achieve this goal. Perhaps the most notable industrial example is the Scanlon Plan, where even in unionized companies, workers and management organize into teams to fulfill the common aim of improving total organization performance.[23]

A few comments must be made on the role of the "person in transition," because this type of person is potentially the most powerful model of all. The person in transition still belongs to the peer group, but his movement out of the group implies that he is embracing some values other than those of the group. If the group trusts him enough, and if it seems clear that these new values are being rewarded by the organization and are rewarding to the transitional person, it is possible that the entire group will change with him in the direction of these new values.[24]

In industry, there is a clear dictum that one way to get ahead is to learn to be like those who are already on the move. Many social service organizations established for the purpose of rehabilitating others, such as Alcoholics Anonymous, use former "patients" as the key change agents in the process of influencing new patients. Perhaps the clearest example of this type of influence comes from Chinese Communist coercive persuasion attempts. Prisoners who were already partly reeducated were assigned to the same cell as the lone newcomer to the prison and proved to be powerful agents of influence (see Schein, pages 284–300).

The power of the person in transition depends very much on whether he is perceived to be "still one of *us*" or is perceived to "have gone over to *them*," particularly in those instances where the peer group is defensively arrayed against the authority. Thus, in the prison, the trusty's influence over inmates is negligible because he has gone too far; he has defected. In the treatment of juvenile delinquent gangs, some therapeutic gains may be achieved if the leader or some respected member of the gang can be induced to accept the psychiatrist. But

---

[23] F. G. Lesieur, *The Scanlon Plan* (New York: Wiley, 1958).

[24] The dynamics of this process are complicated because alongside the trust and faith may exist feelings of jealousy and having been betrayed. The whole problem of sibling rivalry versus learning from a sibling requires further analysis.

if this person accepts therapeutic goals to too great an extent, the others may handle the situation by rejecting him or reducing his status rather than allowing themselves to be influenced by him.

Typology B: Attributes which reflect personal qualities. The second typology is built on the personal qualities of the potential model and the manner in which the potential model presents himself to change targets. We are concerned here with the kinds of qualities which are referred to as *charisma*, and with the kinds of people who seem to inspire, be magnetic, and have a "powerful personality." These qualities may be stable personality characteristics, as in the case of the dedicated leader who trades on his sincerity, conviction, and zeal; or they may be skills learned for the purpose of managing interpersonal relationships, as in the case of the skilled salesman, persuader, or seducer.

Adelson (see pages 335–44) has adapted a typology of primitive healers or witch doctors in his discussion of the kinds of teacher-student relationships which occur in classrooms. The categories he describes can be usefully applied to any potential identification model or change agent. Thus, the change agent can present himself to the change target as a shamam, magician, naturalist, mystic healer, or priest.

The *shaman* communicates to the target a sense of personal power, conviction, autonomy, faith-in-self, and narcissism. He demands allegiance and acceptance of his personal influence on the basis of his power and faith in himself. He stimulates the fatal fascination which others have for the narcissist.

The *magician*, by contrast, purports to produce changes in the target through the manipulation of secret rites and materials to which he has sole access. He elicits trust on the basis of the actual miracles he is able to produce through his magic.

The *naturalist*, too, claims power on the basis of some knowledge he possesses, rather than on some innate personality trait. He differs from the magician in that his knowledge is scientifically verifiable and not secret. His function is to translate natural principles into practical considerations. While presenting a façade of indifference to the change target, he nevertheless is able to communicate that anyone who does not take advantage of the scientific knowledge offered is a fool.

The *mystic healer* functions as a catalyst of the change process. He communicates the assumption that the potential for change is already present in the target and offers the needed help to get the process started. In a sense, he demands change because of his investments in and altruistic concern for the target.

The *priest* presents himself as a gatekeeper, a person who has the official power to control entry into some desired group or desired status. Because he is invested with power from a high source, he is able to specify what the target must learn to achieve membership or status in the desired profession, group, or organization.

Adelson makes an analogy between these types and different kinds of teachers. Equally instructive might be a consideration of psychotherapists in these terms— the powerful personality (shaman) who achieves results through molding patients in his own image; the magician who may use hypnosis, electroshock, and other devices to impress his patients; the naturalist who uses a method such as psychoanalysis because he believes that if the method is followed correctly, the patient will be cured regardless of the particular personality of the therapist; the mystic who relies heavily on his concern and regard for the patient as the primary lever of influence and change; and the priest who dispassionately lays out the requirements for entering the community of the "healthy."

If scanning, positive identification, and defensive identification depend upon the salience of the potential model and the types of feelings he arouses in the target, we can state the following hypotheses. The naturalist is most likely to arouse scanning because he minimizes his own salience. He encourages the target to seek data wherever he can. The priest and magician are most likely to arouse defensive identification because of their power position relative to the target. The mystic healer is most likely to arouse positive identification because of his nonthreatening, altruistic concern for the target. The shaman is most likely to arouse some kind of identification because of his salient position in any relationship. Whether or not the identification will take a positive or negative form will depend on the shaman's particular approach, i.e., the degree of trust or fear he arouses in the target.

Examples of the changing mechanisms

1. Most *institutionalized* influence processes operate through defensive or positive identification and leave little room for scanning. The change target is not expected to discover his own cultural solutions to problems but is expected to benefit from the experience of his elders. If he cannot use symbolic models as guides (those ideal characters he hears about from his parents and teachers or those he reads about), he can always resort to identification with those models who happen to be physically available in the environment.

2. *Planned uninstitutionalized* influence is more difficult to characterize. If we are dealing with situations which involve primarily behavior change, as in the salesman-customer relationship, scanning is not apt to be prevalent, but whatever identification does take place is likely to be only with symbolic models. That is, the salesman may find that his best appeal is to discover who his customer's important identification model is and to link his product with that model (as most advertising attempts to do). For many reasons, the salesman himself is not likely to become a model.

The consultant often finds himself in a situation where, having unfrozen the target, he would like him to engage in scanning to find a solution which best fits his (the target's) needs. The target, however, may be too uncomfortable to search for a solution, preferring instead to seek out the nearest available identification model for emulation. Under some conditions, the consultant may be an adequate model and thus facilitate the influence process; but, under other conditions, this process may produce an uncomfortable situation where the consultant is unable to come up with the ready solution expected by the target, resulting in a weakening of his position as an agent of effective unfreezing. All of us have witnessed cases where consultants were dismissed psychologically on the grounds that they could not handle the client's situation any better themselves. All of us have heard of therapists who were dismissed on the ground that they had "worse" problems than some of their patients or were "unable to bring up their own children."

The change target evidently is very disappointed if he discovers that the change agent is not an adequate positive identification model. Once he has become unfrozen, the target often sees identification as the easiest, even if it is not always the healthiest, influence mechanism. One reason why so many members of the "helping professions" emphasize that the greatest part of their job is to help the client recognize what his problem is, may be the recognition, on their part, that they play a more important role in unfreezing the client than they are able to or want to play in the actual induction of change. At any rate, this remains an important area for further study and conceptual analysis.

3. In the case of *emergent change*, we are least likely to get defensive identification and most likely to get positive identification. Scanning appears to be less probable because friends and lovers often serve as ideal identification models for each other. One may expect scanning to occur, however, in the case where disconfirmation is so severe that the relationship itself is severed. Unless the disconfirmed party can retrospectively discount the disconfirmation, he remains in an unfrozen condition without an immediately relevant identification model. In this instance, he may seek new attitudes and self-perceptions in a wider social network by a systematic search for relevant information about himself.

This example raises the whole issue of whether or not a separation of the unfreezing and changing phases should be built into an effective change strategy for maximum personal growth. The agent of unfreezing inevitably becomes salient in the relationship, yet he may be a poor model. His dilemma is how to keep the change process going without becoming too influential himself as an identification model.

3. Mechanisms of refreezing

Personal and interpersonal reintegration.   Once the target has made a change or been influenced, there still remains the problem of how well the new response fits in with other parts of the personality and whether or not it will be accepted and confirmed by his significant others. One can cite many examples from training programs or psychotherapy of changes which satisfied the trainee or patient but which were rejected by his friends, relatives, and co-workers. One can find examples where, particularly through a process of identification, a person acquired beliefs, attitudes, and values which he later discovered did not fit well with other parts of himself. For any change to become a stable part of the person, it must, at some level, become integrated with other parts of himself and be acceptable to those whose opinions and reactions he values.

In situations of *planned institutionalized* influence, such as socialization and education, refreezing forces are automatically built into the situation, since the responses which the change target is expected to learn are those which the society or group which is doing the influencing defines as basic to its purposes. Thus, any successful change is automatically rewarded by the social environment as well as by the change agent. To the extent that the areas of learning or influence are defined as basic, the person is expected to accommodate other parts of himself to them. In the case of adult socialization, if the new values and attitudes really do not fit, the person has only one alternative—to give up membership in the group or society into which he is being socialized (unless, of course, he can tolerate the dissonance or incongruity).

Refreezing forces are also potentially built into *emergent change* situations. The change agent and/or identification model is usually also a "significant other" who can confirm whatever changes are induced. It is also possible, however, that the changes which a person makes in response to one significant other may give rise to a disconfirmatory response in other relevant people, thus creating further problems for the change target. We often see this exemplified in cases where one member of a family comes under the influence of a doctor, confidant, or other change agent outside the family and begins to change in a direction which threatens the family and is thus rejected by it.

As long as communication channels remain open, the changes resulting from a relationship of lovers or friends are likely to be easily integrated into the personality of both members and into the relationship. There are, however, dramatic instances where changes made by one party produce a greater negative reaction than the original behavior which initiated the change process. A husband gives cues to his wife that her knowledge of politics and world affairs leaves something to be desired. She responds not only by becoming knowledgeable, but by actively participating in political groups with the result that she has little time left for the activities that she and her husband had previously valued. Or, to take another example, a wife disconfirms certain patterns of masculine aggression in her husband. He responds by becoming overly passive and overly solicitous (which she discovers she likes less than the aggression). If the relationship is secure enough, it will allow several cycles of unfreezing, changing, new unfreezing, new changing, etc., until the new behavior is mutually satisfactory and can become refrozen. But, problems can obviously arise when a change is satisfactory to the person making it but unsatisfactory to significant others. In such instances, an unanticipated outcome of the change process may be that the relationship itself is gradually undermined.

Planned uninstitutionalized influence is least predictable with respect to re-freezing because the change agent who is involved in the unfreezing and changing stages is often unrelated to the significant others who must refreeze the change. An excellent example is the evangelist crusades, such as those of Billy Graham, where a high percentage of the people who are converted during the services give up the religion within a matter of days or weeks *unless they are immediately integrated into a local church in their own community.*

Industrial training programs in human relations often produce changes which may disappear and even arouse an adverse reaction in the trainee if his fellow workers disconfirm the new attitudes and behavior learned during training.[25] A salesman can obtain a promise of a purchase from a potential customer only to have the order turned down later because the person's family "talked him out of it."

If the change agent is really concerned about the direction and permanence of change, he must worry not only about providing identification models or other information which will communicate the desired direction of change, but must also make provisions for the adequate refreezing of those changes which do occur. What this means, in practice, is that the change agent must spend some of his time working on the significant others of the change target in order to get them ready for and convinced of the desirability of the change which is being induced in the target. Thus, the consultant may spend a great deal of his time training the client's associates and his organization, even though the client himself is the prime change target. The therapist often discovers that though his role as change agent is adequately institutionalized, the changes he is able to produce do not receive institutionalized support. Thus, the family of a schizophrenic will provide treatment for the patient, but will be unprepared to reinforce and confirm the minor changes which initial treatment may make possible. The therapist, then, is often forced to work with the family and teach them to refreeze the changes which he has induced.

It should, of course, be noted that the mechanism by which the change is induced in the first place, has consequences for the ease or difficulty of refreezing. To the extent that scanning leads to self-selected solutions, it produces changes which are automatically integrated into the person's total personality. From the outset, such solutions have more stability and may, therefore, be more desirable in situations where the change agent has little control over the reactions of significant others. The therapist or consultant attempts to induce changes which fit the person's own needs in the hope that such changes will have a chance of surviving whatever negative reactions they may arouse in others.

Changes produced by positive identification, on the other hand, derive their stability from the stability of the relationship between the target and the model. If the model reinforces the changes and continues to be available to the target, the changes can be long lasting and stable. However, they may not necessarily be integrated into other parts of the target's self, and they may not be accepted by people other than the model.

The problem for the change agent, then, is to assess whether or not the changes which might be induced by identification, will, in fact, fit the person's needs and be reinforced by others. For example, if the consultant observes that his client tends to emulate him and identify with him, he must decide whether

---

[25] E. A. Fleishman, "Leadership Climate, Human Relations Training and Supervisory Behavior." *Personnel Psychology,* Vol. 6 (1953), pp. 205–22. See also E. H. Schein, *Organizational Psychology* (Englewood Cliffs, N.J.: Prentice-Hall, 1970).

to encourage or discourage this process in terms of the above criterion. Similarly, the coach or therapist must decide how much identification to encourage. Of course, if the influence models are also the significant others with whom the target will have a continuous, long-run relationship, then positive identification is a highly functional mechanism of change, and one which will lead readily to refreezing. Thus, when we can, we put change targets into groups in which all the members set a correct example so that identification with any one of them will produce desired changes which will be reinforced.

SUMMARY AND CONCLUSIONS

An attempt has been made in this essay to identify some important dimensions of influence or change induced by interpersonal relationships. We have not dealt with all possible cases of influence or change, but rather have tried to focus on the kinds of changes which are generally associated with interpersonal relationships, namely changes in beliefs, attitudes, and values. The kind of conceptual scheme or model which has been presented is primarily geared toward attitudinal learning and relearning, and contributes little to an understanding of short-run behavioral compliance or reactions and impulses which arise in momentary encounters between people.

The conceptual scheme is organized around the notion that change or influence must be thought of as three separate though overlapping processes—unfreezing, changing, and refreezing. *Unfreezing* involves several basic mechanisms: (1) disconfirmation or lack of confirmation; (2) the induction of guilt anxiety; and (3) the removal of threat or barriers to change. *Changing* can occur through one of two basic mechanisms—identification or scanning. Both are mediated by a process of cognitive redefinition which makes the ultimate attitudinal change possible. *Refreezing* involves the integration of any new responses (attitudes) into the rest of the person's personality and into his significant ongoing relationships.

Several conclusions can be derived from an examination of the change process in terms of this model. *First,* it is apparent that the conceptual definition of *change agent* depends on the phase of the change process under discussion. Some persons may function as disconfirmers, others as inducers of change motives, and others as removers of barriers. Whatever their function, they all facilitate unfreezing. They may not necessarily serve as identification models or make the decisions as to what kinds of models will be available and whether identification or scanning should be encouraged, insofar as any control over the change mechanism can be exerted. Furthermore, the unfreezers and changers are not necessarily the refreezers. Because each phase of the change process is different from the other phases, it is difficult to pinpoint a single set of attributes for the effective change agent which will be suitable for all cases. We have tried to show that the attributes of the effective unfreezer are not the same as those of the effective changer, which in turn, are not the same as those of the effective refreezer.

Second, it should be apparent that a stable change of attitudes or values results from a particular *combination* of several sets of circumstances, *all of which have to be present*. Change is not possible if there is no motivation for change and the induction of such motivation is often a complex process; no change is possible if the person cannot locate solutions by scanning his social field or by finding identification models; and change will not persist unless it is integrated into the personality and into all relationships in which the target is involved. To define influence as just one of these phases is an oversimplification which can only result in conceptual confusion.

Third, within the total range of interpersonal change situations we have selected out four types which have different goals, different outcomes, and involve different combinations of unfreezing, changing, and refreezing mechanisms. These types were labeled *planned* and *unplanned institutionalized influence,* as exemplified by formal and informal socialization, education, and rehabilitation; *planned uninstitutionalized influence,* as exemplified by persuasion, consultation, and coaching; and *emergent change,* as exemplified by those changes which are the unintended by-products of the relationship of lovers, friends, and co-workers. One of the advantages of our conceptual scheme is that it enables us to think about the similarities and differences between these types of change situations.

Fourth, in thinking about actual mechanisms of change, it is important to differentiate two types of identification, one resulting from the change target's need to defend himself against coercive forces from which he cannot escape, and the other based on the target's recognition that the attitudes and responses of certain available models in the environment could offer solutions to the problems he experiences as a result of having been unfrozen. Certain personal characteristics of potential influence models are associated with the latter kind of identification. Two typologies of models were presented—one based on the kind of family situation which the relationship recreates (whether the model is seen as a father, big brother, peer, or person in transition), and one based upon an analysis of primitive healers which deals with the more personal attributes of the change agent. Certain hypotheses were stated about the relative likelihood of identification with the different types of models and the kind of influence each of these types could exert in a relationship.

Finally, the process of refreezing was analyzed. Depending on the goals of the change effort and the means available to the change agent, it makes a considerable difference for the change outcome whether the situation is set up to be one which encourages identification or encourages scanning. We also pointed out the increasing importance of the change agent as an agent of refreezing through his work with the target's "back home" situation in an effort to insure that induced change will be reinforced.

In conclusion, we would like to underscore our conviction that interpersonal influence is an extremely complex process which has not as yet yielded to definitive theoretical analysis. Whether we take reinforcement theory or Gestalt theory from the psychology of learning, or balance theory from the psychology of attitude change, or some theory of growth and change derived from clinical work with patients, we will continue to find examples and processes which somehow are not adequately dealt with by these models. Our strategy has been to face the complexity directly and tolerate some of the ambiguity which a more complex conceptual scheme inevitability brings with it. We eventually hope to deal with this problem by developing an adequate "theory of the middle level" which neither oversimplifies the problem for the sake of elegance, nor overcomplicates it for the sake of clinical richness.

NOTES ON THE READINGS

In selecting readings to illustrate aspects of interpersonal influence and emergent change, we have attempted to avoid articles which are either very well known or which attempt to treat interpersonal relations in terms of oversimplified models.

The first articles deal with planned and unplanned institutionalized influence such as socialization, role training, and political reeducation. The Strauss article deals with socialization processes of the sort found in movement through an organization during the process of one's career. Goffman then explores some of the more intricate dynamics of role redefinition by focusing on a particular kind of role problem—adaptation to failure. These articles deal with adult socialization in the normal pursuit of one's occupation and career.

The next two articles illustrate the dynamics of adult socialization in the political realm, i.e., what happens when someone sets out to deliberately change the political beliefs and behavior of a captive group. These papers should be studied, not only for their informational content about Communist methods of influencing people, but, more importantly, for the perspective they provide us on our own influence institutions. As a number of analysts have pointed out, there are more than casual similarities between Communist coercive persuasion and the kinds of influence which occur in schools, hospitals, prisons, and other "total institutions" in our society.

Our readings turn next to less institutionalized forms of influence. Perhaps the best examples of this type of influence come from therapeutic or educational settings. Frank,[26] for example, has written brilliantly on how therapy can be viewed as essentially a process of persuasion which bears many similarities to other kinds of persuasion. Rather than try to illustrate this aspect with our readings, we have attempted to locate material which illustrates the more common everyday version of seduction and emergent change. Lytle and Wodehouse provide examples of emergent change from two different kinds of life situations—a fraternity, and a resort setting. We then present the paper on identification models by Adelson.

The final two papers in the section deal with special change problems and reflect a growing trend to try to change attitudes and values through the mech-

---

[26] J. D. Frank, *Persuasion and Healing*. Baltimore: John Hopkins Press, 1961.

anism of "behavior change." If the correct *behavior* is emitted, the assumption is made that the attitudes, motives, etc., needed to support such behavior will be learned as well, but that the learning process starts with behavior change. Schwitzgebel gives a general description of the shaping of behavior and Kolb then analyzes how some of these techniques have been applied to motivation training.

Regularized status-passage*

Anselm Strauss

The lives of men and women can—theoretically at least—be traced as a series of passages of status. Insofar as this is so, we most heartily agree with Erikson's striking statement that a sense of identity "is never gained nor maintained once and for all. Like a good conscience, it is constantly lost and regained. . . ."[1]

COACHING

When passages of status are more or less well regulated, those who have gone through the recognized steps stand ready, as I have said, to guide and advise their successors. This guidance is essential, for even regulated passage is perhaps more hazardous than my account has indicated.

In the well known novel, *The Late George Apley*, J. B. Marquand[2] portrays the well-ordered life of George as it follows the traditional Bostonian upper class pattern of growing up and growing old. As a young man, George is in danger of being drawn off the track when he becomes fond of an Irish girl far below him in social position. He is brought to heel through family pressure and by being shown how this incident "really" fits into his entire expected life cycle. Natural as it is for him to dally with such a girl, the "escapade" is not to be treated as a serious venture. The great danger of such an escapade is that through it some George Apley—if not this one—will be drawn off expected paths and lost to family and social class. However, the counsel of elders is requisite to status passages for reasons other than hazard, since all the future steps are clear only

---

* Reprinted with permission of the publisher from *Mirrors and Masks: the Search for Identity* by Anselm Strauss, pp. 109–18. Copyright 1959 by The Free Press, a Corporation.

[1] Erik H. Erikson, "Identity and Totality: Psychoanalytic Observations on the Problem of Youth," *Human Development Bulletin* (Fifth Annual Symposium, Committee on Human Development of the University of Chicago, 1954), p. 57.

[2] John P. Marquand, *The Late George Apley* (New York: Random House, 1936), chap. 8, "The Interlude," pp. 84–92.

to those who have traversed them. Certain aspects of what lies over the horizon are blurred to the candidate, no matter how clear may be his general path. This forces his predecessors not only to counsel and guide him, but to prepare and coach him beforehand. Coaching is an integral part of teaching the inexperienced —of any age.

Once we see this function of "the coach," we are prepared to discuss coaching quite apart from regularized status steps, and within wider contexts than athletics or professional drama. A coaching relationship exists if someone seeks to move someone else along a series of steps, when those steps are not entirely institution-alized and invariant, and when the learner is not entirely clear about their sequences (although the coach is). The football coach attempting to turn out a good half-back, Iago seeking to induce Othello along the path of jealousy, the piano teacher trying to make a concert pianist out of a young man, the revivalist trying to work his audience into a frenzy of conversion, the psychiatrist carefully maneuvering his patient back to better psychological integration, and the confi-dence man manipulating his victim through sequential steps of involvement in an illicit deal: all are instances of coaching relationships, albeit each has different aspects. In each instance there is a man who has yielded himself (whether he knows it or not) to a teacher who guides him along at least partly obscure channels. Since every field in which such teaching goes on has its own prescrip-tions and rules of thumb, my discussion of coaching quite obviously must be very general, and will be pointed particularly toward those changes of identity that take place during coaching.

The general features of the coaching relationship flow from the learner's need for guidance as he moves along, step by step. He needs guidance not merely because in the conventional sense he needs someone to teach him skills, but because some very surprising things are happening to him that require explana-tion. The coach stands ready to interpret his responses, which may otherwise only have the status of ambiguous signs. If you look at something as nonpsychological as learning a physical skill, perhaps you can see the point more easily. The learner leans upon the coach's expert advice, for instance, whether a given muscular movement is going to lead forward, or down a false path; and without the coach he may not even notice his own movement. The coach literally calls attention to new responses: "Look, this is the first time you have managed to do this." Likewise, the coach explains away responses, saying "pay no attention" for what is happening either should be regarded as of no importance or as something that happens only "at this stage." The next steps are pointed out ("Don't worry, wait, this will happen"). In sum: because the sequences of steps are in some measure obscure, and because one's own responses become something out of the ordinary, someone must stand prepared to predict, indicate, and explain the signs.

But the tutor generally assigns himself a far more active role than I have suggested. He does not merely wait for the student to develop new responses; he throws him into situations so as to elicit certain responses from him. This provides an opportunity to indicate, interpret, and predict. Understandably, this involves the coach in a certain kind of duplicity upon occasion (as when a fencing teacher allows his pupil to hit him for the first time); the coach's position also requires that he may have to function like a playwright, arranging episodes, setting scenes, getting supporting characters to act in a certain way. Of course, the pupil, by virtue of his acquisition of new skills or new perspectives, can be counted upon to engage other persons in new interactions. Like the infant who upon learning his first words encounters his parents differently, the learner's recently gained skills will throw him into novel situations. Some outcomes will be gratifying, but, of course, others can be terrifying or at least frightening. The coach utilizes both kinds of outcomes to retain control, occasionally even allowing him his head so as to be able to say—"I told you so, now then you see. . . ." The point is that the untutored can not see until he has tried for himself, just as generally he cannot visualize much of the proper path before hand.

In malevolent kinds of coaching—as in seduction, or in conning by confidence men—the relationship is one of trapper and victim. However, in almost all coaching there appears to be a strong element of inducement, temptation, and behind-the-scenes action. The con man baits, tempts, induces; but so does, although in less obvious ways, the art teacher, the basketball coach, or the psychiatrist. Abstractly stated, the coach not only works on current desires to get action directed along given paths, but seeks to create new desires and aims. He seeks to create a new identity for the pupil—or the victim—and to do this involves him in a variety of canny maneuvers.

In general, we should be struck by the importance of timing in all coaching. Because the pupil is being guided in his moves—muscularly, psychologically, socially—the coach is preoccupied with teaching him certain things at correct places and times. To begin with, the coach may be rejected if he forces too fast a pace, especially at the outset. The pupil may lose face or become frightened or otherwise distressed. In psychiatric coaching the patient may go elsewhere for help or, if the relationship is involuntary as when he is committed to a mental hospital, simply withdraw psychologically. On the other hand, the pupil (whether a patient, victim, or convert) may be lost to his mentor if the latter moves too slowly—lost through boredom, shattering of faith, or other reasons. Of course, the teacher may call attention to his superior experience and wisdom, as well as draw upon the resources of trust placed in him by the other, in order to set the pace; but he does so always at some risk. This risk is unavoidable and can only be minimized by shrewd tactics. The coach has to know when to force his man over a hurdle, and when to let him sidle up to it; when to schedule definite moves, and when to allow a period of relative free play. The coach must skillfully balance between two poles: he must not pressure the student by his own impatience; yet he must force movement at those junctures when the fellow appears ready but reluctant to move, is in fact really "there" but does not realize it.

Crucial tactics in this delicately balanced process are the prescription, the schedule, the challenge, the trial, and the accusation. Prescriptions for action are sometimes called "routines" or "exercises" or "lessons"; they are traditional step-by-step progressions that prepare the way for further movement. When the coaching relationship is well-institutionalized, such routine practices become a very visible and sometimes hampering part of the coaching profession. The schedule is also an integral aspect of the coaching process; notions arise of how fast or how slowly the pupil should move, and at what points he should move slower and faster. There is at least an implicit set of norms governing how quickly he should progress through certain stages. Recently, a psychologist has suggested to a group of psychiatrists how a standardized set of norms might be used to measure the progress of their patients. In the coaching relationship, a considerable potential strain exists because the coach must control his own impulses to standardize schedules too greatly.

Challenges or dares are also an invariant aspect of coaching. Since a person is being asked to relinquish old modes of doing and seeing, he is in effect being asked to do and say and even think things that look risky or dangerous. I recently heard a psychiatrist say to a patient, "It is now time to do. . . . You may fail but you are likely not to; it is a risk worth taking." Of course, there are clever and institutionalized ways of cushioning failure, but the important thing is that the person by meeting the challenge receives an indication of how far he has progressed. His overcoming of a challenge provides a marker, a milestone of his development.

Essential also to coaching is the accusation, hurled or insinuated. The coach will conceive of his pupil on occasion as backsliding, as giving in to old habits, old temptations, and, therefore, must be frankly reprimanded. The pupil will also be accused of loss of faith or trust: "How can you benefit from what I have to teach you if you do not trust me now." From the learner's perspective, the coach may be neglecting his job, ruining one's talents, breaking faith, even engaging in betrayal. Accusations both block the process of learning and are vitally important for those reconciliations that mark turning points on the road forward.

I have mentioned the elements of risk and trust involved in the coaching relationship, although they loom as more obvious in some kinds of relationships than in others. The novice airplane pilot literally puts his life at the disposal of his instructor. In seduction or in confidence games the secret motivations that are involved highlight the risk and danger. Even in such mundane pursuits as piano and voice teaching or training for track meets, the pupil's potential level of performance may be greatly endangered by improper counsel. Insofar as the coaching process also leads to great changes of identity—as in G. B. Shaw's apocryphal drama *Pygmalion*—you, as a pupil, are in large measure ceding an unknown destiny to a mentor who presumably knows where he is taking you. A special danger is that the relationship may be broken off midstream, before "the treatment" is completed, with potential danger to both but particularly to the learner. One of the great and inevitable risks of coaching is precisely that the coach may die, or move away, leaving the student vulnerable in various ways: because he is in a stage of self-imputed personal helplessness, or standing upon the brink of a learning crisis, or not yet properly out of love with the coach ("transference"), or in the midst of meeting a great challenge. But a comparable risk is that the student has the final responsibility of judging when the coaching relationship is genuinely harmful to himself or to his "potential." There is a point beyond which he must not, like Cinderella, stay. The coach may have poor judgment. It is not impossible even that he evinces faulty judgment because he loves or hates his pupil too much; although he may be actually malevolent or merely indifferent. The learner always has an obligation to himself of assessing when he is being harmed and when he is being helped, even in those very traditional situations where the coach is supposed supremely knowledgable.

The reverse side of great risk and danger is trust and faith. To this should be added what the psychoanalysts call "identification"; that is, a very close modeling of self after the other, or after certain of his aspects. The coach is not only a partial model ("do as I do"), but in certain stages may become almost a total model ("be as I am" or "wish to be what I am"). The tutor, of course, may consciously utilize this desire or propensity. On the other hand, in many types of coaching, particularly after the earlier stages of learning, mere imitation is not sufficient for progress.

Let us now consider more explicitly the shifts of identity brought about through coaching, as against the mere acquisition of skill. One cannot, of course, discuss risk, trust, identification, duplicity, challenge, and merely talk of the acquisition of skill. In some coaching, the person may be taken as a *tabula rasa*, as if he had no previous commitments of the kind the coach is now about to build; the task is simply to build upon unimpeded ground. More often this is not a realistic stance for the coach to take. The learner has something to unlearn, to cope with, and this will enter the trajectory of his learning early and often stay with him until very late. This is perhaps another way of saying that the coach must challenge old modes of doing, seeing, and thinking, as well as point out new modes. When the learning and relearning is extreme—and I shall consider a variety of this in the next section—there must be massive and frontal attack upon identities. In less drastic kinds of change, through the agency of coaches, a man is requested also to turn his back upon his past, to discount previous accomplishments, to divest himself of earlier prides, to disidentify himself with old practices, old allies, and even old loves.

One may sometimes observe during the initial sessions of a new coaching relationship how the participants gingerly hold back from much involvement until they are "sure." This is especially true of the student, but the teacher also may have provisos. Traditionally, the early phases may be coached in terms of "make-believe" or "not for keeps"; and institutionally they may take the form of not yet counting the score or recording the performance. All this, in a sense, represents a trial period; one is involved, but without much commitment to his own performance, and can retreat with honor and dignity. It is as if there were a kind of moratorium, during which effort is great but during which both sides ceremonially ignore negative performances. Of course, such a moratorium and such make-believe run all through the coaching process, perhaps particularly during the new phases in cycles of learning, when the person is particularly sensitive to criticism and must be encouraged and must encourage himself to chance certain endeavors. You can see this procedure operating in reverse when young art students are so jealous of their paintings, so serious about their performances, that they bridle when the teacher lays a brush upon their work.

In his fondest moments, the coach may believe that he has total control over the progress of his pupil. But the very character of coaching is likely to set into motion unpredictable changes of identity. The best model for visualizing this learning is not as a steady progression through a series of stages, mostly known to the coach, but rather to imagine a tree with many branches and twigs. The pupil moves along certain branches until he reaches alternatives, and the coach stands ready to guide or channel his movement until the next set of alternatives arises. But the best pupils, like the best children, get out from under the control and the vision of the best teachers, and the best teachers are pleased that this is so. At the outer limits of learning, the stages can no longer be as standardized as at the beginning; and the pupil discovers his own style, whether we are talking of religious conversion, musical composition, or anything else. For the coach, too, the process may be open-ended; he too may end with a different identity. This mutual change may be, as Nelson Foote has suggested, "a winning pattern for each,"[3] but unfortunately it may also be mutually destructive or end happily for one but not for the other.

Something should now be added to counteract the notion that coaching is merely a two-way relationship between a coach and a coached person, for many if not most coaching processes occur in organization or institutional context. Thus the teacher hands on pupils to higher or more famous teachers, saying "I can teach you no more, you are now beyond me—or at least it is said that you are beyond me." Although I shall not develop the point, you ought to recognize that the organizational framework within which the coaching goes on vitally affects the process and outcome of coaching. In some organizational contexts the coach may move his students too quickly (for his own frame, or to get them sponsored jobs), or his coaching may become standardized (because of great numbers of pupils, or because of the excessively strict requirements of the organization) or he may handle his pupils far too impersonally (because of personal tensions engendered by his position, or because of rewards placed upon other activities associated with his position). He may bind his students too closely to himself for their rapid or maximum development (because of his own anxieties created again by his position); or he may fail to sustain proper trust of himself (because close relationships among age ranks are frowned upon in the organization). Since coaching is thus linked with social structure and with the positions and careers of both the coaches and the coached, one can scarcely speak of process as divorced from structure. My discussion of process has been exceedingly

---

[3] Nelson Foote, "Concept and Method in the Study of Human Development," mimeographed manuscript of paper delivered at an Oklahoma conference in Social Psychology.

general and its details must be spelled out in relation to particular structures and worlds. This is a task for meticulous and thoughtful research.

On cooling the mark out:
Some aspects of adaptation
to failure*

Erving Goffman

In cases of criminal fraud, victims find they must suddenly adapt themselves to the loss of sources of security and status which they had taken for granted. A consideration of this adaptation to loss can lead us to an understanding of some relations in our society between involvements and the selves that are involved.

In the argot of the criminal world, the term "mark" refers to any individual who is a victim or prospective victim of certain forms of planned illegal exploitation. The mark is the sucker—the person who is taken in. An instance of the operation of any particular racket, taken through the full cycle of its steps or phases, is sometimes called a play. The persons who operate the racket and "take" the mark are occasionally called operators.

The confidence game—the con, as its practitioners call it—is a way of obtaining money under false pretenses by the exercise of fraud and deceit. The con differs from politer forms of financial deceit in important ways. The con is practiced on private persons by talented actors who methodically and regularly build up informal social relationships just for the purpose of abusing them; white-collar crime is practiced on organizations by persons who learn to abuse positions of trust which they once filled faithfully. The one exploits poise; the other, position. Further, a con man is someone who accepts a social role in the underworld community; he is part of a brotherhood whose members make no pretense to one another of being "legit." A white-collar criminal, on the other hand, has no colleagues, although he may have an associate with whom he plans his crime and a wife to whom he confesses it.

The con is said to be a good racket in the United States only because most Americans are willing, nay eager, to make easy money, and will engage in action

---

* Excerpted from Erving Goffman "On Cooling the Mark Out," reprinted by special permission of The William Alanson White Psychiatric Foundation, Inc., *Psychiatry,* Vol. 15, No. 4 (Nov., 1952), pp. 451–63. Copyright 1952 by The William Alanson White Psychiatric Foundation, Inc.

that is less than legal in order to do so. The typical play has typical phases. The potential sucker is first spotted, and one member of the working team (called the outside man, steerer, or roper) arranges to make social contact with him. The confidence of the mark is won, and he is given an opportunity to invest his money in a gambling venture which he understands to have been fixed in his favor. The venture, of course, is fixed, but not in his favor. The mark is permitted to win some money and then persuaded to invest more. There is an "accident" or "mistake," and the mark loses his total investment. The operators then depart in a ceremony that is called the blowoff or sting. They leave the mark but take his money. The mark is expected to go on his way, a little wiser and a lot poorer.

Sometimes, however, a mark is not quite prepared to accept his loss as a gain in experience and to say and do nothing about his venture. He may feel moved to complain to the police or to chase after the operators. In the terminology of the trade, the mark may squawk, beef, or come through. From the operators' point of view, this kind of behavior is bad for business. It gives the members of the mob a bad reputation with such police as have not yet been fixed and with marks who have not yet been taken. In order to avoid this adverse publicity, an additional phase is sometimes added at the end of the play. It is called cooling the mark out. After the blowoff has occurred, one of the operators stays with the mark and makes an effort to keep the anger of the mark within manageable and sensible proportions. The operator stays behind his team-mates in the capacity of what might be called a cooler and exercises upon the mark the art of consolation. An attempt is made to define the situation for the mark in a way that makes it easy for him to accept the inevitable and quietly go home. The mark is given instruction in the philosophy of taking a loss.

When we call to mind the image of a mark who has just been separated from his money, we sometimes attempt to account for the greatness of his anger by the greatness of his financial loss. This is a narrow view. In many cases, especially in America, the mark's image of himself is built up on the belief that he is a pretty shrewd person when it comes to making deals and that he is not the sort of person who is taken in by anything. The mark's readiness to participate in a sure thing is based on more than avarice; it is based on a feeling that he will now be able to prove to himself that he is the sort of person who can "turn a fast buck." For many, this capacity for high finance comes near to being a sign of masculinity and a test of fulfilling the male role.

It is well known that persons protect themselves with all kinds of rationalizations when they have a buried image of themselves which the facts of their status do not support. A person may tell himself many things: that he has not been given a fair chance; that he is not really interested in becoming something else; that the time for showing his mettle has not yet come; that the usual means of realizing his desires are personally or morally distasteful, or require too much dull effort. By means of such defenses, a person saves himself from committing a cardinal social sin—the sin of defining oneself in terms of a status while lacking the qualifications which an incumbent of that status is supposed to possess.

A mark's participation in a play, and his investment in it, clearly commit him in his own eyes to the proposition that he is a smart man. The process by which he comes to believe that he cannot lose is also the process by which he drops the defenses and compensations that previously protected him from defeats. When the blow-off comes, the mark finds that he has no defense for not being a shrewd man. He has defined himself as a shrewd man and must face the fact that he is only another easy mark. He has defined himself as possessing a certain set of qualitites and then proven to himself that he is miserably lacking in them. This is a process of self-destruction of the self. It is no wonder that the mark needs to be cooled out and that it is good business policy for one of the operators to stay with the mark in order to talk him into a point of view from which it is possible to accept a loss.

In essence, then, the cooler has the job of handling persons who have been caught out on a limb—persons whose expectations and self-conceptions have been built up and then shattered. The mark is a person who has compromised himself, in his own eyes if not in the eyes of others.

Although the term, mark, is commonly applied to a person who is given shortlived expectations by operators who have intentionally misrepresented the facts, a less restricted definition is desirable in analyzing the larger social scene. An expectation may finally prove false, even though it has been possible to sustain it for a long time and even though the operators acted in good faith. So, too, the disappointment of reasonable expectations, as well as misguided ones, creates a need for consolation. Persons who participate in what is recognized as a confidence game are found in only a few social settings, but persons who have to be cooled out are found in many. Cooling the mark out is one theme in a very basic social story.

For purposes of analysis, one may think of an individual in reference to the values or attributes of a socially recognized character which he possesses. Psychologists speak of a value as a personal involvement. Sociologists speak of a value as a status, role, or relationship. In either case, the character of the value that is possessed is taken in a certain way as the character of the person who possesses it. An alteration in the kinds of attributes possessed brings an alteration to the self-conception of the person who possesses them.

The process by which someone acquires a value is the process by which he surrenders the claim he had to what he was and commits himself to the conception of self which the new value requires or allows him to have. It is the process that persons who fall in love or take dope call getting hooked. After a person is hooked, he must go through another process by which his new involvement finds its proper place, in space and time, relative to the other calls, demands, and commitments that he has upon himself. At this point certain other persons suddenly begin to play an important part in the individual's story; they impinge upon him by virtue of the relationship they happen to have to the value in which he has become involved. This is not the place to consider the general kinds of impingement that are institutionalized in our society and the general social relationships that arise: the personal relationship, the professional relationship, and the business relationship. Here we are concerned only with the end of the story, the way in which a person becomes disengaged from one of his involvements.

In our society, the story of a person's involvement can end in one of three general ways. According to one type of ending, he may withdraw from one of his involvements or roles in order to acquire a sequentially related one that is considered better. This is the case when a youth becomes a man, when a student becomes a practitioner, or when a man from the ranks is given a commission.

Of course, the person who must change his self at any one of these points of promotion may have profound misgivings. He may feel disloyal to the way of life that must be left behind and to the persons who do not leave it with him. His new role may require action that seems insincere, dishonest, or unfriendly. This he may experience as a loss in moral cleanliness. His new role may require him to forgo the kinds of risk-taking and exertion that he previously enjoyed, and yet his new role may not provide the kind of heroic and exalted action that he expected to find in it.[1] This he may experience as a loss in moral strength.

There is no doubt that certain kinds of role success require certain kinds of moral failure. It may, therefore, be necessary, in a sense, to cool the dubious neophyte in rather than out. He may have to be convinced that his doubts are a matter of sentimentality. The adult social view will be impressed upon him. He will be required to understand that a promotional change in status is voluntary, desirable, and natural, and that loss of one's role in these circumstances is the ultimate test of having fulfilled it properly.

It has been suggested that a person may leave a role under circumstances that reflect favorably upon the way in which he performed it. In theory, at least, a related possibility must be considered. A person may leave a role and at the same time leave behind him the standards by which such roles are judged. The new thing that he becomes may be so different from the thing he was that criteria such as success or failure cannot be easily applied to the change which has occurred. He becomes lost to others that he may find himself; he is of the twice-born. In our society, perhaps the most obvious example of this kind of termination occurs when a woman voluntarily gives up a prestigious profession in order to become a wife and a mother. It is to be noted that this illustrates an institutionalized movement; those who make it do not make news. In America most other examples of this kind of termination are more a matter of talk than of occurrence. For example, one of the culture heroes of our dinner-table mythology is the man who walks out on an established calling in order to write or paint or live in the country. In other societies, the kind of abdication being considered here seems to have played a more important role. In medieval China, for instance, anchoritic withdrawal apparently gave to persons of quite different

----

[1] Mr. Hughes has lectured on this kind of disappointment, and one of his students has undertaken a special study of it. See Miriam Wagenschein, " 'Reality Shock': A Study of Beginning School Teachers," M.A. thesis, Dept. of Sociology, Univ. of Chicago, 1950.

station a way of retreating from the occupational struggle while managing the retreat in an orderly, face-saving fashion.[2]

Two basic ways in which a person can lose a role have been considered; he can be promoted out of it or abdicate from it. There is, of course, a third basic ending to the status story. A person may be involuntarily deprived of his position or involvement and made in return something that is considered a lesser thing to be. It is mainly in this third ending to a person's role that occasions arise for cooling him out. It is here that one deals in the full sense with the problem of persons' losing their roles.

Involuntary loss seems itself to be of two kinds. First, a person may lose a status in such a way that the loss is not taken as a reflection upon the loser. The loss of a loved one, either because of an accident that could not have been prevented or because of a disease that could not have been halted, is a case in point. Occupational retirement because of old age is another. Of course, the loss will inevitably alter the conception the loser has of himself and the conception others have of him, but the alteration itself will not be treated as a symbol of the fate he deserves to receive. No insult is added to injury. It may be necessary, nonetheless, to pacify the loser and resign him to his loss. The loser who is not held responsible for his loss may even find himself taking the mystical view that all involvements are part of a wider con game, for the more one takes pleasure in a particular role the more one must suffer when it is time to leave it. He may find little comfort in the fact that the play has provided him with an illusion that has lasted a lifetime. He may find little comfort in the fact that the operators had not meant to deceive him.

Secondly, a person may be involuntarily deprived of a role under circumstances which reflect unfavorably on his capacity for it. The lost role may be one that he had already acquired or one that he had openly committed himself to preparing for. In either case the loss is more than a matter of ceasing to act in a given capacity; it is ultimate proof of an incapacity. And in many cases it is even more than this. The moment of failure often catches a person acting as one who feels that he is an appropriate sort of a person for the role in question. Assumption becomes presumption, and failure becomes fraud. To loss of substance is thereby added loss of face. Of the many themes that can occur in the natural history of an involvement, this seems to be the most melancholy. Here it will be quite essential and quite difficult to cool the mark out. I shall be particularly concerned with this second kind of loss—the kind that involves humiliation.

It should be noted, parenthetically, that one circle of persons may define a particular loss as the kind that casts no reflection on the loser, and that a different circle of persons may treat the same loss as a symbol of what the loser deserves. One must also note that there is a tendency today to shift certain losses of status from the category of those that reflect upon the loser to the category of those

---

[2] See, for example, Max Weber, *The Religion of China* (H. H. Gerth, tr.); Glencoe, Ill.: Free Press, 1951; p. 178.

that do not. When persons lose their jobs, their courage, or their minds, we tend more and more to take a clinical or naturalistic view of the loss and a nonmoral view of their failure. We want to define a person as something that is not destroyed by the destruction of one of his selves. This benevolent attitude is in line with the effort today to publicize the view that occupational retirement is not the end of all active capacities but the beginning of new and different ones.

A consideration of consolation as a social process leads to four general problems having to do with the self in society. First, where in modern life does one find persons conducting themselves as though they were entitled to the rights of a particular status and then having to face up to the fact that they do not possess the qualification for the status? In other words, at what points in the structures of our social life are persons likely to compromise themselves or find themselves compromised? When is it likely that a person will have to disengage himself or become disengaged from one of his involvements? Secondly, what are the typical ways in which persons who find themselves in this difficult position can be cooled out; how can they be made to accept the great injury that has been done to their image of themselves, regroup their defenses, and carry on without raising a squawk? Thirdly, what, in general, can happen when a person refuses to be cooled out, that is, when he refuses to be pacified by the cooler? Fourthly, what arrangements are made by operators and marks to avoid entirely the process of consolation?

In all personal service organizations customers or clients sometimes make complaints. A customer may feel that he has been given service in a way that is unacceptable to him—a way that he interprets as an offense to the conception he has of who and what he is. The management therefore has the problem of cooling the mark out. Frequently this function is allotted to specialists within the organization. In restaurants of some size, for example, one of the crucial functions of the hostess is to pacify customers whose self-conceptions have been injured by waitresses or by the food. In large stores the complaint department and the floorwalker perform a similar function.

One may note that a service organization does not operate in an anonymous world, as does a con mob, and is, therefore, strongly obliged to make some effort to cool the mark out. An institution, after all, cannot take it on the lam; it must pacify its marks.

One may also note that coolers in service organizations tend to view their own activity in a light that softens the harsher details of the situation. The cooler protects himself from feelings of guilt by arguing that the customer is not really in need of the service he expected to receive, that bad service is not really deprivational, and that beefs and complaints are a sign of bile, not a sign of injury. In a similar way, the con man protects himself from remorseful images of bankrupt marks by arguing that the mark is a fool and not a full-fledged person, possessing an inclination towards illegal gain but not the decency to admit it or the capacity to succeed at it.

In organizations patterned after a bureaucratic model, it is customary for personnel to expect rewards of a specified kind upon fulfilling requirements of a specified nature. Personnel come to define their career line in terms of a sequence of legitimate expectations and to base their self-conceptions on the assumption that in due course they will be what the institution allows persons to become. Sometimes, however, a member of an organization may fulfill some of the requirements for a particular status, especially the requirements concerning technical proficiency and seniority, but not other requirements, especially the less codified ones having to do with the proper handling of social relationships at work. It must fall to someone to break the bad news to the victim; someone must tell him that he has been fired, or that he has failed his examinations, or that he has been by-passed in promotion. And after the blowoff, someone has to cool the mark out. The necessity of disappointing the expectations that a person has taken for granted may be infrequent in some organizations, but in others, such as training institutions, it occurs all the time. The process of personnel selection requires that many trainees be called but that few be chosen.

When one turns from places of work to other scenes in our social life, one finds that each has its own occasions for cooling the mark out. During informal social intercourse it is well understood that an effort on the part of one person (ego) to decrease his social distance from another person (alter) must be graciously accepted by alter or, if rejected, rejected tactfully so that the initiator of the move can save his social face. This rule is codified in books on etiquette and is followed in actual behavior. A friendly movement in the direction of alter is a movement outward on a limb; ego communicates his belief that he has defined himself as worthy of alter's society, while at the same time he places alter in the strategic position of being able to discredit this conception.

The problem of cooling persons out in informal social intercourse is seen most clearly, perhaps, in courting situations and in what might be called de-courting situations. A proposal of marriage in our society tends to be a way in which a man sums up his social attributes and suggests to a woman that hers are not so much better as to preclude a merger or partnership in these matters. Refusal on the part of the woman, or refusal on the part of the man to propose when he is clearly in a position to do so, is a serious reflection on the rejected suitor. Courtship is a way not only of presenting oneself to alter for approval but also of saying that the opinion of alter in this matter is the opinion one is most concerned with. Refusing a proposal, or refusing to propose, is therefore a difficult operation. The mark must be carefully cooled out. The act of breaking a date or of refusing one, and the task of discouraging a "steady" can also be seen in this light, although in these cases great delicacy and tact may not be required, since the mark may not be deeply involved or openly committed. Just as it is harder to refuse a proposal than to refuse a date, so it is more difficult to reject a spouse than to reject a suitor. The process of de-courting by which one person in a marriage maneuvers the other into accepting a divorce without fuss or undue rancor requires extreme finesse in the art of cooling the mark out.

In all of these cases where a person constructs a conception of himself which cannot be sustained, there is a possibility that he has not invested that which is most important to him in the soon-to-be-denied status. In the current idiom, there is a possibility that when he is hit, he will not be hit where he really lives. There is a set of cases, however, where the blowoff cannot help but strike a vital spot; these cases arise, of course, when a person must be dissuaded from life itself. The man with a fatal sickness or fatal injury, the criminal with a death sentence, the soldier with a hopeless objective—these persons must be persuaded to accept quietly the loss of life itself, the loss of all one's earthly involvements. Here, certainly, it will be difficult to cool the mark out. It is a reflection on the conceptions men have—as cooler and mark—that it is possible to do so.

I have mentioned a few of the areas of social life where it becomes necessary, upon occasion, to cool a mark out. Attention may now be directed to some of the common ways in which individuals are cooled out in all of these areas of life.

For the mark, cooling represents a process of adjustment to an impossible situation—a situation arising from having defined himself in a way which the social facts come to contradict. The mark must therefore be supplied with a new set of apologies for himself, a new framework in which to see himself and judge himself. A process of redefining the self along defensible lines must be instigated and carried along; since the mark himself is frequently in too weakened a condition to do this, the cooler must initially do it for him.

One general way of handling the problem of cooling the mark out is to give the task to someone whose status relative to the mark will serve to ease the situation in some way. In formal organizations, frequently, someone who is two or three levels above the mark in line of command will do the hatchet work, on the assumption that words of consolation and redirection will have a greater power to convince if they come from high places. There also seems to be a feeling that persons of high status are better able to withstand the moral danger of having hate directed at them. Incidentally, persons protected by high office do not like to face this issue, and frequently attempt to define themselves as merely the agents of the deed and not the source of it. In some cases, on the other hand, the task of cooling the mark out is given to a friend and peer of the mark, on the assumption that such a person will know best how to hit upon a suitable rationalization for the mark and will know best how to control the mark should the need for this arise. In some cases, as in those pertaining to death, the role of cooler is given to doctors or priests. Doctors must frequently help a family, and the member who is leaving it, to manage the leave-taking with tact and a minimum of emotional fuss.[3] A priest must not so much save a soul as create one that is consistent with what is about to become of it.

A second general solution to the problem of cooling the mark out consists of offering him a status which differs from the one he has lost or failed to gain but which provides at least a something or a somebody for him to become. Usually the alternative presented to the mark is a compromise of some kind,

---

[3] This role of the doctor has been stressed by W. L. Warner in his lectures at the University of Chicago on symbolic roles in "Yankee City."

providing him with some of the trappings of his lost status as well as with some of its spirit. A lover may be asked to become a friend; a student of medicine may be asked to switch to the study of dentistry;[4] a boxer may become a trainer; a dying person may be asked to broaden and empty his worldly loves so as to embrace the All-Father that is about to receive him. Sometimes the mark is allowed to retain his status but is required to fulfill it in a different environment: the honest policeman is transferred to a lonely beat; the too zealous priest is encouraged to enter a monastery; an unsatisfactory plant manager is shipped off to another branch. Sometimes the mark is "kicked upstairs" and given a courtesy status such as "Vice President." In the game for social roles, transfer up, down, or away may all be consolation prizes.

A related way of handling the mark is to offer him another chance to qualify for the role at which he has failed. After his fall from grace, he is allowed to retrace his steps and try again. Officer selection programs in the army, for example, often provide for possibilities of this kind. In general, it seems that third and fourth chances are seldom given to marks, and that second chances, while often given, are seldom taken. Failure at a role removes a person from the company of those who have succeeded, but it does not bring him back—in spirit, anyway—to the society of those who have not tried or are in the process of trying. The person who has failed in a role is a constant source of embarrassment, for none of the standard patterns of treatment is quite applicable to him. Instead of taking a second chance he usually goes away to another place where his past does not bring confusion to his present.

Another standard method of cooling the mark out—one which is frequently employed in conjunction with other methods—is to allow the mark to explode, to break down, to cause a scene, to give full vent to his reactions and feelings, to "blow his top." If this release of emotions does not find a target, then it at least serves a cathartic function. If it does find a target, as in "telling off the boss," it gives the mark a last-minute chance to re-erect his defenses and prove to himself and others that he had not really cared about the status all along. When a blow-up of this kind occurs, friends of the mark or psychotherapists are frequently brought in. Friends are willing to take responsibility for the mark because their relationship to him is not limited to the role he has failed in. This, incidentally, provides one of the less obvious reasons why the cooler in a con mob must cultivate the friendship of the mark; friendship provides the cooler with an acceptable reason for staying around while the mark is cooled out. Psychotherapists, on the other hand, are willing to take responsibility for the mark because it is their business to offer a relationship to those who have failed in a relationship to others.

It has been suggested that a mark may be cooled out by allowing him, under suitable guidance, to give full vent to his initial shock. Thus the manager of a commercial organization may listen with patience and understanding to the

---

[4] In his seminars, Mr. Hughes has used the term "second-choice" professions to refer to cases of this kind.

complaints of a customer, knowing that the full expression of a complaint is likely to weaken it. This possibility lies behind the role of a whole series of buffers in our society—janitors, restaurant hostesses, grievance committees, floorwalkers, and so on—who listen in silence, with apparent sympathy, until the mark has simmered down. Similarly, in the case of criminal trials, the defending lawyer may find it profitable to allow the public to simmer down before he brings his client to court.

A related procedure for cooling the mark out is found in what is called stalling. The feelings of the mark are not brought to a head because he is given no target at which to direct them. The operator may manage to avoid the presence of the mark or may convince the mark that there is still a slight chance that the loss has not really occurred. When the mark is stalled, he is given a chance to become familiar with the new conception of self he will have to accept before he is absolutely sure that he will have to accept it.

As another cooling procedure, there is the possibility that the operator and the mark may enter into a tacit understanding according to which the mark agrees to act as if he were leaving of his own accord, and the operator agrees to preserve the illusion that this was the case. It is a form of bribery. In this way the mark may fail in his own eyes but prevent others from discovering the failure. The mark gives up his role but saves his face. This, after all, is one of the reasons why persons who are fleeced by con men are often willing to remain silent about their adventure. The same strategy is at work in the romantic custom of allowing a guilty officer to take his own life in a private way before it is taken from him publicly, and in the less romantic custom of allowing a person to resign for delicate reasons instead of firing him for indelicate ones.

Bribery is, of course, a form of exchange. In this case, the mark guarantees to leave quickly and quietly, and in exchange is allowed to leave under a cloud of his own choosing. A more important variation on the same theme is found in the practice of financial compensation. A man can say to himself and others that he is happy to retire from his job and say this with more conviction if he is able to point to a comfortable pension. In this sense, pensions are automatic devices for providing consolation. So, too, a person who has been injured because of another's criminal or marital neglect can compensate for the loss by means of a court settlement.

I have suggested some general ways in which the mark is cooled out. The question now arises: what happens if the mark refuses to be cooled out? What are the possible lines of action he can take if he refuses to be cooled? Attempts to answer these questions will show more clearly why, in general, the operator is so anxious to pacify the mark.

It has been suggested that a mark may be cooled by allowing him to blow his top. If the blow-up is too drastic or prolonged, however, difficulties may arise. We say that the mark becomes "disturbed mentally" or "personally disorganized." Instead of merely telling his boss off, the mark may go so far as to commit criminal violence against him. Instead of merely blaming himself for failure, the mark may inflict great punishment upon himself by attempting suicide, or by acting so as to make it necessary for him to be cooled out in other areas of his social life.

Sustained personal disorganization is one way in which a mark can refuse to cool out. Another standard way is for the individual to raise a squawk, that is, to make a formal complaint to higher authorities obliged to take notice of such matters. The con mob worries lest the mark appeal to the police. The plant manager must make sure that the disgruntled department head does not carry a formal complaint to the general manager or, worse still, to the Board of Directors. The teacher worries lest the child's parent complain to the principal. Similarly, a woman who communicates her evaluation of self by accepting a proposal of marriage can sometimes protect her exposed position—should the necessity of doing so arise—by threatening her disaffected fiancé with a breach-of-promise suit. So, also, a woman who is de-courting her husband must feel lest he contest the divorce or sue her lover for alienation of affection. In much the same way, a customer who is angered by a salesperson can refuse to be mollified by the floorwalker and demand to see the manager. It is interesting to note that associations dedicated to the rights and the honor of minority groups may sometimes encourage a mark to register a formal squawk; politically it may be more advantageous to provide a test case than to allow the mark to be cooled out.

Another line of action which a mark who refuses to be cooled can pursue is that of turning "sour." The term derives from the argot of industry but the behavior it refers to occurs everwhere. The mark outwardly accepts his loss but withdraws all enthusiasm, good will, and vitality from whatever role he is allowed to maintain. He complies with the formal requirements of the role that is left him, but he withdraws his spirit and identification from it. When an employee turns sour, the interests of the organization suffer; every executive, therefore, has the problem of "sweetening" his workers. They must not come to feel that they are slowly being cooled out. This is one of the functions of granting periodic advancements in salary and status, of schemes such as profit-sharing, or of giving the "employee" at home an anniversary present. A similar view can be taken of the problem that a government faces in times of crisis when it must maintain the enthusiastic support of the nation's disadvantaged minorities, for whole groupings of the population can feel they are being cooled out and react by turning sour.

Finally, there is the possibility that the mark may, in a manner of speaking, go into business for himself. He can try to gather about him the persons and facilities required to establish a status similar to the one he has lost, albeit in relation to a different set of persons. This way of refusing to be cooled is often rehearsed in phantasies of the "I'll show them" kind, but sometimes it is actually realized in practice. The rejected marriage partner may make a better remarriage. A social stratum that has lost its status may decide to create its own social system. A leader who fails in a political party may establish his own splinter group.

All these ways in which a mark can refuse to be cooled out have consequences for other persons. There is, of course, a kind of refusal that has little consequence for others. Marks of all kinds may develop explanations and excuses to account in a creditable way for their loss. It is, perhaps, in this region of phantasy that the defeated self makes its last stand.

Brainwashing[*]

Edgar H. Schein

"Brainwashing" is a colloquial term which has been used in reference to the systematic efforts of the Chinese Communists (and by implication the Soviets) to persuade nonbelievers to accept Communist allegiance, commands, and/or doctrine by coercive means. More generally, the term has been applied to any technique designed to manipulate human thought or action against the desire, will, or knowledge of the individual. The word "brainwashing" derives from the Chinese phrase *Hsi Nao*[1] and is most appropriately used in reference to Chinese Communist "thought reform" or "ideological remolding" (*Szu Hsing Koa Tsao*), a program of political indoctrination based on the conception that people who have not been educated in a Communist society have, by definition, incorrect bourgeois attitudes and beliefs, and must therefore be reeducated before they can take their place in a Communist society.[2]

Because of the close connections between Chinese and Soviet Communism and because of the importance which Soviet psychology seems to attach to the works of Pavlov,[3] the assumption has frequently been made that brainwashing is a highly refined adaptation of Pavlovian psychology. From this assumption and

[*] Much of the material in this paper is presented in greater detail in *Coercive Persuasion* (New York: W. W. Norton & Co., 1961). I wish to thank Inge Schneier and Curtis Barker who were my collaborators in preparing that volume and who therefore contributed importantly to this paper. This material was prepared for the 1961 *World Affairs Yearbook* and appears there in slightly condensed form.

[1] E. Hunter, *Brainwashing in Red China* (New York: Vanguard Press, 1951).

[2] R. J. Lifton " 'Thought Reform' of Western Civilians in Chinese Communist Prisons," *Psychiatry*, Vol. 19 (1956), pp. 173–95.

[3] There is some evidence that Pavlov was especially revered during Stalin's later years because of Stalin's personal desires to advance Pavlovian psychology, but that following Stalin's death there has been a steady decline of interest in Pavlov among Soviet psychologists. However, they often find it expedient to translate work which has only remote connections to Pavlovian psychology into Pavlovian terminology or to preface their work with praise of Pavlov, thus giving the impression of a steady monolithic growth of Pavlovianism. See R. C. Tucker, "Stalin and the Uses of Psychology," *World Politics*, Vol. 8 (1956), pp. 455–83; and A. Mintz, "Recent Developments in Psychology in the USSR," *Annu. Rev. Psychol.*, 1958, pp. 453–98, Palo Alto, Calif.

the image of scientific mental destruction which it stimulates has come the conception that brainwashing is a highly dangerous and possibly irresistible weapon against the mind of man.

Studies of Chinese Communist and Soviet methods of confession extraction and indoctrination have shown that they do have some common roots in the secret police methods of the pre-Communist autocracies in both countries and that both are heavily influenced by basic principles of Party organization, but also that they diverge in important respects from each other, and that the common connections to Pavlovian psychology are very doubtful.[4] Where the Soviets have put emphasis on confession extraction to justify public trials prior to eliminating the victim, the Chinese have from the beginning emphasized the role of confession extraction as only one step in the rehabilitation and reform of the prisoner; where the Soviets have traditionally isolated the prisoner and undermined his resistance by depriving him of any social contact, the crux of the Chinese approach has been to immerse the prisoner in a small group of other prisoners who are as, or more, advanced in their reform than he; where Soviet methods have suggested scientific and Machiavellian approaches to interrogation and confession extraction, the Chinese methods have suggested the image of a zealous enthusiastic mass movement sweeping converts into its ranks by virtue of its intrinsic message and have placed reliance on practical knowledge of interpersonal manipulation.

THOUGHT REFORM IN COMMUNIST CHINA

Chinese Communist attempts to reform their enemies—to cure the disease and save the man—were developed initially in response to the weak power position in which the Chinese Communist Party (CCP) found itself. The need to rely on peasants in building the movement, the need to recruit manpower from Kuomintang (KMT) defectors or prisoners of war, the scattering of forces which was necessitated by the guerrilla strategy during the civil war, the opportunity to give political tutelage to uneducated masses over which the CCP had control early in its history, and the requirements of coalition government and united front strategy, all demanded a heavy reliance on persuasion rather than coercion, and resulted in the development of a cadre well versed in the details of Communist ideology and well practiced in the arts of combining persuasion with whatever coercion the power position of the CCP warranted.

Many of the practical methods of persuasion developed were clearly evidenced in the Party Reform movement of the 1940's in which the CCP found itself, instead of physically purging its deviants, engaged in a large-scale effort to revital-

---

[4] See L. E. Hinkle and H. G. Wolff, "Communist Interrogation and Indoctrination of 'Enemies of the State,'" *A.M.A. Arch. Neurol. Psychiat.*, Vol. 76 (1956), pp. 115–74; R. J. Lifton, "Thought Reform" op. cit.; R. A. Bauer, "Brainwashing: Psychology or Demonology?" *J. Soc. Issues*, Vol. 13 (1957), pp. 41–47; E. H. Schein, "Brainwashing and Totalitarianization in Modern Society," *World Politics*, Vol. 11 (1959), pp. 430–41.

ize itself ideologically and to lay down Central Party policy to its scattered forces. These methods included (1) the encouragement of grievances against any and all non-Communist groups or ideas combined with a strong emphasis on highly acceptable positive ideals (e.g., get rid of corrupt landlords to help reconstruct China); (2) heavy reliance on group discussion in an atmosphere demanding of each member a complete exposure of his thought and feeling to the scrutiny and analysis of others; (3) the use of mutual and self-criticism to denigrate and destroy all emotional ties with the past; (4) the teaching of Communist doctrine in a group setting in which the group became a vehicle for the thinking through of ideological material to initially stated conclusions, and in which it was each member's responsibility to find the meaning of the theoretical material for his own concrete case; (5) an unmistakable threat of expulsion from the Party for anyone not willing to reeducate himself.

What is distinctive in this approach is the sophistication of the CCP in the use of social and interpersonal forces in the service of creating a situation in which persuasion was likely to be successful. Given that the individual could be coerced into exposing himself to the kinds of group forces described briefly above, it was highly likely that he would come to accept firmly the premises and attitude which the leaders espoused.

Following the takeover, the CCP approach to organizing and controlling the large Chinese population was to rely on a complex mixture of coercion and persuasion. The leadership's willingness to use terror and coercion was clearly evidenced in the brutality associated with the Land Reform program, in the revival of the *pao chia* system of mutual surveillance, and in the forced conscription or arrest of masses of people who were unwilling to cooperate with the new government. At the same time, a tremendous amount of energy was devoted to propagandizing, educating, indoctrinating, and attempting to convert the Chinese people. The fiction has been constantly maintained that virtually everything the Chinese people are forced to do is done voluntarily and enthusiastically.[5]

To support its attempts to indoctrinate the people, the CCP has made all mass media of communication an extension of the Party propaganda apparatus and has supplemented this apparatus with an elaborate oral agitation network designed to mobilize the support of the large number of illiterates. Such widespread compaigns as "Land Reform" (1950), "Resist America, Aid Korea" (1950), "Three-Anti" (anticorruption, antiwaste, and antibureaucratism in government and Party) (1952), and "Ideological Remolding" (1952, 1957, and 1958) have served to mobilize the Chinese population behind the government and have further facilitated indoctrination. Ideological remolding or thought reform was implemented throughout China through the use of groups devoted to self-criticism, accusation, "grievance telling," discussion, and study. Such groups were usually led by party cadre who reported to higher authorities on the progress of members of the group.

---

[5] A. D. Barnett (ed.), *The United States and the Far East* (New York: Columbia University Press, 1956).

Study groups averaging in size from 10 to 12 were organized in every village, school, factory, prison, and farm, to "rationalize" material presented through reading or lecture and to make it possible for each member to think through how the theoretical point might apply to his own case. "Discussion within the group is often prolonged and intense. Members can and in fact are expected to raise doubts about the official 'correct' view on any subject; but when this happens all other members are expected to argue in favor of the official line. The final objective is mutual agreement and unanimous support of the official line."[6]

Accusation meetings were usually held in neighborhoods, villages, farms, or co-operatives for the purpose of mobilizing grievances against the KMT, landlords, feudalism, and most of all, American imperialism. By having individuals tell their life history and by suitably timing their own accusations, skilled activists could build up emotions in the group to fever pitch which sometimes resulted directly in the trial and perhaps execution of a "cruel landlord" or "corrupt official."

Criticism and self-criticism was often conducted as part of the study group. Everyone in the group was expected to write out a detailed autobiography (the illiterates could always find scribes to whom to dictate their life story) as a basis for pin-pointing sources of reactionary tendencies in his past and as preparations for revealing his "innermost" thoughts to the group. When the life histories were discussed critically in the group, the cadre or activist skillfully blended together political ideology with moralistic principles. Thus, to be a good Communist in the end was tantamount to being unselfish, modest, considerate, willing to take responsibility and so on, each defined, of course, in terms of the person's relationship to the government. To be unselfish, for example, meant to be willing to pay ever higher taxes to the government.

In meetings like these it was usually impossible to hide true feelings under the scrutiny of other group members who were competing with each other in the amount of "help" they could give in uncovering *basic* feelings and attitudes. The growing intimacy of members made it easier for them to see through rationalizations and other defenses, which forced each member into a genuine reappraisal of his own past and heightened the likelihood that he would discover positive features in an ideology which he knew he must accept anyway.

A more intensive form of thought reform was in evidence in the Revolutionary Universities which served as training grounds for cadres.[7] Promising young people would be recruited by methods ranging from elaborate promises of bright futures to virtual forced conscription and put through intensive indoctrination programs of several months' duration. Again a heavy emphasis was given to self-examination and confession in the context of small group discussion, with the aim of producing a genuine severance of all emotional ties to the past and

---

[6] *Ibid.*, p. 127.

[7] W. E. Gourlay, *The Chinese Communist Cadre: Key to Political Control* (Cambridge: Harvard University Russian Research Center, 1952); and R. J. Lifton, "Thought Reform of Chinese Intellectuals: A Psychiatric Evaluation," *J. Soc. Issues*, Vol. 13 (1957), pp. 5–20.

a rebuilding of the student's self-image in terms of the new Communist society. As in other kinds of *rites de passage*, the student ratified his growing new identity by acts such as public denunciation of his father.

For those "students" who proved themselves to be recalcitrant or who needed a more "fundamental" kind of reeducation, as well as for professionals, intellectuals, and party members whose occupations might make their class-consciousness too parochial, there was "reform through labor." Though reform through labor was rationalized as the best way quickly to acquire the proletarian point of view, it seems generally to have been perceived as punishment and to have been viewed as little more than slave labor to be avoided at all costs.

For those individuals (whether Chinese or foreigner) who were accused of, or suspected of, counterrevolutionary activity there were many kinds of prisons. However, it is noteworthy that the thought reform movement also permeated the prison, resulting in the assumption that the inmates should and could be reformed.

Results

The *avowed* purpose of thought reform was to create a "new man" whose basic character and attitudes would be ideally fitted for the Communist society of the future. For the different target groups who became involved in thought reform this usually meant the adoption of certain specific attitudes as well as an underlying set of Communist premises—the peasant has to adopt "correct" attitudes about having his land collectivized, the businessman about having the government expropriate him, the bourgeois reactionary about having to give up his emotional ties to parents, friends, and sometimes spouses, if the latter were considered to be political liabilities. The political prisoner was expected to undergo a more fundamental reevaluation of his past life and to recognize how various of his activities had been harmful to "the people."

The major *implicit* purposes of thought reform appeared to be the creation of obedient citizens and cadres, and the conversion of an entrenched bureaucracy and intelligentsia into an arm of the Communist state. In a sense, thought reform was an elaborate initiation rite which everyone who wished to acquire any status in the new Communist society had to undergo.

The success of the regime in fulfilling its purposes is difficult to evaluate. The visible effect of thought reform in combination with the coercive apparatus upon which it rests had been the creation of massive conformity in all sectors of Chinese society. Almost every visitor to Communist China has been struck by the degree to which all citizens look alike, speak alike, and act alike.[8] It has also been observed that the disciplined efforts of masses of the population have led to a number of tangible accomplishments—increased productivity in some areas

---

[8] R. Guillain, *600 Million Chinese* (New York: Criterion Books, 1957).

of the economy, military success in Korea, and the eradiction of certain vices ("there are no more beggars on the streets of Peking").

There is little doubt that the ascetic, moralistic, and idealistic tone of the message of thought reform has had a strong impact on a serious younger generation bent upon bringing the "New China" into the front ranks of world powers. On the other hand, there are a number of indications that thought reform has not gone deep in influencing attitudes—the burst of criticism which followed Mao's *Let 100 Flowers Bloom* speech, the reports of defectors that group discussion, study, criticism, and self-criticism are engaged in only superficially, and the high number of unreconstructed critics in the political prisons (as estimated by Western repatriates). The safest conclusion is that the effects have been different on different parts of Chinese society and have varied with the skill and sophistication of the cadres responsible for it.

THE INVOLVEMENT OF WESTERN PRISONERS

Westerners became involved with Chinese Communist thought reform in two ways: several hundred European and American professionals, businessmen, and missionaries were arrested on the mainland and subjected to reform in prison, and several thousand United Nations prisoners of war (POW's) encountered a somewhat milder version in the POW camps of North Korea. The arrests on the mainland probably occurred for a number of reasons—to break spy rings which the Communists believed to be operating, to facilitate propaganda operations by discrediting Western efforts in China, to expropriate the properties of Westerners, to collect hostages for political negotiations, and to assert Asian superiority over a group to which the Chinese had felt inferior for so long. It is quite unlikely that any of the arrests occurred in order to subject the prisoner to thought reform; rather the reform was a regular part of prison procedure and had to involve all prisoners. In the case of the POW's also one gets the feeling that thought reform was incidental rather than basic, with the basic purpose being the exploitation of the POW for a variety of propaganda objectives.

TREATMENT OF WESTERN CIVILIANS IN PRISONS

The treatment of civilians in prison varied widely depending upon the location of the prison, the political climate, and the nature of the alleged crime.[9] The most refined thought reform was in evidence in the Peking prison from where came most of the cases of alleged successful brainwashing. The changes in the beliefs, attitudes, and values which the prison regimen produced (which in some cases were substantial and lasting) can only be accounted for by a consideration

---

[9] Schein, *Coercive Persuasion* (1961).

of all the pressures which the total experience generated, even though some of these pressures were incidental to the thought reform program as such.

The initial attitude of the prisoner was important. If he had seen only the good side of Communism, as exhibited in the admirable takeover operation in cities like Peking, he was more likely to accept the "lenient policy" and thus become favorably disposed towards Chinese Communist penal methods. If he had seen the brutal side of Communism as in the Land Reform movement, he was usually predisposed to believe nothing the Communists said and to resist any impulse to be favorably disposed toward them.

Arrest usually followed a period of surveillance and resulted in the prisoner's either being detained in his own house or being taken to some form of prison. He was usually not told the charges against him, yet it was made clear to him that he was considered to be guilty from the moment of arrest on. Once arrested he was expected to come to understand the following version of his predicament: he was in prison because the government considered him a criminal; his crime was obvious to everyone but to him; his first task was to understand the nature of the crime and in this task the authorities and fellow prisoners would do all they could to help him; through analysis of his past behavior he would be shown and would discover how the ultimate consequences of his actions had been harmful to the Chinese people. Once he saw his guilt, he was expected to confess, repent, and reform the undesirable thoughts, attitudes, feelings, and actions which had led to his crimes in the first place.

From the Communist point of view guilt was judged "objectively," which meant that anything which ultimately could have harmed the Chinese people was a crime even if unintended or not acted upon. Thus a prisoner might be considered guilty because of his associations, his alleged intentions, his incorrect thoughts or attitudes, and most importantly, his incorrect social origins. If he was other than proletarian by birth he was considered to have acquired incorrect points of view and attitudes throughout his life which eventually would result in harmful action toward the common people.

From the prisoner's point of view his arrest was unjustified, the accusations of guilt in the initial confrontation with judge or interrogator ridiculous, and the statements about leniency to those who confess meaningless. Only as the full force of the prison regimen made itself felt on him did he come to be able to appreciate intellectually and emotionally what was wanted of him.

The manner in which the prisoner came to be influenced to accept the Communist's definition of his guilt can best be described by distinguishing two broad phases—(1) a process of "unfreezing," in which the prisoner's physical resistance, social and emotional supports, self-image and sense of integrity, and basic values and personality were undermined, thereby creating a state of "readiness" to be influenced; and (2) a process of "changing," in which the prisoner discovered how the adoption of "the people's standpoint" and a reevaluation of himself from this perspective would provide him with a solution to the problems created by the prison pressures. The degree of permanence of the changes in attitude which had occurred would depend on the degree to which these were subsequently integrated with other values and attitudes the prisoner held and were supported by others back home.

Unfreezing

The prisoner's physical strength was undermined by the general inadequacy of the diet, loss of sleep due to intermittent and continuous interrogation, illness, lack of exercise, excessive cold or heat in combination with inappropriate clothing, prolonged standing or squatting during interrogation or as a punishment for infraction of the prison regulations, excessive pain from the wearing of manacles behind the back and ankle chains (which were put on as punishment if the authorities felt that the prisoner was not genuinely trying to reform himself), cuffing and beating by cell mates, and innumerable other events in the prison regimen.

The prisoner's social and emotional supports were undermined by his being completely cut off from any communication with the outside (no incoming or outgoing mail was permitted, and no non-Communist newspapers, etc., were available), by the prohibition of any close emotional relationship with another prisoner except in the context of reform, by the introduction of testimonials of various sorts in the form of confessions by others whom the prisoner respected or simply by surrounding the prisoner with cell mates who were enthusiastic about reforming themselves and who condemned all the values to which he adhered.

The prisoner's image of himself and his sense of integrity or inviolability were undermined primarily by the humiliation, revilement, and brutalization he suffered at the hands of his cell mates in the process of "struggle." Most prisoners were put into a cell containing several Chinese prisoners who were further along in reforming themselves and who saw it as their primary duty to "help" their most backward member to see the truth about himself in order that the whole cell might advance. Each such cell had a leader who was in close contact with the authorities for purposes of reporting on the cell's progress and getting advice on how to handle the Western member. In this setting the cell mates found ways of putting extreme pressure on their unreformed member, particularly since he was often completely dependent upon them for help in feeding himself, eliminating, etc. (especially if he were manacled).

The only thing which would satisfy the cell mates was a sincere confession, but since the prisoner could not guess initially what this meant or what he was to confess, he brought down the full wrath of the others upon his head. They believed in his guilt and felt that only his stubbornness and reactionary tendencies could account for his refusal to confess. The only valid identity granted to him was that of guilty criminal; any attempt to be anything else—a doctor, a missionary, an innocent victim of circumstances—was condemned violently. The fact that this pressure was applied twenty-four hours a day for weeks or months on end must have made it especially potent; there was no private time and no opportunity for retreat.

Other facets of the environment undermined the prisoner's self-image. The prisoner was identified only by number; his every action during the day was carefully prescribed—when to eat, when to go to the toilet, when to wash, etc. The time allotted to these activities was usually far too short to allow for their satisfactory completion (e.g., two minutes for running out to the toilet, eliminating, and returning at a given time of day); he was prohibited from making any decisions—every act had to be preceded by permission from the guard or coordinated carefully with the cell mates (e.g., since sleeping quarters were crowded, prisoners slept huddled together and all had to shift position in unison on an agreed-upon signal); judges and interrogators made a convincing argument that the prisoner could not hope to be released and ever be anything again unless he confessed and repented; the prisoner was often seduced into behavior violating his own self-image, such as making attempts at false confessions or denouncing loved ones. The whole prison atmosphere was completely demeaning.

Some of these same factors also tended to undermine the prisoner's more fundamental values and personality defenses. His state of complete dependency often aroused childhood conflicts and stimulated unconscious guilt; the cell mates constantly rejected and demeaned the prisoner's values, or if there were strong ethical principles, as in the case of priests, showed in many little ways how the person had in his past or was in his present behavior failing to live up to the very values he professed (e.g., pointing out that most missions employed Chinese in "demeaning" jobs such as cooks or houseboys, or that the priest's behavior in the cell was often selfishly motivated).

Guilt was also aroused by the recognition on the part of prisoners that their own middle class values did indeed lead them to subtle prejudices against the working classes and that these prejudices had shown up in their attitudes toward the Chinese prior to imprisonment (e.g., preference for living in fancy quarters, social contacts mostly with the embassy set, etc.). At the same time the values which the Communists professed are so universally valid as to have been unassailable—unselfishness, working for the greater good of humanity, peace, etc.—yet are so difficult to uphold in an absolute sense that the prisoner was constantly having his failures pointed out to him (e.g., taking up too much room while sleeping was considered evidence of selfishness reflecting bad bourgeois attitudes).

Change in attitudes and self-image

The constant threats of death or permanent nonrepatriation led to anxiety and despair which was difficult to cope with. But even more difficult for the prisoner was his increasing recognition that his cell mates really took the lenient policy of the government seriously and were making a genuine attempt to reform themselves. As the cell mates came to be seen as real people rather than merely agents of the prison authorities, the prisoner felt increasingly guilty for his hostility toward them and increasingly committed to trying to understand their point of view. Because his own beliefs, values, and attitudes had been undermined, and because he found himself in an insoluble situation, he became increasingly disposed to trying to find a solution through forming relationships with others who seemed to have found a solution. As his identification with one or more cell mates grew, he came increasingly to understand the basic premises underlying "the people's standpoint," and how he might be perceived to be guilty from this standpoint.

Because the prison experiences had elicited a variety of guilt feelings already, it became possible for the prisoner to attach his guilt feelings increasingly to the crimes which he began to see in his own past behavior, and thus to begin a process of "sincere" confession. He could see that his innocent letters about his trip through a farm area could be giving valuable economic information to the American enemy, that his discussions with people in embassies concerning the morale of students could be used in psychological warfare against the Communists, that his hobnobbing with the embassy set was giving aid and comfort to reactionary forces, or that his failure to join the Communists could be construed as hostility toward them. Once this process of self reevaluation began, the prisoner received all kinds of help and support from the cell mates and once again was able to enter into meaningful emotional relationships with others. His terrible social-emotional isolation was at an end and his role as repentant sinner was given increasing support.

The key elements in this process were (1) the identifications which formed with cell mates, thus making it possible for the prisoner to begin to understand the point of view from which he was judged guilty, and (2) the reevaluation of actual behavior engaged in, which occurred when he applied the scale of values embodied in "the people's standpoint" to his own behavior. The prisoner was not expected to manufacture a false confession, but was expected to see that his actual behavior had in fact been criminal from the Communist point of view.

The intensive self-analysis which accompanied this process often led the prisoner to recognize genuine faults in his own character and as this happened his reform took on a personal as well as political meaning. Some of the prisoners had come to China uncertain of their basic identity and value systems and found in the prison experience an opportunity to arrive at some genuine resolutions of long standing conflicts or to become completely committed to *some* value system.

The group cell as an agent of influence was crucial for several reasons: (1) enforced close contact with others made it likely that strong guilt, anxiety and hostility would be aroused which, in turn, would increase the probability of identification with a cell mate (either as a defense against deeper conflicts or as a solution to the identity crisis which the cell had created); (2) the presence of several others heightened the probability of there being at least one among them who would "see through" and expose any defensive maneuver the prisoner might attempt; (3) the probability was heightened that there would be at least one other cell mate with whom the prisoner could identify because of similar personality or background; (4) once the prisoner began to identify with a cell mate, the group provided many models of how the prisoner was expected to behave and could provide rapid "feedback" in terms of rewarding or punishing his behavior; and (5) the sheer fact of a unanimous group arrayed against the prisoner provided a force which was very difficult to resist psychologically.[10]

Study, interrogation, and trial

The events described thus far were supplemented by study sessions, criticism and self-criticism meetings, and autobiography writing, but these activities did not have genuine impact on the Western prisoner until he had begun the more fundamental self reevaluation described above. If the prisoner was beginning to adopt new attitudes toward himself and others, these activities would be useful in providing rationalizations and a broader conception of what Communism meant, as well as acquainting the prisoner increasingly with Communist semantics.

Throughout his imprisonment, the prisoner was periodically confronted with interrogation sessions and with discussions of his case in the presence of one or more judges. The prisoner's relationship to these authorities was not dissimilar to the heretic's relationships to the inquisitor of the Middle Ages in that the case could only be settled when the prisoner had made a suitable confession, "suitable" being defined by the personal judgment of the authorities, not by law. Psychologically meaningful relationships also grew up with interrogators but not as frequently as with cell mates. Interrogation more often than not was one of the stresses which tended to unfreeze the prisoner and make him increasingly search for a solution to his dilemma.

Once the prisoner began to adopt "the people's standpoint" and to apply this yardstick to his own behavior, he began to be able to confess in a manner which satisfied the authorities. After varying lengths of time, during which he might write and rewrite his confession a half dozen times or more, he would be brought to trial and usually sentenced to imprisonment for a period roughly approximating the length of time he had already spent in prison, to be followed by expulsion from China. The confession, then, usually served as the criterion of the degree of reform, though the authorities also had available to them the reports of the cell chief on the progress which a given prisoner was making. The release of Western prisoners was sometimes dictated more by international negotiations than by degree of reform or the adequacy of the confession. Many prisoners were released who apparently never made a damaging confession, and some were released who made confessions but who obviously did not adopt "the people's standpoint" (as evidenced by their repudiation of the confession following their

---

[10] S. E. Asch, "Effects of Group Pressure upon the Modification and Distortion of Judgments," in *Groups, Leadership, and Men,* Harold Guetzkow (ed.) (Pittsburgh: Carnegie Press, 1951).

release by the Communists). Finally, a number of Western prisoners have been given longer sentences which they are still serving.

Results

The description of coercive persuasion given above applies only to a small number of Western prisoners (the number is difficult to estimate for obvious reasons but is perhaps no larger than 50, taking Americans and Europeans together). The majority of Westerners who were imprisoned either encountered inefficient prisons or were not considered important enough to be reformed. Many of them encountered reform in a superficial fashion—study sessions and criticisms performed as a necessary daily ritual rather than an important psychological activity. Many were never placed into group cells of more reformed prisoners, but were either kept in solitary confinement or placed with other "reactionary" prisoners with whom they were forbidden to communicate in any way whatsoever. Successful brainwashing, in the sense of the repatriate espousing Communist attitudes and reiterating his crimes following release from Communist China, was a rare outcome. Genuine attitude change could only occur if there were already a predisposition in the prisoner and if he encountered a highly effective prison regimen built around the use of the group cell.

Those Americans who exhibited Communist influence at the time of their release into Hong Kong have had varied histories since their release. Several of them have reevaluated their experiences once again after their return home and have ended up wondering how they could ever have believed what they professed to believe toward the end of their imprisonment. Several others have vacillated between sympathy for the Communist position and sympathy for the Western position and are continuing to search for some resolution to their value and attitude conflicts; several have had genuine personality changes built around ethical principles which Communism shares with other value systems, and these individuals have continued to believe that they were guilty of the crimes to which they confessed, that they were indeed treated leniently by the Communists, that the Communist position on matters of basic ethics and values is correct, and that they must continue to live by these principles even if they encounter hostility in the United States. Some have used thought reform as a basis for general personal reform and are grateful to the Chinese for providing this opportunity.

TREATMENT OF PRISONERS OF WAR IN KOREA

The problem which confronted the West with the POW's was not so much their ideological conversion, of which there was virtually none, but rather a variety of collaborative behaviors (such as making radio broadcasts praising the CCP, signing "peace" petitions, asking others to cooperate with the enemy, serving on "peace" committees, making germ warfare confessions, and so on) which the Communists used skillfully to embarrass the United States in particular during the Korean episode.

The American POW was completely unprepared for the political explotiation to which he was subjected, and many of his responses to the Chinese efforts are to be explained primarily by this lack of preparation. Shortly after the UN's entry into Korea the primary expectation on the part of the troops was that capture would result in being tortured, abondoned, or killed by the North Koreans. Subsequent studies of atrocities in Korea substantiated these rumors in that most of the brutal treatment of the POW was the result of North Korean handling."[11]

If a man was captured by the Chinese, however, he found instead of harshness and brutality a friendly welcome, an outstretched hand, and a greeting in broken English of "Welcome," "Congratulations, you have been liberated," or "You have now joined the Fighters for Peace." Because many of the men were unclear about their mission in Korea and resented fighting on foreign soil against an unfamiliar enemy, they were initially receptive to any mention of peace. The Chinese then typically gathered groups of prisoners together at collection points and further explained the "lenient policy": POW's were not viewed as enemy troops, but as misguided, uneducated, or unawakened people who had been "tricked into fighting for an evil capitalist society," and who could be brought to see the truth about the Korean war and the basic validity of Communist peace efforts.

Most of the men were captured during the winter of 1950–51. The first months of captivity were a tough struggle for survival, because of the marginal diet for Western soldiers, the high rate of illness, which was inadequately treated, lack of medical care for the wounded, and extensive exposure to the elements. This combination of circumstances resulted in more than 40 percent of the POW's dying within the first six months of captivity. Psychologically, this was a most difficult time for the POW because the marginal conditions stimulated competition for the scarce resources available, morale was low anyway because of the uncertain future which capture by an Oriental enemy signaled, and the Chinese repeatedly protested that the inadequate supplies of food and medicine resulted from UN bombing of supply lines, not from their own deliberate policy or callousness. They were always highly solicitous and sympathetic, which robbed the prisoners of the opportunity to band together around their common hatred of the enemy. The fact that there were among the large number of prisoners some who from the outset were willing to take advantage of others or to curry the favor of the Chinese created an additional morale problem which the Chinese exacerbated by offering more and better food and medicine to those prisoners who showed a willingness to cooperate with them.

The men were marched north and housed in various kinds of temporary compounds during this winter and were moved into more permanent POW compounds along the banks of the Yalu during the spring of 1951. Shelter, food

---

[11] U.S. Army, *Extract of Interim Historical Report*, Korea War Crimes Division, 1953.

supplies, medical care, and clothing improved sharply with the settling into the permanent compounds, but psychological pressures did not cease because of the manner in which the Chinese organized and operated the camps.

Deliberate disorganization of POW's in permanent camps

The most significant feature of Chinese prison camp control was the systematic destruction of the POW formal and informal group structure which in the end resulted in widespread mutual mistrust among the men, and the necessity for each man to withdraw increasingly into a shell even though he was in the midst of others.

The authority structure of the POW group was destroyed first by segregating all officers and later all noncommissioned officers, thus leaving the mass of prisoners without formal authority of any kind. The prisoners were organized into squads, platoons, and companies, but only the squads were permitted to be commanded by prisoners, and the appointed squad leaders were usually the lowest ranking enlisted men or prisoners who were willing to cooperate with the Chinese. While the ranks were still together the highest ranking officers in a group would sometimes be given the alternative of signing a peace petition and ordering their troops to sign or having their group punished severely. Attempts by these officers to work out compromises which would satisfy the Chinese yet would increase the chances of the survival of their men would often appear to lower ranking officers like collaboration. They would then either overtly or covertly fail to obey orders, thus destroying the chain of command and, in effect, throwing the troops on their own resources.

The informal social structure of the POW group was undermined by a variety of techniques: (1) the Chinese prohibited any form of organized activity not sponsored by themselves, including religious services and recreational activities; (2) emergent leaders were usually discouraged and segregated; (3) extensive use of spies and POW informers made possible close surveillance of all informal activities and the Chinese frequently let POW's know that even their most private conversations and plans were known, thus creating mutual mistrust since no one could be sure that his best friends were not informers; (4) the conduct of interrogations weakened social-emotional ties still further by the frequent presentation to a man of confessions or military information written out by a fellow prisoner; what he usually did not know was that the fellow prisoner had not provided the information voluntarily, but had perhaps agreed to copy it out of some manuals which the Chinese showed him they already possessed; written information of this sort was often widely publicized in camp newspapers to create the impression that collaboration was the rule rather than the exception; (5) the confessions of germ warfare which were coerced from a number of Air Force officers and enlisted men were exploited by forcing several of them to go to the POW camps to give lectures on how they had used germ warfare, usually creating a big impression on the listeners.

As in the case of the civilian prisoner, bonds to loved ones and to the home country were severed by the prohibition of any contact with the outside. Only pro-Communist literature was available in the prison camp libraries; mail was delivered to a prisoner only if it contained bad news or was completely innocuous; if a man inquired about his mail he was usually told that none had arrived, which he was told must mean that his loved ones had abandoned him.

Most of the POW's were forced to write autobiographies and to discuss details of their personal histories during lengthy interrogations. It would be pointed out to a man how any misfortune or difficulty he reported must be the product of the political system under which he grew up, a message which found a responsive chord in the drifters and malcontents and in those prisoners whose enlistment in the Army had, in the first place, been motivated by their failure to achieve any other kind of satisfactory occupational career.

Criticism and self-criticism could not be introduced directly into POW groups without it becoming a mere mockery of what was intended, but it was used effectively to embarrass individual POW's and thereby to weaken the morale of the whole group. For example, most men were required to sign lengthy camp rules shortly after their arrival at a permanent compound. Months later a man might be hauled to the camp commandant's office and accused of a serious crime like expectorating at a forbidden place. He then would be told that to avoid serious punishment he must make a public confession and self-criticism in front of his company or squad. Though the man usually managed to introduce enough idiom into such a procedure to ridicule it, the impact on other POW's of seeing a fellow prisoner humiliate himself was still considerable.

Rewards, threats, and punishments

Rewards and punishments were consistently manipulated to elicit collaborative behavior. Any tendency on the part of a POW to be cooperative with the Chinese was rewarded with increased food rations or luxury items like fresh fruit or cigarettes; any stiffening of resistance was punished with a decrease in food, medicine, or camp privileges, and, if resistance was chronic, led to segregation in special compounds for "reactionaries" in which hard labor was the typical activity. Threats of death or nonrepatriation, occasionally backed by mock executions or severe physical punishment, effectively curbed any violent resistance efforts. The memory of the horrors of the first six months kept alive the knowledge that the Communists were more than willing to let men die or kill them if it suited their purpose.

Prizes of food would be given for essays to be published in the camp newspapers. The winning essay, of course, would invariably be the one which was most pro-Communist. Perhaps the most important award for cooperation with the enemy was the status of "progressive," symbolized by being given a peace dove to wear in the lapel, which made it possible for the POW once again to enter into the meaningful social relationships with others and to obtain a whole range of special privileges such as freedom of movement. For POW's who had not enjoyed any status in the society from which they came, such a status could be very meaningful even though based on cooperation with the enemy.

Lectures and group discussion

To present the Communist point of view and to provide the POW's with suitable reasons why they should cooperate with the Chinese, the political sections of the Red Army units presented daily lectures to be followed by group discussions of the conclusions presented in the lecture. Attendance at both functions was mandatory and the group discussions were monitored by cadres or by "progressives." The content of the lectures was usually crude propaganda around topics like "Who Really Started the Korean War?" and was so full of blatant inaccuracies as to vitiate whatever appeal it might have had (e.g., the statement by the lecturer that "we know that in America very few of you own your own cars"). Certain specific themes like the plea for "peace" inevitably had appeal, however, and POW's found themselves supporting peace activities like signing petitions, inserting peace propaganda into their letters home (they were delivered only if such propaganda were inserted), and serving on peace committees which were formed in each camp.

Results

The most important result was the social disorganization of the POW group which resulted in the bulk of the men withdrawing into an emotional shell and adapting as best they could by cooperating with the Chinese as much as they had to in order to survive, but trying to avoid giving any aid to their propaganda efforts. An important corollary result was the impairment of judgment which resulted from the social-emotional isolation. If a POW could not comfortably discuss his daily affairs with others, seek advice, or consider the consequences of actions he was contemplating, he was cut off from the most important source of validation available to man—the opinions, beliefs, and knowledge of others. Consequently much collaborative behavior occurred because of poor judgment or foresight. The POW's often were unaware how skilled the Communists were in using propaganda and were equally unaware how their behavior might be construed as disloyal. The important point, however, is that collaborative behavior was usually *not* motivated by disloyalty or opportunism, but rather was the complex resultant of attempts to survive in an environment where standards for behavior were extremely difficult to discern.

The extent of this psychological withdrawal showed up clearly in studies of the repatriates. In their observable behavior and on psychological tests they showed marked emotional constriction, inability and unwillingness to get involved with others, and even some impairment of intellectual functioning. It took a period of weeks or months in some cases for the men once again to feel comfortable in close emotional relationships with others.[12]

The Communists were highly successful in managing the prison camps with a minimum of guards. The isolation of the camps, the ready identifiability of Westerners among the North Koreans, the social disorganization of the POW group, and the fact that the armistice talks were going on from early 1951, all militated against extensive escape activities. Numerous escapes were attempted, but in most cases the men were recovered after a fairly short time. On the other hand, the very small percentage of men who were to any degree swayed by the ideological message of the Communists must be considered a dramatic failure of their indoctrination program.

BRAINWASHING: THE VERDICT

The outstanding conclusion one comes away with from a study of these events is that the methods of brainwashing are not diabolical, new, or irresistible. Rather, the Chinese have drawn on their cultural sensitivity to the nuances of interpersonal relationships to put together some highly effective but well-known techniques of indoctrination. Their sophistication about the importance of the small group as a mediator of opinions and attitudes has led to some highly effective techniques of destroying group solidarity, as in the case of the POW's, and of using groups as a mechanism of changing attitudes, as in the political prisons.

---

[12] H. D. Strassman, Margaret B. Thaler, and E. H. Schein, "A Prisoner of War Syndrome: Apathy as a Reaction to Severe Stress," *Amer. J. Psychiat.*, Vol. 112 (1956), pp. 998–1003; E. H. Schein, "The Chinese Indoctrination Program for Prisoners of War," *Psychiatry*, Vol. 19 (1956), pp. 149–72; E. H. Schein, W. F. Hill, H. L. Williams, and A. Lubin, "Distinguishing Characteristics of Collaborators and Resisters among American Prisoners of War," *J. Abnorm. Soc. Psychol.*, Vol. 55 (1957), pp. 197–201; Margaret T. Singer and E. H. Schein, "Projective Test Responses of Prisoners of War Following Repatriation," *Psychiatry*, Vol. 21 (1958), pp. 375–85; E. H. Schein, W. E. Cooley, and M. T. Singer, *A Psychological Followup of Former Prisoners of War of the Chinese Communists* (Cambridge, Mass.: Massachusetts Institute of Technology, Part I, 1960, Part II, 1962).

The special role of guilt in coercive persuasion[*]

E. H. Schein, I. Schneier, and C. H. Barker

One of the primary motives which leads the prisoner to begin a process of change (to begin to allow himself to be influenced) is *guilt*, which he comes to experience in various forms in the prison environment. This experience of guilt results from a combination of external pressures and internal predispositions. From the point of view of the interrogator or judge, criminal guilt is assumed once the prisoner has been arrested, but there are several different bases for such guilt. From the point of view of the prisoner there are a number of predispositions which lead to psychologically distinct types of guilt, though they may not be experienced as different. The purpose of this chapter is to explore these distinctions and thereby to show how the captor's presentation of the nature of guilt begins to unfreeze the prisoner by stimulating in him a sense of guilt, and how the type of guilt which he feels is related to the final outcome of the influence process.

THE CAPTOR'S VIEW OF GUILT

Once arrested, the prisoner must come to understand the following version of his predicament: he is in prison because the government considers him a criminal; his crime is obvious to everyone but to him; his first task is to understand the nature of his crime, and in this task the government will do its best to help him. Analysis of his past will show him how he has been guilty, how the ultimate consequences of his acts have been harmful to the Chinese people. If he is honest with himself he will discover his guilt more rapidly and proceed easily to what is expected of the criminal: admission of guilt by confession, subsequent repentance, and reform of the undesirable thoughts, attitudes, feelings, and actions.

From the moment of his arrival in prison the prisoner has urged upon him

[*] Reprinted from Schein, E. H. with Schneier, I. and Barker, C. H., *Coercive Persuasion* (New York: Norton, 1961), pp. 140–56.

the rationale pf the Chinese authorities by his interrogator, judge, and, most important, his cell mates. He may attempt to defend himself against the accusations of guilt by denying criminal acts or intents, by laughing at their absurdity, or simply by failing to take them seriously, but the total prison regimen as outlined in the previous chapters may convince him that his own concepts of guilt and innocence are incorrect or at least are not shared by the other prisoners or the authorities.

The bases for being judged guilty which he must come to appreciate are the following:

1. *Guilt by association.* The prisoner is guilty if he has associated with any others who are themselves guilty, even if he has not committed any acts "harmful to the Chinese people," or exhibited any intent to do so, or been aware of his association with other guilty parties.[1]

2. *Guilt by intention.* The prisoner is guilty if he exhibits motives which could and probably eventually would lead to actions which would harm the Chinese people; thus the prisoner is at least a potential criminal who must be made to feel his guilt and be punished as social prophylaxis.

3. *Guilt for incorrect attitudes.* The prisoner is guilty if he takes a negative attitude toward the Party or the government or questions any of their decisions, because such an attitude undermines the effectiveness of the "people's representatives" in their programs to help the people; questioning his own guilt or asserting his innocence can be, of course, a further instance of such a negative attitude, thereby proving the government's correctness in the first instance.

4. *Guilt for incorrect thoughts.* The prisoner is guilty if he exhibits thought patterns which reflect bourgeois premises and if he fails to appreciate the validity of Communist premises, even if he does not exhibit intentions or attitudes which could be harmful to the people; it is assumed that wrong thoughts would eventually lead to harmful acts.

5. *Guilt for having knowledge.* The prisoner is guilty if he has knowledge about China which could in any conceivable way be used against the Chinese, no matter how vague or seemingly nonpolitical it might be; if the prisoner is a foreigner such knowledge is particularly suspect because of the presumption that the only possible reason for his remaining in China after the takeover could be the gathering of "intelligence information"; thus activities such as research, casual questioning, and reading all become espionage.

6. *Guilt for harmful action.* The prisoner is guilty if he has committed acts which are harmful to the Chinese people, even if he does not recognize having committed them or does not recognize that they were harmful; seemingly innocuous acts can be defined as seriously harmful by the authorities, e.g., going to a party at a Western embassy is "establishing contact with spies" or actually "passing on information to Western agents"; looking something up in easily available volumes in the library for an attaché at a Western embassy (something

---

[1] Since the guilt of the "others" rests on bases similar to those discussed here, it can be seen that the attribution of guilt to anyone is possible.

he could easily have done himself) is "aiding in espionage activities," and so on.

7. *Guilt for failure to act.* The prisoner is guilty if he has *not* been active in his support of the Party and the government, if he has failed to show his own desire for the welfare of the people, if he has failed to give willingly his own possessions, time, and efforts in behalf of the Communist cause; to stand aside is to condone and support the old status quo.

8. *Guilt for having a characteristic personal fault or faults.* The prisoner is judged guilty if he shows in his behavior in prison some fault, shortcoming, or character defect from the point of view of the idealized image of the "new man"; for example, the prisoner is constantly being shown evidence of his own selfishness, lack of concern for others, class and/or racial prejudice, personal weakness, failure to live up to his own stated ideals, and so on; because the idealized "new man" is morally "perfect" from both a Communist and non-Communist point of view, it is likely that the kinds of faults for which the prisoner is criticized will be perceived by him as faults also.

9. *Guilt for having dangerous social origins.* The prisoner is guilty if he was born into a bourgeois family, if his friends and/or relatives are capitalists, if he was educated under a capitalist system, or if he associated with others of dangerous social origins; it is assumed that various of the consequences described above—incorrect attitudes and thoughts, failure to support the Communist cause, characteristic personal faults, are all due to such social origins; hence incorrect social origins are a primary and incontestable basis for guilt. What makes matters worse for the prisoner is that he cannot deny these origins, they are a matter of fact; he can only deny their effects which is not likely to be convincing.

As one reviews these bases of guilt, one sees that they overlap to a considerable extent and are linked by the underlying assumption that *all situations must be judged by their "objective" results, by their ultimate consequences.* Thoughts, attitudes, intentions, personal characteristics, and even accidents of birth and status must be judged by what they *could* lead to, not by the actual actions they have led to in the past. Thus the person may be guilty without knowing it, and it is the prison's primary task to make the prisoner conscious of his guilt as the prelude to reform. This logic carried to its extreme makes the primary basis of guilt simply the objective fact of having been arrested; arrest is the just consequence of guilt and the presumptive evidence of it.[2]

In general, the agents of influence (judge interrogator, cell mate) presume the guilt of their subject(s). They believe the subject would never have been arrested if he were not considered a threat to the "people." They may not know the precise reason for the subject's guilt or which grounds are justifiably applicable to him. They may not even be convinced that the grounds on which they are arguing are justified. Nonetheless they are able to be persuasive because of their "obvious" sincerity in working for the welfare of the people and in their belief

---

[2] It is an interesting psychological fact that even some prisoners who thought they were arrested unjustly, who saw themselves as innocent, were convinced of the guilt of everyone else in the prison.

that if the subject had not been guilty of something he would not have been arrested. Mistakes are considered unlikely and, in any case, must be made in favor of the system since it defines itself to be in a state of combat.

The frequent allegation that the interrogators, judges, and cell mates are Machiavellian in their tactics is probably based on the prisoner's perception that the agent is willing to manipulate the nature of the accusation to suit the subject's particular vulnerability. Thus the judge may sincerely believe that in some general fashion the prisoner is guilty of harming the people but may not believe the specific charges that he is making against the prisoner. Under the pressure of his job he may end up trying to convince the subject of his guilt rather than trying to ascertain whether he is guilty; and he may be willing in this process to make accusation after accusation until some are found which the subject seems to find difficult to refute. In the end the judge will most likely accept any honest confession drawn from the subject's general sense of guilt, and he will no longer attempt to ascertain facts relevant to the matters confessed to even if some of the confessed facts are incongruous or absurd. If the judge senses, however, that the confession is dishonest, in the sense of being merely an attempt by the prisoner to please him, he will probably be genuinely outraged and continue his efforts to find some basis for guilt which will elicit from the prisoner a genuine confession.

THE PRISONER'S EXPERIENCE OF GUILT

We shall assume at the outset that all socialized people experience a substantial amount of guilt when their behavior, desires, or feelings conflict with the dictates of the moral code or value system they have adopted or when they have not fulfilled some of the expectations held by themselves or by others. Because of their personal history and/or culture some people have stronger drives or make stronger moral demands on themselves than others; they, therefore, experience sharper conflicts and are consequently more guilt-prone than others.

Feelings of guilt are stimulated in the prison situation, both intentionally and inadvertently, by the exacerbation of old conflicts or the creation of new ones. For example, the prison regimen, whether handcuffs and ankle chains are used or not, makes the adult as dependent as a child and arouses some of the childhood conflicts, particularly around problems of authority. Or weakly held values are strengthened by continual emphasis until they begin to conflict with other values, as in the case of the priest for whom the value of unselfishness was sharpened to such a degree that it began to conflict with all efforts on his part to express any self-interest in the service of survival.

The prisoner can come to accept guilt on any one or more of the bases argued "logically" by agents because he does begin to experience guilt in some form. This guilt may be felt primarily as guilt-anxiety, in which case the feeling is present but no psychological basis for it is perceived by the prisoner; or it may be consciously perceived to be related to one or more of the following areas of psychological functioning:

1. *Social guilt.* A recognition on the part of the prisoner that much of what he has had in life has not been earned but has been given to him by accident of birth; thus for a middle-class person to have prejudices against the members of the lower class arouses guilt when he discovers that, in a sense, he has not earned but merely been given his middle-class status.

2. *Ego or identity guilt.* A recognition on the part of the prisoner that he has failed to live up to his image of himself.

3. *Persona guilt.* The feeling of guilt which comes from wearing a mask, from the discovery or recognition of having deliberately or involuntarily deceived another person about oneself, for example, by playing the role of a guilty person while holding reservations.

4. *Loyalty guilt.* A recognition on the part of the prisoner that he has failed in his service to a group with which he is strongly identified or has violated its norms or defiled its image by behaving in a manner not consistent with what is expected of members of that group.

5. *Situational guilt.* Guilt which is aroused by the magnification on the part of others of minor infractions or petty acts which normally do not run counter to the prisoner's basic values or self-image, particularly when they are perceived to have been stimulated by great stress; feelings of guilt in reference to such acts imply that the prisoner has already accepted some of the norms and standards of evaluation of the cellmates and authorities.

These types of guilt are not logically discrete but are important to distinguish if one is to understand some of the psychological processes which characterized the influence process in our subjects. In the remainder of this chapter we shall attempt to illustrate each of these types of guilt by quoting or paraphrasing some of the statements made by our subjects concerning their prison experience.

Social guilt

"Basically, I guess I always felt superior to the Negro. I didn't realize it before, but when I looked back on it from the prison situation, I could see it clearly."

"I realized that I had never done anything for society."

"What I came for [to China] was not so much to study, but to have a good time with the embassy set. To go to parties, and to make my dollar count in a country where help and housing was cheap."

"About ten years ago I was full of ideas of social climbing. I wanted to do some outstanding work so that I might acquire a distinguished social position. I wished to be above other people."

"We've always lived entirely for ourselves—not for others."

These paraphrased statements taken from recent interviews, illustrates most directly what we mean by social guilt. The Communists tried to convince their prisoners that they had actually "harmed the people," or intended harm to them, or had at some time in their lives, as members of a more privileged class, intentionally or unconsciously taken advantage of others, because of inferior "class" status. The struggle meetings, both group criticism and self-criticism sessions, were designed to recall instances of such guilty behavior.

In his recollections, one American repatriate mentions how all foreigners living in China had at least subconscious feelings of superiority to the Oriental. He cites instances where even the unpretentious missionary family from which he came felt itself superior and, despite its low standard of living (lower than that of other foreigners), exploited the Chinese. Today he describes with pleasure, but also with considerable guilt, the gay, luxurious life of the foreign students, the parties, the hobnobbing with the intellectual, social, and political elite of the city.

Even one of the least guilt-prone of our subjects eventually became vulnerable to a sense of social guilt. For two years he had been in prison resisting influence, although making certain behavioral concessions. He recounts how, no matter what the agents tried, he continued to feel no guilt until a general personality crisis was precipitated which led him to "recognize" and accept social guilt.

As I continued my analysis I realized even more how my egotism had slowly developed to where I was incapable of seeing anything which was not to my advantage and where I was oblivious to the plight of others. I remembered how . . . I had looked with revulsion on the poverty around us when I arrived in China. One morning in November, 1948, we had stepped out of the gate of a friend's house where we had spent the night, to find a man stretched out dead on the doorstep, obviously starved to death. It was a shock to both of us and had brought an ugly note into a bright morning. Reflecting on my attitude that day, I realized now that the little sympathy I had felt for the man had been more overshadowed by annoyance over my day being spoiled in such a way. My attitude toward the Korean War had shown the same brutal disregard for the lives of others on a much larger scale.

This subject did not accept "social" guilt before this crisis, not only because he was not particularly guilt-prone but also because he had come from an underdog family, whose sufferings during the depression had made a deep impression on him. As his self-analysis continued, he was led to see the "selfishness" flaw in his character, and thus became ready to accept "social" guilt. Though never a spy in our terms, he said:

Not wanting to harm others was no excuse at all, since a person totally blinded by his own self-interest is incapable of thinking of others, to begin with. If I had not been so blind, I would have been able to see long ago the fallacy in my supposition that my espionage activities had been of service to my country.

Having one's innermost self brought out and dissected under the glaring light of self-criticism was a shattering experience, but the resulting recognition of myself made me determined to overcome the weaknesses in my character which had been the cause of those former mistakes. Thus began the struggle with myself which was to last throughout the rest of my stay in prison and, indeed, goes on even today.

The creation and exploitation of social guilt were possible with almost every prisoner who had already been successfully weakened by other means, even if he was not initially guilt-prone. One reason, among others, is that some evidence of having felt superior can always be dug out and turned into such guilt. The intellectual is vulnerable to accusations such as "you don't mix with the common man; you don't even speak his language." The missionaries who went to China to bring Christianity to the people sometimes lived better than the masses "for whom they were supposed to be an example." If this argument was not convincing, it was pointed out to the missionary that he undoubtedly felt some superiority over the unChristianized heathens.

Thus to have had a feeling of social guilt and to have acknowledged it was to accept some version of this argument: if I have shown a lack of social awareness and have taken no global social responsibility; if I have been prejudiced toward a minority group; if I have felt superior toward anyone because of class origin, in fact felt superior *at all;* if I have been so concerned with my own life as to be unaware of the interests of others or have been too concerned with my own status and ambitions to do things for others, I have been guilty of "a crime against the people."

Ego or identity guilt

. . . Once you have made a false confession you lose heart and self-confidence. If they get you to make another confession, then that lowers resistance even more."

The interviewer asked him, "Why did you make a false confession?"

He said, "Because I thought I would get out if I gave them what they wanted; I thought I would try it." (Apparently the first time he actually tried this was about four months after his imprisonment.)

The interviewer asked what he had confessed to, and he didn't want to tell but later in the conversation it came up. His lie was that he named some sort of organization, which he had made up, for which he had worked. Then he discovered that they had lied to him by telling him that if he made a confession he would get out; and then they didn't release him once they had gotten it. From that time on he decided he was not going to make a false confession. But because he had once made a false confession he began to lose faith in himself. "Why had I given in, why had I lied?" he asked himself. . . . "There is something *degrading* about lying about yourself."

Because this confession undermined this man's self-image of being special, different, even heroic, it drastically lowered his self-esteem. It undermined his self-esteem not only because he had lied but also because he had been unable to resist. Each time he was forced to give in again (he confessed and retracted three or four times), his guilt increased. As his guilt increased, his self-esteem was lowered and his ability to resist making false confessions and believing them became increasingly undermined.

In his explanation of ego guilt he repeated, perhaps without realizing it, the theme: If only I had been what *I thought I was* I would have been able to resist.

After having fought so hard and long to resist, and then having given in because he just wanted the pressure to stop, he could not face the idea that he was so weak as to give in, that he could be willing to lie "just" to relieve the discomfort. Perhaps he began to believe in his own guilt, as argued by the agent, because it was more bearable to believe that he really was a spy and had confessed justifiably than to believe that he was making false confessions about himself just to relieve the unceasing pressures of the agent. It was this man who said on release in Hong Kong:

> I knew in the first place that I was guilty. In order to gain self-respect, one has to confess.

Ego or identity guilt is thus produced by eliciting from the prisoner behavior which is inconsistent with his self-image, by degrading him and/or provoking him into degrading behavior. One priest's attempt to resist such pressure is indicated in the following statement:

> As soon as the door opens we file off quickly to the washing-room at the end of the corridor. With only six or seven places there, we have to wait for our turn. Soap may not be used. You just dip your towel in the trough and pass it over your face and hands. There's a time allowance of two minutes and no more for all the fifteen of us, since twenty eight other cells on this floor have to get through their ablutions in the course of the hour. We come and go back to our cell with the bowed heads of sentenced criminals, though no one has been condemned. The Communist technique sets much store on the outward sign. By subjecting the body to the posture of guilt, the spirit is moulded and brought into a responsiveness indistinguishable from that of domestic animals. That's what's wanted of everyone in the Communist regime. But why does my good friend, Number 1052, bend down lower than the rest, and outdo all by the exaggerated abjection of his posture? It hurts me every time I see this. The line I have adopted is "submissively nonconformist." I keep my eyes cast down like a nun, so that it's impossible to accuse me of breaking the rules by looking about. But I simply won't bow my head. Yet, apart from an occasional "telling-off," I have been left alone in my obstinacy.[3]

The use of handcuffs and ankle chains as punishment for refusal to confess of course insures degradation and dependency and thereby strongly heightens the probability of ego guilt. The provocation of behavior inconsistent with a man's image of himself is also made easier by the fact that in the intimacy of cell life it is not difficult for cell mates to discover those points on which a fellow prisoner is vulnerable.

One of our subjects after a long period of resistance started to make "concessions" in the form of confessions but he did not believe in any of the behavior he had confessed to, i.e., did not feel he had committed any crimes by his own standards. The close relationships which developed in the group cell and the constant argument and harangue from the interrogator led gradually to an intellectual acceptance of the Chinese Communist semantics and to some

---

[3] A. Bonnichon, "Cell 23–Shanghai," *The Month* (1955), p. 4.

identification with cell mates, expressed most clearly in his calling his cell "a sort of home." The cell mates were the first Chinese that the subject felt he had ever known intimately.

Identification with his cell mates made it easier for this man to accept the validity of their definitions of crime. Gradually the acceptance of their definitions led to a habit of conceptualizing his activities and thoughts in terms of them. Finally he came to accept the point of view that he had been guilty of espionage, but then discovered in a newspsper article that repatriated POW's from Korea who had allegedly been brainwashed had been sent to Valley Forge "mental hospital," and concluded that if he stuck to his confession of espionage he would spend the rest of his days following release in an American mental hospital. To avoid this future possibility he decided to rewrite his confession in such a way as to make it seem harmless from an American point of view, and then settled down to await its acceptance by the authorities. After he had waited two months he was called before the investigating judge, at which time he offered to rewrite the confesssion again in the hope of finding a compromise version which would both be acceptable to the Chinese and get him off the hook with the United States. He was met with "cold hostility" and an order to get back to his cell and was most upset by the loathing and disgust in the voice of the judge. He suddenly felt he had been caught red-handed; until then no one and no experience had presented him with direct "proof" of his flaws.

The feeling of having been dishonest with the Chinese made the subject wonder about the core of his character, whether he had any principles at all, and led to a determination to find the causes for his developing the way he had "or he would never have confidence in himself again." For this subject the crisis was precipitated by his acceptance of certain standards of honesty and sincerity *defined by the Chinese cell mates,* and it is these standards he had failed to live up to in his own eyes, in contrast to the first subject mentioned in this section to whom the false confession meant something entirely different. The subject was guilty because his motives for rewriting his confession were selfish, regardless of the truth or falsity of its contents, and because he was acting selfishly he was failing to live up to a self-image of helping "the people." This conflict at the surface must have made contact with a deeper conflict and must have elicited guilt which was attached to impulses and deeds stemming from his earlier life. We cannot guess what these were, but it is clear that the prisoner was able to use the crisis provoked in the prison situation to reexamine more fundamental aspects of his character and to "reform" some of them.

In conclusion, ego or identity guilt, if it was elicited by the imprisonment experience, could range from being relatively superficial to being quite deep and could be the basis for other guilt feelings such as social guilt. To the extent that basic identity components in the prisoner became involved in the intrapsychic conflict the experience of thought reform could lead to fundamental personality or character change.

Persona or face-to-face guilt

"Isolation would have been heaven in that prison. . . . I dreaded it when the others would come [back to the cell] . . . because I knew I would have no peace. . . . Don't mention the word 'help' to me. I never want to hear that again. I had to watch myself, because they would jump on everything I said. But I couldn't avoid saying something, because I just couldn't sit back and withdraw. I'm just that way."

"I'd prepare some answer hours in advance so that I could use [it] if they asked me what I was thinking . . . and I'd feel guilty when I didn't reveal my true opinion, but used a phoney one to make them stop. . . . I'd feel miserable when, after really having made a sincere effort, they didn't believe me. . . . Of course everyone else was *playing a game* of accusations and self-criticism. . . . It was just because everyone was forced to do it. . . . I knew people were forced to play roles. . . . Still I'd feel guilty about playing my roles."

"You could never tell who was play-acting and who wasn't and you couldn't make any kind of a judgment. You didn't have any kind of a relationship with anyone . . . They were not speaking to *you*, they were speaking to *the confessed you* [the masked "you"]. . . . There was no one we could trust. And you always thought someone was going to inform. But there was one person—a cell mate—with whom I once talked . . . we spoke one night when everyone was asleep and he said to me. 'This is the first time I felt that someone didn't speak to me in a role.' He said, 'I am innocent, should I try to make up a crime, do you think it would be a good strategy if I confessed to something, then they will think I have confessed and they will let me go?" Then I answered him frankly and I said, "You must not make any kind of false confession. You must stick to the truth; otherwise you are going to get all confused.' "

This was the only honest conversation and the only private conversation he ever had with anyone in his three and one half years in prison.

Persona or face-to-face guilt is the feeling of guilt which comes from wearing a mask, or from deliberately playing a role which one is aware is not congruent with the self; in short, which comes from deceiving others about oneself. In prison, persona guilt most often resulted when the prisoner, in order to reduce the continued pressure to reform, deliberately began to act as if he were someone he was not, or pretended to opinions which were not his own. In the model reform prison specializing in group struggle meetings, all prisoners were forced initially to wear verbal masks.

This face-to-face deception was more bearable to some than to others. One subject to whom close personal relationships, even with the resented cell mates, were crucial, saw in this type of guilt one of the major stresses of imprisonment. Another subject refers merely to the "embarrassment" of having to manufacture beliefs he did not have. A third subject was hardly affected by this type of deception because he approached human relationships primarily on an intellectual plane: people to him were not really individuals but personified abstractions with whom one relates through ideas (words). In the prison situation, with all his companions hidden behind masks, he was doubly removed from them. Their verbal masks obliterated any clue to their true selves; they were not real people with whom one could have any relationships. Given this definition of the situation and relationships, this prisoner was quite impervious to the group struggle meetings and to cell mate pressures since the screaming, kicking, spitting, and verbal assault came from "ciphers," not real people.

Thus susceptibility to persona or face-to-face guilt depended on the meaning which deception had for the person, how significant others were for him as persons to be concerned about, and how important it was for the person to obtain confirmation of his "real" self from the others in the prison environment.

Loyalty guilt

For an instant, as he stood there, looking out over the street from a window high in Loukawei Prison, there came to him without warning so great a desire to get out of prison that he almost cried out. It would be simple, really. All he had to do was say the word. One single word in answer to one single question and this whole dreadful nightmare existence would come to an end, so that he could walk down a street and be able to turn whichever way he wanted at the corner.

And then there arose in his mind the faces and names of people whom he knew and loved: priests and laymen who had calmly put their lives and freedom on the line, students who had with wide open eyes taken the deliberate step of depriving themselves of a career and the possibility of a decent livelihood, women who had stood dry-eyed and proud as their men, their sons, their brothers, had been marched off to jail, to slave labor camps, to the firing squad. He saw his Chinese fellow Jesuits boldly speaking out against the Red tyranny, knowing that when they went, they would not come back without breaking. "If I do come out, and say anything different from what I have said before and am saying now, have nothing to do with me. . . ."

Shaken and almost sick at the thought of how close he had come to betraying himself and his friends, Father Phillips turned away from the window and moved back toward the door.[4]

Loyalty guilt resulted from behavior, thoughts, or feelings which the prisoner felt to be a violation of the norms of important reference or membership groups or which would sully the image which others held of that group. Thus a priest felt guilty if he committed any actions which were unpriestlike, Marine POW's in Korea felt guilty if they committed un-Marinelike acts, imprisoned Communist sympathizers felt guilty if they were accused of harming rather than helping the people, cell members felt guilty if they violated the norms of the prison cell (assuming they had become identified with it) by refusing to reform themselves. Just as the prison situation could provoke behavior inconsistent with the person's image of himself, so it could provoke behavior inconsistent with his group membership (for example, provoking a priest into a fist fight over some cell privileges). Clearly loyalty guilt and ego guilt overlap to the extent that the person's image of himself to a large extent reflects his perceptions of group membership and identification. A distinction between the two is useful, however,

---

[4] K. Becker, *I Met a Traveler: The triumph of Father Phillips* (New York: Farrar, Strauss and Cudahy, 1958).

because the subjects themselves distinguished quite sharply between the feeling which resulted from violation of self-image and those which resulted from letting down important others. Perhaps loyalty guilt can be thought of as ego guilt plus something more—a sense of failure in someone else's eyes as well as one's own.

Situational guilt

All our subjects made some reference to their commission of "petty" act which their cell mates would catch and exaggerate into an indication of a great bourgeois flaw. From every prison come stories of "great crimes" by Western prisoners—occasional slightly uneven distribution of food or blankets, petty stealing or cheating, accidental use of another's soap, inadvertent selfishness, and so on. This behavior was identified as serious signs of old bourgeois immorality which warranted the moral outrage and sharp attack of the entire cell group. A man who turned a little too far out of "his space" during sleep was told that he did not do so accidentally but because he was selfish. Any "error," even if it did not remotely involve a serious breach of major values, was not overlooked. It was caught, dwelt on, and exaggerated. Thus, no matter how much he tried to get along, the prisoner was likely to find himself being accused of one thing or another all day and night long. The entire prison environment was characterized by constant accusation, making it highly likely that some form of guilt would be stimulated even in the prisoner who was initially not very guilt-prone.

CONCLUSIONS

Regardless of its psychological basis, once guilt was felt the subject became more prone to accepting one or more of the many arguments of the agent concerning his *objective* guilt. The prisoner's subsequent willingness to confess then resulted from his need to attach his feelings of guilt to behavior or thoughts which the authorities sanctioned as crimes, not from having been "broken." In the case of social, persona, or situational guilt his subjectively felt shortcoming coincided with the objectively defined crimes; in the case of ego or loyalty guilt the subject may have been influenced because it was easier for him to accept psychologically the objective crimes he was accused of, and the belief system which defined these as crimes, than to face the weakness in himself which allowed the guilt-provoking behavior to occur in the first place. In the case of guilt-anxiety where the psychological conflict itself was unconscious, the same mechanism may, of course, have applied, in that the prisoner may have accepted objectively defined crimes and attached his guilt to them to prevent his unconscious conflicts from becoming conscious.[5]

We have treated the topic of guilt as an unfreezing force in some detail because it was undoubtedly one of the central forces motivating the prisoner to

---

[5] J. A. M. Meerloo, *The Rape of the Mind* (Cleveland: World Publishing Co., 1956).

change. We wish to reiterate, however, that guilt was not the only force acting on the prisoner tending to unfreeze him; other forces could also start an influence process. On the other hand, the degree of susceptibility to guilt varied sharply from prisoner to prisoner, and many prisoners had effective defenses against guilt which tended to prevent guilt feelings from precipitating major behavior and/or belief changes. Not all prisoners who experienced guilt were unfrozen by it and subsequently influenced. Many of them, like Father Phillips, quoted at the beginning of the section on loyalty guilt, used the small quantity of guilt which the *thought* of giving in stimulated as a defense against actually giving in. Others defended themselves by the usual mechanisms of repression, denial, rationalization, etc., at the psychological level, and by logical argument, or simple refusal to listen at the level of interaction with the agents.

A narrative[*]

Dennis H. Lytle

Dave Spoffard will serve as an excellent example of a fraternity man for a typical four-year college experience. Dave was an outstanding student in high school, where he had graduated third in his class of seventy-six. In addition to his scholastic achievements, he had won a varsity letter in track, was president of the local chapter of a national scholastic honorary, and was voted most likely to succeed in his graduating class. He also had been awarded an MIT scholarship for one half of his freshman year's tuition.

Partially in response to the encouragement of an excellent general science instructor, Dave had developed technical interests early in his high school career. Even though he was not sure of the particular branch in which he was interested, Dave was convinced that engineering was the occupation that he wanted to pursue.

Dave knew only one person in Boston when he arrived for Rush Week, Jim Crosby. Jim was a senior, a member of a fraternity, and had traveled some 50 miles from his home during the summer to see Dave and his parents. It was largely because of Jim that Dave had decided to come to Rush Week. Dave and his parents had previously decided that a fraternity might not be the best thing for him, but Jim had maintained that this was based on experience with the

---

[*] "A Narrative" reprinted in its entirety from an unpublished Bachelor's thesis by Dennis H. Lytle, "The Scholastic Problem in M.I.T. Fraternities," Massachusetts Institute of Technology, 1959. Used by permission.

fraternities of that area. He had assured them that fraternities at MIT were entirely different. He pointed out that fraternity costs were actually cheaper than the costs of dormitory living, and insisted that fraternities encouraged better scholarship by their freshmen than did the dormitories, both by having a minimum average for initiation and by providing upperclassmen tutors in freshman subjects.

Dave and his parents were favorably impressed by Jim, and so they decided that there would be no harm in Dave attending Rush Week, just to get a closer look at the fraternities. Both he and his parents thought that it might be best for Dave to spend some time in the dormitories before coming to a decision between the two, but the final decision was left up to Dave when he arrived at MIT.

Jim met Dave when his train came in and suggested that Dave use his fraternity house as a base of operations during Rush Week, explaining how convenient this would be, since he would be so much closer to the fraternities. The usual procedure was for the freshmen to stay in the dormitories, but they were located on the opposite side of the Charles River from the majority of the fraternities.

Dave saw eleven different fraternities during Rush Week. Everywhere he went he was treated like a king. He found several houses that he liked very much, but none of the others made him feel quite as much at home as Jim's fraternity. The thought of investigating the dormitories was very much present in his mind, but after talking to several men who had lived in the dormitories before pledging, he decided that the fraternities were definitely for him. From this point he did not take long to decide that, of the fraternities, Jim's was the place he wanted to spend his college days. Dave pledged on the last day of Rush Week, and the members of Jim's fraternity were so enthusiastic in their celebration that Dave was overwhelmed, and he was even surer that he had made the correct decision.

There was quite a party at the house that night, and the next morning, which was the start of Freshman Weekend, there were only a couple of brothers in addition to the new pledges at breakfast. Quite a few of the brothers went away during Freshman Weekend, and the pledges stuck pretty much to themselves. Dave heard several of the new pledges remark that there certainly was a letdown after Rush Week, and he actually heard one say that he wasn't sure that he had pledged the right house. The pledges had more of a feeling of belonging, however, when the brothers returned for the opening of school.

The first pledge meeting was held the second Wednesday after school started. The Pledgemaster informed them that the meetings would be held each Wednesday thereafter, and that quizzes would be given each week on the material that had been assigned for study. In addition, the pledges had to carry five nickels at all times to give change to the brothers, to keep the soft drink machine filled at all times, to answer the phone and doorbell on one ring, and to keep the house scrapbook up to date. Each freshman was also required to spend Saturday afternoons working on the physical house.

When the Pledgemaster had finished, another brother, who was introduced as the Scholastic Chairman, spoke for a few minutes about the academic work that the freshmen were expected to do. He explained that they were required to get a minimum term rating of 2.5 to be eligible for initiation.

Later in the same week, a sophomore encouraged Dave to try to be elected to the Freshman Council, which was made up of two representatives from each freshman section. The sophomore explained that this was the place to meet the future leaders of the class, and that it would not take up any more time than the individual desired since there were so many members. Dave ran and was elected section leader from his section. The freshman council met every Friday afternoon for a couple of hours. Dave did not take part in any of the special committees, but he did attend most of the meetings to be able to represent his section.

When the winter track season started in November, Dave decided to try out for the team, especially since he found out that freshman sports could be used to fulfill the required athletic participation.

When his midterm grades were released, they were not as good as he had anticipated, but he was confident that he could improve them before the end of the term by spending a little more time on his studies. He figured out how much time he was spending on the various activities in which he was participating, and discovered that in addition to the time he spent in classes and preparation, he was spending an average of eight hours a week on pledge duties, eight hours a week on track, and two hours a week with the Freshman Council. In addition, there were only two Saturday nights in the term that he had not had a date. He decided that studying on Saturday evenings would be the only way that he would be able to improve his academic work and continue the activities in which he was participating.

Soon after he had started his program of Saturday evening study, several brothers mentioned that they noticed his new practice, and they strongly recommended that he reconsider. They maintained that a person cannot keep up the "grind" all the time without some relaxation and socializing on the weekends. The brothers that spoke to Dave all had above average grades, and since they had more experience than he had, Dave thought that perhaps he had been a little too strict on himself, and decided to date a little more. Pretty soon, he was back in the habit of dating every Saturday night.

When the end of the first term was over, Dave was disappointed when his grades arrrived. He had made B's in Chemistry and Engineering Drawing, C's in Calculus and Humanities, and a D in Physics, giving him a 3.1 term rating out of 5.0. He immediately resolved that this was not the quality of work with which he would be satisfied, and he was determined to perform better next term. He wrote this fact to his parents, whom he knew were disappointed. They replied that they were indeed disappointed, but that they were confident that he would do better the next term since he set his mind to it.

His plans for starting the second term off right were foiled by the fraternity's pre-initiation week activities which took the entire first week of school. The pledges had to perform many tasks, some of a constructive nature, like painting at a children's home, while others were not so constructive, like putting on skits for the benefit of the brothers. There were activities planned for all night every night, so the only sleep that the group got was during the day when they were away from the fraternity house. Following this week, the entire pledge class was initiated, and they all agreed that initiation was worth the trouble they had gone through. Shortly after initiation, the president of the fraternity called a special meeting of the new brothers and briefed them on the duties that they had as freshmen. They still had to tend the coke machine, answer phones during the evening, and spend Saturday afternoons working for the house. There was some grumbling in the group, but the majority realized that the work had to be done by someone, and it was most convenient to fulfill your obligation while you were still a freshman.

The next week, the same sophomore that had spoken to Dave about the Freshman Council suggested that Dave run for Class Secretary. The sophomore explained that the prestige connected with this office would be of great benefit to both Dave and the fraternity, and that people who have potential to be elected to such offices have somewhat of an obligation to the fraternity to try. Dave, even though he was not sure that he was interested, made a genuine effort. He spent much time preparing campaign material and visiting with members of the class. Unfortunately, a member of the Freshman Council who had been much more active on the council, and who had made a wider circle of friends was elected by a narrow margin.

Dave was still competing with the track team, and in addition, was spending about an hour a week working on the undergraduate Public Relations Committee. He decided to work on the PRC when he realized that he would no longer have the Freshman Council the following year.

The second term passed even more rapidly than the first, and when Dave's grades arrived at home during the summer, he found that his marks were a little lower than the previous term, because he had only gotten a C in the Drawing course, and all the other grades were the same.

During the summer, he spent some time considering the course that he would be going into the following term. After much thought and talk with his parents, he decided that he did not want to spend the rest of his life as an engineer, and thought that the best course of study for him would be the course in Industrial Management, where he would have relative freedom to choose an elective program that would give him as much of an engineering background as he needed.

He returned to MIT in early September for Work Week, which precedes Rush Week for fraternities. As the term began, Dave once again was determined to make this the term that he was going to demonstrate that he had what it took to do well at MIT.

At the first house meeting of the new year, Dave was elected Assistant House Manager. This office required that Dave spend about every other Saturday afternoon helping supervise the freshmen in their work. Dave was still working with the PRC, and was attempting to make the Varsity track team. He was determined not to let these activities interfere with his high academic aspirations, however. He spent all of his spare time in the library studying, and would go to the library several nights a week to be able to work better. He disciplined himself very strictly, and was very seldom in "bull sessions," nor did he take "coffee breaks" in the middle of the evenings as did many of the men in the fraternity.

It soon became evident that some of the members of the fraternity did not appreciate the enthusiasm that Dave exhibited for his studies, however. He overheard one person referring to him as a "studying machine," while another said that it didn't seem that Dave valued the company of his fraternity brothers any more. These comments were disturbing to Dave, for though most of the people that he heard making such statements had better grades than he had, they did not approve of the emphasis that he was putting on improving his studies. Dave found that he spent considerable time with a book in his hand, but with his thoughts centered on the disapproval he was receiving. Gradually his afternoons in the library became less frequent, and he found that a little coffee in the middle of the evening helped him relax better during the remainder of the night.

Even though Dave thought that he was putting in as much time on his school work as those around him, his grades remained below average. He slowly became more depressed, and at one time was seriously considering transferring to another school. Maybe he wasn't cut out to be even this much of an engineer. After talking to his faculty advisor, he decided to stay at least until the remainder of that term and come to a final decision during the vacation between terms.

Dave's fraternity brothers were very much opposed to his transferring, and pointed out that men in the lower half of their class at MIT got better jobs than graduates from most other colleges. They were sure that Dave would be robbing himself of a good education if he transferred. Dave considered these points, and since he was not really doing poorly, he concluded that staying was the best thing for him to do.

When the second term began, Dave found that the pre-initiation week was as much a drain on his time as a brother as it was when he was a pledge. During the term that followed, Dave was still on the track team even though he did not make a letter for the indoor season. He was elected secretary of the Public Relations Committee, and was spending about two hours a week in that capacity.

As the track season progressed, and Dave did not seem to be improving much over his high school performance, he began to spend a little less time practicing, and found that the intramural sports were about as much fun, and you could compete in a greater variety of fields without as much time spent in practice. He continued his varsity competition, however, since he still needed the spring's points to complete his athletic obligation.

At the beginning of his junior year, he was elected Social Chairman. During the term that followed, he spent much time developing what was acclaimed as the best social season that the fraternity has seen in some while. When the time for winter track arrived, he decided against participating, having completed the required athletic participation. He continued to be a big supporter of the fraternity intramural teams, however. His grades during this term fell to the lowest point in his college career. He thought that he should buckle down a little more next term.

The second term of his junior year, Dave was nominated to be chairman of the PRC. This was somewhat of a surprise to him, because he had not been doing nearly as much work as some of the other members. He was elected by a narrow margin, so this activity took considerably more time than it had in the past. His second term grades were an improvement over the first term's grades, so both he and his parents were happier.

Dave began interviewing for jobs early in his senior year. Most of the men that he spoke to were very nice, and were interested in his plans, but at the end of the first term all the replies that he had received were polite, but definite, rejections. During the second term of his senior year, Dave and two other seniors rented an apartment near the fraternity house. They thought that such an atmosphere would be much more conducive to studying, and they were all writing theses. It was very convenient, but none of the group got any more done than they had in the fraternity house.

Dave became a little concerned about his thesis toward the end of the term, and at one time was afraid that he was not going to complete it. He was able to finish one day late, however, even though he was not really happy with the job that he had done.

During the last few weeks of school he received a letter from a company that he had visited offering him a position in their technical sales department. Even though he had previously pictured himself in a position that required more technical and analytical ability, Dave had heard many people say that sales was a growing field, so he accepted this job, and joined the company three weeks after he graduated.

As Dave started to work, he looked back on his college days. He was very happy that he had not become so involved in his studies that he missed all the social opportunities that were available at MIT. He was sure that the activities in which he had participated were going to be a genuine asset in his job, and this was especially true of the experiences contributed by fraternity life.

Romance at Droitgate Spa[*]

P. G. Wodehouse

It has been rightly said—and it is a fact on which we pride ourselves—that in the bar parlor of the Angler's Rest, distinctions of class are unknown. Double Best Ports hobnob on terms of the easiest affability with humble Ginger Ales, and I myself have heard a Draught Beer in a Pewter call a Half Bottle of Champagne "old chap" and be addressed in his turn as "old fellow." Once inside that enchanted room, we are all brothers, all equals, from the highest to the lowest.

It was with distress and embarrassment, therefore, that we had watched the Plain Vichy snubbing the friendly overtures of a meek little Milk and Soda, high-hatting him so coldly and persistently that in the end he gave it up and slunk out. Soon afterwards the Vichy also left, explaining that his doctor had warned him not to be out of bed after 10 o'clock at night, and as the door closed behind him we settled down to discuss the unfortunate affair. The Small Bass who had introduced the two men to one another scratched his head ruefully.

"I can't understand it," he said. "I thought they'd have got on so well together. Twin souls, I thought they'd have been."

Mr. Mulliner stirred his hot scotch and lemon.

"What made you think that?"

"Well, they've both just had operations, and they both like talking about them."

"Ah," said Mr. Mulliner, "but what you are forgetting is that while one has been operated on for duodenal ulcer, the other has merely had his tonsils removed."

"What difference would that make?"

"Every difference. There is no sphere of life in which class consciousness is so rampant as among invalids. The ancient Spartans, I believe, were a little standoffish towards their Helots, but not so standoffish as the man who has been

* Reprinted from P. G. Wodehouse, *Crime Wave at Blandings*. By permission of P. G. Wodehouse and Herbert Jenkins, Ltd.

out in Switzerland taking insulin for his diabetes towards the man who simply undergoing treatment from the village doctor for an ingrowing toenail. This is particularly so, of course, in those places where invalids collect in gangs—Bournemouth, for example, or Buxton, or Droitgate Spa. In such resorts the atmosphere is almost unbelievably clique-y. The old aristocracy, the topnotchers with maladies that get written up in the medical journals, keep themselves to themselves pretty rigidly, I can assure you, and have a very short way with the smaller fry."

Mention of Droitgate Spa (said Mr. Mulliner, having ordered a second hot scotch and lemon) recalls to my mind the romance of my distant connection, Frederick Fitch-Fitch, whose uncle, Major General Sir Aylmer Bastable, lived there. It was at Droitgate Spa that the story had its setting, and I have always thought it one that throws a very interesting light on conditions in the class of the community of which we have been speaking.

Frederick at that time was a young man of pleasing manners and exterior who supported life on a small private income, the capital of which was held in trust for him by his uncle, Sir Aylmer; and it was his great desire to induce the other to release this capital so that he could go into the antique business.

For that was where Frederick's heart was. He wanted to buy a half interest in some good Olde Shoppe in the Bond Street neighborhood and start selling walnut tables and things. So every once in a while he would journey down to Droitgate Spa and plead for the stuff, but every time he did so he went away with his dreams shattered. For circumstances had unfortunately so ordered themselves as to make this uncle of his a warped, soured uncle.

Major General Sir Aylmer Bastable, you see, had had an unpleasant shock on coming to settle in Droitgate Spa. The head of a fine old family and the possessor of a distinguished military record, he had expected upon his arrival to be received with open arms by the best people and welcomed immediately into the inner set. But when it was discovered that all he had wrong with him was the gout in the right foot, he found himself cold-shouldered by the men who mattered and thrust back on the society of the asthma patients and the fellows with slight liver trouble.

This naturally soured his disposition a good deal, and his ill humor reacted upon his nephew. Every time Freddie came asking for capital to invest in antique shoppes, he found his uncle smarting from a snub from some swell whom the doctors had twice given up for dead, and so in no mood to part.

And then one day a more serious issue forced itself onto the agenda paper. At a charity matinée Freddie for the first time set eyes on Annabel Purvis. She was the assistant of The Great Boloni, a conjurer who had been engaged to perform at the entertainment, her duties being to skip downstage from time to time, hand him a bowl of goldfish, beam at the audience, do a sort of dance step, and skip back again. And with such winsome grace did she do this that Freddie fell in love at first sight.

It is not necessary for me to describe in detail how my distant connection contrived to make the girl's acquaintance, nor need I take you step by step through his courtship. Suffice it to say that during the cheese and celery course of a luncheon *à deux* some few weeks later Freddie proposed and was accepted. So now it became even more imperative than before that he induce his uncle to release his capital.

It was with a certain uneasiness that he traveled down to Droitgate Spa, for he was fully alive to the fact that the interview might prove a disagreeable one. However, his great love bore him on, and he made the journey and was shown into the room where the old man sat nursing a gouty foot.

"Hullo-ullo-ullo, Uncle!" he cried, for it was always his policy on these occasions to be buoyant till thrown out. "Good morning, good morning, good morning."

"Gaw!" said Sir Aylmer, with a sort of long, shuddering sigh. "It's you, is it?"

And he muttered something which Freddie did not quite catch, though he was able to detect the words "last straw."

"Well," he went on, "what do you want?"

"Oh, I just looked in," said Freddie. "How's everything?"

"Rotten," replied Sir Aylmer. "I've just lost my nurse."

"Dead?"

"Worse. Married. The clothheaded girl has gone off and got spliced to one of the *canaille*—a chap who's never even had so much as athlete's foot. She must be crazy."

"Still, one sees her point of view."

"No, one doesn't."

"I mean," said Freddie, who felt strongly on this subject, "it's love that makes the world go round."

"It isn't anything of the kind," said Sir Aylmer. Like so many fine old soldiers, he was inclined to be a little literal-minded. "I never heard such dashed silly nonsense in my life. What makes the world go round is . . . Well, I've forgotten at the moment, but it certainly isn't love. How the deuce could it?"

"Oh, right ho. I see what you mean," said Freddie. "But put it another way. Love conquers all. Love's all right, take it from me."

The old man looked at him sharply.

"Are you in love?"

"Madly."

"Of all the young cuckoos! And I suppose you've come to ask for money to get married on?"

"Not at all. I just dropped round to see how you were. Still, as the subject has happened to crop up—."

Sir Aylmer brooded for a moment, snorting in an undertone.

"Who's the girl?" he demanded.

Freddie coughed, and fumbled with his collar. The crux of the situation, he realized, had now been reached. He had feared from the first that this was where the good old snag might conceivably sidle into the picture. For his Annabel was of humble station, and he knew how rigid were his relative's views on the importance of birth. No bigger snob ever swallowed a salicylate pill.

"Well, as a matter of fact," he said, "she's a conjurer's stooge."

"A *what?*"

"A conjurer's assistant, don't you know. I saw her first at a charity matinée. She was abetting a bloke called The Great Boloni."

"In what sense, abetting?"

"Well, she stood there upstage, don't you know, and every now and then she would skip downstage, hand this chap a bowl of goldfish or something, beam at the audience, do a sort of dance step and skip back again. You know the kind of thing."

A dark frown had come into Sir Aylmer's face.

"I do," he said grimly. "So! My only nephew has been ensnared by a bally, beaming goldfish-hander! Ha!"

"I wouldn't call it ensnared exactly," said Freddie deferentially.

"I would," said Sir Aylmer. "Get out of here."

"Right," said Freddie, and caught the 2:35 express back to London. And it was during the journey that an idea flashed upon him.

The last of the Fitch-Fitches was not a great student of literature, but he occasionally dipped into a magazine; and everybody who has ever dipped into a magazine has read a story about a hardhearted old man who won't accept the hero's girl at any price, so what do they do but plant her on him without telling him who she is and, by Jove, he falls under her spell completely and then they tear off their whiskers and there they are. There was a story of this nature in the magazine which Freddie had purchased at the newsstand at Droitgate Spa station, and, as he read it, he remembered what his uncle had told him about his nurse handing in her portfolio.

By the time the train checked in at Paddington, his plans were fully formed.

"Listen," he said to Annabel Purvis, who had met him at the terminus, and Annabel said, "What?"

"Listen," said Freddie, and Annabel again said "What?"

"Listen," said Freddie, clasping her arm tenderly and steering her off in the direction of the refreshment room, where it was his intention to have a quick one. "To a certain extent I am compelled to admit that my expedition has been a washout . . ."

Annabel caught her breath sharply.

"No blessing?"

"No blessing."

"And no money?"

"No money. The old boy ran entirely true to stable form. He listened to what I had to say, snorted in an unpleasant manner and threw me out. The old routine. But what I'm working round to is that the skies are still bright and the bluebird on the job. I have a scheme. Could you be a nurse?"

"I used to nurse my Uncle Joe."

"Then you shall nurse my uncle Aylmer. The present incumbent, he tells me, has just tuned out, and he needs a successor. I will phone him that I am despatching immediately a red-hot nurse whom he will find just the same as Mother makes, and you shall go down to Droitgate Spa and ingratiate yourself."

"But how?"

"Why, cluster round him. Smooth his pillow. Bring him cooling drinks. Coo to him, and give him the old oil. Tell him you are of gentle birth, if that's the expression I want. And when the time is ripe, when you have twined yourself about his heart and he looks upon you as a daughter shoot me a wire, and I'll come down and fall in love with you and he will give us his consent, blessing and the stuff. It works."

So Annabel went to Droitgate Spa, and about three weeks later a telegram arrived for Freddie, running as follows:

HAVE INGRATIATED SELF   COME AT ONCE   LOVE AND KISSES   ANNABEL

Within an hour of its arrival, Freddie was on his way to Podagra Lodge, his uncle's residence.

He found Sir Aylmer in his study. Annabel was sitting by his side, reading aloud to him from a recently published monograph on certain obscure ailments of the medulla oblongata. For the old man, though a mere gout patient, had pathetic aspirations towards higher things. There was a cooling drink on the table, and as Freddie entered the girl paused in her reading to smooth her employer's pillow.

"Gaw!" said Sir Aylmer. "You again?"

"Here I am," said Freddie.

"Well, by an extraordinary chance, I'm glad to see you. Leave us for a moment, Miss Purvis. I wish to speak to my nephew here, such as he is, on a serious and private matter. Did you notice that girl?" he said, as the door closed.

"I did, indeed."

"Pretty."

"An eyeful."

"And as good," said Sir Aylmer, "as she is beautiful. You should see her smooth pillows. And what a cooling drink she mixes! Excellent family, too, I understand. Her father is a colonel. Or, rather, was. He's dead."

"Ah well, all flesh is as grass."

"No, it isn't. It's nothing of the kind. The two things are entirely different. I've seen flesh and I've seen grass. No resemblance whatever. However, that is not the point at issue. What I wanted to say was that if you were not a damned fool, that's the sort of girl you would be in love with."

"I am."

"A damned fool?"

"No. In love with that girl."

"What! You have fallen in love with Miss Purvis? Already?"

"I have."

"Well, that's the quickest thing I ever saw. What about your beaming gold-fish?"

"Oh, that's all over. A mere passing boyish fancy."

Sir Aylmer took a deep swig at his cooling drink, and regarded him in silence for a moment.

"Well," he said at length, breathing heavily, "if that's the airy, casual way in which you treat life's most sacred emotions, the sooner you are safely married and settled down, the better. If you're allowed to run around loose much longer, indulging those boyish fancies of yours, I foresee the breach-of-promise case of the century. However, I'm not saying I'm not relieved. I am relieved. I suppose she wore tights, this goldfish girl?"

"Pink."

"Disgusting. Thank God it's all over. Very good, then. You are free, I under-stand, to have a pop at Miss Purvis. Do you propose to do so?"

"I do."

"Excellent. You get that sweet, refined, most-suitable-in-all-respects girl to marry you, and I'll hand over that money of yours, every penny of it."

"I will start at once."

"Heaven speed your wooing," said Sir Aylmer.

And 10 minutes later Freddie was able to inform his uncle that his whirlwind courtship had been successful, and Sir Aylmer said that when he had asked heaven to speed his wooing he had had no notion that it would speed it to quite that extent. He congratulated Freddie warmly and said he hoped that he ap-preciated his good fortune, and Freddie said he certainly did, because his love was like a red, red rose, and Sir Aylmer said, No, she wasn't, and when Freddie added that he was walking on air, Sir Aylmer said he couldn't be, the thing was physically impossible.

However, he gave his blessing and promised to release Freddie's capital as soon as the necessary papers were drawn up, and Freddie went back to London to see his lawyer about this.

His mood, as the train sped through the quiet countryside, was one of perfect tranquillity and happiness. It seemed to him that his troubles were now definitely ended. He looked down the vista of the years and saw nothing but joy and sunshine. If somebody had told Frederick Fitch-Fitch at the moment that even now a V-shaped depression was coming along which would shortly blacken the skies and lower the general temperature to freezing point, he would not have believed him.

Nor when, two days later, as he sat in his club, he was informed that a Mr. Rackstraw was waiting to see him in the small smoking room, did he have an inkling that here was the V-shaped depression in person. His heart was still light as he went down the passage, wondering idly, for the name was unfamiliar to him, who this Mr. Rackstraw might be. He entered the room, and found there a tall, thin man with pointed black moustaches who was pacing up and down, nervously taking rabbits out of his top hat as he walked.

"Mr. Rackstraw?"

His visitor spun round, dropping a rabbit. He gazed at Freddie piercingly. He had bright, glittering, sinister eyes.

"That is my name. Mortimer Rackstraw."

Freddie's mind had flown back to the charity matinée at which he had first seen Annabel, and he recognized the fellow now.

"The Great Boloni, surely?"

"I call myself that professionally. So you are Mr. Fitch? So *you* are Mr. Fitch? Ha! Fiend!"

"Eh?"

"I am not mistaken? You are Frederick Fitch?"

"Frederick Fitch-Fitch."

"I beg your pardon. In that case, I should have said 'Fiend! Fiend!' "

He produced a pack of cards and asked Freddie to take one—any one—and memorize it and put it back. Freddie did so absently. He was considerably fogged. He could make nothing of all this.

"How do you mean—Fiend-Fiend?" he asked.

The other sneered unpleasantly.

"Cad!" he said, twirling his moustache.

"Cad?" said Freddie, mystified.

"Yes sir. Cad. You have stolen the girl I love."

"I don't understand."

"Then you must be a perfect ass. It's quite simple, isn't it? I can't put it any plainer, can I? I say you have stolen . . . Well, look here," said Mortimer Rackstraw. "Suppose this top hat is me. This rabbit," he went on, producing it from the lining, "is the girl I love. You come along and, presto, the rabbit vanishes."

"It's up your sleeve."

"It is not up my sleeve. And if it were, if I had a thousand sleeves and rabbits up every one of them, that would not alter the fact that you have treacherously robbed me of Annabel Purvis."

Freddie began to see daylight. He was able to appreciate the other's emotion.

"So you love Annabel too?"

"I do."

"I don't wonder. Nice girl, what? I see, I see. You worshipped her in secret, never telling your love . . ."

"I did tell my love. We were engaged."

"Engaged?"

"Certainly. And this morning I get a letter from her saying that it's all off, because she has changed her mind and is going to marry you. She has thrown me over."

"Oh, ah? Well, I'm frightfully sorry—deepest sympathy, and all that—but I don't see what's to be done about it, what?"

"I do. There still remains—revenge."

"Oh, I say, dash it! You aren't going to be stuffy about it?"

"I am going to be stuffy about it. For the moment you triumph. But do not imagine that this is the end. You have not heard the last of me. Not by any means. You may have stolen the woman I love with your underhanded chicanery, but I'll fix you."

"How?"

"Never mind how. You will find out how quite soon enough. A nasty jolt you're going to get, my good friend, and almost immediately. As sure," said Mortimer Rackstraw, illustrating by drawing one from Freddie's back hair, "as eggs are eggs. I wish you a very good afternoon."

He took up his top hat, which in his emotion he had allowed to fall to the ground, brushed it on his coat sleeve, extracted from it a cage of lovebirds and strode out.

A moment later he returned, bowed a few times to right and left and was gone again.

To say that Freddie did not feel a little uneasy as the result of this scene would be untrue. There had been something in the confident manner in which the other had spoken of revenging himself that he had not at all liked. The words had had a sinister ring, and all through the rest of the day he pondered thoughtfully, wondering what a man so trained in the art of having things up his sleeve might have up it now. It was in meditative mood that he dined, and only on the following morning did his equanimity return to him.

Able, now that he had slept on it, to review the disturbing conversation in its proper perspective, he came to the conclusion that the fellow's threats had been mere bluff. What, after all, he asked himself, could this conjurer do? It was not as if they had been living in the Middle Ages, when chaps of that sort used to put spells on you and change you into things.

No, he decided, it was mere bluff, and with his complacency completely restored had just lighted a cigarette and fallen to dreaming of the girl he loved, when a telegram was brought to him.

It ran as follows:

COME AT ONCE   ALL LOST   RUIN STARES FACE   LOVE AND KISSES   ANNABEL

Half an hour later, he was in the train, speeding towards Droitgate Spa.

It had been Freddie's intention, on entering the train, to devote the journey to earnest meditation. But, as always happens when one wishes to concentrate and brood during a railway journey, he found himself closeted with a talkative fellow traveler.

The one who interrupted Freddie's thoughts was a flabby, puffy man of middle age, wearing a red waistcoat, brown shoes, a morning coat and a bowler hat. With such a Grade A bounder, even had his mind been at rest, Freddie would have little in common, and he sat chafing while the prismatic fellow prattled on. Nearly an hour passed before he was freed from the infliction of the other's conversation, but eventually the man's head began to nod, and presently he was snoring and Freddie was able to give himself up to his reverie.

His thoughts became less and less agreeable as the train rolled on. And what rendered his mental distress so particularly acute was the lack of informative detail in Annabel's telegram. It seems to him to offer so wide a field for uncomfortable speculation.

"All lost," for instance. A man could do a lot of thinking about a phrase like that. And "Ruin stares face." Why, he asked himself, did ruin stare face? While commending Annabel's thriftiness in keeping the thing down to twelve words, he could not help wishing that she could have brought herself to spring another twopence and be more lucid.

But of one thing he felt certain. All this had something to do with his recent visitor. Behind that mystic telegram he seemed to see the hand of Mortimer Rackstraw, that hand whose quickness deceived the eye, and he knew that in lightly dismissing the other as a negligible force he had been too sanguine.

By the time he reached Podagra Lodge, the nervous strain had become almost intolerable. As he rang the bell, he was quivering like some jelly set before a diet patient, and the sight of Annabel's face as she opened the door did nothing to alleviate his perturbation. The girl was obviously all of a twitter.

"Oh, Freddie!" she cried. "The worst has happened."

Freddie gulped.

"Rackstraw?"

"Yes," said Annabel, "But how did you know about him?"

"He came to see me, bubbling over a good deal with veiled menaces and what not," explained Freddie. He frowned and eyed her closely. "Why didn't you tell me you had been engaged to that bird?"

"I didn't think you would be interested. It was just a passing girlish fancy."

"You're sure? You didn't really love this blighted prestidigitator?"

"No, no. I was dazzled for a while, as any girl might have been, when he sawed me in half, but then you came along and I saw that I had been mistaken and that you were the only man in the world for me."

"Good egg," said Freddie, relieved.

He kissed her fondly and, as he did so, there came to his ears the sound of rhythmic hammering from somewhere below.

"What's that?" he asked.

Annabel wrung her hands.

"It's Mortimer!"

"Is he here?"

"Yes. He arrived on the one-fifteen. I locked him in the cellar."

"Why?"

"To stop him going to the Pump Room."

"Why shouldn't he go to the Pump Room?"

"Because Sir Aylmer has gone there to listen to the band and they must not meet. If they do, we are lost. Mortimer has hatched a fearful plot."

Freddie's heart seemed to buckle under within him. He had tried to be optimistic, but all along he had known that Mortimer Rackstraw would hatch some fearful plot. He could have put his shirt on it. A born hatcher.

"What plot?"

Annabel wrung her hands again.

"He means to introduce Sir Aylmer to my uncle Joe. He wired to him to come to Droitgate Spa. He had arranged to meet him at the Pump Room, and then he was going to introduce him to Sir Aylmer."

Freddie was a little fogged. It did not seem to him much of a plot.

"Now that I can never be his, all he wants is to make himself unpleasant and prevent our marriage. And he knows that Sir Aylmer will never consent to your marrying me if he finds out that I have an uncle like Uncle Joe."

Freddie ceased to be fogged. He saw the whole devilish scheme now—a scheme worthy of the subtle brain that could put the ace of spades back in the pack, shuffle, cut three times, and then produce it from the inside of a lemon.

"Is he so frightful?" he quavered.

"Look," said Annabel simply. She took a photograph from her bosom and extended it towards him with a trembling hand. "That is Uncle Joe, taken in the masonic regalia of a Grand Exalted Periwinkle of the Mystic Order of Whelks."

Freddie glanced at the photograph and started back with a hoarse cry. Annabel nodded sadly.

"Yes," she said. "That is how he takes most people. The only faint hope I have is that he won't have been able to come. But if he has ——"

"He has," cried Freddie, who had been fighting for breath. "We traveled down in the train together."

"What!"

"Yes. He must be waiting in the Pump Room now."

"And at any moment Mortimer will break his way out of the cellar. The door is not strong. What shall we do?"

"There is only one thing to do. I have all the papers . . ."

"You have no time to read now."

"The legal papers, the ones my uncle has to sign in order to release my money. There is just a chance that if I rush to the Pump Room I may get him to put his name on the dotted line before the worst happens."

"Then rush," cried Annabel.

"I will," said Freddie.

He kissed her quickly, grabbed his hat, and was off the mark like a jack rabbit.

A man who is endeavoring to lower the record for the distance between Podagra Lodge, which is in Arterio-Sclerosis Avenue, and the Droitgate Spa Pump Room has little leisure for thinking, but Freddie managed to put in a certain amount as his feet skimmed the pavement. And the trend of his thought was such as to give renewed vigor to his legs. He could scarcely have moved more rapidly if he had been a character in a two-reel film with the police after him.

And there was need for speed. Beyond the question, Annabel had been right when she had said that Sir Aylmer would never consent to their union if he found out that she had an uncle like her Uncle Joe. Uncle Joe would get right in amongst him. Let them but meet, and nothing was more certain than that the haughty old man would veto the proposed nuptials.

A final burst of speed took him panting up the Pump Room steps and into the rotunda where all that was best and most refined in Droitgate Spa was accustomed to assemble of an afternoon and listen to the band. He saw Sir Aylmer in a distant seat and hurried towards him.

"Gaw!" said Sir Aylmer. "You?"

Freddie could only nod.

"Well, stop puffing like that and sit down," said Sir Aylmer. "They're just going to play 'Poet and Peasant.' "

Freddie recovered his breath.

"Uncle____" he began. But it was too late. Even as he spoke, there was a crash of brass and Sir Aylmer's face assumed that reverent, doughlike expression of attention so familiar in the rotundas of cure resorts.

"Sh," he said.

Of all the uncounted millions who in their time have listened to bands playing "Poet and Peasant," few can ever have listened with such a restless impatience as did Frederick Fitch-Fitch on this occasion. Time was flying. Every second was precious. At any moment disaster might befall. And the band went on playing as if it had taken on a life job. It seemed to him an eternity before the final oom-pom-pa.

"Uncle," he cried, as the echoes died away.

"Sh," said Sir Aylmer testily, and Freddie, with a dull despair, perceived that they were going to get an encore.

Of all the far-flung myriads who year in and year out have listened to bands playing the "Overture" to *Raymond*, few can ever have chafed as did Frederick Fitch-Fitch now. This suspense was unmanning him, this delay was torture. He took the papers and a fountain pen from his pocket and toyed with them nervously. He wondered dully as he sat there how the opera *Raymond* had ever managed to get itself performed, if the "Overture" was as long as this. They must have rushed it through in the last five minutes of the evening as the audience groped for its hats and wraps.

But there is an end to all things, even to the "Overture" from *Raymond*. Just as the weariest river winds somewhere safe to sea, so does this "Overture" eventually finish. And when it did, when the last notes faded into silence and the conductor stood bowing and smiling with that cool assumption, common to all conductors, that it is they and not the perspiring orchestra who have been doing the work, he started again.

"Uncle," he said, "may I trouble you a moment . . . These papers."

Sir Aylmer cocked an eye at the documents.

"What papers are those?"

"The ones you have to sign, releasing my capital."

"Oh, those," said Sir Aylmer genially. The music had plainly mellowed him. "Of course, yes. Certainly, certainly. Give me . . ."

He broke off, and Freddie saw that he was looking at a distinguished, silvery-haired man with thin, refined features, who was sauntering by.

"Afternoon, Rumbelow." he said.

There was an unmistakable note of obsequiousness in Sir Aylmer's voice. His face had become pink, and he was shuffling his feet and twiddling his fingers. The man to whom he had spoken paused and looked down. Seeing who it was that had accosted him, he raised a silvery eyebrow. His manner was undisguisedly supercilious.

"Ah, Bastable," he said distantly.

A duller man than Sir Aylmer Bastable could not have failed to detect the cold hauteur in his voice. Freddie saw the flush on his uncle's face deepen. Sir Aylmer mumbled something about hoping that the distinguished-looking man was feeling better today.

"Worse," replied the other curtly. "Much worse. The doctors are baffled. Mine is a very complicated case." He paused for a moment, and his delicately chiseled lip curled in a sneer. "And how is the gout, Bastable? Gout! Ha, ha!"

Without waiting for a reply, he passed on and joined a group that stood chatting close by. Sir Aylmer choked down a mortified oath.

"Snob!" he muttered. "Thinks he's everybody just because he's got telangiecstasis. I don't see what's so wonderful about having telangiecstasis. Anybody could have . . . What on earth are you doing? What the devil's all this you're waving under my nose? Papers? Papers? I don't want any papers. Take them away, sir!"

And before Freddie could burst into the impassioned plea which trembled on his lips, a commotion in the doorway distracted his attention. His heart missed a beat, and he sat there, frozen.

On the threshold stood Mortimer Rackstraw. He was making some enquiry of an attendant, and Freddie could guess only too well what that enquiry was. Mortimer Rackstraw was asking which of those present was Major General Sir Aylmer Bastable. Attached to arm, obviously pleading with him and appealing to his better self, Annabel Purvis gazed up into his face with tear-filled eyes.

A moment later, the conjurer strode up, still towing the girl. He halted before Sir Aylmer and threw Annabel aside like a soiled glove. His face was cold and hard and remorseless. With one hand he was juggling mechanically with two billiard balls and a bouquet of roses.

"Sir Aylmer Bastable?"

"Yes."

"I forbid the banns."

"What banns?"

"Their banns," said Mortimer Rackstraw, removing from his lips the hand with which he had been coldly curling his moustache and jerking it in the direction of Annabel and Freddie, who stood clasped in each other's arms, waiting for they knew not what.

"They're not up yet," said Annabel.

The conjurer seemed a little taken back.

"Oh?" he said. "Well, when they are, I forbid them. And so will you, Sir Aylmer, when you hear all."

Sir Aylmer puffed.

Mortimer Rackstraw shook his head and took the two of clubs from it.

"A bounder, maybe," he said, "but not tight. I have come here, Sir Aylmer, in a spirit of altruism to warn you that if you allow your nephew to marry this girl the grand old name of Bastable will be mud."

Sir Aylmer started.

"Mud?"

"Mud. She comes from the very dregs of society."

"I don't," cried Annabel.

"Of course she doesn't," cried Freddie.

"Certainly she does not," assented Sir Aylmer warmly. "She told me herself that her father was a colonel."

Mortimer Rackstraw uttered a short, sneering laugh and took an egg from his left elbow.

"She did, eh? Did she add that he was a colonel in the Salvation Army?"

"What!"

"And that before he saw the light he was a Silver Ring bookie, known to all the heads as Rat-Faced Rupert, the Bermondsey Twister?"

"Good God!"

Sir Aylmer turned to the girl with an awful frown.

"Is this true?"

"Of course it's true," said Mortimer Rackstraw. "And if you want further proof of her unfitness to be your nephew's bride, just take a look at her Uncle Joe, who is now entering left-center.

And Freddie, listless now and without hope, saw that his companion of the train was advancing towards them. He heard Sir Aylmer gasp and was aware that Annabel had stiffened in his arms. He was not surprised. The sun, filtering through the glass of the rotunda, lit up the man's flabby puffiness, his morning coat, his red waistcoat and his brown shoes, and rarely if ever, thought Freddie, could the sun of Droitgate Spa have shone on a more ghastly outsider.

There was nothing, however, in the newcomer's demeanor to suggest that he felt himself out of place in the refined surroundings. His manner had an easy self-confidence. He sauntered up and without *gêne* slapped the conjurer on the back and patted Annabel on the shoulder.

" 'Ullo, Mort. 'Ullo, Annie, my dear."

Sir Aylmer, who had blinked, staggered and finally recovered himself, spoke in a voice of thunder.

"You, sir! Is this true!"

"What's that, old cock?"

"Are you this girl's uncle?"

"That's right."

"Gaw!" said Sir Aylmer.

He would have spoken further, but at this point the band burst into "Pomp and Circumstance" and conversation was temporarily suspended. When it became possible once more for the human voice to make itself heard, it was Annabel's Uncle Joe who took the floor. He had recognized Freddie.

"Why, I've met you," he said. "We traveled down in the train together. Who's this young feller, Annie, that's huggin' and squeezin' you?"

"He is the man I am going to marry," said Annabel.

"He is not the man you are going to marry," said Sir Aylmer.

"Yes, I am the man she is going to marry," said Freddie.

"No, you're not the man she is going to marry," said Mortimer Rackstraw.

Annabel's Uncle Joe seemed puzzled. He appeared not to know what to make of this conflict of opinion.

"Well, settle it among yourselves," he said genially. "All I know is that whoever does marry you, Annie, is going to get a good wife."

"That's me," said Freddie.

"No, it isn't," said Sir Aylmer.

"Yes, it is," said Annabel.

"No, it's not," said Mortimer Rackstraw.

"Because I'm sure no man," proceeded Uncle Joe, "ever had a better niece. I've never forgotten the way you used to come and smooth my pillow and bring me cooling drinks when I was in the hospital."

There was the sound of a sharp intake of breath. Sir Aylmer, who was saying, "It isn't, it isn't, it isn't," had broken off abruptly.

"Hospital?" he said. "Were you ever in a hospital?"

Mr. Boffin laughed indulgently.

"Was I ever in a hospital! That's a good 'un. That would make the boys on the medical council giggle. Ask them at St. Luke's if Joe Boffin was ever in a hospital. Ask them at St. Christopher's. Why, I've spent most of my life in hospitals. Started as a child with Congenital Pyloric Hypertrophy of the Stomach and never looked back."

Sir Aylmer was trembling violently. A look of awe had come into his face, the look which a small boy wears when he sees a heavyweight champion of the world.

"Did you say your name was Joe Boffin?"

"That's right."

"Not *the* Joe Boffin. Not the man there was that interview with in the Christmas number in the *Lancet?*"

"That's me."

Sir Aylmer started forward impulsively.

"May I shake your hand?"

"Put it there."

"I am proud to meet you, Mr. Boffin. I am one of your greatest admirers."

"Nice of you to say so, ol' man."

"Your career has been an inspiration to me. Is it really true that you have Thrombosis of the Heart *and* Vesicular Emphysema of the Lungs?"

"That's right."

"And that your temperature once went up to 107.5?"

"Twice. When I had Hyperpyrexia."

Sir Aylmer sighed.

"The best I've ever done is 102.2."

Joe Boffin patted him on the back.

"Well, that's not bad," he said. "Not bad at all."

"Excuse me," said a well-bred voice.

It was the distinguished-looking man with the silvery hair who had approached them, the man Sir Aylmer has addressed as Rumbelow. His manner was diffident. Behind him stood an eager group, staring and twiddling their fingers.

"Excuse me, my dear Bastable, for intruding on a private conversation, but I fancied . . . and my friends fancied . . ."

"We all fancied," said the group.

"That we overheard the name Boffin. Can it be, sir, that you are Mr. *Joseph* Boffin?"

"That's right."

"Boffin of St. Luke's?"

"That's right."

The silvery-haired man seemed overcome by a sudden shyness. He giggled nervously.

"Then may we say—my friends and I—how much . . . We felt we would just like . . . Unwarrantable intrusion, of course, but we are all such great admirers . . . I suppose you have to go through a good deal of this sort of thing, Mr. Boffin . . . people coming up to you, I mean, and . . . perfect strangers, I mean to say . . ."

"Quite all right, old man, quite all right. Always glad to meet the fans."

"Then may I introduce myself? I am Lord Rumbelow. These are my friends, the Duke of Mull, the Marquis of Peckham, Lord Percy . . ."

" 'Ow are you, 'ow are you? Come and join us, boys. My niece, Miss Purvis."

"Charmed."

"The young chap she's going to marry."

"How do you do?"

"And his uncle, Sir Aylmer Bastable."

All heads were turned towards the Major General. Lord Rumbelow spoke in an awed voice.

"Is this really so, Bastable? Your nephew actually going to marry Mr. Boffin's niece? I congratulate you, my dear fellow. A most signal honor." A touch of embarrassment came into his manner. He coughed. "We were just talking about you, oddly enough, Bastable, my friends and I. Saying what a pity it was that we saw so little of you. And we were wondering—it was the Duke's suggestion—if you would care to become a member of a little club we have—quite a small affair—rather exclusive, we like to feel—the Twelve Jolly Stretcher Cases. . . ."

"My dear Rumbelow!"

"We have felt for a long time that our company was incomplete without you. So you will join us? Capital, capital! Perhaps you will look in there tonight? Mr. Boffin, of course," he went on deprecatingly, "would, I am afraid, hardly condescend to allow himself to be entertained by so humble a little circle. Otherwise——"

Joe Boffin slapped him affably on the back.

"My dear feller, I'd be delighted. There's nothing stuck up about me."

"Well, really! I hardly know what to say . . ."

"We can't all be Joe Boffins. That's the way I look at it."

"The true democratic spirit."

"Why, I was best man at a chap's wedding last week, and all he'd got was emotional dermatitis."

"Amazing! Then you and Sir Aylmer will be with us tonight? Delightful. We can give you a bottle of lung tonic which I think you will appreciate. We pride ourselves on our cellar."

A babble of happy chatter had broken out, almost drowning the band, which was now playing the "Overture" to *William Tell,* and Mr. Boffin, opening his waistcoat, was showing the Duke of Mull the scar left by his first operation. Sir Aylmer, watching them with a throbbing heart, was dizzily aware of a fountain pen being thrust into his hand.

"Eh?" he said. "What? What's this? What, what?"

"The papers," said Freddie. "The merry old documents in the case. You sign here, where my thumb is."

"Eh? What? Eh? Ah, to be sure, Yes, yes, yes," said Sir Aylmer, absently affixing his signature.

"Thank you, Uncle, a thousand——"

"Quite, quite. But don't bother me now, my boy. Busy. Got a lot to talk about to these friends of mine. Take the girl away and give her a sulfur water."

And, brushing aside Mortimer Rackstraw, who was offering him a pack of cards, he joined the group about Joe Boffin. Freddie clasped Annabel in a fond embrace. Mortimer Rackstraw stood glaring for a moment, twisting his moustache. Then he took the flags of all nations from Annabel's back hair and with a despairing gesture strode from the room.

The teacher as a model*

Joseph Adelson

Discussions of the Good Teacher are likely to leave us more uplifted than enlightened. The descriptions we read generally amount to little more than an assemblage of virtues; we miss in them a sense of complexity and ambiguity that we know to characterize the teacher's work. Here are some paradoxes to help us get going: a teacher may be a good teacher yet not serve as a model to any of his students; he may inspire his students and yet fail to influence them; he may influence them without inspiring them; he may be a model for them and yet not be an effective teacher; and so on. To say all of this is to make the point—an obvious one but generally overlooked in the more solemn and global discussions of the Teacher—that charisma, competence and influence do not necessarily go hand in hand. A great many college teachers, perhaps most of them, are "good" teachers—good in the sense that they are conscientious and devoted, that they are lucid, articulate and fair-minded lecturers, and that more often than not they succeed in illuminating the subject matter. Their students learn from them, often learn very much; yet these teachers ultimately do not make much of a difference in their students' lives beyond the learning they impart. At another extreme we have those rare teachers who stir and enchant their students, and yet who may be spectacularly inept in teaching subject matter. I think now of a former colleague of mine, in some ways a truly great man, who is so ebullient, erratic and distractable, so easily carried away by the rocketing course of his thought, that his students—even the bright ones—just sit there, benumbed, bewildered and finally enthralled. They know themselves to be close to a Presence and are willing to suffer incoherence to join vicariously in that demonic enthusiasm.

What we must do, plainly, is to recognize the pluralism in teaching—the many styles of influence, the many modes of connection that bind student and teacher to each other. Teaching styles are so diverse that they can be categorized in a

* Excerpted from Joseph Adelson, "The Teacher as a Model," reprinted from *The American Scholar*, Vol. 30, No. 3 (Summer, 1961), pp. 383–406. Copyright © 1961 by the United Chapters of Phi Beta Kappa. By permission of the publishers.

great many different ways. The grouping I want to try out was suggested by the yet unpublished work of Merrill Jackson, an anthropologist who has been doing a cross-cultural study of the healer's role. He has isolated five distinct modes of healing: shamanism, magic, religion, mysticism and naturalism. Here is an abbreviated description of these types: the shaman heals through the use of personal power, using craft, charm and cunning; the magician heals through his knowledge of arcane and complex rules, and his ability to follow ritual precisely; the priest claims no personal power, but achieves his healing capacity as an agent or vessel of an omnipotent authority; the mystic healer relies on insight, vision and wisdom, through which he cures the sick soul; the naturalist (the present-day physician) is impersonal, empirical, task-oriented.

You may be struck, as I was, by the reflection that these separate modes of healing in some sense persist to this day. While the present-day type of healing is naturalistic (and in fact it is a common complaint that medical specialists are *too* impersonal, and do not give enough attention to the patient as a human being), we nevertheless find that the physician's relation to the patient is often patterned on an older style. Thus we have those physicians who follow the shamanistic mode, in that they implicitly define healing as a struggle between disease on the one hand and their own cunning and power on the other; or those for whom medicine involves a ritualistic following of rules; or those who claim no personal charisma, but define themselves to the patient as humble servants of a Godhead, in this case Modern Medical Science. This typology may be a useful one for treating other forms of interaction, such as those that obtain between teacher and student. For example, those teachers who define themselves primarily as experts in subject-matter are roughly equivalent to naturalistic healers, in that the relationship to the client is in both cases impersonal and task-oriented. In any case, it is worth trying; I want to use Jackson's schema to consider in detail three types of teachers.

THE TEACHER AS SHAMAN

Here the teacher's orientation is narcissistic. The public manner does not matter; this type of teacher is not necessarily vain or exhibitionistic; he may in fact appear to be withdrawn, diffident, even humble. Essentially, however, he keeps the audience's attention focused on himself. He invites us to observe the personality in its encounter with the subject matter. He stresses charm, skill, *mana*, in the self's entanglement with ideas. When this orientation is combined with unusual gifts, we have a *charismatic* teacher, one of those outstanding and memorable personalities who seem more than life-size. The charismatic teacher is marked by power, energy and commitment: by power we mean sheer intellectual strength or uncommon perceptiveness and originality; by energy we mean an unusual force or vivacity of personality; and by commitment a deep absorption in the self and its work. Generally, all of these qualities are present to some degree: energy without power turns out to be mere flamboyance; power without energy or commitment is likely to be bloodless, arid, enervating.

This tells us only part of the story. In that group of teachers whom we term narcissistic we find considerable variation in the degree of impact on the student. In some cases the narcissistic teacher's impression on us is strong but transient; he moves us, but the spell does not survive the moment. We admire him as we admire a great performer, in his presence we dream of doing as well ourselves. But when the occasion is past we return to our mundane selves, out of the spell, unchanged, uninfluenced. In other instances, we may find the teacher's narcissism at the least distasteful and at times repelling, Something in it warns us to keep our distance, to remain wary and uncommitted.

What makes the difference? I am not sure that we know, but I think we will understand it better when we know more about variations in narcissism. There is a narcissism that makes a hidden plea to the audience; it cries out: "Look how wonderful I am! Admire me! Love me!" There is also a narcissism that is vindictive and vengeful; it says: "I love myself. Who needs you?" In either case the audience, or at least a good share of it, seems to sense the infantile source and quality of the teacher's narcissism, senses the petulance or anxiety that informs the teacher's manner, and keeps itself from becoming involved.

There is another and rarer form of narcissism that affects us quite differently from these. It is directed neither toward nor against the audience; it is autonomous, internally fed, sustaining itself beyond the observer's response to it. The best description of its appeal remains Freud's:

> It seems very evident that one person's narcissism has a great attraction for those others who have renounced part of their own narcissism and are seeking after object-love; the charm of a child lies to a great extent in his narcissism, his self-sufficiency and inaccessibility, just as does the charm of certain animals which seem not to concern themselves about us, such as cats and the large beasts of prey. . . . It is as if we envied them their power of retaining a blissful state of mind—an unassailable libido-position which we ourselves have since abandoned.

It is this form of narcissism—ingenuous, autonomous—that, when it is joined to other qualities, makes the teacher memorable. This orientation invites us to identification, to share in its bounty, to seek its protection and care or to join its omnipotence. Yet teachers of this kind are most problematic. They tempt us into regressions. We may come to feel them to be too exalted to serve as models for us. Or we may feel defeated by them before we begin, thinking that anything we achieve will be only second-rate, that we can never grow up enough to equal them.

THE TEACHER AS PRIEST

The priestly healer claims his power not through personal endowment, but through his office; he is the agent of an omnipotent authority. Do we have a parallel to this in teaching? I would say it is the teacher who stresses not his personal virtures, but his membership in a powerful or admirable collectivity, for example, physics, psychoanalysis, classical scholarship. The narcissistic teacher to some degree stands apart from his discipline and seems to say: "I am valuable in myself." The priestly teacher says: "I am valuable for what I belong to. I represent and personify a collective identity."

It is difficult to generalize about this mode of teaching, since the teacher's behavior toward the student varies so much with the nature of the collectivity. It is one thing when the collectivity is coterminous with a subject-matter, and another when it is an enclosed or beleaguered sect within a discipline (for example, the various "schools" within sociology and psychology). Collectivities differ in their openness, their degree of organization, their status vis-à-vis other groups. Some are easy to enter, while others are closed; some are loose and informal, bound by common interest and camaraderie, and others are stratified and formal; some are marginal in status, while others are secure, entrenched elites. Other differences involve the teacher's status in the collectivity: the undergraduate teacher may proselytize, seeking recruits among the promising students; the graduate-professional school teacher will first indoctrinate, then examine and finally ordain the recruit.

To illustrate the teacher's activity in the priestly mode, I will refer to the more enclosed and differentiated collectivities. We generally find the following elements: *Continuity.* The collectivity defines itself along a temporal dimension. It has a version of the past and a vision of the future. In the past there were Great Ancestors whose qualities and trials established the collective identity. There is a program for the immediate future as well as a prophecy of the distant future. One of the teacher's tasks is to help the student absorb the sense of the collective past and accept the common blueprint for the future. *Hierarchy.* Generally (although not always) the collectivity is stratified in prestige and authority. The teacher's personal authority depends in some part on his position on the ladder of authority. While the teacher is superordinate to the student, he in turn is subordinate to more elevated figures. The student internalizes the group's system of hierarchy, and learns that he is beholden not only to his teacher but to other members of the hierarchy. One of the distinctive features of this mode of teaching is that both teacher and student may share a common model or group of models, either exalted contemporaries or Great Ancestors. *Election.* When the group is an elite, when membership in it is desirable and hard to achieve, we generally will find that emphasis is placed on discipline, the enduring of trials and self-transformation. The educational process is in some degree an extended rite of passage; the teacher's role is to prepare the student for the trials he will endure, and to administer the tests that will initiate him. *Mission.* The collectivity often offers a utopian view of the future (especially when it is powerless and competitive) as well as a program for achieving dominance and instituting reforms. In these cases, the teacher's work is informed by missionary zeal;

the student is expected to absorb the group's sense of mission and in turn to recruit and socialize others once he himself has achieved office.

There is no question of the potency of the priestly mode of teaching. It achieves its effectiveness for a great many different reasons. Teacher and student are generally in a close relationship to each other. The student is encouraged to model his *activity* after the teacher's, very much as in those charming experiments on imprinting, where the baby duck follows the decoy. We also find a good deal of close coaching, both of behavior and ideology. In most cases the teaching is, both positive and negative—that is, the student is trained not only to develop new behaviors, but also is required to eliminate competing or discordant responses. Generally the student is given an unambiguous ideal of character and behavior (he may be allowed, as part of the strategy of training, to feel uncertain whether he is meeting this ideal, but the ideal itself is usually clear cut enough). In some instances the collectivity offers an encompassing doctrine, and the student is exhorted to re-interpret his experiences in the vocabulary of the doctrine; and when this is not the case, the training itself demands so complete a commitment of time and energy that the student's ideational world narrows to include only the collectivity and its concerns. The teacher customarily enjoys a great deal of power in relation to the student, which reinforces the latter's dependency. The student's tie to the collectivity is further reinforced by his close association with peers—rivals, fellow-aspirants, fellow-sufferers—who share his trials, sustain him in moments of doubt, restore his flagging spirits and keep alive his competitive drive. Finally, this mode of teaching is effective because it offers to the student a stake in a collective, utopian purpose, and also a promise of such tangible rewards as power, position, money, intellectual exclusiveness.

Less obviously, but quite as important, the collectivity makes its appeal to the student in helping him to resolve internal confusions. His participation allows a distinct identity choice; it supports that choice by collective approval; it reduces intellectual and moral ambiguity. A great many advantages also accrue to the collectivity; over the short run, at least, it is helped in achieving its aims by its capacity to recruit a cadre of devoted, disciplined believers. (The history of my own field, psychology, has been decisively influenced by the ability of certain schools to select and organize students in the "priestly" framework, an ability that has very little to do with intellectual merit.) But we also must recognize that this mode of education possesses some deadly disadvantages, both to the student and the group. The student purchases direction, force and clarity, but does so by sacrificing some share of his own development; in some important ways he is no longer his own man. For the collectivity, the danger is in a loss of flexibility and innovation. (We have a perfect example in the history of the psychoanalytic movement. Through the 1930's it was, in its policies of recruitment and training, the most cosmopolitan of groups, a circumstance that produced an extraordinary boldness and vivacity of thought. Since its capture by American psychiatry it has developed a priestly mode of education, the result being a severe loss in intellectual scope and energy. It has now settled into its own Alexandrian age, repeating itself endlessly, living off its intellectual capital, affluent yet flatulent, an ironic example of the failure of success.)

The dominance of this mode of teaching in the graduate and professional schools, while regrettable, is probably inevitable. It is more disturbing to note its steady encroachment in undergraduate education. For many college teachers the introductory courses have less value in themselves than as a net in which to trap the bright undergraduate, while the advanced courses increasingly serve only to screen and socialize students for what the faculty deems "the great good place"—namely, the graduate school. Furthermore, academic counseling at the freshman and sophomore level frequently produces a guerrilla warfare between disciplines, each seeking to capture the promising talents for itself, and without too much regard for the student's needs and interests. If matters are not worse than they already are, it is not because the disciplines have any genuine concern for the undergraduate or for liberal ideals of education, but because the leviathans have managed to neutralize each other's demands. Even so, the pressure of required courses and prerequisites serves to force the student into premature career commitment, while the onerous demands on his time (especially in the laboratory sciences, but also and increasingly in other fields) keep him from trying anything else.

THE TEACHER AS MYSTIC HEALER

The mystic healer finds the source of illness in the patient's personality. He rids his patient of disease by helping him to correct an inner flaw or to realize a hidden strength. The analogy here—perhaps it is a remote one—is to the teacher I will term *altruistic*. He concentrates neither on himself, nor the subject-matter, nor the discipline, but on the student, saying: "I will help you become what you are." We may recall Michelangelo's approach to sculpture: looking at the raw block of marble, he tried to uncover the statue within it. So does the altruistic teacher regard his unformed student; this type of teacher keeps his own achievement and personality secondary; he works to help the student find what is best and most essential within himself.

At this point we are uncomfortably close to the rhetoric of the college brochure. This is what the colleges tell us they do; and yet we know how very rarely we find altruistic teaching. Why is it so rare? For one thing, it is a model-less approach to teaching; the teacher points neither to himself nor to some immediately visible figure, but chooses to work with his students' potential and toward an intrinsically abstract or remote ideal. For another, this mode of teaching demands great acumen, great sensitivity—the ability to vary one's attack according to the phase of teaching and to the student—now lenient, now stern, now encouraging, now critical.

But the reason that the altruistic mode is so rarely successful lies deeper than these. The mode is selfless; it demands that the teacher set aside, for the moment at least, his own desires and concerns to devote himself without hidden ambivalence to the needs of another. In short, the teacher's altruism must be genuine; and altruism, as we know, is a fragile and unsteady trait, all too frequently reactive, born out of its opposite. If the teacher's selflessness is false, expedient or mechanical, if it comes out of a failure in self-esteem, or if it gives way to an underlying envy—and, in the nature of things, these are real and ever-present possibilities—then the teaching at best will not come off and at the worst may end in damaging the student.

Some years ago I taught at an excellent progressive college that, quite unwittingly, induced some of its younger faculty to opt for a pseudo-altruistic mode of teaching. The college was committed to the ideal of student self-realization, and this was not, I should say, the usual pious cant, but a conscious, deliberate aim that showed itself in day-to-day planning and policy. In pursuit of this ideal, the college authorities stressed altruistic teaching; it was held that talent, productivity and eminence were of only secondary importance in the hiring and firing of faculty, that teaching talent *per se* was primary. Here things went seriously awry; for a variety of reasons, the college managed to attract an astonishing proportion of charismatic teachers—either men of established reputation, or ambitious and talented young men on the way up, but in either case men of great vitality, self-confidence and self-absorption. The presence of these teachers produced a star system: the students, quite naturally, adored them; and they gave the college its distinctive tone—febrile, impassioned.

When a young teacher was hired by the college it was quite natural for him to gravitate to the charismatic mode of teaching. But sometimes it did not work out for him—he did not have, or felt that he did not have, the necessary resources of talent, drive and "personality." If he wanted to survive at the college (or so he believed) he had to carve out a niche for himself, or even better, make himself indispensable. He had to find a new style, and he was likely to choose altruism, whether or not it really suited him. He played the role of the teacher who had given up his own ambitions to put himself at the service of youth. In some cases, I suspect, this role was chosen coolly and cynically, the teacher reasoning, quite correctly, that the college authorities would find it embarrassing to fire someone who was so true a believer in the college's ideology; in other cases the teacher adopted this role gradually and without deliberation, waking up one morning, so to speak, to discover that this had been his métier all along.

Expedient altruism very rarely came off, either for the teacher or his students. The latter sometimes showed an uncanny, although largely, unconscious, sensitivity in these matters—they could sense that the pseudo-altruist was somehow not quite the real thing. They might deem him "nice," "friendly" and "very helpful," but they said so in a forced or lukewarm way that often concealed a polite disdain. The teacher's manner was often so artificial and oversolicitous that students, I think, were made uneasy by it, feeling that they did not really merit all that elaborate concern. This type of teacher tended to attract the marginal and unmotivated students, primarily because he was reputed to be soft. The more serious students continued to prefer the charismatic teacher, however difficult and demanding he might occasionally be; and this was so, I think, not only because of his greater gifts, but also because they would cleave only to someone who showed them that he loved himself.

Expedient altruism produced most of the time a kind of dead-level mediocrity in teaching; students were not much influenced, but neither were they damaged. It was a very different matter when this mode was chosen not as a survival technique but to perform some obscure personal restitution, when the teacher loved his students to avoid hating them, helped them to avoid harming them. As I suggested before, this equilibrium is ordinarily too delicate to sustain, and in fact I know of no examples where the students of the reactively altruistic teacher did not in some way suffer from a breakthrough of envy or sadism on the teacher's part. I remember one man, widely known to be lovable, who was warm and encouraging to his students and who, when their backs were turned, would write the most damning letters of recommendation for them. In another more spectacular instance a particularly sanctimonious advocate of good teaching was fired when his own major students petitioned the college to do so. It turned out that he had the habit of helping his students by being "sincerely frank" with them, expositing their "weak points" at great length and in excruciating detail, and so managing to wound and humiliate them deeply.

This last anecdote reminds us of what might otherwise escape our attention, that the teacher may sometimes serve as a negative or *anti-model.* Here student uses teacher as a lodestar, from which he sails away as rapidly as he can, seeming to say: Whatever he is, I will not be; whatever he is for, I will be against. Teachers who exercise this power of revulsion are, in their own way, charismatic types; indeed, the teacher who is charismatically positive for some will be negative for others. He breeds disciples or enemies; few remain unmoved. If we follow a student's development closely enough we generally discover both positive and negative models; the decision to be or become like someone goes hand in hand with a negative choice of identity and ideal.

An even more important topic on the negative side of modeling concerns the teacher whose value changes—the *disappointing* model. I would not have thought this to be so important—it does not come up in casual conversations on modeling; but close interviewing frequently brings to light examples of disappointments in the model.

Let me suggest why this may be so. It may be trite and facile to say so, but we are led again to the importance of the Oedipal motif, especially where we find a close relationship between teacher and student. These apprenticeships tend to be colored by the student's earlier tie to the father; they repeat or complete the Oedipal interaction. For most of us—and for some of us acutely—one outcome of the Oedipal situation was our coming to feel disappointed by the father. When we were very young, we thought him to be grand and omnipotent; then we learned better, and for some this was a galling discovery. In these cases the close tie to an esteemed teacher has the meaning of a second chance, an opportunity to relive and master that early disenchantment. The attempt to cure disappointment, however, generally leads to its repetition. The student must keep up the fiction of his teacher's perfection; any flaw, any failing in the teacher, must be denied out of existence. It is too hard a position to maintain, and sooner or later the discovery of some defect in the now idealized teacher will send the student into a state of acute disappointment.

When the student uses his relation to the teacher in this repetitive way, he is especially vulnerable to any failure in the teacher's work or character. In the main, students are not so vulnerable; they learn to be realistic about their teachers, enough so that they are spared any strong sense of disappointment. Indeed, they manage it so well that we are likely to remain unaware that it *is* a problem, that even the "normal" student undergoes at some time some crisis, however minor, concerning the clay feet of an intellectual idol. I remember a poignant moment when talking to a young man who was telling me of his admiration for a brilliant teacher. After working for this man for some time, it dawned on him that the teacher was in some respects petty, petulant and vain. At first, he told me, he had a hard time reconciling these traits with the man's great intellectual gifts; but then he was able to recognize that the two really had nothing to do with each other. What was poignant—painful in fact—was that the student told me this in a strained, bluff, overly hearty manner that spoke tellingly of the struggle it had been to accept it.

The student's responses to disappointment depend not only on his susceptibility but also on the type of flaw he discovers in the teacher. It makes a difference whether or not the failing is *role-relevant*. It puts a greater strain on the student when the model's fault involves role performance than when it is unrelated to how the teacher does his work. In the latter instance the student can more easily compartmentalize his view of the teacher.

Probably the most difficult type of failure for the student to accept is a moral one. By "moral" I do not mean, primarily, the teacher's living up to conventional standards in pleasure-seeking; rather I mean such qualities as integrity, fairness, ethical sensitivity, courage. The student is not overly demoralized to discover that his model's ego qualities are not quite what he thought or hoped they were, that his teacher is not as intelligent, penetrating or perceptive as he first appeared to be. It is, indeed, part of the student's maturation that he learn to tolerate this fact, just as the child in growing up learns to give up his belief that the parents are omnicompetent. But a moral failure is not so easily accepted and, if it is serious enough in nature, is likely to be a disheartening or even a shattering experience. When we think of the teacher as a model, we think naturally of the teacher as an ego ideal—an avatar of virtue—and take for granted, and thus ignore, the superego aspects. Yet some teachers influence us primarily because they embody the moral ideal of the role, or because they represent the unpleasant necessities of work, duty or intellectual honesty. Edward Tolman played such a role for graduate students (and faculty too, I imagine) at Berkeley; many of us were not deeply influenced by him intellectually, but all of us were profoundly touched by his integrity and humility. And Freud has told us how, many years later, he could still recall an incident of his student days when, arriving late to work, he was "overwhelmed by the terrible gaze of his [Brucke's] eyes." Most of us do our work in the silent presence of some such gaze, terrible or (nowadays) merely reproachful.

The teacher's life is as filled with moral tension and ambiguity as any other, but the moral dimension is most visibly operative in areas that do not affect the student (such as departmental politics); consequently, moral issues do not ordinarily become problematic in the teacher-student relationship. But when they do, we become intensely aware of their tacit importance. I know of only one clear-cut occurrence of this kind: a group of students in one of the sciences discovered that their teacher—ordinarily full of pieties about the holy obligations of the scientist—was not entirely responsible in his handling of evidence; he was not guilty of outright fabrication but of cutting, fitting and suppressing data to fit the needs of the study. Not all of the students were distraught by his discovery—here again vulnerability varies—but some were entirely demoralized and in one case a student (who had been sitting on the fence) decided to give up research altogether and choose an applied career.

Those of us who were at the University of California during the loyalty oath troubles had a unique opportunity to observe how the moral qualities of our teachers, ordinarily taken for granted and so overlooked, could assume overweening importance in a moment of moral crisis. It was an uncanny time for us: with one part of ourselves we lived in the routine of things, concerned with courses, prelims, dissertations; and all the while our inner, central attention was elsewhere, held in a fretful preoccupation with the morality play in which our teachers were involved. We wondered how things would turn out, of course, but beyond and deeper than that the intimate, compelling question was whether our models would behave honorably. Most of them did not; although for a time we kept ourselves from recognizing this, largely by allying ourselves psychically with the very few who acted heroically while ignoring the very many who did not. It taught us, on the one hand, that moral courage is possible and, on the other, that it is uncommon. All in all, it was a quick and unpleasant education. Perhaps it is just as well for all of us, teachers and students alike, that serious moral examination occurs so rarely.

Operant shaping[*]

Ralph Schwitzgebel

Man is used to feeling superior to animals even when the animals perform complex tasks. B. F. Skinner (1938, pp. 339–340) once trained a rat to pull a string to obtain a marble from a rack which it then carried with its forepaws across a cage and dropped in a tube in order to receive a pellet of food. Most people are likely to view this as a mere stunt or joke.

An experiment with more serious social implications has been conducted by William Cumming (1966). By using operant shaping techniques, he trained pigeons to recognize small, defective electronic components (diodes) as they passed by on a mock assembly line. After passing inspection, the components were fed into a large machine that then assembled these components into commercial products.

Thus far, nothing seems too serious until one is told that the pigeons did this inspection job very well, in fact, better than the men in the factory on the assembly line. The birds inspected approximately one thousand parts per hour, and Bird 119 could inspect at this rate continuously for four hours. Longer sessions of inspections were not tried because the human operator checking this bird's work was unable to continue at this rate. The bird showed no fatigue; in fact, its performance tended to improve rapidly the longer it worked.

In addition to inspecting electronic components better than their human competitors, pigeons cost very little (not over five dollars for the best), eat very little, require very little sleep, if any, and have been known to work for days, even weeks and months without stopping. Furthermore, as Cumming notes, they will work for "chicken feed." But, as the possibility of replacing men with pigeons on the regular assembly line appeared increasingly imminent, organized labor objected. After all, it is embarrassing enough to be replaced by a machine; to be replaced by a pigeon is unbearable. Thus in this company,[1] men are still sent to do a pigeon's job.

TECHNIQUES OF SHAPING

Perhaps the solution to the problem of use of pigeons in factories is not to leave pigeons unemployed, but to train men to reach higher levels of skill and accomplishment than pigeons. One effective procedure for developing new behaviors in both men and animals is *operant shaping*. Because operant shaping is a special form of *operant conditioning*, it is helpful to understand a few very general concepts commonly used in operant conditioning theory.

During operant conditioning, a specific behavior is followed by a prearranged environmental event that reinforces (or in popular language, "rewards") the behavior. The reinforcer may be food, money, or verbal praise. The behavior is known as a *response*. A group of very similar responses, such as the responses required to operate identical levers, is known as an *operant*. The term operant emphasizes the fact that the responses "operate" upon the environment to produce reinforcing consequences.

The frequency of a response prior to conditioning is called the *operant level* of the response. An environmental event is a reinforcer if it follows a response and increases the frequency of that response over its earlier operant level. It is clear that a response cannot be reinforced if it is not emitted by the subject. Operant shaping is used to obtain responses that would otherwise occur either very rarely or never.

Operant shaping involves reinforcing successively closer approximations to the desired response until that response is emitted. For example, let us assume that we want to shape a behavior in a student involving the scratching of his right ear with his right hand. Though one might have to wait quite a long time for this behavior to occur naturally, with shaping techniques and, of course, a willing student, this response can usually be obtained at high rates of frequency in ten to fifteen minutes.

Staats and Staats (1964) have described the procedure used to shape an ear touching response in a student. Essentially, the experimenter begins by waiting for any movement of the student. If the student becomes restless and moves in his chair, the experimenter reinforces this movement. Initially, the experimenter reinforces any movements that occur so that the general class of "movements" becomes reinforced and increases in frequency. During these general movements, the student will probably move his right shoulder. The experimenter then reinforces this shoulder movement as well as general movements of the upper body and right side. Then as the shoulder movements become more frequent, the experimenter reduces the reinforcement of general movements (differential rein-

---

[1] The name of the company is withheld by request. Management and public relations problems also occurred in a similar experiment using pigeons as quality control inspectors to locate faulty capsules for a drug manufacturer (Verhave, 1966).

forcement) until all movements that are clearly not tending toward the desired, final response are not longer reinforced.

As movements of the right shoulder become more frequent, movements of the right arm are likely to occur. These movements are then strengthened, leading to more movements of the right hand, some of which may be toward the head. These are then reinforced until the ear is touched.

Sidman (1962, pp. 173–74) has suggested some useful principles in the shaping process.

1. Reinforce the behavior immediately. If the reinforcement is delayed, even by a fraction of a second, it is likely to be preceded by some behavior other than that which the experimenter intended to reinforce.

2. Do not give too many reinforcements for an approximation of the desired final response. Behavior that is initially reinforced must ultimately be extinguished as we move closer to the end point. If we reinforce intermediate forms of behavior too much, these once-reinforced but now-to-be-discarded responses will continue to intrude and will unduly prolong the shaping process . . .

3. Do not give too few reinforcements for an approximation of the desired final response. This is the most common difficulty in shaping behavior; the experimenter moves too fast. He abandons a response before he has reinforced it enough and, as a consequence, both the response and the variations which stem from it extinguish before he can mold the next closer approximation to the final behavior. The subject may then return to his original behavior, as if he had never gone through a shaping process at all . . .

4. Carefully specify the response to be reinforced in each successive step. Before abandoning one response and reinforcing the next approximation to the final behavior, the experimenter must watch the subject closely to determine what behavior is available for reinforcement.

Thus far, even with these principles, the ability to shape behavior is still very much an art rather than a clearly specified routine.[2] Basically, the same procedures that are used to shape a rat to carry marbles or a pigeon to inspect electronic components can be used to train people to drive a car or ski. The reinforcers used in these shaping procedures are usually those that have indirect or secondary reinforcing potential.

Use of secondary reinforcers

There are two general categories of reinforcers: *primary reinforcers* and *secondary reinforcers*. A primary reinforcer is a stimulus that does not depend upon a prior history of conditioning. Water and food are typical examples of primary reinforcers. A secondary reinforcer is a neutral stimulus which has been closely and consistently associated with a primary reinforcer so that it acquires reinforc-

---

[2] For example, the amount of reinforcement a response requires before shifting the reinforcement to a new response may depend upon the operant level of that response. Based upon this assumption, some statistical formulae are being developed, known as shaping indexes, to guide the shaping of human vocal responses (cf. Lane, Kopp, Sheppard, Anderson, and Carlson, 1967). However, very little work has been done in the area of human operant behavior discussed here.

ing potential. This is accomplished by presenting the neutral stimulus immediately prior to the primary stimulus.

If a green light is turned on immediately preceding the presentation of a primary reinforcer, such as food, to a hungry rat, the light will acquire reinforcing potential. Later, even though all food is withheld, the rat will press a bar to turn on the light.[3]

A secondary reinforcer, however, tends to loose its reinforcing potential for an animal rather quickly if it is not eventually followed by a primary reinforcer. The process during which reinforcement is no longer given is referred to as *extinction*. The rate at which a response declines in frequency during extinction depends to a large extent upon the previous type and rate of reinforcement. Responses previously reinforced by secondary reinforcers usually declines in frequency more rapidly than those responses previously reinforced by primary reinforcers.

Secondary reinforcers that are paired with more than one primary reinforcer are called *generalized reinforcers*. Money, social approval, and affection are sometimes considered generalized reinforcers for humans because they have been closely associated with several primary reinforcers.

The importance of secondary reinforcement in operantly shaping behavior may be seen in a simple example offered by Holland and Skinner (1961). The objective of the shaping process was to get a dog to touch a doorknob with his nose. The dog was first taught to respond to a secondary reinforcer, the sound of a dimestore noisemaker cricket. This was done by clicking the noisemaker and immediately tossing a bit of food into the dog's dish. When this sound became a secondary reinforcer, the process of shaping was begun.

Successive approximations to the terminal response, touching the doorknob, were immediately reinforced by clicking the noisemaker. Initially, any movement of the dog was reinforced by a click, then gradually only those movements toward the door and doorknob were reinforced. Finally, when the dog's nose touched the doorknob he was given a piece of food.

The use of the click as a secondary reinforcer was important because the dog needed to be reinforced immediately, but tossing the dog a piece of meat would have made the dog move his head toward the floor. Thus movement of his head toward the floor rather than movement toward the doorknob would have been reinforced and the terminal response of touching the doorknob would not have been obtained as soon if at all. In shaping, the reinforcer should not interfere with the behavior being shaped. The click served as an easily administered and noninterfering secondary reinforcer.

---

[3] Secondary reinforcers are also sometimes known as "conditioned reinforcers." This implies that a neutral stimulus acquires its reinforcing potential through a conditioning process. This assumption needs more experimental investigation before it can be completely accepted (cf. Hill, 1968). Secondary reinforcers may also become reinforcing because of the "information" which they provide about the likelihood of subsequent reinforcement (Hendry, 1969).

Chaining

Shaping can be used to produce not only one response but also a series or chain of responses. A series of secondary reinforcers can be constructed so that an animal will press a level to obtain a green light, then press another level to obtain a white light then to press a third level to obtain food. *Chaining* is accomplished by following a response with a stimulus that acts as a secondary reinforcer and as a signal that "sets the occasion" for the next response. Under these conditions, an animal will work to receive a series of secondary reinforcers if they are eventually followed by a primary reinforcer.

Most behavior is actually a chain of smoothly performed responses. The pressing of a lever by an animal to obtain food is a series of responses involving at least the animal's rising, pressing, and lowering which is followed by seizing the food and eating it. If a secondary reinforcer which is usually present in this chain is eliminated, the entire chain of responses may be disrupted (Keller and Shoenfeld, 1950).

The shaping of chains of responses is often done, even inadvertently, in the daily life situations of humans. Little Jonathan, for example, decides that he wants a jelly sandwich. He follows his mother around the house whining, "I want a sandwich," which his mother attempts to ignore. Occasionally she says, "No, you can't have a sandwich," or some similar statement, but the whining continues. He begins to tug and hang on her skirt. In desperation to avoid further annoyance, she gives Little Jonathan his sandwich. His mother has successfully shaped a chain of responses made up of whining, tugging, and eating. If Little Jonathan merely says, "I want a sandwich," he does not get one. If he only whines or tugs at her skirt, he does not get one. But, if he does all these annoying things in proper sequence, he does get a sandwich. That mothers can successfully shape this, as well as other chains of annoying responses, is evidenced by the fact that the world is filled with whining cookie collectors.

Response chains may be weakened by at least three procedures. One procedure is to eliminate a stimulus that usually precedes one of the responses in the chain (e.g., hide the jar of jelly that initiates the request for the jelly sandwich). Another procedure is to withhold reinforcement of the terminal response (e.g., do not give Jonathan the sandwich). These two procedures involve primarily extinction. A third procedure is to shape responses that compete with the response chain to be eliminated (e.g., teach Jonathan to make his own sandwich).

Although shaping procedures have been fairly clearly demonstrated in the experimental laboratory, their application to humans in daily life situations requires considerable extrapolation. Only by allowing some imprecision and many unverified assumptions can one say that operant conditioning procedures are applicable to humans in their natural milieu. To a large extent, the reasoning is by analogy rather than by deduction. Nevertheless, these analogies have permitted the development of techniques for changing human behavior which have produced rather striking results.

A CASE STUDY: SHAPING THE ATTENDANCE OF DELINQUENTS IN TREATMENT PROGRAMS

Earlier in this chapter, it was suggested that a student's behavior might be shaped so that he would scratch his right ear with his right hand. This could be accomplished within ten to fifteen minutes. While watching such demonstrations, a student of the slightly rebellious type might well ask the professor, "Why not just tell the student to scratch his ear and save all the time and effort?" The question would be a good one. If a person can perform the terminal behavior (if the behavior is in his *behavioral repertoire*), it is usually more efficient just to ask him to behave in a certain way. If the behavior is not in the person's behavioral repertoire or if he is not cooperative, shaping may be necessary.

Delinquents are ideal subjects upon which to test the power of shaping procedures because they will not cooperate with a professor merely to be polite or to earn a better mark in a psychology class. (A colleague of ours once remarked that it was very understandable why psychology did not work with real people— psychologists usually test their theories on unusual organisms such as white rats and college undergraduates.) To test shaping procedures, a project was set up to obtain the attendance and cooperation of delinquents in therapy-like situations such as talking into a tape recorder and taking psychological tests (Schwitzgebel, 1964). Most of the boys had extensive court records and had spent time in reform school or prison. They were also generally known as serious "troublemakers" in the community.

In general, the shaping procedure was as follows. Delinquents who did not know the experimenter were met on the street corner or in the typical meeting places of delinquents and offered a part-time job of talking into a tape recorder as an experimental subject. The job paid from one dollar up to two dollars an hour for, on the average, two or three hours a week. The subject was invited to bring a friend or two along, look over the laboratory situation, then make up his mind as to whether he wanted to participate. During this initial conversation, he would be casually offered a cigarette, free games on a pinball machine, or food as a reinforcer of his attention. The experimenter, the subject, and his friends would then ride the subway back to the laboratory where they were immediately offered a Coke and more to eat. The delinquents were generally willing to come along with the experimenter because they were bored and apparently had nothing more interesting to do.

At the laboratory, the subject and his friends would usually play with the tape recorder, ask numerous questions about the electronic equipment and the secretaries, and play with a white rat used in experiments. They would then participate in an informal, tape-recorded interview. At the conclusion of the interview, the subject would be given an unexpected "bonus" of one dollar.

If the subject seemed willing and able to keep appointments, he was scheduled to meet the experimenter at the laboratory at his convenience the following day.

If the subject missed this meeting or if the experimenter decided that the boy could not keep appointments, the experimenter went out to meet him the following day at the original meeting place. One subject, for example, who was initially met in a pool room failed to arrive at the laboratory for his second interview. The experimenter then went back to the pool room and spent considerable time there for the next several days and found the subject. The boy appeared glad to see the experimenter and both of them rode the subway back to the laboratory. The third meeting was arranged for the next day at the same time outside of the subway entrance nearest the pool room. When the subject arrived at this location, he was immediately reinforced by being offered a cigarette and was complimented by the experimenter. The experimenter paid the subway fares. The fourth meeting was arranged inside the subway station after the toll gate. (Part of the previous day's wage was paid to the subject in the form of subway tokens which he could not easily spend elsewhere.) The next meeting was arranged just outside the subway exit nearest this laboratory. Finally, the subject was met at the laboratory.

This arrangement of meetings at locations increasingly close to the laboratory did, of course, appear strange to the subject. He was honestly told at the second meeting that delinquents often have trouble arranging their schedules and getting to appointments on time. This shaping procedure was being used as part of an experiment to see if it could make his attendance less difficult and more reliable.

The attitude of the experimenters toward the attendance problem is also very important. The problem of delinquent nonattendance was considered to be very different from the problem of nonattendance at therapy sessions by middle-class neurotic patients. If a middle-class person pays for therapy and then fails to attend, it may be a sign of the severity of his problem. He has had much experience with keeping appointments and recognizes their importance to himself and to the therapist. If a delinquent fails to attend a meeting, he may just have been doing something more interesting at the time and not have realized the importance of the meeting to the experimenter.

If a subject failed to attend, this was interpreted to mean that the shaping procedure was inadequate, that the boy had forgotten about the meeting, or that the laboratory situation was not attractive enough for him. The solution to this was to improve the shaping procedure and the incentive, set a time for another meeting, and let each boy know that no matter how many meetings he missed he was still welcome.

Unless a boy was in jail or had a severe physical or mental disability, his failure to attend was not seen as his fault but the fault of inadequate techniques. In one extreme case of nonattendance, the experimenter and a project assistant, a very attractive girl with long blond hair, drove to the boy's home located in a low-rent housing project in a new, white convertible, the kind most highly prized by the delinquent subculture. The boy, who was standing on the corner with

352 *Interpersonal dynamics*

his friends, was immediately impressed (or, more accurately, stunned) and eagerly came along to the laboratory for the ride. Afterwards, the boy commented to the experimenter, "It was just like out of the movies when you drove up."

Of twenty-five delinquent subjects in this project, only two failed to develop reliable attendance patterns within fifteen or fewer meetings. One of these boys was arrested and went to reform school. The other boy took a job that took up most of his available hours.

It could be argued, and should be, that at least some of the delinquents in this experiment would have attended the meetings at the laboratory without the use of shaping procedure. To test the usefulness of the shaping procedure more carefully, a second experiment was conducted. Fifteen boys between the ages of fifteen and nineteen were met in a pool room and were told about an "opportunity" to participate in some research. The pool room was a well known meeting place for delinquents. The proposed research involved getting some very brief questionnaires filled out by local businessmen. (This task was selected in order to encourage delinquents to contact businessmen, of whom they are usually frightened, and to ask them for jobs.) The boys would be paid fifty cents for each questionnaire completed.

The boys were asked to come to a church office about twelve blocks away the next day if they were interested. Most of the boys were clearly not interested and were hesitant to talk with the research assistant, a college senior.[4] Two of the boys said that they might stop by the office the following day, but they did not show up. None of the boys were willing to offer their names or telephone numbers.

The boys who were contacted and showed no interest in the project were designated as the subjects in the experiment. (The two boys who said they might show up were eliminated as they were considered too cooperative to be included in this study). The goal was to shape the attendance of the remaining thirteen boys. The research assistant returned to the pool hall the next day with mimeographed questionnaires and a pocket full of change. He met many boys he had seen the previous day and offered each of them fifty cents for getting the manager of the pool hall to fill out the questionnaire and sign it. The manager had previously indicated his willingness to participate. The boys vacillated between perceiving the entire situation as a "gag" and questioning the assistant as to whether the questionnaire would get the manager into trouble. In the assistant's own words (Solomon, 1966):

After some intensive verbal prodding, I finally got three boys to ask [the manager] for his signature; though each boy took his own sheet, they approached [the manager] together as if there were some security in numbers. By this time many more boys had gathered around to see what all the commotion was about. The boys returned with the signature and following Sidman's advice,[5] I immediately gave them fifty cents each. This seemed

---

[4] We wish to thank Richard J. Solomon for his excellent help and pioneering spirit.

[5] See Sidman as quoted earlier in this chapter.

to change the entire complexion of the crowd. Formerly reluctant members of the [experimental] group who were not even interested enough to question me about the project became the first to ask for a chance to "get a signature." Luckily for my pocketbook, I had only a few more mimeographed sheets with me which I gave to those who asked first.

A time was set up for meeting the boys at the church office the next day. None of the boys showed up. The behavior had not yet been adequately shaped and all of the thirteen subjects had thus twice failed to attend. The research assistant then returned three more times to the pool hall with more questionnaires and money. He gave special attention to those subjects who seemed to be least interested. At the fifth scheduled meeting, six subjects showed up at the pool room and three arrived at the church office near the scheduled time. On one occasion, a boy, thinking that he was supposed to meet the research assistant at the church, arrived at the church early, waited for a while, then realizing his error hurried back to the pool room in time to keep the original meeting.

After three more meetings, the following pattern emerged: Nine of the thirteen delinquents who had previously failed to attend now arrived regularly at the church office, three attended occasionally, and one did not attend at all. Thus, this small experiment tends to confirm the possibility that delinquent attendance and cooperation can be shaped even in activities that delinquents initially reject.

Although delinquent subjects may arrive dependably at a laboratory or church office, their arrival may not be prompt. It may be as many as several hours early or late. The next step in the project was to shape prompt arrival.[6] This was achieved primarily through the use of cash "bonuses" as reinforcers. For example, a subject might arrive an hour late for the tenth meeting. The experimenter would welcome him, mention that this was much better than the previous day when he was an hour and a half late. For the "good effort" the boy was given a twenty-five cent cash bonus. The next day the boy might arrive within fifteen minutes of the appointed time—hoping perhaps for a dollar bonus. The experimenter might mention nothing about his arrival, but the boy would be likely to call attention to the fact and ask about his bonus. It would then be explained that the employee can always expect to receive the basic wage but that bonuses depend entirely on the amount of money the experimenter happens to possess and on his feelings at the time. The boy might be disappointed until, later in the hour, he receives a fifty cent bonus for, say, showing curiosity about the meaning of a recurring dream. He might then realize that he could never be sure what he might receive a bonus for or what the bonus would be, but in general the whole thing seemed to be an interesting game. At the following meeting, the experimenter might take the subject to a restaurant for a sandwich if he arrived still more promptly.

Using the procedures we have outlined, it was possible to shape arrival to

[6] It should be noted that shaping attendance involves both spacial and temporal dimensions. In most laboratory experiments the temporal dimension is ignored; the animal is merely placed in the cage or the subject, usually a cooperative undergraduate, arrives on time.

FIGURE 1

Arrival times of experimental subject S_2 for initial twenty-two meetings

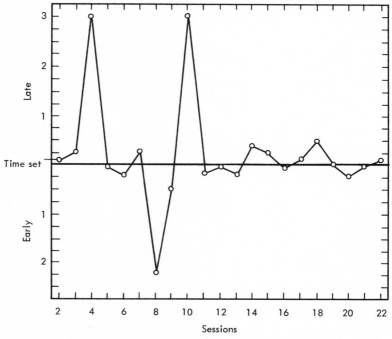

Source: R. Schwitzgebel and D. A. Kolb. "Inducing behaviour change in adolescent delinquents." *Behaviour Research and Therapy,* 1964, 1, 297–304.

within a few minutes of the scheduled time for most subjects. Figure 1 shows the arrival times for a typical subject, S_2, for the first twenty-two meetings.

In a subsequent study of youthful offenders ranging in age from twelve to twenty one years, the subjects showed a group mean of thirty-eight minutes late during the first four meetings (Schwitzgebel, 1969). One group of these subjects then received reinforcers (bonuses) contingent on prompt attendance while a matched group of subjects received none. They received bonuses for other socially desirable behaviors (e.g., putting Coke bottles away at the end of an interview). Both groups improved in the promptness and dependability of their attendance over the first twenty meetings. The contingent-reinforcement group, however, had a significantly lower mean discrepancy between appointment time and arrival time (11.2 minutes) than the group without contingent reinforcement (15.6 minute mean discrepancy).

It should be noted that bonuses were not offered immediately following each more prompt arrival by the subjects in this study as is customarily done in shaping new responses. This might have been a more effective procedure. On the other hand, a certain amount of intrigue and adventure throughout the period of shaping might have served as a reinforcer. Also, it is possible that the experimenters inadvertantly greeted a subject more enthusiastically or treated him more considerately than usual when he arrived close to the scheduled time. This may have served as an implicit but consistent reinforcer.

Although the shaping procedures discussed here may sound somewhat rigid, they were not carried out in a harsh or mechanistic manner. Rather, the subjects were genuinely liked by the research staffs, and the experiments were carried out in a spirit of enthusiasm. This attitude may have significantly contributed to the positive results.

An interesting experiment by Rosenthal (1966, pp. 165–176) points to the importance of the experimenter's attitude in shaping behavior. Laboratory rats were randomly assigned to two groups of experimenters. One group of experimenters received rats that were arbitrarily labeled "bright"; the other group of experimenters received rats that were arbitrarily labeled "dull." There was, in fact, no difference in the learning ability of the rats because they all came from the same carefully controlled animal colony. Experimenters who thought their rats were "bright" and expected positive performance shaped the behavior of their rats to press a bar considerably better than those experimenters who thought their rats were "dull." The experimenters had "biased" the results.

Evidence from Rosenthal's experiment also suggested that those experimenters who worked with the supposedly "bright" rats felt more relaxed and were more friendly and enthusiastic. They handled the animal more and observed the animal's behavior more closely than those experimenters who thought they were working with the "dull" rats. This closer observation by the experimenters working with the "bright" rats could allow more accurate and rapid reinforcement of those behaviors approximating the terminal response, bar pressing. In the same manner, experimenters who expect positive performance from delinquents and are friendly and enthusiastic may be more successful in shaping behavior than experimenters who expect failure. In a broader sense, that which is called experimenter bias in the laboratory may be called therapeutic skill in the clinic.

DEVELOPMENT OF COOPERATIVE AND FRIENDLY BEHAVIOR

Shaping procedures have been used to modify a wide range of behaviors. Children have been trained to eat (White, 1959), use the toilet (Marshall, 1966), follow orders (Davison, 1964), read (Staats, 1968), speak (Risley and Wolf, 1966), wear glasses (Wolf, Risley, and Mees, 1964), and use experimental equipment (Ferster and DeMyer, 1961). Of broader social significance, however, is the use of shaping procedures to develop cooperation. However, work in this area is still at a very exploratory level.

Some researchers have been moderately successful in developing cooperative responses in the higher apes (cf., Crawford, 1935). Under carefully designed conditions, even rats have been trained to cooperate so that both will avoid shock and obtain adequate food—though this involves using intense electric shock and a severe deprivation of food (Daniel, 1942). It is encouraging to note that Wolfe (1939) found that cooperative responses were somewhat more frequent in children than in apes when both were tested in similar experimental situations.

In the study by Wolfe and Wolfe, some cooperative responses were probably in the behavioral repertoires of the children prior to the experiment. In a study of four mute schizophrenic children by Hingtgen and Trost (1966), cooperative behavior had to be carefully developed by making reinforcement contingent on behaviors that successively approximated cooperation. The reinforcers were coins that could be put into a vending machine to obtain candy. The subjects were seen in pairs and the shaping procedure was divided into four phases.

During the first phase, reinforcement was given when one subject approached, then accidentally touched, then deliberately touched the other subject with his hand. In the second phase, reinforcement was given only when there was physical contact by hand also accompanied by a simple vocalization. Reinforcement during the third phase required vocalization plus contact with both hands. During the fourth phase, reinforcement was contingent upon both subjects making a vocal response and touching each with both hands.

A high frequency of cooperative responses was shaped in approximately forty-six sessions. Only one coin was given for each cooperative response and this resulted in frequent competitive behavior such as pushing, tugging, pinching, and hugging to prevent the other from getting the coin. In short, they began to act like typical children—laughing and smiling when cooperative behavior was developing well and expressing anger when cooperation was not developing well. These new responses generalized from the laboratory to the ward and home.

Although competition may not be the exact behavioral opposite of cooperation (cf., Lindsley, 1966), competitive behavior may need to be reduced in order to construct the social situation necessary for the reinforcement of cooperative responses. For example, Dennis, a seven year old boy at a state training school, was so aggressive that he was not allowed to associate with the other children in the institution (Bostow and Bailey, 1969). He was given tranquilizing drugs and was sometimes tied to a door in a hallway where he was able to strike only occasional passersby. During the treatment program, each time he bit, kicked, scratched, or butted his head against another person he was placed in a small "timeout" booth for two minutes. Alternatively, each time two minutes elapsed without such aggressive behavior, Dennis was given a small amount of milk or carbonated beverage or a bite of cookie. Within this situation of alternative contingencies, the frequency of aggressive behaviors rapidly declined and within a week he was allowed to associate with the other children for increasing periods of time. Occasionally during the periods of reinforcement, he would approach other children to hug and embrace them. It is likely that some of the effectiveness of this procedure resulted from the combined use of both punishment and reinforcement contingencies.

One of the early attempts to develop cooperation in pairs of children was by Azrin and Lindsley in 1956. Their experiment followed closely an earlier experiment by Skinner (1953, p. 306) in which cooperative responses had been developed in a pair of pigeons. Essentially, Azrin and Lindsley placed two children at opposite ends of a table. At each end of the table, there were three holes and a stylus in front of each child as shown in Figure 2. The children were told that

FIGURE 2
Apparatus used for the reinforcement of cooperation between children

Source: N. H. Azrin and O. R. Lindsley, "The reinforcement of cooperation between children." *Journal of Abnormal and Social Psychology,* 1956, 52, 100–102.

they could play the game any way that they wanted to and were shown how to put the styli into the holes. They were also shown some jelly beans that would fall into a cup on the table.

If the styli were placed in directly opposite holes, a red light flashed on the table and a jelly bean fell into the cup. Although the children were not told about this requirement, all ten teams of children (two children in each team) learned to cooperate within the first ten minutes. Leader-follower relationships generally lasted throughout the experiment. When reinforcement was temporarily terminated, cooperative behavior clearly declined in frequency. When reinforcement was again initiated following this period of extinction, the earlier rate of cooperation was almost immediately restored.

Using more elaborate equipment and experimental controls, Lindsley (1966) induced cooperation and competition in teams of adult subjects by changing only the contingencies of reinforcement. In teams with a history of cooperation, the induced competition was eventually changed into complex patterns of cooperation, usually involving alternating leadership so that each gave the other equal opportunity for individual reinforcement. Lindsley also noted that "altruistic gifts are not accepted as debts unless the donor provided the gifts by sacrificing reinforcement to himself. In other words, an unavoidable gift, one with no other alternative, is not responded to as a gift" (p. 495).

ADVANTAGES AND LIMITATIONS OF SHAPING

There is no doubt that shaping procedures can be used to develop new behaviors that were not previously in a person's repertoire. Whether shaping is the most efficient procedure to use depends on a number of factors. Surely, shaping is inefficient, comparatively speaking, if a new behavior can be obtained merely by asking the subject to perform it. For example, a subject will usually display more assertive or cooperative behaviors in a social situation if he is asked to do so and is assured that such behaviors are appropriate and acceptable. The fact that it is difficult to discuss the desired behavior with a rat or pigeon surely does not preclude such discussion with a human.

There is fairly consistent evidence that a person's awareness of the conditions of reinforcement can greatly improve his performance if he wants his performance to improve (e.g., Spielberger and DeNike, 1966). In fact, a person's belief about the conditions under which reinforcements will be given may influence rates of behavior more than the contingencies of reinforcement actually in effect (e.g., Kaufman, Baron, and Kopp, 1966; Dulany, 1968). This should not be too surprising because we often see people behaving in ways that will not produce results they expect—which is usually another way of saying that they do not accurately perceive the contingencies of reinforcement.

When shaping procedures are successfully used, it is often not clear, especially in the case of children, whether the subject did not know what the contingencies of reinforcement were for the appropriate behavior, knew the contingencies but chose not to participate, or wished to participate, but lacked the required behavior.

Behavior change methods that emphasize shaping procedures to obtain a desired behavior often assume a behavioral deficit. Although this may be true, it should not be assumed without clear evidence that the subject was aware of the reinforcement contingencies previously associated with the desired behavior and that the shaping procedures have not changed the previous reinforcement contingencies. This last possibility is particularly likely in natural settings because as the subject displays the desired behavior other people may observe and interact with him more frequently, thus increasing the frequency of reinforcers associated with the desired behavior. Attention and praise may be effective reinforcers easily overlooked in the natural environment, especially when the researcher is used to observing more tangible reinforcers such as food or coins.

A study of the social development of a child by Buell, Stoddard, Harris, and Baer (1968) illustrates this possibility nicely. Polly, a three year old girl, showed no cooperative play with other children, rarely used the outdoor play equipment, and would hang onto the teachers. The behavior change technique focused exclusively on getting Polly to play on the outdoor equipment by placing her on it each day and holding her there at least thirty seconds (a procedure called "priming"). She was reinforced for staying on the equipment by the teacher's interest and approval. Equipment use by Polly as well as behaviors such as touching other children, using children's names, and cooperative play were carefully observed before, during, and after this technique was used. Not only did Polly's use of the outdoor equipment markedly increase, but so did the child-oriented behaviors of touching, cooperative play, and use of names although these behaviors were not deliberately shaped or reinforced.

One can agree with the researchers in this study that the collateral development of these social behaviors resulted from Polly's increased contact with peers and availability to peer group reinforcement. Thus changing the reinforcement contingencies for one behavior produced changes in that behavior which in turn changed the contingencies for collateral behaviors. If these collateral behaviors were also being shaped, an investigator could be easily misled to believe that shaping produced the behavior change rather than the changed contingencies of peer group reinforcement.

Another factor to be considered in the analysis of the effectiveness of shaping procedures is the availability of alternative procedures that may be used to produce new behaviors. Modeling is a particularly likely alternative. If a subject already has available the basic components of a new behavior, he may be able to imitate a new behavior quite readily. Shaping the new behavior is likely to take longer, require more effort, and involve more exposure to physical or social risk. In this regard, Bandura (1969, pp. 143–144) appropriately notes:

In laboratory investigations of learning processes experimenters usually arrange comparatively benign environments in which errors will not produce fatal consequences for the organism. In contrast, natural settings are loaded with potentially lethal consequences that unmercifully befall anyone who makes hazardous errors. For this reason, it would be exceedingly injudicious to rely primarily upon trial-and-error and successive approximation methods in teaching children to swim, adolescents to drive automobiles, or adults to master complex occupational and social tasks. If rodents, pigeons, or primates toiling in contrived situations could likewise get electrocuted, dismembered, or bruised for errors that inevitably occur during early phases of learning, few of these venturesome subjects would ever survive the shaping process.

On the other hand, if the new behavior requires the learning of many new, internal, physiological cues, as in water skiing, modeling procedures may be much reduced in their effectiveness. It is, of course, sometimes possible to combine procedures, such as shaping and modeling, to increase the rate of behavior change.

Another combination of behavior change procedures that is often useful is shaping and extinction. The nonreinforcement of one behavior may facilitate the shaping of an incompatible or competing behavior. This was illustrated in the earlier case of Dennis who was placed in a "timeout" room following aggressive behavior and positively reinforced when his behavior was nonaggressive or friendly. Because friendly responses are generally incompatible with aggressive responses, the shaping of friendly responses may reduce aggressive responses—in somewhat the same manner as whistling can be reduced by reinforcing the eating of crackers, an incompatible behavior.

Not many carefully designed treatment programs have incorporated the extinction of one behavior and the systematic reinforcement of an incompatible behavior. An exception is a study by Wahler (1969) in which parents were taught to isolate their children in a bedroom for five minutes immediately following "oppositional" (destructive and stubborn) behavior and reinforce cooperative behavior by parental approval and play. The changes in behavior were marked and stable, the spontaneous approaches of the children to their parents increased, and the social reinforcement value of the parents was enhanced.

An increasing number of studies are using parents or paraprofessional personnel to shape and reinforce behavior (e.g., Marshall, 1966; Patterson, 1965; Wagner, 1968; Wolf, Risley, and Mees, 1964). If verbal instructions to the parents are not adequate, a gradual, step-by-step training procedure, including videotape feedback, can be used to shape the parents' behavior which will in turn modify the child's behavior (Bernal, Young, and Shannon, 1970). Thus it may eventually become possible to change behavior on a much broader scale than is now possible with only the use of highly trained professionals.

SUMMARY

During operant conditioning, a specific behavior is followed by a prearranged environmental event that reinforces that behavior. A reinforcer, such as food, money, or verbal praise, increases the frequency (probability) of the behavior. The behavior is called a response and a group of similar responses is known as an operant.

Operant shaping is a special form of operant conditioning. It is a procedure used to develop new behaviors which are not in the subject's behavioral repertoire. During operant shaping, successively closer approximations to the new, desired behavior are reinforced until the new behavior is finally emitted.

A primary reinforcer is a stimulus that does not require the subject to have a prior history of conditioning or learning in order for the stimulus to act as a reinforcer. Food and water are typical examples of primary reinforcers. A secondary reinforcer is a neutral stimulus which has been closely associated with a primary reinforcer often enough so that it acquires reinforcing potential. Secondary reinforcers which are associated with more than one primary reinforcer over a period of time are known as generalized reinforcers. Typical generalized reinforcers for humans are money, social approval, and affection. They are frequently used in the shaping of human behavior and the maintenance of high levels of behavioral activity.

Shaping procedures have been used to develop a wide range of behaviors such as eating, speaking, reading, and cooperating with others. In one demonstration project, juvenile delinquents were met on street corners and in pool rooms and their participation in therapy programs was shaped through the use of generalized reinforcers. The shaping of human behavior does not need to be done in a harsh and mechanistic manner. In fact, shaping appears to be most successful when it is done with enthusiasm by the experimenter and with a positive attitude toward the subjects.

Shaping generally seems most effective if the subject is aware of the shaping procedure and its objective. If, however, the subject has available the basic components of a new behavior but has never integrated them, demonstrating and modeling the behavior to the subject and then asking him to imitate may be more effective than shaping. Sometimes shaping and modeling procedures can be combined. Shaping procedures can often be taught readily enough so that parents or paraprofessional personnel can assist the therapist in changing a patient's behavior in natural settings outside of the clinic or laboratory.

BIBLIOGRAPHY

Azrin, N. H. and Lindsley, O. R. The reinforcement of cooperation between children. *Journal of Abnormal and Social Psychology*, 1956, *52*.

Bandura, A. *Principles of Behavior Modification*. New York: Holt, Rinehart and Winston, 1969.

Bernal, M. E., Young, S., and Shannon, G. Application of a procedure for modification of brat behaviors. Unpublished manuscript, Neuro-psychiatric Institute, University of California, Los Angeles, 1970.

Bostow, D. F. and Bailey, J. B. Modification of severely disruptive and aggressive behavior using brief time-out and reinforcement procedures. *Journal of Applied Behavior Analysis*, 1969, *2*.

Buell, J., Stoddard, P., Harris, F. R., and Baer, D. M. Collateral development of accompanying reinforcement of outdoor play in a preschool child. *Journal of Applied Behavior Analysis*, 1968, *1*.

Crawford, M. P. Cooperative behavior in chimpanzees. *Psychological Bulletin*, 1935, *32*.

Cumming, W. W. A bird's eye glimpse of men and machines. In R. Ulrich, T. Stachnik, and J. Mabry (eds.), *Control of Human Behavior*. Glenview, Ill.: Scott, Foresman and Co., 1966.

Daniel, W. J. Cooperative problem solving in rats. *Journal of Comparative Psychology*, 1942, *34*.

Davison, G. C. A social learning therapy programme with an autistic child. *Behavior Research and Therapy*, 1964, *2*.

Dulany, D. E. Awareness, rules and propositional control: a confrontation with S.R. behavior therapy. In T. R. Dixon and D. L. Horton (eds.), *Verbal Behavior and General Behavior Theory*. Englewood Cliffs, N.J.: Prentice-Hall, 1968.

Ferster, C. B. and DeMeyer, M. K. The development of performance in autistic children in an automatically controlled environment. *Journal of Chronic Disease*, 1961, *13*.

Hendry, D. P. (ed.). *Conditioned Reinforcement*. Homewood, Ill.: The Dorsey Press, 1969.

Hill, W. F. Sources of evaluative reinforcement. *Psychological Bulletin*, 1968, *68*.

Hingtgen, J. N. and Trost, F. C., Jr. Shaping cooperative responses in early childhood schizophrenics: II reinforcement of mutual physical contact and vocal responses. In R. Ulrich, T. Stachnik, and J. Mabry (eds.), *Control of Human Behavior*. Glenview, Ill.: Scott, Foresman and Co., 1966.

Holland, J. G. and Skinner, B. F. *The Analysis of Behavior*. New York: McGraw-Hill, 1961.

Kaufman, A., Baron, A., and Kopp, R. E. Some effects of instruction on human operant behavior. *Psychonomic Monograph Supplement*, 1966, *1*.

Keller, F. S. and Schoenfeld, W. N. *Principles of Psychology*. New York: Appleton-Century-Crofts, 1950.

Lane, H., Kopp, J., Sheppard, W., Andersons, T., and Carlson, D. Acquisition, maintenance, and retention in the differential reinforcement of vocal duration. *Journal of Experimental Psychology Monograph Supplement*, 1967, *74*, 2, Part 2.

Lindsley, O. R. Experimental analysis of cooperation and competition. In T. Verhave (ed.), *The Experimental Analysis of Behavior: Selected Readings*. New York: Appleton-Century-Crofts, 1966.

Marshall, G. R. Toilet training of an autistic eight year old through conditioning therapy: a case report. *Behavior Research and Therapy*, 1966, *4*.

Patterson, G. R. An application of conditioning techniques to the control of a hyperactive child. In L. P. Ullmann and L. Krasner (eds.), *Case Studies in Behavior Modification*. New York: Holt, Rinehart and Winston, 1965.

Risley, T. and Wolf, M. M. Experimental manipulation of autistic behaviors and generalization into the home. In R. Ulrich, T. Stachnik, and J. Mabry (eds.), *Control of Human Behavior*. Glenview, Ill.: Scott, Foresman and Co., 1966.

Rosenthal, R. *Experimenter Effects in Behavioral Research*. New York: Appleton-Century-Crofts, 1966.

Schwitzgebel, R. K. *Streetcorner Research: An Experimental Approach to the Juvenile Delinquent*. Cambridge, Mass.: Harvard University Press, 1964.

Schwitzgebel, R. K. Development of an electronic rehabilitation system for parolees. *Law and Computer Technology*, 1969, *2*.

Schwitzgebel, R. K. Issues in the use of an electronic rehabilitation system with chronic recidivists. *Law and Society Review,* 1969, *3.*

Sidman, M. Operant techniques. In A. J. Bachrach (ed.), *Experimental Foundations of Clinical Psychology.* New York: Basic Books, 1962.

Skinner, B. F. *The Behavior of Organisms: An Experimental Analysis.* New York: Appleton-Century-Crofts, 1938.

Skinner, B. F. *Science and Human Behavior.* New York: Macmillan, 1953.

Solomon, R. J. Use of operant conditioning procedures to shape delinquent attendance. Unpublished manuscript. Harvard University, 1966.

Spielberger, C. D. and DeNike, L. D. Descriptive behaviorism versus cognitive theory in verbal operant conditioning. *Psychological Review,* 1966, *73.*

Staats, A. W. *Learning, Language, and Cognition.* New York: Holt, Rinehart and Winston, 1968.

Staats, A. W. and Staats, C. K. *Complex Human Behavior.* New York: Holt, Rinehart and Winston, 1964.

Verhave, T. The pigeon as a quality control inspector. In R. Ulrich, T. Stachnik, and J. Mabry (eds.), *Control of Human Behavior.* Glenview, Ill.: Scott, Foresman and Co., 1966.

Wagner, M. K. Parent therapists: an operant conditioning method. *Mental Hygiene,* 1968, *52.*

Wahler, R. G. Oppositional children: a quest for parental reinforcement control. *Journal of Applied Behavior Analysis,* 1969, *2.*

White, R. W. Motivation reconsidered: the concept of competence. *Psychological Review,* 1959, *66.*

Wolf, M. M., Risley, T., and Mees, H. Application of operant conditioning procedures to the behavior problems of an autistic child. *Behavior Research and Therapy,* 1964, *1.*

Wolfe, D. L. and Wolfe, H. M. The development of cooperative behavior in monkeys and young children. *Journal of Genetic Psychology,* 1939, *55.*

Changing achievement motivation[*]

David A. Kolb

The hundreds of studies on achievement motivation, or *n* Achievement as it is technically called, are largely the result of the efforts of David McClelland who developed a new theory of motivation, a new means of measuring social motives through the use of projective tests and a technology for changing motivation through psychological education. Prior to this work, there was the commonly accepted notion, especially among psychoanalytically oriented therapists, that human motivations were determined largely during childhood and remained fixed throughout the person's lifetime. In reviewing this work, McClelland (1965, p. 332) noted two unusual sources of behavior change that encouraged him to consider more carefully whether in fact motivations could be changed later in life.

Oddly enough we were encouraged by the successful efforts of two quite different groups of "change agents"—operant conditioners and missionaries. Both groups have been "naive" in the sense of being unimpressed by or ignorant of the state of psychological knowledge in the field. The operant conditioners have not been encumbered by any elaborate theoretical apparatus; they do not believe motives exist anyway, and continue demonstrating vigorously that if you want a person to make a response, all you have to do is elicit it and reward it (cf. Bandura and Walters, 1963, pp. 238 ff). They retain a simple faith in the infinite plasticity of human behavior in which one response is just like any other and any one can be "shaped up" (strengthened by reward)—presumably even an "achievement" response as produced by a subject in a fantasy test . . . Like operant conditioners, the missionaries have gone ahead changing people, because they have believed it possible. While the evidence is not scientifically impeccable, common-sense observation yields dozens of cases of adults whose motivational structure has seemed to be quite radically and permanently altered by the educational efforts of Communist Party, Mormon, or other devout missionaries.

McClelland's approach to changing achievement was based on research studies that showed how achievement motivated people behaved. To understand the motivation training techniques it is helpful to first understand something about achievement motivation and how it is measured.

To measure achievement motivation, McClelland made a creative integration of Freudian and Hullian theories of motivation. According to Freud, motivation is evident in the fantasy lives of individuals. Dream interpretation is one principal method psychoanalysts use to discover a person's motivations, hidden conflicts, and wishes. Henry Murray's Thematic Apperception Test (TAT) is a second, widely used method of eliciting fantasies of individuals by having them make up stories to a set of ambiguous pictures. Both of these clinical approaches, however, lacked a rigorous quantitative method of determining the strength and extent to which motives were operating in a person's life. Here McClelland integrated the Hullian experiment perspective with the Freudian view. Consistent with the Hullian notion of drive-reduction, an attempt was made to qualify human motivation objectively as reflected in TAT responses.

The first task in devising a method of measuring motivation was to vary the intensity of a human motive and to measure its effects on imagination or fantasy. Just as Hull had experimentally manipulated drive states in animals (e.g., he increased the hunger drive by depriving animals of food for varying lengths of time) McClelland began by experimentally manipulating the strength of food motivation in humans. He obtained TAT stories from groups of Navy men who differed in the number of hours during which they had gone without food. The experiments, performed at the U.S. Submarine Base in New London, Connecticut, showed that different degrees of hunger were reflected in different amounts of food imagery in the TAT stories. In other words, fantasy TAT stories could be used to measure the strength of motivation (Atkinson and McClelland, 1948).

McClelland then used the same strategy to study achievement motivation. The intensity of achievement motivation was varied by giving different instructions to groups of individuals just before they wrote their TAT stories. One group was told that people who did well on the fantasy test were creative intelligent leaders. It was assumed that these instructions would arouse achievement thoughts. The TAT responses of this group were compared to TAT responses of a group given "neutral" instructions and to a third group who were given "relaxed" instructions. The specific kinds of thoughts which were present in the achievement group TAT's and absent in the "neutral" and "relaxed" set of TAT's became the operational definition of achievement motivation (McClelland, Atkinson, Clark, and Lowell, 1953).

Subsequent research with this measure of achievement motivation indicated that individuals with high n Achievement showed certain consistent patterns of behavior:

1. These individuals preferred situations in which they had personal responsibility for the outcomes of events rather than situations, like gambling, where events were determined by chance (French, 1958; McClelland, et at., 1953).

2. They chose goals for themselves that were realistic but challenging as opposed to goals that were either too easy or too risky (McClelland, 1958; Atkinson and Litwin, 1960; Atkinson, 1958).

3. They sought situations where they could obtain immediate concrete feedback to determine how well they were doing (French, 1958; Moss and Kagan, 1961).

These findings, corroborated by other research in such diverse areas as child-rearing and management, began to indicate that high achievement motivation was a key factor in the successful strivings for excellence which characterize the entrepreneur. Achievement motivation also appeared to influence task-oriented behavior. Lowell (1952) assigned subjects to two experimental groups depending upon whether they scored high or low in achievement motivation as reflected in six imaginary stories told by the subjects. The groups were then given the task of unscrambling and rearranging letters into meaningful words. The group that scored high in achievement motivation performed at a significantly higher level on this task than the group that scored low on achievement motivation.

This relationship between achievement motivation and entrepreneurship led McClelland to study the impact of achievement motivation on the broader problem of economic development. Weber (1904) had observed the relationship between the pervasiveness of the Protestant ethic and the rise of capitalism. McClelland suggested a social-psychological interpretation for Weber's hypothesis. The Protestant ethic represented a stress upon independence, self-reliance, and hard work—the achievement values which McClelland had shown to produce entrepreneurial activity. McClelland reasoned further that increases and decreases in these cultural values should herald subsequent increases and decreases in economic activity. Potentially, this hypothesis provided a psychological explanation for the economic flourishing and decay of nations throughout history.

The research documenting this interpretation of economic history has been presented in great detail in McClelland's book, *The Achieving Society* (1961). Only two key studies presented in this book will be described here. In the first, the average productivity of the twelve Protestant countries in the temperate zone was compared to the average economic productivity of the thirteen Catholic countries in the temperate zone. The measure used to compare economic productivity was the kilowatt hours of electricity consumed per capita. There was a striking difference in favor of the Protestant countries. In the second key study,

McClelland obtained measures of the level of achievement motivation in twenty-two countries both in 1925 and in 1950 by counting the frequency of achievement themes in samples of third and fourth grade reading books. Three measures of the gain in economic productivity were obtained for the period 1925 to 1950: (1) change in national income as measured in international units per capita; (2) change in kilowatt hours per capita of electricity produced; and (3) a combination of the above two measures of change. Levels of achievement motivation in 1925 and 1950 were found to be correlated with the degree of deviation from expected economic gains. The level of achievement motivation in 1925 predicted the rate of economic development from 1925 to 1950.

This striking confirmation of achievement motivation theory was extended in several subsequent research studies. Levels of achievement motivation were measured in the literature of Spain and England from the 1600's through the 1800's. In both cases, the rise and fall of achievement motivation preceded the rise and fall of economic productivity by about 25 to 50 years. Similar relationships were obtained for achievement motivation levels and economic productivity in Greece from 900 to 100 B.C. and pre-Incan Peru from about 800 B.C. to 700 A.D. (McClelland, 1961, ch. 4).

ACHIEVEMENT MOTIVATION TRAINING FOR BUSINESSMEN AND POTENTIAL ENTREPRENEURS

The above findings raised an interesting theoretical issue with important practical implications. Was there a causal relationship between achievement motivation and entrepreneurial behavior; and if so, would it be possible to increase an individual's achievement motivation and thereby increase his entrepreneurial success? To answer this question McClelland and his coworkers set about the task of designing a training course to increase achievement motivation. Rather than rely on any single theory of behavior change in designing the course they chose to draw their training techniques from a wide variety of psychological theories—learning theory, education, mass media research, theories of attitude change, motivation theory, and psychotherapy. Twelve propositions were drawn from these theories to describe how the course should be designed and run (McClelland, 1965). These propositions are summarized below under the headings: Goal-Setting, Motive Syndrome, Cognitive Supports, and Group Supports.

Major propositions

Goal-setting. The three propositions in this group focus on inducing confidence commitment, and the measurement of change in the attainment of goals. Proposition 1 states that the more reasons the person has in advance about the possibility and desirability of change, the more likely he is to change. This notion has wide support in the psychological literature: the Hawthorne effect (in business), the "Hello-Goodbye" effect (in therapy), "experimenter bias" studies (in experimental psychology), and prestige-suggestion studies (in attitude change), among others, all support the contention that belief in the possibility and desirability of change is influential in changing a person. Among the means used to create this belief in course participants have been the presentation of research findings on the relationship of *n*-Achievement to entrepreneurial success, the suggestive power of membership in an experimental group designed to show an effect, and the prestige of a university. This prestige "pitch" is given before the course proper begins. Later in the course, participants make a public commitment to seeking specific achievement goals.

Proposition 8 (numbered as in McClelland, 1965b) states that the more an individual commits himself to achieving specific goals related to the motive, the more the motive is likely to influence his future thought and action. Proposition 9 states that motive change is more likely to occur if a person keeps a record of his progress toward his goal. Thus, in the course, reinforcement is built into the goal-setting procedure by having course participants establish methods of measuring just how well they are doing at any given time. This is the kind of regular, concrete feedback that is especially important to people with high achievement motivation and that fits well into operant conditioning theory.

Motive syndrome.   A *motive*, as defined here, is a pattern or cluster of goal-directed thoughts typically associated with certain action strategies. Because both thoughts and actions occur in specific, real-life contexts, the motive syndrome is the integration of thoughts, actions, and contexts. Proposition 3 states that the more an individual clearly conceptualizes the motive to be acquired, the more likely he will be to employ that motive. In the achievement motivation courses, therefore, participants are given the TAT and then taught to score their own stories. In this way, they learn what the achievement motive is, and evaluate just how much of the motive they have upon entering the course. After learning the scoring system, participants are encouraged to use those labels in coding their own thinking in everyday situations. Similarly, participants learn the action strategies of people with high achievement motivation through playing illustrative games, analyzing case studies and discussing everyday life situations as a group. This portion of the course is based upon two other propositions. The more a person can link the motive to related actions, the more likely it is that the motive will be acquired (Proposition 4). The more a person can transfer and apply the newly conceptualized motive to events in his daily life, the more likely the motive will be increased (Proposition 5). These propositions derive from experimental and educational research on the generalization and transfer of training.

Cognitive supports.   The research on attitude and opinion change demonstrates that thoughts and actions can be affected through rational discussion and dialogue. Thus, to increase a particular motive, it is also important to explore rationally how that motive is consistent with the demands of reality (Proposition 2), how it will be an improvement in a person's self-image (Proposition 6), and how it is consistent with the dominant cultural values (Proposition 7). The more a person sees these consistencies and possible improvements, the more likely it is that the motive will be increased. In the *n*-Achievement courses, these connections are fostered through an extensive presentation of the research showing the relationship between *n*-Achievement and entrepreneurial success; self-confrontation, meditation, and individual counseling; and group discussions of *n*-Achievement in relation to the folk lore, religious books, and the expressed values of the culture.

Group support. Cognitive learning and practice alone are not sufficient to increase motivation; affective factors are important as well. Thus the *n*-Achievement courses also encourage change in affect through several different procedures. Typically, the course leaders assume a nondirective, warm, accepting role consistent with the emphasis on warmth and support of client-centered therapists (Proposition 10). Although the instructors lead discussions and often present information, generally their role is to support open exploration by course members. The choice of whether or not to employ *n*-Achievement in one's own life is left to the participants.

In addition, this emotional, personal confrontation is encouraged by giving the course in "retreat" settings which dramatize the importance of self-study (Proposition 11). Finally, emotional group supports are fostered by encouraging the group members to continue group activities. In this way, the ideas and feelings are kept salient through the new reference group after the course has ended (Proposition 12).

Applications

The first achievement motivation training course was conducted for executives of a major American corporation. The course was five days long and was given to sixteen successful middle level managers. At first blush, this seems like something akin to selling iceboxes to Eskimos because it is difficult to imagine individuals who should be more achievement motivated than successful executives in an exceptionally successful corporation. It was felt, however, that "even a moderate increase in the strength of achievement motivation would lead to more effective performance, which would be reflected by objective measures such as rate of advancement" (Aronoff and Litwin, 1971, p. 218). To test this hypothesis, the sixteen men who participated in the achievement motivation training course were .matched with sixteen other similar executives who participated in the corporation's regular four week management development course. Two years later the two groups were compared on an index of advancement in the company which ranged from −1 (demotion) to +2 (more than one promotion in the two year period and/or a large salary increase). The achievement trained group moved from an average advancement of .55 in the two years before the course to .88 in the two years after the course. The management development group showed a decrease in the rate of advancement from .64 to .27 during this same period. Though these results must be interpreted cautiously because of the small sample size, it appears that the achievement training produced a marked increase in advancement for the course participants at a time when the careers of their peers seemed to be tapering off.

To test his theory of achievement motivation, entrepreneurship, and economic development further, a program of research on achievement motivation training was initiated in developing countries. Training courses were run in Spain, Mexico, Japan, Italy, and India. The Indian training courses were given as part of a research design which allowed a scientific assessment of the impact of the training on entrepreneurial behavior and economic indicators (McClelland and Winter, 1969). Seventy-six businessmen running small businesses in the towns of Kakinada and Vellore participated in a ten day achievement motivation training course. Table 1 shows how the course affected the entrepreneurial activities

TABLE 1
Percentage of entrepreneurs classified as "active" (+2) during two year periods

Type of group	Before course, 1962–64	After course, 1964–66
A. Kakinada—trained in n-Achievement (N = 51)[a]	18%	55%[b]
B. Kakinada—untrained Controls (N = 22)	18%	18%
C. Rajahmundry—untrained Controls (N = 35)	26%	31%[c]
D. Vellore—trained in n-Achievement (N = 25)	17%	44%[d]
E. Vellore—Untrained Controls (N = 16)	13%	19%[e]
X. All Trained in n-Achievement (N = 76)	18%	51%[g]
Y. All Untreated Controls (N = 73)	22%	25%[i]

Source: After D. McClelland and D. G. Winter, *Motivating Economic Achievement.* New York: Free Press, 1969. p. 213.

[a] Slight variations in the N because of deaths, unavailability of data, etc.

[b] Significant at $<.001$ by chi square analysis, group A & B difference significant at $<.01$.

[c] Difference between controls before and after, not significant. Significant difference compared to Kakinada trained entrepreneurs, $<.05$.

[d] Significant at $<.05$.

[e] Difference between controls before and after not significant. Not significant versus Vellore trained.

[f] Significant at $<.001$.

[g] Difference between group X and Y, significant at $<.001$.

of these trained businessmen in comparison to similar, untrained businessmen. (Percent "active" indicates how many men reported entrepreneurial activities such as promotions or salary increases above 25 per cent, starting a new business, and/or expanding the business.) In all cases, the trained business groups showed substantial and significant increases in entrepreneurial activity in the two years after training while the control groups remained near their initial levels. In addition, McClelland and Winter demonstrated that the trained businessmen achieved significant improvements in other aspects of entrepreneurial performance. They worked longer hours, made more definite attempts to start new businesses, and actually started more businesses. They also made more investments, employed more workers, and showed greater percentage increases in the gross income of their firms. Thus by all measures they became better entrepreneurs than their untrained counterparts and more effective than they themselves were before they participated in achievement motivation training.

In the U.S., Timmons (1971) has reported similar positive results from the application of achievement motivation training in two programs designed to stimulate black capitalism—one in Oklahoma and one in Washington, D.C. In both programs a one week achievement training program produced significant increases in business activity for course participants when they were compared to untrained counterparts in their respective communities six months after the training. Timmons (1971, p. 80) makes the following comments about achievement motivation training for entrepreneurs.

1. . . . it appears that the training does not achieve such results by deep seated transformation of the motivation or personality of the individual. Rather, in numerous instances, the training affects participants by stimulating, building on, or facilitating a latent potential for entrepreneurial activity.

2. The training program has an apparent catalytic effect of providing a basis for collaborative activities in the form of joint ventures and partnerships.

3. The unusual turnaround of a business . . . suggests that persistent entrepreneurial behavior, in combination with the problem-solving techniques acquired in the training course, can appreciably help to overcome complex and stubborn internal management situations.

4. Entrepreneurial training is apparently effective in generating a common concern among the trainer for community betterment as a criterion for exploring or initiating a new venture.

ACHIEVEMENT MOTIVATION TRAINING IN EDUCATIONAL SETTINGS

At the same time that achievement motivational training courses were being conducted to increase the entrepreneurial activity of the businessmen, similar courses were being conducted to see if achievement motivation training could measurably improve the academic achievement of underachievers and potential school dropouts. Although correlational studies between achievement motivation and academic achievement usually show only a small positive relationship (Atkinson, 1958; McClelland, et al., 1953; Ulinger and Stevens, 1960), it seemed that achievement training might have a positive affect on the academic performance of the underachiever. Kolb (1965) tested this hypothesis by giving an achievement motivation training course to twenty high school boys who attended an Ivy League special six week summer school for underachieving students at a university. Thirty-seven boys at the same summer school served as control subjects. A year and a half later, the achievement trained boys had improved significantly more in their grade average than had the other boys in the summer school. The amount of change as a result of achievement motivation training, however, was very much a function of the boys' social class. High socio-economic status (SES) boys showed a great deal of improvement in grade average while low SES boys did not (see Figure 1). This difference seemed due to the fact that high

FIGURE 1

Changes in high school grades as a function of social class comparing achievement motivation trained and control group subjects

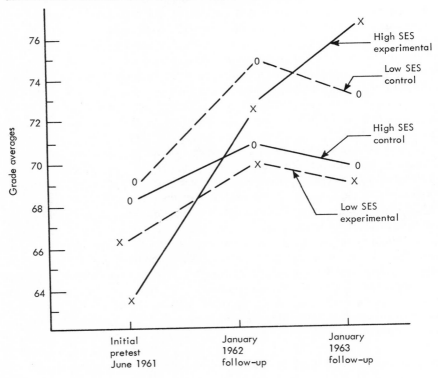

SES boys lived in a class environment where achievement values were encouraged while the class environment of lower class boys did not encourage their newly acquired achievement orientation.

In a study by Alschuler (1967), two residential *n*-Achievement courses were given to twenty-one high school juniors. These students were among a group of fifty-six students identified by school personnel as the "most difficult" students in school. Most of the students were potential drop-outs and had a long history of discipline problems. Interestingly, many of their characteristic behavior patterns were demonstrated during the residential course, to the dismay of the course leaders who were less able to control the students than their high school teachers. Given this unfavorable immediate feedback, the results of a one year follow-up study are particularly surprising. Only one student (4.7 percent) in the experimental group dropped out of school while eight students (22.2 percent) in the matched control group of thirty-six dropped out of school. The experimental group also showed a statistically significant increase on their average (mean) grade level. The grades of the experimental group increased even though they tended to be taking more difficult courses than before. No equivalent change in the level of aspiration was indicated in the course choices of the control group.

In discussing their new school and extracurricular activities, most of the boys who participated in achievement training described new personal interests that led them into their activities. In contrast, very few of the boys in the control group attributed their new activities to their own motives. Instead, they cited the influence and pressure of others as reasons for their activities. Thus, they reflected a continued lack of internal motivation in contrast to the *n*-Achievement boys who showed a new sense of autonomy and control over their own lives.

SUMMARY

The achievement motivated person is a hard working person who seeks personal responsibility, who sets realistic but challenging personal goals and who seeks feedback about the effects of his efforts. As such he tends to do particularly well in those situations which allow for personal control and innovation, particularly entrepreneurial business situations. Historical studies have shown that the level of achievement concern in a nation's cultural values may be related to the rise and fall of the nation's economy. In Spain and England, for example, levels of achievement motivation as reflected by the nation's literature proceeded the rise and fall of the country's economic productivity by about 25 to 50 years. On an individual level, businessmen in various countries who have received achievement motivation training have shown significant improvements in their business performance as compared to businessmen who were not trained.

Achievement motivation training involves an integration of individual and group tasks. The individual is asked to set clear goals of achievement for himself and is encouraged to develop confidence and commitment to these goals. He is also taught to think about achievement in everyday situations and to imitate and develop achievement strategies by reading case studies, playing illustrative games, and observing achievement motivated role model. Much of this is done in a group context with leaders who are warm and supportive while the group encourages individual self-exploration and change.

In both business and educational settings, achievement training appears to be a workable technique for increasing achievement oriented behavior. In these areas, motivation training has produced measurable change in behavior that have been maintained over time. There are potentially great benefits to be gained from this approach to behavior change, both through the specific applications of achievement motivation training techniques and through the wider application of this general approach to behavior change.

BIBLIOGRAPHY

Alschuler, A. S. The achievement motivation development project: a summary and review. Unpublished paper, Harvard Graduate School of Education, 1967.
Aronoff, J. and Litwin, G. H. Achievement motivation training and executive advancement. *Journal of Applied Behavioral Science*, 1971, 7.

Atkinson, J. W. (ed.). *Motives in Fantasy, Action and Society.* Princeton, N.J.: Van Nostrand, 1958.

Atkinson, J. W. and Litwin, G. H. Achievement motive and test anxiety conceived as motivation approach success and motive to avoid failure. *Journal of Abnormal and Social Psychology,* 1960, *60.*

Atkinson, J. W. and McClelland, D. C. The projective expression of needs II. The effect of different intensities of the hunger drive on thematic apperception. *Journal of Experimental Psychology,* 1948, *38.*

Bandura, A. and Walters, R. H. *Social Learning and Personality Development.* New York: Holt, Rinehart and Winston, 1963.

French, E. G. Effects of the interaction of motivation and feedback on task performance. In J. W. Atkinson (ed.), *Motives in Fantasy, Action and Society.* Princeton, N.J.: Van Nostrand, 1958.

Kolb, D. A. Achievement motivation training for under-achieving high school boys. *Journal of Personality and Social Psychology,* 1965, *1.*

Lowell, E. L. The effect of need for achievement on learning and speed of performance. *Journal of Psychology,* 1952, *33.*

McClelland, D. C. Risk taking in children with high and low need for achievement. In Atkinson, J. W. (ed.), *Motives in Fantasy, Action and Society.* Princeton, N.J.: Van Nostrand, 1958.

McClelland, D. C. *The Achieving Society.* Princeton, N.J.: Van Nostrand, 1961.

McClelland, D. C. Toward a theory of motive acquisition. *American Psychologist,* 1965, *20.*

McClelland, D. C., Atkinson, J. W., Clark, R. W., and Cowell, E. L. *The Achievement Motive.* New York: Appleton-Century-Crofts, 1953.

McClelland, D. C. and Winter, D. G. *Motivating Economic Achievement.* New York: Free Press, 1969.

Moss, H. A. and Kagan, J. Stability of achievement and recognition-seeking behaviors from early childhood through adulthood. *Journal of Abnormal and Social Psychology,* 1961, *62.*

Timmons, J. A. Black is beautiful—is it bountiful? *Harvard Business Review,* Nov.–Dec., 1971.

Uhlinger, C. A. and Stephens, M. W. Relation of achievement motivation to academic achievement in students of superior ability. *Journal of Educational Psychology,* 1960, *51.*

Weber, M. *The Protestant Ethic and the Spirit of Capitalism.* (1st ed. 1904.) T. Parsons (translator). New York: Scribner, 1930.

Part IV

The instrumental relationship

INTRODUCTION

In this part we should like to consider a type of relationship which is central to our lives—the instrumental or work relationship. While it is true that man does not live by bread alone, it is equally true that bread (or some other product) is vital to his life; and often that bread is obtained through a process of interaction with other people.[1] An "instrumental relationship may be defined as any relationship of two or more persons which has as its ultimate function the performance of a task.

The main portion of this essay will be concerned with some of the issues relevant to the *work* relationship. In the closing part, a special case will be considered: that of the "creative relationship," where the desired output is some sort of new, innovative product such as a creative solution to a problem or an artistic work.

BACKGROUND

Until recently, most of the attention to man's work was centered on its more technical and formalistic aspects. Problems of the work setting, the proper rules structure, the nature of the technical operations required, etc., received the major focus of attention. In other words, work was generally conceived as being something which an isolated individual or single person performed. Only recently has there been a shift of emphasis toward recognition of the fact that work itself involves a relationship between people.

We may mark the Hawthorne Studies of Elton May and his associates[2] as the beginning of a shift of interest toward the interpersonal aspects of the work

---

[1] In this context, we are considering work to be an end in itself, not just a sublimation of other needs or a diversion of aggressive or hostile impulses.

[2] F. J. Roethlisberger and W. J. Dickson, *Management and the Worker* (Cambridge: Harvard University Press, 1939).

process and a movement toward adding more flesh to man's skeletal conception of task interaction. From these studies to the present there has been a continual increase in the amount of research effort and interest directed toward this area, especially toward such phenomena as group norms and their growth, problems in communication between individuals and groups,[3] and resistances to change in work and interaction routines.[4]

THE BASIS FOR INSTRUMENTAL RELATIONSHIPS

We now turn to a simple but fundamental question, the answer to which should provide us with a clearer image of our topic: Why is an instrumental *relationship* necessary, desirable, useful, or practicable in a given task situation? There seem to be several rather basic answers to this question.

1. For a number of reasons, one person may not be able to do the work alone. There may be too much to do, too much time pressure, or some other constraint; so help from another person is needed to complete the task. Or there may be a set of complementary skills required for completion, such as in certain kinds of problem-solving situations which require members to have varied bits of knowledge or different skills. Or, there may be too many activities required simultaneously to permit their performance by one individual, even if he does have the requisite abilities. Too much to do, too little time, too many skills required, too many things to do at once. These factors may be summarized as follows: Man needs the help of others when his activities or instrumental goals become so large or complex that they prohibit his obtaining them by himself. This is clearly one major source of human work organizations, and of most other organizations that have some sort of output as a goal.

2. Those who perform a service for others generally must enter into a relationship with the recipient of the service, even though that relationship may be quite "fleeting" and only minimally cooperative.[5]

3. The relationship may be of value as an end in itself—it may simply be more

---

[3] A. Bavelas, "Communication Patterns in Task-Oriented Groups," D. Lerner and H. D. Lasswell (eds.), *The Policy Sciences* (Stanford, Calif.: Stanford University Press, 1951), pp. 193–202; also H. Guetzkow and H. A. Simon, "The Impact of Certain Communication Nets upon Organization and Performance in Task-Oriented Groups," *Management Science*, Vol. 1 (1955), pp. 233–50.

[4] L. Coch and J. R. P. French, "Overcoming Resistance to Change," *Human Relations*, Vol. 1 (1947), pp. 512–32.

Much of the research and thinking done on the work process today may also be considered under the field of "organization theory." For extensive bibliographies specifically related to this field, see C. Argyris, *Personality and Organization* (New York: Harper Bros., 1957); P. Blau and W. R. Scott, *Formal Organizations: A Comparative Approach* (San Francisco: Chandler Pub. Co., 1962); J. G. March and H. A. Simon, *Organizations* (New York: John Wiley & Sons, 1958). For collections of articles, see M. Haire (ed.) *Modern Organization Theory* (New York: John Wiley & Sons, 1959); J. C. March (ed.), *Handbook of Organizations* (Chicago: Rand McNally, Inc., 1963); and James D. Thompson (ed.), *Approaches to Organizational Design* (Pittsburgh: University of Pittsburgh Press, 1966).

[5] See the article by Davis in this part.

satisfying to work with others than to work alone.[6] There appear to be wide individual variations in the degree of importance placed on satisfaction of relational needs.[7] As Rosenberg[8] found, some people hold as one of their major criteria for choice of work the opportunity to perform their work in relationships with others, while others expressed little or no specific interest in this aspect of different occupations.

4. A work relationship may also be formed in order to reduce competition which, if continued, could be harmful to both parties. When two newsboys on the same corner decide to work together at rush hour, with one handing out papers and the other collecting money, this decision may come in part from a belief that together they will sell more than they would separately. It may also be motivated by anxiety stemming from each's fear that he may be completely driven out of business by the other. The actual danger of this happening may be real or fantasied, but the force toward getting together can act in either case.

5. The example just cited implies an ultimately cooperative relationship. The relationship may also be formed *in order to compete*. This is evidently the case with Lee and Yang, the Nobel Prize winning physicists,[9] who help to keep their interest high by racing each other to different kinds of solutions. Even in this type of competitive relationship, however, there is an implicit agreement to cooperate in the competition.[10]

6. Finally, an instrumental relationship may result when the distribution of power between the partners is so uneven that one can control the other and keep him in the relationship for the controller's own ends. The prototype of this is, of course, the master-slave relationship, which has lost its importance in the United States but still exists in some other cultures.

To summarize, we have presented six bases for the formation of an instrumental relationship: (1) to *break down* a task that is too large, complex, etc., to be performed alone; (2) to have someone for whom to perform a *service;* (3) for the satisfaction of *interacting* with another person; to either (4) *avoid* the costs or (5) *gain* the benefits of *competition;* and (6) because one who holds power over another wishes to accomplish certain goals through the other. Two final comments are needed to clarify this list. First, a specific relationship may be initiated for any one or for a *mixture* of these reasons. Second, a relationship may be formed for one reason but may become important for other reasons as it changes over time.

---

[6] See Roy, "Banana Time," in this part.

[7] For a systematic measuring of these needs see William Schutz, *FIRO–B: A Three-Dimensional Theory of Interpersonal Behavior* (New York: Rinehart, 1958).

[8] M. Rosenberg. *Occupations and Values* (Glencoe, Ill.: Free Press, 1957).

[9] "Profiles, A Question of Parity," *New Yorker Magazine* (May 12, 1962), pp. 49–104.

[10] The mere fact of remaining together in the relationship may not *always* indicate an agreement to cooperate. There may be other forces keeping the parties together. An interesting case of this is the small-group experimental setting where the subjects' decisions to participate in the experiment create a commitment to remain in the group even though the task demands continued competition.

TYPES OF INSTRUMENTAL RELATIONSHIPS

Having considered the reasons for the formation of instrumental relationships, let us move on to the question of how we might *classify* relationships. Two basic dimensions will be used here to illustrate how we can make distinctions.[11] Both dimensions relate to the personal orientation of the parties in the relationship. The first dimension is concerned with the trust orientation of the parties toward each other. For simplicity, the two alternatives will be called *friendly* and *antagonistic.* In the friendly orientation, the dominant assumptions people hold toward each other are positive. On the whole, person A trusts the other person, B, and does not fear that B will strive to fulfill some vested interest of his own at A's expense. Conversely, in the antagonist orientation there is a negative set and a sense of mistrust—that A must be on his toes lest B use an opening to some personal advantage that A considers inappropriate and harmful to himself.

The second dimension is concerned with whether ends to be obtained in the relationship will be joint or individual. The two possibilities here are a *cooperative* orientation, where the effort of each member is seen as collaborative and useful to the other, and a *competitive* orientation, where attainment of goals by one member is seen as a threat to the goal attainment of the other.[12]

These two dimensions, then, provide us with four logical types of instrumenal relationship: (*a*) friendly cooperation; (*b*) antagonistic competition; (*c*) friendly competition; (*d*) antagonistic cooperation. Each of these will be briefly described in turn.

a) Friendly cooperation. In this type of instrumental relationship the general orientation of the parties is one of generally positive feelings toward one other and help is given and received in the process of moving toward what is usually a common goal. One example of this type might be two mechanical engineers trying to solve a heat transfer problem.

b) Antagonistic competition. This is the opposite of friendly cooperation and might be considered by many not to be a relationship at all. We consider it to be such by using "relationship" to mean that one person's actions must be recognized and responded to by the other, and vice versa. In this type, the personal orientations of the participants are generally negative, including disrespect, mistrust, and often hostility. The individual efforts are not seen as contributing toward any common end. An interesting example of this type is the relationship between a dance musician and his audience, where the competition is for a curious mixture of power, self-esteem, enjoyment, and artistic taste.[13]

---

[11] These are, of course, only two out of many different dimensions that might be used to develop typologies of instrumental relationships.

[12] This dimension is basically the same as Deutsch's orientation variable which hinges on what he calls "promotive interdependence" in cooperative situations. " 'Promotive interdependence' specifies a condition in which individuals are so linked together that there is a positive correlation between their goal attainments." M. Deutsch, "Cooperation and Trust: Some Theoretical Notes," *Nebraska Symposium on Motivation,* 1962 (Lincoln: University of Nebraska Press), pp. 275–319.

[13] Howard Becker, "The Professional Dance Musician," *American Journal of Sociology,* Vol. 57

c) Friendly competition. This is a mixed case, where the parties have a basically positive personal orientation toward one another, even though at some level they are using their individual efforts to compete with one another. An example already cited earlier is quite appropriate here: the case of Lee and Yang, who race each other to problem solutions. Another would be professional golfers opposing each other in a tournament where they are essentially competing for a prize and often still feel quite close and trusting toward one another, playing under an elaborate system of courtesies and other norms. That this is the case is illustrated by the exceptions (the very stir they cause proves the point), such as the antagonism between Gary Player and Gay Brewer in a 1967 British golf tournament. They had slipped into an Antagonistic-Competition mode.

d) Antagonistic cooperation.[14] This is the other mixed case, where there is a negative personal orientation of the parties toward each other, even though

FIGURE 1

Orientation to contributions

		Cooperative	*Competitive*
Orientation to other party	*Friendly*..........	(*a*) Friendly Cooperation	(*c*) Friendly Competition
	Antagonistic.......	(*d*) Antagonistic Cooperation	(*b*) Antagonistic Competition

there also exists ostensibly an orientation of cooperation or pooling of efforts in pursuit of a group goal. A good example of this type of relationship is that of a student discussion group trying to arrive at solutions to assigned cases. In some of these groups, the participants cooperate in a general polite manner, but they are actually holding back their best ideas for individual use at a later date.[15]

Figure 1 presents these basic dimensions. Once again it should be noted that instrumental relationships do not necessarily occur in these "pure" types. Any

---

(Sept. 1951), pp. 136–44. Becker also raises the question of *which* relationship is chosen for analysis of instrumental activities like services—the relationship between performer and client, or the one between performer and colleagues. It would appear that in most cases of antagonistic-competitive performer-client relationships the performer also has simultaneously a more supportive relationship with his own colleagues.

[14] This term was originally suggested by David Riesman.

[15] Robert Ardrey provides a fascinating chapter describing the antagonistic-cooperative orientation in certain groups of animals and men—the society of inward antagonism which he calls "the noyau." In fact, these groups reverse the axes of our typology and are really "cooperatively antagonistic," where the antagonism is the output and they need one another to continue the process. See Robert Ardrey, *The Territorial Imperative* (New York: Atheneum, 1966), Chap. v.

given relationship may have elements of any or all of these types in it, in varying strengths.

By way of illustrating the possible implication of this typology, we may consider the six bases of a work relationship presented above and ask whether relationships formed for different reasons would tend to be found in specific cells of Figure 1.

1. Relationship formed to reduce complexity. We would expect the majority of these relationships to be found in cell (*a*), Friendly Cooperation, since they are generally formed voluntarily to accomplish some sort of joint goal that cannot be obtained singly. There will also be some cases of (*d*) Antagonistic Cooperation, as when the task demands that people work together who would ordinarily not choose to associate; and cases of (*c*) Friendly Competition, as in the Yang-Lee case noted above, where the participants compete within a limited framework while agreeing to pool their output in the end.

2. Service relationship. This may fall into any one of the four cells, depending on the nature of the roles involved. Important here would be such elements as the expectations of each party for the other and the type and length of contact between the parties.[16]

3. Relationship formed for interaction. This relationship would generally fall in cell (*a*), Friendly Cooperation, and secondarily in cell (*c*), Friendly Competition. The very nature of its formation indicates that when it ceased to have a friendly and trusting orientation it would not satisfy its original function and would tend to break down.

4. Relationship to avoid competition. This type will by definition fall into the two cooperative cells. It may result in Friendly Cooperation, but there is also a good chance for an orientation of Antagonistic-Cooperation, especially if feelings of mistrust, hostility, and the like that were built up during the competitive phase were not adequately worked through when the switch was made from competition to cooperation.

5. Relationship to gain effects of competition. The predominant orientation here would be cell (*c*), Friendly Competition, especially since there has usually been a Friendly Cooperative orientation prior to the decision to compete. If the orientation changed over time to an antagonistic one, we could assume that the basis for the relationship had also changed.

6. Relationship formed because of the power one holds over another. This would result in a generally antagonistic orientation, in cells (*d*) or (*b*). This orientation is caused on the one hand by the controller's feelings that he *must* use his power to obtain desired performance from the controlled person and therefore he cannot trust the controlled to do it on his own, and on the other hand by the controlled's feelings of hostility for being controlled and his feelings that he cannot trust the controller's interests to be the same as his own. This

---

[16] See Davis' article in this part for an example of a service relationship which is characterized by a mix of antagonistic cooperation and competition.

relationship is probably most often found to be a *mixture* of Antagonistic Cooperation and Competition, as in the case of a chain-gang convict who both produces some sort of work and sabotages his foreman by explicitly following some directive which he knows from his experience to be incorrect.

PROBLEMS IN THE RELATIONSHIP AND THEIR SOLUTION

Now that we have considered formation of the instrumental relationship and one possible typology, let us move on to the kinds of problems that must be solved if the relationship is to continue once it has been formed.

Our basic assumption, following several different authors,[17] is that there are two fundamental problem areas which must be dealt with in an instrumental relationship: (*a*) problems concerning the *task* involved and operations for its performance, and (*b*) problems concerning the *maintenance* of the relationship or control of its "socioemotional" state.[18] In making this assumption we are also more generally asserting that a system has two needs, both of which must be met to some minimum degree and balanced with each other if the system is to continue. Members must therefore enact roles during the life of the group which carry out these functions or meet these needs.[19]

Task issues, generally, are concerned with how to proceed in performing the task—what goals are to be set for the relationship; how influence and control are to be distributed for decision making; which strategies, division of labor, and the like are to be used; what actual operations are to be used and how they will be carried out; and feedback on past performance. Note that these task areas are more relevant for shared communication in some types of instrumental relationships than they are in others. For instance, they would be of prime consideration in most relationships formed specifically to get help in doing a certain job. On the other hand, for a relationship that was formed for the relational value itself, task problems may at times be suppressed to a great extent. Intermediate between these two would be the service relationship, which would

---

[17] The "Task" and "Socioemotional" distinction has been closely associated with Bales and his associates; these are similar to the leadership functions of "initiating structure" and "consideration" associated with the Ohio State studies. See E. A. Fleishman, "Leadership Climate, Human Relations Training, and Supervisory Behavior," *Personnel Psychology,* Vol. 6 (1953), pp. 205–22; and A. W. Halpin and B. J. Winer, "A Factorial Study of the Leader Behavior Descriptions," in R. M. Stogdill and W. M. Coons (eds.) *Leader Behavior: Its Description and Measurement,* Bureau of Business Research Monog. 88 (Columbus Ohio State University, 1957). This section is also influenced by the formulations of the National Training Laboratories concerning task and maintenance functions in a group. See L. P. Bradford, J. R. Gibb, and K. D. Benne, *T-Group Theory and Laboratory Method* (New York: Wiley, 1964).

[18] Another way of making the division would be (1) technical or content aspects of the job itself; (2) the area of structure—division of labor, who does which parts of (1); (3) the socioemotional problems listed as (*b*) above. However, for simplification of the considerations which follow, our purposes are best served by combining (1) and (2) under the general heading of task problems.

[19] For an enumeration of the forms which these roles may take, see K. D. Benne and P. Sheats, "Functional Roles of Group members," *Journal of Social Issues,* Vol. 4 (1948), pp. 41–60.

have certain task areas defined as being the responsibility of the service person and *not* appropriate for sharing with the client.

Maintenance issues, on the other hand, are oriented more specifically toward the relationship itself and its continuance; that is, these issues most often have to do with tensions that result from either just being together or from trying to do a task. They can be characterized by such questions as: How close or distant are the partners with each other, and how do they want to be? How do members *feel* about each other? How shall hostility and other *disruptive feelings* be handled in the relationship? What effect will *transference* phenomena (reacting to the partner in terms of people in earlier relationships) have on the relationship? How will *evaluations* of one another be handled?[20]

For each of these two sets of problems the basic process for solution is one of *information transaction* between the parties. The basic idea is that task and maintenance functions are accomplished through a *feedback* process where information is exchanged concerning the state of the task, the relationship, or the individuals involved.[21] This exchange serves both to change these states and to trigger other kinds of action which change the system. For instance, if one partner in a relationship tells the other that he dislikes having to do all the detail work, this might then create a situation where the *distribution* of work may be rearranged to be more satisfactory to both parties or more realistic in terms of abilities. Task performance might improve as a result of this process. Then information must be exchanged again, and the general process is repeated.[22]

These transactions may be verbal, such as the sharing of ideas or personal feelings at a particular moment, or they may be nonverbal, such as actual physical action that is taken. The transactions may also be *intended*, as when one party to the relationship tells the other that they might be able to accomplish more if they divided up the work, or they may be *unintended*, as when the same statement about work division is made and the listener gets two other messages that the sender is unaware he is transmitting—(*a*) that the sender does not trust the listener in certain work areas and (*b*) that he does not feel that he can discuss it openly with the listener, for whatever reasons.

RELATIONSHIP BETWEEN TASK AND MAINTENANCE PROBLEMS

There are many ways in which task operations affect maintenance of the relationship. *First*, decisions and arrangements concerning the power distribution

---

[20] For a view of this area which is not limited to the instrumental relationship, see the essay on "Emotional Modalities" which introduces Part I of this volume. See also Henry C. Smith, *Sensitivity to People* (New York: McGraw-Hill, 1966).

[21] For a fuller description of this feedback process and one author's view of the effect that it can have on an instrumental relationship, see Chris Argyris, *Interpersonal Competence and Organizational Effectiveness* (Homewood, Ill.: Richard D. Irwin, 1962), especially pp. 38–54.

[22] Related to this feedback process, but more general, is the function of *reality testing* which may be performed by these information transactions between parties to a relationship. See the essay which introduces Part V of this volume.

may strongly affect both parties if (*a*) the one with less power feels hostile toward the one with more power, or (*b*) if either has less commitment because of the unequal distribution, or (*c*) if it is equally distributed and one party feels ambivalent about this because of his previous relationships, which have all been unbalanced.[23] *Second,* decisions, ideas, plans, etc., and the process by which they are produced will affect the participants' evaluations of one another, and these impressions will affect each's feelings about the other and his own feelings about and perception of himself in the situation.[24]

Third, just general interaction and contact in performance of a task may tend to increase the participant's feelings for one another as a result of a continuing increase in information held about each other.[25] *Fourth,* the giving or receiving of help on a particular task may affect one's sense of self-esteem, the status that one confers on the other, and one's desire to continue in the relationship.[26] *Finally,* the general trustworthiness which one exhibits in working on the task may have a strong effect on the other's perception of him as trustworthy in other areas of the relationship.[27]

There may be points where task and maintenance considerations come into conflict. It may be necessary because of time limitations to overemphasize completion of the task, even to the detriment of the relationship itself. This is especially likely if the relationship must meet some external standard such as showing a profit.[28] Or it may be necessary to discuss maintenance in order to break out of a situation which has become locked on one task element which will remain unproductive, as when an argument over appropriate meeting times must be considered in terms of the influence or control each party is exerting before a final decision can be made. In this case a maintenance problem is blocking progress and must be dealt with, even if it is an apparent digression from work on the schedule.

In the other direction, as well as helping loosen a persistent problem situation,

---

[23] It should be pointed out here that although the question of power and influence distribution is not emphasized in this essay, it is a major concern of many writers who have developed normative theories of organization. See such writers as C. Argyris, *Integrating the Individual and the Organization* (New York: John Wiley, 1964); R. Likert, *New Patterns of Management* (New York: McGraw-Hill Book Co., 1961); and *The Human Organization* (New York: McGraw-Hill, 1967); D. McGregor, *The Human Side of Enterprise* (New York: McGraw-Hill Book Co., 1960); and the synthesizing article by W. G. Bennis, "Leadership Theory and Administrative Behavior: The Problem of Authority," *Administrative Science Quarterly,* Vol. 4 (1959), pp. 260–301.

[24] For a broader perspective on this view, see the classics by C. H. Cooley, *Human Nature and the Social Order* (New York: Scribner, 1902) and G. H. Mead, *Mind, Self and Society* (Chicago: University of Chicago Press, 1935).

[25] G. C. Homans, *The Human Group* (New York: Harcourt, Brace, 1950).

[26] See Homans' article in this Part.

[27] For an experimental analysis of trust as a variable in the relationship, see M. Deutsch, "Cooperation and Trust, *Interpersonal Dynamics,* 1st ed."

[28] There is a trap here, however. The relationship may be ignored in order to meet some external standard in the short run, and the resulting deterioration in the state of the relationship may then cause failure of task performance in the long run. See Likert's (*New Patterns*) analysis of the differences in how this problem is handled by effective and ineffective leaders of work groups.

discussion of the relationship may drive out all task considerations and contribute to anxiety-motivated flight from the task at hand.[29] This would be exemplified by the case of a partnership that spent all its time talking, for instance, about the effects the partners had on one another, thereby preventing them from making any decisions or producing anything. The motive here would generally be an avoidance of the possibility of making mistakes or failing in some task situation.[30]

Implied but not explicitly stated above is the notion that the conflict between task and maintenance may be reduced by a higher-order maintenance element: a commitment or climate in the relationship which allows a free and open interchange about the *state* of a relationship and how the task and maintenance functions themselves are being performed. This climate allows the relationship and its parties to learn from their experience and grow toward more effective attainment of their goals since this type of information transaction determines in part the effectiveness of transactions in both of the basic problem areas.[31]

DEALING WITH TASK AND MAINTENANCE PROBLEMS IN THE DIFFERENT TYPES OF RELATIONSHIPS

In this section, we would like to make some predictions about tendencies toward effective information sharing about task and maintenance issues in the four types of relationships described above. These tendencies would be a factor in whether the relationship would be productive and/or would continue.

a) Friendly cooperation. The tendency here would be toward being able to deal with both task and maintenance issues as they are appropriate. The friendly (high trust) orientation would promote the taking of risk as far as raising tawdry or difficult issues is concerned,[32] and the cooperative orientation would provide a basic motivation—wanting to do better as a team—which could be related in the partner's minds to a striving and sharing together (about the task) rather than separately.

b) Antagonistic competition. In this case, the tendency would be toward low willingness to deal with both maintenance and task issues. The low trust level would make risk taking more difficult, and the open competition would orient the persons toward not dealing with task issues, since any information shared

---

[29] M. S. Olmstead, "Orientation and Role in the Small Group," *American Sociological Review*, Vol. 19 (December 1954), pp. 741–51.

[30] Although exclusive focus on maintenance may also be motivated by a general hunger for closer, more involving relationships than are characteristic of our society today, this hunger would account for part of the rapid growth in T-group activity since its inception in 1947. See Bradford, Gibb, and Benne, *T-Group Theory.*

[31] This implication may be seen as moving toward normative theory and away from description. See again the essay on "Towards Better Interpersonal Relationships" which introduces Part V of this volume.

[32] See Argyris' article in this Part.

might help the other and consequently hurt one's self. Information that is shared is often calculated to mislead or distort, thus pushing the two persons (or groups, or nations) father apart.[33]

   c) Friendly competition.   In this instance, the basically positive orientation toward one another would promote dealing with maintenance issues. However, talking about the task would be more questionable, since the competitive situation again means that information sharing might mean a lost advantage. Individuals would probably experience some conflict over how to proceed on the task and would be drawn toward seeking out "safe" moments when the task can be talked about without hurting one's own position—such as professional football players on opposing teams discussing crucial plays *after* the game or at the *end* of a season. The competitive element makes it hard for them to change what they are doing *in process.*

   d) Antagonistic cooperation.   In this other mixed case, dealing with maintenance would tend to be low owing to negative feelings and mistrust (poor climate for risk taking), and dealing with the task would probably be moderate. There is a pull toward task discussions because of the partners' interdependence, but this pull could "run down" over time as untended maintenance problems build up. Motivation toward the task goal could become less potent than desires to get out of the relationship or to protect one's self from the other person. Unsatisfactory superior-subordinate relationships often fit this pattern.

   By way of summarizing these predictions, we should note one striking pattern: There is a clear trend toward "the rich get richer and the poor get poorer."[34] In Friendly Cooperation, where tensions and difficulties would tend to be lower than the other three, the tendencies are toward freer discussion of both task and maintenance. Conversely, in Antagonistic Cooperation, for instance, a good deal of tension is generated by the process of working together, and the situation is loaded against dealing with it, thus allowing the problems to build, making it still more difficult to share information and so on.

   From this view, we can see why in recent years a good deal of interest has been generated in the process of helping a relationship through a third party (consultant, counselor, etc.).[35] An "outsider" can often observe patterns and can communicate information that is too risky for the partners to raise. This sharing may provide them with a view of reality that they can use to break out of their downward spiral. Third-party help often occurs in the context of a larger process of organizational improvement or "organization development."

---

[33] See Blake's article on intergroup competition in this part.

[34] This point was clarified through a discussion with Tim Hall.

[35] See R. Beckhard, "The Confrontation Meeting," *Harvard Business Review,* Vol. *45,* No. 2 (March–April 1967); R. R. Blake, Jane S. Mouton and R. L. Sloma, "The Union-Management Intergroup Laboratory," *Journal of Applied Behavioral Science,* Vol. 1, No. 1 (Spring 1965); F. I. Steele, "Consultants and Detectives," *Journal of Applied Behavioral Science;* Vol. 5, No. 2 (1969); R. W. Walton, *Third-Party Consultation* (Reading, Mass.: Addison-Wesley, 1969).

THE ORGANIZATION DEVELOPMENT PROCESS

In the last ten years, a growth in concern for more systematic integration of task and maintenance work in organizations has led to the birth of a new area in the applied behavioral sciences: organization development, or OD, as it is now called. The fundamental assumption behind OD is that organizations need a regular, natural process of self-correction and self-renewal in order to promote an effective use of internal resources and an adaptive relationship with the surrounding environment.

Although OD is often discussed in programmatic terms, it is first and foremost a *process*—a process of planned change whose emphasis varies as situations and problems change, but whose major purpose remains the promotion of changes which help the system's members use their resources more fully. The process of improvement is a continuous one, and it implies a more positive direction of growth than does the term "maintenance" which we used above (although we do intend for this term to imply the development of the potential of a relationship, not just a holding to a particular level of competence or intimacy).

The roots of the OD process are deep in the behavioral sciences.[36] Many of the early OD practitioners (Richard Beckhard, Edgar Schein, Robert Blake and Jane Mouton, Warner Burke, Sheldon Davis, etc.) were involved in the laboratory method of experienced-based education. Although OD still retains laboratory training methods for many activities (e.g., team building sessions or problem-confrontation meetings), the process has expanded far beyond the interpersonal sphere. It now includes such change targets as authority structures, sociotechnical systems, physical settings, and relations between a system and its environment.[37]

Even with this expansion, however, interpersonal work relationships are a central focus in OD work today, both as a tool for change and as an outcome of the OD process. Building better work relationships permits more disclosure and freer problem solving in an atmosphere of trust. This freedom of action facilitates more systematic handling of such organizational issues as the need for more responsive decision structures. In the other direction, changes in structure, technology, or physical settings can result in improved working relationships with less energy being drained off in unnecessary stress from conflicting expectations and demands.

This two-way influence process illustrates the most important lesson to be learned from the OD process: interpersonal relationships in organizations are one subsystem of the total set of factors that, taken together, result in work experiences that range from efficient and satisfying to inefficient and frustrating. Attempts to change work relationships without attention being paid to supporting

---

[36] A good overview of the history of OD and its varieties in practice can be obtained through the Addison-Wesley "Series in Organization Development," which published a six book set in 1969 and a three book set in 1973.

[37] For a quick survey of these approaches, see Harvey Hornstein, Barbara B. Bunker, W. Warner Burke, Marion Gindes, and Roy Lewicki (eds.), *Social Intervention: A Behavioral Science Approach* (New York: The Free Press, 1971).

variables, such as structure or reward systems, are likely to be neutralized by the system. Conversely, attempts to change structural variables without accompanying development of the relational skills needed by members to carry out the changes are likely falter through incomplete applications and half-trials. An effective OD process works at a number of levels, and tries to build continuous processes which integrate interpersonal experiences with the settings in which they take place.

THE CREATIVE RELATIONSHIP

Let us now consider a special case—that of the *creative* relationship. By a creative relationship we mean a relationship whose main expected product is some new, unusual, original combination of elements that is found to be useful by some group at some time.[38] The output can involve music, drama, painting, sculpture, and other visual art forms; architectural products combining form and function; ingenious solutions to business-related problems; new experiences in an affective relationship; new solutions to pressing problems of international cooperation and interaction[39] advances in scientific knowledge, theory, organizations of concepts, and so on.

From this list it can be seen that this "type" of relationship really cuts across many of the categories found in this book and may exist simultaneously in any of them at a given time. The reason for its inclusion in this section is that there is a *product* of some sort involved. It is, however, the *creative* aspect of this product that is of importance at this point. At the same time we do not mean to deny the fact that the instrumental aspects of a relationship may have a marked effect on the creative output of the relationship. This effect is interestingly demonstrated in an article by Becker,[40] who analyzes the role of the professional dance musician. In it he illustrates vividly the tensions of dance musicians, who resent the fact that they are forced to satisfy the requirements of an instrumental relationship with their audience because the audience response determines the economic criterion of success or failure. The musicians feel that the need to satisfy an audience prevents development of a creative relationship with that audience and severely handicaps them in their efforts to be creative, spontaneous artists with expressional integrity.

Background

By and large, the interpersonal aspects of creativity have been neglected in social science[41] and even in the humanities. Even for those who have been

---

[38] M. I. Stein, "Creativity and Culture," *Journal of Psychology,* Vol. 36 (1953), pp. 311–22.

[39] See Blake's article in this Part.

[40] Included in the two previous editions of this book.

[41] For an illustration of the scope of work in the general area of creativity, see the bibliographic collection by M. I. Stein and S. J. Heinze, *Creativity and the Individual* (Chicago: Graduate School of Business, University of Chicago, and Glencoe, Ill.: Free Press, 1960).

students of this area, the issue that has preoccupied most of them has been group versus individual problem solving, with no clear-cut evidence emerging that would be of general application to different kinds of groups and situations.[42]

The same formulation of the issue has pervaded areas other than the academic. The technique of "brainstorming" grew up in the American business world as an effort to stimulate creativity, especially in the pursuit of advertising themes. Then Taylor and his associates did their well-known experiment on brainstorming versus individual idea-production. Some real doubt was cast upon the efficacy of the group-creation process with the finding that ad hoc groups of individuals whose ideas were pooled *after the fact* did better than the real groups whose members interacted with one another.[43]

In general, this result confirms the belief of those whose basic orientation toward creativity is that it must be an individual phenomenon. For example, C. P. Snow, in summing up his point of view on science and its values in *The Search,* has Fane say, with regard to the proposed concept of a *team* to do the research in a new institute, that "I'm inclined to think we want more individuals in research, not less . . . I don't believe very much in these teams of yours for solving problems . . . and even if I did, I think I'd prefer that a few things in life were left to the individual man."[44]

With a few exceptions, psychoanalysts have also tended to ignore the interpersonal aspects of creativity. Ernest Schachtel is one of the exceptions, but he, too, emphasizes the inhibitory side of interpersonal relations. He illuminates quite effectively what he feels are the interpersonal sources of man's blocks to experiencing in actual terms that which happens to and around him.[45] His thesis is that as people grow and are socialized into the ways of their society, they begin to experience phenomena in terms of the categories which they are taught. Subsequently they do not nesessarily experience phenomena in ways which are most appropriate for the reality inself. Schachtel sees this socialization as a source of stereotyped or rigidly structured cognitions denying the experiential process. This leads to an attenuation of fresh ideas, phenomena, and concepts available to man.

His most striking point is a description of how people experience events in categories or terms which they anticipate will best serve to describe the event or experience to others and in terms which are most appropriate for themselves in the actual situation.

Even when Schachtel mentions the relationship with the psychoanalyst as one way to break down certain of the systematized schemata that have been built

---

[42] I. Lorge, D. Fox, J. Davitz, and M. Brenner, "A Survey of Studies Contrasting the Quality of Group Performance and Individual Performance," *Psych. Bulletin,* Vol 55, No. 5 (1958), p. 337.

[43] D. W. Taylor, P. C. Berry, and C. H. Block, "Does Group Participation When Using Brainstorming Facilitate or Inhibit Creative Thinking?" *Administrative Science Quarterly,* Vol. 3 (1958), pp. 23–47.

[44] C. P. Snow, *The Search* (New York: Charles Scribner's Sons, 1958), p. 226.

[45] E. G. Schachtel, "On Memory and Childhood Amnesia," in P. Mullahy (ed.), *A Study of Interpersonal Relations* (New York: Hermitage Press, 1949).

up by people to view their world, he merely mentions it in passing but does not deal with the actual aspects of the relationship that might help in this process.

In a *New Yorker* profile[46] the reporter wrote about Yang and Lee, the two Nobel Prize winning physicists who have produced some good results while working as a team. Yet in the process no investigation was made into the elements or factors which made this relationship a creative one. The author's only note on the relationship itself was that it was "unusual" for two physicists to work closely together and to produce results such as theirs. Wilson's article on the Strayhorn-Ellington relationship (in the second edition of this book) is better in this regard, but still a far cry from an in-depth analysis of what really makes the difference in creative relationship.

One gets the general feeling in each of these examples, as in many others that could be presented, that creativity is viewed as being of necessity an individual process, and, therefore, a relationship has no relevance to it; or if it does, it is one of inhibition only. An essay by Gardner Murphy[47] is one counter to this orientation—although in very general terms. It is his thesis that not only is a relationship not necessarily antithetical to the creative process, but that it may be vital to creativity, given the nature of our rapidly changing society. From this he concludes that man's real task may be to deal with the reality of the existence of interpersonal relationships rather than to reject or deny that they have any part in the creative process.

Henry Murray, in an article entitled "Unprecedented Evolutions,"[48] also calls for a new look at the possibilities for creative relationships, especially with respect to the kinds of international problems which threaten the very continuation of life itself on this planet. It is his view that the solutions to these kinds of problems may in fact be the result of creative "synthesism" or combination of diverse points of view in relationships.

What is the creative process itself?

For the moment, let us consider one model of the creative process, that presented by Henry Murray.[49] He distinguishes what he considers to be the four necessary conditions for creativity: (*a*) the circulation of combinable entities; (*b*) permeable boundaries between categories, spheres of interest, the conscious and the unconscious, etc.; (*c*) periodic decompositions—de-differentiations and disintegrations (or reexaminations of what has already been done—and discarding if necessary); and (*d*) favorable conditions for new combinations.

---

[46] *New Yorker Magazine*, "Profiles," May 12, 1962.

[47] Gardner Murphy, "Creativeness in Our Own Era," *Human Potentialities* (New York: Basic Books, Inc., 1958). Chap. x.

[48] Henry Murray, "Unprecedented Evolutions," *Daedalus*, Vol. 90, No. 3 (1961).

[49] H. Murray, "Vicissitudes of Creativity," In H. H. Anderson (ed.), *Creativity and Its Cultivation*, Interdisciplinary Symposia of Creativity, Michigan State University, 1957–58 (New York: Harper & Bros.; 1959), pp. 110–18.

In general, the process seems to be that of "mixing it up," or of having as wide as possible a conception on the part of those involved of the alternatives available or potentially available, plus favorable conditions for becoming aware of new "paths" even after having traveled part way down one that originally appeared to be fruitful.

Effects of interpersonal relationships on the creative process

The kinds of processes that we have described above as being most relevant to creativity include experimentation, innovation, regeneration, risk taking, starting over, questioning of assumptions, relief from anxiety, etc. What is the relationship between these processes and interpersonal phenomena? In general, most of these processes would seem to vary with the strength of *perceived threat* in different situations. More specifically, creative processes would be undermined in situations where anxiety is aroused concerning loss of one's status, inclusion in the relationship, or basic welf-worth and sense of self-esteem. When these kinds of threats are perceived, then internally or externally produced alternatives (relating to a particular problem *or* to a more general style of operation) are reduced, often with no awareness on the part of the individual that this limiting has taken place.[50]

For the relationship to facilitate creativity, therefore, a climate must be created which reduces perceived threat and makes creativity the norm.[51] However, when creativity becomes the only acceptable product, new anxiety will be generated in the participants over their relative status or sense of self-worth if they are not able to be creative 100 percent of the time. This new anxiety may again limit alternatives. To avoid this new anxiety the relationship must develop a climate of mutual support and reduced competitiveness.

Thus, the two necessary elements of a creative relationship appear to be (*a*) appropriate norms toward creativity and innovation *plus* (*b*) a shared feeling of acceptance of the individual as an individual in the relationship.[52] This acceptance should include a willingness to allow and help him to be himself in the relationship, to grow as a result of it, and to make the most of his experiences as they occur for him. There is good evidence that for most creative people, such as Darwin or Freud, there is a small but strong reference group supporting them, even in the face of much larger opposition from the total society.

These are not the only variables relevant to a creative relationship. The interpersonal competence of the individual members may allow a broader spectrum of thought and action to come into play in combination than either member had by himself. Individual differences are also important in determining the

---

[50] See Schachtel's discussion of "childhood amnesia," "On Memory."

[51] See W. J. J. Gordon, *Synectics: The Development of Creative Capacity* (New York: Harper & Bros., 1961).

[52] Carl Rogers, "The Characteristics of a Helping Relationship," *On Becoming a Person* (Boston: Houghton Mifflin, 1961).

extent to which this kind of climate effectively releases these potential abilities. An individual who is immobilized by the mere presence of others, regardless of the immediate atmosphere that his partner attempts to foster, may be quite inappropriate for collaborative creative endeavors, and should be recognized as such. This does not rule out the possibility of the relationship serving as a change environment in which such an individual can express himself more freely, thereby allowing a more creative output, which in turn may further free him from former inhibitions. The question of how this circular process can be initiated is beyond the scope of this paper, but satisfactions coming from relating per se early in the relationship may be a crucial element here.

THE READINGS

The readings that follow illustrate both this essay's concepts and many others related to work relationships. Homans provides a general framework for interpersonal transactions and their development over time in the work setting. Roy describes a participant-observation study of the manner in which relationships and play can offset some of the negative aspects of boring, repetitive tasks. Davis analyzes the alienation resulting from the short time-structure of the service provided by cabdrivers.

Blake's reading confronts the major problem area of intergroup relations, considering both sources of difficulty and strategies for improving relations between groups. Steele discusses the impact of the physical setting on social interaction at work, while Argyris provides numerous examples of the way in which interpersonal values and resultant behavioral styles can influence the climate and performance of an executive group.

In the area of organization development, Harrison presents a model for the negotiation of a shared set of role expectations between members of a work relationship, and Sherwood and Glidewell indicate a process by which this negotiation can be made a recurring part of organizational life. On the creative relationship, Gibb analyzes those features of the interpersonal climate that support or block experimentation and risk-taking.

Social behavior as exchange*

George C. Homans

THE PROBLEMS OF SMALL-GROUP RESEARCH

This essay will hope to honor the memory of Georg Simmel in two different ways. So far as it pretends to be suggestive rather than conclusive, its tone will be Simmel's; and its subject, too, will be one of his. Because Simmel, in essays such as those on sociabilty, games, coquetry, and conversation, was an analyst of elementary social behavior, we call him an ancestor of what is known today as small-group research. For what we are really studying in small groups is elementary social behavior: what happens when two or three persons are in a position to influence one another, the sort of thing of which those massive structures called "classes," "firms," "communities," and "societies" must ultimately be composed.

As I survey small-group research today, I feel that, apart from just keeping on with it, three sorts of things need to be done. The first is to show the relation between the results of experimental work done under laboratory conditions and the results of quasi-anthropological field research on what those of us who do it are pleased to call "real-life" groups in industry and elsewhere. If the experimental work has anything to do with real life—and I am persuaded that it has everything to do—its propositions cannot be inconsistent with those discovered through the field work. But the consistency has not yet been demonstrated in any systematic way.

The second job is to pull together in some set of general propositions the actual results, from the laboratory and from the field, of work on small groups—propositions that at least sum up, to an approximation, what happens in elementary social behavior, even though we may not be able to explain why the propositions should take the form they do. A great amount of work has been done, and more appears every day, but what it all amounts to in the shape of a set of propositions from

* Reprinted in its entirety from George C. Homans, "Social Behavior as Exchange," *American Journal of Sociology*, Vol. 63, No. 6 (May, 1958), pp. 597–606. The University of Chicago Press, used by permission.

which, under specified conditions, many of the observational results might be derived, is not at all clear—and yet to state such a set is the first aim of science.

The third job is to begin to show how the propositions that empirically hold good in small groups may be derived from some set of still more general propositions. "Still more general" means only that empirical propositoins other than ours may also be derived from the set. This derivation would constitute the explanatory stage in the science of elementary social behavior, for explanation *is* derivation.[1] (I myself suspect that the more general set will turn out to contain the propositions of behavioral psychology. I hold myself to be an "ultimate psychological reductionist," but I cannot know that I am right so long as the reduction has not been carried out.)

I have come to think that all three of these jobs would be furthered by our adopting the view that interaction between persons is an exchange of goods, material and nonmaterial. This is one of the oldest theories of social behavior, and one that we still use every day to interpret our own behavior, as when we say, "I found so-and-so rewarding"; or "I got a great deal out of him"; or, even, "Talking with him took a great deal out of me." But, perhaps just because it is so obvious, this view has been much neglected by social scientists. So far as I know, the only theoretical work that makes explicit use of it is Marcel Mauss's *Essai sur le don*, published in 1925, which is ancient as social science goes.[2] It may be that the tradition of neglect is now changing and that, for instance, the psychologists who interpret behavior in terms of transactions may be coming back to something of the sort I have in mind.[3]

An incidental advantage of an exchange theory is that it might bring sociology closer to economics—that science of man most advanced, most capable of application, and, intellectually, most isolated. Economics studies exchange carried out under special circumstances and with a most useful built-in numerical measure of value. What are laws of the general phenomenon of which economic behavior is one class?

In what follows I shall suggest some reasons for the usefulness of a theory of social behavior as exchange and suggest the nature of the propositions such a theory might contain.

AN EXCHANGE PARADIGM

I start with the link to be behavioral psychology and the kind of statement it makes about the behavior of an experimental animal such as the pigeon.[4] As a pigeon explores its cage in the laboratory it happens to peck a target, whereupon

[1] See R. B. Braithwaite, *Scientific Explanation* (Cambridge: Cambridge University Press, 1953).

[2] Translated by I. Cunnison as *The Gift* (Glencoe, Ill.: Free Press, 1954).

[3] In social anthropology D. L. Oliver is working along these lines, and I owe much to him. See also T. M. Newcomb, "The Prediction of Interpersonal Attraction," *American Psychologist*, XI (1956), 575–86.

[4] B. F. Skinner, *Science and Human Behavior* (New York: Macmillan Co., 1953).

the psychologist feeds it corn. The evidence is that it will peck the target again; it has learned the behavior, or, as my friend Skinner says, the behavior has been reinforced, and the pigeon has undergone *operant conditioning.* This kind of psychologist is not interested in how the behavior was learned: "learning theory" is a poor name for this field. Instead, he is interested in what determines changes in the rate of emission of learned behavior, whether pecks at a target or something else.

The more hungry the pigeon, the less corn or other food it has gotten in the recent past, the more often it will peck. By the same token, if the behavior is often reinforced, if the pigeon is given much corn every time it pecks, the rate of emission will fall off as the pigeon gets *satiated.* If, on the other hand, the behavior is not reinforced at all, then, too, its rate of emission will tend to fall off, though a long time may pass before it stops altogether, before it is *extinguished.* In the emission of many kinds of behavior the pigeon incurs *aversive stimulation,* or what I shall call "cost" for short, and this, too, will lead in time to a decrease in the emission rate. Fatigue is an example of a "cost." Extinction, satiation, and cost, by decreasing the rate of emission of a particular kind of behavior, render more probable the emission of some other kind of behavior, including doing nothing. I shall only add that even a hard-boiled psychologist puts "emotional" behavior, as well as such things as pecking, among the unconditioned responses that may be reinforced in operant conditioning. As a statement of the propositions of behavioral psychology, the foregoing is, of course, inadequate for any purpose except my present one.

We may look on the pigeon as engaged in an exchange—pecks for corn—with the psychologist, but let us not dwell upon that, for the behavior of the pigeon hardly determines the behavior of the psychologist at all. Let us turn to a situation where the exchange is real, that is, where the determination is mutual. Suppose we are dealing with two men. Each is emitting behavior reinforced to some degree by the behavior of the other. How it was in the past that each learned the behavior he emits and how he learned to find the other's behavior reinforcing we are not concerned with. It is enough that each does find the other's behavior reinforcing, and I shall call the reinforcers—the equivalent of the pigeon's corn— *values,* for this, I think, is what we mean by this term. As he emits behavior, each man may incur costs, and each man has more than one course of behavior open to him.

This seems to me the paradigm of elementary social behavior, and the problem of the elementary sociologist is to state propositions relating the variations in the values and costs of each man to his frequency distribution of behavior among alternatives, where the values (in the mathematical sense) taken by these variables for one man determine in part their values for the other.[5]

I see no reason to believe that the propositions of behavioral psychology do

---

[5] *Ibid.,* pp. 297–329. The discussion of "double contingency" by T. Parsons and E. A. Shils could easily lead to a similar paradigm (see *Toward a General Theory of Action* [Cambridge, Mass.: Harvard University Press, 1951], pp. 14–16).

not apply to this situation, though the complexity of their implications in the concrete case may be great indeed. In particular, we must suppose that, with men as with pigeons, an increase in extinction, satiation, or aversive stimulation of any one kind of behavior will increase the probability of emission of some other kind. The problem is not, as it is often stated, merely what a man's values are, what he has learned in the past to find reinforcing, but how much of any one value his behavior is getting him now. The more he gets, the less valuable any further unit of that value is to him, and the less often he will emit behavior reinforced by it.

THE INFLUENCE PROCESS

We do not, I think, possess the kind of studies of two-person interaction that would bear out these propositions or fail to do so. But we do have studies of larger numbers of persons that suggest that they may apply, notably the studies by Festinger, Schachter, Back, and their associates on the dynamics of influence. One of the variables they work with they call *cohesiveness*, defined as anything that attracts people to take part in a group. Cohesiveness is a value variable; it refers to the degree of reinforcement people find in the activities of the group. Festinger and his colleagues consider two kinds of reinforcing activity: the symbolic behavior we call "social approval" (sentiment), and activity valuable in other ways, such as doing something interesting.

The other variable they work with they call *communication* and others call *interaction*. This is a frequency variable; it is a measure of the frequency of emission of valuable and costly verbal behavior. We must bear in mind that, in general, in one kind of variable is a function of the other.

Festinger and his co-workers show that the more cohesive a group is, that is, the more valuable the sentiment or activity the members exchange with one another, the greater the average frequency of interaction of the members.[6] With men, as with pigeons, the greater the reinforcement, the more often is the reinforced behavior emitted. The more cohesive a group, too, the greater the change that members can produce in the behavior of other members in the direction of rendering these activities more valuable.[7] That is, the more valuable the activities that members get, the more valuable those that they must give. For if a person is emitting behavior of a certain kind, and other people do not find it particularly rewarding, these others will suffer their own production of sentiment and activity, in time, to fall off. But perhaps the first person has found their sentiment and activity rewarding, and, if he is to keep on getting them, he must make his own behavior more valuable to others. In short, the propositions

[6] K. W. Back, "The Exertion of Influence through Social Communication," in L. Festinger, K. Back, S. Schachter, H. H. Kelley, and J. Thibaut (eds.), *Theory and Experiment in Social Communication* (Ann Arbor: Research Center for Dynamics, University of Michigan, 1950), pp. 21–36.

[7] S. Schachter, N. Ellerston, D. McBride, and D. Gregory, "An Experimental Study of Cohesiveness and Productivity," *Human Relations*, IV (1951), pp. 229–38.

of behavioral psychology imply a tendency toward a certain proportionality between the value to others of the behavior a man gives them and the value to him of the behavior they give him.[8]

Schachter also studied the behavior of members of a group toward two kinds of other members, "conformers" and "deviates."[9] I assume that conformers are people whose activity the other members find valuable. For conformity is behavior that coincides to a degree with some group standard or norm, and the only meaning I can assign to *norm* is "a verbal description of behavior that many members find it valuable for the actual behavior of themselves and others to conform to." By the same token, a deviate is a member whose behavior is not particularly valuable. Now Schachter shows that, as the members of a group come to see another member as a deviate, their interaction with him—communication addressed to getting him to change his behavior—goes up, the faster the more cohesive the group. The members need not talk to the other conformers so much; they are relatively satiated by the conformers' behavior: they have gotten what they want out of them. But if the deviate, by failing to change his behavior, fails to reinforce the members, they start to withhold social approval from him: the deviate gets low sociometric choice at the end of the experiment. And in the most cohesive groups—those Schachter calls "high cohesive-relevant"—interaction with the deviate also falls off in the end and is lowest among those members that rejected him most strongly, as if they had given him up as a bad job. But how plonking can we get? These findings are utterly in line with everyday experience.

PRACTICAL EQUILIBRIUM

At the beginning of this paper I suggested that one of the tasks of small-group research was to show the relation betweek the results of experimental work done under laboratory conditions and the results of field research on real-life small groups. Now the latter often appear to be in practical equilibrium, and by this I mean nothing fancy. I do not mean that all real-life groups are in equilibrium. I certainly do not mean that all groups must tend to equilibrium. I do not mean that groups have built-in antidotes to change: there is no homeostasis here. I do not mean that we assume equilibrium. I mean only that we sometimes *observe* it, that for the time we are with a group—and it is often short—there is no great change in the values of the variables we choose to measure. If, for instance, person A is interacting with B more than with C both at the beginning and at the end of the study, then at least by this crude measure the group is in equilibrium.

Many of the Festinger-Schachter studies are experimental, and their propositions about the process of influence seem to me to imply the kind of proposition

---

[8] Skinner, *Science and Human Behavior*, p. 100.

[9] Schachter, "Deviation, Rejection, and Communication," *Journal of Abnormal and Social Psychology*, XLVI (1951), pp. 190–207.

that empirically holds good of real-life groups in practical equilibruim. For instance, Festinger et al. find that, the more cohesive a group is, the greater the change that members can produce in the behavior of other members. If the influence is exerted in the direction of conformity to group norms, then, when the process of influence has accomplished all the change of which it is capable, the proposition should hold good that, the more cohesive a group is, the larger the number of members that conform to its norms. And it does hold good.[10]

Again, Schachter found, in the experiment I summarized above, that in the most cohesive groups and at the end, when the effort to influence the deviate failed, members interacted little with the deviate and gave him little in the way of sociometric choice. Now two of the propositions that hold good most often of real-life groups in practical equilibrium are precisely that the more closely a member's activity conforms to the norms the more interaction he receives from other members and the more liking choices he gets from them too. From these main propositions a number of others may be derived that also hold good.[11]

Yet we must ever remember that the truth of the proposition linking conformity to liking may on occasion be masked by the truth of other propositions. If, for instance, the man that conforms to the norms most closely also exerts some authority over the group, this may render liking for him somewhat less than it might otherwise have been.[12]

Be that as it may, I suggest that the laboratory experiments on influence imply propositions about the behavior of members of small groups, when the process of influence has worked itself out, that are identical with propositions that hold good of real-life groups in equilibrium. This is hardly surprising if all we mean by equilibrium is that all the change of which the system is, under present conditions, capable has been effected, so that no further change occurs. Nor would this be the first time that statics has turned out to be a special case of dynamics.

PROFIT AND SOCIAL CONTROL

Though I have treated equilibrium as an observed fact, it is a fact that cries for explanation. I shall not, as structural-functional sociologists do, use an assumed equilibrium as a means of explaining, or trying to explain, why the other features of a social system should be what they are. Rather, I shall take practical

---

[10] L. Festinger, S. Schachter, and K. Back, *Social Pressures in Informal Groups* (New York: Harper & Bros., 1950), pp. 72–100.

[11] For propositions holding good of groups in practical equilibrium see G. C. Homans, *The Human Group* (New York: Harcourt, Brace & Co., 1950), and H. W. Riecken and G. C. Homans, "Psychological Aspects of Social Structure," in G. Lindzey (ed.), *Handbook of Social Psychology* (Cambridge, Mass.: Addison-Wesley Publishing Co., 1954), II, pp. 786–832.

[12] See Homans, *Human Group*, pp. 244–48, and R. F. Bales, "The Equilibrium Problem in Small Groups," in A. P. Hare, E. F. Borgatta, and R. F. Bales (eds.) *Small Groups* (New York: A. A. Knopf, 1953), pp. 450–56.

equilibrium as something that is itself to be explained by the other features of the system.

If every member of a group emits at the end of, and during, a period of time much the same kinds of behavior and in much the same frequencies as he did at the beginning, the group is for that period in equilibrium. Let us then ask why any one member's behavior should persist. Suppose he is emitting behavior of value A_1. Why does he not let his behavior get worse (less valuable or reinforcing to the others) until it stands at $A_1 - \Delta A$? True, the sentiments expressed by others toward him are apt to decline in value (become less reinforcing to him), so that what he gets from them may be $S_1 - \Delta S$. But it is conceivable that, since most activity carries cost, a decline in the value of what he emits will mean a reduction in cost to him that more than offsets his losses in sentiment. Where, then, does he stablize his behavior? This is the problem of social control.[13]

Mankind has always assumed that a person stabilizes his behavior, at least in the short run, at the point where he is doing the best he can for himself under the circumstances, though his best may not be a "rational" best, and what he can do may not be at all easy to specify, except that he is not apt to think like one of the theoretical antagonists in the *Theory of Games*. Before a sociologist rejects this answer out of hand for its horrid profit-seeking implications, he will do well to ask himself if he can offer any other answer to the question posed. I think he will find that he cannot. Yet experiments designed to test the truth of the answer are extraordinarily rare.

I shall review one that seems to me to provide a little support for the theory, though it was not meant to do so. The experiment is reported by H. B. Gerard, a member of the Festinger-Schachter team, under the title "The Anchorage of Opinions in Face-to-Face Groups."[14] The experimenter formed artificial groups whose members met to discuss a case in industrial relations and to express their opinions about its probable outcome. The groups were of two kinds: high-attraction groups, whose members were told that they would like one another very much, and low-attraction groups, whose members were told that they would not find one another particularly likable.

At a later time the experimenter called the members in separately, asked them again to express their opinions on the outcome of the case, and counted the number that had changed their opinions to bring them into accord with those of other members of their groups. At the same time, a paid participant entered into a further discussion of the case with each member, always taking, on the probable outcome of the case, a position opposed to that taken by the bulk of the other members of the group to which the person belonged. The experimenter counted the number of persons shifting toward the opinion of the paid participant.

---

[13] Homans, *Human Group*, pp. 281–301.
[14] *Human Relations*, VII (1954), pp. 313–25.

TABLE 1
Percentage of subjects changing toward someone in the group

	Agree-ment	Mild Disagree-ment	Strong Disagree-ment
High attraction.....................	0	12	44
Low attraction.....................	0	15	9

The experiment had many interesting results, from which I choose only those summed up in Tables 1 and 2. The three different agreement classes are made up of people who, at the original sessions, expressed different degrees of agreement with the opinions of other members of their groups. And the figure 44, for instance, means that, of all members of high-attraction groups whose initial opinions were strongly in disagreement with those of other members, 44 percent shifted their opinion later toward that of others.

In these results the experimenter seems to have been interested only in the differences in the sums of the rows, which show that there is more shifting toward the group, and less shifting toward the paid participant, in the high-attraction than in the low-attraction condition. This is in line with a proposition suggested earlier. If you think that the members of a group can give you much—in this case, liking—you are apt to give them much—in this case, a change to an opinion in accordance with their views—or you will not get the liking. And, by the same token, if the group can give you little of value, you will not be ready to give it much of value. Indeed, you may change your opinion so as to depart from agreement even further, to move, that is, toward the view held by the paid participant.

So far so good, but, when I first scanned these tables, I was less struck by the difference between them than by their similarity. The same classes of people in both tables showed much the same relative propensities to change their opinions, no matter whether the change was toward the group or toward the paid participant. We see, for instance, that those who change least are the high-attraction, agreement people and the low-attraction, strong-disagreement ones. And those who change most are the high-attraction, strong-disagreement people and the low-attraction, mild-disagreement ones.

TABLE 2
Percentage of subjects changing toward the paid participant

	Agree-ment	Mild Disagree-ment	Strong Disagree-ment
High attraction.....................	7	13	25
Low attraction.....................	20	38	8

How am I to interpret these particular results? Since the experimenter did not discuss them, I am free to offer my own explanation. The bahavior emitted by the subjects is opinion and changes in opinion. For this behavior they have learned to expect two possible kinds of reinforcement. Agreement with the group gets the subject favorable sentiment (acceptance) from it, and the experiment was designed to give this reinforcement a higher value in the high-attraction condition than in the low-attraction one. The second kind of possible reinforcement is what I shall call the "maintenance of one's personal integrity," which a subject gets by sticking to his own opinion in the face of disagreement with the group. The experimenter does not mention this reward, but I cannot make sense of the results without something much like it. In different degrees for different subjects, depending on their initial positions, these rewards are in competition with one another: they are alternatives. They are not absolutely scarce goods, but some persons cannot get both at once.

Since the rewards are alternatives, let me introduce a familiar assumption from economics—that the cost of a particular course of action is the equivalent of the foregone value of an alternative[15]—and then add the definition: Profit = Reward – Cost.

Now consider the persons in the corresponding cells of the two tables. The behavior of the high-attraction, agreement people gets them much in the way of acceptance by the group, and for it they must give up little in the way of personal integrity, for their views are from the start in accord with those of the group. Their profit is high, and they are not prone to change their behavior. The low-attraction, strong-disagreement people are getting much in integrity, and they are not giving up for it much in valuable acceptance, for they are members of low-attraction groups. Reward less cost is high for them, too, and they change little. The high-attraction, strong-disagreement people are getting much in the way of integrity, but their costs in doing so are high, too, for they are in high-attraction groups and thus foregoing much valuable acceptance by the group. Their profit is low, and they are very apt to change, either toward the group or toward the paid participant, from whom they think, perhaps, they will get some acceptance while maintaining some integrity. The low-attraction, mild-disagreement people do not get much in the way of integrity, for they are only in mild disagreement with the group, but neither are they giving up much in acceptance, for they are members of low-attraction groups. Their rewards are low; their costs are low too, and their profit—the difference between the two—is also low. In their low profit they resemble the high-attraction, strong-disagreement people, and, like them, they are prone to change their opinions, in this case, more toward the paid participant. The subjects in the other two cells, who had medium profits, display medium propensities to change.

If we define profit as reward less cost, and if cost is value foregone, I suggest that we have here some evidence for the proposition that change in behavior

---

[15] G. J. Stigler, *The Theory of Price* (rev. ed.; New York: Macmillan, 1952), p. 99.

is greatest when perceived profit is least. This constitutes no direct demonstration that change in behavior is least when profit is greatest, but if, whenever a man's behavior brought him a balance of reward and cost, he changed his behavior away from what got him, under the circumstances, the less profit, there might well come a time when his behavior would not change further. That is, his behavior would be stabilized, at least for the time being. And, so far as this were true for every member of a group, the group would have a social organization in equilibrium.

I do not say that a member would stabilize his behavior at the point of greatest conceivable profit to himself, because his profit is partly at the mercy of the behavior of others. It is a commonplace that the short-run pursuit of profit by several persons often lands them in positions where all are worse off than they might conceivably be. I do not say that the paths of behavioral change in which a member pursues his profit under the condition that others are pursuing theirs too are easy to describe or predict; and we can readily conceive that in jockeying for position they might never arrive at any equilibrium at all.

DISTRIBUTIVE JUSTICE

Yet practical equilibrium is often observed, and thus some further condition may make its attainment, under some circumstances, more probable than would the individual pursuit of profit left to itself. I can offer evidence for this further condition only in the behavior of subgroups and not in that of individuals. Suppose that there are two subgroups, working close together in a factory, the job of one being somewhat different from that of the other. And suppose that the members of the first complain and say: "We are getting the same pay as they are. We ought to get just a couple of dollars a week more to show that our work is more responsible." When you ask them what they mean by "more responsible," they say that, if they do their work wrong, more damage can result, and so they are under more pressure to take care.[16] Something like this is a common feature of industrial behavior. It is at the heart of disputes not over absolute wages but over wage differentials—indeed, at the heart of disputes over rewards other than wages.

In what kind of proposition may we express observations like these? We may say that wages and responsibility give status in the group, in the sense that a man who takes high responsibility and gets high wages is admired, other things equal. Then, if the members of one group score higher on responsibility than do the members of another, there is a felt need on the part of the first to score higher on pay too. There is a pressure, which shows itself in complaints, to bring the *status factors*, as I have called them, into line with other. If they are in line, a condition of *status congruence* is said to exist. In this condition the workers may

---

[16] G. C. Homans, "Status among Clerical Workers," *Human Organization*, XII (1953), pp. 5–10.

find their jobs dull or irksome, but they will not complain about the relative position of groups.

But there may be a more illuminating way of looking at the matter. In my example I have considered only responsibility and pay, but these may be enough, for they represent the two kinds of thing that come into the problem. Pay is clearly a reward; responsibility may be looked on, less clearly, as a cost. It means constraint and worry—or peace of mind foregone. Then the proposition about status congruence becomes this: If the costs of the members of one group are higher than those of another, distributive justice requires that their rewards should be higher too. But the thing works both ways: If the rewards are higher, the costs should be higher too. This last is the theory of *noblesse oblige*, which we all subscribe to, though we all laugh at it, perhaps because the *noblesse* often fails to *oblige*. To put the matter in terms of profit: though the rewards and costs of two persons or the members of two groups may be different, yet the profits of the two—the excess of reward over cost—should tend to equality. And more than "should." The less-advantaged group will at least try to attain greater equality, as, in the example I have used, the first group tried to increase its profit by increasing its pay.

I have talked of distributive justice. Clearly, this is not the only condition determining the actual distribution of rewards and costs. At the same time, never tell me that notions of justice are not a strong influence on behavior, though we sociologists often neglect them. Distributive justice may be one of the conditions of group equilibrium.

EXCHANGE AND SOCIAL STRUCTURE

I shall end by reviewing almost the only study I am aware of that begins to show in detail how a stable and differentiated social structure in a real-life group might arise out of a process of exchange between members. This is Peter Blau's description of the behavior of sixteen agents in a federal law-enforcement agency.[17]

The agents had the duty of investigating firms and preparing reports on the firms' compliance with the law. Since the reports might lead to legal action against the firms, the agents had to prepare them carefully, in the proper form, and take strict account of the many regulations that might apply. The agents were often in doubt what they should do, and then they were supposed to take the question to their supervisor. This they were reluctant to do, for they naturally believed that thus confessing to him their inability to solve a problem would reflect on their competence, affect the official ratings he made of their work, and so hurt their chances for promotion. So agents often asked other agents for help and advice, and, though this was nominally forbidden, the supervisor usually let it pass.

---

[17] Peter M. Blau, *The Dynamics of Bureaucracy* (Chicago: University of Chicago Press, 1955), pp. 99–116.

Blau ascertained the ratings the supervisor made of the agents, and he also asked the agents to rate one another. The two opinions agreed closely. Fewer agents were regarded as highly competent than were regarded as of middle or low competence; competence, or the ability to solve technical problems, was a fairly scarce good. One or two of the more competent agents would not give help and advice when asked, and so received few interactions and little liking. A man that will not exchange, that will not give you what he has when you need it, will not get from you the only thing you are, in this case, able to give him in return, your regard.

But most of the more competent agents were willing to give help, and of them Blau says:

A consultation can be considered an exchange of values: both participants gain some-thing, and both have to pay a price. The questioning agent is enabled to perform better than he could otherwise have done, without exposing his difficulties to his supervisor. By asking for advice, he implicitly pays his respect to the superior proficiency of his colleague. This acknowledgment of inferiority is the cost of receiving assistance. The consultant gains prestige, in return for which he is willing to devote some time to the consultation and permit it to disrupt his own work. The following remark of an agent illustrates this: "I like giving advice. It's flattering, I suppose, if you feel that others come to you for advice."[18]

Blau goes on to say: "All agents like being consulted, but the value of any one of very many consultations became deflated for experts, and the price they paid in frequent interruptions became inflated."[19] This implies that, the more prestige an agent received, the less was the increment of value of that prestige; the more advice an agent gave, the greater was the increment of cost of that advice, the cost lying precisely in the foregone value of time to do his own work. Blau suggests that something of the same sort was true of an agent who went to a more competent colleague for advice: the more often he went, the more costly to him, in feelings of inferiority, became any further request. "The re-peated admission of his inability to solve his own problems . . . undermined the self-confidence of the worker and his standing in the group."[20]

The result was that the less competent agents went to the more competent ones for help less often than they might have done if the costs of repeated admissions of inferiority had been less high and that, while many agents sought out the few highly competent ones, no single agent sought out the latter much. Had they done so (to look at the exchange from the other side), the costs to the highly competent in interruptions to their own work would have become exorbi-tant. Yet the need of the less competent for help was still not fully satisfied. Under these circumstances they tended to turn for help to agents more nearly like themselves in competence. Though the help they got was not the most

---

[18] *Ibid.*, p. 108.

[19] *Ibid.*, p. 108.

[20] *Ibid.*, p. 109.

valuable, it was of a kind they could themselves return on occasion. With such agents they could exchange help and liking, without the exchange becoming on either side too great a confession of inferiority.

The highly competent agents tended to enter into exchanges, that is, to interact with many others. But, in the more equal exchanges I have just spoken of, less competent agents tended to pair off as partners. That is, they interacted with a smaller number of people, but interacted often with these few. I think I could show why pair relations in these more equal exchanges would be more economical for an agent than a wider distribution of favors. But perhaps I have gone far enough. The final pattern of this social structure was one in which a small number of highly competent agents exchanged advice for prestige with a large number of others less competent and in which the less competent agents exchanged, in pairs and in trios, both help and liking on more nearly equal terms.

Blau shows, then, that a social structure in equilibrium might be the result of a process of exchanging behavior rewarding and costly in different degrees, in which the increment of reward and cost varied with the frequency of the behavior, that is, with the frequency of interaction. Note that the behavior of the agents seems also to have satisfied my second condition of equilibrium: The more competent agents took more responsibility for the work, either their own or others', than did the less competent ones, but they also got more for it in the way of prestige. I suspect that the same kind of explanation could be given for the structure of many "informal" groups.

SUMMARY

The current job of theory in small-group research is to make the connection between experimental and real-life studies, to consolidate the propositions that empirically hold good in the two fields, and to show how these propositions might be derived from a still more general set. One way of doing this job would be to revive and make more rigorous the oldest of theories of social behavior—social behavior as exchange.

Some of the statements of such a theory might be the following. Social behavior is an exchange of goods, material goods but also non-material ones, such as the symbols of approval or prestige. Persons that give much to others try to get much from them, and persons that get much from others are under pressure to give much to them. This process of influence tends to work out at equilibrium to a balance in the exchanges. For a person engaged in exchange, what he gives may be a cost to him, just as what he gets may be a reward, and his behavior changes less as profit, that is, reward less cost, tends to a maximum. Not only does he seek a maximum for himself, but he tries to see to it that no one in his group makes more profit than he does. The cost and the value of what he gives and of what he gets vary with the quantity of what he gives and gets. It is surprising how familiar these propositions are; it is surprising, too, how propositions about the dynamics of exchange can begin to generate the static thing we call "group structure" and, in so doing, generate also some of the propositions about group structure that students of real-life groups have stated.

In our unguarded moments we sociologists find words like "reward" and "cost" slipping into what we say. Human nature will break in upon even our most elaborate theories. But we seldom let it have its way with us and follow up systematically what these words imply.[21] Of all our many "approaches" to social behavior, the one that sees it as an economy is the most neglected, and yet it is the one we use every moment of our lives—except when we write sociology.

"Banana time"—Job satisfaction and informal interaction[*]

Donald F. Roy

This paper undertakes description and exploratory analysis of the social interaction which took place within a small work group of factory machine operatives during a two-month period of participant observation. The factual and ideational materials which it presents lie at an intersection of two lines of research interest and should, in their dual bearing, contribute to both. Since the operatives were engaged in work which involved the repetition of very simple operations over an extra-long workday, six days a week, they were faced with the problem of dealing with a formidable "beast of monotony." Revelation of how the group utilized its resources to combat that "beast" should merit the attention of those who are seeking solution to the practical problem of job satisfaction or employee morale. It should also provide insights for those who are trying to penetrate the mysteries of the small group.

Convergence of these two lines of interest is, of course, no new thing. Among the host of writers and researchers who have suggested connections between "group" and "joy in work" are Walker and Guest, observers of social interaction on the automobile assembly line.[1] They quote assembly-line workers as saying,

---

[21] *The White-Collar Job* (Ann Arbor: Survey Research Center, University of Michigan, 1953), pp. 115–27.

[*] Excerpted from Donald F. Roy, "Banana Time," *Human Organization*, Vol. 18, No. 4 (Winter, 1959–60), pp. 158–168. Used by permission.

[1] Charles R. Walker and Robert H. Guest, *The Man on the Assembly Line* (Cambridge: Harvard University Press, 1952).

"We have a lot of fun and talk all the time,"[2] and, "If it weren't for the talking and fooling, you'd go nuts."[3]

My account of how one group of machine operators kept from "going nuts" in a situation of monotonous work activity attempts to lay bare the tissues of interaction which made up the content of their adjustment. The talking, fun, and fooling which provided solution to the elemental problem of "psychological survival" will be described according to their embodiment in intragroup relations. In addition, an unusual opportunity for close observation of behavior involved in the maintenance of group equilibrium was afforded by the fortuitous introduction of a "natural experiment." My unwitting injection of explosive materials into the stream of interaction results in sudden, but temporary, loss of group interaction.

My fellow operatives and I spent our long days of simple, repetitive work in relative isolation from other employees of the factory. Our line of machines were sealed off from other work areas of the plant by the four walls of the clicking room. The one door of this room was usually closed. Even when it was kept open, during periods of hot weather, the consequences were not social; it opened on an uninhabited storage room of the shipping department. Not even the sounds of work activity going on elsewhere in the factory carried to this isolated work place. There were occasional contacts with "outside" employees, usually on matters connected with the work; but, with the exception of the daily calls of one fellow who came to pick up finished materials for the next step in processing, such visits were infrequent.

Moreover, face-to-face contact with members of the managerial hierarchy were few and far between. No one bearing the title of foreman ever came around. The only company official who showed himself more than once during the two-month observation period was the plant superintendent. Evidently overloaded with supervisory duties and production problems which kept him busy elsewhere, he managed to pay his respects every week or two. His visits were in the nature of short, businesslike, but friendly exchanges. Otherwise, he confined his observable communications with the group to occasional utilization of a public address system. During the two-month period, the company president and the chief chemist paid one friendly call apiece. One man, who may or may not have been of managerial status, was seen on various occasions lurking about in a manner which excited suspicion. Although no observable consequences accrued from the peculiar visitations of this silent fellow, it was assumed that he was some sort of efficiency expert, and he was referred to as "The Snooper."

As far as our work group was concerned, this was truly a situation of laissez-faire management. There was no interference from staff experts, no hounding by time-study engineers or personnel men hot on the scene of efficiency or good human relations. Nor were there any signs of industrial democracy in the form

---

[2] *Ibid.*, p. 77.
[3] *Ibid.*, p. 68.

of safety, recreational, or production committees. There was an international union, and there was a highly publicized union-management cooperation program; but actual interactional processes of cooperation were carried on somewhere beyond my range of observation and without participation of members of my work group. Furthermore, these union-management get-togethers had no determinable connection with the problem of "touching out" a twelve-hour day at monotonous work.

Our work group was thus not only abandoned to its its own resources for creating job satisfaction, but left without that basic reservoir of ill-will toward management which can sometimes be counted on to stimulate development of interesting activities to occupy hand and brain. Lacking was the challenge of intergroup conflict, that perennial source of creative experience to fill the otherwise empty hours of meaningless work routine.[4]

The clicking machines were housed in a room approximately thirty by twenty-four feet. They were four in number, set in a row, and so arranged along one wall that the busy operator could, merely by raising his head from his work, freshen his reveries with a glance through one of three large barred windows. To the rear of one of the end machines sat a long cutting table; here the operators cut up rolls of plastic materials into small sheets manageable for further processing at the clickers. Behind the machine at the opposite end of the line sat another table which was intermittently the work station of a female employee who performed sundry scissors operations of a more intricate nature on raincoat parts. Boxed in on all sides by shelves and stocks of materials, this later locus of work appeared a cell within a cell.

The clickers were of the genus punching machines; of mechanical construction similar to that of the better-known punch presses, their leading features were hammer and block. The hammer, or punching head, was approximately eight inches by twelve inches at its flat striking surface. The descent upon the block was initially forced by the operator, who exerted pressure on a handle attached to the side of the hammer head. A few inches of travel downward established electrical connection for a sharp, power-driven blow. The hammer also traveled, by manual guidance, in a horizontal plane to and from, and in an arc around, the central column of the machine. Thus the operator, up to the point of establishing electrical connections for the sudden and irrevocable downward thrust, had flexibility in maneuvering his instrument over the larger surface of the block. The latter, approximately twenty-four inches wide, eighteen inches deep, and ten inches thick, was made, like a butcher's block of inlaid hardwood; it was set in the machine at a convenient waist height. On it the operator placed his materials, one sheet at a time if leather, stacks of sheets if plastic, to be cut with steel dies on assorted sizes and shapes. The particular die in use would be moved, by hand, from spot to spot over the materials each time a cut was made;

[4] Donald F. Roy, "Work Satisfaction and Social Reward in Quota Achievement: An Analysis of Piecework Incentive," *American Sociological Review*, Vol. XVIII (October 1953), 507–14.

less frequently, materials would be shifted on the block as the operator saw need for such adjustment.

Introduction to the new job, with its relatively simple machine skills and work routines, was accomplished with what proved to be, in my experience, an all-time minimum of job training. The clicking machine assigned to me was situated at one end of the row. Here the superintendent and one of the operators gave a few brief demonstrations, accompanied by bits of advice which included a warning to keep hands clear of the descending hammer. After a short practice period, at the end of which the superintendent expressed satisfaction with progress and potentialities, I was left to develop my learning curve with no other supervision than that afforded by members of the work group. Further advice and assistance did come, from time to time, from my fellow operatives, sometimes upon request, sometimes unsolicited.

THE WORK GROUP

Absorbed at first in three related goals of improving my clicking skill, increasing my rate of output, and keeping my left hand unclicked, I paid little attention to my fellow operatives save to observe that they were friendly, middle-aged, foreign-born, full of advice, and very talkative. Their names, according to the ways they addressed each other, were George, Ike, and Sammy.[5] George, a stocky fellow in his late fifties, operated the machine at the opposite end of the line; he, I later discovered, had emigrated in early youth from a country in Southeastern Europe. Ike, stationed at George's left, was tall, slender, in his early fifties, and Jewish; he had come from Eastern Europe in his youth. Sammy, number three man in the line, and my neighbor, was heavy set, in his late fifties, and Jewish; he had escaped from a country in Eastern Europe just before Hitler's legions had moved in. All three men had been downwardly mobile as to occupation in recent years. George and Sammy had been proprietors of small businesses; the former had been "wiped out" when his uninsured establishment burned down; the latter had been entrepreneuring on a small scale before he left all behind him to flee the Germans. According to his account, Ike had left a highly skilled trade which he had practiced for years in Chicago.

I discovered also that the clicker line represented a ranking system in descending order from George to myself. George not only had top seniority for the group, but functioned as a sort of leadman. His superior status was marked in the fact that he received five cents more per hour than the other clickermen, put in the longest workday, made daily contact, outside the workroom, with the superintendent on work matters which concerned the entire line, and communicated to the rest of us the directives which he received. The narrow margin of superordination was seen in the fact that directives were always relayed in the superintendent's name; they were on the order of, "You'd better let that go now, and get

---

[5] All names used are fictitious.

on the green. Joe says they're running low on the fifth floor," or, "Joe says he wants two boxes of the 3-die today." The narrow margin was also seen in the fact that the superintendent would communicate directly with his operatives over the public address system; and, on occasion, Ike or Sammy would leave the workroom to confer with him for decisions or advice in regard to work orders.

Ike was next to George in seniority, then Sammy. I was, of course, low man on the totem pole. Other indices to status differentiation lay in informal interaction, to be described later.

With one exception, job status tended to be matched by length of workday. George worked a thirteen-hour day, from 7 A.M. to 8:30 P.M. Ike worked eleven hours, from 7 A.M. to 6:30 P.M.; occasionally he worked until 7 or 7:30 for an eleven and a half- or a twelve-hour day. Sammy put in a nine-hour day, from 8 A.M. to 5:30 P.M. My twelve hours spanned from 8 A.M. to 8:30 P.M. We had a half hour for lunch, from 12 to 12:30.

The female who worked at the secluded table behind George's machine put in a regular plant-wide eight-hour shift from 8 to 4:30. Two women held this job during the period of my employment; Mable was succeeded by Baby. Both were Negroes, and in their late twenties.

A fifth clicker operator, an Arabian *emigré* called Boo, worked a night shift by himself. He usually arrived about 7 P.M. to take over Ike's machine.

THE WORK

It was evident to me, before my first workday drew to a weary close, that my clicking career was going to be a grim process of fighting the clock, the particular timepiece in this situation being an old-fashioned alarm clock which ticked away on a shelf near George's machine. I had struggled through many dreary rounds with the minutes and hours during the various phases of my industrial experience, but never had I been confronted with such a dismal combination of working conditions as the extra-long workday, the infinitesimal cerebral excitation, and the extreme limitation of physical movement. The contrast with a recent stint in the California oil fields was striking. This was no eight-hour day of racing hither and yon over desert and foothills with a rollicking crew of "roustabouts" on a variety of repair missions at oil wells, pipelines, and storage tanks. Here there were no afternoon dallyings to search the sands for horned toads, tarantulas, and rattlesnakes, or to climb old wooden derricks for raven's nests, with an eye out, of course, for the tell tale streak of dust in the distance which gave ample warning of the approach of the boss. This was standing all day in one spot beside three old codgers in a dingy room looking out through barred windows at the bare walls of a brick warehouse, leg movements largely restricted to the shifting of body weight from one foot to the other, hand and arm movements confined, for the most part, to a simple repetitive sequence of place the die, _____ punch the clicker, _____ place the die, _____ punch the clicker, and intellectual activity reduced to computing the hours to quiting time. It is true that from time to time a fresh stack of sheets would have to be substituted for the clicked-out old one; but the stack would have been prepared by someone else, and the exchange would be only a minute or two in the making. Now and then a box of finished work would have to be moved back out of the way and an empty box brought up, but the moving back and the bringing up involved only a step or two. And there was the half hour for lunch, and occasional trips to the lavatory or the drinking fountain to break up the day into digestible parts. But after each momentary respite, hammer and die were moving again: click, _____ move die, _____ click, _____ move die.

Before the end of the first day, Monotony was joined by his twin brother, Fatigue. I got tired. My legs ached, and my feet hurt. Early in the afternoon I discover a tall stool and moved it up to my machine to "take the load off my feet." But the superintendent dropped in to see how I was "doing" and promptly informed me that "we don't sit down on this job." My reverie toyed with the idea of quitting the job and looking for other work.

The next day was the same: the monotony of the work, the tired legs and sore feet and thoughts of quitting.

THE GAME OF WORK

In discussing the factory operative's struggle to "cling to the remnants of joy in work," Henri de Man makes the general observations that "it is psychologically impossible to deprive any kind of work of all its positive emotional elements," that the worker will find *some* meaning in any activity assigned to him, a "certain scope for initiative which can satisfy after a fashion the instinct for play and the creative impulse," that "even in the Taylor system there is found luxury of self-determination."[6] De Man cites the case of one worker who wrapped 13,000 incandescent bulbs a day; she found her outlet for creative impulse, her self-determination, her meaning in work by varying her wrapping movements a little from time to time.[7]

So did I search for *some* meaning in my continuous mincing of plastic sheets into small ovals, fingers, and trapezoids. The richness of possibility for creative expression previously discovered in my experience with the "Taylor system"[8] did not reveal itself here. There was no piecework, so no piecework game. There was no conflict with management, so no war game. But, like the light bulb wrapper, I did find a "certain scope for initiative," and out of this slight freedom to vary activity, I developed a game of work.

The game developed was quite simple, so elementary, in fact, that its playing was reminiscent of rainy-day preoccupations in childhood, when attention could

---

[6] Henri de Man, *The Psychology of Socialism* (New York: Henry Holt, and Company, 1927), pp. 80–81.

[7] *Ibid.*, p. 81.

[8] Roy, "Work Satisfaction."

be centered by the hour on colored bits of things of assorted sizes and shapes. But this adult activity was not mere pottering and piddling; what it lacked in the earlier imaginative content, it made up for in clean-cut structure. Fundamentally involved were: (a) variation in color of the materials cut, (b) variation in shapes of the dies used, and (c) a process called "scraping the block." The basic procedure which ordered the particular combination of components employed could be stated in the form: "As soon as I do so many of these, I'll get to do those." If, for example, production scheduled for the day featured small, rectangular strips in three colors, the game might go: "As soon as I finish a thousand of the green ones, I'll click some brown ones." And, with success in attaining the objective of working with brown materials, a new goal of "I'll get to do the white ones" might be set. Or the new goal might involve switching dies.

Scraping the block made the game more interesting by adding to the number of possible variations in its playing; and, what was perhaps more important, provided the only substantial reward, save for going to the lavatory or getting a drink of water, on days when work with one die and one color of material was scheduled. As a physical operation, scraping the block was fairly simply; it involved application of a coarse file to the upper surface of the block to remove roughness and unevenness resulting from the wear and tear of die penetration. But, as part of the intellectual and emotional content of the game of work, it could be itself a source of variation in activity. The upper left-hand corner, and so on until the entire block had been worked over. Then, on the next round of scraping by quadrants, there was the possibility of a change of color or die to green trapezoid or white oval pieces.

Thus the game of work might be described as a continuous sequence of short-range production goals with achievement rewards in the form of activity change. The superiority of this relatively complex and self-determined system over the technically simple and outside-controlled job satisfaction injections experienced by Milner at the beginner's table in a shop of the feather industry should be immediately apparent:

> Twice a day our work was completely changed to break the monotony. First Jennie would give us feathers of a brilliant green, then bright orange or a light blue or black. The "ohs" and "ahs" that came from the girls at each change was proof enough that this was an effective way of breaking the monotony of the tedious work.[9]

But a hasty conclusion that I was having lots of fun playing my clicking game should be avoided. These games were not as interesting in the experiencing as they might seem to be from the telling. Emotional tone of the activity was low, and intellectual currents weak. Such rewards as scraping the block or "getting to do the blue ones" were not very exciting, and the stretches of repetitive movement involved in achieving them were long enough to permit lapses into obsessive reverie. Henri de Man speaks of "clinging to the remnants of joy in

---

[9] Lucille Milner, *Education of An American Liberal* (New York: Horizon Press, 1954), p. 97.

work," and this situation represented just that. How tenacious the clinging was, how long I could have "stuck it out" with my remnants, was never determined. Before the first week was out this adjustment to the work situation was complicated by other developments. The game of work continued, but in a different context. Its influence became decidedly subordinated to, if not completely overshadowed by, another source of job satisfaction.

INFORMAL SOCIAL ACTIVITY OF THE WORK GROUP: TIMES AND THEMES

The change came about when I began to take serious note of the social activity going on around me; my attentiveness to this activity came with growing involvement in it. What I heard at first, before I started to listen, was a stream of disconnected bits of communication which did not make much sense. Foreign accents were strong and referents were not joined to coherent contexts of meaning. it was just "jabbering." What I saw at first, before I began to observe, was occasional flurries of horseplay so simple and unvarying in pattern and so childish in quality that they made no strong bid for attention. For example, Ike would regularly switch off the power at Sammy's machine whenever Sammy made a trip to the lavatory or the drinking fountain. Correlatively, Sammy invariably fell victim to the plot by making an attempt to operate his clicking hammer after returning to the shop. And, as the simple pattern went, this blind stumbling into the trap was always followed by indignation and reproach from Sammy, smirking satisfaction from Ike, and mild paternal scolding from George. My interest in this procedure was at first confined to wondering when Ike would weary of his tedious joke or when Sammy would learn to check his power switch before trying the hammer.

But, as I began to pay closer attention, as I began to develop familiarity with the communication system, the disconnected became connected, the nonsense made sense, the obscure became clear, and the silly actually funny. And, as the content of the interaction took on more and more meaning, the interaction began to reveal structure. There were "times" and "themes," and roles to serve their enaction. The interaction had subtleties, and I began to savor and appreciate them. I started to record what hitherto had seemed unimportant.

Times

This emerging awareness of structure and meaning included recognition that the long day's grind was broken by interruptions of a kind other than the formally instituted or idiosyncratically developed disjunctions in work routine previously described. These additional interruptions appeared in daily repetition in an ordered series of informal interactions. They were, in part, but only in part and in very rough comparison, similar to those common fractures of the production process known as the coffee break, the coke break, and the cigarette break. Their distinction lay in frequency of occurrence and in brevity. As phases of the daily series, they occurred almost hourly, and so short were they in duration that they disrupted work activity only slightly. Their significance lay not so much in their function as rest pauses, although it cannot be denied that physical refreshment was involved. Nor did their chief importance lie in the accentuation of progress points in the passage of time, although they could perform that function far more strikingly than the hour hand on the dull face of George's alarm clock. If the daily series of interruptions be likened to a clock, then the comparison might best be made with a special kind of cuckoo clock, one with a cuckoo which can provide variation in its announcements and can create such an interest in them that the intervening minutes become filled with intellectual content. The major significance of the interactional interruptions lay in such a carryover of interest. The physical interplay which momentarily halted work activity would initiate verbal exchanges and thought processes to occupy group members until the next interruption. The group interactions thus not only marked off the time; they gave it content and hurried it along.

Most of the breaks in the daily series were designated as "times" in the parlance of the clicker operators, and they featured the consumption of food or drink of one sort or another. There was coffee time, peach time, banana time, fish time, coke time, and, of course, lunch time. Other interruptions, which formed part of the series but were not verbally recognized as times, were window time, pickup time, and the staggered quitting times of Sammy and Ike. These latter unnamed times did not involve the partaking of refreshments.

My attention was first drawn to this times business during my first week of employment when I was encouraged to join in the sharing of two peaches. It was Sammy who provided the peaches; he drew them from his lunch box after making the announcement, "Peach time!" On this first occasion I refused the proffered fruit, but thereafter regularly consumed my half peach. Sammy continued to provide the peaches and to make the "Peach time!" announcement, although there were days when Ike would remind him that it was peach time, urging him to hurry up with the mid-morning snack. Ike invariably complained about the quality of the fruit, and his complaints fed the fires of continued banter between peach donor and critical recipient. I did find the fruit a bit on the scrubby side but felt, before I achieved insight into the function of peach time, that Ike was showing poor manners by looking a gift horse in the mouth. I wondered why Sammy continued to share his peaches with such an ingrate.

Banana time followed peach time by approximately an hour. Sammy again provided the refreshment, namely, one banana. There was, however, no four-way sharing of Sammy's banana. Ike would gulp it down by himself after surreptitiously extracting it from Sammy's lunch box, kept on a shelf behind Sammy's work station. Each morning, after making the snatch, Ike would call out, "Banana time!" and proceed to down his prize while Sammy made futile protests and denunciations. George would join in with mild remonstrances, sometimes scolding Sammy for make so much fuss. The banana was one which Sammy brought for his own consumption at lunch time; he never did get to eat his banana, but kept bringing one for his lunch. At first this daily theft startled and amazed me. Then I grew to look forward to the daily seizure and the verbal interaction which followed.

Window time came next. It followed banana time as a regular consequence of Ike's castigation by the indignant Sammy. After "taking" repeated references to himself as a person badly lacking in morality and character, Ike would "finally" retaliate by opening the window which faced Sammy's machine, to let the "cold air" blow in on Sammy. The slandering which would, in its echolatic repetition, wear down Ike's patience and forbearance usually took the form of the invidious comparison: "George is a good daddy! Ike is a bad man! A very bad man!" Opening the window would take a little time to accomplish and would involve a great deal of verbal interplay between Ike and Sammy, both before and after the event. Ike would threaten, make feints toward the window, then finally open it. Sammy would protest, argue, and make claims that the air blowing in on him would give him a cold; he would eventually have to leave his machine to close the window. Sometimes the weather was slightly chilly, and the draft from the window; unpleasant; but cool or hot, windy or still, window time arrived each day. (I assume that it was originally a cold season development.) George's part in this interplay, in spite of the "good daddy" laudations, was to encourage Ike in his window work. He would stress the tonic values of fresh air and chide Sammy for his unappreciativeness.

Following window time came lunch time, a formally designated half-hour for the midday repast and rest break. At this time, informal interaction would feature exchanges between Ike and George. The former would start eating his lunch a few minutes before noon, and the latter, in his role as straw boss, would censure him for malobservance of the rules. Ike's off-beat luncheon usually involved a previous tampering with George's alarm clock. Ike would set the clock ahead a few minutes in order to maintain his eating schedule without detection, and George would discover these small daylight saving changes.

The first "time" interruption of the day I did not share. It occurred soon after I arrived on the job, at eight o'clock. George and Ike would share a small pot of coffee brewed on George's hot plate.

Pickup time, fish time, and coke time came in the afternoon. I name it pickup time to represent the official visit of the man who made daily calls to cart away boxes of clicked materials. The arrival of the pickup man, a Negro, was always a noisy one, like the arrival of a daily passenger train in an isolated small town. Interaction attained a quick peak of intensity to crowd into a few minutes all communications, necessary and otherwise. Exchanges invariably included loud depreciations by the pickup man of the amount of work accomplished in the clicking department during the preceding twenty-four hours. Such scoffing would be on the order of "Is that all you've got done? What do you boys do all day?"

These devaluations would be countered with allusions to the "soft job" enjoyed by the pickup man. During the course of the exchanges news items would be dropped, some of serious import, such as reports of accomplished or impending layoffs in the various plants of the company, or of gains or losses in orders for company products. Most of the news items, however, involved bits of information on plant employees told in a light vein. Information relayed by the clicker operators was usually told about each other, mainly in the form of summaries of the most recent kidding sequences. Some of this material was repetitive, carried over from day to day. Sammy would be the butt of most of this newscasting, although he would make occasional counter-reports on Ike and George. An invariable part of the interactional content of pickup time was Ike's introduction of the pickup man to George. "Meet Mr. Papeatis!" Ike would say in mock solemnity and dignity. Each day the pickup man "met" Mr. Papeatis, to the obvious irritation of the latter. Another pickup time invariably would bring Baby (or Mable) into the interaction. George would always issue the loud warning to the pickup man: "Now I want you to stay away from Baby! She's Henry's girl!" Henry was a burly Negro with a booming bass voice who made infrequent trips to the clicking room with lift-truck loads of materials. He was reputedly quite a ladies' man among the colored population of the factory. George's warning to "Stay away from Baby!" was issued to every Negro who entered the shop. Baby's only part in this was to laugh at the horseplay.

About mid-afternoon came fish time, George and Ike would stop work for a few minutes to consume some sort of pickled fish which Ike provided. Neither Sammy nor I partook of this nourishment, nor were we invited. For this omission I was grateful; the fish, brought in a newspaper and with head and tail intact, produced a reverse effect on my appetite. George and Ike seemed to share a great liking for fish. Each Friday night, as a regular ritual, they would enjoy a fish dinner together at a nearby restaurant. On these nights Ike would work until 8:30 and leave the plant with George.

Coke time came late in the afternoon, and was an occasion for total participation. The four of us took turns in buying the drinks and in making the trip for them to a fourth floor vending machine. Through George's manipulation of the situation, it eventually became my daily chore to go after the cokes; the straw boss had noted that I made a much faster trip to the fourth floor and back than Sammy and Ike.

Sammy left the plant at 5:30, and Ike ordinarily retired from the scene an hour and a half later. These quitting times were not marked by any distinctive interaction save the one regular exchange between Sammy and George over the former's "early washup." Sammy's tendency was to crowd his washing up toward five o'clock, and it was George's concern to keep it from further creeping advance. After Ike's departure came Boo's arrival. Boo's was a striking personality productive of a change in topics of conversation to fill in the last hour of the long workday.

Themes

To put flesh, so to speak, on this interactional frame of "times," my work group had developed various "themes" of verbal interplay which had become standardized in their repetition. These topics of conversation ranged in quality from an extreme of nonsensical chatter to another extreme of serious discourse. Unlike the times, these themes flowed one into the other in no particular sequence of predictability. Serious conversation would suddenly melt into horseplay, and vice versa. In the middle of a serious discussion on the high cost of living, Ike might drop a weight behind the easily startled Sammy, or hit him over the head with a dusty paper sack. Interaction would immediately drop to a low comedy exchange of slaps, threats, guffaws, and disapprobations which would invariably include a ten-minute echolalia of "Ike is a bad man, a very bad man! George is a good daddy, a very fine man!" Or, on the other hand, a stream of such invidious comparisons as followed a surreptitious switching-off of Sammy's machine by the playful Ike might merge suddenly into a discussion of the pros and cons of saving for one's funeral.

"Kidding themes" were usually started by George or Ike, and Sammy was usually the butt of the joke. Sometimes Ike would have to "take it," seldom George. One favorite kidding theme involved Sammy's alleged receipt of $100 a month from his son. The points stressed were that Sammy did not have to work long hours, or did not have to work at all, because he had a son to support him. George would always point out that he sent money to his daughter; she did not send money to him. Sammy received occasional calls from his wife, and his claim that these calls were requests to shop for groceries on the way home were greeted with feigned disbelief. Sammy was ribbed for being closely watched, bossed, and henpecked by his wife, and the expression "Are you man or mouse?" became an echolalic utterance, used both in and out of the original context.

Ike, who shared his machine and the work scheduled for it with Boo, the night operator, came in for constant invidious comparison on the subject of output. The socially isolated Boo, who chose work rather than sleep on his lonely night shift, kept up a high level of performance, and George never tired of pointing this out to Ike. It so happened that Boo, an Arabian Moslem from Palestine, had no use for Jews in general; and Ike, who was Jewish, had no use for Boo in particular. Whenever George would extol Boo's previous night's production, Ike would try to turn the conversation into a general discussion on the need for educating the Arabs. George, never permitting the development of serious discussion on this topic, would repeat a smirking warning, "You watch out for Boo! He's got a long knife!"

The "poom poom" theme was one that cause no sting. It would come up several times a day to be enjoyed as unbarbed fun by the three older clicker operators. Ike was usually the one to raise the question, "How many times you go poom poom last night?" The person questioned usually replied with claims of being "too old for poom poom." If this theme did develop a goat, it was I. When it was pointed out that I was a younger man, this provide further grist for the poom poom mill. I soon grew weary of this poom poom business, so dear to the hearts of the three old satyrs, and, knowing where the conversation would inevitably lead, winced whenever Ike brought up the subject.

I grew almost as sick of a kidding theme which developed from some personal information contributed during a serious conversation on property ownership and high taxes. I dropped a few remarks about two acres of land which I owned in one of the western states, and from then on I had to listen to questions, advice, and general nonsensical comment in regard to "Danelly's farm."[10] This "farm" soon became stocked with horses, cows, pigs, chickens, ducks, and the various and sundry domesticated beasts so tunefully listed in "Old McDonald Had a Farm." George was a persistent offender with this theme. Where the others seemed to be mainly interested in statistics on livestock crops, etc., George's teasing centered on a generous offering to help with the household chores while I worked in the fields. He would drone on, *ad nauseam,* "when I come to visit you, you will never have to worry about the housework, Danelly. I'll stay around the house when you go out to dig the potatoes and milk the cows, I'll stay in and peel potatoes and help your wife do the dishes." Danelly always found it difficult to change the subject on George, once the latter started to bear down on the farm theme.

Another kidding theme which developed out of serious discussion could be labelled "helping Danelly find a cheaper apartment." It became known to the group that Danelly had a pending housing problem, that he would need new quarters for his family when the permanent resident of his temporary summer dwelling returned from a vacation. This information engendered at first a great deal of sympathetic concern and, of course, advice on apartment hunting. Development into a kidding theme was immediately related to previous exchanges between Ike and George on the quality of their respective dwelling areas. Ike lived in "Lawndale," and George dwelt in the "Woodlawn" area. The new pattern featured the reading aloud of bogus "apartment for rent" ads in newspapers which were brought into the shop. Studying his paper at lunchtime, George would call out, "Here's an apartment for you, Danelly! Five rooms, stove heat, $20 a month, Lawndale Avenue!" Later, Ike would read from his paper, "Here's one! Six room, stove heat, dirt floor, $18.50 a month! At 55th and Woodlawn." Bantering would then go on in regard to the quality of housing or population in the two areas. The search for an apartment for Danelly was not successful.

Serious themes included the relating of major misfortunes suffered in the past by group members. George referred again and again to the loss, by fire, of his business establishment. Ike's chief complaints centered around a chronically ill wife who had undergone various operations and periods of hospital care. Ike spoke with discouragement of the expenses attendant upon hiring a housekeeper for himself and his children; he referred with disappointment and disgust to a

---

[10] This spelling is the closest I can come to the appellation given me in George's broken English and adopted by other members of the group.

teen-age son, an inept lad who "couldn't even fix his own lunch. He couldn't even make himself a sandwich!" Sammy's reminiscences centered on the loss of a flourishing business when he had to flee Europe ahead of Nazi invasion.

But all serious topics were not tales of woe. One favorite serious theme which was optimistic in tone could be called either "Danelly's future" or "getting Danelly a better job." It was known that I had been attending "college," the magic door to opportunity, although my specific course of study remained some-what obscure. Suggestions poured forth on good lines of work to get into, and these suggestions were backed with accounts of friends, and friends of friends, who had made good via the academic route. My answer to the expected question, "Why are you working here?" always stressed the "lots of overtime" feature, and this explanation seemed to suffice for short-range goals.

There was one theme of especially solemn import, the "professor theme." This theme might also be termed "George's daughter's marriage theme"; for the recent marriage of George's only child was inextricably bound up with George's connection with higher learning. The daughter had married the son of a professor who instructed in one of the local colleges. This professor theme was not in the strictest sense a conversation piece; when the subject came up George did all the talking. The two Jewish operatives remained silent as they listened with deep respect, if not actual awe, to George's accounts of the Big Wedding which, including the wedding pictures entailed an expense of $1,000. It was monologue, but there was listening, there was communication, the sacred communication of a temple, when George told of going for Sunday afternoon walks on the Midway with the professor, or of joining the professor for a Sunday dinner. Whenever he spoke of the professor, his daughter, the wedding, or even the new son-in-law, who remained for the most part in the background, a sort of incidental like the wedding cake, George was complete master of the interaction. His manner, in speaking to the rank-and-file of clicker operators, was indeed that of master deigning to notice his underlings. I came to the conclusion that it was the professor connection, not the straw-boss-ship or the extra nickel an hour, which provided the fount of George's superior status in the group.

If the professor theme may be regarded as a cream of verbal interaction, the "chatter themes" should be classed as the dregs. The chatter themes were hardly themes at all; perhaps they should be labelled "verbal states," or "oral autisms." Some were of doubtful status as communication; they were like the howl or cry of an animal responding to its own physiological state. They were exclamations, ejaculations, snatches of song or doggerel, talkings-to-oneself, mutterings. Their classification as themes would rest on their repetitive character. They were echolalic utterances, repeated over and over. An already mentioned example would be Sammy's repetition of "George is a good daddy, a very fine man! Ike is a bad man, a very bad man!" Also, Sammy's repetition of "Don't bother me! Can't you see I'm busy? I'm a very busy man!" for ten minutes after Ike had dropped a weight behind him would fit the classification. Ike would shout "Mamariba!" at intervals between repetition of bits of verse such as:

Mama on the bed,
Papa on the floor,
Baby in the crib
Says giver some more!

Sometimes the thee operators would pick up one of these simple chatterings in a sort of chorus. "Are you man or mouse? I ask you, are you man or mouse?" was a favorite of this type.

So initial discouragement with the meagerness of social interaction I now recognized as due to lack of observation. The interaction was there, in constant flow. It captured attention and held interest to make the long day pass.

The cabdriver and his fare:
Facets of a fleeting relationship[*]

Fred Davis[1]

Even in an urban and highly secularized society such as ours, most service relationships, be they between a professional and his client or a menial and his patron, are characterized by certain constraints on too crass a rendering and consuming of the service.[2] That is to say, in the transaction, numerous interests besides that of simply effecting an economic exchange are customarily attended to and dealt with. The moral reputation of the parties,[3] their respective social standing, and the skill and art with which the service is performed[4] are but a few of the noninstrumental values which are usually incorporated into the whole act.

Tenuous though such constraints may become at time, particularly in large cities where anonymous roles, only segmentally related, occur in great profusion; it is at once evident that for them to exist at all something approximating a

[*] Reprinted in its entirety from Fred Davis, "The Cabdriver and His Fare: Facets of a Fleeting Relationship," *American Journal of Sociology*, Vol. 65, No. 2 (Sept. 1959), pp. 158–65. Used by permission of The University of Chicago Press.

[1] This article is based largely on notes and observations made by me over a six-month period in 1948 when I worked as a cabdriver for one of the larger taxicab firms in Chicago. I am greatly indebted to Erving Goffman, Everett C. Hughes, and Howard S. Becker for their comments and criticisms.

[2] Talcott Parsons, *The Social System* (Glencoe, Ill.: Free Press, 1951), pp. 48–56.

[3] Erving Goffman, *The Presentation of Self in Everyday Life* (Edinburgh: University of Edinburgh Social Science Research Centre, 1956), pp. 160–62.

[4] Everett C. Hughes, *Men and Their Work* (Glencoe, Ill.: Free Press, 1958), pp. 88–101.

community must be present. Practitioners and clients must be sufficiently in communication for any untoward behavior to stand a reasonable chance of becoming known, remarked upon, remembered, and, in extreme cases, made public. And, whereas the exercise of sanctions does not necessarily depend on a community network[5] that is closely integrated (or one in which there is a total identity of values and interests), it does depend on there being some continuity and stability in the relationships that make up the network, so that, at minimum, participants may in the natural course of events be able to identify actions and actors to one another.[6] It is mainly, though not wholly, from this vantage point that big city cabdriving as an occupation is here discussed, particularly the relationship between cabdriver and fare and its consequences for the occupational culture.[7] Approximating in certain respects a provincial's caricature of the broad arc of social relations in the metropolis, this relationship affords an extreme instance of the weakening and attenuation of many of the constraints customary in other client-and-patron-oriented services in our society. As such, its analysis can perhaps point up by implication certain of the rarely considered preconditions for practitioner-client relations found in other, more firmly structured, services and professions.

In a large city like Chicago the hiring of a cab by a passenger may be conceived of in much the same way as the random collision of particles in an atomic field. True, there are some sectors of the field in which particles come into more frequent collision than others, for example, downtown, at railroad depots, and at the larger neighborhood shopping centers. But this kind of differential activity within the field as a whole provides little basis for predicting the coupling of any two specific particles.

To a much more pronounced degree than is the case in other client-and-patron-oriented services, the occupation of cabdriver provides its practitioners with few, if any, regularities by which to come upon, build up, and maintain a steady clientele. The doctor has his patients, the schoolteacher her pupils, the janitor his tenants, the waitress her regular diners; and in each case server and served remain generally in some continuing or renewable relationship. By contrast, the cabdriver's day consists of a long series of brief contacts with unrelated persons of whom he has no foreknowledge, just as they have none of him, and whom he is not likely to encounter again.

Furthermore, by virtue of the differential spatial, social, and organizational arrangements of the community, it is also likely that the clients of these other

    [5] Because it better delineates the boundaries and linkages of informal sanctioning groups found in large cities, the term "network" is used here to qualify the more global concept of "community." See Elizabeth Bott, *Family and Social Network* (London: Tavistock, 1957), pp. 58–61.

    [6] Robert K. Merton, "The Role Set: Problems in Sociological Theory," *British Journal of Sociology*, VIII, No. 2 (June 1957), 114.

    [7] Parallel studies of this aspect of occupational culture are: Hughes, *Men and Their Work*, pp. 42–55; Howard S. Becker, "The Professional Dance Musician and His Audience," *American Journal of Sociology*, LVII (September, 1951), 136–44; Ray Gold, "Janitor versus Tenants: A Status-Income Dilemma," *American Journal of Sociology*, LVII (March, 1951), 486–93.

practitioners will, in some manner at least, know one another and be related to one another in ways that often transcend the simple circumstance of sharing the same services: they may also be friends, kin, neighbors, or colleagues. For this reason the clientele of most practitioners is something more than an aggregate of discrete individuals; it is, as well, a rudimentary social universe and forum to which the practitioner must address himself in other than purely individual terms.[8]

The cabdriver, by comparison, has no such clientele. He has no fixed business address, and his contacts with passengers are highly random and singular. To a striking degree he is a practitioner without reputation because those who ride in his cab do not comprise, except perhaps in the most abstract sense, anything approximating a social group. They neither know nor come into contact with one another in other walks of life, and, even if by chance some do, they are unaware of their ever having shared the services of the same anonymous cab-driver. Even were the driver deliberately to set out to build up a small nucleus of steady and favored passengers, the time-space logistics of his job would quickly bring such a scheme to naught. Unable to plot his location in advance or to distribute time according to a schedule, he depends on remaining open to all comers wherever he finds himself. Much more so than other classes of service personnel, cabdrivers are both the fortuitous victims and the beneficiaries of random and highly impersonal market contingencies.

This set of circumstances—fleeting, one-time contact with a heterogeneous aggregate of clients, unknown to one another—exerts an interesting influence on the role of cabdriver.

Unable, either directly through choice or indirectly through location, to select clients, the cabdriver is deprived of even minimal controls. His trade therefore exposes him to a variety of hazards and exigencies which few others, excepting policemen, encounter as frequently; for example: stick-ups, belligerent drunks, women in labor, psychopaths, counterfeiters, and fare-jumpers. Unlike the police-man's however, his control over them is more fragile.

Nor, incidentally, is the cabdriver's social status or level of occupational skill of much help in inducing constraint in fares. Patently, his status is low, in large part precisely because, unlike the professional and other practitioners command-ing prestige, he can hardly be distinguished from his clients in task-relevant competence. Not only is the operation of a motor car a widely possessed skill, but a large portion of fares have, for example, a very good idea of the best routes to their destination, the rules and practices of the road, and the charges for a trip. Though they are rarely as adept or sophisticated in these matters as the cabdriver, the discrepancy is so small that many think they know the driver's job as well as he does. Periodically, a cabdriver will boldly challenge a difficult and critical passenger to take over the wheel himself. Others, wishing to impress on the fare that theirs is a real service requiring special talent and skill, will resort

---

[8] Merton, "The Role Set," pp. 110–12.

to darting nimbly in and out of traffic, making neatly executed U-turns and leaping smartly ahead of other cars when the traffic light changes.

Goffman[9] speaks of a category of persons who in some social encounters are treated as if they were not present, whereas in fact they may be indispensable for sustaining the performance. He terms these "non-persons" and gives as an example a servant at a social gathering. Although cabdrivers are not consistently approached in this way by fares, it happens often enough for it to become a significant theme of their work. Examples are legion. Maresca[10] tells of the chorus girl who made a complete change from street clothing into stage costume as he drove her to the theater. More prosaic instances include the man and wife who, managing to suppress their anger while on the street, launch into a bitter quarrel the moment they are inside the cab; or the well-groomed young couple who after a few minutes roll over on the back seat to begin petting; or the businessman who loudly discusses details of a questionable business deal. Here the driver is expected to, and usually does, act as if he were merely an extension of the automobile he operates. In actuality, of course, he is acutely aware of what goes on in his cab, and, although his being treated as a nonperson implies a degraded status, it also affords him a splendid vantage point from which to witness a rich variety of human schemes and entanglements.

The fleeting nature of the cabdriver's contact with the passenger at the same time also makes for his being approached as someone to whom intimacies can be revealed and opinions forthrightly expressed with little fear of rebuttal, retaliation, or disparagement. And though this status as an accessible person is the product of little more than the turning inside-out of his nonperson status—which situation implies neither equality nor respect for his opinion—it nevertheless does afford him glimpses of the private lives of individuals which few in our society, apart from psychiatrists and clergy, are privileged to note as often or in such great variety. It is probably not a mistaken everyday generalization that big city cabdrivers, on their part, feel less compunction about discussing their own private lives, asking probing questions, and "sounding off" on a great many topics and issues than do others who regularly meet the public, but less fleetingly.[11]

In cabdriving, therefore, propriety, deference, and "face" are, in the nature of the case, weaker than is the case in most other service relationships. This absence contributes to a heightened preoccupation with and focusing on the purely instrumental aspect of the relationship which for the driver is the payment he receives for his services. This perhaps would be less blatantly the case were it not for the gratuity or tip. For the noncab-driving company driver, the sum

---

[9] Goffman, *The Presentation*, p. 95.

[10] James V. Maresca, *My Flag Is Down* (New York: Dutton, 1945). Essentially the same incident is related by an unidentified cabdriver on the documentary recording of Tony Schwartz, *The New York Taxi Driver* (Columbia Records, ML 5309, 1959).

[11] CF. Schwartz, *Taxi Driver*. In fact, these characteristic qualities, with a work-adapted, bittersweet admixture of cynicism and sentimentality, comprise the core of the personality widely imputed to cabdrivers by the riding public. Cf. Hughes, *Men and Their Work*, pp. 23–41.

collected in tips amounts roughly to 40 percent of his earnings. Considering, for example, that in Chicago in the late forties a hard-working cabdriver, who worked for ten hours a day, six days a week, would on the average take home approximately seventy-five dollars a week including tips, the importance of tipping can readily be appreciated. For the family man who drives, tips usually represent the difference between a subsistence and a living wage. Also, tips are, apart from taxes, money "in the clear," in that the driver does not have to divide them with the company as he does his metered collections.[12] Sum for sum, therefore, tips represent greater gain for him than do metered charges.

It would probably be incorrect to hold that pecuniary considerations are the sole ones involved in the cabdriver's attitude toward the tip. Yet in such tip-sensitive occupations as cabdriving, waitering, and bellhopping to suggest[13] that the tip's primary significance is its symbolic value as a token of affection or appreciation for a service well performed would be even wider of the mark. Vindictive caricatures abound among cabdrivers, as they do among waiters, waitresses, and bellhops, of the "polite gentleman" or "kind lady" who with profuse thanks and flawless grace departs from the scene having "stiffed" (failed to tip) them. In occupations where the tip constitutes so large a fraction of the person's earnings, the cash nexus, while admittedly not the only basis upon which patrons are judged, is so important as to relegate other considerations to a secondary place. Will the fare tip or will he "stiff?" How much will he tip? The answers remain in nearly every instance problematic to the end. Not only is there no sure way of predicting the outcome, but in a culture where the practice of tipping is neither as widespread nor as standardized as in many Continental countries, for example, the driver cannot in many cases even make a guess.

No regular scheme of work can easily tolerate so high a degree of ambiguity and uncertainty in a key contingency. Invariably, attempts are made to fashion ways and means of greater predictability and control; or, failing that, of devising formulas and imagery to bring order and reason in otherwise inscrutable and capricious events. In the course of a long history a rich body of stereotypes, beliefs, and practices[14] has grown up whose function is that of reducing uncertainty, increasing calculabilty, and providing coherent explanations.

A basic dichotomy running through the cabdriver's concept of his client work is of regular cab users and of noncab users, the latter referred to as "jerks," "slobs," "yokels," "public transportation types," and a host of other derogatory terms. The former class, though viewed as quite heterogeneous within itself, includes all who customarily choose cabs in preference to other forms of local

---

12 In Chicago in 1948 the company driver's share of the metered sum was 42½ percent. Since that time the proportion has been increased slightly.

13 Cf. William F. Whyte, *Human Relations in the Restaurant Industry* (New York: McGraw-Hill Book Co., 1948), p. 100.

14 Cf. here and in the section to follow the pertinent remarks of Hughes on "guilty knowledge" developed by those in a service occupation with reference to their clientele. Hughes, *Men and Their Work*, pp. 81–82.

transportation, are conversant with the cab-passenger role, and, most of all, accept, if only begrudgingly, the practice of tipping. By comparison, the class of noncab users includes that vast aggregate of persons who resort to cabs only in emergencies or on special occasions, and are prone too often to view the hiring of a cab as simply a more expensive mode of transportation.

Take, for example, the familiar street scene following a sudden downpour or unexpected breakdown in bus service, when a group of individuals cluster about a bus top, several dart from the curb now and then in hope of hailing a cab. Such persons are almost by definition noncab users or they would not be found at a bus stop in the rain; nor would they be keeping an eye out for a possible bus. A potential fare in this predicament is to the cabdriver a foul-weather friend, and drivers are on occasion known to hurtle by in spiteful glee, leaving the supplicant standing.

He who hires a cab only on special occasions, frequently to impress others or, perhaps, himself alone, is another familiar kind of noncab user. Writing of his experiences as a London cabdriver, Hodge relates a by no means uncommon encounter:

> But tonight is different. Perhaps the Pools have come up for once. Anyhow, he's got money. He signals me with exaggerated casualness from the cinema entrance. . . . She steps in daintily, the perfect lady, particularly where she puts her feet. As soon as she's safely inside, he whispers the address . . . and adds, as one man of the world to another, "No hurry, driver." Then he dives in with such utter *savoire faire, comme il faut,* and what not, that he trips over the mat and lands face first on the back seat.[15]

Perhaps the most obvious kind of nonuser is the person who, after hailing a cab, will ask the driver some such question as, "How much will it cost to take me to 500 Elm Street?" By this simple inquiry this person stands revealed as one who takes a narrow view of cab travel and from whom not much, if anything, can be expected by way of tip. On the other hand, regular cab users demonstrate in a variety of ways that for them this is a customary and familiar mode of travel. The manner in which they hail a cab, when and how they announce their destination, the ease with which they enter and exit, how they sit—these, and more, though difficult to describe in precise detail, comprise the Gestalt.

There exists among drivers an extensive typology of cab users, the attributes imputed to each type having a certain predictive value, particularly as regards tipping. Some of the more common and sharply delineated types are:

The sport.   The cabdriver's image of this type combines in one person whose attributes of character which he views as ideal. While the Sport's vocation may be any one of many, his status derives more from his extravocational activities, e.g., at the race track, prize fight, ball games, popular restaurants, and bars. He is the perennial "young man on the town." Gentlemanly without being aloof, interested without becoming familiar, he also is, of course, never petty. Most of all, his tips are generous, and even on very short rides he will seldom tip less than a quarter. A favorite success story among cabdrivers describes

---

[15] Herbert Hodge, "I Drive a Taxi," *Fact,* No. 22 (January 1939), pp. 28–29.

at length and in fine detail the handsome treatment accorded the driver on an all-night tour with a Sport.[16]

The blowhard.   The Blowhard is a false Sport. While often wearing the outer mantle of the Sport, he lacks the real Sport's casualness, assured manners, and comfortable style. Given to loquaciouness, he boasts and indiscriminately fabricates tales of track winnings, sexual exploits, and the important people he knows. Often holding out the promise of much by way of tip, he seldom lives up to his words.

The businessman.   These are the staple of the cab trade, particularly for drivers who work by day. Not only are they the most frequently encountered; their habits and preferences are more uniform than those of any other type: the brisk efficiency with which they engage a cab, their purposefulness and disinclination to partake of small talk. Though not often big tippers, they are thought fair. Thus they serve as something of a standard by which the generosity or stinginess of other is judged.

The lady shopper.   Although almost as numerous as businessmen, Lady Shoppers are not nearly as well thought of by cabdrivers. Ther stereotype middle-aged woman, fashionably though unattractively dressed, sitting somewhat stiffly at the edge of her seat and wearing a fixed glare which bespeaks her conviction that she is being "taken for a ride." Her major delinquency, however, is undertipping; her preferred coin is a dime, no more or less, regardless of how long or arduous the trip. A forever repeated story is of the annoyed diver, who, after a grueling trip with a Lady Shopper, hands, the coin back, telling her, "Lady, keep your lousy dime. You need it more than I do."[17]

Live ones.[18]   Lives Ones are a special category of fare usually encountered by the cabdriver who works by night. They are, as a rule, out-of town conventioneers or other revelers who tour about in small groups in search of licentious forms of entertainment: cabarets, burlesques, trip-tease bars, pick-up joints, etc. As often as not, they have already had a good deal to drink when the cabdriver meets them, and, being out-of-towners they frequently turn to him for recommendations on where to go. In the late forties an arrangement existed in Chicago whereby some of the more popular Near North Side and West Madison Street "clip joints" rewarded cabdrivers for "steering" Live Ones to their establishments. Some places paid fifty cents "a head"; others a dollar "for the load." As do the many other who regularly cater to Live Ones—e.g., waitresses, bartenders, female bar companions (B-girls), night-club hosts and hostesses, entertainers, prostitutes—cabdrivers often view them as fair game. And while their opportunies for pecuniary exploitation are few and more limited than those open, for example, to B-girls and night-club proprietors, many drivers feel less inhibited about padding charges and finagling extras from Live Ones then they do from other fares. Often extravagant in their tips because

---

[16] As in the past, the Sport still serves as something of a hero figure in our culture, particularly among the working classes. A type midway between the Playboy and the Bohemian, his unique appeal rests perhaps on the ease and assurance with which he is pictured as moving between and among social strata, untainted by upper-class snobbishness, middle-class conventionality and lower-class vulgarity. In *The Great Gatsby*, Fitzgerald gives us a penetrative exposition of the myth of the Sport and its undoing at the hands of the class system.

[17] The stereotype of women as poor tippers is widely shared by other tip-sensitive occupations. Cf. Frances Donovan, *The Woman Who Waits* (Boston: Badger, 1920).

[18] The term "Live Ones" is employed in a variety of pursuits as apparently diverse as retail selling, night-club entertainment, traveling fairs, and panhandling. Generally it designates persons who are "easy touches," eager to succumb to the oftentimes semifraudulent proposals of the operator, Cf. W. Jack Peterson and Milton A. Maxwell, "The Skid Row Wino," *Social Problems,* V (Spring 1958), 112.

of high spirits and drink, Live Ones are also frequently careless and forget to tip altogether. Knowing that Live Ones are out to "blow their money" anyway, many drivers believe they are justified in seeing to it that they are deprived of a small portion.

Although the cab culture's typology of fares stems in a large part from the attempt to order experience, reduce uncertainty, and further calculability of the tip, it is questionable of course as to how accurate or efficient it is. For, as has often been remarked, stereotypes and typologies have a way of imparting a symmetry and regularity to behavior which are, at best, only crudely approximated in reality. Too often it happens, for example, that a fare tabbed as a Sport turns out to be a Stiff (nontipper), that a Blowhard matches his words with a generous tip, or that a Lady Shopper will give fifteen or even twenty cents. The persistence of the typology, therefore, has perhaps as much to do with the cabdriver's *a posteriori* reconstructions and rationalizations of fare behavior as it does with the typology's predictive efficiency.

To protect and insure themselves against an unfavorable outcome of tipping, many drivers will, depending upon circumstances, employ diverse tactics and stratagems (some more premeditated than others) to increase the amount of tip or to compensate for its loss should it not be forthcoming. Certain of these are listed below. It should be understood, however, that in the ordinary instance the driver makes no attempt to manipulate the fare, believing resignedly that in the long run such means bear too little fruit for the effort and risk.

Making change.   Depending on the tariff and the amount handed him, the driver can fumble about in his pockets for change, or make change in such denominations as often to embarrass a fare into giving a larger tip than he had intended. The efficacy of this tactic depends naturally on the determination and staying power of the fare, qualities which many fares are averse to demonstrate, particularly when it comes to small change.

The hard-luck story.   This is usually reserved for young persons and others who, for whatever reason, evidence an insecure posture vis-à-vis the driver. Typically, the hard-luck story consists of a catalogue of economic woes, e.g., long and hard hours of work, poor pay, insulting and unappreciative passengers, etc. In "confiding" these to the fare, the driver pretends to esteem him as an exceptionally sympathetic and intelligent person who, unlike "the others," can appreciate his circumstances and act accordingly. Most drivers, however, view the hard-luck story as an unsavory form of extortion, beneath their dignity. Furthermore, while it may work in some cases, its potential for alienating tips is probably as great as its success at extracting them.

Fictitious charges.   The resort to fictitious and fraudulent charges occurs most commonly in those cases in which the driver feels that he has good reason to believe that the fare will, either through malice or ignorance, not tip and when the fare impresses him as being enough of a non-cab user as not to know when improper charges are being levied. Once, when I complained to a veteran cabdriver about have been "stiffed" by a young couple, newly arrived in Chicago, to whom I had extended such extra services as carrying luggage and opening doors, I was told: "Wise up kid! When you pick up one of these yokels at the Dearborn Station carrying a lot of cheap straw luggage on him, you can bet ninety-nine times out of a hundred that he isn't going to tip you. Not that he's a mean guy or anything, but where he comes from, they never heard of tipping. What

I do with a yokel like that is to take him to where he's going, show him what the fare is on the meter, and tell him that it costs fifteen cents extra for each piece of luggage. Now, he doesn't know that there's no charge for hand luggage, but that way I'm sure of getting my tip out of him."

The "psychological" approach.   Possibly attributing more art to their trade than is the case, some drivers are of the opinion that a cab ride can be tailored to fit a passenger in much the same way as can a suit of clothes. One cabdriver, boasting of his success at getting tips, explained: "In this business you've got to use psychology. You've got to make the ride fit the person. Now, take a businessman. He's in a hurry to get some place and he doesn't want to lot of bullshit and crapping around. With him you've got to keep moving. Do some fancy cutting in and out, give the cab a bit of a jerk when you take off from the light. Not reckless, mind you, but plenty of zip. He likes that.[19] With old people, it's just the opposite. They're more afraid than anyone of getting hurt or killed in a cab. Take it easy with them. Creep along, open doors for them, help them in and out, be real folksy. Call them 'Sir' and 'Ma'am' and they'll soon be calling you 'young man.' They're suckers for this stuff, and they'll loosen up their pocketbooks a little bit."

In the last analysis, neither the driver's typology of fares nor his stratagems further to any marked degree his control of the tip. Paradoxically, were these routinely successful in achieving predictability and control, they would at the same time divest the act of tipping of its most distinguishing characteristics—of its uncertainty, variability, and of the element of revelation in its consummation. It is these—essentially the problematic in human intercourse[20]—which distinguish the tip from the fixed service charge. And though another form of remuneration might in the end provide the cabdriver with a better wage and a more secure livelihood, the abrogation of tipping would also lessen the intellectual play which uncertainty stimulates and without which cabdriving would be for many nothing more than unrelieved drudgery.

That the practice of tipping, however, expressly befits only certain kinds of service relationships and may under slightly altered circumstances easily degenerate into corruption or extortion is demonstrated, ironically enough, by the predicament of some cabdrivers themselves. To give an example: In the garage out of which I worked, nearly everyone connected with maintenance and assignment of cabs expected tips from drivers for performing many of the routine tasks associated with their jobs, such as filling a tank with gas, changing a tire, or adjusting a carburetor. Although they resented it, drivers had little recourse but to tip. Otherwise, they would acquire reputations as "stiffs" and "cheapskates," be kept waiting interminably for repairs, and find that faulty and careless work had been done on their vehicles. Particularly with the dispatcher did the perversion of the tipping system reach extortionate proportions. His power derived from the assignment of cabs; to protect themselves from being assigned "pots" (cabs that would break down in the middle of the day), drivers tipped him fifty cents at the beginning of every week. Since nearly every driver tipped the dispatcher

---

[19] Cf. Hodge, "I Drive a Taxi," p. 17.
[20] Cf. Donovan, *The Woman Who Waits*, p. 262.

and since there were more drivers than good cabs, a certain numbers of drivers would still be assigned "pots." Some, wishing to insure doubly against this would then raise the bribe to a dollar and a half a week, causing the others to follow suit in a vicious spiral. If little else, this shows how the tip—as distinguished from the gift, honorarium, inducement, or bribe—depends for its expressive validity on there not being a too close, long sustained, or consequential relationship between the parties to a service transaction.

Among service relationships in our society, that between the big city cabdriver and his fare, due to the way in which they come into contact with each other, is especially subject to structural weakness.

The relationship is random, fleeting, unrenewable, and largely devoid of socially integrative features which in other client and patron oriented services help sustain a wider range of constraints and controls between the parties to the transaction. (Much the same might be said of such service occupations as waitress, bellhop and hotel doorman, the chief difference being, however, that these operate from a spatially fixed establishment, which in itself permits of greater identifiability, renewability, and hence constraint in one's relationship to them.) As a result, the tendency of the relationship is to gravitate sharply and in relatively overt fashion toward those few issues having to do with the basic instrumental terms of the exchange. The very fact of tipping, its economic centrality and the cab culture's preoccupation with mastering its many vagaries reflect in large part the regulative imbalance inherent in the relationship.

By inference, this analysis raises anew questions of how to account for the many more formidable and apparently more binding practitioner-client constraints found in other personal service fields, in particular the professions. To such matters as career socialization, colleague groups, socially legitimated skill monopolies, and professional secrecy there might be added a certain safe modicum of continuity, stability, and homogeneity of clientele.[21] For, given too great and random a circulation of clients among practitioners, as might occur for example under certain bureaucratic schemes for providing universal and comprehensive medical service, the danger is that informal social control networks would not come into being in the community, and, as in big city cabdriving, relations between servers and served would become reputationless, anonymous, and narrowly calculative.

---

[21] William J. Goode, "Community within a Community: The Professions," *American Sociological Review*, XXII, No. 2 (April 1957), 198–200, and Eliot Freidson, "Varieties of Professional Practice," draft version of unpublished paper, 1959.

Psychology and the crisis of statesmanship*

Robert R. Blake

Resolution of conflict between groups of people—whether between nations, between management and labor, the departments of a business or university, or between social agencies within a community setting—requires the exercise of statesmanship. Permanent resolutions may be brought about through a realistic approach to the source of conflict. Whatever the circumstances, however, attempts at resolutions involve psychological aspects. Statesmen are confronted with designing psychological structures that can contribute to the handling of differences. Occasionally statesmen are successful. Too frequently they fail.

Fundamental divisions between groupings of peoples confront us today. They affirm that the problem of statesmanship is crucial. On the international scene there rages a full-blown cold war. The first satellite appears in the sky and is described here as a "hunk of iron." Two weeks later the sputnik cocktail is available: one part of vodka and two of sour grape juice. Within social groupings segregation and integration constitute burning issues of the hour. Troops, not statesmanship, prevent the eruption of conflict. On the economic front, a fundamental breach separates labor and management on basic issues regarding the organization of work, even on ways toward bringing an end to the current recession. Bickering among military services goes on unabated. Religious differences split groups and generate the very rivalry and discord the precepts of religion are intended to diminish or obliterate. There seems no end. Some divisions produce constructive competitiveness and are healthy. Many are not. The result is unwanted and unnecessary friction that blocks more basic pursuits.

Secret negotiations in smoke-filled rooms, in palaces, or on yachts; slick operators pulling strings and making deals; and blind resistance with bland refusal to examine issues have not served too well in managing or relieving differences

* Reprinted from *American Psychologist*, Vol. 4 (1959), pp. 87–94. This article was originally presented as the Presidential Address, Southwestern Psychological Association, 1958. Appreciation expressed to Muzafer Sherif and Jane Srygley Mouton for suggestions regarding this manuscript.

between groupings of peoples. Statemanship in all fields is faltering. Without theory, statesmen lack clear-cut guides for planning and action. Yet principles of behavior are involved. Some have been identified through psychological research. The resurgence of statesmanship is contingent on the effective use of such knowledge. My purpose is to examine approaches for resolving differences between groups against the background of psychological theory and research. Research in this area is only in the early stages of development, but it does provide guide lines for clarifying the nature and the scope of the problems and for identifying solutions that may bring permanent reduction in intergroup conflicts.

APPROACHES TO THE MANAGEMENT OF INTERGROUP DISPUTES

When groups stand opposed, four ways of terminating the conflict are possible: (*a*) isolate the groups and eliminate contact between them; (*b*) unite them into one group, even if it means "cracking their heads together"; (*c*) join the contest, let the more powerful annihilate the weaker: "Right will prevail"; and (*d*) maintain the identity of each group and through functional relations seek resolution by interaction, discussion, and decision. Except for rare instances the first three: isolationism, enforced unification, and extinction all contain significant negative components more repugnant than the conflict they seek to relieve. They will not be commented upon further. The fourth way holds genuine promise. It seems so obvious. "When you have a difference, sit down and talk it through. If not that, tell it to a neutral person and let him decide." Yet the path that seeks resolution through interaction, discussion, and decision itself is permeated with subtle difficulties. Here is where true statesmanship enters, for to take cognizance of the psychological characteristics of various approaches is to increase the probability of successful resolution of intergroup conflict.

RESOLUTION OF DIFFERENCES THROUGH INTERACTION, DISCUSSION, AND DECISION

Six fundamental approaches to the reduction of intergroup tensions through interaction are: negotiations by group members, use of the "good offices" of an intermediary, exchange of persons, handing the conflict to judges, the use of special decision-making panels to plot solutions that involve specific common goals, and intergroup therapy. Each is examined below from the standpoint of research evidence when available and, where not, from the point of view of field experience and logical analysis. The goal is to provide a general orientation to problems of intergroup relations.

Negotiations by group members

Negotiations by representatives. Solutions are sought most commonly through negotiations carried on by representatives, either the leaders themselves or persons specifically designated to negotiate. The United Nations is an example on the international level. Within universities and companies, members of departments are called together as committees where each participant is expected to represent his department in the resolution of matters that affect it. Bargaining teams in labor-management negotiations also are composed in this way. A key for evaluating this approach is found in the fact that the representative is a *member* of the group he represents. He knows the problem from an ingroup point of view.

As background for evaluating the representational approach, consider the following. Two or more groups stand opposed on a critical issue. Each has a preferred solution which its members support. Both solutions are publicly known in advance of negotiations. Representatives meet. Frequently, the interaction develops into a win-lose contest, with each representative maintaining his group's position while attempting to provoke the other representative to capitulate. The representative who exerts influence on the opposing representative and in doing so obtains their acceptance of his group's position may be accorded a "hero" reaction within his group or bringing it victory (Blake and Mouton, 1958). On the other hand, the representative who relinquishes his group's position, thus giving victory to the opposition, often is treated as disloyal or as "traitorous" by members of his own group. The representative who wins stands to enjoy increased status within his group, and he senses it. The representative who capitulates loses prestige and is confronted with possible ostracism. He knows that, too (Roethlisberger, 1945). It is probable that the more cohesive the group and the more basic the issue in the life of the group, the more the "hero" or "traitor" reaction is magnified, since the hero has supported the group's position and the traitor has deviated from it in a significant manner (Schachter, 1951).

"Deadlock" is one result of the traitor threat. If a representative cannot win, through deadlocking the issue he can avoid losing. Through deadlocking, a traitor reaction can be avoided, but representatives of both sides stand to suffer reduction in membership status relative to the increased power accompanying victory. Another alternative to defeat is "compromise": give as little as possible and get as much, or create the appearance that both sides have yielded some, but with neither suffering defeat. Unfortunately, such compromises often may be mechanical and brittle, constituting artificial solutions rather than real resolutions.

When negotiations take a win-lose turn, as they often do if preferred positions constitute public standards announced in advance, then quest for resolution by representatives may be replete with obstacles. The core of the difficulty seems to be that representatives are "committed" people. From the standpoint of their own group membership they are not entirely "free" to act in accord with "fact," or even to engage in compromise, if to do so would be interpreted by group members as "defeat." To a degree the limitations noted here may be reduced when representatives are freed to negotiate without prior instructions. Even then, however, they may be "expected" to act in certain ways even though formal instructions have not been placed on them.

The critical limitation in seeking resolutions through representatives seems to be in the "conflict of interest" aspect. For the representative to suffer defeat may be for him to place his membership status in jeopardy, while by gaining victory he may enhance his membership position. In the negotiation situation though, logical considerations may require that the representative renounce his group's prior position in order to gain a valid resolution of the intergroup problem. Where there is conflict of interest, the situation is such that ingroup loyalty can overwhelm logic.

Negotiations through summit conference. When negotiations by representatives fail, the plea is heard: "If only the *leaders* would get together, that would do more good than any other one step that could be taken." Let us examine this one. It is tricky. On first glance it appears to be a most practical and concrete approach. If leaders cannot agree, who can?

Modern history shows that summit conferences on the international scene have resulted in something less than complete success to either side. One has only to recall Yalta, Potsdam, and Geneva within the recent past for examples. White House conferences on education, social welfare, and so on have fared little better. Repeated parlays by the Joint Chiefs of Staff have not resulted in satisfactory unification of military activity.

Leaders face the inherent limitations of any representataive in negotiating. A further consideration in this approach is related to the source from which the leader's power is derived. To the degree he is an autocratic leader, with power to regulate followers through control of their physical, economic, or political systems, he also has power to negotiate and to commit. Why? The logic is that he can go against existing standards and norms within his group, still retain his power, and enforce the changes to which he has committed himself. Not so when leadership power is derived through an elective system. Evidence suggests that under elective conditions the leader may be even *less* free to negotiate than are other group members. It may be that the norms for leadership are more exacting and require greater responsibility than for others within the group (Harvey, 1953; Whyte, 1943). Then too, Kelley and Volkart (1952) have demonstrated an inverse correlation between evaluation by a person of his membership in a group and his susceptibility to communication on topics opposed to group norms. Also, O. J. Harvey (1953) has shown that middle and lower status group members have higher expectations for leaders than for other members and that the leader shares their expectations for his own performance. A leader, in other words, seems to be more subject to regulation by his own group than other members are. Efforts to change leaders, and other members as well, which would make them deviate from these norms will encounter strong resistances (Cartwright, 1951).

When prevailing leadership has failed to bring about resolution or when it has made no attempt in this direction, according to Pelz (1951) the result may be increased frustration of the group expectations and consequent loss of influence by the leader. Under these conditions the suggestion to "get new leaders" frequently is heard. Leaders do come and go, and often a new leader will try, by traditional means, to accomplish what predecessors have failed to attain. No less frequently does a new leader fail. He stands in the same or a similar relationship to accepted standards and norms within his group as did the old one. The Merei study (1949) suggests his difficulty. Strong leaders were brought into groups whose traditions and standards already had been formed. To exert leadership influence within the group, they had first to *accept* the very positions they sought to change. In other words the "fresh" approach soon dies under the impact of prevailing conditions. The rule seems to be that, rather than "a new broom sweeping clean," the "new look" is rapidly transformed into an old wheeze.

The use of intermediaries

An approach in some respects comparable with the use of representatives or with the search for resolution of intergroup conflict through formal leaders involves the intermediary. Intermediaries usually hold membership in neither of the contending groups, but are from an outside organization or a level in an organization higher than the groups which are in conflict. The intermediary is expected to pass between the groups and to aid in the reduction of conflict through identifying areas of agreement, clarifying areas of disagreement, and developing proposals designed to ease tensions which are acceptable to both sides in a controversy. The intermediary, in other words, supplies a critical link of communication. He can pierce the boundaries which otherwise constitute barriers to communication. Usually he acts without formal authority. His success is based primarily on the goodwill and confidence that his reputation and his status as one who belongs to neither group creates.

The intermediary role needs experimental evaluation before a critical appraisal of its advantages and limitations can be given. History contains examples of conspicuous successes and outstanding failures of this approach. From a logical point of view it does appear, however, to have the advantage of increasing communication between contending groups. It has the further advantage that final responsibility for resolution rests, not on the judgment of the intermediary, but on attitudes within the competing groups themselves. A major limitation is in the fact that many situations of intergroup conflict are such that there is no organization outside or above the groups which are in disagreement which can arrange the appointment and acceptance from both sides of an intermediary.

A further disadvantage is possibly of greater importance. Basic communication between groups is not necessarily improved through actions of an intermediary, since arrangements for intergroup communication are likely to remain the same after his departure or as they were before his services were employed. The result is that *conditions* similar to those responsible for the initial eruption of conflict may remain unchanged. In a sense the intermediary role is better suited to the relief of symptoms than to the correction of basic causes.

Exchange of persons

An approach said to have implications for resolving intergroup differences in the long-term view involves exchange of persons across the boundaries of the competing groups. The idea is that exposure on a people-to-people basis for the purpose of getting to know others, their institutions, and cultural products can serve to increase understanding as a background for future cooperation. The appeal is that if people will but look and see with their own eyes they will penetrate their prejudices and stereotypes. Educational exchanges from student activities to the Fulbright fellowship program are examples in the academic field. Examples from business and industry include exchanges of industrial productivity teams between the United States and Europe as well as the pattern in business of rotating personnel from one position to another in the effort to develop managers who have a company orientation rather than a provincial, departmental point of view. There may be other advantages to this approach aside from its contribution to the resolution of intergroup differences, but that is the aspect being considered here.

Findings from a half-dozen experiments involving exchanges between political and racial groupings point to two general conclusions (Ram and Murphy, 1952; Saenger, 1953). One is that people-to-people interaction across groups may serve to make those whose attitudes initially are pro, more pro, and those who initially are anti, more anti. Rather than being subject to fundamental alteration it appears that attitudes and convictions which already are established undergo intensification, though there is some evidence that changes related to the specific conditions of interaction may appear.

A second generalization is based on the observation that social, political, and economic attitudes, rather than being determined solely on an individual personality basis, are significantly anchored in reference groups. If, through an exchange experience, an individual's attitudes shift in a direction away from those formerly held, on return to his group he is subject to confrontation from his peers for expressing attitudes contrary to those accepted by them. The Bennington study (Newcomb, 1943) is an outstanding early example of the extent to which individuals express attitudes which maintain congruency with attitudes anchored in their group memberships. French and Zajonc (1957) have carried the analysis of the problem further, presenting evidence which suggests that when an individual is faced with an intergroup norm conflict the attitudes expressed are those which are most congruent with situational factors. That is to say, an individual who is under exchange-of-persons conditions, and moves from one group to another, is more prone to express attitudes consistent with the views of the group in which he is located. Another consideration is that contact between groups does not always lead to a lessening of conflict. A study in the Near East shows that ingroups may be most hostile to those groups with which they come in closest contact (Dodd, 1935).

While exchange programs as approaches for resolving intergroup conflict leave much to be desired, two implications can be drawn. One is that those who initially are neutral are most susceptible to influence. Without preformed attitudes there is a real possibility that the increased exposure provided can result in a more objective appraisal of experiences. It is from an awareness of this consideration that the most intensive efforts by both sides in the cold war are concentrated on the so-called uncommitted people. The effort is to move them away from a neutral position on the argument of the "immorality of neutrality."

The other implication is that plans involving the exchanges of *groups* may create a favorable background for future intergroup resolution, where person-to-person programs fail. The reason is that, when individuals undergo new experiences as a *group*, attitudes anchored at the group level may themselves be subject to modification. Refusal by an individual to maintain altered attitudes then constitutes deviation from the group norms with consequent rejection confronting the individual who refuses to change (Schachter, 1951). Thus reinforcement of changed attitudes comes about through group membership.

The use of "judges"

Resolution of differences is sought through judges, persons trained to evaluate materials relevant to the issue under examination. Since judges hold membership in neither of the competing groups, they are not subject to the conflict of interest situation described above; therefore, they can be "fair." The Supreme Court and federal and state legal systems all are based on gaining resolution through the use of judges. Because of the judge's "outside" position, contestants are expected to accept the outcome as an impartial one.

Do they? The answer depends on where you sit. It is likely to be "Yes," if the decision favors your group; "No," if it goes against the position your group embraces. Listen to the following remarks from exploratory studies (Harvey, 1957; Human Relations Training Laboratory, 1958). They are reactions toward "neutral" judges from those defeated by his decision.

The judge is biased, unfair, and incompetent . . . he has no grasp of the problem . . . he does not possess the intelligence prerequisite to be fair and unbiased . . . he doesn't seem to know too much about the subject . . . he didn't take enough time.

In other words, when group members are committed to their position and a judge decides against it, either the group is wrong or the judge is wrong. In their initial reactions group members have *little* doubt as to which: it is the judge. Results from several sources suggest that the stronger the commitment of a group to its solution, the more relevant the problem to the life of the group, and the more cohesive the group, the greater the negative reactions to a judge whose decision defeats them. Even though obligated to accept the verdict, attitudes remain more or less consistent with convictions held prior to the rendering of the judgment.

When intergroup competition has been generated for study purposes under laboratory training conditions with resolution of the conflict placed in the hands of a judge, a delayed reaction of considerable importance has been noted among members within some defeated groups (Human Relations Training Laboratory, 1958). Though the initial reaction in the defeated group toward the judge is as noted above, "it's the judge who is at fault," a delayed reaction among some members is, "it's our group which is at fault." Such a reaction seems to arise among the members who were the least committed to the group's position before the issue was submitted. Rather than venting their frustrations from defeat on the judge, they discharge it by aggressive attacks on other group members. A consequence is that the group tends to "splinter," to loose its former degree of cohesion and to disrupt.

When the judge renders a verdict favoring a group's position, two things are evident. The judge is experienced as being fair and unbiased all right, because the judgment he proclaims "only proves that we were right in the first place." He is experienced as being a *good* judge because he sees the situation as members themselves see it. "If there was any doubt in our minds before, his ruling eliminated it. Now we know we're right." Resolutions thus attained may have administrative consequences, particularly if the judge's decision is reinforced by sanctions. To those who lose, the resolution retains an arbitrary, mechanical quality. Losers comply because the ground rules require it, but they remain unconvinced.

By comparison with a representative or a leader a judge is not gripped in the vise of a conflict-of-interest situation. Yet the judge is as suspect by those whose position he defeats as is the representative who goes against his group. The inherent difficulty is that the judge's decision may carry little force in comparison with the strength of the group's commitment to its position. The defeated frequently are not moved to alter their position.

Common goals with crisscross panels

A situation favoring resolution is present when both of the opposing sides are confronted with a common goal which can only be reached through interdependent effort. This set of circumstances has confronted social agencies in raising operating budgets. Competing with one another was found to be less than successful, but when agencies came together and agreed on a superordinate goal which could only be reached through joint effort, greater success was achieved. Each group maintained its identity, and yet through embracing a common goal, the area of conflict was eliminated and one of cooperation was created. Another example of a new grouping designed to achieve a common goal is the proposed single agency to take the place of competing individual services in the development and coordination of approaches to outer space. Control of military uses of atomic energy and programs for world reduction of arms constitute goals at the international level which have been dreamt about but not yet realized. Companies that have introduced cost concern programs on a common goal basis have found this approach quite successful (Hood, 1957). Only recently, however, has experimental work been oriented toward a more systematic assessment of the approach.

In three highly ingenious studies Sherif, who originally formulated the problem discussed here, has explored a variety of ways of relieving differences between contending groups (Sherif, 1958; Sherif and Sherif, 1953, 1956). Groups were placed in competition on a win-lose basis. Unsuccessful in relieving the tensions thus produced were contacts between members, contacts between leaders, and preaching and coercion. More fruitful was the solution of competing groups joining together in order to defeat a third, outside group, but in this way the area of conflict was widened. The most appropriate way found was that of confronting contending groups with a common problem which could be resolved only through their joint efforts. Once a superordinate goal was accepted as a challenge by high status members of both sides then mutual efforts by individuals, with less regard for primary group affiliations, became more common. Contending groups started to pull together, and contacts between members turned to positive purposes instead of serving as occasions for accusations and mutual irritations.

Several conditions are necessary for employing the superordinate goal approach. Both sides must *desire* a genuine solution, and the mere presence of friction is not by any means indicative that they do. The absence of such requisite problem-solving motivation precludes the success of any approach. In addition there is a need for a single definition of the problem developed by both sides without a prior statement of preferred solutions. This way avoids commitments which are prone to become irreversible when one side appears to be losing, and strategies for dealing with the "loss of face" problem become unnecessary. Fundamental conditions for successful resolution are present when both of these considerations have been met.

A limitation in employing the superordinate goal approach is in the fact that all members of competing groups rarely are able to combine efforts toward attaining superordinate goals. There is need of a way for representatives to interact toward the attainment of superordinate goals which can provide freedom of action without the status reduction that occurs with going against one's own group's position.

There is a possibility which avoids difficulties encountered by other methods. Each side develops a list of nominees whom they consider qualified to represent them with respect to one particular source of friction. Next, from the list of nominees, members of both groups elect a decision-making panel through voting on representatives from *both* sides. The final panel contains members who represent their own group and yet who simultaneously represent the other group as well.

By the conditions of their selection, being jointly elected, representatives are more free to confront the problem without facing the hero-traitor dynamic that arises from the usual unilateral group orientation. Why? The reason is that group members from both sides experience such representatives as oriented toward a "fair" solution. Even when they go against a prevailing standard of their group the action is experienced as more "legitimate" that when they do so as unilateral representatives. Furthermore, representatives themselves are motivated to examine issues from the frames of reference of both groups, rather than from that of their own group alone.

The crisscross panel is a way of approaching the resolution of intergroup disputes that is currently under experimental evaluation. The procedure constitutes but an extension of democratic methods to the solution of problems. Even now a modification of it is employed to settle labor-management disputes which have gone into deadlock. The method provides the possibility of progress toward reduction of intergroup conflict, whether the point of application involves disputes between nations, labor-management, government agencies, departments of a company organization, or between social agencies within a community.

Intergroup therapy

A final possibility remains when other approaches fail. It is based on therapeutic conceptions that deal with problems of relationship. The *unit* of therapy, rather than being focused on the individual, the interpersonal level, or the group, is comprised of competing groups in *relationship* with one another. The rationale is that groups may hold perceptions and stereotypes of one another which are distorted, negative, or so hidden that they prevent functional relationships from arising between them. Only *after* basic problems of relationships have been eliminated is effective interaction possible. If the contending groups are so large as to eliminate the possibility of interchange among all members simultaneously, segments of groups may be employed, with the procedure repeated until fundamental sources of intergroup animosity have been neutralized.

One procedure of intergroup therapy is to bring contending groups together as *groups*. In private each discusses and seeks to agree on its perception and attitudes toward the other and its perceptions of itself as well. Then *representatives* of both groups talk together in the presence of other group members from both sides who are obligated to remain silent. During this phase representatives are responsible for accurate communication of the picture that each group has constructed of the other and of itself. They are free to ask questions for clarification of the other group's point of view, but ground rules prevent them from giving rationalizations, justifications, etc. The reason for using representatives is that communication remains more orderly and responsibility is increased for them to provide an accurate version of the situation. Members of both groups then discuss *in private* the way they are perceived by each other in order to develop understanding of the discrepancies between their own view of themselves and the description of them by the other side. Finally, again working through representatives, each helps the other to appreciate bases of differences, to correct *invalid* perceptions, and to consider alternative explanations of past behavior. Fundamental value conflicts not based on distortions also can be identified and examined; then suggestions can be developed for ways of working on problems which can result in solutions apart from basic value conflicts.

Intergroup therapy is relatively unexplored, although it has been tried with success in industrial settings on several occasions. Many problems, themselves subject to solution through the superordinate goal approach, cannot even be faced until deeper animosities *between* groups have been resolved or at least explored and neutralized. If emotion-laden negative attitudes and stereotypes are dealt with first, it becomes increasingly possible in a second phase to formulate and work toward the attainment of a superordinate goals as described above.

Now to return to my thesis. Statesmanship is faltering. Many problems of tremendous import continue to be handled by statesmen on an intuitive basis—a paradox in a world where scientific method has advanced understanding so far. Approaches frequently are used which fail to recognize the psychological characteristics of people and the dilemmas confronting them when engaging in discussion intended to resolve intergroup disputes. What are some of the psychological characteristics of people that must be considered?

Take, for example, the situation of a typical representative. In negotiation he is faced with a fundamental conflict of interest. Stephen Decatur in 1816 said: "Our country! In her intercourse with foreign nations, may she always be in the right; but our country, right or wrong!" In this remark he was identifying the dilemma facing all representatives of groups which are in competition, whether leaders or other members. If to yield or to compromise means defeat, it exposes the responsible person to rejection and ostracism by his peers. To resist and gain victory can lead to his acclamation as a hero. The consequence is that representatives are motivated to win, or at least to avoid defeat, even though a realistic solution of an intergroup problem may be sacrificed in the process. An intermediary who holds membership in neither group may be employed to develop solutions acceptable to both groups. This approach, which has some positive merits, when it is possible to appoint an intermediary from some outside group, may be successful in resolving a specific problem but is likely to do little to effect resolution of basic cleavages between groups, since lines of communication supplied by the action of this intermediary are likely to be eliminated after his departure.

Resolution of conflict through the action of judges also suffers a critical limitation. Rendering a judgment which defeats a side does not convince the vanquished protagonists of the error of their ways. Further, the force to implement the verdict is not within the group but must be added from the outside. Neither understanding, nor acceptance, nor commitment, but coercion is likely to be the force which prevents the extension of conflict. The limitations of this procedure frequently outweigh its possible merits for the simple reason that punitive action, or the threat of it, is basic to enforcement.

There is another way which seems more constructive. Acting with respect to common goals, representatives can be selected through a crisscross election method in such a way as to free them to confront the problem more squarely, rather than trying to "win" from a partisan point of view. When this is done, subscribing to the outcome is an obligation within *both* groups. It can occur through acceptance and commitment, without coercion. Concrete application should begin with problems of lesser significance at low levels in order to permit an assessment of the method and the development of skill in using it in specific situations. Then, with success, the procedure can be applied to more important problems at higher levels until issues of substance and significance are being dealt with in a constructive manner.

When an approach to resolution of intergroup problems through superordinate goals cannot be made because of negative, emotionally saturated perceptions, attitudes, and stereotypes, a possibility of solution still remains. Through insertion of a preliminary phase involving the concepts of intergroup therapy, conditions favoring problem solving may be created. If the approach "unblocks" intergroup relationships, then the actions required by superordinate goal considerations can be introduced.

Theory of behavior relating to individuals in group situations and relations between groups is basic to the enlightened practice of statemanship. It provides guidelines for planning and action. The outcome of the crisis of our times may well rest on whether or not statesmen can design situations for the resolution of intergroup disputes which are sound. Introduction of a psychological point of view may constitute a condition for survival.

REFERENCES

Blake, R. R. and Mouton, Jane S. "Heroes and Traitors: Two Patterns of Representing Groups in a Competitive Situation," *International Journal of Sociometry* (1958).

Cartwright, D. "Achieving Change in People: Some Applications of Group Dynamics Theory," *Human Relations* Vol. 4 (1951), pp. 381–92.

Dodd, S. C. "A Social Distance Test in the Near East," *American Journal of Sociology,* Vol. 41 (1935), pp. 194–204.

French, J. R. P., Jr. and Zajonc, R. B. "An Experimental Study of Cross-Cultural Norm Conflict," *Journal of Abnormal and Social Psychology,* Vol. 54 (1957), pp. 218–24.

Harvey, J. "Subjective Reactions to a Judge as a Function of His Verdict." Unpublished manuscript, University of Texas, 1957.

Harvey, O. J. "An Experimental Approach to the Study of Status Relations in Informal Groups," *American Sociological Review,* Vol. 18 (1953), pp. 357–67.

Hood, R. *Concern for Costs.* Ann Arbor: Survey Research Center, University of Michigan, 1957.

Human Relations Training Laboratory, *Proceedings.* Taos, N.M.: Human Relations Training Laboratory, 1958.

Kelley, H. H. and Volkart, E. H. "The Resistance to Change of Group-Anchored Attitudes," *American Sociological Review,* Vol. 17 (1952), pp. 453–65.

Merei, F. "Group Leadership and Institutionalization," *Human Relations,* Vol. 2 (1949), pp. 23–39.

Newcomb, T. M. *Personality and Social Change.* New York: Dryden, 1943.

Pelz, D. C. "Leadership within a Hierarchical Organization," *Journal of Social Issues,* Vol. 7 (1951), pp. 49–55.

Ram, P. and Murphy, G. C. "Recent Investigations of Hindu-Muslim Relations in India," *Human Organization,* Vol. 11 (1952), pp. 13–16.

Roethlisberger, F. J. "The Foreman: Master and Victim of Double Talk," *Harvard Business Review,* Vol. 23 (1945), pp. 283–98.

Saenger, G. *The Social Psychology of Prejudice.* New York: Harper, 1953.

Schachter, S. "Deviation, Rejection, and Communication," *Journal of Abnormal and Social Psychology,* Vol. 46 (1951), pp. 190–207.

Sherif, M. "Reduction of Intergroup Conflict," *American Journal of Sociology,* Vol. 53 (1958), pp. 349–56.

Sherif, M. and Sherif, Carolyn W. *Groups in Harmony and Tension.* New York: Harper, 1953.

Sherif, M. and Sherif, Carolyn W. *An Outline of Social Psychology,* 2d ed. New York: Harper, 1956.

Whyte, W. F. *Street Corner Society.* Chicago: University of Chicago Press, 1943.

Physical settings and social interaction[*]

Fred I. Steele

In my consultation and research on the impact of the physical setting on behavior in organizations, I have identified six dimensions which represent the basic functions that settings play for people. These dimensions were intended to be specific enough to capture major pieces of human experience with the environment, yet broad enough to result in a manageable number of categories, so that they would be a practical diagnostic tool. The dimensions are[1]:

---

[*] Adapted from Chapter 5, "Social Contact," in F. I. Steele, *Physical Settings & Organization Development,* Reading, Mass.: Addison-Wesley Publishing Co., Inc., 1973.

[1] Although I will not present a long derivation here, I should note that these categories were inspired by two main sources: Maslow's theory of basic human needs, and my own and others' observations of the activities in which people engage in different settings, including their complaints about the inadequacies of the settings for their needs.

1. *Security and shelter*—protection from harmful or unwanted stimuli from your surroundings, such as a roof protecting you from the rain or a thick wall keeping sounds out of your room so you can sleep at night.

2. *Social contact*—arrangements of facilities and spaces that permit or promote social interaction, such as a garden apartment's central bank of mailboxes where people come face-to-face with one another fortuitously.

3. *Symbolic identification*—the messages sent by settings which tell someone what a person, group, or organization is like, such as a person decorating his office.

4. *Task instrumentality*—appropriate facilities and layouts that are useful for tasks that are being done in a particular setting, such as a soundproof room for taping records.

5. *Pleasure*—the place itself provides pleasure or gratification to those who use it, such as hikers greatly enjoying the views they have visiting the Olympic Peninsula in Washington.

6. *Growth*—the setting providing a stimulus for the user's growth, such as when a person learns something new about himself from the feelings he has while he is lost in a dark woods overnight.

Each of these dimensions is discussed in some detail in *Physical Settings and Organization Development.* The emphasis of this reading will be on the impact of settings on interpersonal contact, with the majority of examples drawn from work organizations.

To understand this dimension, we must look at two aspects: first, the impact of the setting in terms of the amount and quality of the social contacts it provides; and second, what kinds of contact the users *want* and the goodness of fit between this and the actual impact of the setting. In explaining these aspects, I will look at three properties of the setting: arrangements of facilities, locations of people relative to one another and to activities, and the amount of mobility allowed by a setting.

INFLUENCE OF FACILITIES ARRANGEMENTS

There are several kinds of impact that spatial arrangements have on the amount of interpersonal interaction. One influence, first identified by Humphrey Osmond, is the "sociopetal" or "sociofugal" aspect of settings. These impacts are, respectively, the tendency of arrangements to bring people together (as in a small doctor's waiting room or in sitting around a small card table), or to push them apart (as in airport waiting rooms or large living rooms where furniture is far apart). Sommer provides a very moving description of the mental hospital setting in which sociofugal space was so graphically and proudly designed in as an "improvement."

Most of the chairs on this ward stood in straight lines along the walls, but there were several rows back-to-back in the center; around several columns there were four chairs, each chair facing a different direction! . . . With as many as 50 ladies in the large room, there were rarely more than one or two brief conversations. The ladies sat side by side against the newly painted walls in their new chrome chairs and exercised their options of gazing down at the newly tiled floor or looking up at the new florescent lights. [Further on, he says] The arrangement of furniture is left to the ward staff who do not realize the therapeutic potential for furniture arrangement. Ward geography is taken for granted, and a chair becomes something to sweep around rather than a necessary tool for social interaction.[2]

Imagine yourself trying to *maintain* your sanity in that kind of setting, let alone trying to improve from an already shaky position!

I should add that there is another factor which allows this arrangement to be distancing: Not only mental patients, but most of us, tend to take our spatial arrangements as we find them. Unless the furniture is actually bolted down (as is, unfortunately, often the case, especially in universities), a given arrangement can only remain sociofugal if people assume it is fixed. This is an example of what I call "Pseudofixed Feature Space"—settings that are treated as fixed, even though they are changeable.

In another series of experiments, Sommer[3] found in his studies of seating arrangements that an across-corner arrangement was preferred for seated conversations, with across the table being second and side-by-side least preferred. Settings that only allow side-by-side seating, such as many classrooms or terminal waiting rooms, will tend to reduce contact, particularly between people who are not in adjacent seats.

This last point raises the issue of fixed versus variable seating arrangements. Classrooms that have fixed seats make it difficult for individual students to relate to anyone but the teacher at the front or the students on either side, and even they are often too close for comfortable conversation. On the other hand, movable furniture when combined with group norms which support changing the arrangements when appropriate can facilitate different amounts of interaction as they are desired.

A recent structural example of this flexibility is a living room designed for my Prickley Mountain, Vermont, house by Thomas Luckey. The room has *no* furniture but is *all* furniture, that is, plywood forms covered with foam rubber and carpeted. Any of it can be sat on, walked on, etc. People can arrange themselves in many different patterns. My use of this space for different social activities has confirmed that interaction is facilitated by wide choice about how to arrange oneself. Conversely, it is also easy to find a fairly private spot when that feels appropriate.

The arrangement of furniture in offices is an obvious area where the above ideas need to be applied. Spaces can be arranged to keep people apart or bring them together, depending on where chairs, sofas, desks, files, etc., are placed.

---

[2] Robert Sommer, *Personal Space: The Behavioral Basis of Design* (Englewood Cliffs, N.J.: Prentice-Hall, 1969), pp. 78–79.

[3] Robert Sommer, "Small Group Ecology", *Psychological Bulletin*, Vol. *67*, No. 2, 1967.

Occupants of offices often use their "props" to regulate the distance between themselves and others. As Hall[4] summarizes the impact of this effect, he says,

Business and social discourse conducted at the far end of social distance (seven to twelve feet) has a more formal character than if it occurs inside the close phase (four to seven feet). Desks in the offices of important people are large enough to hold visitors at the far phase of social distance. Even in an office with standard-sized desks, the chair opposite is eight or nine feet away from the man at the desk. At the far phase of social distance, the finest details of the face, such as the capillaries of the eye, are lost.

As the above paragraph suggests, arrangements affect not only the *quantity* but the *quality* of social contact. Steinzor[5] noted that in discussion groups, when a man finished speaking, the next speaker tended to be someone *across* from him rather than *adjacent* to him. From this, he formulated the "expressive contact hypothesis" that since visual contact could be made more easily with those across (who can be seen without turning or without violating social distance norms by looking at them from too close), people are more likely to be aware of, and, therefore, responsive to, those across from them.

In the office situation, the implication would be that in both group sessions and individual work activities in a common area, people will tend to be more aware of others whom they can see easily than those whom they cannot see. Physical arrangements obviously play a major role in who can be seen by whom. We must also note, however, that the social setting also affects this contact process. Hearn[6] found that the type of leadership in a group affected the responsiveness pattern. With minimal leadership, Steinzor's effect was duplicated. But with a strong leader present, responses tended to come from adjacent people. This is a nice example of joint influence of the physical and social environments. Sommer[7] summarizes it this way:

Based on the studies of dominance described earlier, we can hypothesize that with a strong leader close by, the individual restricts his gaze to adjacent seats, but when leadership is weak or absent, he can look anywhere and the stimulus value of people opposite becomes heightened.

To repeat, the Steinzor effect illustrates that the arrangement of facilities affects both the amount and quality of contact that people can have. Although we tend to talk about contact as simply present or absent, the fact is that there are different kinds of contact: temporary, constant, surface, intimate, playful, work-oriented, open, closed, and so on. Facilities should also be analyzed in terms of the kinds of contact they facilitate.

For example, although there are no hard data, preliminary interviews indicate

---

[4] E. T. Hall, *The Hidden Dimension* (Garden City, New York: Doubleday, 1966), p. 115.

[5] B. Steinzor, "The Spatial Factor in Face-to-Face Discussion Groups," *Journal of Abnormal and Social Psychology*, vol. 45, 1950.

[6] Gordon Hearn, "Leadership and the Spatial Factor in Small Groups," *Journal of Abnormal and Social Psychology*, vol. 54, 1957.

[7] Sommer, *Personal Space* p. 61.

that one outcome of the open room seating arrangements of the office landscape plan is that while general interaction of a group tends to go up through greater visibility and ease of movement, social contacts of a more intimate nature tend to go down. As people feel more doubts about the privacy of their conversations, both visually and verbally, they tend to make the conversations less personal, even though there are more of them.

Of course, we would expect this influence to be mediated by the social structure, just as it was in the Hearn study. When the group climate is such that people do not mind being overheard, then an open-office layout can enhance both general and intimate contact. For instance, the vice president of a small company described their executive office:

We decided to have both our desks in the same space, with a wall only half-way across. The president and I are in much better touch with what we are doing as a top management team. We know what commitments and contacts are being made. But it wouldn't work if we hadn't decided at the beginning not to have secrets from one another!

RELATIVE LOCATIONS

At a slightly larger scale, interaction is also affected by the relative locations of different facilities, people, and activity areas. For instance, social group membership has been shown to be heavily influenced by locational variables. In a study conducted in a married-students housing project it was found that friendship patterns were affected by two major factors: sheer distance between houses (a 4–5 house separation seemed to be about the limit for a regular friendship), and the direction in which the houses, and, therefore, their entrances, faced. People who lived in houses whose entrances faced each other on a court tended to become a cohesive social group. People whose house fronts were turned, for appearance sake, toward the street, had less than half as many friends in the project as did those who lived in houses facing the courtyard.[8]

The investigators also found that people who lived near entries, stairways, and mailboxes made more friends and had a more active social life. I have observed the same phenomenon at my Vermont home. The people that live next to the mailboxes (which are all in one location) have described to me their feeling of centrality in the community. The same effect is common in work organizations, where some people are located in much more high-contact positions than others. One girl I interviewed recognized this effect most clearly when her situation had changed:

My social life has changed drastically since my desk was moved to the end of a dead-end corridor. I used to be right near the entrance to the whole place and saw almost everyone as they came in and out. I don't have so many interruptions now, but I also have fewer conversations. I also eat lunch by myself more, when groups forget to include me. I like the whole feeling less than before.

---

[8] L. Festinger, S. Schacter, and K. Back, *Social Pressures in Informal Groups: A Study of Human Factors in Housing* (New York: Harper), 1950.

Leavitt found a similar pattern in his study of communication networks. People in central positions in a star-shaped network tended to be more satisfied with the task than those in peripheral positions. Group leadership was also highly correlated with centrality of position.[9]

Another locational factor that influences interaction is the presence or absence of *central gathering spaces*—places that are not "owned" by anyone, such as a desk is, but are likely to be used by many members of a system or community. For a setting to be good for accidental or informal contact, it needs several characteristics. One is that it be central—that is, that people would naturally pass through it on their way to other places. A second is that there be places to sit or come to rest comfortably. Third, people need to be able to stop there, and converse or watch others, without blocking the flow of vehicular or foot traffic by their stopping. As I recently observed, a bulletin board in a busy narrow hallway is almost useless, since no one can stop there long enough to read it or chat with others about the notices without clogging up the whole hallway.

An example from the community sphere of a good central space is Sproule Plaza at the University of California at Berkeley. It has all of the above features, plus good weather which adds to the comfort of just "hanging around." I am convinced that this space was a major factor in the connections that led to the Free Speech Movement. Even though the demonstrators complained of alienation from the huge university, they were able to come together for common action in ways that most student bodies never do. Without Sproule Plaza this coming together would have been much more difficult, if not impossible.

The nature of work tasks and their associated technologies often affect locations in which people do their work, and thereby also influence the amount of social contact they have with one another. In the classic Hawthorne studies, the existence of a single room set up for the experiment promoted contact among the members of the group. The opposite effect often occurs as well. Blauner[10] describes a miners' union in England that demanded "hazard pay" when changes in work technology required them to work in isolation from one another. The point was not just that physical danger increased, but that it was psychologically more stressful to work alone.

Finally, location influences interaction not only when people are isolated *from* one another, but also when they are isolated *with* one another for long periods of time. Altman and Haythorn[11] found that experimental pairs in isolation from all other contacts developed specific patterns of interpersonal contact that helped them maintain a manageable climate during their forced interaction. Territorial behavior with bed and chair (identifying a piece of furniture as exclusively one's own to use) tended to reduce conflicts; those pairs that did not develop territorial

---

[9] H. Leavitt, "Some Effects of Certain Communication Patterns on Group Performance," *Journal of Abnormal and Social Psychology*, vol. 46, 1950.

[10] Robert Blauner, *Alienation and Freedom* (Chicago: University of Chicago Press), 1964.

[11] I. Altman and W. Haythorn, "The Ecology of Isolated Groups," *Behavioral Science*, vol. 12, no. 3, 1967.

norms tended to last a shorter time in the experiment than those that did.

Topics of conversation are also influenced by isolation together. As a submarine officer put it,

On a two-month cruise, certain topics are just not talked about, as a way of keeping friction down. I found this out the hard way by being more vocal since I wasn't a career officer. I learned after my first cruise, though. You know you've got to be with those guys for a long time, it's just not worth it to take the chance of a permanent blow-up.

Other occupational groups have reported the same self-monitoring of group behavior, including polar explorers, weather station personnel, and oil explorers. I have heard a family describe the same process when they were on a camping trip. It is clear that forced interaction in a closed setting has a big influence on the quality of social contact that occurs there.

MOBILITY

The last effect of settings on social contact that I will discuss here is the extent to which physical mobility is allowed or required in a setting. In general, the more free people are to move around, the more likely they are to come in contact with one another, especially if they are not adjacent to each other in their regular seats or work stations.

The nature of the technology of a particular kind of work often has a major impact on physical mobility. For instance, Blauner points out that on automobile assembly lines the combination of noise and fixed work positions produces a sense of powerlessness in the workers and retards group formation. The operators have very little contact with their co-workers as long as the belt is bringing their work to them in a steady flow.[12] He contrasts this with automated chemical process plants, where operators do have freedom to move as they choose. They have both greater contact with other operators and more opportunity to see where their work fits into the whole process of the plant. Blauner also shows the limits of mobility, however, in his description of textile workers tending "acres" of machines in an automated plant. They have great mobility but little real freedom to contact one another, since they must move swiftly to deal with problems over a large number of machines. They have only fleeting contact with one another, although this is slightly more than they would have if they were locked into one position. No mobility and forced mobility can both reduce contact.

One of the most interesting examples of the impact of mobility on social contact is the new 747 jumbo jet. The increased size over conventional airliners has allowed structural features such as more aisle space and inclusion of lounge areas. This change in physical setting has increased mobility, with some interesting social effects:

---

[12] Blauner, *Alienation and Freedom*, p. 114.

In flight, passengers behave differently on board a jumbo than on a smaller jet. "A gregariousness has set in that we did not reckon on," says Pan Am president Najeeb Halaby. Passengers wander up and down the two aisles, try to help the stewardessess, or invade the first-class flight lounge on the deck.[13]

The most important long-run effect of increased jet size may well be on the nature of air travel as a social experience, rather than simply on the number of people carried per trip.

CHOICE ABOUT CONTACT

I would like to close this section on settings and social contact with the issue of how you decide whether the social effects of a particular setting are good or not. At heart, this depends upon *who* the users are, what they *want* in the way of contact, and what the relevant social system *needs* in the way of minimum contact of members in order to survive.

For instance, let us return for a moment to the case of the 747 jet. Zinsser (1970) raises some questions (which I personally share) about whether the new layout may *force* contact, and remove the traveler's choice to be alone if he wishes.

But all that we really want from the 747 is to get there in reasonable comfort and to be left alone just what we always wanted from the ocean liners and never got. . . . Perhaps we should want it otherwise. As the number of our fellow passengers increases, so should our ability to enjoy their company and to feel a little less alone. Yet when all is said (by the pilot) and done (by the stewardess), flight is still a solitary encounter with our own emotions.[14]

In other words, the limited mobility of earlier planes allowed many people who preferred solitude to get it with little effort. Now that movement around the plane is easier, the "solitaries" will have to work harder to maintain their aloneness—the space is not helping them as much.

Decisions about settings design and contact are usually made by someone who has a particular vested interest in the outcome. Sommer provides a graphic example:

Cafe patrons around the world may be in for an unpleasant surprise. Furniture designer Henning Larsen was consulted by Copenhagen cafe owners whose customers lingered endlessly over coffee. Larsen developed a chair that exerts disagreeable pressure on the spine if occupied for over a few minutes. The Larsen chair is now being marketed in New York and other cities.[15]

---

[13] "Jumbo Beats the Gremlins," *Time*, July 13, 1970.

[14] William Zinsser, "As Jumbo Jets Arrive and Liners Depart, Must Shuffleboard Roll on Forever?" *Life*, January 23, 1970.

[15] Sommer, *Personal Space*, p. 121.

We could well expect the Larsen chair to show up in company lounges where employees take their breaks. The point is that it would be ordered by the office management, not by the employees who would be using it. It was the cafe owners who decided that prolonged conversation was no good, not the patrons of the cafe.

A similar process occurs around the *use* of existing structures. I recently heard of a new midwestern high school that was designed with a very effective central forum. Early experiences in the new school showed that it was used as a catch-all gathering place much like the Sproule Plaza pattern I described earlier. This interaction, however, was a threat to the administration of the school, given the nature of the shaky relationship between authority and students in schools today. To keep students from getting together too long, they now station staff members in the forum to move students along. They have outlawed "hanging out" in a perfect hanging-out space.

Finally, it is sometimes hard to tell where *preferences* for a particular level of social contact leave off and the *effects* of particular settings on those preferences begin. A person may prefer a certain intensity of contact with others because he has spent long periods in a setting that provided that kind of contact. The example given from E. T. Hall earlier of Americans' preferences for private rooms and offices fits this pattern.

Interpersonal barriers to decision making*

Chris Argyris

The actual behavior of top executives during decision-making meetings often does not jibe with their attitudes and prescriptions about effective executive action. The gap that often exists between what executives say and how they behave helps create barriers to openness and trust, to the effective search for alternatives, to innovation, and to flexibility in the organization. These barriers are more destructive in important decision-making meetings than in routine meetings, and they upset effective managers more than ineffective ones.

The barriers cannot be broken down simply by intellectual exercises. Rather, executives need feedback concerning their behavior and opportunities to develop self-awareness in action. To this end, certain kinds of questioning are valuable; playing back and analyzing

---

* "Interpersonal Barriers to Decision Making," by Chris Argyris, *Harvard Business Review* (March–April 1966), © 1966 by the President and Fellows of Harvard College; all rights reserved.

FIGURE 1
Nature of the study

The six companies studied include: (1) an electronics firm with 40,000 employees, (2) a manufacturer and marketer of a new innovative product with 4,000 employees, (3) a large research and development company with 3,000 employees, (4) a small research and development organization with 150 employees, (5) a consulting-research firm with 400 employees, and (6) a producer of heavy equipment with 4,000 employees.

The main focus of the investigation reported here was on the behavior of 165 top executives in these companies. The executives were board members, executive committee members, upper-level managers, and (in a few cases) middle-level managers.

Approximately 265 decision-making meetings were studied and nearly 10,000 units of behavior analyzed. The topics of the meetings ranged widely, covering investment decisions, new products, manufacturing problems, marketing strategies, new pricing policies, administrative changes, and personnel issues. An observer took notes during all but 10 of the meetings; for research purposes, these 10 were analyzed "blind" from tapes (i.e., without ever meeting the executives). All other meetings were taped also, but analyzed at a later time.

The major device for analyzing the tapes was a new system of categories for scoring decision-making meetings.[1] Briefly, the executives' behavior was scored according to how often they—owned up to and accepted responsibility for their ideas or feelings; opened up to receive others' ideas or feelings; experimented and took risks with ideas or feelings; helped others to own up, be open, and take risks; did not own up; were not open; did not take risks; and did not help others in any of these activities.

A second scoring system was developed to produce a quantitative index of the *norms* of the executive culture. There were both positive and negative norms. The positive norms were:

1. *Individuality,* especially rewarding behavior that focused on and valued the uniqueness of each individual's ideas and feelings.
2. *Concern* for others' ideas and feelings.
3. *Trust* in others' ideas and feelings.

The negative norms were:

1. *Conformity* to others' ideas and feelings.
2. *Antagonism* toward these ideas and feelings.
3. *Mistrust* of these ideas and feelings.

In addition to our observations of the men at work, at least one semistructured interview was conducted with each executive. All of these interviews were likewise taped, and the typewritten protocols served as the basis for further analysis.

[1] For a detailed discussion of the system of categories and other aspects of methodology, see my book, *Organization and Innovation* (Homewood, Illiniois, Richard D. Irwin, Inc., 1965).

tape recordings of meetings has proved to be a helpful step; and laboratory education programs are valuable.

These are a few of the major findings of a study of executive decision making in six representative companies. The findings have vital implications for management groups everywhere; for while some organizations are less subject to the weaknesses described than are others, *all* groups have them in some degree. In this article I shall discuss the findings in detail and examine the implications for executives up and down the line. (For information on the company sample and research methods used in the study, see Figure 1.)

WORDS VERSUS ACTIONS

According to top management, the effectiveness of decision-making activities depends on the degree of innovation, risk taking, flexibility, and trust in the executive system. (Risk taking is defined here as any act where the executive risks his self-esteem. This could be a moment, for example, when he goes against the group view; when he tells someone, especially the person with the highest power, something negative about his impact on the organization; or when he seeks to put millions of dollars in a new investment.)

Nearly 95 percent of the executives in our study emphasize that an organization is only as good as its top people. They constantly repeat the importance of their responsibility to help themselves and others to develop their abilities. Almost as often they report that the qualities just mentioned—motivation, risk taking, and so on—are key characteristics of any successful executive system. "People problems" head the list as the most difficult, perplexing, and crucial.

In short, the executives vote overwhelmingly for executive systems where the contributions of each executive can be maximized and where innovation, risk taking, flexibility, and trust reign supreme. Nevertheless, the *behavior* of these same executives tends to create decision-making processes that are *not* very effective. Their behavior can be fitted into two basic patterns:

Pattern A—thoughtful, rational, and mildly competitive. This is the behavior most frequently observed during the decision-making meetings. Executives following this pattern own up to their ideas in a style that emphasizes a serious concern for ideas. As they constantly battle for scarce resources and "sell" their views, their openness to others' ideas is relatively high, not because of a sincere interest in learning about the point of view of others, but so they can engage in a form of "one-upmanship"—that is, gain information about the others' points of view in order to politely discredit them.

Pattern B—competitive first, thoughtful and rational second. In this pattern, conformity to ideas replaces concern for ideas as the strongest norm. Also, antagonism to ideas is higher—in many cases higher than openness to ideas. The relatively high antagonism scores usually indicate, in addition to high competitiveness, a high degree of conflict and pent-up feelings.

Exhibit 1 summarizes data for four illustrative groups of managers—two groups with Pattern A characteristics and two with Pattern B characteristics.

Practical Consequences

In both patterns executives are rarely observed:

Taking risks or experimenting with new ideas or feelings;
Helping others to own up, be open, and take risks;
Using a style of behavior that supports the norm of individuality and trust as well as mistrust;
Expressing feelings, positive or negative.

EXHIBIT 1
Management groups with Pattern A and Pattern B characteristics

| | PATTERN A | | | | | | PATTERN B | | | |
| | Group 1: 198 units* | | Group 2: 143 units* | | Group 3: 201 units* | | Group 4: 131 units* | |
Units characterized by:	Number	Percent	Number	Percent	Number	Percent	Number	Percent
Owning up to own ideas and feelings	146	74	105	74	156	78	102	78
Concern for others' ideas and feelings	122	62	89	62	52	26	56	43
Conformity to others' ideas and feelings	54	27	38	26	87	43	62	47
Openness to others' ideas and feelings	46	23	34	24	31	15	25	19
Individuality	4	2	12	8	30	15	8	6
Antagonism to others' ideas and feelings	18	9	4	3	32	16	5	4
Unwillingness to help others own up to their ideas	5	2	3	2	14	7	4	3

* A unit is an instance of a manager speaking on a topic. If during the course of speaking he changes to a new topic, another unit is created.

These results should not be interpreted as implying that the executives do not have feelings. We know from the interviews that many of the executives have strong feelings indeed. However, the overwhelming majority (84%) feel that it is a sign of immaturity to express feelings openly *during decision-making meetings*. Nor should the results be interpreted to mean that the executives do not enjoy risk taking. The data permit us to conclude only that few risk-taking actions were *observed* during the meetings. (Also, we have to keep in mind that the executives were always observed in groups; it may be that their behavior in groups varies significantly from their behavior as individuals.)

Before I attempt to give my views about the reasons for the discrepancy between executives' words and actions, I should like to point out that these results are not unique to business organizations. I have obtained similar behavior patterns from leaders in education, research, the ministry, trade unions, and government. Indeed, one of the fascinating questions for me is why so many different people in so many different kinds of organizations tend to manifest similar problems.

WHY THE DISCREPANCY?

The more I observe such problems in different organizations possessing different technologies and varying greatly in size, the more I become impressed with the importance of the role played by the values or assumptions top people hold on the nature of effective human relationships and the best ways to run an organization.

Basic values

In the studies so far I have isolated three basic values that seem to be very important:

1. *The significant human relationships are the ones which have to do with achieving the organization's objective.* My studies of over 265 different types and sizes of meetings indicate that executives almost always tend to focus their behavior on "getting the job done." In literally thousands of units of behavior, almost none are observed where the men spend some time in analyzing and maintaining their group's effectiveness. This is true even though in many meetings the group's effectiveness "bogged down" and the objectives were not being reached because of interpersonal factors. When the executives are interviewed and asked why they did not spend some time in examining the group operations or processes, they reply that they were there to get a job done. They add: "If the group isn't effective, it is up to the leader to get it back on the track by directing it."

2. *Cognitive rationality is to be emphasized; feelings and emotions are to be played down.* This value influences executives to see cognitive, intellectual discussions as "relevant," "good," "work," and so on. Emotional and interpersonal

discussions tend to be viewed as "irrelevant," "immature," "not work," and so on.

As a result, when emotions and interpersonal variables become blocks to group effectiveness, all the executives report feeling that they should *not* deal with them. For example, in the event of an emotional disagreement, they would tell the members to "get back to facts" or "keep personalities out of this."

3. *Human relationships are most effectively influenced through unilateral direction, coercion, and control, as well as by rewards and penalties that sanction all three values.* This third value of direction and control is implicit in the chain of command and also in the elaborate managerial controls that have been developed within organizations.

Influence on operations

The impact of these values can be considerable. For example, to the extent that individuals dedicate themselves to the value of intellectual rationality and "getting the job done," they will tend to be aware of and emphasize the intellectual aspects of issues in an organization and (consciously or unconsciously) to suppress the interpersonal and emotional aspects, especially those which do not seem relevant to achieving the task.

As the interpersonal and emotional aspects of behavior become suppressed, organizational norms that coerce individuals to hide their feelings or to disguise them and bring them up as technical, intellectual problems will tend to arise.

Under these conditions the individual may tend to find it very difficult to develop competence in dealing with feelings and interpersonal relationships. Also, in a world where the expression of feelings is not valued, individuals may build personal and organizational defenses to help them suppress their own feelings or inhibit others in such expression. Or they may refuse to consider ideas which, if explored, could expose suppressed feelings.

Such a defensive reaction in an organization could eventually inhibit creativity and innovation during decision making. The participants might learn to limit themselves to those ideas and values that were not threatening. They might also decrease their openness to new ideas and values. And as the degree of openness decreased, the capacity to experiment would also decrease, and fear of taking risks would increase. This would reduce the *probability* of experimentation, thus decreasing openness to new ideas still further and constricting risk taking even more than formerly. We would thereby have a closed circuit which could become an important cause of loss of vitality in an organization.

SOME CONSEQUENCES

Aside from the impact of values on vitality, what are some other consequences of the executive behavior patterns earlier described on top management decision making and on the effective functioning of the organization? For the sake of brevity, I shall include only examples of those consequences that were found to exist in one form or another in all organizations studied.

Restricted commitment

One of the most frequent findings is that in major decisions that are introduced by the president, there tends to be less than open discussion of the issues, and the commitment of the officers tends to be less than complete (although they may assure the president to the contrary). For instance, consider what happened in one organization where a major administrative decision made during the period of the research was the establishment of several top management committees to explore basic long-range problems:

As is customary with major decisions, the president discussed it in advance at a meeting of the executive committee. He began the meeting by circulating, as a basis for discussion, a draft of the announcement of the committees. Most of the members' discussion was concerned with raising questions about the wording of the proposal:

"Is the word *action* too strong?"
"I recommend that we change 'steps can be taken' to 'recommendations can be made.' "
"We'd better change the word 'lead' to 'maintain.' "

As the discussion seemed to come to an end, one executive said he was worried that the announcement of the committees might be interpreted by the people below as an implication "that the executive committee believes the organization is in trouble. Let's get the idea in that all is well."

There was spontaneous agreement by all executives: "Hear, hear!"

A brief silence was broken by another executive who apparently was not satisfied with the concept of the committees. He raised a series of questions. The manner in which it was done was interesting. As he raised each issue, he kept assuring the president and the group that he was not against the concept. He just wanted to be certain that the executive committee was clear on what it was doing. For example, he assured them:

"I'm not clear. Just asking."
"I'm trying to get a better picture."
"I'm just trying to get clarification."
"Just so that we understand what the words mean."

The president nodded in agreement, but he seemed to become slightly impatient. He remarked that many of these problems would not arise if the members of these new committees took an overall company point of view. An executive commented (laughingly), "Oh, I'm for motherhood too!"

The proposal was tabled in order for the written statement to be revised and discussed further during the next meeting. It appeared that the proposal was the president's personal "baby," and the executive committee members would naturally go along with it. The most responsibility some felt was that they should raise questions so the president would be clear about *his* (not *their*) decision.

At the next meeting the decision-making process was the same as at the first. The president circulated copies of the revised proposal. During this session a smaller number of executives asked questions. Two pushed (with appropriate care) the notion that the duties of one of the committees were defined too broadly.

The president began to defend his proposal by citing an extremely long list of examples, indicating that in his mind "reasonable" people should find the duties clear. This comment and the long list of examples may have communicated to others a feeling that the president was becoming impatient. When he finished, there was a lengthy silence. The president then turned to one of the executives and asked directly, "Why are you worried about this?" The executive explained, then quickly added that as far as he could see the differences were not major ones and his point of view could be integrated with the president's by "changing some words."

The president agreed to the changes, looked up, and asked, "I take it now there is common agreement?" All executives replied "yes" or nodded their heads affirmatively.

As I listened, I had begun to wonder about the commitment of the executive committee members to the idea. In subsequent interviews I asked each about his view of the proposal. Half felt that it was a good proposal. The other half had reservation ranging from moderate to serious. However, being loyal members, they would certainly do their best to make it work, they said.

Subordinate gamesmanship

I can best illustrate the second consequence by citing from a study of the effectiveness of product planning and program review activities in another of the organizations studied:

It was company policy that peers at any given level should make the decisions. Whenever they could not agree or whenever a decision went beyond their authority, the problem was supposed to be sent to the next higher level. The buck passing stopped at the highest level. A meeting with the president became a great event. Beforehand a group would "dry run" its presentation until all were satisfied that they could present their view effectively.

Few difficulties were observed when the meeting was held to present a recommendation agreed to by all at the lower levels. The difficulties arose when "negative" information had to be fed upward. For example, a major error in the program, a major delay, or a major disagreement among the members was likely to cause such trouble.

The dynamics of these meetings was very interesting. In one case the problem to present was a major delay in a development project. In the dry run the subordinates planned to begin the session with information that "updated" the president. The information was usually presented in such a way that slowly and carefully the president was alerted to the fact that a major problem was about to be announced. One could hear such key phrases as:

"We are a bit later than expected."
"We're not on plan."
"We have had greater difficulties than expected."
"It is now clear that no one should have promised what we did."

These phrases were usually followed by some reassuring statement such as:

"However, we're on top of this."
"Things are really looking better now."
"Although we are late, we have advanced the state of the art."
"If you give us another three months, we are certain that we can solve this problem."

To the observer's eyes, it is difficult to see how the president could deny the request. Apparently he felt the same way because he granted it. However, he took nearly 20 minutes to say that this shocked him; he was wondering if everyone was *really* doing everything they could; this was a serious program; this was not the way he wanted to see things run; he was sure they would agree with him; and he wanted their assurances that this would be the final delay.

A careful listening to the tape after the meeting brought out the fact that no subordinate gave such assurances. They simply kept saying that they were doing their best; they had poured a lot into this; or they had the best technical know-how working on it.

Another interesting observation is that most subordinates in this company, especially in presentations to the president, tended to go along with certain unwritten rules:

1. Before you give any bad news, give good news. Especially emphasize the capacity of the department to work hard and to rebound from a failure.

2. Play down the impact of a failure by emphasizing how close you came to achieving the target or how soon the target can be reached. If neither seems reasonable, emphasize how difficult it is to define such targets, and point out that because the state of the art is so primitive, the original commitment was not a wise one.

3. In a meeting with the president it is unfair to take advantage of another department that is in trouble, even if it is a "natural enemy." The sporting thing to do is say something nice about the other department and offer to help it in any way possible. (The offer is usually not made in concrete form, nor does the

department in difficulty respond with the famous phrase, "What do you have in mind?")

The subordinates also were in agreement that too much time was spent in long presentations in order to make the president happy. The president, however, confided to the researcher that he did not enjoy listening to long and, at times, dry presentations (especially when he had seen most of the key data anyway). However, he felt that it was important to go through this because it might give the subordinates a greater sense of commitment to the problem!

Lack of awareness

One of our most common observations in company studies is that executives lack awareness of their own behavioral patterns as well as of the negative impact of their behavior on others. This is not to imply that they are completely unaware; each individual usually senses some aspects of a problem. However, we rarely find an individual or group of individuals who is aware of enough of the scope and depth of a problem so that the need for effective action can be fully understood.

For example, during the study of the decision-making processes of the president and the vice presidents of a firm with nearly 3,000 employees, I concluded that the members unknowingly behaved in such a way as *not* to encourage risk taking, openness, expression of feelings, and cohesive, trusting relationships. But subsequent interviews with the 10 top executives showed that they held a completely different point of view from mine. They admitted that negative feelings were not expressed, but said the reason was that "we trust each other and respect each other." According to 6 of the men, individuality was high and conformity low; where conformity was agreed to be high, the reason given was the necessity of agreeing with the man who is boss. According to eight of the men, "We help each other all the time." Issues loaded with conflict were not handled during meetings, it was reported, for these reasons:

"We should not discuss emotional disagreements before the executive committee because, when people are emotional, they are not rational."

"We should not air our dirty linen in front of the people who may come in to make a presentation."

"Why take up people's time with subjective debates?"

"Most members are not acquainted with all the details. Under our system the person who presents the issues has really thought them through."

"Prediscussion of issues helps to prevent anyone from sandbagging the executive committee."

"Rarely emotional; when it does happen, you can pardon it."

The executive committee climate or emotional tone was characterized by such words as:

"Friendly."

"Not critical of each other."

"Not tense."

"Frank and no tensions because we've known each other for years."

How was I to fit the executives' views with mine? I went back and listened to all the interviews again. As I analyzed the tapes, I began to realize that an interesting set of contradictions arose during many of the interviews. In the early stages of the interviews the executives tended to say things that they contradicted later; Exhibit 2 contains examples of contradictions repeated by six or more of the ten top executives.

EXHIBIT 2
Contradictory statements

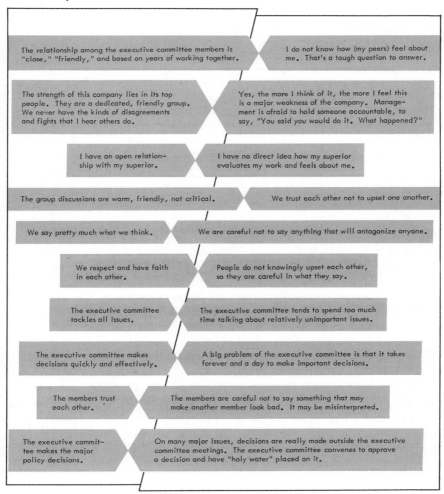

The relationship among the executive committee members is "close," "friendly," and based on years of working together.

I do not know how (my peers) feel about me. That's a tough question to answer.

The strength of this company lies in its top people. They are a dedicated, friendly group. We never have the kinds of disagreements and fights that I hear others do.

Yes, the more I think of it, the more I feel this is a major weakness of the company. Management is afraid to hold someone accountable, to say, "You said you would do it. What happened?"

I have an open relationship with my superior.

I have no direct idea how my superior evaluates my work and feels about me.

The group discussions are warm, friendly, not critical.

We trust each other not to upset one another.

We say pretty much what we think.

We are careful not to say anything that will antagonize anyone.

We respect and have faith in each other.

People do not knowingly upset each other, so they are careful in what they say.

The executive committee tackles all issues.

The executive committee tends to spend too much time talking about relatively unimportant issues.

The executive committee makes decisions quickly and effectively.

A big problem of the executive committee is that it takes forever and a day to make important decisions.

The members trust each other.

The members are careful not to say something that may make another member look bad. It may be misinterpreted.

The executive committee makes the major policy decisions.

On many major issues, decisions are really made outside the executive committee meetings. The executive committee convenes to approve a decision and have "holy water" placed on it.

What accounts for these contradictions? My explanation is that over time the executives had come to mirror, in their behavior, the values of their culture (e.g., be rational, nonemotional, diplomatically open, and so on). They had created a culture that reinforced their own leadership styles. If an executive wanted to behave differently, he probably ran the risk of being considered a deviant. In most of the cases the executives decided to forgo this risk, and they behaved like the majority. These men, in order to live with themselves, probably had to develop various defenses and blinders about their acquiescence to an executive culture that may not have been the one they personally preferred and valued.

Incidentally, in this group there were two men who had decided to take the other route. Both men were viewed by the others as "a bit rough at the edges" or "a little too aggressive."

EXHIBIT 3

How the executive committee was rated by 25 executives below it

	Low	*Moderate*	*High*
Characteristic rated:			
Openness to uncomfortable information*	12	6	4
Risk taking	20	4	1
Trust	14	9	2
Conformity	0	2	23
Ability to deal with conflict	19	6	0

* Three executives gave a "don't know" response.

To check the validity of some of the findings reported, we interviewed the top 25 executives below the executive committee. If our analysis was correct, we knew, then they should tend to report that the members of the executive committee were low in openness to uncomfortable information, risk taking, trust, and capacity to deal with conflicts openly, and high in conformity. The results were as predicted (see Exhibit 3).

Blind spots

Another result found in all organizations studied is the tendency for executives to be unaware of the negative feelings that their subordinates have about them. This finding is not startling in view of the fact that the executive problem-solving processes do not tend to reward the upward communication of information about interpersonal issues that is emotionally laden and risky to communicate. To illustrate:

In one organization, all but one of the top executive committee members reported that their relationships with their subordinates were "relatively good to excellent." When asked how they judged their relationships, most of the executives responded with such statements as: "They do everything that I ask for willingly," and "We talk together frequently and openly."

The picture from the middle management men who were the immediate subordinates was different. Apparently, top management was unaware that:

—71% of the middle managers did not know where they stood with their superiors; they considered their relationships as ambiguous, and they were not aware of such important facts as how they were being evaluated.

—65% of the middle managers did not know what qualities led to success in their organizations.

—87% felt that conflicts were very seldom coped with; and that when they were, the attempts tended to be inadequate.

—65% thought that the most important unsolved problem of the organization was that the top management was unable to help them overcome the intergroup rivalries, lack of cooperation, and poor communications; 53% said that if they could alter one aspect of their superior's behavior, it would be to help him see the "dog eat dog" communication problems that existed in middle management.

—59% evaluated top management effectiveness as not too good or about average; and 62% reported that the development of a cohesive management team was the second most important unsolved problem.

—82% of the middle managers wished that the status of their function and job could be increased but doubted if they could communicate this openly to the top management.

Interestingly, in all the cases that I have observed where the president asked for a discussion of any problems that the top and middle management men present thought important, the problems mentioned above were never raised.

Rather, the most frequently mentioned problem (74% of the cases) was the overload problem. The executives and managers reported that they were overloaded and that the situation was getting worse. The president's usual reply was that he appreciated their predicament, but "that is life." The few times he asked if the men had any suggestions, he received such replies as "more help," "fewer meetings," "fewer reports," "delay of schedules," and so on. As we will see, few of these suggestions made sense, since the men were asking either for increases in costs or for a decrease in the very controls that the top management used to administer the organization.

Distrust and antagonism

Another result of the behavior patterns earlier described is that management tends to keep promotions semisecret and most of the actual reasons for executive changes completely secret. Here is an example from an organization whose board we studied in some detail over a period of two years:

The executives complained of three practices of the board about which the board members were apparently unaware: (1) the constant alteration of organizational positions and charts, and keeping the most up-to-date versions semiconfidential; (2) shifting top executives without adequate discussion with all executives involved and without clearly communicating the real reasons for the move; and (3) developing new departments with product goals that overlapped and competed with the goals of already existing departments.

The board members admitted these practices but tended not to see them as being incompatible with the interests of the organization. For example, to take the first complaint, they defended their practice with such statements as: "If you tell them everything, all they do is worry, and we get a flood of rumors"; "The changes do not *really* affect them"; and, "It will only cut in on their busy schedule and interrupt their productivity."

The void of clear-cut information from the board was, however, filled in by the executives. Their explanations ranged from such statements as "They must be changing things because they are not happy with the way things are going" to "The unhappiness is so strong they do not tell us." Even the executives who profited from some of these moves reported some concern and bewilderment. For example, three reported instances where they had been promoted over some "old-timers." In all cases they were told to "soft-pedal the promotion aspect" until the old-timers were diplomatically informed. Unfortunately, it took months to inform the latter men, and in some cases it was never done.

There was another practice of the board that produced difficulties in the organization:

Department heads cited the board's increasing intervention into the detailed administration of a department when its profit picture looked shaky. This practice was, from these subordinates' view, in violation of the stated philosophy of decentralization.

When asked, board members tended to explain this practice by saying that it was done only when they had doubts about the department head's competence, and then it was always in the interests of efficiency. When they were alerted about a department that was not doing well, they believed that the best reaction was to tighten controls, "take a closer and more frequent look," and "make sure the department head is on top of things." They quickly added that they did not tell the man in question they were beginning to doubt his competence for fear of upsetting him. Thus, again we see how the values of deemphasizing the expression of negative feelings and the emphasizing of controls influenced the board's behavior.

The department heads, on the other hand, reported different reactions. "Why are they bothered with details? Don't they trust me? If not, why don't they say so?" Such reactions tended to produce more conformity, antagonism, mistrust, and fear of experimenting.

Still another board practice was the "diplomatic" rejection of an executive's idea that was, in the eyes of the board, offbeat, a bit too wild, or not in keeping with the corporate mission. The reasons given by the board for not being open about the evaluation again reflected adherence to the pyramidal values. For example, a board member would say, "We do not want to embarrass them," or "If you really tell them, you might restrict creativity."

This practice tended to have precisely the impact that the superiors wished to *avoid*. The subordinates reacted by asking, "Why don't they give me an opportunity to explain it?" or "What do they mean when they suggest that the 'timing is not right' or 'funds are not currently available'?"

Processes damaged

It is significant that defensive activities like those described are rarely observed during group meetings dealing with minor or relatively routine decisions. These activities become most noticeable when the decision is an important one in terms of dollars or in terms of the impact on the various departments in the organization. *The forces toward ineffectiveness operate most strongly during the important decision-making meetings.* The group and organizational defenses operate most frequently when they can do the most harm to decision-making effectiveness.

Another interesting finding is that the more effective and more committed executives tend to be upset about these facts, whereas the less effective, less committed people tend simply to lament them. They also tend to take on an "I told them so" attitude—one of resignation and noninvolvement in correcting the situation. In short, it is the better executives who are negatively affected.

WHAT CAN BE DONE?

What can the executive do to change this situation?

I wish that I could answer this question as fully as I should like to. Unfortunately, I cannot. Nevertheless, there are some suggestions I can make.

Blind alleys

First, let me state what I believe will *not* work.

Learning about these problems by listening to lectures, reading about them, exploring them through cases is not adequate; an article or book can pose some issues and get thinking started, but—in this area, at least—it cannot change behavior. Thus, in one study with 60 top executives:

Lectures were given and cases discussed on this subject for nearly a week. A test at the end of the week showed that the executives rated the lecturers very high, liked the cases, and accepted the diagnoses. Yet when they attempted to apply their new-found knowledge outside the learning situation, most were unable to do so. The major problem was that they had not learned how to make these new ideas come to life in their behavior.

As one executive stated, pointing to his head: "I know up here what I should do, but when it comes to a real meeting, I behave in the same old way. It sure is frustrating."[1]

Learning about these problems through a detailed diagnosis of executives' behavior is also not enough. For example:

I studied a top management group for nearly four months through interviews and tape recordings of their decision-making meetings. Eventually, I fed back the analysis. The

---

[1] See my article, "Explorations in Interpersonal Competence II," *Applied Behavioral Science,* Vol. 1, No. 3, 1965, p. 255.

executives agreed with the diagnosis as well as with the statement by one executive that he found it depressing. Another executive, however, said he now felt that he had a clearer and more coherent picture of some of the causes of their problems, and he was going to change his behavior. I predicted that he would probably find that he would be unable to change his behavior—and even if he did change, his subordinates, peers, and superiors might resist dealing with him in the new way.

The executive asked, "How can you be so sure that we can't change?" I responded that I knew of no case where managers were able to alter successfully their behavior, their group dynamics, and so forth by simply realizing intellectually that such a change was necessary. The key to success was for them to be able to show these new strategies in their behavior. To my knowledge, behavior of this type, groups with these dynamics, and organizational cultures endowed with these characteristics were very difficult to change. What kind of thin-skinned individuals would they be, how brittle would their groups and their organizations be if they could be altered that easily?

Three of the executives decided that they were going to prove the prediction to be incorrect. They took my report and studied it carefully. In one case the executive asked his subordinates to do the same. Then they tried to alter their behavior. According to their own accounts, they were unable to do so. The only changes they reported were (1) a softening of the selling activities, (2) a reduction of their aggressive persuasion, and (3) a genuine increase in their asking for the subordinates' views.

My subsequent observations and interviews uncovered the fact that the first two changes were mistrusted by the subordinates, who had by now adapted to the old behavior of their superiors. They tended to play it carefully and to be guarded. This hesitation aggravated the executives, who felt that their subordinates were not responding to their new behavior with the enthusiasm that they (the superiors) had expected.

However, *the executives did not deal with this issue openly.* They kept working at trying to be rational, patient, and rewarding. The more irritated they became and the more they showed this irritation in their behavior, the more the subordinates felt that the superiors' "new" behavior was a gimmick.

Eventually, the process of influencing subordinates slowed down so much that the senior men returned to their more controlling styles. The irony was that in most cases the top executives interpreted the subordinates' behavior as proof that they needed to be needled and pushed, while the subordinates interpreted the top managers' behavior as proof that they did not trust their assistants and would never change.

The reason I doubt that these approaches will provide anything but temporary cures is that they do not go far enough. If changes are going to be made in the behavior of an executive, if trust is to be developed, if risk taking is to flourish, he must be placed in a different situation. He should be helped to (a) expose his leadership style so that he and others can take a look at its true impact; (b) deepen his awareness of himself and the dynamics of effective leadership; and (c) strive for these goals under conditions where he is in control of the amount, pace, and depth of learning.

These conditions for learning are difficult to achieve. Ideally, they require the help of a professional consultant. Also, it would be important to get away from the organization—its interruptions, pressures, and daily administrative tensions.

Value of questions

The executive can strive to be aware that he is probably programmed with a set of values which cause him to behave in ways that are not always helpful to others and which his subordinates will not discuss frankly even when they believe he is not being helpful. He can also strive to find time to uncover, through careful questioning, his impact on others. Once in a while a session that is focused on the "How am I doing?" question can enlighten the executive and make his colleagues more flexible in dealing with him.

One simple question I have heard several presidents ask their vice presidents with success is: "Tell me what, if anything, I do that tends to prevent (or help) your being the kind of vice president you wish to be?" These presidents are careful to ask these questions during a time when they seem natural (e.g., performance review sessions), or they work hard ahead of time to create a climate so that such a discussion will not take the subordinate by surprise.

Some presidents feel uncomfortable in raising these questions, and others point out that the vice presidents are also uncomfortable. I can see how both would have such feelings. A chief executive officer may feel that he is showing weakness by asking his subordinates about his impact. The subordinate may or may not feel this way, but he may sense that his chief does, and that is enough to make him uncomfortable.

Yet in two companies I have studied where such questions were asked, superiors and subordinates soon learned that authority which gained strength by a lack of openness was weak and brittle, whereas authority resting on open feedback from below was truly strong and viable.

Working with the group

Another step that an executive can take is to vow not to accept group ineffectiveness as part of life. Often I have heard people say, "Groups are no damned good; strong leadership is what is necessary." I agree that many groups are ineffective. I doubt, however, of either of the two leadership patterns described earlier will help the situation. As we have seen, both patterns tend to make the executive group increasingly less effective.

If my data are valid, the search process in executive decision making has become so complicated that group participation is essential. No one man seems to be able to have all the knowledge necessary to make an effective decision. If individual contributions are necessary in group meetings, it is important that a climate be created that does not discourge innovation, risk taking, and honest leveling between managers in their conversations with one another. The value of a group is to maximize individual contributions.

Interestingly, the chief executive officers in these studies are rarely observed making policy decisions in the classic sense, viz., critical selections from several alternatives and determination of future directions to be taken. This does not mean that they shy away from taking responsibility. Quite the contrary. Many report that they enjoy making decisions by themselves. Their big frustration comes from realizing that most of the major decisions they face are extremely complex and require the coordinated, honest inputs of many different executives. They are impatient at the slowness of meetings, the increasingly quantitative nature of the inputs, and, in many cases, their ignorance of what the staff groups did to the decision inputs long before they received them.

The more management deals with complexity by the use of computers and quantitative approaches, the more it will be forced to work with inputs of many different people, and the more important will be the group dynamics of decision-making meetings. If anyone doubts this, let him observe the dry runs subordinates go through to get a presentation ready for the top. He will observe, I believe, that much data are included and excluded by subordinates on the basis of what they believe those at the top can hear.

In short, *one of the main tasks of the chief executive is to build and maintain an effective decision-making network.* I doubt that he has much choice *except* to spend time in exploring how well his group functions.

Such explorations could occur during the regular workday. For example:

> In one organization the president began by periodically asking members of his top group, immediately after a decision was made, to think back during the meeting and describe when they felt that the group was not being as effective as they wished. How could these conditions be altered?
>
> As trust and openness increased, the members began to level with each other as to when they were inhibited, irritated, suppressed, confused, and withholding information. The president tried to be as encouraging as he could, and he especially rewarded people who truly leveled. Soon the executives began to think of mechanisms they could build into their group functioning so they would be alerted to these group problems and correct them early. As one man said, "We have not eliminated all our problems, but we are building a competence in our group to deal with them effectively if and when they arise."

Utilizing feedback

Another useful exercise is for the superior and his group members to tape-record a decision-making meeting, especially one which is expected to be difficult. At a later date, the group members can gather and listen to the tape. I believe it is safe to say that simply listening to the tape is an education in itself. If one can draw from skilled company or outside help, then useful analyses can be made of group or individual behavior.

Recently, I experimented with this procedure with an "inside" board of directors of a company. The directors met once a month and listened to tape recordings of their monthly board meetings. With my help they analyzed their behavior, trying to find how they could improve their individual and group effectiveness. Listening to tapes became a very involving experience for them. They spent nearly four hours in the first meeting discussing less than ten minutes of the tape.

"Binds" created. One of the major gains of these sessions was that the board members became aware of the "binds" they were creating for each other and of the impact they each had on the group's functioning. Thus:

Executive A was frequently heard antagonizing Executive B by saying something that B perceived as "needling." For example, A might seem to be questioning B's competence. "Look here," he would say, "anyone who can do simple arithmetic should realize that. . . ."

Executive B responded by fighting. B's way of fighting back was to utilize his extremely high capacity to verbalize and intellectualize. B's favorite tactic was to show A where he missed five important points and where his logic was faulty.

Executive A became increasingly upset as the "barrage of logic" found its mark. He tended to counteract by (a) remaining silent but manifesting a sense of being flustered and becoming redfaced; and/or (b) insisting that his logic *was* sound even though he did not express it in "highfalutin language" as did B.

Executive B pushed harder (presumably to make A admit he was wrong) by continuing his "barrage of logic" or implying that A could not see his errors because he was upset.

Executive A would respond to this by insisting that he was not upset. "The point you are making is so simple, why, anyone can see it. Why should I be upset?"

Executive B responded by pushing harder and doing more intellectualizing. When Executive A eventually reached his breaking point, he too began to shout and fight.

At this point, Executives C, D, and E could be observed withdrawing until A and B wore each other out.

Progress achieved. As a result of the meetings, the executives reported in interviews, board members experienced fewer binds, less hostility, less frustration, and more constructive work. One member wondered if the group had lost some of its "zip," but the others disagreed. Here is an excerpt from the transcript of one discussion on this point:

Executive A: My feeling is, as I have said, that we have just opened this thing up, and I for one feel that we have benefited a great deal from it. I think I have improved; maybe I am merely reflecting the fact that you [Executive B] have improved. But at least I think there has been improvement in our relationship. I also see signs of not as good a relationship in other places as there might be.

I think on the whole we are much better off today than we were a year ago. I think there is a whole lot less friction today than there was a year ago, but there's still enough of it.

Now we have a much clearer organization setup; if we were to sit down here and name the people, we would probably all name exactly the same people. I don't think there is much question about who should be included and who should not be included; we've got a pretty clean organization.

Executive B: You're talking now about asking the consultant about going on with this week's session?

Executive A: It would be very nice to have the consultant if he can do it; then we should see how we can do it without him, but it'd be better with him.

Executive B: But that's the step, as I understand it, that should be taken at this stage. Is that right?

Executive A: Well, I would certainly favor doing something; I don't know what. I'm not making a specific recommendation; I just don't like to let go of it.

Executive C: What do you think?

Executive D: I'm not as optimistic as A. I wonder if anybody here agrees with me that maybe we haven't made as much progress as we think. I've personally enjoyed these experiences, and I'd like to see them continued.

Executive A: Would you like to venture to say why I think we have made progress and why I might be fooled?

Executive D: Well, I think maybe you are in the worst position to evaluate progress because if the worst possible thing that can happen is for people to no longer fight and struggle, but to say, "yes, sir," you might call that progress. That might be the worst thing that could happen, and I sort of sense some degree of resignation—I don't think it's progress. I don't know. I might be all alone in this. What do you think?

Executive C: On one level it is progress. Whether it is institutional progress and whether it produces commensurate institutional benefits is a debatable question. It may in fact do so. I think it's very clear that there is in our meetings and in individual contact less heat, less overt friction, petulance, tension, than certainly was consistently the case. Do you agree?

Executive D: Yes, I think so.

Executive C: It has made us a great deal more aware of the extent and nature of the friction and clearly has made all of us intent on fighting less. There's some benefit to it; but there are some drawbacks.

Executive A: Well, if you and D are right, I would say for that reason we need more of the program.

Laboratory training

Another possibility is for the executive to attend a program designed to help increase competence in this area, such as laboratory education and its various offshoots ("T-groups," the "managerial grid," "conflict management labs," and so on[2]). These learning experiences are available at various university and National Training Laboratory executive programs. They can also be tailor-made for the individual organization.

I believe outside programs offer the better way of becoming acquainted with this type of learning. Bear in mind, though, that since typically only one or two executives attend from the same organization, the biggest payoff is for the individual. The inside program provides greater possibilities for payoff to the organization.

At the same time, however, it should also be kept in mind that in-house programs *can* be dangerous to the organization. I would recommend that a thorough study be made ahead of time to ascertain whether or not a laboratory

---

[2] For detailed discussions of such variations see my article, "T-Groups for Organizational Effectiveness," *Harvard Business Review* March–April 1964, p. 60; R. R. Blake, J. S. Mouton, L. B. Barnes, and L. E. Greiner, "Breakthrough in Organization Development," *Harvard Business Review* November–December 1964, p. 135; and Edgar Schein and Warren Bennis, *Personal and Organizational Change Through Laboratory Methods* (New York, Wiley, 1965).

educational experience would be helpful to company executives individually and to the organization.

Open discussion

I have never observed a group whose members wanted it to decay. I have never studied a group or an organization that was decaying where there were not some members who were aware that decay was occurring. Accordingly, one key to group and organizational effectiveness is to get this knowledge out into the open and to discuss it thoroughly. The human "motors" of the group and the organization have to be checked periodically, just as does the motor of an automobile. Without proper maintenance, all will fail.

Role negotiation: A tough-minded approach to team development

*Roger Harrison**

The development of psychological mindedness among business executives has been associated with a philosophical trend in behavioral science which is concerned primarily with human relations. It tends to be egalitarian rather than elitist, oriented toward the development of persons rather than task efficiency, and concerned with feelings, attitudes and interpersonal relationships rather than with power and authority or knowledge and competence. In its application to human relations in work, practitioners in this tradition tend to work for the development in the organization of openness of communication, collaborative relationships based on mutual trust, and democratic decision making in small groups. The assumption underlying such approaches is that people will function effectively in work settings if they can be taught to treat one another with trust, openness, acceptance and understanding. McGregor's Theory Y and Argyris's Interpersonal Competence are representative of the human relations tradition in behaviorial theory and the T group exemplifies its application to managerial education and organization development.

* Roger Harrison is Vice President of Development Research Associates, Inc., of Newton Centre, Massachusetts and practices organization development and training in London, England.

A competing behavioral philosophy which has enjoyed considerable influence in some quarters may be termed achievement oriented. It is oriented towards production and achievement, finding interest and challenge in work using one's skills and knowledge. Practitioners work to develop the individual's abilities and creativity and his willingness to accept and exercise personal responsibility for decisions, productivity and quality. Herzberg's and McClelland's theories of the motivation to work are representative of this school of thought. Management by Objectives, Achievement Motivation Training and Job Enrichment are typical interventions flowing from these theories, as is the conscious attempt to push responsibility and decision making down to lower levels in the organization.

The underlying assumption here is that men work effectively when they are given opportunities to achieve, create, learn, accept responsibility. Human relations tend to be ignored or relegated to a lesser status (e.g. Herzberg's "hygiene factors").

Both of these dominant approaches may be termed tender minded, in that they tend to assume that people at work will be collaborative and productive if only the barriers to their doing so are removed. Competition, conflict and the struggle for power tend to be explained away. They may be seen as the result of frustration of basic needs for achievement, growth and relatedness. They may be explained as deriving from misperception of basically collaborative situations (seeing the situation as "win-lose" rather than as "win-win"), or as forced by roles in organizations which require people to compete. Competition, conflict and the struggle for power thus are seen as derivative, symptomatic *effects*, rather than as basic, ubiquitous *causes*. The problem of organizational change is seen as one of *releasing* human potential for collaboration and productivity, rather than as one of controlling or checking greed, competitiveness and exploitation.

I have worked in and from time to time contributed to the tender minded approaches of behavioral science to the problems of management and organization. My hopes and values are still with these optimistic and growth oriented views of the nature of man, but my experience increasingly convinces me that these approaches are incomplete and to some extent naive in that they fail to deal realistically or effectively with powers and coercion. I increasingly see these latter processes as highly significant forces for both change and stability in organizations, and it begins to seem strange to me that behavioral scientists have so little that is constructive to say to managers about these forces. Most of what we have to say is negative: For example, we point out the restrictive effect of power differences on upward communication in the organization. But we are strangely silent when it comes to the *use* of power and coercion, as though power corrupts not only those who have it, but also those who study its use and function. Often we seem to be trying to convince managers not only that the use of their power is immoral, but that it is ineffective as well. We also imply to managers that their view of organizational reality is faulty. We tell them that what is most *real* is not the competitiveness, exploitation, coercion and control which they experience, but rather the drives toward openness, collaboration, productivity and responsibility which we see lying hidden and untapped in the humans who make up the organization. In some managerial education of which the T group is an example, we may encourage the manager to act in the organization as though our reality was actual and his was not. The results of the manager's acting on this teaching have been reported by my clients as painful and dangerous.

My growing conviction is that my clients have a more accurate and reality based map of the forces affecting them in their organizational lives than do my academic colleagues. Among other things, their map usually charts power and influence, and whether people are on their side or against them. Clearly marked are indications as to whom one can be open and honest with, and who will use the information you give against you. My clients do not chart an organizational world which is safe for openness, collaboration, creativity and personal growth.

I do not mean to imply that the more optimistic behavioral science approaches to business are so naive as to claim the world is quite safe for the processes they try to promote. What I am concerned about is the failure to work with the forces which *are* in ascendance. In this paper I shall present a modest program for working with human problems in organizations which does work directly with issues of power, competitiveness and coercion. The use of this method also involves an attempt to work from the clients' views of their problems and situations without making initial assumptions about what their "real" needs are, either for interpersonal relationships or for challenging and stimulating work.

This program which is called Role Negotiation makes one basic assumption: that most people in organizations prefer a fair negotiated settlement to a state of unresolved conflict. To operate the program a modest but significant risk is called for from the participants: They must be specific about what changes in behavior, authority, responsibility, etc., they wish to obtain from others in the situation. If the participants take the risk asked of them and do specify quite concretely the changes desired on the part of others, then significant changes in work group effectiveness can usually be obtained. I shall outline the rather simple series of steps in this program and then discuss why I think it represents a useful alternative to more tender minded approaches. For the sake of illustration we shall assume that a consultant is working with a natural work group of five to seven people which includes a boss and his subordinates, two levels in the formal organization.

PHASE 1: WARM UP

As in any team development work, some low threat activities are needed to reduce the mistrust of the consultant, establish his credibility and areas of competence and bring the group to talk more easily about work problems with the consultant. This phase may last a few minutes or several months, depending upon how sophisticated and confident the group is in the use of behavioral science resources. With one group this may take the form of long lunch and dinner meetings in which the consultant is probed and tested for soundness on a wide range of topics which may seem to have little to do with team development. The group appears to be trying indirectly to find out whether the consultant is "enough like us" to be trusted. Another group may wish to hear the consultant lecture on behavioral science topics and may then critically challenge and argue with him on the points which he raises. Another may wish to discuss problems which they have with other groups and levels in the organization before they deal with their internal difficulties. With other, more ready groups this phase may be dispensed with almost immediately in favor of the actual team development work. But I seldom work with any group which does not have some need to test me as a person and as a professional before serious work can begin. When I try to hurry this stage too much it usually results in ineffective work in the next phases.

PHASE 2: CONTRACT SETTING

This phase merges naturally with the previous one, and there is often no clear dividing line between them. Its purpose is to get clear between the group and the consultant what each may expect from the other. This is a critical step in the change process. It controls and channels everything which happens afterwards. I work toward a contract with the following provisions which it is helpful to get written down as a first practice step in the rather formal way of working which I try to establish.

1. It is not legitimate for the consultant to press or probe anyone's *feelings*. We are concerned about work: who does what, how and with whom. How people feel about their work or about others in the group is their own business, to be introduced or not according to their own judgment and desire. The expression or nonexpression of feelings is not part of the contract. The consultant agrees to adopt a laissez faire role with respect to expression of feelings.

2. Openness and honesty about *behavior* are expected and essential for the achievement of results. This means

a. that the consultant will ask for full disclosure about *what* work people do, *how* they do it, and *with whom* they do it; and

b. that the consultant will probe for people to be specific and concrete in expressing their expectations and demands for the *behavior* of others. Each team member is expected to be open and specific about what he wants others to do *more* or *do better* or *do less* or maintain unchanged.

3. No expectation or demand is adequately communicated until it has been *written down* and is clearly understood by both sender and receiver, or will any change process be engaged in until this has been done.

4. The full sharing of expectations and demands does not constitute a completed change process. It is only the precondition for change to be agreed through negotiation. It is unreasonable for anyone in the group, boss or subordinate, to expect that any change will take place merely as a result of communicating a

demand or expectation. Unless a team member is willing to change his own behavior in order to get what he wants from the other(s), he is likely to waste his and the group's time talking about the issue. When a member makes a request or demand for changed behavior on the part of another, the consultant will always ask what quid pro quo (something for something) he is willing to give in order to get what he wants. This goes for the boss as well as for the subordinates. If the boss can get what he wants simply by issuing orders or clarifying expectations from his position of authority, he probably does not need a consultant or a change process.

5. The change process is essentially one of bargaining and negotiation in which two or more members each agree to change behavior in exchange for some desired change on the part of the other. This process is not complete until the agreement can be *written down* in terms which include the agreed changes in behavior and make clear what each party is expected to give in return.

6. Threats and pressures are neither illegitimate nor excluded from the negotiation process. However, group members should realise that overreliance on the negative quid pro quo usually results in defensiveness, concealment, decreased communication and retaliation, and may lead to breakdown of the negotiation. The consultant will do his best to help members to accomplish their aims with positive incentives wherever possible.

During the discussion of the contract, I try to help participants see that each member has power and influence in the group, both positively to reward and collaborate with others, and negatively to resist, block or punish. Each uses his power and influence to create a desirable and satisfying work situation for himself. When this process takes place covertly and/or only partly consciously, people often takes place covertly and/or only partly consciously, people often use much time and energy in it unproductively. It is unproductive because people are often unsure about others' desires and intentions. This makes it difficult to judge how a particular pressure or proffered reward will be responded to. We often judge others' wants and needs as though they were as our own. We "do unto others as we would have them do unto us," and because they are not in all respects like us, our ignorance results in ineffectiveness. We make guesses about how others will respond to our attempts to influence their behavior, and when the guesses are wrong we have no option other than to continue the laborious process of trial and error, slowly building up our knowledge of what is and is not effective with each other person through a clumsy and not very systematic experimentation.

In stable, slowly changing organizational situations, this trial and error process may be satisfactory, because people do learn how to influence one another given a sufficient period of contact. When situations and personnel change more rapidly (over periods of months rather than years), then this most primitive learning process does not do the job fast enough. The more fluid the system, the more important it is to develop information rapidly which will permit people to influence one another effectively. I try to get my clients to see that if information about desires and intentions is equally shared, then they will all increase the effectiveness of their influence attempts. Further, when others try to influence them the proffered quid pro quo will be more likely to be one which they really want and need. Following the terms of the contract will then not only have the effect of resolving current problems but also of increasing knowledge within the group of how effectively to influence one another. The intended effect is that the *total amount of influence of group members on one another should increase.* There is no intention that the amount of influence one member exerts relative to that of another should change or stay the same. This is left free to vary, but the consultant so conducts himself that opportunities to increase one's influence within the system are as nearly equal as possible.

PHASE 3: DIAGNOSIS

The next stage in the Role Negotiation process is for the group and the consultant to develop a shared understanding of how work actually gets done in the group. In diagnosis, I focus on decision making and communication, as these are the vehicles by which power and influence are exercised in the organization. Any of the following activities may be helpful in clarifying work processes.

1. Find out and list what are the major *kinds* of decisions which are made by members of the group.

2. For each type of decision, list *who* is involved, in order of the influence which each has on the final outcome.

3. Draw an organization chart in which the vertical dimension indicates the number and importance of decisions in which the individual plays a key role.

4. Connect members on the chart by "communication lines" as follows:

  a.═══════ frequent communication on important matters
  b._____ regular communication on important matters
  c._ _ _ _ _ _ occasional communication on important matters

5. Add arrows to the above lines, indicating who generally initiates the communication.

6. Discuss the organization chart, raising questions about how the work of the group is conducted and decisions made (e.g. how many layers are involved in decisions? why? why are some people involved or left out of some decisions? is this the kind of organization the group members feel is most effective? if not, how should it be different?)

These diagnostic activities are useful for the consultant if he does not know the group's operations and relationships very well, and they serve as a second warm up activity for the group. They are somewhat less personal and threatening than the more confronting diagnostic activities to which we turn next.

7. Ask each person by himself to consider the organization charts and the lists of decisions and to reflect on his satisfactions and dissatisfactions with the

way business is conducted within the group. What things would he change if he could? What things would he particularly like to keep as they are? Who and what would have to change in order to improve things?

Each member is asked to take a paper, one piece for each other member of the group, and to consider and list for each person things which influence the writer's work effectiveness. For each person he makes three lists.

a. Those things which the other person should do *more* or do *better*.
b. Those things which the other should do *less*.
c. Those things the other does which facilitate the writer's effectiveness and should not be changed.

These lists are exchanged so that each person has all the lists which pertain to his work behavior. Each member makes a master list for himself on a large piece of (flip chart) paper on which he shows the behavior which each other person desires him to do *more* or *better*, *less*, or *continue* unchanged. These are posted so that the entire group can peruse and refer to each list. Each member is allowed to question the others who have sent messages about his behavior, querying the what? why? and how? of their requests, but no one is allowed a rebuttal, defence or even a yes or no reply to the messages he has received. The consultant intervenes in the discussion to make sure that only clarification is taking place and that argument, discussion and decision making about issues is not engaged in at this stage.

The purpose of this rather rigid and formal control on communication by the consultant is to make sure that the group does not have a negative problem solving experience and that members do not get polarized on issues or take up extreme positions which they will feel impelled to defend in order to save face. Communication is controlled in order to prevent escalation of actual or potential conflicts. The strategy is to channel the energy which has been generated or released by the sharing of demands and expectations into successful problem solving and mutual influence. The consultant intervenes to inhibit hostile and destructive expression at this point and later to facilitate constructive bargaining and negotiation of mutually beneficial agreements. This initial sharing of desires and change goals leads to a point at which the team development process is most vulnerable, because if sufficient anger and defensiveness are generated by the problem sharing, the consultant will not be able to hold the negative processes in check long enough for the development of the positive problem solving spiral on which the process depends for its effectiveness. However, my guess is that groups in which the latent anger is too great will usually avoid the team development activity altogether; at any rate, such an uncontrollable breakthrough of hostility has not yet occurred in my experience with the method. My concern over the negative possibilities is in part responsible for the slow, deliberate and rather formal development of the confrontation of issues within the group.

PHASE 4: NEGOTIATION

After each member has had an opportunity to clarify the messages he has received, the group proceeds to the selection of issues for negotiation. The consultant begins this phase by reemphasizing that unless a quid pro quo can be offered in return for a desired behavior change, there is little point in having a discussion about it: *unless behavior changes on both sides the most likely prediction is that the status quo will continue.* (It can be argued that this is an extremely conservative point of view and that behavior does in fact change between men of good will simply as a result of an exchange of views. While I do not deny that this occurs, I do not assume it in my practice and I allow myself to be pleasantly surprised when it happens!).

Each participant is asked to indicate two or more issues on which he particularly wants to get some change on the part of another. He is also asked to select one or more issues on which he feels it may be possible for him to move in the direction desired by others. He does this by marking his own flip chart and those of the other members. In effect, each person is indicating the issues upon which he most wants to exert influence and those on which he is most willing to accept influence. With the help of the consultant the group then goes through the lists to select the "most negotiable issues," those where there is a combination of a high desire for change on the part of an initiator and a willingness to negotiate on the part of the person whose behavior is the target of the change attempt. The consultant asks for a group of two or more persons who are involved in one such issue to volunteer for a negotiation demonstration before the rest of the group.

The negotiation process consists of the parties making contingent offers to one another of the form, "if you do X, I will do Y." The negotiation ends when all parties are satisfied that they will receive a reasonable return for whatever they are agreeing to give. The consultant asks that the agreement be formalized in writing which states specifically and concretely what each party is going to give and receive in the bargain. He also asks the participants to discuss openly what sanctions can be applied in the case of nonfulfillment of the bargain by one or another party. Often this involves no more than reversion to the status quo, but it may involve the application of pressures and penalties as well.

After the negotiation demonstration the members are asked to select other issues they wish to work on. A number of negotiations may go on simultaneously, the consultant being involved at the request of any party to any negotiation. All agreements are published to the entire group, however, and questioned by the consultant and the other members to test the good faith and reality orientation of the parties in making them. Where agreement proves impossible, the consultant and other group members try to help the parties find further incentives (positive or, less desirably, coercive) which they may bring to bear to encourage agreement.

This process is, of course, not so simple as the bare bones outlined here. All kinds of difficulties can occur, from bargaining in bad faith, to refusal to bargain at all, to dangerous escalation of conflict. In my experience, however, group members tend to be rather wise about the issues they can and cannot deal with, and I refrain from pushing them to negotiate issues they feel are unresolvable. My aim is to create a beginning to team development with a successful experience which group members will see as a fruitful way of improving their effectiveness and satisfaction. I try to go no further than the members feel is reasonable.

PHASE 5: FOLLOW UP

At the conclusion of a team development cycle as outlined above, I suggest that the group test the firmness of the agreements they have negotiated by living with them awhile before trying to go further. We can then get together later to review the agreement, renegotiate ones which have not held or which are no longer viable, and continue the team development process by dealing with new issues. Hopefully, the group will eventually take over the conduct of the Role Negotiation activity and the consultant's role will whither away. This can occur when the group has developed sufficient control over the dangers, avoidances and threats involved in the negotiation process that they no longer need third party protection or encouragement. However, I do not claim any greater success than my tender minded colleagues in freeing clients from dependence on my services. What I do find is that there is less backsliding between visits in teams I have worked with using this method than when I have applied more interpersonally oriented change interventions. The agreements obtained through Role Negotiation seem to have more "teeth" in them than those which rely on the softer processes of interpersonal trust and openness. This is not a description of the world as I wish it to be; it is how I find it.

THE DYNAMICS OF ROLE NEGOTIATION

Role Negotiation intervenes directly into the relationships of power, authority and influence within the group. The change effort is directed at the work relationships among members. It encourages members to attempt to change their roles vis-à-vis one another, hence the name, Role Negotiation. Role Negotiation avoids probing into the likes and dislikes of members for one another and their personal feelings about one another. In this it is more consonant with the task oriented organizational norms of impersonality than are more interpersonal interventions. I have found that groups with whom I have had difficulty working when I focused on interpersonal issues dropped their resistance and returned willingly to problem solving when I shifted my approach to Role Negotiation. Clients seem more at home with problems of power and influence than they do with interpersonal issues. They feel more competent and less dependent upon the skill and trustworthiness of the consultant in dealing with these issues, and so they are ready to work sooner and harder. I also find my own skill not so central to the change process as it is when I am dealing with interpersonal issues. Because clients are less dependent upon the consultant, I suspect that the amount of skill and professional training which is required to conduct Role Negotiation is less than for more sensitive approaches.

This is not to say that Role Negotiation poses no threat to organization members. The consultant asks participants to be open about matters which are often covert in normal life. The effect of a thorough Role Negotiation is to expose the *real* power and influence of organization members, and this may be either more or less than they would wish to have known. Both those who bluff and those who operate behind the scenes may feel their positions threatened by the open discussion of influence processes which is the stuff of Role Negotiation. Persons who rely upon their formal authority and status for personal security may be discomfited by the revelation that some others in the group pay only lip service to the formal authority and are more concerned about what they can get away with than about the rules and regulations. Conversely, these latter may feel it is to their advantage to conceal their true assessment of the realities of power and influence behind an appearance of loyal compliance. The processes of diagnosis and negotiation run counter to the political practices of concealment and deception. Resistance to negotiation develops when openness about needs, intentions and goals is felt to show weakness or expose one to manipulation or exploitation. For this reason it is likely that groups which are engaged in really serious internal political or power struggles will find it quite difficult to engage effectively in Role Negotiation.

I have, however, had success in working with groups in which more minor forms of politicking were going on. As mentioned above, members tend to limit the issues dealt with to those which they feel are safe. These provide a foothold for an opening up of communication and constructive problem solving. As members become more confident and adept with the process, they can bring more touchy issues into the arena. The method does not require that members proceed to expose issues more rapidly than they feel is to their advantage. Nor does the consultant try to establish a norm (or myth) of trust and good will. Rather he encourages members to deal with those issues they can tackle and to be aware of the limitations placed on this process by competition for personal advantage. The hope is that members will find gradually that they can achieve more for themselves by open negotiation than they can by private competition and that the more constructive process will in time replace the more restrictive and limiting one. This is a hope, not a promise. However, my experience convinces me that Role Negotiation is less sensitive and vulnerable to mistrust and seeking for personal advantage than approaches to team development which deal directly with interpersonal and emotional issues.

Role Negotiation is vulnerable, however, in two ways. One is the failure of rewards and sanctions to motivate the agreed upon behavior. This may occur when the bargaining was conducted at a rather superficial level or in bad faith (where there is a partly or wholly conscious intention to subvert the agreement). In such a case the incentives are simply not strong enough. Or it may happen that one party to the agreement continues to keep his part of the bargain even though the other defaults on his. This happens when the injured party is unwilling to precipitate open conflict. These are the kinds of issues we can expect to encounter in follow up sessions to the original Role Negotiation.

Another vulnerability is to external interventions which upset the balance of give and take achieved during a successful negotiation. Others, outside or inside the organization may change so as to reward or punish behavior which was the subject of negotiation, making it less attractive to adhere to the original agreement. This may eventually make it necessary to widen the scope of the team development effort beyond the boundaries of the original team. A model for Intergroup Role Negotiation is, of course, practical. Indeed, the processes described in this paper have been applied to intergroup conflict resolution for much longer than they have been used for team development. An outcome of Role Negotiation as a team development approach is the development of skill in the processes of issue definition and negotiation which are useful in dealing with intergroup conflict. In this, Role Negotiation has an advantage over team development approaches based on openness, trust and caring. These latter tend to be ineffective in the intial stages of intergroup problem solving, when the groups are often oriented almost exclusively toward competition.

THE ECONOMICS OF ROLE NEGOTIATION

One disadvantage of interpersonal approaches to team development is that the level of skill and experience demanded of the consultant is very high indeed. Managers are not confident in dealing with these issues. Because they feel at risk they reasonably want to have as much safety and skill as money can buy. The great demand for skilled consultants on interpersonal and group processes has created an extreme shortage and a meteoric rise in consulting fees. It seems unlikely that the supply will soon catch up with the demand.

The shortage of highly skilled workers in team development argues for deskilling the requirements for effective consultant performance. Examples of deskilled approaches to team development are Robert Blake's Managerial Grid and Ralph Coverdale's training programs in group effectiveness, both of which steer away from deeper emotional issues within the team. I see Role Negotiation as another way of reducing the skill requirements for the consultant in team development. I hope and believe that Role Negotiation can be practiced by management development specialists with substantial experience in group work, a fair degree of personal sensitivity and familiarity with behavioral science concepts. I do not think it demands professional training in the behavioral sciences or the ability to conduct T groups.

A SUMMARY COMPARISON OF ROLE NEGOTIATION WITH HUMAN RELATIONS ORIENTED APPROACHES

The following comparison highlights the differences between the Role Negotiation approach and the tender minded interpersonal approaches which I feel are direct competitors with it. The differences have been highlighted rather than the similarities to define more sharply the Role Negotiation approach.

Human Relations Approach	Role Negotiation
Assumes people collaborate naturally if we remove the barriers of suspicion, mistrust and stereotyped perception. At bottom, people's interests are similar and compatible. They will tend to be trustworthy, mutually supportive, and helpful if they are given a chance.	Assumes people have truly different and sometimes opposed interests. Conflict and competition are normal, natural states of affairs. People will try to maximize what they perceive to be their own interests. If it is to their advantage, they can be expected to be exploitative, untrustworthy and competitive.
The effective alternative to competition is trust, openness and voluntary collaboration.	The effective alternative to competition and mistrust is a negotiated agreement based on enforceable guarantees of mutual observance.
Diagnosis of difficulties focuses on the perceptions, needs, attitudes and feelings of persons toward one another's personal style.	Diagnosis of difficulties focuses on the rights, powers, privileges, demands and requirements which incumbents of roles have with respect to one another.
Resolution of interpersonal difficulties is approached by working toward understanding and acceptance of one another's needs, attitudes and feelings.	Resolution of differences is approached by working toward negotiated settlement of differences based on a quid pro quo.
The targets of change are interpersonal relationships: trust, confidence, openness, acceptance and understanding among persons.	The targets of change are working relationships: duties, responsibilities, authority, accountability of persons in roles.
The forces maintaining changes come from the desire of persons to maintain satisfying relationships of openness, caring and trust.	The forces maintaining changes come from the ability and willingness of parties to an agreement to administer and withhold rewards and sanctions for others' compliance with or violation of negotiated agreements.
Changes are vulnerable to 1) erosion of trust and openness when persons follow organizational norms and requirements for impersonal behavior toward one another; 2) role requirements which are incompatible with trust, collaboration and caring;	Changes are vulnerable to 1) failure of the original agreement to be based on sufficiently potent rewards and sanctions; 2) unwillingness or inability of either party to apply rewards or sanctions to enforce agreements;

3) competition between commitment to tasks and commitment to persons when these compete for scarce time and personal resources.

3) imbalance of rewards and sanctions caused by third party interventions from parties outside the agreement.

TOWARD AN INTEGRATION OF THE HUMAN RELATIONS AND ROLE NEGOTIATION APPROACHES

I have in this paper contrasted the human relations and Role Negotiation approaches. In doing so I have emphasized the differences between them in order to highlight the unique characteristics of the Role Negotiation methods and give them a promising and attractive image. Yet it seems to me that the two approaches may bear an organic and developmental relationship to each other, in which the Role Negotiation methods lay the groundwork for effective and lasting work at the interpersonal and emotional levels. I believe that the process of getting responsibility, authority, accountability and competition for rewards under control and subject to agreement forms the necessary basis for resolution of interpersonal problems. If we try to skip this more mundane step, the harder, tougher issues pose a continual threat to resolutions based on tender minded assumptions. I think that if we can achieve stable, viable resolutions of the hard issues they may then form a realistic basis for the trust and openness without which interpersonal problem solving is impossible.

Role Negotiation may now facilitate the transition towards a greater depth and interpersonal confrontation. For example, I have used it in this way in a T group where the managers (strangers to each other) were uneasy about dealing directly with interpersonal issues. The Role Negotiation focused on behavior changes which members wanted from one another. The structural support and the emphasis on behavior rather than upon feelings reduced the threat of dealing with interpersonal issues. The emphasis on the quid pro quo as a basis for negotiated change legitimized resistance to change and provided individuals with protection against group conformity pressures. I and the participants felt the method provided a safe and effective way of moving into interpersonal issues. As the T group members developed more confidence, they found they could do without the structure and the extra safety. It had served its purpose.

This experience did not take place in an ongoing work group. The members did not have ambitions and goals as competitive as those I commonly find in client groups. It would be pleasant to think that a stable resolution of differences based on Role Negotiation could indeed pave the way for members to deal openly and understandingly with one another as persons. At present this is only a hope on my part. A tough minded approach continues to form the basis for effective work with the problems presented by my clients.

Planned renegotiation: A norm-setting OD intervention[*]

John J. Sherwood and John C. Glidewell

Organization development has been described as "an educational process by which human resources are continuously identified, allocated, and expanded in ways that make these resources more available to the organization, and therefore, improve the organization's problem-solving capabilities." The concept of planned renegotiation describes a procedure by which controlled change can enter an organization in such a way that resources become more available to the organization. It is derived from a clear and simple theory of how roles are established and changed.

The theory itself is a norm-setting intervention because it is intended to become part of the normative structure of an organization, and as such to become part of the language, rhetoric, and expectations of members of the organization. Furthermore, the use of these concepts in successful problem-solving leads to the learning of behavioral skills by insight, reinforcement, and imitation. As we often like to hear Lewin say, there is nothing as practical as a good theory. Where the concept of planned renegotiation becomes part of the norms of an organization, it can constitute the heart of an OD effort.

THE MODEL

The model describes how social systems—that is, relations between persons and relations between groups—are established and become stabilized so that work can get done, and how change can enter the system. The model is cyclical, and it includes four phases.

1. Sharing information and negotiating expectations. When persons begin to establish a relationship which they expect may endure over some period of

* Copyright © 1971 by John J. Sherwood and John C. Glidewell. Appeared previously as Paper No. 338, Institute for Research in the Behavioral, Economic, and Management Sciences, Purdue University, November 1971.

time—as brief as a preemployment interview or as long lasting as a marriage or an appointment to the U.S. Supreme Court—they first exchange information. They share information about themselves and they exchange expectations, which are usually implicit and unspecified, about how each is to behave with the other(s). They are essentially trading information and establishing expectations about how a "member" of this relationship, or a member of this group, is going to behave.

Once a sufficient exchange of information occurs, so that uncertainty is reduced to an acceptable level and the behaviors of the parties are more or less predictable, and if the relationship is seen as enduring sometime into the future, then commitment to these shared expectations takes place.

2. Commitment. Once commitment to a set of shared expectations takes place, then each member's role is defined, and each member knows for the most part what is expected of him and for the most part what he can expect from the others. The strength of each individual's commitment and the range of his behavior encompassed by his role are both measures of the importance or centrality to him of this particular relationship. The more important the relationship, the more evidence of commitment is required and the more behaviors—including attitudes, values, and perceptions—are embraced by the role expectations. With commitment comes stability.

3. Stability and productivity. When there is commitment to a set of shared expectations, these expectations govern the behavior of group members and provide stability within the relationships—that is, for the most part you do what I expect of you and for the most part I do what you expect of me. This stability in the relationships leads to the possibility that work can now get done. While stability does not guarantee productivity, it is necessary for productive work to occur. The energy of the principals is now available for other things, since their relationships are sufficiently predictable that they no longer required sustained attention.

Commitment to a set of shared expectations then governs behavior during a period of stability—but invariably, sooner or later, disruption occurs.

4. Disruption. Disruption occurs because of a violation of expectations by the principals or because of external intrusion into the system. It is assumed that disruption is inevitable, only the duration of the period of stability varies, because (a) information is never completely shared during the initial period when expectations are negotiated; and (b) individuals, groups, and organizations are viewed as open systems—i.e., they change as a consequence of transactions with their environment.

Disruptions may be external in origin, such as a new person assigned to a work group, a loss of personnel, an assignment of a new task or higher quota, a budgetary cut and reallocation of resources, or reorganization of personnel and subsequent reassignment of duties. The first child born into a marriage is an example of a new input into the relationship which is likely to lead to the violation of previously established expectations. Disruptions may also be internal in origin, such as, the sharing of information which was not made available earlier when expectations were being negotiated. Persons also change as a consequence of new experiences, training, and education. When the changed person returns to the unchanged role, expectations may be violated leading to a disruption of the relationship.

It is at the point of disruption that change can enter the system, for it is at this time that expectations are no longer fixed. New information can now enter the system, and the renegotiation of expectations can occur. Once again the system recycles through: (1) sharing information and renegotiating expectations, then (2) commitment to a set of expectations, which governs behavior during a period (3) of stability and productivity, when, for the most part, you do what I expect of you and I do what you expect of me, until (4) disruption once again occurs, because of a violation of expectations by the principals or because of external intrusion into the system. With disruption change can once again enter the system, as it cycles from renegotiation through disruption, and yet another opportunity for renegotiation (see Figure 1).

The paradox is that the very moment the system is most open to change there are strong inhibiting forces working to return things "to the way they used to be," because of anxiety accompanying the uncertainty which characterizes the system at the time it is in a state of disruption.

When a disruption of expectations occurs, uncertainty follows—because I can no longer depend on your doing what I expect of you, and my own role is also unclear to me—and with uncertainty the principals become anxious. The anxiety is uncomfortable. The quickest and surest way to reduce that anxiety is for the relationship to return once again "to the way things used to be." This is often a ritualized commitment to prior expectations, such as a perfunctory apology, handshake, or embrace, without admitting the new information into the system, which is now available since it gave rise to the disruption. This new information would form the basis for renegotiating the expectations governing the relationship. The relationship remains closed to change, when the parties deal with the uncertainty and anxiety produced by disruption by returning to the original level of sharing expectations without renegotiation—for example, the pledge, "it won't happen again," or the admonition, "don't let it happen again," or the reaffirmation of the way things used to be, "let's be gentlemen" or "I'm sorry, I was wrong, everything is now okay . . . nothing is changed!"

It is during the period of disruption, when the parties are uncertain about their roles and the future of the relationship and are therefore anxious, that the system must be held open if change is to enter. If new information is allowed to enter the relationship and is treated in a problem-solving way, it can provide the basis for renegotiating the expectations governing the relationship. The newly renegotiated expectations are, therefore, more likely to be in line with the current realities of the situation, and once commitment occurs, the period of stability is likely to be more enduring before the next ensuing disruption.

If the parties share this model as a part of their language and their mutual expectations, these concepts are likely to help them by increasing their tolerance for the uncertainty and the accompanying anxiety which surround their relationship while expectations are held open during renegotiation. Through continued use of these concepts, the behavioral skills of the parties also increase, thereby facilitating the renegotiation process.

FIGURE 1

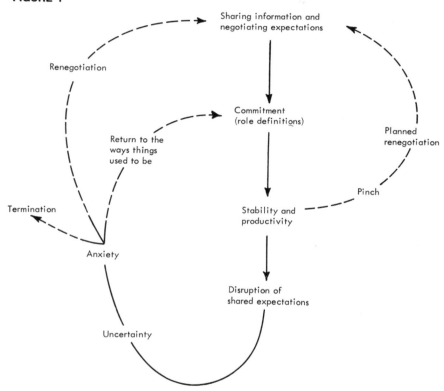

The theory predicts that disruption without renegotiation leads to an increasing frequency and intensity of disruptions. When each disruption is not treated as a new source of information and a new opportunity for adjustment of expectations and change, but rather as a disagreeable state that cannot be tolerated due to the urgency to return "to the way things used to be," then the source of the disruption is never satisfactorily remedied, improved, or even ameliorated. If the problem or difficulty in the relationship is never addressed directly, it is likely to persist and add to the intensity of future disruptions precipitated by new problems entering the relationship.[1] The more inflexible the system—a two-person relationship, a group, an organization, or a community—the more likely a final disruptive event will be explosive and destructive. Such a relationship is likely to be terminated in a manner which is destructive to the parties involved.

Whenever disruption occurs the possibility of terminating the relationship is always an alternative solution. Termination is more likely to be a constructive, problem-solving solution, when it is a consequence of renegotiation. Termination is more likely to result in the destructive loss of resources, when one or more of the following are present: (1) The disruption is unplanned and explosive, (2) the system is rigid and inflexible, or (3) the parties have little or no prior experience in renegotiating adjustments to changing conditions.

PLANNED RENEGOTIATION

The model states that relationships cycle through (1) the sharing of information and negotiation of expectations, through (2) commitment to (3) stability and productivity to (4) disruption and the possibility of renegotiation and therefore change. It has also been assumed that it is difficult to hold the system open for renegotiation because of the uncertainty and anxiety that prevails at that time. These concepts then provide a way to introduce controlled change by *anticipating* disruption and renegotiating expections *in advance*. This is known as planned renegotiation.

Where this simple model of how roles are established and how they change is available to the parties and where they have skills in sharing their reactions, feelings, and perceptions about their relationship, change can be introduced in a controlled and systematic way through planned renegotiation. This is less stressful than renegotiation under conditions of disruption. Both the model and the concept of planned renegotiation thus become parts of the relationship—so that "whenever I feel a pinch," that pinch is shared and the possibility of renegotiation is raised. A *pinch* is a signal of the possibility of an impending disruption and it describes a sense of loss of freedom within one's current role (see Figure 1). The The felt loss of freedom may be due to a sense of expanded resources or to subtle constriction of expectations by others. In either case, there is the possibility of resources lost to the system.

Some examples of pinches which raise the possibility of renegotiation are:

—"I think I am now ready to go to New York on a buying trip without you."

—"I find that I am defensive with you, because you judge others so harshly. I don't want you judging me that way."

---

[1] The intensity of future disruptions is not likely to be increased where problems or difficulties in a relationship are handled by reducing commitment to the relationship. In this case, an apparent "return to the way things used to be" is actually a withdrawal of commitment. Over time such a strategy leads to an atrophied relationship. (In the *Marriage Grid*, Houston: Gulf Publishing Co., 1971, by Jane Mouton and Robert Blake, this is a 1 : 1 orientation, e.g., "Home is where I eat, sleep, and keep my things.")

—"While I will continue to do all the drafting work, I would like to do some engineering work on this project."

—"I think that I somehow have to know all the answers, because no one in this group ever admits that they don't know something. I, therefore, bluff my way along."

—"We are always talking about how bright we all are, and as a consequence I am becoming more and more cautious about the ideas I choose to share lest they appear anything but brilliant."

—"I have to begin saying no to you or you have to stop adding to my workload. I will be unable to meet the commitments I have already made unless something is changed."

—"I like you a lot, and I suddenly realize that I am very hesitant to disagree with you for fear that you will then dislike me."

When the question of renegotiation of expectations is raised "when I feel a pinch," the parties have more *choice* and more control over change. They are subject to fewer negotiations "under fire," and they are less often victims of crises and pressures to return to the way things used to be.

IMPLICATIONS AND DISCUSSION

Planned renegotiation is likely to be a successful norm-setting invervention in an organization where there is some prior commitment to the concept of organization development, so that persons are neither so closed that differences are ignored and inappropriately smoothed over nor so competitive that differences are exploited by subversive rivalry.

On the other hand, people need concepts to guide their behavior. Organization development efforts often involve skill training in interpersonal relations, or process consultation, or prescriptions to do things differently—such as, "be open"—with training in interpersonal skills, but without an adequate theoretical framework that provides concepts to guide behavior. The tools of Gestalt therapy help people expand their own awareness of themselves and make more data available to the system. But what to do with data when more available? The planned renegotiation model supplies a framework for guilding more productive working relationships with information generated through organization development efforts.

Similarly, participative management systems need information from all levels of supervision in order to function effectively. But once the information is generated, how is it to be handled: The planned renegotiation model provides a framework for allowing new information to change the system, where such change is agreeable to all parties involved.

The theory underlying the concept of planned renegotiation is clear and simple and straightforward. Theoretical elaborations have been purposely avoided. It is intended that the concepts become part of the language or organizational life. Persons can be trained in the skills of planned renegotiation. It is important that people learn to detect pinches before disruptions develop. A pinch is felt by an individual, whereas a disruption is experienced by all parties involved in the relationship. It is, therefore, incumbent upon an individual who feels a pinch also to take responsibility for raising the question of renegotiation with the other(s), rather than asserting that it is someone else's problem or responsibility. At the same time, it is important he understand that when he experiences a pinch, this is going to make him anxious. When a pinch is shared and renegotiation considered, then others become anxious as well. People get anxious both because of the uncertainty which is introduced into the relationship, and because they are never sure whether they will personally be better off after the renegotiation is completed than they were before. When people work with this model, they learn that anxiety becomes controlled and tolerable when there is a commitment to problem-solving. There remains nevertheless a risk each time the relationship is opened for examination and renegotiation.

In the first few attempts at renegotiation within the model, people are simultaneously working on two problems: (1) trying out a problem-solving model and developing skills and procedures for its use; and (2) working on the pinch that gave rise to the renegotiation. Over time both skills and procedures develop, as does confirmation of the model and its usefulness to the parties involved (or its lack of usefulness).

Based on the assumption that "most people in organizations prefer a fair negotiated settlement to a state of unresolved conflict," Harrison[2] has developed a very sound procedure for changing role relationships. It should be useful to those who would like to try planned renegotiation in a formally structured and specifically programmed way. Harrison calls his procedure "role negotiation." It is a detailed program for exchanging expectations and demands for the behavior of others in terms of what each wants others (a) to do more or do better, (b) to do less, or (c) to remain unchanged. These expectations are written, so as to be clearly understood by both sender and receiver. When one person makes a request or demand for changed behavior on the part of another, he must specify a quid pro quo he is willing to give in order to get what he wants. The process is complete when an agreement is written which specifies the agreed upon changes in behavior and makes clear what each party is expected to give in return, including a discussion of possible sanctions for noncompliance. The procedures are clear and simple, if a bit mechanical, and they require a consultant in the early stages to establish the rules and to moderate their use.

There are various other ways organizations might make use of the concept of planned renegotiation. An organization might design a "renegotiating arena," where the principals commit themselves not to leave the field until a satisfactory set of mutual expectations is established.[3] A skilled third party consultant might be available to them.

---

[2] See Roger Harrison, "Role Negotiation: A Tough Minded Approach to Team Development," the preceding article in this Part.

[3] The method, "Meetings for Two" in Fordyce and Weil (1971, pp. 114–16), is a highly structured session designed to provide the opportunity to renegotiate expectations in a two-person relationship without the benefit of a theoretical model. While a third party is not required, the procedure is so highly structured that the presence of a third person seems almost essential.

The question is sometimes raised, if planned renegotiation is encouraged, won't this lead to the termination of some relationships that would not otherwise terminate? Yes, it probably will. Where relationships are terminated by choice, this is likely to be an outcome which is more healthy for the individuals and more productive for the organization over the long run, than to retain members who are essentially "captive."

While the theory of how roles are established and changed seems to be interpersonal in focus and appears to concentrate on the modification of behavior in one-to-one situations, the concepts also describe the relation of a person to a group or the relations of all members of a group to one another—e.g., task group, committee, subordinates reporting to one supervisor, family, etc. Relations between groups are also subject to disruption and renegotiation as well, e.g., relations between departments, branch offices, or project teams.[4]

Rather than a theory of interpersonal affairs, the theory is better described as a description of the establishment and change of *relations* between elements of a social system—persons or groups. The theory is more encompassing that it first might seem, it can include some of the major realities of organizational life, such as the power of economics and legitimate authority and the competition between persons or groups for scarce resources. A subordinate can certainly raise the question of renegotiation with his supervisor, and help him learn to use the model. Issues of authority can be subjects of renegotiation. Where individuals or groups are highly competitive, renegotiation can take the form of more open bargaining rather than secretive, and sometimes subversive, rivalry.

While all of us need concepts to guide our behavior, it would seem that the model of how roles are established and changed and the concept of planned renegotiation would be particularly useful for those who frequently enter and work with temporary systems. The more fluid and changing the system, the more important it is to be able to develop means of producing information rapidly which then permits people to appropriately influence one another and to accept appropriate influence. Furthermore, working within this model even within an enduring and established relationship is likely to help a person develop those behavioral skills which are effective in life in temporary systems. These concepts are also probably useful to those who play a mediating role as a third party consultant to others in conflict.

SUMMARY

This paper is based on the assumption that people need concepts to guide their behavior. A clear and simple model of how roles are established and changed is presented—relationships cycle through (1) the sharing of information and the negotiation of expectations, then (2) commitment to a set of expectations, which

---

[4] Several persons have reported that this model is also useful for negotiating change in the behavior of a single person (intrapersonal change). Persons have talked to themselves about themselves and held dialogs in a Gestalt fashion between "how I am now" and "how I would like to be," followed by commitment to a new set of expectations, stability, disruption, and renegotiation.

governs behavior during a period (3) of stability and productivity, when, for the most part you do what I expect of you and I do what you expect of me, until (4) disruption occurs and the possibility of change enters the system. This theory itself is a norm-setting intervention into an organization when it becomes a part of the normative structure, language, and expectations of members of the organization.

The concept of planned renegotiation is derived from this model and represents a procedure by which controlled change can enter an organization, thereby freeing and expanding resources for problem-solving. This enhances an organization's internal flexibility which is one important criterion of organizational effectiveness.

With a statement such as planned renegotiation, people have more choice in their lives and are less likely to be victims "of the way things used to be . . ."

Defensive communication*

Jack R. Gibb

One way to understand communication is to view it as a people process rather than as a language process. If one is to make fundamental improvements in communication, he must make changes in interpersonal relationships. One possible type of alteration—and the one with which this paper is concerned—is that of reducing the degree of defensiveness.

Defensive behavior is defined as that behavior which occurs when an individual perceives threat or anticipates threat in the group. The person who behaves defensively, even though he also gives some attention to the common task, devotes an appreciable portion of his energy to defending himself. Besides talking about the topic, he thinks about how he appears to others, how he may be seen more favorably, how he may win, dominate, impress, or escape punishment, and/or how he may avoid or mitigate a perceived or an anticipated attack.

Such inner feelings and outward acts tend to create similarly defensive postures in others, and if unchecked, the ensuing circular response becomes increasingly destructive. Defensive behavior, in short, engenders defensive listening, and this in turn produces postural, facial, and verbal cues which raise the defense level of the original communicator.

Defense arousal prevents the listener from concentrating upon the message.

---

* Reprinted by permission from *ETC: A Review of General Semantics,* Vol. XXII, No. 2; copyright 1965, by the International Society for General Semantics.

Not only do defensive communicators send off multiple value, motive, and affect cues, but also defensive recipients distort what they receive. As a person becomes more and more defensive, he becomes less and less able to perceive accurately the motives, the values, and the emotions of the sender. My analyses of tape-recorded discussions revealed that increases in defensive behavior were correlated positively with losses in efficiency in communication.[1] Specifically, distortions became greater when defensive states existed in the groups.

The converse, moreover, also is true. The more "supportive" or defense reductive the climate, the less the receiver reads into the communication distorted loadings which arise from projections of his own anxieties, motives, and concerns. As defenses are reduced, the receivers become better able to concentrate upon the structure, the content, and the cognitive meanings of the message.

In working over an eight-year period with recordings of discussions occurring in varied settings, I developed the six pairs of defensive and supportive categories presented in Table 1. Behavior which a listener perceives as possessing any of

TABLE 1

Categories of behavior characteristic of supportive
and defensive climates in small groups

Defensive Climates	Supportive Climates
1. Evaluation	1. Description
2. Control	2. Problem Orientation
3. Strategy	3. Spontaneity
4. Neutrality	4. Empathy
5. Superiority	5. Equality
6. Certainty	6. Provisionalism

the characteristics listed in the left-hand column arouses defensiveness, whereas that which he interprets as having any of the qualities designated as supportive reduces defensive feelings. The degree to which these reactions occur depends upon the personal level of defensiveness and upon the general climate in the group at the time.[2]

Speech or other behavior which appears evaluative increases defensiveness. If by expression, manner of speech, tone of voice, or verbal content the sender seems to be evaluating or judging the listener, then the receiver goes on guard. Of course, other factors may inhibit the reaction. If the listener thought that the speaker regarded him as an equal and was being open and spontaneous, for example, the evaluativeness in a message would be neutralized and perhaps not even perceived. This same principle applies equally to the other five categories of potentially defense-producing climates. The six sets are interactive.

---

[1] J. R. Gibb, "Defense Level and Influence Potential in Small Groups," in L. Petrullo and B. M. Bass (eds.), *Leadership and Interpersonal Behavior* (New York: Holt, Rinehart and Winston, 1961), pp. 66–81.

[2] J. R. Gibb, "Sociopsychological Processes of Group Instruction," in N. B. Henry (ed.), *The Dynamics of Instructional Groups* (Fifty-ninth Yearbook of the National Society for the Study of Education, Part II, 1960), pp. 115–35.

Because our attitudes toward other persons are frequently, and often necessarily, evaluative, expressions which the defensive person will regard as nonjudg-
mental are hard to frame. Even the simplest question usually conveys the answer
that the sender wishes or implies the response that would fit into his value system.
A mother, for example, immediately following an earth tremor that shook the
house, sought for her small son with the question: "Bobby, where are you?" The
timid and plaintive "Mommy, I didn't do it" indicated how Bobby's chronic mild
defensiveness predisposed him to react with a projection of his own guilt and
in the context of his chronic assumption that questions are full of accusation.

Anyone who had attempted to train professionals to use information-seeking
speech with neutral effect appreciates how difficult it is to teach a person to say
even the simple "Who did that?" without being seen as accusing. Speech is so
frequently judgmental that there is a reality base for the defensive interpretations
which are so common.

When insecure, group members are particularly likely to place blame, to see
others as fitting into categories of good or bad, to make moral judgments of their
colleagues, and to question the value, motive, and affect loadings of the speech
which they hear. Since value loadings imply a judgment of others, a belief that
the standards of the speaker differ from his own causes the listener to become
defensive.

Descriptive speech, in contrast to that which is evaluative, tends to arouse
a minimum of uneasiness. Speech acts which the listener perceives as genuine
requests for information or as material with neutral loadings are descriptive.
Specifically, presentations of feelings, events, perceptions, or processes which do
not ask or imply that the receiver change behavior or attitude are minimally
defense producing. The difficulty in avoiding overtone is illustrated by the problems of news reporters in writing stories about unions, Communists, Negroes,
and religious activities without tipping off the "party" line of the newspaper. One
can often tell from the opening words in a news article which side the newspaper's
editorial policy favors.

Speech which is used to control the listener evokes resistance. In most of our
social intercourse someone is trying to do something to someone else—to change
an attitude, to influence behavior, or to restrict the field of activity. The degree
to which attempts to control produce defensiveness depends upon the openness
of the effort, for a suspicion that hidden motives exist heightens resistance. For
this reason, attempts of nondirective therapists and progressive educators to
refrain from imposing a set of values, a point of view, or a problem solution upon
the receivers meet with many barriers. Since the norm is control, noncontrollers
must earn the perceptions that their efforts have no hidden motives. A bombard-
ment of persuasive "messages" in the fields of politics, education, special causes,
advertising, religion, medicine, industrial relations, and guidance has bred cynical
and paranoid responses in listeners.

Implicit in all attempts to alter another person is the assumption by the change
agent that the person to be altered is inadequate. That the speaker secretly views

the listener as ignorant, unable to make his own decisions, uninformed, immature, unwise, or possessed of wrong or inadequate attitudes is a subconscious perception which gives the latter a valid base for defensive reactions.

Methods of control are many and varied. Legalistic insistence on detail, restrictive regulations and policies, conformity norms, and all laws are among the methods. Gestures, facial expressions, other forms of nonverbal communication, and even such simple acts as holding a door open in a particular manner are means of imposing one's will upon another and hence are potential sources of resistance.

Problem orientation, on the other hand, is the antithesis of persuasion. When the sender communicates a desire to collaborate in defining a mutual problem and in seeking its solution, he tends to create the same problem orientation in the listener, and of greater importance, he implies that he has no predetermined solution, attitude, or method to impose. Such behavior is permissive in that it allows the receiver to set his own goals, make his own decisions, and evaluate his own progress—or to share with the sender in doing so. The exact methods of attaining permissiveness are not known, but they must involve a constellation of cues and they certainly go beyond mere verbal assurances that the communicator has no hidden desires to exercise control.

When the sender is perceived as engaged in a stratagem involving ambiguous and multiple motivations, the receiver becomes defensive. No one wishes to be a guinea pig, a role player, or an impressed actor, and no one likes to be the victim of some hidden motivation. That which is concealed also may appear larger than it really is, with the degree of defensiveness of the listener determining the perceived size of the suppressed element. The intense reaction of the reading audience to the material in the *Hidden Persuaders* indicates the prevalence of defensive reactions to multiple motivations behind strategy. Group members who are seen as "taking a role," as feigning emotion, as toying with their colleagues, as withholding information, or as having special sources of data are especially resented. One participant once complained that another was "using a listening technique" on him!

A large part of the adverse reaction to much of the so-called human relations training is a feeling against what are perceived as gimmicks and tricks to fool or to "involve" people, to make a person think he is making his own decision, or to make the listener feel that the sender is genuinely interested in him as a person. Particularly violent reactions occur when it appears that something is trying to make a stratagem appear spontaneous. One person has reported a boss who incurred resentment by habitually using the gimmick of "spontaneously" looking at his watch and saying, "My gosh, look at the time—I must run to an appointment." The belief was that the boss would create less irritation by honestly asking to be excused.

Similarly, the deliberate assumption of guilelessness and natural simplicity is especially resented. Monitoring the tapes of feedback and evaluation sessions in training groups indicates the surprising extent to which members perceive the strategies of their colleagues. This perceptual clarity may be quite shocking to the strategist, who usually feels that he has cleverly hidden the motivational aura around the gimmick.

This aversion to deceit may account for one's resistance to politicians who are suspected of behind-the-scenes planning to get his vote, to psychologists whose listening apparently is motivated by more than the manifest or content-level interest in his behavior, or to the sophisticated, smooth, or clever person whose "oneupmanship" is marked with guile. In training groups the role-flexible person frequently is resented because his changes in behavior are perceived as strategic maneuvers.

In contrast, behavior which appears to be spontaneous and free of deception is defense reductive. If the communicator is seen as having a clean id, as having uncomplicated motivations, as being straightforward and honest, and as behaving spontaneously in response to the situation, he is likely to arouse minimal defense.

When neutrality in speech appears to the listener to indicate a lack of concern for his welfare, he becomes defensive. Group members usually desire to be perceived as valued persons, as individuals of special worth, and as objects of concern and affection. The clinical, detached, person-as-an-object-of-study attitude on the part of many psychologist-trainees is resented by group members. Speech with low affect that communicates little warmth or caring is in such contrast with the affect-laden speech in social situations that it sometimes communicates rejection.

Communication that conveys empathy for the feelings and respect for the worth of the listener, however, is particularly supportive and defense reductive. Reassurance results when a message indicates that the speaker identifies himself with the listener's problems, shares his feelings, and accepts his emotional reactions at face value. Abortive efforts to deny the legitimacy of the receiver's emotions by assuring the receiver that he need not feel badly, that he should not feel rejected, or that he is overly anxious, though often intended as support giving, may impress the listener as lack of acceptance. The combination of understanding and empathizing with the other person's emotions with no accompanying effort to change him apparently is supportive at a high level.

The importance of gestural behavioral cues in communicating empathy should be mentioned. Apparently spontaneous facial and bodily evidences of concern are often interpreted as especially valid evidence of deep-level acceptance.

When a person communicates to another that he feels superior in position, power, wealth, intellectual ability, physical characteristics, or other ways, he arouses defensiveness. Here, as with the other sources of disturbance, whatever arouses feelings of inadequacy causes the listener to center upon the affect loading of the statement rather than upon the cognitive elements. The receiver then reacts by not hearing the message, by forgetting it, by competing with the sender, or by becoming jealous of him.

The person who is perceived as feeling superior communicates that he is not willing to enter into a shared problem-solving relationship, that he probably does not desire feedback, that he does not require help, and/or that he will be likely to try to reduce the power, the status, or the worth of the receiver.

Many ways exist for creating the atmosphere that the sender feels himself equal to the listener. Defenses are reduced when one perceives the sender as being willing to enter into participative planning with mutual trust and respect. Differences in talent, ability, worth, appearance, status, and power often exist, but the low defense communicator seems to attach little importance to these distinctions.

The effects of dogmatism in producing defensiveness are well known. Those who seem to know the answers, to require no additional data, and to regard themselves as teachers rather than as co-workers tend to put others on guard. Moreover, in my experiment, listeners often perceived manifest expressions of certainty as connoting inward feelings of inferiority. They saw the dogmatic individual as needing to be right, as wanting to win an argument rather than solve a problem, and as seeing his ideas as truths to be defended. This kind of behavior often was associated with acts which others regarded as attempts to exercise control. People who were "right" seemed to have low tolerance for members who were "wrong"—that is, those who did not agree with the sender.

One reduces the defensiveness of the listener when he communicates that he is willing to experiment with his own behavior, attitudes, and ideas. The person who appears to be taking provisional attitudes, to be investigating issues rather than taking sides on them, to be problem solving rather than debating, and to be willing to experiment and explore tends to communicate that the listener may have some control over the shared quest of or the investigation of the ideas. If a person is genuinely searching for information and data, he does not resent help or company along the way.

CONCLUSION

The implications of the above material for the parent, the teacher, the manager, the administrator, or the therapist are fairly obvious. Arousing defensiveness interferes with communication and thus makes it difficult—and sometimes impossible—for anyone to convey ideas clearly and to move effectively toward the solution of therepeutic, educational, or managerial problems.

Part V

Toward better interpersonal relationships

This is our pad
we all have a ball here
we don't have much bread but
bread is really not very important
when you have good relationships
          From Suzuki Beane

Social scientists, more often than not, are reluctant to expose their own value-systems. To make matters worse, the idea of a "good" *relationship* is slightly foreign, even distasteful, to many students of human behavior who can regard only individual skin boundaries as "real." We will have to forego both of these biases in what follows.

Until now we have either consciously avoided or only vaguely implied two important aspects of interpersonal relationships. The first has to do with the word "better" in our title; "better" implies improvement, and improvement implies a desired state, that is, a "good" state. So we will be dealing here with the normative side of interpersonal relationships, with notions about "good and bad," "healthy and sick." We aim to make explicit the values that govern our own choices and styles of interpersonal relationships.

Secondly, if we can envision a good relationship, then we have to ask: what kinds of personal competencies and what kinds of environmental conditions are conducive to the development and maintenance of these relationships?

In short, this essay and the readings that follow are concerned with (1) a vision of ideal interpersonal relations, and (2) the most effective way to reach that state. Let us start with the normative question: what is a *good* relationship?

I. NORMATIVE ASPECTS OF INTERPERSONAL RELATIONSHIPS

1. A framework for evaluating interpersonal relationships

Can we establish a single criterion of goodness or badness which would be relevant for all interpersonal relationships? Consider the following: customer-salesman, psychiatrist-patient, husband-wife, manager-foreman, guard-inmate, lover-mistress, nurse-doctor. Or take the following kinds of relationships: puppy love, friendship, a crush, an affair; rivals, enemies, boyfriends, fraternity brothers, colleagues, cousins, siblings; or conditions like enforced, contractual, clandestine, accidental, "stuffy," informal, creative, chronic, stable. Or take the following settings: bureaucracy, fraternity, family, board of education, classroom. Does goodness mean the same thing for all of these? Obviously not.

We have to ask: "good for what?" As a starting analytic point let us say that all interpersonal relationships are oriented toward some *primary goal*, that is, some goal or function whose presence is necessary for the relationship to exist and whose absence would seriously undermine it. For example, if two friends stop satisfying each others' affiliative needs, the relationship would end. If two research collaborators can no longer do good research together, they will drift to more productive partners or work on their own. When the pupil can no longer learn from the teacher or the teacher thinks he can no longer impart new knowledge, the relationship will draw to a close. Thus, the *raison d'être* of the relationship, the salient reason for its formation, serves as a framework for evaluation.

On this basis we can characterize four distinct types of relationships: *Type A:* a relationship formed for the purpose of fulfilling *itself*, such as love, marriage, friendship. The main transaction in the relationship is "feelings" and for that reason we will refer to Type A as *expressive-emotional*.[1]

A *Type B* relationship exists in order to establish "reality," but of two distinct kinds. The content of the interpersonal transaction for one kind of Type B (1) is information about the "self" or about the relationship. This could include interpersonal "feedback" or reflected appraisals. The content of the interpersonal transaction for the other kind of Type B (2) encompasses information about the environment or a "definition of the situation." The former kind (1) exists in order to understand the relationship and the "self;" the latter (2) exists in order to comprehend social realities. An example of (1) might be a pair of friends who help each other find their identity. The other (2) can often be observed in social groups, say a fraternity, where the norms of the group establish certain social realities: e.g. "what courses or professors are best," "what kind of girls are the best 'dates,'" etc. In either case (1) or (2) we refer to Type B as *confirmatory*.[2]

A *Type C* relationship is formed for the purpose of *change* or *influence*. Thus

---

[1] Essentially, this book is organized around the four types of relationships. For example, the "expressive-emotional" is treated in Part I, etc.

[2] See the essay introducing Part II for a complete treatment of these types of relationships.

one or both parties to the relationship come together to create a change in each other or the relationship. The change may entail anything from acquiring new behaviors to attitude change. The main transaction between the change-agent and change-target is information about the desired state to be achieved and feedback on how the target is doing. Examples of change are psychiatrist-patient, teacher-student, parent-child, etc.[3]

A *Type D* relationship is formed in order to achieve some goal or task: a conductor and his violin section or a foreman and his workers or collaborators on a research project are all examples of Type D. We will call this type, *instrumental;* the main coin of interpersonal exchange is information *about the task.*[4]

Before continuing our analysis, we should mention that these four types can rarely, if ever, be observed in "pure" form; the purpose of a relationship cannot be so simple or monolithic. A couple, for example, may marry not only for the relationship itself (Type A) but for some instrumental purpose as well (Type D). We know of two anthropologists whose marriage was based on "love" and the need to work together. And we know of many co-workers, engaged in instrumental activities who permit—even desire—the relationship itself to take priority over the task. Conversely, there are partners in business, often brothers, whose relationship has become increasingly contractual rather than familial. And Type B, confirmatory relationships are, of course, a category of the more general types, particularly Type C, change relationships. In any case, we have never seen a purely "confirmatory" relationship. So we are not dealing with mutually exclusive types, but with overlapping categories with multiple functions. Despite this qualification, we do want to stress for analytical purposes that every relationship is formed—indeed, is caused—in order to realize one primary function.

Now we are in a better position to answer the question raised earlier on: what is a good relationship? Let us now turn to Figure 1. This diagram shows the four types of relationships ordered down the vertical axis. In column (1) we have listed the content of the interpersonal transactions. In column (2) we have listed the various criteria for a good relationship. This is based on our main assertion, only implied until now, that a relationship is considered good to the extent that it fulfills its primary function. Thus to determine whether a Type A relationship is good, we have to estimate if it is mutually *satisfying* to the participants; that is: do they have the desired relationship? For Type B there are two kinds of criteria depending on whether or not the exchange concerns the establishing of an interpersonal or self reality or whether or not the relationship was used to apprehend external reality. If (1), then we observe confirmation, some agreement about the relationship. If (2), then we observe consensus, some agreement about the definition of the situation. For .Type C the desired change is the main criterion; for Type D, productivity (or creativity) is the key. *Satisfaction, confirmation* (and *consensus*), *desired change,* and *productivity* are the terms which can be applied to the goodness of a relationship, depending upon its unique function.

---

[3] See the essay introducing Part III for a complete treatment of these types of relationships.

[4] See the essay introducing Part IV for a detailed treatment of Type D.

FIGURE 1
Multiple criteria framework for evaluating interpersonal relationships

	(1) The content of the interpersonal transaction	(2) Criteria for good relationships	(3) Outcomes of good relationships	(4) Outcomes of bad relationships
Type A: Emotional-Expressive	Feelings	Mutual satisfaction	"Solidarity"	Alienation Ambivalence Hostility
Type B: Confirmatory	Information about self: 1) Interpersonal feedback; reflected appraisals Information about environment: 2) Definitions of the situation	1) Confirmation 2) Consensus	1) Integrated identity Self-actualization Consensus about reality 2) Cognitive mastery Consensus about reality	1) Disconfirmation 2) Anomie
Type C: Change-Influence	Information about desired goal and progress toward achieving goal	Desired change	Growth Termination Internalization	Resistance Interminable dependence
Type D: Instrumental	Information about task	Productivity Creativity	Competence Output	Inadequate Low output

2. Outcomes of good and bad relationships

If the primary function of a relationship is fulfilled—what we have been calling a *good* relationship—we can expect a positive outcome; if not, then a negative one. What are the outcomes of good and bad relationships? Columns (3) and (4) list these.

A. For Type A, solidarity is the indicator of a good relationship, and *ambivalence, alienation,* or *chronic hostility* are the indicators of a bad relationship. Let us say a word or two more about "solidarity," a term which has had the recent misfortune of connoting "togetherness." What we have in mind is closer to Murray's Dionysian couple:

> . . . engaged now and again in unpremeditated, serious yet playful, dramatic outbursts of feeling, wild imagination, and vehement interaction, in which one of them—sometimes Adam, sometimes Eve—gave vent to whatever was pressing for expression. Walpurgis was the name they gave to episodes of this insurgent nature . . . each of the two psyches, through numberless repetitions, discharged its residual as well as emergent and beneficient dispositions, until nearly every form of sexuality and nearly every possible complementation of dyadic roles had been dramatically enacted . . . and all within the compass of an ever mounting trust in the solidarity of their love, evidenced in the Walpurgis episodes by an apparently limitless mutual tolerance of novelty and emotional extravagance.[5]

In our view, then, solidarity encompasses a wide range of complex emotions as well as the capacity for the individuals to risk the confrontation of their emotional vicissitudes; at the same time they must remain together despite and because of their own anxieties and appetites.

B. It might be useful to state with greater clarity than before the two classes of relationships we are grouping in Type B. Both have to do with comprehending reality, one an *interpersonal* reality that develops from the interactions between the participants and serves to define the boundaries of self-hood and of the interpersonal relationship. The "self" is born in the communicative acts and, according to this symbolic-interactionist position, "we begin to see each other as others see us" and begin to "take the role of the other." Thus, the formation, definition, and evaluation of the self emerge from the successive interactions we have with significant others.[6]

The other class of Type B has to do with apprehending some element in the environment, an item "x," let us say, for which we require interpersonal support in order to "understand" it. This is identical to Festinger's idea concerning the attainment of "social reality."[7] He asserts that opinions, attitudes, and beliefs—as differentiated from physical realities, which could be proved or disproved by

---

[5] H. A. Murray, "Vicissitudes of Creativity," in H. H. Anderson (ed.), *Creativity and Its Cultivation,* Interdisciplinary Symposia on Creativity, Michigan State University, 1957–58 (New York: Harper & Bros., 1959), pp. 110–18.

[6] For a recent discussion stemming from this tradition of Mead and Cooley see H. D. Duncan, *Communication and Social Order* (New York: Bedminister Press, 1962).

[7] L. Festinger, "Informal Social Communication," *Psychological Review,* Vol. 57 (1950), pp. 271–82.

physical means—need anchorage in a socially valued group. Thus, one powerful motive for people to come together in interpersonal relationships is to "make sense," to order, to develop cognitive mastery over the outside world. As Festinger says: "An opinion, a belief, an attitude is correct, valid, and proper to the extent that it is anchored in a group of people with similar beliefs, opinions, and attitudes."[8]

To this extent we are all "conformists;" that is, all of us need interpersonal evidence to attain cognitive control over our environments.

Let us come back now to the possible outcomes of good and bad Type B relationships. If we consider the interpersonal class, (1), then in a good relation-ship, an integrated "personal identity" or self-actualization and self-enhancement would emerge as well as a realistic relationship; in the external (2) case, cognitive mastery over some salient aspect of the environment would emerge. In either case *the outcomes of goodness in Type B is the consensus and confirmation regarding the perception of reality.*

This increased perception of reality that comes about through consensus or confirmation—regardless of its *validity*—has a tremendous liberating effect leading to a self-expansiveness and self-acceptance in (1) and a high degree of morale and confidence in (2).

A bad Type B (1) would consist of chronic refutation and dissonance and therefore probably not last. Farber[9] writes movingly of his experience with a patient who refused to confirm him (Farber)—by simply not getting "well;" that is, by not acting like a patient should. We have all experienced and witnessed situations like this where a group or person has denied self or role confirmation to another, consciously or not: students who won't learn, children who won't obey, audiences who won't approve, followers who won't be influenced, and friends who won't share or confirm our delusions about self, and in fact, stubbornly transmit cues counter to our own self-image.[10]

A bad Type B (2) exists when the parties to a relationship cannot agree on or make sense about external realities. It is most graphically described in the words of Kafka where even the reader gets fooled into thinking that the Kafkaesque world *is* more eerie and ambiguous than "real life." The fact of the matter is that the *world* is no more or less complicated but *people* cannot arrive at any agreement about it. So it is a world without "norms," without clear-cut references —evolved out of a shared frame of reference—necessary to establish consensus about "reality." The ability to predict future events, the need to reduce uncer-

---

[8] *Ibid.,* p. 273.

[9] L. Farber, "Therapeutic Despair," *Psychiatry,* Vol. 21 (February 1958), pp. 7–20.

[10] Recently, some evidence has been gathered which shows the effects of role confirmation and refutation on a group of nurses. (J. E. Berkowitz and N. H. Berkowitz, "Nursing Education and Role Conception," *Nursing Research,* Vol. 9 [1960], "briefs.") It was felt that the patients who responded to treatment were confirming the nurses' role and those patients who responded to treatment were refuting the nurses' role. The hypothesis, supported by the data, was: patients who were disconfirmers would not be liked or treated as well by the nursing staff as those patients who were role-confirmers.

tainty—all these matters we call "cognitive mastery"—are essential for man's security. It is one of the main reasons (and costs) for interpersonal relationships, for without it, relationships devolve into *anomie*, a disoriented, ambiguous, uncertain world.

There is a special case of a bad outcome for a Type B that bears some attention. Imagine a situation where two or more people come together and confirm their own relationship but seriously distort some aspect of "social reality." Let us take an example from literature. In Thomas Mann's story, "The Blood of the Walsungs,"[11] the twin brother and sister seriously misperceive (but agree on) the outside world and withdraw further and further into the nest of their own distortions. The fact that they hold a unique and different view from most people tends to further intensify their alienation, for the only support they can find is restricted. This form of social withdrawal has been observed, for example, among apocalyptic messianic groups.[12]

This distortion of and rejection by the outside world—always linked with libidinal contraction and intensification—leads to a state of affairs Slater calls "social regression."[13]

The tandem alcoholism of the married couple in the movie, "Days of Wine and Roses," as well as the bizarre and autistic games played by George and Martha in Albee's play, "*Who's Afraid of Virginia Woolf?*[14] are both good examples of this phenomenon. Sometimes this type of relationship resembles "solidarity," like the Walpurgis experiences reported above, but they are always different by nature. "Social regression" flourishes only in a social vacuum and when there is a powerful motive to distort external reality. Solidarity can last only if there is some realistic connection with the outside world.

C. A Type C relationship is defined by its pivotal concern with the acquisition or modification of behavior or attitudes, as imparted by a change-agent (A) to some change target (B). It is true that changes occur in the other types of relationship discussed, but only spontaneously and adventitiously. Type C encompasses primarily the class of change-inductions that are planned; for example, it would include primarily relationships resulting in changes due to formal course work (teacher-student or work partner in "lab"), and only incidentally the informal or unplanned kinds of relationships such as those which occur in "bull-session" groups. Type C covers a wide range of relationships, from parent-child to psychiatrist-patient, from coach-pupil to warden-inmate.[15]

---

[11] Thomas Mann, *Stories of Three Decades* (New York: Knopf, 1936), pp. 279–319.

[12] L. Festinger, H. W. Riecken, Jr., and S. Schachter, *When Prophecy Fails* (Minneapolis: University of Minnesota, 1956); also J. A. Hardyck and M. Braden, "Prophecy Fails Again: A Report of a Failure to Replicate," *J. of Abn. Soc. Psychol.*, Vol. 65 (1962), pp. 136–41.

[13] P. Slater, "On Social Regression," *American Soc. Review*, Vol. 28 (1963), pp. 339–64.

[14] E. Albee, *Who's Afraid of Virginia Woolf?* (New York: Atheneum, 1963).

[15] The reader is referred back to the essay introducing Part III where change relationships are treated in detail.

In addition to this emphasis on change, growth, and learning, an analysis of Type C further reveals two unique characteristics. First, these relationships are almost always oriented toward termination (graduation, parole, or death). An "interminable" psychoanalysis is considered deplorable, while an "interminable" marriage is considered honorable. Second, Type C reveals a special kind of relationship between the change-agent (A) and the target (B) which we refer to as "tilted." In other words we expect A to influence B, to "give to" B, to teach B more—than the other way around. As a rule students learn from teachers, patients from psychiatrists, pupils from coaches.[16] Thus the interpersonal exchange is slanted and less reciprocal, by definition, than other types. With these preliminary considerations out of the way, let us turn to the indicators of a good and bad Type C relationship.

A good Type C leads to three distinct, but related, outcomes. First, there is consensus between A and B that the desired growth or change or influence has been attained. Second, the relationship has reached a state wherein its continuation, while possibly helpful, will not lead to significant advances. It must end. Third, the client must have internalized the learning process, such that the process of learning begun in the relationship can continue. Thus *growth, termination,* and *internalization* are the indicators of a good Type C relationship.

The reverse of these criteria serve to signify badness. Dissatisfaction with B's rate of progress on the part of either A or B is a common indicator. The frequently heard remark: "I must change my teacher-therapist-coach-trainer; we're not getting anywhere" is an example. Second, the relationship cannot be extended indefinitely. That is, there must be some point at which the hoped-for changes will occur. Without this explicit termination point, both A and B can possibly get trapped in a false dream where the original and primary purpose of the relationship gets sidetracked.[17] Third, the target must be able to use what he has learned in an autonomous fashion; that is, without undue dependence on the change-agent. Patients who are forever returning to their therapists are not "cured"; acting students who suffer immobilizing stage fright unless their coach is watching from the wings are not "trained." We do not mean to imply that in a good Type C relationship the client has nothing more to learn and never returns for further training; we do mean that the client is relatively free of dependence and has learned how to continue the process on his own.

D. Instrumental relationships, Type D, are formed in order to produce or create: a song, an idea, a car, a formula, a dress. It encompasses the range of relationships involved in those activities which function in order to produce a

---

[16] We have omitted those exceptional, but highly interesting, cases where B can influence A more than A can influence B. More often than not, these are perverse, given our definition of Type C. Teachers may indeed learn from students, but this is different from exploitation and "stealing ideas." Analysts may "use" countertransference productively for the patient's ultimate health, but this is different than cashing in on stock tips or sexual exploitation.

[17] What often happens in these cases is that both partners in the relationship shift consciously or unconsciously to another type of relationship; the ski-instructor who marries his student, for example, is a switch from C to A. We will return to this point later.

"good or service."[18] It is ordinarily what people "do for a living"; it is certainly what most people do to earn enough for other types of relationships. As the need for interdependence and collaboration increases—that is to say: as specialization increases—this form of relationship will grow in importance and will call for more searching examination. It may be already the most ubiquitous form of interpersonal relationship in an industrialized society such as ours.

These are two main indicators of a good instrumental relationship; *competence* and *output*. The latter is objectively measured, usually in the form of a productivity rate: stories sold *per* year, pages typed *per* day, articles published *per* year, bolts attached *per* minute, profits earned *per* quarter, etc. Because of the relative ease of measuring output, instrumental relationships are often easier to judge as good or bad.

Less objective than output, but equally important from our point of view, is the way participants engaged in an instrumental relationship manage their work. Decision making, problem solving, coordination, quality of collaboration, energy expenditure: these are some of the elements in the complex factor we refer to as *competence*.[19]

A bad instrumental relationship exists, then, if either competence or output is unsatisfactory relative to certain norms. One would expect that these two factors would be positively correlated, but there is inadequate evidence to make this assertion.[20]

3. Aberrations, anomalies, and confusions in interpersonal relationships

Before going on to section two of this essay, where we will discuss the personal and environmental conditions for attaining good interpersonal relations, it might be useful to pause briefly to pursue some suggestive leads which the foregoing analysis provides. These have to do with those relationships which seem "special"

---

[18] Unaccounted for here are those instrumental relationships we associate with the service industries, such as some customer salesman relationships, cabbie-passenger, receptionist-customer. We have ignored this class of relationships for two reasons. First because this type of relationship rarely involves more than a brief encounter in a transient setting. Second because there is a peculiar lack of reciprocity. The waitress is instrumentally involved with the diner, but he is not involved instrumentally with her—and typically he has only a "service" relationship to her. This is a difficult class of problems for our analytic scheme to handle. Temporary relationships, such as games, vacation trips, etc., are examined brilliantly in a recent essay by M. Miles, "On Temporary Systems," manuscript (New York: Columbia University, 1963); see also A. R. Anderson and O. K. Moore, *Autotelic Folk-Models* (New Haven: Sociology Department, Yale University, 1959).

[19] Time and space considerations do not allow for a complete discussion of these issues. They go far beyond the purposes of this essay. The so-called "criterion problem" has perplexed industrial psychologists and students of organizational behavior for some time and we do not aim to settle any issues with this inadequate discussion. For a fuller statement, see W. G. Bennis "Towards a 'Truly' Scientific Management: The Concept of Organization Health," *General Systems Yearbook* (Ann Arbor: Mental Health Research Institute, 1962).

[20] C. Argyris, *Interpersonal Competence and Organizational Effectiveness* (Homewood, Ill.: Irwin-Dorsey Press, 1962); R. Likert, *New Patterns of Management* (New York: McGraw-Hill Book Co., Inc., 1961).

or irregular, relationships which capture the imagination, which attract the public eye, which fascinate.[21] Often they are puffed-up beyond all recognition by the popular press; at times they seem bizarre and/or perverse. In any case, they seem to be the stuff of romance, tragedy, farce and dreams—of fiction and plays— rather than "real life." In fact, we will suggest that they represent a class of problems, latent in all interpersonal relationships: *problems arising out of (a) transformations, (b) conflicts and ambiguities, and (c) deceit regarding the goal of the relationship.* Our multiple criteria framework (Figure 1) can provide the necessary analytic framework for this analysis.

a) Collusive transformations. In the musical comedy, "How to Succeed in Business without Really Trying," a chorus of secretaries cry out in shock and anger at one of their number who, on the verge of marrying her boss, decides to break the engagement. Their disappointment, and the audience's, is clear: the girl is about to destroy their constant dream, a cherished image they all hold and which partly keeps them at work. This fascination for secretaries who marry bosses, teachers who marry students, actresses who marry their leading men, analysts who marry their patients, we usually think of as "romantic" or morbid, depending on our orientation. In fact, it represents a joint decision—not neces- sarily conscious—where a relationship shifts from one modality to another. We call this "collusive transformation."

One of the most interesting examples of this can be seen in Shaw's "Pygma- lion." Henry Higgins and Eliza Doolittle enter into a Type C relationship in order to alter her manners and "character," but end up with an incipient Type A relationship. Every bit of drama and comedy is derived from this shift: whether or not Eliza will return to Higgins, how Colonel Pickering, Mr. Doolittle, and Higgins' mother perceive the relationship,[22] how the Type A emphasis becomes more pivotal without awareness on the part of Eliza or Higgins, etc. Another interesting example of the same shift (Type C to Type A) can be seen in the Rodgers and Hammerstein musical, "The King and I." The tension and drama of the play evolved from a collusive shift from a change (Type C) to an expressive- emotional (Type A) relationship. Romance, according to our analysis, can always be reduced to a collusive transformation, shifting from any type, to Type A.

An interesting example of another style of collusive transformation (Type A to B) can be seen in the play and movie, "Tea and Sympathy." A friendly relationship develops between the wife of an instructor and his student. The student becomes increasingly morose concerning doubts about his masculinity. The wife of the instructor, toward the end of the drama, decides to shift her

---

[21] Again, we are constrained by our lack of concepts for a relationship. We can talk of a charismatic person; how about a charismatic "interperson"? or bizarre "interperson"? Don't married couples and types of relationships have "character" at least as much as a person does? Don't couples have a "presentation of a unit" as much as an individual has a "presentation of self"? A primitive start on such a language was made by Shepard and Bennis ("A Theory of Training by Group Methods," *Human Relations,* Vol. 9 [1956], pp. 403–44). Much more needs to be done.

[22] For a discussion of class or hierarchy as a determining feature in interpersonal relationships, see Duncan, *Communication and the Social Order.*

relationship with the boy in order to *confirm* his manhood. The play ends as she removes her blouse in preparation for the rites of passage.

Other styles of collusive transformations can be observed, though possibly with less frequency than the shift to Type A. A Type A to any other type is perhaps the rarest, though Danny Kaye and Sylvia Fine, his ex-wife, still collaborate on his musical numbers (going from A to D).

b) Conflict or unclarity. There is a class of relationships which can end only in one of two ways, depending upon one's orientation: if one is observing, then absurdity; if one is participating, then despair. It must end because the relationship is construed and entered into for different reasons. Turgenev's "A Month in the Country," provides an example. A young tutor falls madly in love with the mother of his charges—because she is a "lady." She in turn loves him because his love rejuvenates her. To the audience this is the absurd love of age and youth.

A more striking example comes from the recent novella, *One Hundred Dollar Misunderstanding.*[23] A young college boy—middle-class and pompous—propositions and goes to bed with a fourteen year-old Negro prostitute. He refuses to pay her her one hundred dollar fee because he näively thinks she went to bed with him because she "found him attractive." The entire book is based on this misperception of the relationship.

One other case, also from recent fiction, comes from James Baldwin's *Another Country.*[24] A young man enters into a relationship with a married woman in order to assert or confront his masculinity (Type B), she gets involved for love (Type A). The relationship was constructed on conflicting purposes and shortly dissolved. Baldwin writes: "But it was only love which could accomplish the miracle of making a life bearable—only love, and love itself mostly failed; and he had never loved her. He had used her to find out something about himself. And even this was not true. He had used her in the hope of avoiding a confrontation with himself. . . ."[25]

c) Deceit. The Negro prostitute in the example above was not dissembling; she was not "conning" the boy like a B-girl at the bar of some café who insinuates unimaginable sexual adventures awaiting the "unsuspecting" victim if he only continues to buy her more *ersatz* whiskey. The girl made it perfectly clear to the boy that she was a "pro" and that she was interested in him only as a client.[26]

---

[23] R. Gover, *One Hundred Dollar Misunderstanding* (New York: Grove Press, 1961).

[24] J. Baldwin, *Another Country* (New York: Dell, 1963).

[25] *Ibid.,* p. 340.

[26] It's difficult to know who's dissembling to whom in such cases, and for what reasons. It's perfectly obvious, in most situations, that these B-girls are using sex as a come-on, as a inducement. It is perfectly obvious to the reader in *One Hundred Dollar Misunderstanding* that the girl is a prostitute. It is hard to believe that the "mark" is oblivious to these cues or that he is unconscious of them. Most likely, he simply doesn't tell himself what is really going on because this doesn't conform to his self-image, at least his *ideal* self-image. It's a bit like cheating at solitaire; one knows one is acting not altogether "proper" but at the same time, one doesn't have to admit it fully. We discussed this in reference to self-rating inventories or personality tests in the essay introducing Part I. The point is worth stating again. Most people don't cheat on tests and they rarely "try" even if they know they are the only ones who will see the results. But they do play "against themselves," that is dissemble slightly—not fully—in order to "come out the way you want to."

But in the case of the B-girl or the con-man or in any relationship of an exploitative kind, the relationship is jointly and publicly formed for one reason, but privately formed for another reason by one of the parties to the relationship: the teacher who makes "friends" with the ninth grade girl because she was told that the youngster is a "problem"; the opportunistic starlet who manages to "fall in love" with every director; the young executive who marries the boss's daughter for power; the psychologist who asks the college sophomore to do some work but in fact is using him as an experimental subject; and so on. All of these are basically exploitative, the basis of the "con-game."

If we sharpen our focus on the exploitative relationship, we will be able to make some interesting distinctions. As we conceive it, this relationship is always characterized by its *double meaning* to one, and only one, participant. So we are not talking about *joint mystification* where both parties enter into it for a professed reason, while each conceals a more basic, identical one. Comedy movies of the 1930's were made of this stuff: Girl meets Boy in fancy hotel on the Riviera; each pretends gigantic wealth and amorous interest in the other; each intends to use the other instrumentally. The movies usually end, after successively hilarious misunderstandings, in a collusive (and explosive) transformation to Type A.

We are not talking about *unconscious exploitation*, either of a collusive nature where both parties are involved in it or where only one participant is unconsciously involved. The boss's daughter marries the young executive because she unconsciously wants her father replaced; the man marries the daughter because he also unconsciously wants the father replaced. They are "in love," but under false pretenses; i.e., unconsciously for other reasons.

Finally, exploitative relationships must be distinguished from *conscious collusion*, wherein A and B come together for a professed type of relationship which both know to be other than their real purpose. A middle-aged woman goes to a dance-instructor for the expressed purpose of learning new dance steps. In fact, the woman knows she continues her lessons for other reasons, of an expressive-emotional kind, while he continues to see her for instrumental, not change, reasons. They both know that the other knows his or her reasons for their relationship. Thus, it continues, each of them satisfying a different pivotal goal than the other.

There are other classes of irregularities and anomalies which our approach cannot account for and others that it can. We hope we have demonstrated, however, that if we focus attention on the primary function of a relationship and relate this to transformation, clarity, conflict, and deceit, it is possible to illuminate some relationships which we ordinarily consider bizarre or perverse, or at least, "irregular."

Before turning to section two, let us summarize our approach and propose some conclusions. Our approach to the normative issues—of good and bad—is a *functional* one. If a relationship satisfies its functions, then it is good; if not, then it is bad. Inasmuch as there are *four* primary functions for relationships, our approach has been based on *multiple criteria*. Evidence is adduced for goodness (or health) by certain outcomes presented in Figure 1. Irregularities and anomalies can be derived by analyzing confusions, transformations, conflicts, and deceit with regard to primary functions.

The final point we want to make, by way of conclusion, has to do with the outcomes of goodness we presented in Figure 1: solidarity, confirmation and reality, growth, and competence. They cannot be, or should they be, restricted so neatly to their "own" type of relationship as portrayed. An instrumental relationship, devoid of change or solidarity, would be arid. A change relationship, devoid of competence or confirmation, would become stagnant. And so on. *All* of the outcomes must be involved, to some degree, in all relationships.

FIGURE 2

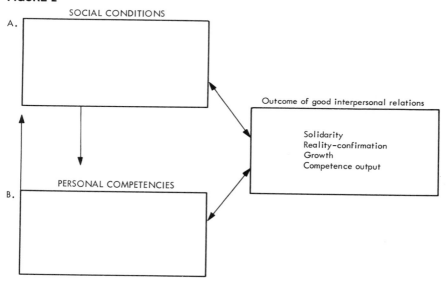

Figure 2 reveals the substance of the remainder of the essay. We start from the assumption that the fabric of our social environment and the personal competencies of the individuals involved determine the success of the interpersonal relationship. We hope to articulate these conditions in the most general way so that they encompass *any social milieu* where interpersonal dynamics occur.

All relationships exist in some social context—a group, an organization, a community, an institution. Whatever we call it—environment or society—it provides a texture within which our relationships are embedded and by which they are governed. To some degree the goodness and badness of interpersonal relationships are dependent on the conditions of the social setting. In any case, relationships do not exist in a vacuum. We intend now to explore the *social conditions* upon which our relationships are based. In Section B we shall examine the personal conditions that determine the quality of relationships.

A. The social conditions

Our vision of a "social architecture" conducive to forming and maintaining good interpersonal relationships consists of three sets of "blueprints." One set has to do with (1) "system-characteristics," the social processes which govern behavior. The others are (2) values and (3) goals.

II. SOCIAL AND PERSONAL CONDITIONS OF GOOD INTERPERSONAL RELATIONS

1. *System characteristics*

A system is simply a set of mutually dependent elements or parts in interaction. We propose that good interpersonal relationships can only occur in certain kinds of systems, specifically ones which have the following characteristics:

a) The System should be "open." Allport has pieced together four criteria of open systems:

(1) There is intake and output of both matter and energy. (2) There is the achievement and maintenance of steady (homeostatic) states, so that the intrusion of outer energy will not seriously disrupt internal form and order. (3) There is generally an increase of order over time, owing to an increase in complexity of and differentiation of parts. (4) Finally, at least at the human level, there is more than mere intake and output of matter and energy; *there is extensive transactional commerce with the environment.*[27]

The importance of the open system for us is its emphasis on the transactions between system and environment. A closed system, on the other hand, is defined as one which is isolated and self-contained: "Like a decaying bridge," Allport says, "it sinks into thermodynamic decay."[28]

Because an open system negotiates, merges, connects with its environments it contains a number of unique potentialities. Because it confronts unexpected stimuli, it can learn from external inputs; this allows for varied inputs and experiences, incongruities and surprises. These exogenous infusions, as well as providing productive energy and inputs, also work to challenge the system. If the system can "adapt" and cope with these external stresses, it can continually develop new patterns, possibilities and shapes—like a kaleidoscope with an infinite variety of designs. But these environmental transactions may also create insurmountable problems to the open system. New inputs may occur, for example, which are ignored by the system or inadequately managed. If the system fails

---

[27] Gordon Allport, *Personality and Social Encounter* (Boston: Beacon Press, 1960), p. 43. Emphasis added.

[28] *Ibid.*, p. 42.

to adjust to the environment it loses its integrity or it collapses and decays.[29]

The cost of closed and open systems should be clear. In one case, we have a system which *contacts* the environment. In the closed system case, there is practically no contact. Thus the closed system is adjustive, preservative, programed, but insulative. We are opting for the strains of the open system: adaptive, restorative, unprogramed, permeable, but stressful.

b) ***The influence structure should be balanced and characterized by interdependence.*** When we talk of influence we shall be less abstract than we were in our discussion of an open system; for influence encompasses the ways in which people exert power and express subordination. In social systems this governs an important part of the interactions. People are made to do things by fiat, order, and command; or by fear, intimidation, and coercion; or by persuasion, reward, and attraction. And people respond to these forces by surrender, rebellion, "apeing," consent, agreement, consensus, avoiding, denying, dissembling, complying, and obeying. Whatever system we observe, there is some structure of influence.

One of the main problems in most influence structures is *hierarchy:* a formal or informal arrangement whereby some person—a boss, teacher, a policeman—tells other people what to do. When the subordinates do what they are told and do it well, they are rewarded; when they do not do it or do it poorly, the rewards are withheld or punishment is applied. Our world view is partly based on this simple Law of Effect.[30] Party leaders, managers, teachers, parents, dictators, ministers all employ it.

Influence of this simple reward-and-punishment type is ubiquitous, tending more often than not to be dysfunctional. For example, one of its problems is that subordinates spend an awesome amount of time in an attempt to divine what they think the influencing agent, the authority, wants. Whether or not the subordinates guess correctly and act appropriately is problematical; what is not problematical is the fruitless complexity of the search. As one of our M.I.T. students put it recently: "We seem to spend about 75 percent of our time solving the professor, and 25 percent, the problem."[31]

Another problem with the traditional form of influence has to do with the assumptions bosses hold about subordinates. If one assumes that people are lazy, dumb, dishonest, passive, and simple hedonists—as the more traditional theories

---

[29] There are many ways for an open system to regress or decay: through complacency, poor reality-testing, and internal strains which reduce external commerce. The "causal texture of the environment" is another crucial variable which F. E. Emery and E. L. Trist ("The Causal Texture of Organizational Environments," paper presented at the International Congress of Psychology, Washington, D.C., 1963) have recently analyzed.

[30] The Law of Effect can be summarized by saying that people tend to repeat behaviors which are rewarded and stop behaviors which are punished: "Spare the rod and spoil the child."

[31] The reader must be warned of our oversimplified discussion of this issue. We are compressing, but not, we hope, distorting the problem. Some of these issues are treated in more detail in the essay introducing Part III of this volume. For a thorough treatment, see W. G. Bennis, "Leadership Theory and Administrative Behavior: The Problem of Authority," *Administrative Science Quarterly*, Vol. 4 (1959), pp. 259–301; and D. McGregor, *The Human Side of Enterprise* (New York: McGraw-Hill, 1960).

of hierarchial influence imply—then directive and coercive controls are probably necessary. Of course, the coercive controls produce the very behavior they assume, and thus we have a classic example of a self-fulfilling prophecy. An additional irony is that even people who are inadequate, passive, and inert rarely respond positively to unilateral subordination.

A number of behavioral scientists have been concerned with influence structures in a variety of settings: classroom, work place, research lab, family, office. Their recommendations are phrased in different ways but all point toward a more balanced and interdependent influence structure; from "informational-interdependent"[32] to "internalization";[33] from "Theory Y"[34] to "autotelic folk-models."[35] But the moral and practical impact is the same: influence is appropriate to the degree (1) that there is a collaborative—not authoritarian—relationship; (2) that people act on "credible" information; and (3) that self-determination plays a crucial role in the influence structure.

These three factors define what we mean by *interdependence*. The concept can be further elaborated and summarized this way: Influence, of an interdependent type, involves a joint effort toward reaching some mutually determined goal which requires complementary skills and information. This collaborative interaction evolves from the press of task demands and personnel resources, not from formal status, personal tyranny, or bureaucratic code. Interdependence involves an integration between authority and the subordinate—not freedom from either. Freedom and autonomy are limited only by credible information, task requirements, and self-impositions. Restrictions to freedom are certainly never due to extrinsic rewards in the social system we are envisaging, but only to internal rationalizations. Finally, interdependence does not imply "permissiveness" or "protectiveness"; such terms indicate only the shallow indulgencies of a pseudodemocratic system.

c) Decisions should be made by consensus. We can distinguish influence from decision making in an arbitrary fashion. The former was defined exclusively in terms of hierarchy, the power dimension. Decision making, on the other hand, encompasses two sets of activities: (1) procedures for conflict resolution and (2) procedures for choosing and evaluating alternatives. The criterion for these two activities can be briefly summarized as the *principle of consensus*.

Consensus is a *portmanteau* term which tends to mean all things to all people. To the "true-believer" consensus is democracy, if not truth. To the skeptic, it is an uninformed majority and a cowed minority. To the innocent, it is a "unanimous vote." The problem is not only a conceptual one, though consensus *is* a

---

[32] O. J. Harvey, D. E. Hunt, and H. M. Schroder, *Conceptual Systems and Personality Organization* (New York: Wiley, 1961).

[33] H. C. Kelman, "Compliance, Identification, and Internalization; Three Processes of Attitude Change," *Journal of Conflict Resolution*, Vol. 2 (1958), pp. 51–60.

[34] McGregor, *The Human Side.*

[35] Anderson and Moore, *Autotelic Folk-Models.*

protean and elastic idea. The fact is that it also bootlegs in an emotional and moral cargo, difficult to untangle from conceptual fuzziness.[36]

To us, consensus is a procedure for deciding among alternatives in interpersonal (or group) situations. This procedure must fulfill the following conditions: (1) It must include only those items which are salient to the membership and for which the membership has evidenced a distinctive competence. (2) If there is a conflict or difference, it must be resolved by valid and credible data, publicly shared and communicated; differences are never resolved by impersonal orders, rank, or personal vicissitudes. (3) If differences exist, they are always to be faced and dealt with, rather than avoided or denied. (4) There should be as much involvement and participation in the decision making process as salience and competence permits.

These are stringent criteria for consensus and only possible, perhaps, under unique conditions. But they are guidelines and may hold genuine promise.

d) The communication structure should maximize clarity. Every system requires some mechanism for transmitting, receiving, and storing information. The ideal communication structure must function to maintain clarity, economy, and relevance. Three conditions should be realized for this: (1) Information must be transmitted in the most unambiguous fashion possible in order to insure cognitive clarity. (2) Information should be transmitted only to the relevant parts of the system. (3) Information must not be filtered or distorted because of status anxieties or threat to the organization.

This last point is probably the most crucial and vexing of the three. How does a system guarantee valid (undistorted) upward communication if the information may displease or contradict the boss or teacher? A story circulating about Samuel Goldwyn takes its humor from this theme. Apparently Goldwyn called his staff together and was reported to have said: "Now, look: I want each and every one of you to tell me what's wrong with our operation here—even if it means losing your job!"[37]

And how does a system guarantee valid information and feedback from its

---

[36] It should be remembered tha consensus *is* a moral as well as practical issue. The fact that we favor it morally (an ultimately for pragmatic reasons—under certain conditions) is not related to its empirical validation—which is problematical. There are many conditional qualifiers to be made for the effective operation of consensus or any kind of group decision making. The interested reader should consult Krech, Crutchfield, and Ballachey, *Individual in Society* (New York: McGraw-Hill Book Co., Inc., 1962), Chap. 13.

[37] A more serious example of this same phenomenon can be inferred from research by E. P. Torrance, "Some Consequences of Power Differences on Decision Making in Permanent and Temporary Three-Man Groups," *Research Studies, State College of Washington*, Vol. 22 (1954), pp. 130–40. Here we see how subordinates in the military not only censored the communication of the right answer when they had it, but also allowed the authority to answer incorrectly when they, the subordinates, knew the correct answer. What permits a situation to develop where subordinates let superiors make mistakes when they know better and for superiors to assume that they, and never subordinates, have the key to intelligent action?

environment when these threaten the system's existence? Emery and Trist[38] have observed such cases where organizations misperceive or ignore environmental cues. This leads inexorably to an organizational demise, either by suicide or annihilation. Surely organizations, like individuals, have ways of distorting reality —or "selective inattention"—for who would dare to forecast doom, death, struggle, or any profound change when it's easier to deny, delay, or distort the truth?

e) *The system must have adequate reality-testing mechanisms.* These problems cannot be settled satisfactorily by providing only an adequate communication structure, whose main function is clarity and relevance. We need an additional mechanism, some way to guarantee adequate determinations of the internal state of the system as well as the boundaries relevant to the system and what is going on outside the boundaries. In short, every system requires some formal mechanism for establishing "truth" about its internal and external relationships and functioning. Most systems possess mechanisms that are either inadequate and convenient, or adequate and inconvenient. An example of the former is the (useless and illusory) bookkeeping statistics kept by some business firms. The latter can be seen when a system finds itself imperiled, too late to effect a "comeback." Emery and Trist, for example, tell of a case in which a canning company—going ahead in a major expansion—failed to recognize certain trends (frozen foods, Common Market, etc.) and continued to fail to recognize them until it was too late. "The managing director and indeed most of the other senior people were removed."[39]

What is most needed is some formal agency to ascertain and measure the relevant values connected with the system, not only for the present but for the changing future.

Open-system, interdependence, consensus, clarity, and *reality:* These are the idealized set of system characteristics we propose. There is a final one, only implied: that there be a "principle of appropriateness" which essentially determines the validity of the action. For example, it is not at all certain that interdependence and consensus is always appropriate. Some people and some situations, require different styles. Even "clarity" is not *always* desirable; sometimes a boss may have to employ "ambiguity" as a weapon or tool, and so on. We encourage these system-characteristics to be employed, but they should be used appropriately—not with a dogmatic or Utopian vengeance. Let us now turn to the second set of conditions of our social architecture.

2. Values

We will define values as those standards or directives upon which we base our decisions and to which we are committed. They are inherent in all systems for they govern to a great extent, the way people interact. They help to shape

[38] "The Causal Texture."
[39] *Ibid.*, p. 4.

how "close" people get, how power and influence are enforced, how work gets accomplished, how truth is revealed, and so on. Values permit or preclude certain system characteristics; values stress and understress certain dimensions of institutional life. (If the system characteristics and the value system are discordant, one must be modified or the system will fragment.) Values make possible the "identity" of a system, the possibilities and limitations of its actions. It follows that values are important, not just "academic."[40]

In combing the literature and in examining our own superegos we have arrived at five values that affirm the system characteristics described in the previous section. The first is *openness* in interpersonal expression; to "speak what we feel, not what we ought to say." This openness implies the free expression of observations, feelings, ideas, associations, opinions, evaluations; free expression of thoughts and feelings *without*, however, threatening or limiting others. Obviously, there are precautions and choices which must be taken;[41] openness can be destructive, too. The important thing to register here, even with these qualifications, is that the system should encourage the expression of feelings, rather than their suppression.

Closely related to openness is the value of *experimentalism*, the willingness to expose new ideas and to translate ideas into action. Experimentalism implies risk taking, uncertainty, "sticking one's neck out," as distinguished from "playing it safe," conservatism, etc.

In order for openness and experimentalism to exist, another value must accompany them. We will call this *threat-reduction*, to signify values which can be characterized by a climate which allows mistakes readily, tolerates failures without retaliation or renunciation, encourages a sense of responsible risk taking without fear.

A number of writers have identified a similar, if not identical, value in discussions of the social conditions for learning or creativity: Carl Rogers' "psychological safety"[42] or Harold Lasswell's "warmly indulgent relation."[43] And Anderson and Moore[44] suggest that a good learning environment must be "cut off" from the more serious aspects of society's activities. They mean that a person should be allowed to make mistakes without dire consequences either to himself or society.

The fourth value we propose for our idealized system is *integration* or fusion between man's emotional needs and the system's rational goals. What is required

---

[40] For a penetrating analysis of the role of value in institutions, see P. Selznick, *Leadership in Administration* (Evanston, Ill.: Row Peterson, 1957).

[41] Uninhibited expression of feelings may be as dysfunctional and as phony as the uninhibited suppression of them. There is no easy formula for the right balance. It depends on the legitimacy of feelings, and the personalities, skill, insights of the participants. See the papers by Argyris and Bennis on this part for points of view on this matter.

[42] Carl Rogers, "Toward a Theory of Creativity," in H. Anderson (ed.), *Creativity and Its Cultivation* (New York: Harper & Bros., 1959), pp. 69–82.

[43] Harold Lasswell, "The Social Setting of Creativity," in *ibid.*, pp. 203–21.

[44] *Autotelic Folk-Models.*

FIGURE 3

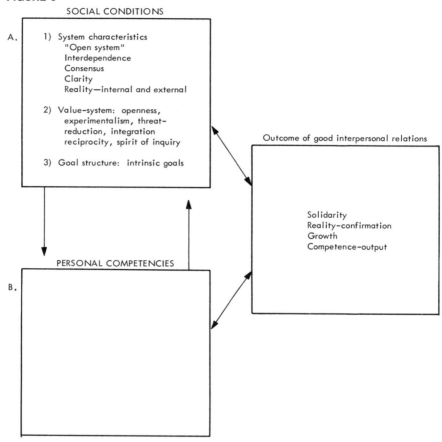

is the understanding that man is not only head and hands, but also heart. The value system must encourage reciprocation between the emotions of the participants and the intellective press of the environment.[45]

The fifth and final value has to do with what we call a *spirit of inquiry,* or unflinching curiosity to look at the way things are, a boldness with which to look at the processes which govern the behavior of the system. This value provides the security for the preservation of all other values for it insures the continual

[45] C. Argyris (*Personality and Organization* [New York: Harper & Bros., 1957]) and more recently H. Levinson ("Reciprocation: The Relationship between Man and Organization," invited address, American Psychological Association, Division of Industrial Psychology, 1963) have been examining this issue. The reader is referred to their works for a more thorough discussion.

scrutiny of so-called "givens," and questions the legitimacy of "received notions" and the hallowed, but hobbling, "past." This process of inquiry, turned inside and outside, what we are calling a "spirit of inquiry," provides the impulse for appropriate choices and adaptability.

3. *Characteristics of goal.* The final consideration in this analysis of the social conditions required for good interpersonal relations is the *goal.* We want to stress only one aspect here. The goal should be *intrinsically* rewarding and should contain its *own sources of motivation.* In other words, the goal should contain enough valence or reward for the individual so that exogenous rewards are unnecessary.[46]

Figure 3 summarizes the social conditions for good interpersonal relations. We should say, before going on, that our remarks on the social architecture deserve more elaboration and qualification than we provide. Whatever unqualified exaggerations still exist can be blamed on the very nature of social Utopias.

B. The personal competencies

Assume that we are dealing with a population of mature adults reasonably motivated for interaction. What are the competencies (or capacities) that would lead to good interpersonal relationships? We are biased toward those capacities that tend to deepen and widen the *emotional interchange* as well as *increase understanding:*

1. *Capacity to receive and send information and feelings reliably.* This not only includes the ability to *listen* and *perceive* accurately and fully, but other qualities as well. For example, it includes *sensitivity,* meaning a lowered threshold or heightened alertness to salient interpersonal events; that is, an active and creative awareness, not simply a passive absorption.

2. *Capacity to evoke the expression of feelings.* Most anybody can listen passively to someone; the kind of listening that makes a difference is where the other is unafraid to express a thought, a belief, a feeling ordinarily reserved for autistic reveries or denied to the self. Just as we *maintain* a certain threshold to human experience, we also communicate our threshold, and quite often "stop" or inhibit the other.[47]

3. *Capacity to process information and feelings reliably and creatively.* This means that we can conceptualize and order our interpersonal experience, that we can obstract and play with various combinations of interpersonal exchanges and arrive at some diagnosis. Points 1 and 2 have to do with *sensitivity;* this point has to do with adequate *diagnosis.*

---

[46] McGregor, *The Human Side.*

[47] An unexplored, but important, area for research is the role of the *listener* in interpersonal relations. There are "charismatic listeners" and "dull listeners"; there are listeners who evoke deep, meaningful human encounters and others who foreclose them. Why? We should know more about this.

4. *Capacity to implement a course of action.* A diagnosis may indicate a certain behavior; say the girl really requires more dominance or the boy needs to be included more but doesn't know how to ask for it. What is required are *action*-skills. Diagnostic sensitivity without remedial action may be no more disastrous than action without diagnosis, but it is often sadder. *Behavioral flexibility plus* diagnostic sensitivity raises the prospects for better interpersonal relations.

5. *Capacity to learn in each of the above areas.* It is far easier to talk of the *blocks* to learning—and "learning how to learn" in the interpersonal area— than to suggest some positive steps. Nevertheless, let us try. First, the individual must attempt to develop an attitude of "observant participation"; that is, a frame of mind that permits and encourages a constant analysis and interpretation of his interpersonal experiences. People simply do not learn from experience alone; it is experience observed, processed, analyzed, interpreted, and verified that we learn from. This constant scrutiny of one's own and other's behavior causes some stiltedness at first[48] and may interfere with spontaneity, but gaining any new skill causes this initial uneasiness.

This constant review and reflection is difficult, for it asks the individual to consider data that may be not only "new" (i.e., unnoticed until now) but also contradictory to the way the person ordinarily likes to see himself. Socrates once said that "the unexamined life isn't worth living." Modern psychiatry would tell him that the examined life is no fun either.

In any case, learning is simply not possible without continual surveillance and appraisal. And this examination is not possible without the possibility of gaining validating (or disconfirming) data from one's personal environment.

How these capacities are developed; how individuals learn "empathy," or learn to "identify" or learn to listen and perceive more realistically; how individuals learn to make connections, to induce trust, to permit other people to understand them and vice-versa, to develop an observant-participating orientation; how human beings can become more sensitive: these are all questions that deserve better answers than we now have.

We are, almost all of us, equally in the dark on this issue. And society seems reluctant to consider or provide viable methods for satisfying the enormous curiosity about, and the will to enhance, interpersonal relations. Two roads, only, seem available. We have the "how-to-do" approach symbolized by the Sunday rotogravure personality test; on the other hand, we have a long-term bout with psychotherapy, where the person is defined as "ill."

Please do not misunderstand. Psychoanalysis is irreplaceable as a healing force in our society; even "do-it-yourself" personality tests may help to engender curiosity. But certainly a society such as ours which is placing increasing emphasis

---

[48] Exposure to almost anyone undergoing the early days of psychoanalysis or a human relations training laboratory, such as those conducted by the National Training Laboratory, is sufficient indication of a spastic, "overserious," rather mannered self-examination. To the outsider it is Theater of the Absurd. The insider sympathizes with what the outsider is missing.

FIGURE 4

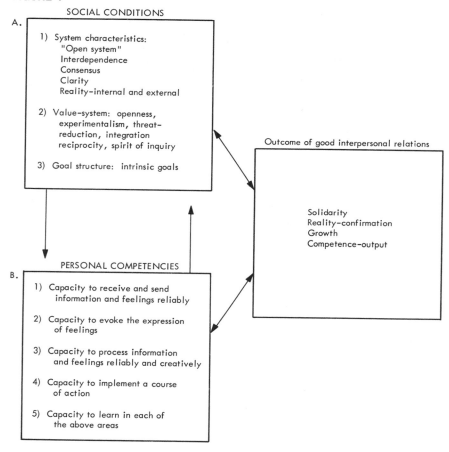

on interpersonal skills and knowledge requires more institutional avenues for fulfillment than these.[49]

This book, alas, also fails to do more than scratch the surface. Learning about interpersonal relations by *reading* about them is almost a contradiction in terms. One learns by doing and examining. But even that last sentence is hollow for this is hard work.

Figure 4 represents the summary of our essay. It was our intention to derive

---

[49] The National Training Laboratory in this country and Tavistock Institute in England have developed the methodology of "human relations training" to a genuinely professional level. We feel this is an encouraging sign and will be a development that will increase its momentum in and import on our society. We still await, however, a sound statement on "positive mental health" that will legitimize the idea of *enhancement* as well as cure (E. H. Schein, and W. G. Bennis, *Personal and Organizational Change through Group Methods* [New York: Wiley, 1964]).

a set of criteria to represent good interpersonal relations and to speculate on the social conditions and personal competencies which lead in that direction.

The readings in this section touch in one way or another on all three boxes in Figure 4. The article by Robert White emphasizes the personal and interpersonal evasions and responsibilities for maximizing healthy relationships. Carl Roger's article develops some of his very personal and significant ideas and ideals regarding the proper learning environment for interpersonal competence. Argyris, Jourard, and Clark stress the interaction between interpersonal skills and competence. Bennis discusses the values of "Laboratory Training" where he stresses the "rule of appropriateness." Studs Terkel's piece graphically describes a root cause of alienation in the work place and suggests a simple remedy in the interchange between two human beings. Walton's reading looks at worker alienation from an organizational perspective and describes some innovative attempts to counter it.

Sense of interpersonal competence: Two case studies and some reflections on origins*

Robert W. White

Every interaction with another person can be said to have an aspect of competence. Acts directed toward another are intended, consciously or unconsciously, to have an effect of some kind, and the extent to which they produce this effect can be taken as the measure of competence. When interactions are casual, when we are merely "passing the time of day," the element of competence may be minimial, although even in such cases we are surprised if we produce no effect at all, not even an acknowledging grunt. When matters of importance are at stake, the aspect of competence is bound to be larger. If we are seeking help or offering it, trying to evoke love or giving it, warding off aggression or expressing it, resisting influence by others or trying to exert influence, the effectiveness of our behavior is a point of vital concern. In extreme cases interpersonal acts may

---

* From Robert W. White, *The Study of Lives in Interpersonal Dynamics*, pp. 73 and 90. Reprinted by permission of the Publishers, Atherton Press. Copyright © 1964, Atherton Press, New York. All rights reserved.

have virtually no purpose beyond the testing or display of competence. This is true when dominance over others has become an autonomous end, when "throwing one's weight around" and taking command of situations is done simply for the joy of being effective—a joy that is undoubtedly all the greater when it counteracts a fear that one is not effective.

In the main, competence is not the most distinctive feature of interpersonal behavior, and its significance is sometimes overlooked. If the transaction involves an important need, our attention is drawn to the gratification or frustration of that need rather than to the background theme of effectiveness in dealing with people. Yet this background theme is always there, and we should always try to reckon with it. When a child wants to go to the circus but cannot persuade his parents to take him, he suffers a frustration of those urges that draw children to the circus—curiosity, excitement, adventure—and he may also be wounded by the revealed shortcoming of parental love, especially if it signifies that a sibling, taken to the circus the year before, is more warmly loved. But implicit in the whole situation is a setback to his sense of competence in dealing with his parents. He has failed to elicit their sympathetic interest in his heartfelt desires; he has failed to secure their cooperation in satisfying those desires. Along with his more direct frustrations, he has suffered a decrement of confidence in his ability to make himself effective in the human environment.

Competence means capacity, fitness, or ability. The competence of a living organism means its fitness or ability to carry on those transactions with the environment which result in its maintaining itself, growing, and flourishing. In the human case, effectiveness in dealing with the environment is achieved largely through learning. The child's attempts to remove his pains and gratify his needs, and especially his playful explorations and manipulations during the spare time between such crises, build up in him a knowledge of the effects they can have on him.[1] To describe it neurologically, competence is an achieved state of affairs in the nervous system which makes effective action possible; and it can be approximately measured in some of its aspects by tests of aptitude, intelligence, and achievement. The subjective side of this can be called sense of competence. We know that for various reasons one's sense of competence does not correspond exactly to actual competence as estimated by others, though it is always related to it. Abilities to deal with physical surroundings and to control one's body effectively are matters of no small importance to the child, but the central significance of the human environment confers a corresponding significance on the sense of interpersonal competence.[2]

In clinical work, sense of competence has been widely recognized in negative forms: feelings of helplessness, inhibition of initiative, the inferiority complex.

---

[1] These points are developed in detail in Robert W. White, "Motivation Reconsidered: The Concept of Competence," *Psychological Review*, Vol. 66 (1959), pp. 297–333.

[2] The expression "interpersonal competence" has been used in a much more inclusive sense than the one intended here by Nelson N. Foote and Leonard S. Cottrell, *Identity and Interpersonal Competence* (Chicago: University of Chicago Press, 1955).

The positive side has perhaps been poisoned for many of us by that hastily conceived dream figure of perfect mental health who has attained invulnerable self-confidence and serene self-esteem—obviously a conceited fool. But the extreme cases, real or fictional, should not draw attention away from sense of competence at the daily operating level. Our best insight comes from the ordinary phenomenon of confidence, which is an aspect of virtually every act. We can detect it by horse sense; that, at least, is what horses do when inexperienced riders are on their backs. A horse can apparently deduce from the first few physical contacts with the novice that the situation is right for a little fun along the bridle path or an unscheduled return to the stable. Similarly, though with less whimsical intent, a teacher making the acquaintance of a new class will notice how the children approach each activity. At the crafts table, for instance, she will see behavior ranging from picking things up quickly and using them firmly, through all grades of tentativeness and uncertainty, to hanging back or turning completely away. If the tools had horse sense, they could rate the confidence of the children who picked them up.

We can detect the influence of sense of competence in the judgments we are constantly making, often half-consciously, about what we can and cannot do. We can step across this puddle but not the next one; we can build rough shelves in the playroom but not a finished bookcase for the living room; we would be glad to paint and shift the scenery for the play but not to act or promote the sale of tickets; we undertake with relative equanimity to criticize a fault in a subordinate but suffer no small anxiety when the boss calls a meeting to criticize long-range company policy. How do we know so well what we can and cannot do? Since in the beginning we could not do any of these things, even step across the smallest puddle, it is safe to say that we have learned it all through experience. Past actions, successful and unsuccessful, have taught us the ranges of our effectiveness. Sense of competence is the result of cumulative learning, and it is ever at work influencing the next thrust of behavior.

INTERPERSONAL INCOMPETENCE IN SCHIZOPHRENIA

The schizophrenic, we are repeatedly told, withdraws from reality. This phrase has performed miracles in obscuring our understanding of the schizophrenic disorder. For company-hungry Americans it is a wicked thing to withdraw, a sign of secret pride and an evil sense of superiority; and this judgment seems to be verified if the patient entertains grandiose fantasies of his own importance. The implication of the phrase is that the patient has a happy, secret place to which he can retire, a utopia of lovely fantasies which draw him like a magnet when the going gets rough in the responsible adult world. But surely this is the daydream of slightly weary responsible citizens rather than the experience of schizophrenic patients, whose jumbled world is often full of suffering and pain.

A small change in the formulation may, it seems to me, bring us closer to the psychological truth. The patient, let us say, gives up in his attempts to make himself effective in his human environment. He does so because he has always felt his influence upon it to be small and because even his modest hopes have been shattered by recent disappointments. One aspect of the disorder, in other words, is a chronic weakness in sense of interpersonal competence, which leads under stress to a surrender of effort in actuality and thus to a loss of control over dreamlike ideation. This is not, of course, the whole story of schizophrenia, which may have constitutional and biochemical aspects, as well as peculiarities in the direction and control of impulses; but I believe that it expresses correctly a significant aspect of the disorder. Even in the paradoxical case in which the patient fancies himself to have the power of Napoleon, his sense of actual interpersonal competence is often enough represented by a docile conformity to hospital routines.

It is often said that schizophrenic patients have strong latent dependent needs. To this we must add that they feel remarkably incompetent to obtain satisfaction of their needs. They may, like a borderline case beautifully described by Rickers-Ovsiankina and Riggs,[3] view the human environment as a mysterious puzzlebox to which they have not found the key; they may ask the therapist to tell them what he knows about the inscrutable business of handling people. They show their low expectations by breaking off the therapeutic relation if there is even a hint of indifference on the part of the therapist. They feel themselves to be at the mercy of what other people do to them, even to the point of entertaining delusions of hostile intent and of humanly inspired influencing machines. They see no way to set these things right.

Why do schizophrenics find the human environment so intractable? Clues are now coming in from the study of disorders very early in childhood. It is characteristic of autistic children that they do not interact with the human environment. Often they look around people rather than at them, and it is extremely difficult to draw them into games such as pat-a-cake or rolling a ball back and forth.[4] Kanner[5] and Ritvo and Provence[6] point out that in some cases this lack of interaction is specific to the human environment; with inanimate objects the child plays in relatively normal fashion. There are two possible reasons for this state of affairs: what Erikson has called a "lack of sending power in the child";[7] and what Kanner, Eisenberg, and others have described as cold, preoc-

---

[3] Maria A. Rickers-Ovsiankina and Margaret M. Riggs, "To Be or Not To Be: A Schizophrenic Personality," in A. Burton and R. E. Harris (eds.) *Clinical Studies of Personality* (New York: Harper & Brothers, 1955), Chap. 4.

[4] Beata Rank, "Adaptation of the Psychoanalytic Technique for the Treatment of Young Children with Atypical Development," *American Journal of Orthopsychiatry*, Vol. 19 (1949), pp. 130–39.

[5] Leo Kanner, "Autistic Disturbances of Affective Contact," *The Nervous Child*, Vol. 2 (1943), pp. 217–50.

[6] Samuel Ritvo and Sally Provence, "Form Perception and Imitation in Some Autistic Children," *Psychoanalytic Study of the Child* (New York: International Universities Press, 1953), VIII, 155–61.

[7] Erik H. Erikson, *Childhood and Society* (New York: W. W. Norton, 1950).

cupied, mechanical attitudes in the parents.[8] Whatever may be the relative influence of the two factors, the result is that the child does not experience his own effort as having any effect on the human environment; therefore, it draws his interest no more than furniture, over which he has no influence. If the human environment inspires anxiety, lack of interest may be frozen into an inhibition of interest.

These observations suggest that one of the factors contributing to schizophrenia, with its fragile social confidence, is a bad start in eliciting response from the human environment. And they further suggest the more general formulation that *sense of interpersonal competence develops through effort and its efficacy in human interactions.* This provides us with a clue to the kinds of events that are likely to be important for development.

DEVELOPMENTAL CRISES OF INTERPERSONAL CONFIDENCE

Interaction with the human environment is a continuous process, but like any other form of development, it tends to have dramatic moments and critical peaks. It is misleading, I believe, to identify these peaks with Freud's stages of psychosexual development; the growth of competence is not captured by these affective crises, however important they may be.[9] I shall not undertake here a systematic sketch of development; let it suffice just to mention some of the situations that are likely to be critical.

One of these is the situation of play with the parents apart from the satisfying of bodily needs. Does the child show initiative, and do the parents respond with pleasure and interest, or do they find it a bit of a bore? Another is the situation created by the child's early steps toward independence, as when he undertakes to feed himself. Is he eager and persistent in these attempts? Do they meet maternal acquiescence, or do they produce irritation at the slow progress and messy spilling? The theme of independence continues through various stages, as manipulation and locomotion permit the child to explore larger and perhaps more dangerous spheres. Another crisis may occur over the expression of will through language. The often observed period of negativism, which we must now interpret interactively as probable negativism on both sides, comes when the child is first capable of issuing verbal commands and offering verbal defiance. How vigorously does he pursue these investigations and to what extent will his parents think it necessary to "break his will" and assert their own? Then there is the question of justice, which is often sharpest in disputes between siblings. Can the child plead his cause and be heard, or does he feel that nothing is effective, either because of favoritism or because of a blanket injunction against quarreling?

---

[8] Leon Eisenberg, "The Fathers of Autistic Children," *American Journal of Orthopsychiatry*, Vol. 27 (1957), pp. 715–24.

[9] Robert W. White, "Competence and the Psychosexual Stages of Development," *Nebraska Symposium on Motivation* (Lincoln, Nebraska: University of Nebraska Press, 1960), pp. 97–141.

In all these situations the interaction is mainly between child and parents, but new crises occur when the child ventures into play with other children. Is he able to influence the course of interaction, dominate the play, and keep his toys; or does he have to follow unwillingly and lose a few of his possessions? Can he cut an effective figure in competitive activities and thus elicit the respect of his contemporaries? Can he become something of a persuasive force and exert a share of leadership in serious pursuits? These issues extend all the way into adolescence, when a further crisis may arise from the revitalized problem of confidence with the other sex. And, of course, the problems continue even later, as we have seen by pursuing our two subjects into their late twenties.

In 1938 Murray wrote as the opeining words of *Explorations in Personality* "Man is today's great problem." If "today" is moved forward to 1963 the statement is only the more true. The study of lives must set for itself the goal of understanding development in all its significant aspects. If sense of interpersonal competence develops through effort and its efficacy in human interactions, we shall not fully understand today's great problem without uncovering this theme in the life history.

Goals and meta-goals of laboratory training*

Warren G. Bennis

By "laboratory training" I mean essentially those human relations training activities associated with the National Training Laboratories in this country and with Tavistock in England. Although there are variations in the training programs offered, they usually involve an attention to interpersonal, group, organizational, and change processes derived from psychological and psychiatric disciplines. T-groups, sensitivity or group dynamics training are often used as examples of the laboratory method insofar as they all attempt to use *experienced behavior* of the group members to generate meaningful learning.[1]

I think there is general agreement about the goals of laboratory education.

---

* Warren G. Bennis, "Goals and Meta-Goals of Laboratory Training," *Human Relations Training News*, National Training Laboratories, Washington, D.C., Vol. 6, No. 3 (Fall, 1962), pp. 1–4. Used by permission.

[1] See L. Bradford, J. Gibb, and K. Benne (eds.), *T-Group Theory and Laboratory Method* (New York: Wiley, 1964) and Edgar H. Schein and Warren G. Bennis, *Personal and Organizational Change through Group Methods* (New York: Wiley, 1965).

The "take-home" booklets, the promotional material, the opening lectures of laboratories generally reflect this consensus. And while there are some variations of the stated goals, depending on the staff and participant composition (e.g., Church Laboratory, School Administrator Laboratory, and so on), they usually include objectives such as these: (*a*) self-insight, or some variation of learning related to increased self-knowledge; (*b*) understanding the conditions which inhibit or facilitate effective group functioning; (*c*) understanding interpersonal operations in groups; and (*d*) developing skills for diagnosing individual, group, and organizational behavior.

But beyond these explicit goals, there rests another set of learnings which shall be referred to as "meta-goals" (or "values," if you would prefer). These meta-goals transcend and shape the articulated goals. They are "in the air" at every laboratory and undoubtedly guide staff decisions ranging from laboratory design to trainer interventions. More crucial is the realization that the meta-goals, if internalized, lead to a set of values which may run counter to the participant's sponsoring ("back-home") organization. I would like to suggest four pivotal meta-goals for discussion; the hope being that, if reasonable, they can be integrated into future human relations training more explicitly.

1. EXPANDED CONSCIOUSNESS AND RECOGNITION OF CHOICE

Extracting men in organizations from their day-to-day preoccupations and transplanting them into a culture where they are urged to observe and understand personality and group dynamics creates conditions where "givens" become choices—or at least create potentials for choice. Laboratory training—if anything —is a device which deroutinizes, which slows down for analysis, processes which are "taken for granted." It is a form of training which questions received notions and attempts to "unfreeze" role expectations (the Lewinian re-educational and change process of "unfreezing, restructuring, and refreezing"). The impulse for this cognitive restructuring comes about primarily because the control mechanisms taken for granted in institutionalized behavior are decisively absent in a laboratory. I am referring to control mechanisms which serve to regulate behavior, such as mission, authority patterns, norms regulating intimacy and control, decision apparatus, communication, traditions, and precedents. The ambiguity of norms, of behavioral constraints, of anticipatory rewards, creates what Lewin referred to as a "primitivization" of behavior due to the regressive climate. And the happy necessity of this human existence, to paraphrase T. S. Eliot, is for men to find things out for themselves, i.e., to create order, clarify one's identity, establish norms and a sense of community. In fact, one can look at laboratory training as the formation of norms and structure which build a community—except that, unlike most communities, the constituent members are present at its birth.

There are many analogies to this process; psychotherapy, perhaps, is the most obvious. According to one of its proponents, Karl Menninger, a regressive situation is evoked whereby the patient is deliberately forced to reexperience situations which bind and immobilize present choices. The indoctrination and socialization practices of many institutions, particularly "total institutions" where attempts are made to reshape normative patterns, bear a close resemblance to this unfreezing process. The "insight culture" of mental hospitals,[2] the "coercive persuasion" and "thought control"[3] programs used in Korean P.O.W. camps, military indoctrination programs,[4] and even some management development programs[5] are all to some degree exemplars.

Laboratory training, then, realizes its meta-goal of "expanded consciousness and recognition of choice points" by way of a very complicated process: extracting participants from their day-to-day preoccupations, cultural insulation, and deroutinization. Parallel to and combined with this unfreezing process is an emphasis on awareness, sensitivity, and diagnosis, all of which encourage the participant to think about his behavior—most particularly to think about how he chooses to behave.

2. A "SPIRIT OF INQUIRY"

Closely related to the meta-goals of choice—and, in fact, only conceptually separable—is an attitude of inquiry associated with science. It is a complex of human behavior and adjustment that has been summed up as the "spirit of inquiry" and includes many elements. The first may be called the hypothetical spirit, the feeling for tentativeness and caution, the respect for probable error. Another is experimentalism, the willingness to expose ideas to empirical testing. The exigencies of the laboratory situation help to create this orientation. For the ambiguous and unstructured situation creates a need to define and organize the environment. In addition, the participants are prodded and rewarded by staff members to question old, and try new, behaviors; they are reinforced by concepts to probe, to look at realities unflinchingly, to ask "why."

Again this bears a kinship with the methodology—although *not*, notably, the symbolic interpretive system—of psychoanalysis. Nevitt Sanford has said in this connection that it appears ". . . most notably in Freud's psychoanalytic method of investigation and treatment. (This method is, in my view, Freud's greatest, and it will be his most lasting contribution. By the method, I mean the whole contractual arrangement according to which both therapist and patient become investigators, and both objects of careful observation and study; in which the therapist can ask the patient to face the truth because he, the therapist, is willing

---

[2] Alfred Stanton and Morris S. Schwartz, *The Mental Hospital* (New York: Basic Books, 1954).

[3] Edgar H. Schein, *Coercive Persuasion* (New York: W. W. Norton, 1961).

[4] Sanford M. Dornbusch, "The Military Academy as an Assimilating Institution," *Social Forces,* May, 1955, pp. 316–21.

[5] Edgar H. Schein, "Management Development as a Process of Influence," *Industrial Management Review, M.I.T.,* May, 1961.

to try to face it in himself; in which investigation and treatment are inseparable aspects of the same humanistic enterprise.)"

In laboratory training all experienced behavior is a subject for questioning and analysis, limited only by the participants' threshold of tolerance to truth and new ideas.

Metagoals, the "spirit of inquiry" and the "recognition of choice," imply that curiosity about and making sense of human behavior are as legitimate and important (if not as "sanitary") as nonhuman phenomena. (I have always been perplexed and sometimes annoyed at observing the most gifted and curious natural scientists and engineers stop short of asking "why" when it touched on the human condition. Part of laboratory education, I suspect, it to expand the range of curiosity and experimental attitude to "people.")

3. AUTHENTICITY IN INTERPERSONAL RELATIONS

An important imperative in laboratory training has to do with the relatively high valuation of feelings: their expression and their effects. The degree to which participants can communicate feelings and in turn evoke valid feelings from other members is regarded as an important criterion of group growth. One theory postulates that "group development involves the overcoming of obstacles to valid communication,"[6] i.e., where valid communication is defined as interpersonal communication free—as far as humanly possible—of distortion.

Authenticity, "leveling," and "expressing feelings" comprise an important part of the laboratory argot, all of which can be summed up in a passage from *King Lear:* "Speak what we feel, not what we ought to say."

This tendency toward authenticity should not be surprising when we consider that so much time and attention are devoted to the analysis of interpersonal behavior, to understanding the effects of a participant's behavior on other group members. Measurements of changes during these training programs, indeed, suggest personal growth resembling that seen in psychotherapy;[7] i.e., the participant, as he knows himself, will be much the same person as he is known to others.[8]

4. COLLABORATIVE CONCEPTION OF THE AUTHORITY RELATIONSHIP

Permeating the atmosphere of laboratory training is a concept of the authority relationship which differs substantially from the legalistic Weberian emphasis on legitimacy of position. The contractual elements are understressed, and the

---

[6] Warren G. Bennis and Herbert A. Shepard, "A Theory of Group Development," *Human Relations* Vol. 4 (1956).

[7] Richard L. Burke and Warren G. Bennis, "Changes in Perception of Self and Others During Human Relations Training," *Human Relations* Vol. 2 (1961), pp. 165–82.

[8] Marie Jahoda, *Current Concepts of Positive Mental Health* (New York: Basic Books, 1958).

collaborative and interdependent elements are accentuated. In McGregor's writings we can identify the major elements in this conception of authority: (*a*) Management by objective, i.e., the requirements of the job are set by the situation (they need not be seen by either party as personal requirements established by the superior),[9] so that the authority relationship is viewed as a collaborative process where superior and subordinate attempt to develop ground rules for work and productivity; (*b*) the recognized interdependence between subordinates and superiors; (*c*) the belief that subordinates are capable of learning *self-control*, i.e., to internalize and exercise standards of performance congruent with organizational objectives without reliance on controls from exogenous sources.

Underlying this conception of authority is the "double reference" held toward superiors and subordinates based on person and role ingredients. For the subordinate and superior have to view each other as *role incumbents* with a significant power differential (even taking into account the interdependence) as well as *human beings* with strengths and weaknesses. Most theories of organization deny the personality elements of role and thereby fail to come to terms with the basic antagonism and tension between role and personality in organizational behavior.

How this conception of authority is internalized during laboratory training is beyond the scope of this paper; moreover, the process is not altogether clear. Readings and lectures cover the material somewhat, and identification with staff members undoubtedly contributes. But most important is the realization that *the teaching-learning process of laboratory training is a prototype of the collaborative conception of authority.* Putting it differently, we can say that learning is accomplished through the requirements of the situation and a joint, collaborative venture between the trainer and participants. Also, there is the belief that participants can exercise self-control in the learning process; i.e., the participant accepts influence on the basis of own evaluation rather than reliance on outside controls, such as rewards and punishments. Internalization, through credibility—rather than compliance, through exogenous controls—is the type of social influence employed in laboratory training.[10] It is precisely this form of influence which holds for the collaborative conception of authority we have been discussing.

These four meta-goals, then—expanded consciousness and recognition of choice, spirit of inquiry, authenticity in interpersonal relations, and a collaborative conception of authority—represent what I think to be the most important results gained from laboratory training. (Another important metagoal not discussed here is the professionalization of the manager's role.)

It is interesting that critics of this approach regularly misconstrue or fail to understand these meta-learnings. Dubin, in an otherwise thoughtful analysis of this training, wonders whether it doesn't train managers to be "other-directed,"

---

[9] Douglas M. McGregor, *The Human Side of Enterprise* (New York: McGraw-Hill, 1960).

[10] This formulation of social influence is taken from Herbert Kelman's "Processes of Opinion Change," *Public Opinion Quarterly* (Spring, 1961), reprinted in Warren G. Bennis, Kenneth D. Benne, and Robert Chin (ed.), *The Planning of Change* (New York: Holt, Rinehart, and Winston, 1961), pp. 509–17.

or to become "permissive leaders."[11] From other sources, charges are made about "togetherness," brainwashing, and "group-thinking." It is not entirely the fault of the critics, for the writing in the field has generally stressed the purely "group dynamics" aspects while slighting the meta-goal emphasis presented here.

I think we trainers, too, have colluded in this misunderstanding from time to time. We become preoccupied with matters of "expressing feelings" or "shared leadership" or "manipulative behavior" or "giving feedback" or "democratic functioning," or with "people who talk too much *vs.* people who remain silent" or with "cohesive versus fragmented groups," and so on. These are, of course, legitimate matters and should concern trainers. But they've gained a hegemony which I want to question.

For I care much less about a participant's learning that he talked too much and will, in the future, talk less, than I do about his recognizing that choice exists and that there are certain clear consequences of under- or overparticipation. I care much less about producing a "cohesive" group than I do about members' understanding the "costs" and gains of cohesiveness, when it's appropriate and worth the cost and when it may not be. I care far less about developing shared leadership in the T Group than I do about the participants' recognizing that a choice exists among a wide array of leadership patterns. In short, I care far more about developing *choice and recognition of choice points than I do about change.* Change, I think, is the participants' privilege, but choice is something trainers must emphasize. (This goes right across the board. I will try doggedly to create valid conditions for "giving and receiving feedback," for example. I will doggedly insist that the members "experience" it so that they have a basis for choice. Then I will just as doggedly insist that a choice remain open, to continue or not, to modify or not.)

Emphasizing the meta-goals has another importance with respect to organizational change. For they represent what the participant internalizes and transfers to his organization. "Everything the child learns in school he forgets," goes an old French maxim, "but the education remains." Similarly the metagoals remain. These internalized learnings have profound implications for the individual and for the organization because they deeply affect and modify the value and motivational commitments which determine the individual's orientation to his role. I think we have to keep them explicitly in mind in our training and in our future designs.

---

[11] Robert F. Dubin, "Psyche, Sensitivity, and Social Structure," in Robert T. Tannenbaum, Irving W. Weschler, and Fred M. Massarik, *Leadership and Organization* (New York: McGraw-Hill, 1961), pp. 401–15.

This is me*

Carl R. Rogers

I would like to take you inside, to tell you some of the things I have learned from the thousands of hours I have spent working intimately with individuals in personal distress.

I would like to make it very plain that these are learnings which have significance for *me*. I do not know whether they would hold true for you. I have no desire to present them as a guide for anyone else. Yet I have found that when another person has been willing to tell me something of his inner directions this has been of value to me, if only in sharpening my realization that my directions are different. So it is in that spirit that I offer the learnings which follow. In each case I believe they became a part of my actions and inner convictions long before I realized them consciously. They are certainly scattered learnings, and incomplete. I can only say that they are and have been very important to me. I continually learn and relearn them. I frequently fail to act in terms of them, but later I wish that I had. Frequently, I fail to see a new situation as one in which some of these learnings might apply.

They are not fixed. They keep changing. Some seem to be acquiring a stronger emphasis, others are perhaps less important to me than at one time, but they are all, to me, significant.

I will introduce each learning with a phrase or sentence which gives something of its personal meaning. Then I will elaborate on it a bit. There is not much organization to what follows except that the first learnings have to do mostly with relationships to others. There follow some that fall in the realm of personal values and convictions.

I might start off these several statements of significant learnings with a negative item. *In my relationships with persons I have found that it does not help,*

---

* Excerpted from "This is Me," *On Becoming a Person* (Boston: Houghton Mifflin Co., 1961), pp. 15–27. Used by permission.

in the long run, to act as though I were something that I am not. It does not help to act calm and pleasant when actually I am angry and critical. It does not help to act as though I know the answers when I do not. It does not help to act as though I were a loving person if actually, at the moment, I am hostile. It does not help for me to act as though I were full of assurance, if actually I am frightened and unsure. Even on a very simple level I have found that this statement seems to hold. It does not help for me to act as though I were well when I feel ill.

What I am saying here, put in another way, is that I have not found it to be helpful or effective in my relationships with other people to try to maintain a façade, to act in one way on the surface which I am experiencing something quite different underneath. It does not, I believe, make me helpful in my attempts to build up constructive relationships with other individuals. I would want to make it clear that while I feel I have learned this to be true, I have by no means adequately profited from it. In fact, it seems to me that most of the mistakes I make in personal relationships, most of the times in which I fail to be of help to other individuals, can be accounted for in terms of the fact that I have, for some defensive reason, behaved in one way at a surface level, while in reality my feelings run in a contrary direction.

A second learning might be stated as follows—*I find I am more effective when I can listen acceptantly to myself, and can be myself.* I feel that over the years I have learned to become more adequate in listening to *myself* so that I know, somewhat more adequately than I used to, what I am feeling at any given moment—to be able to realize *I am* angry; or that I *do* feel rejecting toward this person; or that I feel very full of warmth and affection for this individual; or that I am bored and uninterested in what is going on; or that I am eager to understand this individual; or that I am anxious and fearful in my relationship to this person. All of these diverse attitudes are feelings which I think I can listen to in myself. One way of putting this is that I feel I have become more adequate in letting myself *be* what I *am*. It becomes easier for me to accept myself as a decidedly imperfect person, who by no means functions at all times in the way in which I would like to function.

This must seem to some like a very strange direction in which to move. It seems to me to have value because the curious paradox is that when I accept myself as I am, then I change. I believe that I have learned this from my clients as well as within my own experience—that we cannot change, we cannot move away from what we are, until we thoroughly *accept* what we are. Then change seems to come about almost unnoticed.

Another result which seems to grow out of being myself is that relationships then become real. Real relationships have an exciting way of being vital and meaningful. If I can accept the fact that I am annoyed at or bored by this client or this student, then I am also much more likely to be able to accept his feelings in response. I can also accept the changed experience and the changed feelings which are then likely to occur in me and in him. Real relationships tend to change rather than to remain static.

So I find it effective to let myself be what I am in my attitudes; to know when I have reached my limit of endurance or of tolerance, and to accept that as a fact; to know when I desire to mold or manipulate people, and to accept that as a fact in myself. I would like to be as acceptant of these feelings as of feelings of warmth, interest, permissiveness, kindness, understanding, which are also a very real part of me. It is when I do accept all these attitudes as a fact, as a part of me, that my relationship with the other person then becomes what it is, and is able to grow and change most readily.

I come now to a central learning which has had a great deal of significance for me. I can state this learning as follows: *I have found it of enormous value when I can permit myself to understand another person.* The way in which I have worded this statement may seem strange to you. Is it necessary to *permit* oneself to understand another? I think that it is. Our first reaction to most of the statements which we hear from other people is an evaluation, or judgment, rather than an understanding of it. When someone expresses some feeling or attitude or belief, our tendency is, almost immediately, to feel "That's right"; or "That's stupid"; "That's abnormal"; "That's unreasonable"; "That's incorrect"; "That's not nice." Very rarely do we permit ourselves to *understand* precisely what the meaning of his statement is to him. I believe this is because understanding is risky. If I let myself really understand another person, I might be changed by that understanding. And we all fear change. So as I say, it is not an easy thing to permit oneself to understand an individual, to enter thoroughly and completely and empathically into his frame of reference. It is also a rare thing.

To understand is enriching in a double way. I find when I am working with clients in distress, that to understand the bizarre world of a psychotic individual, or to understand and sense the attitudes of a person who feels that life is too tragic to bear, or to understand a man who feels that he is a worthless and inferior individual—each of these understandings somehow enriches me. I learn from these experiences in ways that change me, that make me a different and, I think, a more responsive person. Even more important perhaps, is the fact that my understanding of these individuals permits them to change. It permits them to accept their own fears and bizarre thoughts and tragic feelings and discouragements, as well as their moments of courage and kindness and love and sensitivity. And it is their experience as well as mine that when someone fully understands those feelings, this enables them to accept those feelings in themselves. Then they find both the feelings and themselves changing. Whether it is understanding a woman who feels that very literally she has a hook in her head by which others lead her about, or understanding a man who feels that no one is as lonely, no one is as separated from others as he, I find these understandings to be of value to me. But also, and even more importantly, to be understood has a very positive value to these individuals.

There is another learning which has had importance for me. *I have found it enriching to open channels whereby others can communicate their feelings, their private perceptual worlds, to me.* Because understanding is rewarding, I would like to reduce the barriers between others and me so that they can, if they wish, reveal themselves more fully.

In the therapeutic relationship there are a number of ways by which I can make it easier for the client to communicate himself. I can by my own attitudes create a safety in the relationship which makes such communication more possible. A sensitiveness of understanding which sees him as he is to himself, and accepts him as having those perceptions and feelings, helps too.

But as a teacher also I have found that I am enriched when I can open channels through which others can share themselves with me. So I try, often not too successfully, to create a climate in the classroom where feelings can be expressed, where people can differ—with each other and with the instructor. I have also frequently asked for "reaction sheets" from students—in which they can express themselves individually and personally regarding the course. They can tell of the way it is or is not meeting their needs, they can express their feelings regarding the instructor, or can tell of the personal difficulties they are having in relation to the course. These reaction sheets have no relation whatsoever to their grade. Sometimes the same sessions of a course are experienced in diametrically opposite ways. One student says, "My feeling is one of indefinable revulsion with the tone of this class." Another, a foreign student, speaking of the same week of the same course says, "Our class follows the best, fruitful and scientific way of learning. But for people who have been taught for a long, long time, as we have, by the lecture type, authoritative method, this new procedure is ununderstandable. People like us are conditioned to hear the instructor, to keep passively our notes and memorize his reading assignments for the exams. There is no need to say that it takes long time for people to get rid of their habits regardless of whether or not their habits are sterile, infertile and barren." To open myself to these sharply different feelings has been a deeply rewarding thing.

I have found the same thing true in groups where I am the administrator, or perceived as the leader. I wish to reduce the need for fear or defensiveness, so that people can communicate their feelings freely. This has been most exciting, and has led me to a whole new view of what administration can be. But I cannot expand on that here.

There is another very important learning which has come to me in my counseling work. I can voice this learning very briefly. *I have found it highly rewarding when I can accept another person.*

I have found that truly to accept another person and his feelings is by no means an easy thing, any more than is understanding. Can I really permit another person to feel hostile toward me? Can I accept his anger as a real and legitimate part of himself? Can I accept him when he views life and its problems in a way quite different from mine? Can I accept him when he feels very positively toward me, admiring me and wanting to model himself after me? All this is involved in acceptance, and it does not come easy. I believe that it is an increasingly common pattern in our culture for each one of us to believe, "Every other person must feel and think and believe the same as I do." We find it very hard to permit our children or our parents or our spouses to feel differently than we do about particular issues or problems. We cannot permit our clients or our students to differ from us or to utilize their experience in their own individual ways. On a national scale, we cannot permit another nation to think or feel differently than we do. Yet it has come to seem to me that this separateness of individuals, the right of each individual to utilize his experience in his own way and to discover his own meanings in it,—this is one of the most priceless potentialities of life. Each person is an island unto himself, in a very real sense; and he can only build bridges to other islands if he is first of all willing to be himself and permitted to be himself. So I find that when I can accept another person, which means specifically accepting the feelings and attitudes and beliefs that he has a real and vital part of him, then I am assisting him to become a person, and there seems to me great value in this.

The next learning I want to state may be difficult to communicate. It is this. *The more I am open to the realities in me and in the other person, the less do I find myself wishing to rush in to "fix things."* As I try to listen to myself and the experiencing going on in me, and the more I try to extend that same listening attitude to another person, the more respect I feel for the complex processes of life. So I become less and less inclined to hurry in to fix things, to set goals, to mold people, to manipulate and push them in the way that I would like them to go. I am much more content simply to be myself and to let another person be himself. I know very well that this must seem like a strange, almost an Oriental point of view. What is life for it we are not going to do things to people? What is life for if we are not going to mold them to our purposes? What is life for if we are not going to teach them the things that *we* think they should learn? What is life for if we are not going to make them think and feel as we do? How can anyone hold such an inactive point of view as the one I am expressing? I am sure that attitudes such as these must be a part of the reaction of many of you.

Yet the paradoxical aspect of my experience is that the more I am simply willing to be myself in all this complexity of life and the more I am willing to understand and accept the realities in myself and in the other person, the more change seems to be stirred up. It is a very paradoxical thing—that to the degree that each one of us is willing to be himself, then he finds not only himself changing, but he finds that other people to whom he relates are also changing. At least this is a very vivid part of my experience, and one of the deepest things I think I have learned in my personal and professional life.

Let me turn now to some other learnings which are less concerned with relationships, and have more to do with my own actions and values. The first of these is very brief. *I can trust my experience.*

One of the basic things which I was a long time in realizing, and which I am still learning, is that when an activity *feels* as though it is valuable or worth doing, it *is* worth doing. Put another way, I have learned that my total organismic sensing of a situation is more trustworthy than my intellect.

All of my professional life I have been going in directions which others thought were foolish, and about which I have had many doubts myself. But I have never regretted moving in directions which "felt right," even though I have often felt lonely or foolish at the time.

I have found that when I have trusted some inner nonintellectual sensing, I have discovered wisdom in the move. In fact, I have found that when I have followed one of these unconventional paths because it felt right or true, then in five or ten years many of my colleagues have joined me, and I no longer need to feel alone in it.

As I gradually come to trust my total reactions more deeply, I find that I can use them to guide my thinking. I have come to have more respect for those vague thoughts which occur in me from time to time, which *feel* as though they were significant. I am inclined to think that these unclear thoughts or hunches will lead me to important areas. I think of it as trusting the totality of my experience, which I have learned to suspect is wiser than my intellect. It is fallible I am sure, but I believe it to be less fallible than my conscious mind alone. My attitude is very well expressed by Max Weber the artist, when he says, "In carrying on my own humble creative effort, I depend greatly upon that which I do not yet know, and upon that which I have not yet done."

Very closely related to this learning is a corollary that, *evaluation by others is not a guide for me.* The judgments of others, while they are to be listened to, and taken into account for what they are, can never be a guide for me. This has been a hard thing to learn. I remember how shaken I was, in the early days, when a scholarly, thoughtful man who seemed to me a much more competent and knowledgeable psychologist than I, told me what a mistake I was making by getting interested in psychotherapy. It could never lead anywhere, and as a psychologist I would not even have the opportunity to practice it.

In later years it has sometimes jolted me a bit to learn that I am, in the eyes of some others, a fraud, a person practicing medicine without a license, the author of a very superficial and damaging sort of therapy, a power seeker, a mystic, etc. And I have been equally disturbed by equally extreme praise. But I have not been too much concerned because I have to feel that only one person (at least in my lifetime, and perhaps ever) can know whether what I am doing is honest, thorough, open and sound, or false and defensive and unsound, and I am that person. I am happy to get all sorts of evidence regarding what I am doing and criticism (both friendly and hostile) and praise (both sincere and fawning) are a part of such evidence. But to weigh this evidence and to determine its meaning and usefulness is a task I cannot relinquish to anyone else.

In view of what I have been saying the next learning will probably not surprise you. *Experience is, for me, the highest authority.* The touchstone of validity is my own experience. No other person's ideas, and none of my own ideas, are as authoritative as my experience. It is to experience that I must return again and again, to discover a closer approximation to truth as it is in the process of becoming in me.

Neither the Bible nor the prophets—neither Freud nor research—neither the revelations of God nor man—can take precedence over my own direct experience.

My experience is the more authoritative as it becomes more primary, to use the semanticist's term. Thus the hierarchy of experience would be most authoritative at its lowest level. If I read a theory of psychotherapy, and if I formulate a theory of psychotherapy based on my work with clients, and if I also have a direct experience of psychotherapy with a client, then the degree of authority increases in the order in which I have listed these experiences.

My experience is not authoritative because it is fallible. It is the basis of authority because it can always be checked in new primary ways. In this way its frequent error or fallibility is always open to correction.

Now another personal learning. *I enjoy the discovering of order in experience.* It seems inevitable that I seek for the meaning or the orderliness or lawfulness in any large body of experience. It is this kind of curiosity, which I find it very satisfying to pursue, which has led me to each of the major formulations I have made. It led me to search for the orderliness in all the conglomeration of things clinicians did for children, and out of that came my book on *The Clinical Treatment of the Problem Child.* It let me to formulate the general principles which seemed to be operative in psychotherapy, and that has led to several books and many articles. It has led me into research to test the various types of lawfulness which I feel I have encountered in my experience. It has enticed me to construct theories to bring together the orderliness of that which has already been experienced and to project this order forward into new and unexplored realms where it may be further tested.

Thus I have come to see both scientific research and the process of theory construction as being aimed toward the inward ordering of significant experience. Research is the persistent disciplined effort to make sense and order out of the phenomena of subjective experience. It is justified because it is satisfying to perceive the world as having order, and because rewarding results often ensue when one understands the orderly relationships which appear in nature.

So I have come to recognize that the reason I devote myself to research and to the building of theory is to satisfy a need for perceiving order and meaning, a subjective need which exists in me. I have, at times, carried on research for other reasons—to satisfy others, to convince opponents and skeptics, to get ahead professionally, to gain prestige, and for other unsavory reasons. These errors in judgment and activity have only served to convince me more deeply that there is only one sound reason for pursuing scientific activities, and that is to satisfy a need for meaning which is in me.

Another learning which cost me much to recognize, can be stated in four words. *The facts are friendly.*

It has interested me a great deal that most psychotherapists, especially the psychoanalysts, have steadily refused to make any scientific investigation of their therapy, or to permit others to do this. I can understand this reaction because I have felt it. Especially in our early investigations I can well remember the anxiety of waiting to see how the findings came out. Suppose our hypotheses were *dis*proved! Suppose we were mistaken in our views! Suppose our opinions were not justified! At such times, as I look back, it seems to me that I regarded the facts as potential enemies, as possible bearers of disaster. I have perhaps been slow in coming to realize that the facts are *always* friendly. Every bit of evidence one can acquire, in my area, leads one that much closer to what is true. And being closer to the truth can never be a harmful or dangerous or unsatisfying thing. So while I still hate to readjust my thinking, still hate to give up old ways of perceiving and conceptualizing, yet at some deeper level I have, to a considerable degree, come to realize that these painful reorganizations are what is known as *learning*, and that though painful they always lead to a more satisfying, because somewhat more accurate, way of seeing life. Thus at the present time one of the most enticing areas for thought and speculation is an area where several of my pet ideas have *not* been upheld by the evidence. I feel if I can only puzzle my way through this problem that I will find a much more satisfying approximation to the truth. I feel sure the facts will be my friends.

Somewhere here I want to bring in a learning which has been most rewarding, because it makes me feel so deeply akin to others. I can word it this way. *What is most personal is most general.* There have been times when in talking with students or staff, or in my writing, I have expressed myself in ways so personal that I have felt I was expressing an attitude which it was probable no one else could understand, because it was so uniquely my own. Two written examples of this are the Preface to *Client-Centered Therapy* (regarded as most unsuitable by the publishers), and an article on "Persons or Science." In these instances I have almot invariably found that the very feeling which has seemed to me most private, most personal, and hence most incomprehensible by others, has turned out to be an expression for which there is a resonance in many other people. It has led me to believe that what is most personal and unique in each one of us is probably the very element which would, if it were shared or expressed, speak most deeply to others. This has helped me to understand artists and poets as people who have dared to express the unique in themselves.

There is one deep learning which is perhaps basic to all of the things I have said thus far. It has been forced upon me by more than twenty-five years of trying to be helpful to individuals in personal distress. It is simply this. *It has been my experience that persons have a basically positive direction.* In my deepest contacts with individuals in therapy, even those whose troubles are most disturbing, whose behavior has been most antisocial, whose feelings seem most abnormal, I find this to be true. When I can sensitively understand the feelings which they are expressing, when I am able to accept them as separate persons in their own right, then I find that they tend to move in certain directions. And what are these directions in which they tend to move? The words which I believe are most truly descriptive are words such as positive, constructive, moving toward self-actualization, growing toward maturity, growing toward socialization. I have come to feel that the more fully the individual is understood and accepted, the more he tends to drop the false fronts with which he has been meeting life, and the more he tends to move in a direction which is forward.

I would not want to be misunderstood on this. I do not have a Pollyanna view of human nature. I am quite aware that out of defensiveness and inner fear individuals can and do behave in ways which are incredibly cruel, horribly destructive, immature, regressive, antisocial, hurtful. Yet one of the most refreshing and invigorating parts of my experience is to work with such individuals and to discover the strongly positive directional tendencies which exist in them, as in all of us, at the deepest levels.

Let me bring this long list to a close with one final learning which can be stated very briefly. *Life, at its best, is a flowing, changing process in which nothing is fixed.* In my clients and in myself I find that when life is richest and most rewarding it is a flowing process. To experience this is both fascinating and a little frightening. I find I am at my best when I can let the flow of my experience carry me in a direction which appears to be forward, toward goals of which I am but dimly aware. In thus floating with the complex stream of my experiencing, and in trying to understand its everchanging complexity, it should be evident that there are no fixed points. When I am thus able to be in process, it is clear that there can be no closed system of beliefs, no unchanging set of principles which I hold. Life is guided by a changing understanding of an interpretation of my experience. It is always in process of becoming.

I trust it is clear now why there is no philosophy or belief or set of principles which I could encourage or persuade others to have or hold. I can only try to live by *my* interpretation of the current meaning of *my* experience, and try to give others the permission and freedom to develop their own inward freedom and thus their own meaningful interpretation of their own experience.

If there is such a thing as truth, this free individual process of search should, I believe, converge toward it. And in a limited way, this is also what I seem to have experienced.

Healthy personality and self-disclosure[*]

Sidney M. Jourard

For a long time, health and well-being have been taken for granted as "givens," and disease has been viewed as the problem for man to solve. Today, however, increasing numbers of scientists have begun to adopt a reverse point of view: Disease and trouble are coming to be viewed as the givens, and specification of positive health and its conditions as the important goal. Physical, mental, and social health are values representing restrictions on the total variance of being. The scientific problem here consists in arriving at a definition of health, determining its relevant dimensions, and then identifying the independent variables of which these are a function.

Scientists, however, are supposed to be hard-boiled, and they insist that phenomena, in order to be counted "real," must be public. Hence, many behavioral scientists ignore man's self, or soul, since it is essentially a private phenomenon. Others, however, are not so quick to allocate man's self to the limbo of the unimportant, and they insist that we cannot understand man and his lot until we take his self into account.

I probably fall into the camp of these investigators who want to explore health as a positive problem in its own right and who, further, take man's self seriously —as a reality to be explained and as a variable which produces consequences for weal or woe. In this chapter, I would like more fully to explore the connection between positive health and the disclosure of self. Let me commence with some sociological truisms.

Social systems require their members to play certain roles. Unless the roles are adequately played, the social systems will not produce the results for which they have been organized. This flat statement applies to social systems as simple as one developed by an engaged couple and to those as complex as a total nation among nations.

* Talk given November 20, 1958, at a meeting of the North Florida Section of the American Personnel and Guidance Association and published in *Mental Hygiene*, Vol. 43 (1959).

Societies have socialization "factories" and "mills"—families and schools— which serve the function of training people to play the age, sex, and occupational roles which they shall be obliged to play throughout their life in the social system. Broadly speaking, if a person plays his roles suitably, he can be regarded as a more or less normal personality. *Normal personalities, however, are not necessarily healthy personalities* (Jourard, 1958, pp. 16–18).

Healthy personalities are people who play their roles satisfactorily and at the same time derive personal satisfaction from role enactment; more, they keep growing and they maintain high-level physical wellness (Dunn, 1959). It is probable enough, speaking from the standpoint of a stable social system, for people to be normal personalities. But it is possible to be a normal personality and be absolutely miserable. We would count such a normal personality unhealthy. In fact, normality in some social systems—successful acculturation to them—reliably produces ulcers, piles, paranoia, or compulsiveness. We also have to regard as unhealthy those people who have never been able to enact the roles that legitimately can be expected from them.

Counselors, guidance workers, and psychotherapists are obliged to treat—with both patterns of unhealthy personality—those people who have been unable to learn their roles and those who play their roles quite well, but suffer the agonies of boredom, frustration, anxiety, or stultification. If our clients are to be helped, they must change, and change in *valued* directions. A change in a valued direction may arbitrarily be called growth. We have yet to give explicit statement to these valued directions for growth, though a beginning has been made (Fromm, 1947; Jahoda, 1958; Jourard, 1958; Maslow, 1954; Rogers, 1958). We who are professionally concerned with the happiness, growth, and well-being of our clients may be regarded as professional lovers, not unlike the Cyprian sisterhood. It would be fascinating to pursue this parallel further, but for the moment let us ask instead what this has to do with self-disclosure.

To answer this question, let's tune in on an imaginary interview between a client and his counselor. The client says, "I have never told this to a soul, doctor, but I can't stand my wife, my mother is a nag, my father is a bore, and my boss is an absolutely hateful and despicable tyrant. I have been carrying on an affair for the past 10 years with the lady next door, and at the same time I am a deacon in the church." The counselor says, showing great understanding and empathy, "Mm-humm!"

If we listened for a long enough period of time, we would find that the client talks and talks about himself to this highly sympathetic and empathic listener. At some later time, the client may eventually say, "Gosh, you have helped me a lot. I see what I must do and I will go ahead and do it."

Now this talking about oneself to another person is what I call self-disclosure. It would appear, without assuming anything, that self-disclosure is a factor in the process of effective counseling or psychotherapy. Would it be too arbitrary an assumption to propose that people become clients *because they have not disclosed themselves in some optimum degree to the people in their life?*

An historical digression: Toward the end of the 19th century, Joseph Breuer, a Viennese physician, discovered (probably accidentally) that when his hysterical patients talked about themselves, disclosing not only the verbal content of their memories, but also the feelings that they had suppressed at the time of assorted "traumatic" experiences, their hysterical symptoms disappeared. Somewhere along the line, Breuer withdrew from a situation which would have made him Freud's peer in history's hall of fame. When Breuer permitted his patients "to be," it scared him, one gathers, because some of his female patients disclosed themselves to be quite sexy, and what was probably worse, they felt quite sexy toward him. Freud, however, did not flinch. He made the momentous discovery that the neurotic people of his time were struggling like mad to avoid "being," to avoid being known and, in Allport's (1955) terms, to avoid "becoming." He learned that his patients, when they were given the opportunity to "be"—which free association on a couch is nicely designed to do—would disclose that they had all manner of horrendous thoughts and feelings which they did not even dare disclose to themselves, much less express in the presence of another person. Freud learned to permit his patients to be, through permitting them to disclose themselves utterly to another human. He evidently did not trust anyone enough to be willing to disclose himself vis-à-vis; so he disclosed himself to himself on paper (Freud, 1955) and learned the extent to which he was himself self-alienated. Roles for people in Victorian days were even more restrictive than today, and Freud discovered that when people struggled to avoid being and knowing themselves, they got sick. They could only become well and stay relatively well when they came to know themselves through self-disclosure to another person. This makes me think of Georg Groddeck's magnificent *Book of the It (Id)* in which, in the guise of letters to a naive young woman, Groddeck shows the contrast between the *public self*—pretentious role playing—and the warded off but highly dynamic *id*—which I here very loosely translate as "real self."

Let me at this point draw a distinction between role relationships and interpersonal relationships—a distinction which is often overlooked in the current spate of literature that has to do with human relations. Roles are inescapable. They must be played or else the social system will not work. A role by definition is a repertoire of behavior patterns which must be rattled off in appropriate contexts, and all behavior which is irrelevant to the role must be suppressed. But what we often forget is the fact that it is a *person* who is playing the role. This person has a self, or I should say he *is* a self. All too often the roles that a person plays do not do justice to all of his self. In fact, there may be nowhere that he may just *be* himself. Even more, the person may not *know* his self. He may, in Horney's (1950) terms, be self-alienated. This fascinating term, "self-alienation," means that an individual is estranged from his real self. His real self becomes a strange, a feared and distrusted stranger. Estrangement, alienation from one's real self, is at the root of the "neurotic personality of our time" so eloquently described by Horney (1936). Fromm (1947) referred to the same phenomenon as a socially patterned defect. Self-alienation is a sickness which is so widely shared that no one recognizes it. We may take it for granted that all the clients whom we encounter are self-alienated to a greater or lesser extent. If you ask anyone to answer the question, "Who are you?" the answer will generally be, "I am a psychologist," "a businessman," a "teacher," or what have you. The respondent will probably tell you the name of the role with which he feels most closely identified. As a matter of fact, the respondent spends a great part of his life trying to discover who he is, and once he has made some such discovery, he spends the rest of his life trying to play the part. Of course, some of the roles—age, sex, family, or occupational roles—may be so restrictive that they fit a person in a manner not too different from the girdle of a 200-pound lady who is struggling to look like Brigitte Bardot. There is Faustian drama all about us in this world of role playing. Everywhere we see people who have sold their soul, or their real self, if you wish, in order to be a psychologist, a businessman, a nurse, a physician, a this or a that.

Now, I have suggested that no social system can exist unless the members play their roles and play them with precision and elegance. But here is an odd observation, and yet one which you can all corroborate just by thinking back over your own experience. It is possible to be involved in a social group such as a family or a work setting for years and years, playing one's roles nicely with the other members—and never getting to know the *persons* who are playing the other roles. Roles can be played personally and impersonally, as we are beginning to discover. A husband can be married to his wife for 15 years and never come to know her. He knows her as "the wife." This is the paradox of the "*lonely* crowd" (Riesman, 1950). It is the loneliness which people try to counter with "togetherness." But much of today's "togetherness" is like the "parallel play" of two-year-old children, or like the professors in Stringfellow Barr's (1958) novel who, when together socially, lecture *past* one another alternately and sometimes simultaneously. There is no real self-to-self or person-to-person meeting in such transactions. Now what does it mean to know a person, or, more accurately, a person's self? I don't mean anything mysterious by "self." All I mean is the person's subjective side— what he thinks, feels, believes, wants, worries about—the kind of thing which one could never know unless one were told. *We get to know the other person's self when he discloses it to us.*

Self-disclosure, letting another person know what you think, feel, or want is the most direct means (though not the only means) by which an individual can make himself known to another person. Personality hygienists place great emphasis upon the importance for mental health of what they call "real-self being," "self-realization," "discovering oneself," and so on. An operational analysis of what goes on in counseling and therapy shows that the patients and clients discover themselves through self-disclosure to the counselor. They talk, and to their shock and amazement, the counselor listens.

I venture to say that there is probably no experience more horrifying and terrifying than that of self-disclosure to "significant others" whose probable reactions are assumed, but not known. Hence the phenomenon of "resistance."

This is what makes psychotherapy so difficult to take and so difficult to administer. If there is any skill to be learned in the art of counseling and psychotherapy, it is the art of coping with the terrors which attend self-disclosure and the art of decoding the language, verbal and nonverbal, in which a person speaks about his inner experience.

Now what is the connection between self-disclosure and healthy personality? Self-disclosure, or should I say "real" self-disclosure, is both a symptom of personality health (Jourard, 1958, pp. 218–21) and at the same time a means of ultimately achieving healthy personality. The discloser of self is an animated "real-self be-er." This, of course, takes courage—the "courage to be." I have known people who would rather die than become known. In fact, some did die when it appeared that the chances were great that they would become known. When I say that self-disclosure is a symptom of personality health, what I mean really is that a person who displays many of the other characteristics that betoken healthy personality (Jourard, 1958; Maslow, 1954) *will also display the ability to make himself fully known to at least one other significant human being.* When I say that self-disclosure is a means by which one achieves personality health, I mean something like the following: It is not until I *am* my real self and I act my real self that my real self is in a position to grow. One's self grows from the *consequence of being.* People's selves stop growing when they repress them. This growth arrest in the self is what helps to account for the surprising paradox of finding an infant inside the skin of someone who is playing the role of an adult. In a fascinating analysis of mental disease, Jurgen Ruesch (1957) describes assorted neurotics, psychotics, and psychosomatic patients as persons with selective atrophy and overspecialization in various aspects of the process of communication. This culminates in a foul-up of the processes of knowing others and of becoming known to others. Neurotic and psychotic symptoms might be viewed as smoke screens interposed between the patient's real self and the gaze of the onlooker. We might call the symptoms "devices to avoid becoming known." A new theory of schizophrenia has been proposed by a former patient (Anonymous, 1958) who "was there," and he makes such a point.

Alienation from one's real self not only arrests one's growth as a person; it also tends to make a farce out of one's relationships with people. As the ex-patient mentioned above observed, the crucial "break" in schizophrenia is with *sincerity,* not reality (Anonymous, 1958). A self-alienated person—one who does not disclose himself truthfully and fully—can never love another person nor can he be loved by the other person. Effective loving calls for knowledge of the object (Fromm, 1956; Jourard, 1958). How can I love a person whom I do not know? How can the other person love me if he does not know me?

Hans Selye (1950) proposed and documented the hypothesis that illness as we know it arises in consequence of stress applied to the organism. Now I rather think that unhealthy *personality* has a similar root cause, and one which is related to Selye's concept of stress. It is this. Every maladjusted person is a person who has not made himself known to another human being and in consequence does not know himself. Nor can he be himself. More than that, *he struggles actively to avoid becoming known by another human being.* He *works* at it ceaselessly, 24 hours daily, and it is work! The fact that resisting becoming known is *work* offers us a research opening, incidentally (cf. Dittes, 1957; Davis and Malmo, 1950). I believe that in the effort to avoid becoming known, a person provides for himself a cancerous kind of stress which is subtle and unrecognized but none the less effective in producing, not only the assorted patterns of unhealthy personality which psychiatry talks about, but also the wide array of physical ills that have come to be recognized as the stock in trade of psychosomatic medicine. Stated another way, I believe that *other people come to be stressors to an individual in direct proportion to his degree of self-alienation.*

If I am struggling to avoid becoming known by other persons then, of course, I must construct a false public self (Jourard, 1958, pp. 301–2). The greater the discrepancy between my unexpurgated real self and the version of myself that I present to others, then the more dangerous will other people be for me. If becoming known by another person is threatening, then the very presence of another person can serve as a stimulus to evoke anxiety, heightened muscle tension, and all the assorted visceral changes which occur when a person is under stress. A beginning already has been made, demonstrating the tension-evoking powers of the other person, through the use of such instruments as are employed in the lie detector, through the measurement of muscle tensions with electromyographic apparatus, and so on (Davis and Malmo, 1950; Dittes, 1957).

Students of psychosomatic medicine have been intimating something of what I have just finished saying explicitly. They say (cf. Alexander, 1950) the ulcer patients, asthmatic patients, patients suffering from colitis, migraine, and the like, are chronic *repressors* of certain needs and emotions, especially hostility and dependency. Now when you repress something, you are not only withholding awareness of this something from yourself, you are also withholding it from the scrutiny of the other person. In fact, the means by which repressions are overcome in the therapeutic situation is through relentless disclosure of self to the therapist. When a patient is finally able to follow the fundamental rule in psychoanalysis and disclose everything which passes through his mind, he is generally shocked and dismayed to observe the breadth, depth, range, and diversity of thoughts, memories, and emotions which pass out of his "unconscious" into overt disclosure. Incidentally, by the time a person is that free to disclose in the presence of another human being, he has doubtless completed much of his therapeutic sequence.

Self-disclosure, then, appears to be one of the means by which a person engages in that elegant activity which we call real-self-being. But is real-self-being synonymous with healthy personality? Not in and of itself. I would say that real-self-being is a necessary but not a sufficient condition for healthy personality. Indeed, an authentic person may not be very "nice." In fact, he may seem much "nicer" socially and appear more mature and healthy when he is *not* being his real self than when he is his real self. But an individual's "obnoxious" but authentic self can never grow in the direction of greater maturity until the person has become acquainted with it and begins to *be* it. Real-self-being produces consequences which, in accordance with well-known principles of behavior (*cf.* Skinner, 1953), produce changes in the real self. Thus, there can be no real growth of the self without real-self-being. Full disclosure of the self to at least one other significant human being appears to be one means by which a person discovers not only the breadth and depth of his needs and feelings, but also the nature of his own self-affirmed values. There is no necessary conflict, incidentally, between real-self-being and being an ethical or nice person, because for the average member of our society, self-owned ethics are generally acquired during the process of growing up. All too often, however, the self-owned ethics are buried under authoritarian morals (Fromm, 1947).

If self-disclosure is one of the means by which healthy personality is both achieved and maintained, we can also note that such activities as loving, psychotherapy, counseling, teaching, and nursing are impossible of achievement without the disclosure of the client. It is through self-disclosure that an individual reveals to himself and to the other party just exactly who, what, and where he is. Just as thermometers and sphygmomanometers disclose information about the real state of the body, self-disclosure reveals the real nature of the soul, or self. Such information is vital in order to conduct intelligent evaluations. All I mean by evaluation is comparing how a person is with some concept of optimum. You never really discover how truly sick your psychotherapy patient is until he discloses himself utterly to you. You cannot help your client in vocational guidance until he has disclosed to you something of the impasse in which he finds himself. You cannot love your spouse or your child or your friend unless those persons have permitted you to know them and to know what they need in order to move toward greater health and well-being. Nurses cannot nurse patients in any meaningful way unless they have permitted the patients to disclose their needs, wants, worries, anxieties, and doubts, and so forth. Teachers cannot be very helpful to their students until they have permitted the students to disclose how utterly ignorant and misinformed they presently are. Teachers cannot even provide helpful information to the students until they have permitted the students to disclose exactly what they are interested in.

I believe we should reserve the term inter*personal* relationships to refer to transactions between "I and thou" (Buber, 1937), between *person* and *person*, not between role and role. A truly personal relationship between two people involves disclosure of self one to the other in full and spontaneous honesty. The data that we have collected up to the present time have shown us some rather interesting phenomena. We found (Jourard and Lasakow, 1958), for example, that the women we tested in universities in the Southeast were consistently higher self-disclosers than men; they seem to have a greater capacity for establishing person-to-person relationships, inter*personal* relationships, than men. This characteristic of women seems to be a socially patterned phenomenon which sociologists (Parsons and Bales, 1955) refer to as the *expressive* role of women in contradistinction to the instrumental role which men universally are obliged to adopt. Men seem to be much more skilled at *im*personal, *instrumental* role playing. But public health officials, very concerned about the sex differential in morality rates, have been wondering what it is about being a man which makes males die younger than females. Do you suppose that there is any connection whatsoever between the disclosure patterns of men and women and their differential death rates? I have already intimated that withholding self-disclosure seems to impose a certain stress on people. Maybe "being manly," whatever that means, is slow suicide!

I think there is a very general way of stating the relationship between self-disclosure and assorted values such as healthy personality, physical health, group effectiveness, successful marriage, effective teaching, and effective nursing. It is this. A person's self is known to be the immediate determiner of his overt behavior. This is a paraphrase of the phenomenological point of view in psychology (Combs and Snygg, 1959). Now, if we want to understand anything, explain it, control it, or predict it, it is helpful if we have available as much pertinent information as we possibly can. Self-disclosure provides a source of information which is relevant. This information has often been overlooked. Where it has not been overlooked, it has often been misinterpreted by observers and practitioners through such devices as projection or attribution. *It seems to be difficult for people to accept the fact that they do not know the very person whom they are confronting at any given moment.* We all seem to assume that we are expert psychologists and that we know the other person, when in fact we have only constructed a more or less autistic concept of him in our mind. If we are to learn more about man's self, then we must learn more about self-disclosure—its conditions, dimensions, and consequences. Beginning evidence (cf. Rogers, 1958) shows that actively accepting, empathic, loving, nonpunitive response—in short, love—provides the optimum conditions under which man will disclose, or expose, his naked quivering self to our gaze. It follows that if we would be helpful (or should I say *human*) we must grow to loving stature and learn, in Buber's terms, to confirm our fellow man in his very being. Probably, this presumes that we must *first* confirm our *own* being.

REFERENCES

Alexander, F. *Psychosomatic Medicine.* New York: Norton, 1950.

Allport, G. *Becoming.* New Haven: Yale University Press, 1955.

Anonymous. "A New Theory of Schizophrenia," *Journal of Abnormal and Social Psychology,* Vol. 57 (1958), pp. 226–36.

Barr, S. *Purely Academic.* New York: Simon & Schuster, 1958.

Buber, M. *I and Thou.* New York: Scribners, 1937.

Combs, A. and Snygg, D. *Individual Behavior.* 2nd ed. New York: Harper, 1959.

Davis, F. H. and Malmo, R. B. "Electromyographic Recording during Interview," *American Journal of Psychiatry,* Vol. 107 (1950), pp. 908–16.

Dittes, J. E. "Extinction during Psychotherapy of GSR Accompanying 'Embarrassing' Statements," *Journal of Abnormal and Social Psychology*, Vol. 54 (1957), pp. 187–91.

Dunn, H. L. "High-Level Wellness for Man and Society," *American Journal of Public Health*, Vol. 49 (1959), pp. 786–92.

Freud, S. *The Interpretation of Dreams.* New York: Basic Books, 1955.

Fromm, E. *Man for Himself.* New York: Rinehart, 1947.

————. *The Art of Loving.* New York: Harper, 1956.

Horney, K. *The Neurotic Personality of Our Time.* New York: Norton, 1936.

————. *Neurosis and Human Growth.* New York: Norton, 1950.

Jahoda, Marie. *Current Concepts of Positive Mental Health.* New York: Basic Books, 1958.

Jourard, S. M. *Personal Adjustment: An Approach through the Study of Healthy Personality.* New York: Macmillan, 1958.

Jourard, S. M. and Lasakow, P. "Some Factors in Self-Disclosure," *Journal of Abnormal and Social Psychology*, Vol. 56 (1958), pp. 91–98.

Maslow, A. H. *Motivation and Personality.* New York: Harper, 1954.

Parsons, T. and Bales, R. F. *Family, Socialization, and Interaction Process.* Glencoe, Ill.: Free Press, 1955.

Riesman, D. *The Lonely Crowd.* New Haven: Yale University Press, 1950.

Rogers, C. R. "The Characteristics of a Helping Relationship," *Personal Guidance Journal*, Vol. 37 (1958), pp. 6–16.

Ruesch, J. *Disturbed Communication.* New York: Norton, 1957.

Selye, H. *The Physiology and Pathology of Exposure to Stress.* Montreal: Acta, 1950.

Skinner, B. F. *Science and Human Behavior.* New York: Macmillan, 1953.

The nature of competence-acquisition activities and their relationship to therapy[*]

Chris Argyris

I have been asked to discuss the objectives and nature of the group work that is called laboratory education (T-groups or sensitivity training). This is not an easy task because there is a great variety of learning activities that go under the

---

[*] Invited paper for Association for Research in Nervous and Mental Diseases, December, 1967, New York.

same label. Another problem is that the underlying theory has only recently begun to be developed.[1]

The most useful solution seemed to be to focus on the theory that underlies much of these dynamics, a theoretical framework which may be called *competence acquisition*.[2]

The objective of competence acquisition is to provide the participants with opportunities to diagnose and increase their interpersonal competence. Interpersonal competence is the ability to cope effectively with interpersonal relationships. Three criteria of effective interpersonal coping are:

a) The individual perceives the interpersonal situation accurately. He is able to identify the relevant variables plus their interrelationships.

b) The individual is able to solve the problems in such a way that they remain solved. If, for example, interpersonal trust is low between A and B, they may not have been said to solve the problem competently unless and until it no longer recurs (assuming the problem is under control).

c) The solution is achieved in such a way that A and B are still able to work with each other at least as effectively as when they began to solve their problem.

The test of interpersonal competence therefore is not limited to insight and understanding. The individual's interpersonal competence is a function of his ability (and the ability of the others involved) to solve interpersonal problems. This criterion implies that to test the interpersonal competence developed in a learning situation, the individual(s) must show that the learning has transferred beyond the learning situation. The aim, therefore, is to change behavior and attitudes in such a way that observable changes can be found in solving interpersonal problems outside the learning situations. Transfer of learning is a central aspiration in competence acquisition.

REQUIREMENTS FOR THE TRANSFER OF LEARNING

Providing the conditions for the maximum transfer of learning is extremely difficult in the interpersonal area. First, it takes much practice to develop interpersonal skills because they are complex and because much unfreezing is usually required. If the individual is to be internally committed to the new learning he must have come to the conclusion that his old modes of behavior were no longer effective. This conclusion needs to be based on actual experiences in the learning situation where he used his old modes of behavior and found them wanting.

Second, the individual must develop new modes of behavior that are also tested and found more effective than the old. These new modes of behavior must

---

[1] Edgar H. Schein and Warren G. Bennis, *Personal and Organizational Change through Group Methods* (New York: Wiley, 1965), and L. P. Bradford, J. R. Gibb, and K. D. Benne (eds.), *T-Group Theory and Laboratory Method* (New York: Wiley, 1964).

[2] Such a differentiation is discussed in Chris Argyris, "On the Future of Laboratory Education," *Journal of Applied Behavioral Science* (June 1967).

have been practiced enough so that the individual feels confident in his ability to use them.

Third, the individual must develop new modes of adjunct behavior that may be called for if he uses the new modes of behavior. For example, if the individual learns to express his feelings of anger or love more openly, he may also have to develop new competence in dealing with individuals who are threatened by such openness.

It is important, therefore, for the individual to learn how to express these feelings in such a way that he minimizes the probability that his behavior will cause someone else to become defensive, because then the environment could become threatening. This suggests a fourth criterion: namely, the probability that A will behave in an interpersonally competent manner is not only a function of his own confidence in his abilities to do so; it is also a function of the others' confidence and willingness to behave in an interpersonally competent manner. For example, the writer's interpersonal competence scores have been found to vary immensely, depending upon the situation in which he is placed. Quantitatively, his scores have ranged from 150 to 390 where the lowest score obtained is 10 and the highest 390.[3] Interpersonal competence, therefore, is an interpersonal or situational ability and not simply an individual or personal ability. This does not mean that each individual cannot learn skills that will help him behave more competently. It means that such skills are necessary but not sufficient.

Finally, the probability is very low that an individual can be taught everything he needs to know in order to behave competently in most situations in which he will be placed. The variance and complexity of life is too great to predict it adequately ahead of time. Therefore, *the most important requirement in obtaining transfer of learning is to generate, along with the knowledge of any specific behavior, the basic skills needed to diagnose new situations effectively and those needed to develop cooperation with others involved to generate the competent behavior appropriate to the situation.*

Experience in, and theory relevant to, competence acquisition suggest that there are several key elements in the learning situation if these five requirements are to be fulfilled. The individuals must learn how to (1) communicate with each other in a manner that generates minimally distorted information; (2) give and receive feedback that is directly capable of validation and minimally evaluative; (3) perform these skills in such a way that self-acceptance and trust among individuals tends to increase; and (4) create effective groups in which problem solving may occur.

MINIMALLY DISTORTED INFORMATION

It seems self-evident to state that the information needed for competent problem solving should not be distorted. Altering behavior on the basis of dis-

---

[3] Chris Argyris, *Organization and Innovation* (Homewood, Ill.: Irwin, 1965).

torted feedback would tend to make the individuals distorted, which, in turn, would tend to increase the probability that future feedback would be given or received in a distorted manner.

Self-awareness and self-acceptance

The minimum requirement that each individual must meet if he is to provide minimally distorted information is to manifest a relatively high degree of *self-awareness* and *self-acceptance*. The more an individual is aware and accepting of those aspects of his self which are operating in a given situation, (1) the higher the probability that he will discuss them with minimal distortion, and (2) the higher the probability that he will listen with minimal distortion. For example, if A is aware and accepting of his predisposition to control others, he will tend to listen to the impact that he is having upon others without distorting what others are saying. Moreover, he will also tend to provide another controlling individual with feedback that is minimally distorted by his own similar problem in that area.

How is the individual to increase his self-awareness and self-acceptance? By receiving minimally distorted feedback from others about his impact upon them and their willingness to be accepting and understanding of his behavior, even though *he* may not be. Thus we have an interpersonal bind. Helpful feedback depends partially upon self-awareness and self-acceptance, yet these two factors depend upon helpful feedback!

How is this circular process broken into? This is a key task of the educator. Presumably he has (relatively speaking) a higher degree of self-awareness and self-acceptance against which the individuals can interact. His bind is that if he is not careful he can easily become the focus of attention. Everyone will tend to turn to him for valid information. This dependency could lead to awareness but hardly to confidence on the part of the learners will turn to each other as resources. In doing so, the educator makes two important assumptions about each individual. Each is assumed to have a constructive intent. Each is capable of learning from others *if* he receives the kind of information that is helpful and *if* the proper group atmosphere is developed.

Acceptance and trust of others

One of the major initial tasks of the educator is to create conditions under which the learners can become aware of and test the validity of these two assumptions. If these two assumptions are not validated for each individual in the learning situation, the processes of competence acquisition will not be highly effective. This test is very difficult to make during the early stages because most of the learners are expecting the educator to control their learning, to tell them what to do, to provide them with agendas, etc. If he behaves in any other way, he may easily be perceived as hostile, noncaring, or ineffective.

One reason a T-group experience usually begins with the withdrawal of the expected directive leadership, agenda, status, etc., is in order that the staff member may emphasize that he really means to help them come to trust in each other's intention to be constructive, in their capabilities to learn, and to develop an effective group. The point is made forcefully at the outset, not because the educator enjoys the drama of his apparent withdrawal and the resulting social weightlessness, but because he has learned that such behavior on his part is so strange that individuals do not tend to believe him unless he behaves this way with purpose and thrust. The educator strives not to be seduced from this stance by accusations of being perplexing, cruel, or ineffective. His major response during this period is, in effect, "I can understand that you may feel that if I have any concern for you I will help you out of this predicament. But may I point out again that I am assuming that a deeper predicament is to learn to rely on all of our strengths and not to become focused primarily on me?"

As soon as the learners realize that the educator means what he says, they usually turn to each other for help "to get the group moving." Those who begin to take the lead also expose their behavior, which becomes the basis for learning because it provides material to be diagnosed and discussed. Thus Mr. A may dislike the initial social weightlessness and may appoint himself as chairman. He may, somewhat demandingly, begin to define an agenda. The educator may eventually use this "here and now" situation to help the members explore their feelings about Mr. A. This could lead Mr. A to realize the impact he has had on others. It could also help the others to explore their different reactions to Mr. A (some welcome his behavior and some dislike it), as well as their feelings about beginning to be open. Another task would be for the members to explore the group process. For example, how was the decision made to develop an agenda? Did Mr. A check to see if he had the commitment of the members? What happens to decisions made unilaterally?

The point is that no matter which approach is taken, the educator uses the "here and now" to maximize their feelings of responsibility for their learning. It is primarily *their* behavior that they explore. It is *their* behavior that defines the goal. It is *their* responsibility to choose whether they will learn from the situation and if so, how, and how much. To be sure, early in the history of this type of learning, some people resent the fact that the educator does not prevent them from going in what he "knows" will be an ineffective direction. However, as the members see the importance of being self-responsible, as they feel the internal confidence that is developed from experiencing self-responsibility, as they come to trust others in the group, they become much more understanding of the educator's strategy not to interfere. Indeed, by the end of the first week, it is not uncommon for group members to caution an educator against too early intervention on his part to "pull them out of a difficulty." They have come to trust their capacity to do this and to value the intrinsic satisfaction that goes along with such learning. Moreover, they may have also begun to learn how it is for them, in another situation, to "withdraw" in order to help others help themselves.

Conditions for psychological success

The word "withdraw" is placed in quotation marks because it is not true that the educator withdraws in the sense of becoming uninvolved or being nondirective. The withdrawal from the expected leadership style is purposive action. The educator is deeply involved in creating the kind of environment which, if the learners decide to enter, will lead to important learning. What is that environment? The answer to this question identifies one of the underlying characteristics of competence acquisition mentioned at the outset. *No matter what is being learned substantively, it should be learned in such a way that it is accompanied by feelings of psychological success and confidence in self and others, and the group.*

The educator manipulates the environment (*never* the people) so that the individuals, if they decide to enter the environment, are offered frequent opportunities to (1) define their own learning goal, (2) develop their paths to the goal, (3) relate the goal and the paths to their central needs, and (4) experience a challenge in achieving the goal that stretches their present level of abilities.[4]

The educator is actively striving to create the learning conditions which will lead them to an increase in trust and confidence in themselves and in their group. As the trust of self, others, and group increases, the probability of giving and receiving valid information increases and so does the probability of self-awareness and self-acceptance, which in turn increases the predisposition for more experiences of psychological success.

GIVING AND RECEIVING HELPFUL INFORMATION

Feedback may be undistorted but not very helpful in creating behavioral change, self-acceptance, and an effective group. In order for information to be most helpful it should be directly verifiable and minimally evaluative.

Directly verifiable information

It is important to distinguish between information that can be verified directly by self and others versus information that can be validated by reference to some conceptual scheme. The first type of feedback includes categories of behavior that are directly *observable*,[5] the second utilizes categories that are inferred. The more the information used in the learning situations is composed of *inferred* categories that refer to a conceptual scheme, the greater the dependence of the individuals upon the conceptual scheme if they are to verify the information that they are using. If, for example, the conceptual scheme is a clinical framework,

---

[4] Kurt Lewin, Tamara Dembo, Leon Festinger, and Pauline Sears, "Levels of Aspiration" in J. M. V. Hung (ed.), *Personality and Behavior Disorders* (New York: Ronald, 1944), pp. 333–78.

[5] I am indebted to Dr. Alvan R. Feinstein (Yale Medical School) for clarifying this distinction and recommend to the reader his book, *Clinical Judgment* (Williams and Wilkins, 1967).

then the individuals must turn to the educator for help because he knows the scheme. (Indeed, is not a great part of therapy learning the conceptual scheme of the therapist?) This dependence *decreases* the *probability* of experiencing psychological success, trust in others and in the group, because the key to success, trust, and effectiveness lies in knowing the conceptual scheme, which is in the mind of the therapist. For example, if B learns from the therapist that his hostility is probably an attempt to deal with authority figures and that the transference phenomenon is actively present, he will be unable to verify these inferences unless he learns the conceptual scheme used by the therapist. Moreover, even if he learns the scheme, B will soon find that he is using inferred categories for which relatively unambiguous tests are not available. He is being diagnosed, "interpreted," and advised with the use of concepts that he understands vaguely and which have minimal operational actions to test their validity. He may indeed come to feel that the very process of testing the therapist's inference could be interpreted as resistance.

Information, therefore, should be as far as possible directly verifiable. However, to generate information that is directly verifiable by nonprofessionals as well as professionals requires that it remain as close to observable data as possible. For example, B learns that when he behaves in X manner (asks questions, evaluates others), A feels attacked. B then can turn to the group and check to see if they see him behaving in X manner and, if so, whether they also feel attacked. He may learn that some see him behaving in X manner and some see him behaving in Y manner. He may learn that some feel attacked and some do not. Finally, he may learn that, of those who do *not* feel attacked, several feel this way because X type of behavior is not threatening to them. Others may find Y type of behavior threatening.

One of the crucial learnings that B obtains is that his behavior is rarely perceived in a unitary fashion and that its impact varies widely. He may then ask the members to describe what kind of behavior they would not have found threatening. This information may lead B to alter his behavior. It may also lead him to decide to behave in X or Y manner but, the next time, show awareness that his behavior is having a differential impact.

In the section above we distinguished two kinds of inferred categories. One that was related to a formal theoretical framework (he is projecting; she is ambivalent) and the other that was related to the personal values of the individual (he is nice; she is sweet). There is a third way that formal or personal theory may be used.

There are many writers who are beginning to stress the use of more directly observable categories. For example, the therapist may say to the client, "I think you are kidding yourself; it sounds like you would like to kill that individual, you are so angry."

The function of such *attributive* interventions is to attribute something to the person, which the therapist infers exists, about which the client is more or less unaware. Such an intervention may use relatively observable categories, but they are based upon a theoretical framework. Thus, if the patient asks, "Why do you say I am kidding?" he may receive a reply, "Because you are denying such and such." Or, if he asks, "Why do you think I want to kill so and so?" he may receive a reply "You sounded very angry, and I felt that you were afraid to say what you truly felt." It now becomes apparent that the former intervention was based upon the concept of denial, the latter on a concept of some category of psychological blockage.

Any intervention that attributes something to the client that he has not already mentioned (in some directly verifiable form) is based upon the therapist's inferences about the inner states of the client. Such an invention is also of the inferred variety even though it may be initially placed in the language of observed categories.

Telling the client what may be "inside" himself, "causing" his problems, even if *correct*, will tend to lead to psychological failure, because the client, if he is to be rational and self-responsible, must assign the primary responsibility for the insight to the therapist. It was the therapist who guessed correctly what was "in" the client. If the therapist, however, intervenes and gives the raw data from which he infers the client is unaware or not expressing openly that he is kidding himself or wants to kill someone, then the client is able to judge for himself the possible validity of the inference.

This comment should emphasize that the meaning of "here and now" in competence acquisition is significantly different from the meaning of "here and now" in many psychotherapeutic activities. Some psychotherapists tend to use the "here and now" to help the client discover the unconscious structure active in the present but created in the past. Others use "here and now" data to help the client see that he uses the relationship to involve the therapist as a more or less unconscious object. Finally, others use the "here and now" data to generate enough evidence to make an interpretation to the patient, such as that he may be projecting, or that he may be identifying with such and such a person, etc.[6]

In all these examples the "here and now" data are used to help the professional generate interpretations that go much beyond the directly verifiable, observed category. This point cannot be made too strongly. To date, the overwhelming number of psychotherapists' works read by the author has led him to the conclusion that, unlike his emphasis on observed categories, they use interpretations of the "here and now" variety which are composed of *inferred* categories:[7]

Minimally evaluative feedback

The second major characteristic of helpful information is that it is minimally evaluative of the recipient's behavior. There are two reasons for this. First, such

---

[6] For illustrations, see Henry Ezriel, "Notes on Psychoanalytic Group Therapy: II. Interpretation and Research." *Psychiatry*, Vol. 15 (May, 1952), pp. 119–26.

[7] William Glasser may be closer to this view, but he gives examples in terms of "there and then." *Reality Therapy* (New York: Harper & Row, 1965), p. 75 ff.

information reduces the probability of making the receiver defensive, thereby creating conditions under which accurate listening will be increased. Thus laboratory education does not value the communication of all information. It values that openness which will help the individuals receiving feedback to learn. Second, minimally evaluative information describes them as good or bad. This places the responsibility for evaluation, if there is to be any, on the individual trying to learn about himself. He, and only he, has the responsibility of deciding whether he plans to change his behavior. Again, placing the responsibility on the individual increases the probability that if he changes, since it is his decision, he will tend to experience a sense of psychological success.

This does not mean that evaluation is harmful. Evaluation of behavior and effectiveness is necessary and essential. The point is that one ought, as far as possible, to create conditions under which the individual makes his own evaluation and then asks for confirmation or disconfirmation. If the individual first makes his own evaluation, then even if it is negative, a confirmation by others of his negative quality can lead to growth and inner confidence in one's capacity to evaluate oneself correctly.[8]

This implies that an individual should take the initiative in seeking confirmation and that he should "own up" with his evaluations before others do so. "Going first," if it is to be successful, requires that several conditions be met. First, the individual should be unconflicted and accepting about his evaluation of himself. If he is not, others will sense it and may tend to withhold their true feelings. This tendency to withhold, in turn, will be a function of their view of the individual's strength to receive accurately and use effectively the evaluative comments that he is requesting. Thus, "going first" requires less courage and more competence. The individual has created, by his behavior, the conditions under which others would trust him to use their evaluative feedback competently.

THE EFFECTIVE GROUP AND ITS USE FOR INDIVIDUAL CHANGE

A careful analysis of the activities described above will suggest that competence acquisition requires the development of effective groups. For example, the individual requires minimally distorted and immediately capable of validation feedback. If he is to understand his impact upon others, then he needs to receive valid information from others. In order to obtain valid information, the others should be minimally defensive. Assuming that the selection process has eliminated those who are so defensive that they cannot learn from others (see next section), then the major source for defensiveness becomes the group. If the members cannot decide on a sequence of topics acceptable to all—who will receive the first feedback—or if they are unable to judge the constructive intent of the members, then their problem solving could become so ineffective that they would become frustrated with, and angry at, each other. Under these conditions,

---

[8] Chris Argyris, *Interpersonal Competence and Organizational Effectiveness* (Homewood, Ill.: Irwin, 1962), pp. 140–43.

minimally distorted, immediately verifiable information will rarely be generated. *Although competence acquisition focuses on helping individuals become more interpersonally competent, the very nature of personality (its incompleteness without others, the need for consensual validation, etc.) makes an effective group central to the learning processes.*

This conclusion leads naturally to two questions. What is an effective group? How can one utilize an effective group to facilitate individual growth?

Beginning with the former question, four major dimensions of group effectiveness are:

1) The members focus on defining group goals that "satisfy" the needs and utilize the important abilities of the individual members. Adequate time is spent to make certain that the goals represent a challenge to the group as well as to the individuals and that the members are internally committed to the achievement of the goals.

2) Attention is paid, whenever it is necessary, to the group processes. For example, are the members' contributions additive? Do the members focus on the history of the group in order to learn from its successes and failures, from its internal conflicts, from its problem solving? Are the members owning up to their ideas and feelings? Are they open to new ideas and feelings? Are they experimenting and taking risks?

3) Norms are generated that reward the individuality of each member, that show respect and concern for the members' ideas and feelings, that facilitate and maintain a sense of trust.

4) Leadership is shared so that each member is leading the group when his skills are the most pertinent to the achievement of the group goals.

The next question is, how may an effective group be used as a medium for individual behavioral change? Cartwright, on the basis of a review of the literature, suggests several conditions under which a group may be a more effective medium for change.[9]

There needs to be a strong sense of belonging to the same group, including a *reduction* of the normal gap between teacher and student, doctor and patient, etc., so that the faculty and students feel as members of one group in matters involving their growth. This means that the staff member must strive to become a member of the group without giving up his expertise. This is a difficult task because, as we have seen, so many of the members come to the group with different expectations. As was pointed out above, the staff member strives to develop membership by withdrawing initially and dramatically creating a situation in which the members must turn to each other as resource people. As their trust and confidence in themselves and in their group increases, their need to see the staff member as a godlike, distant figure decreases.

A second way to earn genuine membership was also described above. The staff

---

[9] Dorwin Cartwright, "Achieving Change in People: Some Applications of Group Dynamics Theory," *Human Relations*, Vol. 4 (1951), pp. 381–93.

member makes as many of his contributions as possible be minimally distorted, at the level of observed categories, and focused on how he sees the world (and not what is "in" others, or what "the" group is doing). This makes every one of his contributions subject to verification by the other members. The point is that every other member must learn how to use effectively both of these strategies. As they do, they will begin to feel closer to each other, including the staff member. Indeed, one of the crucial ways in which a staff member earns his membership is by making several interventions which are not verifiable or are found to be in error. This helps the group to realize that he is not infallible and that the staff member needs *them* to check his own effectiveness.

As the members begin to trust their selves and each other, as their group functioning becomes more effective, the group becomes more attractive to each member. As the group becomes more attractive, it meets the second conditions defined by Cartwright. The more attractive the group is to its members, the greater is the influence that the group can exert on its members.

Cartwright also suggests a third condition; namely, that a strong pressure for change in the group can be established by creating shared perceptions by the members of the need for change. Again, examples of how a staff member creates opportunities for these pressures to develop were described in the previous section. If the staff member creates, at the outset, an opportunity for the members to "take over," and if in behaving they exhibit interpersonally incompetent behavior, it will lead to their becoming frustrated. If they feel a need to be competent and their intent is constructive, then these experiences will become a major source of shared perception of the need for their change.

If the staff member follows the strategy of helping the members develop their own plans, define their own learning goals, generate their own level of aspiration (psychological success), then we have created the fourth condition mentioned by Cartwright. Information relating to the need for change, plans for change, and consequences of change must be shared by all relevant people in the group.

We conclude, therefore, that individual learning cannot be separated from group effectiveness, and (happily) the conditions required for each are overlapping but highly consonant. This suggests that the arguments of individual versus group learning may be off the mark. Moreover, it may not make much sense to plan a learning experience that focuses on only one level of learning. Both levels of learning must be experienced to some degree of effectiveness if learning is to occur at either level. One may wish *to begin* at the group or individual level, but if a whole learning experience is to be developed, the interdependencies of each on the other must be brought out and mastered. This is especially relevant if we think of the criterion of transfer of learning. When an individual finds himself in a situation outside of the learning context, the members of that situation will not focus on individual or group phenomena simply because that is what *he* learned to do in *his* laboratory. Under these conditions the individual may feel frustrated and experience a greater sense of failure than the members who had never attended a laboratory, since their level of aspiration, related to their interpersonal competence, may be realistically lower than his.

Another implication is that the learning experience should last long enough and be designed in such a way that the learners can be exposed to "pairs" of interpersonal and group phenomena. Moreover, one may predict that if the staff chooses to ignore the individual or the group phenomena during the learning experiences, the learners will have to make up the deficiency in their own informal way. For example, a recent delegation to a Leicester-Tavistock conference reported that they spent many off hours discussing their learning about their personal competence and about the usefulness of the experience: two topics never scheduled formally (and rarely informally) by the faculty. A group experience recently conducted by the writer, which never got to group phenomena during the formal sessions, led many members to spend many of their informal hours focusing on that subject.

COMPETENCE AND SURVIVAL ORIENTATION LEAD TO OPEN AND CLOSED SYSTEMS

At the beginning of this paper two assumptions of competence acquisition were defined. They were that the individuals have (1) a constructive intent and (2) a genuine desire to learn, to become interpersonally more competent. It was noted that the less the constructive intent to learn, the less the conditions of competence acquisition apply. Why would individuals have different degrees of willingness to learn?

A detailed discussion of this question would lead beyond the main thrust of this paper. However, a brief note is necessary in order to build the position. Individuals can be described as predisposed or oriented toward increasing their competence or toward protecting themselves in order to survive. Maslow describes the former as growth motivation, the latter as deficiency motivation.[10] The more the individual is competence-oriented, the more he will tend to focus on those activities that enlarge his self and increase his self-acceptance and confidence. The individual becomes more an *open* system. In the area of interpersonal relations, the activities involved in the growth and acceptance of self may be conceptualized as the seeking of a sense of interpersonal competence.[11]

Developing a sense of interpersonal competence is intrinsically satisfying; it provides much of the motivation for growth and learning in interpersonal relationships. However, the individual will tend to be free to focus on competence acquisition only to the extent that he feels his survival problems are resolved (i.e., they do not control his present behavior). Thus human beings "graduate" into

---

[10] A. H. Maslow, *Personality and Motivation* (New York: Harper & Row, Pub., Inc. 1954.

[11] Robert W. White, "Motivation Reconsidered: The Concept of Competence," *Psychological Review*, Vol. 66 (1959), pp. 297–334.

and, once having done so, strive to maintain, competence acquisition orientation. They will return to survival orientation only when they experience threat. A survival orientation is primarily one of the protection of the self. The individual, through the use of defense mechanisms, withdraws, distorts, or attacks the environment. In all cases the end result is to reduce the probability that the individual will learn from the environment. This, in turn, begins to make the individual more closed and less subject to influence. The more closed the individual becomes, the more his adaptive reactions will be controlled by his internal system. But since his internal system is composed of many defense mechanisms, the behavior will not tend to be functional or economical. The behavior may eventually become compulsive, repetitive, inwardly stimulated, and observably dysfunctional. The individual becomes more of a *closed* system. The greater the proportion of the individual's behavior that falls into this category (closed), the more he approximates the condition that Kubie has described as neurotic behavior.

It is important to emphasize that individuals are *not* being viewed as either closed or open. People are not open or closed. Nor is all openness effective and all closedness ineffective. An individual may be quite open in learning about his authority relationships but not his capacity to create mistrust. Another individual may be open to learning more about how to express his feelings and suddenly become closed when he realizes he has reached the point that further expression of feelings could lead to an uncontrollable state. He prefers to postpone further expression of feelings until he has learned to manage the new feelings that he has expressed.

The important point, from a theory of learning, is that the educator and the client need to be able to differentiate between that learning which evolves around problems and issues about which the individual is more or less open or closed. Each state of affairs requires different interventions with which to encourage learning. Thus, as we shall see in a moment, it may be necessary to use inferred evaluative interventions under certain conditions if the individual is to gain insight and unfreeze. However, if one is to go beyond insight and unfreezing, then one will have to utilize competence-oriented learning conditions. These learning conditions may be inhibited if mixed with too strong a component of interventions designed to unfreeze closed (survival-oriented) behavior. The problem is *not* that it may be difficult for the educator to cope with; he may be competent to shift from one level of intervention to another. The problem is the group. Until the members become much more competent, they will find the mixture confusing. One of the basic reasons is that interventions designed to unfreeze closed behavior tend not to create conditions for psychological success, directly verifiable information, minimally evaluative feedback, and effective group functioning. The members will feel challenged enough to learn how to be competent in terms of these conditions. Moreover, they will feel the pressure stemming from the reality that their learning experience is limited in time.

Openness and closedness are affected by:

1) The situation in which the individual is placed. If the situation is confirma-

bly threatening, then closedness may be a functional response. Individuals may become more closed for social reasons. Empirical evidence has been presented that there seems to be a general tendency for people to create social systems that are closed and reward survival orientation.[12] It is therefore possible for the indiviudal to behave in a closed manner because it makes sense; it is functional in a closed system. This type of closedness we will call *external* to indicate that it comes primarily from the social system. An individual who is closed for external reasons has not internalized the systemic values to such a point that he cannot differentiate closedness from openness. He is able to go back and forth from more open to more closed behavior depending upon the situation. In a T-group, for example, an externally clased individual will resist openness initially until he can assure himself that the T-group is truly an open system.

The individual whose survival orientation stems from personal reasons may be called *internally* closed. This individual is unable to become open when he is provided with a situation in which openness is relevant and functional. He generalizes that the world is threatening far beyond the situation where threats have existed or do exist.

2) The duration of the threat. A threat could produce momentary closedness if it is of short duration, or it could produce long-lasting closedness if it lasts for a long period of time.

3) The parts of the personality affected by the threat. The degree of closedness will tend to vary if the source of threat is related to inner, peripheral, or central aspects of the self. Peripheral aspects are those that have a low potency for the individual, while inner aspects tend to have a high potency. We assume that one must pass through the peripheral in order to arrive at the inner aspects.

The central aspects can be peripheral or inner. The key differentiating property is that change in a central part will tend to create changes in the surrounding parts, be they inner or peripheral.

4) Whether or not the source of the threat is from within or from without. The problems in dealing with threat that an individual faces are very different when the threat emanates from within than when the threat comes from the external environment.

5) Finally, the degree of control the system is able to manifest (in our case, individuals) over the threat. The less the control over the threat, the greater the probability that the individual will become closed. Closedness will also increase as the potency of the parts involved increases and as the duration of the threat increases.

It should be clear, therefore, that it is a gross oversimplification to think of open and closed individuals. What is more likely is that individuals are more or less closed or open, both in terms of degree and in terms of time. The more an individual seeks the processes of competence acquistion, the more open he may

---

[12] Chris Argyris, *Interpersonal Competence and Organizational Effectiveness* (Homewood, Ill.: The Dorsey Press, 1962); *Organization and Innovation* (Homewood, Ill.: Irwin, 1964); and "Interpersonal Barriers to Decision Making," *Harvard Business Review* (March–April 1966), pp. 84–97.

be said to be. The more an individual resists these processes, the more closed he may be said to be. *The point to be emphasized is the hypothesis that the more open an individual can be, the more he can learn from competence-acquisition activities; the more closed, the more he may need therapy, at least as the initial step toward competence acquisition.*

To summarize, the probability of learning to behave more competently *and* to transfer this learning beyond the learning situation increases:

1) *As the client's* self-awareness and self-acceptance increases; as his acceptance and trust of others increases.

2) As the *educator* is able to create, in the learning situation, conditions of (*a*) psychological success, (*b*) directly verifiable information, (*c*) minimally evaluative feedback, and (*d*) effective group functioning (group goals are congruent with member needs, attention to group processes, norms of individuality, concern, trust, and shared leadership).

3) *As these conditions for effective learning* feed back to help increase and strengthen the individual's self-awareness and self-acceptance and his acceptance and trust of others, which, in turn, increase the probability that

4) the *members* will take increasing responsibility and manifest greater competence in creating conditions of effective learning which

5) provide the *members* and educator opportunity to practice and deepen their competence as well as their confidence in creating the conditions elsewhere.

Some readers may wonder if we are suggesting that feelings of pain, fear, self-accusation should not occur in the learning session. Is this learning experience one that emphasizes "sweetness and light"?

One of the problems is that we are limited by space. However, two points should be made. Anyone who has experienced, either as an educator or a member, the difficulty in creating conditions for effective learning, the embarrassment of realizing how incompetent one can be, the blindness of one's own impact upon others, or the capacity to unintentionally prevent the reception of valid feedback can testify to the existence of feelings of pain, fear, and confrontation of reality.

The second and more important point is that the strategy presented in this paper suggests that the educator should not focus directly on creating such feelings as pain, fear, etc. He should focus, as much as possible, on creating the conditions described above. If, while he does this, fear, pain, anguish, and frustration occur (and they will occur), he helps the members to express these feelings and to understand the basis of such fears. Past experience suggests two important causes of these feelings are (1) the awareness of one's blindness to (2) the degree of one's interpersonal incompetence. The awareness of such conditions provides internal motivation for further work on increasing one's interpersonal competence.

Dealing with psychological tensions[1*]

Carl R. Rogers

The behavioral sciences have made modest but real progress in learning to deal with psychological tensions within the individual; with tensions between individuals; with tensions between small groups. We have practical skills which permit us to create deep and harmonious relationships in a group of diverse individuals. We have even made a small beginning in dealing with international tensions on a simulated basis.

What is needed is a concerted effort—an interdisciplinary task force—to push out the boundaries of such knowledge and to apply these growing skills to existing tensions—interracial, international, and other.

It is often said that atomic force may blow our whole civilization, our whole way of life, off this terrestrial globe. No sensible man can deny that this is a frightening possibility. Yet the way in which the problem is stated is frequently inaccurate. It is not atomic energy which is the crucial element in such potential destruction. The crucial element is the fear or hate or panic or greed or pride of some very human beings who will trigger that holocaust, if it comes. It will be the unresolved tensions between groups of individuals which will stoke the fires of those feelings.

So the desperate problem we are facing is not, in my estimation, "How can we stop nuclear war?" The crucial issue is, "How can we resolve the psychological tensions which divide individuals, groups, and nations?" It is on this problem that I would like to focus. I wish to call your attention to the highly significant learnings which are beginning to accumulate in the behavioral sciences in regard to dealing with psychological tensions.

---

[1] Address given to the 21st Annual Institute on World Affairs, San Diego State College, August 16, 1963.

* Reprinted in its entirety from Carl R. Rogers, "Dealing with Psychological Tensions," *Journal of Applied Behavioral Science*, vol. 1, no. 1, 1965, pp. 6–24.

A MODEL FOR UNDERSTANDING TENSION SITUATIONS

Let me start out by indicating that tension situations are, viewed from a basic perspective, not so complicated as they sometimes appear. International tensions, for example, seem incredibly complex when we try to understand the differences between Russia and the United States, between the United States and Cuba, or between the Arabs and the Jews. It seems even more difficult to try to understand the problems and tensions which exist between the government of South Africa and the Bantus. We find ourselves involved in national, racial, economic, historical, and other factors. We see the same complexity when we look at the tensions between Negroes and whites in the United States at the present time. Yet, psychologically, there is a great deal of similarity among all these widely divergent and highly complex tensions. I would like to suggest a very simple pattern or model which, from a psychological perspective, would encompass almost all tensions—whether interpersonal, marital, interracial, intergroup, or international.

If you will examine almost any tension situation, I believe that you will find that it is based on the following fundamental statements which are held with conviction and belief by the parties involved in the tension. In their simplest form, the two statements are: "I am right and you are wrong"; "I am good and you are bad." The aspect which we frequently fail to realize is that these statements are usually held with real conviction by each of the two opposing parties in the situation. What creates tension is the head-on collision between these two sets of irreconcilable attitudes and beliefs.

It is very hard for us as fallible human beings to recognize that the conviction and certitude which we feel about our own rightness and our own goodness in any given tension situation is usually equaled by the certitude of our opponent's conviction that *he* is the one who is right and good. Consequently, where such a situation of opposing beliefs exists, we have all of the ingredients for a deep and continuing tension, whether we are talking about the differences between a man and his wife or differences between the Communist world and the Western world.

What I am saying is that any of the tension situations about which we are concerned boils down to an essentially simple psychological pattern, in which almost identical attitudes are held by the two parties. It may help if you think of one or two real situations of difference and stress and tension—perhaps the violent marital discord of some couple you know, and a sharp international disagreement of which you have some knowledge. Now think of these actual differences in terms of the pattern I have just described. Does not each party hold to the belief that "I am correct and accurate and sound in my view of the situation, my perception of its elements, my interpretation of its meaning"? "My view is the right and true one. You are unfortunately mistaken and inaccurate in your view of the situation and in your analysis of what it means. Your view is false and wrong, yet you stubbornly hold to it." Again I would ask whether these actual tension situations you are considering do not also contain the following element of further value judgment. "I am honest and straightforward and fundamentally good in my approach to our relationship and its problems. Unfortunately, you are none of these things. You are essentially bad and evil and untrustworthy in your approach to the whole situation. My motives are good. Yours are not." I wonder whether you will not agree with me that these views, held in essentially identical fashion by each party to the dispute, characterize almost every serious tension situation, whether between individuals, groups, or nations.

NEW KNOWLEDGE FOR DEALING WITH TENSION

Are such situations essentially hopeless? Must we helplessly stand by to wait and see whether the conflict inexplicably dies down or whether the two parties engage in attempts at mutual destruction? My answer is a strongly negative one. The theme of my remarks is that the young and relatively unrecognized behavioral sciences have a beginning knowledge of how to cope with such mutual antagonism, conflict, and distrust, but that little attention is being paid to this knowledge. Let me see whether I can state in very brief form the kinds of knowledge which are available—knowledge which certainly needs to be expanded, verified, and modified but, above all, needs to be applied and used.

In the first place, we have a very considerable knowledge of how to deal with conflict and tension *within* the individual. The whole field of psychotherapy is concerned with tensions very similar to those which I have described. The individual who comes for therapy feels that there is within him this decent and reasonable self which is at war with vague, bad, false, wrong forces underneath the surface which he cannot understand. He feels there is real danger that these forces may overwhelm his known, proper outward self. Therapy is an attempt to help the individual reconcile these opposing forces. What we have learned in dealing with these inner tensions has a great deal of relevance for the intergroup and international tensions which plague the world.

In the second place, we have some knowledge of how to deal with deep, individual, face-to-face tensions between two people. If I as a psychologist am asked to deal with a crucial tension situation in which two individuals are shouting at each other, expressing differences which seem fundamental and extreme, I have a basic knowledge of how to deal with that situation in a way that has a high probability of reducing the tension. I cannot guarantee success, but there is knowledge available to me both in practice and in research which would make the likelihood of my being effective in the situation very considerable.

There is knowledge available on how to deal with tensions between two small groups. If, for example, there are two small groups deeply antagonistic to each other (in which the individuals are speaking for themselves, not as representatives of some other constituency), I as a behavioral scientist would have available to me a body of knowledge and experience which would make it quite probable that I could deal with this situation in a way in which tensions would be reduced and conflict very possibly resolved.

Let me indicate another area of practical knowledge in dealing with psychological tensions. We know how to create deeply harmonious relationships in a group of very diverse individuals. If a number of persons with divergent attitudes, opinions, beliefs, and convictions is willing to devote as much as two intensive weeks of meeting together, and if a facilitator trained in group dynamics and group process is available to these people, then I can say with considerable assurance that by the end of the two weeks the individuals will feel that they are in meaningful communication with one another, that they will be finding the interpersonal relationships significant, that they will have developed a much greater degree of trust in the other individuals in the group, that they will be experiencing a real harmony together, and that they will regard the whole experience as extremely valuable.

Still another very new area of knowledge in the behavioral sciences has to do with simulated national groups. If small groups are formed and each one is made into a "nation" with its own resources, military forces, economic strengths and weaknesses, its own history of allies and enemies, experimentation can be done on "international" tensions. It has been found that in these simulated international situations, which become very real to the participants, certain "international" strategies lead to a reduction of tension and others to a heightening of tension and eventual "war." Such experiments are in their beginning. Nevertheless, they represent a hopeful source of new knowledge which almost certainly will develop with further experimentation and research.

This is a condensed overview of some of the knowledge available in the behavioral sciences for dealing with tension—tension which ranges from conflicts existing within an individual to tensions which exist between nations. I would like now to take each of the five areas of knowledge I have indicated and spell out in somewhat more detail the meaning of the statements I have just made.

REDUCTION OF INDIVIDUAL TENSIONS

Let me speak first about tensions internal to the individual. One of the most common problems with which, as a psychotherapist, I deal is the individual who is at war within himself. As he so frequently tells me, outwardly he is an acceptable person, able to make a living, awarded some degree of recognition by the world. But he feels inwardly that he is a fraud—worthless, incompetent, full of bad impulses and evil intentions. His strongest feeling is, "If people ever come to know me as I really *am*, they would completely reject me."

As a therapist, I have learned to accept each of these flatly contradictory perceptions and feelings. My pattern of response often is, "You see yourself as worthy, effective, and normal; and yet, at the same time, you feel that you are unworthy, bad, incompetent, abnormal." When he discovers that, unlike most others he has known, I have no desire to convince him of one perception or the other, he feels much more free of threat and can begin to explore his attitudes and experiences much more fully—the specific ways in which he feels worthwhile and the elements which make him feel unworthy. I think of one young man who, in this exploration, talked more and more about the fact that he just "went blank" at crucial points: his mind failed to function; he became confused and almost disoriented; he flubbed important examinations; and he was unable to carry out important duties. I was unable to see why this seemed to him such conclusive evidence of a bad and evil aspect of his nature until he expressed more and more of his relationship to his father and to others in authority. Finally, I ventured tentatively, "I wonder whether what you are telling me is that you have, through this 'blankness,' found a surefire way of defeating all of those who want to control you and mold you into the image they have fashioned for you?" After a moment of silence in which he seemed to be digesting this, he broke into wildly uncontrollable laughter, which was very embarrassing to him—and, I admit, very puzzling to me. Then haltingly, and with some feeling of shame, he recognized that not only were my statements accurate but that the wild laughter was a full experiencing, for the first time in his life, of the glee he had felt in defeating his father and everyone else through these outwardly distressing periods of "blankness."

Following this, in subsequent interviews, came the slower and more difficult recognition that these two parts of himself could each be accepted, that they could live comfortably in one person, that they were not fundamentally incompatible. He began to see that it was not true that one part of him was bad, another part good; one part right, and one wrong. More specifically, he came to realize that he could work openly for approval of others and could strive for recognition but that he could also resist control by others, that he could do what *he* wished and not simply what others expected or demanded of him. The two elements of his emotional life, which had seemed so incompatible that they were not even in touch with each other, were experienced now as being elements which could perhaps live comfortably within one person.

We know a great deal about this kind of change within the individual. Recent research enables us to define and measure certain attitudes within the therapist which facilitate such a resolution of tension (Rogers, 1962). Other studies have given us both a theoretical picture of the process by which such change comes about and empirical evidence of such a process and its relationship to improved adjustment [Rogers, 1961 (b)]. With a great deal more certainty than would have been possible a decade or two ago, we can specify the psychological conditions which will enable a conflicted person to change and the process he will go through in changing. We have, in other words, a body of reasonably solid knowledge about the constructive reduction of tension situations which exist within the individual. We know that when the individual is able to confront such internal tension, this process can lead to a higher level of psychological integration [Rogers, 1961 (a)]. We have developed a considerable empirical skill in bringing about this process.

TENSION BETWEEN INDIVIDUALS

If we turn to discord which exists between two individuals, we may seem a bit closer to the interests of those whose focus is on international relationships. How is it possible to meet such a tension situation in a constructive way? Here again most of our knowledge comes from practice and research in the field of counseling and psychotherapy, and you will find many parallels to what I have been saying about conflicts *within* the individual.

When two persons are in serious discord, whether we are speaking of a discordant marital relationship, friction between an employer and an employee, a formal and icy dispute between two diplomats, or tension growing out of some other base, we tend to find certain very common elements.

1. The attitudes and beliefs are those of the model I described earlier; and they are rigidly, not tentatively, held. In such a dispute there is no doubt at all but that I am right and you are wrong. I am on the side of the angels, and you belong with the forces of darkness.

2. There is a breakdown of communication. You do not hear what I say, in any understanding way; and I am unwilling and unable to hear what you are really saying. As Rapaport says: "The futility of most debates as means of modifying outlooks can be traced to the unwillingness or inability of the opponents to listen to one another" (1960, p. 289).

3. There are distortions in perception. The evidence which is taken in by my senses—your words, your actions, your responses to my words and actions—is trimmed and shaped by my needs to fit the views of you which I already hold. Evidence which is clearly and openly contradictory to my rigidly held views is conveniently ignored or made acceptable by being grossly distorted. Thus a real gesture toward reconciliation on your part can be perceived by me as only another deceitful trick.

4. Implicit in all this is the element of distrust. While whatever *I* do is obviously done with honorable intent, whatever *you* do is equally obviously done with an underlying evil intent, no matter how sweetly reasonable it may appear on the surface. Hence, from the perspective of each opponent, the whole relationship is shot through with suspicion and mistrust.

I believe I am correct in saying that in any serious two-person dispute, these four elements are invariably present and often make the situation appear hopeless. Yet there are knowledge and skill available which can be applied to such a situation.

If there is to be progress in reducing this kind of tension, we have learned that the first necessity is a facilitative listener—a person who will listen empathically and will understand the attitudes of each disputant from his own point of view. When an individual feels that he is thoroughly accepted and thoroughly understood, he finds it less necessary to hold rigidly to his own beliefs and attitudes. Again, to use Rapaport's words, "Conveying assurance of understanding is the first step in the removal of threat" (1960, p. 291).

The next step in tension reduction is that the individual begins to explore his attitudes more fully, with less rigidity and less defensiveness. When he finds himself understood, there is a real release of tension and, following this, more searching of self and less distortion in attitudes. With this lessened tension the individual comes to explore aspects of his thinking which he has not fully investigated on a conscious level. He begins to bring into the picture elements which he has previously been reluctant to consider or has denied completely.

Gradually out of this exploration comes the development of an awareness of patterns and motives. This is the kind of thing which in therapy has been termed "insight." The individual comes to recognize that not all of his motives are those that he has proclaimed and that some of his attitudes and behaviors are not so fully justified as he has been maintaining to his opponent and to the world.

As this recognition of hitherto unsuspected motives and patterns develops, there is now a change in the perception of the situation. With the degree of relaxation of tension which has developed, each person in the dispute can come to recognize that the problem may be viewed in more than one way. This recognition that the previous convictions are perceptions and not facts is an extremely important element in change. As a matter of fact, the situation is nearly resolved when each party to the dispute can say, "I perceive the situation this way, and this seems right to me. You perceive the situation that way, and that seems right to you." Thus, a union official whose initial statement had been that "management people are a bunch of so-and-so's"—comes, through such a process, to change his attitude. First, his picture of the situation was, "We are right. Management is all wrong. The situation is impossible." After a few interviews he perceives the problem in new terms which could be summarized as follows: "Management has faults. We have faults. The only people who help are those who honestly face the reality of each dispute. That is very hard to do. I don't know whether it can be done." Note how radically the pattern has changed. No longer is he correct and good, his opponent mistaken and bad. There can be little question that this new conception of the problem is more realistic than the first and that the problem itself is more soluble when seen in these more accurate terms.

TENSION BETWEEN GROUPS

The behavioral scientist has learned that dealing with friction and antagonism between two groups involves very similar principles. To choose one example from many, Muench describes the way in which he dealt with an industry which had asked him for help. Labor-management relationships were extremely bad, and tension was high. He says: "Although many times both management and the union committee attempted to induce me into taking sides or acting as an arbitrator, I conceived of my role as a consultant attempting to get an impartial overview of current problems and possible leads toward their solution. Because tensions were so great and communication so meager between the opposing parties, I determined to approach each person and group with a relatively unstructured, open-ended, psychotherapeutic-type session in which primary concern was with crystallizing issues, pinpointing areas of difference, and recognizing the feelings and attitudes which colored every issue" (1960, p. 166).

As he thus listened with understanding, he found that the three primary difficulties were ineffective communication, mutual distrust, and differing perceptions of the same issue. For instance, the company saw itself as a firm believer in collective bargaining. The union saw the company as always having its mind definitely made up in advance, always certain it was right, and clearly unwilling to bargain. Muench began to modify these difficulties: first, by providing a model of empathic listening in his own behavior and by training both labor and management representatives in this attitude; and second, by reducing both mistrust and distorted perception through the better communication which emerged. The result was not a company without problems, but a company in which the attitudes and skills of genuine listening and real communication made problems soluble. The pattern of tension, of "right-good versus wrong-bad," had been sharply modified.

I think it is not too much to say that if any two groups are willing to be in the same room together, each willing to voice its beliefs, attitudes, and feelings toward the other, then a facilitator, skilled in the theory and practice of communication, can bring about a reduction in tension and a trend toward the resolution of problems.

It should be noted, however, that I am talking of groups in which the members are speaking for themselves. I believe much less progress has as yet been made in dealing with group tensions when the spokesmen of the two parties are not free to speak as individuals, but can present only the "line" to which they are previously committed by their constituents. Since many large industrial disputes and most international disputes are of this variety, this is a serious deficiency. Yet there is every reason to suppose that it, too, would yield to a concerted scientific attack.

THE T GROUP—AN INSTRUMENT FOR TENSION REDUCTION

I should like now to talk about a new development in the behavioral science field, one in which I am currently very much interested. It is an extremely potent way of bringing about close, honest, deep, positive human relationships; and yet the means of achieving this goal appear so simple that unless you have had such an experience you are not likely to believe what I am about to say. I am speaking of the phenomenon variously known as the unstructured workshop, the "T" group, the "basic encounter" group. Let me describe one instance from my own recent experience.

A group of business executives was brought together for a week-long conference on leadership. As a large part of the program, they were scheduled to spend 30 hours of the week in continuing groups of 12 to 15 members. I was the facilitator of one such group. I said very simply at the outset that we could use this group for any purpose we wished, that there was absolutely no agenda. One might suppose that with such an opening, one group might discuss business, another golf, another devote itself to telling dirty stories. But the amazing thing is that, given this kind of freedom, safety, and permission, such a group tends, I believe, almost invariably to devote itself to exploring its own current interpersonal relationships, to getting to know one another more deeply and vitally in the here-and-now. To be sure, there is an uncertain milling about at first, and in this particular group I found myself responding to and accepting the attitudes of uncertainty and uneasiness which occurred. But then feelings began to emerge —feelings of veiled criticism toward some member of the group, feelings of dissatisfaction with self. Gradually, the experience acquired a dynamics and a motive power of its own; and my own part in the group became much less that of a leader and more that of a participant. Where at first it seemed impossible that we could profitably spend five or six hours a day together, now the meetings seemed too short. Where feelings first were veiled, now they were out in the open. Sharp hostilities between members developed and were expressed. Warmly sensitive and tender reactions, quite unlike those of everyday life, were also expressed. The most accurately descriptive term is that the relationships became *real*—and hence meaningful. It was most impressive that as time went on, the group found it unbearable that any member should live behind a mask, a façade. The polite words, the intellectual understanding of one another and of the relationships, the smooth coin of tact and cover-up—amply satisfactory for interactions outside—were not good enough. Gently at times, almost savagely at others, the group *demanded* that the individual be himself, that his feelings not be hidden, that he remove the mask of ordinary social intercourse. Does this sound turbulent and upsetting? It definitely was. Yet through it there developed a silken bond of reality-to-relationship which bound us closer than we had ever been before. Individuals developed ability to understand one another—not politely, but in depth, sensing the pain and the hopes and the struggles of the other. They came to appreciate the other person—not the pseudoappreciation of "I value you when you behave in ways that I approve," but the real appreciation of "I value you as you *are*, with your likes and your dislikes, your virtues and your faults, your strengths and your weaknesses."

I am sure you must feel that I exaggerate. Let me quote from a letter from a workshop member written one month after the conference (Gilbreath, 1963). He speaks of the difficult and depressing circumstances he has met during that month and adds, "I have come to the conclusion that my experiences with you have profoundly affected me and I am truly grateful. This is different from personal therapy. None of you *had* to care about me, none of you needed to seek me out and let me know of things you thought would help me, none of you *had* to let me know that I was of help to you—yet you did, and as a result, it has far more meaning than anything else I have so far experienced. When I feel the need to hold back and not live spontaneously, for whatever reason, I remember that 12 persons just like those before me now said to let go and be congruent, to be myself and, of all unbelievable things, they even loved me more for it. This has given me the *courage* to come out of myself many times since then. Often, it seems, my very doing of this helps the others to experience similar freedom."

Lest you think such reactions represent a peculiarly American overenthusiasm, let me quote from the report of a member of a similar workshop conducted in Australia. He speaks of "the pace and quality of movement, movement into relationship, depth of involvement, expression of feelings and meanings related to other individuals in the group, heightened sensitivity to other group members, to what was happening in the group as a whole, and to the multiple personal relationship evolving within it" (Barrett-Lennard, 1963).

At greater length, a member of a workship in Great Britian (called a Study Group there) describes something of what occurred in her group. She tells of how they came to know the many facets of each individual. "The funny man revealed his tragedy; the conventional one, his originality. . . . Everyone, I think, suffered a sea change into something rich and strange" (Rioch, unpublished paper). She speaks of the depth of expression. "The themes which ran through the group discussions were the most important ones imaginable: the individual and the community; dependency and autonomy; loneliness and shared experience; riotous impulse and responsibility; love and hate; birth, death, and rebirth. These themes were not discussed in an intellectual way; we experienced them and expressed what we experienced" (Rioch, unpublished paper). She sums up: "In the Study Group, most of us felt at first very strong conflict between ourselves as individuals and the strangers who constituted the group. Or, one might say that we felt a strong sense of isolation, alienation, and unease in the group. But as time went on, it became clearer and clearer that in seeking ourselves, our own interest, our own individual identity, we found it more and more in the interrelationships of the group and not—to steal a phrase from Alan Watts—in a 'skin-encapsulated ego' . . . I do not mean that this experience liberated us once and for all from the conflicts of our individual claims versus the world outside us. But it did give a glimpse of what such liberation could be like" (Rioch, unpublished paper).

You may well be asking what all this has to do with worldwide tensions. Of what significance is it that psychologists and psychiatrists have learned the simple conditions which cause a group of people to develop *real* relationships with one another—communicative relationships with both positive and negative feelings in them, but with a closeness of personal regard rarely seen in our modern world?

The reason for my stress on this recent discovery—and I think it is important enough to be labeled that—is that I believe these essentially simple conditions release and make evident man's deep hunger to be at one and the same time deeply and uniquely himself and deeply in relationship with another. Martin Buber has put this very well indeed. "Man wishes to be confirmed in his being by man, and wishes to have a presence in the being of the other . . . secretly and bashfully he watches for a YES which allows him to be and which can come to him only from one human person to another" (1957, p. 104). We have learned how to set up a group experience which allows the individual to *be* and to have a presence in the being of another. It is upon this hunger and this need that we must and can rely in the constructive resolution of interpersonal as well as international tensions.

INTERNATION SIMULATION

If we turn our attention away from the individual and the small group, we may well ask, What does behavioral science have to contribute to an understanding of procedures which would reduce tensions in international situations? Here an exciting experimental study conducted by Crow and Solomon at the Western Behavioral Sciences Institute in La Jolla (Crow and Solomon, 1963; Solomon, 1963) gives us a clue to the answers. In a new type of procedure called "internation simulation," originally developed by Dr. Harold Guetzkow, five sovereign "nations" were initiated, each composed of three persons—a central decision maker or chief of state, a secretary of defense, and a secretary of state. Each of these "nations" was informed of its own resources, its military forces, and its economic and other problems, especially in relation to one another. In a development which was distressingly parallel to the real world, the tensions increased among the five nations to a point where explosive nuclear conflict seemed very likely. The tensions became so real that members could not sleep at night, so busy were they in thinking up ways to defeat their enemies. At this point, the chief of state of one of the "nations" was secretly instructed to utilize the strategy suggested by Charles Osgood (1962), a psychologist, for graduated reciprocation in tension reduction, otherwise known as GRIT. He announced publicly to the "world" that he was embarking on a "march to peace," in which he would take steps especially designed to reduce world tension. His country would announce these steps before they were taken and the date on which they would be taken. True to his word, he began a series of preannounced steps in the diplomatic, economic, military, cultural, and scientific areas. He started with low-risk moves in each of these areas, granting some small concession such as making exchange of students freely possible. Then, as tension appeared to be subsiding, he cautiously moved to steps which involved more risk, such as closing an overseas military base, with enemy inspection to confirm that the base had indeed been closed. His actions along these lines stirred distrust and suspicion both in his own colleagues and in the other nations of the "world." Both the members of his own "nation" and his allies became very greatly disturbed and said that this "march toward peace" must be modified. The leader found that he did indeed have to have fortitude to carry out the policy of GRIT. Nevertheless, as time went on, the "enemy" countries gradually realized that to keep "world" support and to maintain the satisfaction of their own people, they must reciprocate. Their distrust of his various actions slowly decreased. Consequently, a series of reciprocal tension-reducing actions occurred in the "enemy" countries. At this point, the research had to be terminated for lack of time.

Without giving undue importance to this beginning research on an important matter, the study has shown that national problems can be simulated on a small and laboratory scale, that the participants can become deeply and emotionally involved, that different strategies produce very different reactions in other "countries," and that there are some strategies already developed which seem definitely to reduce "world" tensions. This is an exceedingly hopeful development, and it will, I trust, be followed by a whole series of experiments patterned along similar lines.

Your reaction to this experiment may well be one of scorn. How can we learn anything from "nations" composed of three persons, in an artificial setting? Yet we all applaud the U.S. Corps of Engineers when, at very considerable cost, it constructs miniature replicas of portions of the Mississippi River. On a small scale, in a laboratory setting, it can study ways of dealing with this monarch of the waters in its alternate moods of raging, destructive torrent or apathetic, useless trickle. It can construct levees, dams, jetties, underwater wing dams to control and deepen the channel. It can try out flood conditions and drought conditions. On the basis of experience with the model, millions upon millions of dollars have been invested in changing the river into a well-behaved channel of commerce and usefulness. Should we not be willing to invest at least an equal amount of laboratory experimentation on a problem which has far more potential for destruction and for good?

I have, I hope, indicated that the behavioral sciences have made significant beginnings in practice, theory, and research having to do with the reduction of psychological tensions. Such knowledge is spotty and incomplete. It has serious gaps. Yet it is a beginning.

The point which appalls me, however, is that there is no concerted effort to exploit, develop, and utilize such knowledge. I suspect this is due to the fact that the behavioral sciences have not yet gained the status and prestige of the physical sciences, and hence have not yet earned the confidence of the people, of organizations and agencies, and of the government.

Let me remind you of two analogies which might point the way to a sound course of action. During the war, when it became possible to create synthetic rubber in a test tube, millions of dollars and an army of talent were turned loose on the problem of using that finding, of developing it into a practical, economical procedure. Also, when the splitting of the atom was hardly more than a laboratory theory, the vast Manhattan Project was initiated to take this basic knowledge and turn it into the incredible enterprise which created the atomic bomb.

Does it not seem reasonable that our beginning knowledge of tension reduction between people and groups should be similarly enlarged and developed? Here we have one of the most crucial problems of the world today—and we are making no organized attempt to enlarge our knowledge of how to deal with it.

A PROPOSAL

I would like to present a tentative proposal. It would begin with a recognition that the tensions, frictions, antagonisms which divide individuals, groups, and nations constitute a truly explosive situation which may mean disaster for our civilization. To meet this urgent need, a task force should be organized of individuals whose knowledge would contribute to the solution of the problem. This would include psychologists and psychiatrists skilled in group and individual therapy, workers in the field of group dynamics, sociologists and anthropologists, political scientists, experimental psychologists—a complete interdisciplinary team chosen for their research and practical skills. They would be given support adequate to the importance of the problem. They would be charged with the task of developing the basic theory, the laboratory and applied research, the pilot demonstrations—all having to do with the resolution of psychological tensions. They would be asked to serve as consultants to the diplomats of the State Department, to the Peace Corps, to the agencies administering foreign aid, to the various governmental and private agencies dealing with racial tensions. They would thus be involved not only in theory and basic research but in the application of any available knowledge to the practical resolution of existing tensions and the improvement of communication in human relationships. The organization of such a task force does not seem to me an impossible dream, and the importance of its payoff cannot be exaggerated.

Such a program could provide a channel by which our infant scientific knowledge in this area could develop into a flood of know-how. It would provide, it seems to me, the greatest possibility that we might be able to deal constructively with the vast tensions which the world culture can no longer afford—the strife between races, the disputes between labor and management, the cold wars of tension between nations. It would take only a comparatively small amount of money, of effort, to set such an enterprise in motion. The question is, Will we choose to undertake it?

REFERENCES

Barrett-Lennard, G. T.   Personal correspondence with author. July 1963.

Buber, M.   Distance and relation. *Psychiatry,* 1957, **20,** 104.

Crow, W. J., and L. N. Solomon.   A simulation study of strategic doctrines. La Jolla: *Western Behavioral Sciences Institute Reports,* 1963.

Gilbreath, S.   Personal communication. 1963.

Muench, G. A.   A clinical psychologist's treatment of labor-management conflicts. *Personnel Psychol.,* Summer 1960, **13,** 165–72.

Osgood, C. E.   *An alternative to war or surrender.* Urbana: University of Illinois Press, 1962.

Rapaport, A.   *Fights, games and debates.* Ann Arbor: The University of Michigan Press, 1960.

Rioch, M. J. The Leicester conference. Unpublished paper, 1963.

Rogers, C. R. *On becoming a person*. Boston: Houghton Mifflin, 1961, Chapter 18, "A tentative formulation of a general law of interpersonal relationships." (a)

Rogers, C. R. The process equation of psychotherapy. *Amer. J. Psychother.*, 1961, **15**, 27–45. (b)

Rogers, C. R. The interpersonal relationship: The core of guidance. *Harv. Educ. Review*, Fall 1962, **32**, 416–29.

Solomon, L. N. Reducing tensions in a test-tube world. *War/peace report*, July 1963, **3**, 7, 10–12.

Task group therapy: Goals and the client system[1*]

James V. Clark

My practice as a consultant has brought me into intimate contact with many groups of organizationally related people struggling to improve their relations to one another and to their tasks. Being allowed to help them in this process is not only a considerable privilege, it is immensely stimulating and exciting. And one of the things it stimulates most is my desire to understand the process better so that I can help in it more. Moreover, the process itself is becoming so widespread that we are suddenly confronted with the necessity of training many more practitioners more quickly than we could have dreamed of even a few years ago.

The processes of social and organizational change and consultation are enormously complex. These processes have to do with job and organizational design, with attempting to correlate the requirements of the external environment to the internal organization, and so on. But my focus in this paper, as my focus as a practitioner, is on what happens within and between people who work together that facilitates more fully functioning behavior in themselves and in their groups.

For the purposes of identification I call this aspect of organizational change "task group therapy." While I realize it has some drawbacks as a label, I find

---

[1] An earlier version of this paper was presented at the "Existentialism and Group Process" workshop at the 1966 meeting of the Los Angeles Group Psychotherapy Association.

* Used by permission of the author. Footnotes deleted.

that it has some utility in sharpening attention on an aspect of practice that is often overlooked and misunderstood.

My first plunge into this area was in 1959 when I joined with several of my colleagues at the Harvard Business School (Professors Barnes, Lawrence, Katz, Orth and Seiler) on a project involving a large team of engineers, designers and draftsmen in a machinery manufacturing corporation. We might have been less nervous had we been as aware as we could have been that others had preceeded us. In fact, UCLA's Human Relations Research Group had described just such an effort in a 1955 *Harvard Business Review* article. Moreover, this group had conceptualized it even earlier, in a 1954 article for *Personnel.* Of course, others were starting to work in the same area—Shepard and Blake at ESSO, Beckhard and others. And Argyris was soon to start his extensive researches in the area.

All of these people were beginning to use T group and sensitivity training types of procedures with groups of employees who had everyday relationships with each other. Of course, the idea caught hold; practice proliferated and widely varying concepts and methods developed. This paper, however, will not summarize them.

BACKGROUND

There are three major changes in psychology and psychotherapy which are of critical importance for the practice of task group therapy.

The first of these, and perhaps the most fundamental, is the shift from the Freudian conception of man to the "Maslovian," a shift which focuses attention on man's capacities to be fully functioning. This shift is profound. Rather than regarding man as basically little better than animal-like, it regards him as derivatively acting less than fully human. Such a reconception directs the therapist toward helping open up hidden forces of greatness and good rather than toward closing down on presumed forces of pettiness and evil. In this context, the therapist is a liberator, not one who simply helps "unbalanced" people to get "balanced" again.

The second major shift is away from interpretive therapies and toward experiential ones. Here the work of Perls focusing on the here and now, and of Rogers focusing on the behavior of the psychotherapist were of fundamental importance. The work of Jourard and of Culbert is relevant in this regard in that the importance of therapists continuing and sharing their growth with their patients is underscored. Research at UCLA on personality change in sensitivity training groups shows consistently that individual changes of members is strongly determined by the therapeutic behavior they experience in one another, regardless even of whether they experience those behaviors in the official group leader. This whole trend of research and thinking suggests to the task group therapist that it is not primarily his accurate and perceptive insights but rather the qualities of being fully human, as expressed by himself and members of his group, that determine individual changes in groups. This recognition opens up the immensely optimistic possibility that therapeutic growth processes do not require an educated "pregrown" therapist in order to occur. They can be stimulated to occur between normal, untrained human beings expressing normal human capacities for genuineness, listening and regard.

Thus the art of therapy (the "therapeuti" were an ancient Egyptian group who practiced *healing*) is something all can be helped to practice. "Therapy," therefore, has two meanings in the phrase "task group therapy;" the outside therapist or consultant helps the task group members to become more therapeutic.

The third major change has to do with reconceiving psychotherapy as a social process. The prevailing model of the psychotherapeutic process was, until recently, that psychotherapy was a "one-person phenomenon, nonsocial, though influenced by an external agent, the psychoanalyst." It is only recently that a great surge of interest has arisen in an alternative conception, "that the psychotherapeutic process can be viewed as a two-or-more person, true social phenomenon." Because individual psychoanalysis came first and because Freud and his early followers were so seminal and impactful, many have tended to assume that individual psychotherapy, and particularly psychoanalysis, was *deeper* than other kinds of therapy.

This assumption is more "up for grabs" at the present time than ever before. For one thing, the whole concept of depth is being looked at; Levy, in his exhaustive analysis of psychological interpretation has stated that it "has only one defensible meaning: the complexity of the *inferential* link between the event and our statements about it." He states further that the concept of depth is most typically invoked to "account for any discrepancy between the patient's accounting for his situation and the therapist's.

The most ferment in this area is going on at the level of practice, however. As Haley says, in a charming and insightful paper the shift to family therapy has largely been underground for two reasons, "those using this method have been too uncertain about their techniques and results to commit themselves to print (therapists of individuals have not let this dissuade them) and there has apparently been a fear of charges of heresy because the influence of family members has been considered irrelevant to the nature and cure of psychopathology in a patient." Haley points out that the family therapist, on the other hand, argues that "psychopathology in the individual is a product of the way he deals with intimate relations, they way they deal with him, and the way other family members involve him in their relations with each other. Further, the appearance of symptomatic behavior in an individual is necessary for continued functioning of a particular family system. Therefore, changes in the individual can only occur if the family system changes." As Haley observes, psychoanalysis has always maintained that the function of symptoms is to maintain an *intra*psychic balance and that from that point of view, family relations are peripheral to the problems psychotherapy must resolve. He says that "the argument that the symptoms of an individual maintain the balance of his *family* system rather than maintain a balance of intrapsychic forces is a . . . major change in psychiatric thinking." He concludes that what makes both individual and family therapy successful is to be discovered at the level of similarities in behavior between the two-person social system called individual therapy and the three-or-more person social system called family therapy.

This conceptual shift has been discussed by a growing number of writers. For example, Parloff observes that psychiatric emphasis in general is moving in ever-widening circles away from the individual: from the intrapsychic structure of the individual to the relationship between patient and parent to the family as a subcultural unit and to the total cultural context. And, in an enlightening book, the British psychoanalyst R. D. Laing says that the extension of psychiatric thinking to a whole "nexus" of self and other selves and of the interaction between those selves "reflects one of the most significant theoretical and methodological developments in the psychiatry of the last two decades. Over this period, there has been growing dissatisfaction with any theory or study of the individual which artificially isolates him from the context of his life, interpersonal and social. The inadequacy of what we might call *monadic* psychology has become increasingly apparent."

So, from this standpoint, the task group therapist can see that his client is a system of people and that it is this *system* that he is trying to help change. His immediate outcomes then are not necessarily individual changes. As a practical matter, he often can't stay around that long. He is trying to change what happens *between* people so that after he leaves, individual growth will continue as an outcome of new kinds of social transactions.

This paper attempts to integrate these three major revisions in psychological thought with the practice of task group therapy. The form of that integration is probably already apparent. The way I view it, task group therapy (or any natural group therapy) is an effort to release man's potential for being more fully human through changing his social systems in such a way that the therapeutic, growth-producing behaviors of confrontation, genuineness, listening and regard for others are allowed to be expressed and experienced. This paper is essentially an elaboration on that view.

In summary, then, it has been useful to me to identify task group therapy as a subfield and to place that subfield in relationship to the other natural group therapies such as family therapy and therapeutic community therapy and to the emerging field of organizational change. That is, task group therapy is a field whose tendrils engage contemporary psychology, psychiatry, conjoint family therapy, family theory, religious philosophy (Martin Buber is frequently quoted by natural group therapists of many persuasions) and organizational change practice just as early T-group conceptualization was rooted in the social psychological and educational theory and practice that were contemporary to it (and which are still relevant and important).

At the outset, however, let me say that the ways in which task group therapy does and will manifest itself as a field are not fixed at the present time. It may produce a set of concepts and practices that highlight aspects of the more usual organizational interventions or it may delineate a specific role for one member of an organizational development or "social architecture" team. In this regard Trist has already stated the necessity for self-actualizing behaviors on the part of individuals working on the critical "metaproblems" of our newly emerging post-industrial society.

Therefore, as with any other field we may one day have task group therapy specialists as well as others who make use of task group therapy theory and technique in their own more general practice. For me personally, the most accurate statement I can make is that the role of the task group therapist is the way in which he works with the greatest sense of contribution, involvement and commitment.

In this paper I will spell out this approach as best I can at the present time, stating its goals, clients, methods, concepts of intervention, risks, and present and future uses.

GOALS

The goal of task group therapy is to help groups construct and maintain social and technical *systems* which support their members' expressing their *individual* authentic beings.

Many theologians and psychotherapeutic theorists, of course, are interested in man developing his capacities for faith, commitment, creativity, love and health. Perhaps, however, because of their deep seated commitment to the development of the individual, few such writers have concentrated on how social systems outside the therapist's office can be created to support such development. Indeed, one even hears the argument that social systems are inherently antithetical to man's highest functioning. But, as I have stated elsewhere, it is not one's membership in a group per se that determines individuation, it is one's membership in a special kind of group, one whose behavior, norms and values support individuation.

Even as clinical psychology and theology have often concentrated on individual development to the exclusion of social system, so have many organizational consultants, in their concentration on the characteristics of the system and on the role behaviors required by that system, often failed to see how the capacities of individuals to act autonomously, to choose and to relate are central to that system's functioning. It is my position, however, that the task group therapist needs to join with those who ask us to see the interrelations between the individual and his social system, to recognize even that the abstraction we call "personality" is hard indeed to extricate from social system: hard to isolate conceptually or in practice. Although having as his deepest value, man's search for authenticity, as Bugental has named it, the task group therapist has an intense concern with people's expression of that search in such a way that social and sociotechnical systems get created which accomplish valid social ends and support it.

On the other hand he invites his fellow management consultants to view such things as, for example the entrepreneurial function of the business, so neglected in management theory and education as Drucker has warned us, as an arena in which man must confront existential givens and be helped not to flee from his own faith, commitment and creativity. He sees such common symptoms as the endemic absense of effective goal setting and performance evaluation as involving resistances to the experiencing of existential guilt and loneliness. He is willing to help a group whose market position is deteriorating rapidly to look at why it pushes unwanted products at the public and to go into what it means to really *feel* and incorporate into one's awareness one's contingency, the fact that one's future is in the hands of unknown and unknowable forces and that not to encounter the uncertainties of the market place is often a way of pretending the world is more predictable than it is. Every kind of ineffective organizational behavior is likely to be made worse, or perhaps even caused, by groups and individuals functioning in a constricted manner. He, therefore, calls out to his colleagues to stop separating "personal growth" (or personal constriction) from "task work." Personal growth and task work are compartmentalized only to their mutual detriment. Each of the everyday activities of the work world—accounting, planning, goal setting, evaluating, scheduling and so on—is an opportunity to confront one's existence in a more fully functioning manner.

Therefore, the task group therapist agrees with that part of contemporary psychology that is saying that psychological depth is not the inferential depth of inherent evil and original sin, or even inherent homeostasis; it is the depth of *experiencing* in the everyday here and now the ways in which we both move toward and resist the awful and awesome potentialities in the world and in us. And this resistance, at work, expresses itself in the development of sociotechnical systems which do not maximize involvement, creativity, viability, adaptability, and so on and, as such, inhibit such work-oriented behavior as risk taking, control of quality and efficiency, long range planning, and so on.

The goal, then, the psychosocial goal, if you like, of task group therapy is to create effective sociotechnical systems which support the kind of human encounters in which there is greater likelihood that people's authentic beings will be expressed in relation to one another and their work. Parenthetically, it is interesting to speculate that this may be a somewhat less than exclusive goal of task group therapy in the future. As our society, supports more leisure and abundance, it may someday happen that our work will be the construction of noneconomic communities for the purpose of individuation. Already, institutions such as Esalen Institute at Big Sur, California, and nearly two dozen similar institutions elsewhere are springing up in this form and at least one large economic organization has abandoned profit maximization as a goal for the maximization of natural and human resources. But for the present, task group therapy is primarily concerned with work in formal organizations designed to accomplish some task, and I will now turn to a discussion of the typical problem the task group therapist encounters there.

THE CLIENT: SELF-DEFEATING TASK GROUPS

Behavior patterns

There are two kinds of behaviors I typically encounter when I actually enter a task group. One is avoidance. The members avoid each other around tasks they could do better together, usually maintaining that "group-think" or "management by committees" stifle "individuality." If individual members have been in such a group for a long time they often appear bored and sometimes even look a little sad. If pressed to name tasks they could do better together they either can't think of them or say that they tried that once a long time ago and it didn't work. (Around this kind of group it is particularly important to examine the organizational design variables before starting to work; it is possible they really should be in some other organizational configuration then the one they are in.)

If the group does meet together, it tends to show the characteristics of the other main type of group behavior I usually see. In fact, it is the more common. I call it "self-defeating." No matter what gets started in such groups at the individual or group level, inevitably and inexorably, the new behavior gets stopped. Once, while working with a self-defeating group, I realized I had just had a long, vivid fantasy of one of those adult toys that was on the market a few years ago, the square black box with a lid and a button, the pushing of which produced a whirring noise and a hand which came slowly up out of the opening lid and whose sole function was to press the button which returned the whole box to closed silence. It seemed to me then, and it still does, that this little box is the totem for self-defeating groups.

By the way, such groups do not always look the same. They do not always look deadly or tense, for example. The members may joke a lot, look jovial or even friendly. It may be that self-defeating behaviors are widely dispersed or limited to one man. They may be heavy ("Well, we tried that long ago before you were ever a department manager") or light ("Hey, that reminds me of a funny situation I saw on TV last night"). It may come from high ranking members never listening to or constantly interrupting low ranking ones. It may come in a variety of packages but the outcome is always the same, self-defeating task behavior. Effective work and creative growth do not occur.

Argyris's research has shown that this kind of behavior is rather more widespread than some of us might have thought. In nearly 300 top-level decision-making meetings involving companies of several different sizes and missions, his data showed that the executives were only rarely observed taking risks or experimenting with new ideas or feelings, helping others to be open or take risks, behaving in such a way as to support a norm of individuality and trust as well as mistrust, or expressing feelings, positive or negative. He also discovered that the same executive believed that the "effectiveness of decision-making activities depends on the degree of innovation, risk taking, flexibility and trust in the executive system." Thus the men talked and believed in a model for their own behavior which they hardly ever actually implemented. In the meetings few members risked disagreeing with the president, fewer still evidenced much sense of commitment to the plans they agreed to support, and the groups appeared to delay and avoid making joint decisions. In interviews after the meetings executives reported many feelings of discomfort concerning how little they knew about what their peers and superiors felt about them, about the time wasted in avoiding real decisions and in discussing unimportant issues and how careful the members were to say nothing which rocked the boat. In short, the data showed that most of the top level decision-making groups spent most of the time having rational appearing meetings which were in fact almost completely determined by the members' needs to suppress feelings. In this regard, Argyris also observed that the members of these groups were quite convinced that the expression of feelings was not relevant to work, inappropriate, and a waste of time.

The situations described by Argyris have been observed many times over by myself and others, and the societal norms concerning the suppression of feelings are well known. Before I read Argyris' description three years ago, however, I had supposed such behaviors characterized only groups who perceived themselves in serious trouble. What differentiates Argyris' groups from the ones I have worked with is not their behavior, however, but only the extent to which the members were aware of their behavior, or at least were aware of the pain they felt in such situations and were willing to undergo something as out of the ordinary as task group therapy to relieve that pain. Members may feel that pain personally ("I'm not getting anywhere and neither are any of the other men around here. We're all stuck in the glue.") or organizationally ("We aren't setting goals, making plans, developing new products or making money and we can't seem to really change."). Either way, when a task group therapist is brought in someone is either hurting or impatient about his growth and development, but the group's behavior usually shows much the same thing as seen in Argyris' groups.

Parenthetically, abnormal families (families that have one or more antisocial or seriously disturbed members) exhibit similar characteristics. They take much longer to make decisions, the family decisions are more often different from what the member's individually wanted and the members show a marked tendency to hold back self-revealing statements, and to remain silent and noncommittal.

In summary, I believe that the feelings of uncertainty encountered by anyone approaching the boundary line between what is familiar and what is strange will produce a pronounced increase in behavior which is designed to anchor him in structured relations with others. In other words, when his task is fairly well bounded, he can be relatively free and open with others but when his task is suddenly filled with uncertainties, he locks into highly structured and patterned relationships with others.

One sees these overstructured interpersonal behaviors often at the top of an organization wherever a top executive group must plan new paths and forsake old ones. Or in members of two separate departments (sales and engineering or research and development) who are suddenly required to relate in more effective ways than "us guys" versus "those guys." One will surely see it when metagroups, such as urban coalitions, regional pollution boards and the like bring together different organizations to solve overarching societal problems beyond the capacities of any one group to solve. Or in some organizational group suddenly required to invent or collaborate in executing some extraordinary organizational or institutional change. In short, any task group when facing change or the threat of change will tend to have an increase in "gamey" interpersonal behavior.

Typically, such structured and repetitive interpersonal behavior is either dominating or submissive, or more often both. An outsider in the presence of these behaviors experiences an oppressive sense of impotence and boredom as he watches people operating at one "speed" and in one style only, regardless of what the stimulus or situation is. One feels a great sense of constriction in one of these groups.

I first began to think about this several years ago when I was consulting with a firm that had great success in the response of its bench workers to increased opportunities for interaction, mutual influence and technical contribution but dismal failure in the response of its vice presidents to the same kind of opportunities. Product innovation was falling behind, costs were overly high, market position was receding, as were sales, and little if any long range planning or joint problem solving was going on in executive council meetings. There the president talked, analyzed and criticized, and the subordinates said as little as possible to him and next to nothing with one another. Since that time I have seen Argyris's observation that this kind of self-defeating behavior is much less frequent in groups working on fairly repetitive tasks, and I have seen the same thing myself. As I thought about these observations I recalled how apparently productive an average classroom is—no interpersonal trouble, polite and serious behavior, books get read, papers written, exams passed. And I contrasted this with what happens when the same teacher and the same students shift to a sensitivity training context. As Bion and many others have observed, the group promptly fills the leadership vacuum created by the staff member with pairing, fighting or withdrawal behaviors. People who appeared serious, mature and competent now appear flustered, upset, immature and incompetent. This analogy makes it clear that the average classroom, the average assembly job, and perhaps even the average middle management task are all wellbounded. To be told one has the freedom to build a total machine or instrument or to work on a given section of a coal seam without set procedures or to do some term project in a creative and innovative way, or whatever, is very different from learning one has the freedom to run a whole institution any way one wants and relate to subordinates any way one thinks best and plan for the future in any way one thinks necessary and settle on the direction one believes an entire organization should take in the future. In such situations, the interpersonal "games" or styles people have adapted over the years but which rarely cause "trouble" flourish. People flee from the anxious uncertainty of defining themselves in an unstructured world to the more soothing certainty of predictable interpersonal behavior. Put differently, an executive feels more comfortable (not necessarily the same as "pleasant") when he seeks to figure out what his boss wants all the time and is afraid to have any ideas of his own than when he confronts an unpredictable and incomprehensible situation; carves out a policy recommendation and set of actions to deal with it and offers his plan to the executive council with full willingness to accept responsibility for its failure. In short, the uncertainty of the task situation has caused the group members to turn their attention away from the task and to enter into all the kinds of structured and repetitive interpersonal behavior patterns which focus attention almost exclusively on one another instead.

Communication patterns. Because these repetitive interpersonal behavior patterns require the same responses to a variety of stimuli, the communication patterns found in such groups are characterized by a great deal of incongruence. That is, members are frequently observed saying one thing and behaving in such a way as to imply they are meaning something quite different. The shouted statement, "Goddamn it, I'm not mad, I'm only interested in the facts!" is frequently quoted as an example of an incongruent communication.

Tannenbaum's work on pluralistic ignorance among executives is relevant here. In informal surveys of hundreds of middle- and upper-level managers in training programs, he and others have found that approximately 70 percent of these managers report that they try to hide feelings of personal self-doubt and inadequacy from their colleagues at work. In a more detailed study of 50 executives in an advanced management class, he and his associates showed that the executives evidenced a significant error in estimating the extent of their fellow students' self assertiveness, social independence, feelings of self adequacy, emotional independence and sociability. These data certainly point to the existence of a widespread situation that would have to lead to incongruence; if nearly everybody feels inadequate at work, and nearly everybody assumes that nobody else does, suppression and denial of feelings and, therefore, incongruent speech must be rampant in executive discussions.

Argyris' research certainly shows that it is, although he labeled such speech "imbalance behavior." He describes such behavior by an example, "individual A would say to B, 'I believe in people having their say, but in this case, x is true. You're wrong and you'd better change your mind if you wish to succeed here.' . . . If B is to believe the plus-minus character of A's behavior it would communicate to him contradictory messages. On the one hand, it implies that A believes in individuality, yet he creates conditions of conformity for B." His findings show imbalance scores to account for around a third of all communication behavior in executive meetings, and that such scores significantly decrease during programs showing various degrees of what I call task group therapy.

It is clear that what Argyris calls imbalance communication behavior is similar to what the communication theorists at the Palo Alto Mental Research Institute have been calling the "double-bind" behavior they believe to be an important factor in the development of schizophrenia. That is, when a child grows up in a family whose communication patterns contain a great deal of double-binds, he is likely to exhibit schizophrenic behavior. One explication of this theory stated the following conditions as necessary in both the senders and receivers for a double-bind pattern to occur.

1) In a double-bind situation, a person is faced with a significant communication involving a pair of messages, of different level or logical type, which are related but incongruent with each other.

2) Any attempt to leave the field is blocked.

3) It is, therefore, important to respond adequately to the communication situation, which includes responding to its duality and contradiction.

4) An adequate response is difficult to achieve because of the concealment, denial, and inhibition inherent in or added to the basic contradictory pair of messages.

Two examples come to mind which will illustrate. In one, a mother is visiting her schizophrenic son in a mental hospital. They are in a visiting room together. The son, who appears physically comfortable, is wearing a short-sleeved sweater. The mother, looking warm to an observer, is wearing a wool suit. The window is closed. The mother says in a solicitous voice, "You look like you need fresh air, darling. Open the window." Now the son can surely see his mother looking warm and can feel that he himself is comfortable. Yet there is his mother telling him in an apparently kindly tone that he "needs fresh air." He doesn't move. She then says, angrily, "You're no better here than you were at home. You still don't see how much I love you." So, he is in a double-bind. If he does what he wants and leaves the window closed, his mother is angry at him for not understanding how much she "loves him." If he follows her orders, and acts against his own will, he will receive her approval for knowing that she loves him—an impossible situation to which he responds with a kind of cowering silence while his eyes dart around the room looking for escape.

Another example is from a recent group I was in. A young man newly promoted to management was told that he should feel free to call on his boss any time for help and instruction. When he did, he found two things consistently. Either the boss would forget the meeting or, if he remembered, would spend most of this time answering the telephone. The young subordinate did not feel helped and instructed. When he finally in task group therapy, summoned his courage to comment on this double-bind, and the feelings it engendered in him (he had "given up" and was losing interest in his work) the boss told him that he was imagining things, that he hadn't forgotten any meetings and still wanted to help the subordinate. The subordinate retreated, shaken, and was silent for several sessions.

Notice in both instances that the "real" problem occurred not solely because of the original double-bind, but because it is not considered legitimate to talk about it. In both examples, the authority figure effectively told the subordinates (the ones who cannot "leave the field") that they were simply imagining things and shouldn't feel or talk that way. It is this point that is the "final straw" of the double-bind. After all, double-binds—incongruent statements where people talk one way and look like they feel a different way—are commonplace. What produces the mentally disturbed child or the self-defeating group is not then the original double-bind alone but rather its reinforcement by another double-bind structure on a wider scale. In executive task groups, the widespread denial that feelings exist performs the same function; the system, that is, constantly denies its members the right to perceive or respond to the original double-bind messages which constitute such a large percentage of its behavior. (Recall that Argyris found that one third of all statements were "imbalance.")

In both these areas—self-defeating executive groups and disturbed families— the denial of feelings is seen clearly in the extent to which the power figures in each situation mask their difficulties from themselves and others. Argyris has shown that superiors constantly overestimate the trust and openness they afford subordinates and thus consistently underestimate the amount of confusion and negative feelings their subordinates have about them; and Lidz has stated that in disturbed families "considerable "masking" of potential sources of conflict occurred, creating an unreal atmosphere in which what was said and admitted differed from what was actually felt and admitted." These are all aspects of what Wynne has called "pseudo-mutuality" and he states that pseudoagreement is the method *par excellence* for driving a controversy underground and, as such, is particularly dangerous.

Functionality of incongruent communication.   Spoken of sociologically, each of these social systems develops a set of norms which govern "membership" in the system, and whose function it is to produce cohesion in that system. It is thus clear that congruent communication, in which the same feelings were expressed verbally and nonverbally in the same act, would be socially dysfunctional for such systems; it would produce the disequilibrium of open conflict. In fact, these norms demanding incongruent communications from members are so widespread in our society that any group of strangers coming together immediately behaves in terms of them. In this regard, Bobele and I have observed in our research on self awareness and natural therapeutic relationships that people who show measurably more congruent behavior at the beginning of a sensitivity training group of strangers are isolated by that group *permanently,* and hence never establish the natural therapeutic relationships our UCLA researches have shown correlate with changes in self awareness. In fact, such early deviants are the only people showing statistically significant *declines* in self awareness over the life of a group.

Another aspect of the function of incongruent behavior for the social system is at present only an interesting speculation, and that has to do with scapegoating. As has already been suggested in this essay, seriously disturbed children are becoming more and more to be seen as a function of the family system in which they live, a point made clearly in a lucid paper on "The Emotionally Disturbed Child as the Family Scapegoat" by Vogel and Bell. There they contend that disturbed spouses cover their deep fears about their marital relationship by joining together (unconsciously) around the production of a seriously disturbed child.

Looking back, I can recall one or more scapegoats in many task group therapy situations I have been in. In one group, for example, the scapegoating included two members of a seven-man group. It was noted, after several hours of task group therapy, that the president never critized four of his subordinates, but nearly always criticized the two others. The four never criticized the president, but frequently criticized the same two the president did. The two never criticized anyone, although they did not care for each other very much. Parenthetically, one had severe ulcerative colitis and the other a history of heart disease. One man rarely spoke at the beginning of task group therapy, and the other spoke in a very confusing and incongruent way, a way which often earned him the scorn and criticism of the president.

In another group of ten members one man in particular was scapegoated, but privately. In the group, no one spoke to him for a long time other than the task group therapist, and the executive in charge of the group admitted him to membership in the therapy program largely because of the therapist's urging. He showed, parenthetically, symptoms of chronic alcoholism and these symptons had become troublesome on the job, although no one had ever spoken to him about it. When he did speak in the early stages of the group, he was often confusing and incongruent. By the way, it is extremely difficult for the task group therapist not to get embedded in the same patterns as the group he is working with, and the mistake I made with these men was to get too angry at their incongruence too soon, thus damaging our relationship at the beginning.

One fact stands out around these scapegoats and their social function which interests me; when, in task group therapy, they were helped to express their feelings of anger and/or inadequacy and uncertainty, they generated a tremendous amount of affection. It was as if their cohesive function was multiplied rather than diminished during task group therapy as they became more congruent, and more capable of commenting on and responding to the double-binds they were placed in (more capable of "metacommunicating" as the Palo Alto communication theorists would say). In some cases, but not all, leaders showed a considerable amount of affection for the scapegoat, and in two cases came explicitly to the realization that they criticized the scapegoat for precisely the same behaviors they had come to realize were an important part of themselves. Clearly this whole issue of scapegoating, or of producing what the conjoint family therapists wisely call an "identified patient," merits much investigation in executive task groups.

SUMMARY

What we have seen so far in this section, then, is that self-defeating behavior characterizes those task groups facing the most uncertainty, that this behavior is self-defeating in terms of group members' needs both to relate in satisfying and necessary ways to their tasks and to each other, and that the double-binding incongruent communication patterns associated with them are strikingly similar to those observed in severely disturbed families.

Earning one's bread[*]

Studs Terkel

Why do people work?

To make money, of course. To survive the day. The razor of necessity cuts close. The job is often a chore, rarely a delight. To earn one's bread by the sweat of one's brow is the lot of mankind. So The Scriptures tell us. So the President echoes. So echo answers echo with a righteous and resounding Amen. No matter how demeaning the task, no matter how it dulls the senses and breaks the spirit, one *must* work—or else.

Lately, though, there has been a questioning of this "work ethic," especially by the young. Strangely enough, it has touched off profound grievances in others, hitherto silent and anonymous.

Unexpected precincts are being heard from in a show of discontent by blue collar and white. Communiques are alarming concerning absenteeism in auto plants. On the evening bus, the tense, pinched faces of young file clerks and elderly secretaries tell us more than we care to know. On the expressways, middle-management men pose without grace behind their wheels, as they flee city and job.

In all, there is more than a slight ache. And there dangles the impertinent question: Ought there not be another increment, earned though not yet received, to one's daily work—an acknowledgement of a man's *being?*

Steve Hamilton is a professional baseball player. At 37, he is near the end of his career as a pitcher for the San Francisco Giants. "A lot of us are popular

---

[*] Courtesy of Publishers-Hall Syndicate.

heroes. People recognize you on the street. I've never been a big star, I've done about as good as I can with the equipment I have. I played with Mickey Mantle and now I'm playing with Willie Mays. People always recognize them. But for someone to recognize me, it really made me feel good. I think everybody gets a kick out of feeling special."

Mike Fitzgerald was born the same year as Hamilton. He is a laborer in a steel mill. "I feel like the guys who built the Pyramids. Somebody built 'em. Somebody built the Empire State Building, too. There's hard work behind it. I would like to see a building, say the Empire State, with a foot-wide strip from top to bottom, and the name of every bricklayer on it, the name of every electrician. So when a guy walked by, he could take his son and say: 'See, that's me over there on the 45th floor. I put that steel beam in.' Picasso can point to a painting. I think I've done harder work than Picasso and what can I point to? Everybody should have something to point to.

"It's the nonrecognition by other people that gets you. Everybody says for a housewife to be called *just* a housewife is degrading. It is also degrading to be called *just* a laborer. The difference is that a man goes out and maybe gets smashed. I work so damn hard, I just want to come home and sit down and lay around. It isn't that the workingman is dumb. He's just tired, that's all.

"If my kid ever goes to college, I want him to have a little respect for those 'dumb somebodies,' to realize that his dad is one of those 'dumb somebodies.' This is why I work. Every time I see a young guy walk by with a shirt and tie and dressed up real sharp, I'm looking at my kid. That's it."

Sharon Atkins is a good twenty years older than Mike's kid. She's 24. She's been to college and acridly observes: "The first myth that blew up in my face is that a college education will get you a worthwhile job."

For the past two years, she's been a receptionist at an advertising agency. "I didn't look at myself as 'just a dumb broad' at the front desk, who took phone calls and messages. I thought I was something else. The office taught me differently." She was having a fairly intelligent discussion" with some clients, until they discovered the nature of her job. "Two of them just stopped the conversation and turned around to find other people with name tags. I wasn't worth bothering with, I wasn't rejected because of what I had to say or the way I talked, but simply because of my function.

I was being treated as just a piece of equipment, like the telephone. So I made up another name for my job—'communications control.'

"Just to fill in time at this boring job, I write letters to myself and to other people and never mail them. I call it the land of no-phone, where there is no machine telling me where I have to be every minute. This crummy little machine with buttons on it . . . You're just a little machine yourself. A monkey can do what I do.

"Until recently, I'd cry in the morning. I didn't want to get up. You tremble when you hear the first ring. After that, nothing. Unless there is somebody on the phone who is either very kind or very nasty. The rest are just non. They don't exist, they're just voices."

She experiences a single moment of triumph each day: at one minute to five. She turns off the machine.

Among her contemporaries, there is no such rejection: job and status have no meaning. Blue collar or white, teacher or cabbie, her friends judge her and themselves by their *beingness.* Nora Watson, a young journalist, recounts a party game: Who Are You? Older people respond with their job titles: I'm a copywriter. I'm an accountant. The young say: I'm me, my name is so-and-so. Frank Donner, a middle-aged journalist, observes: Older people *always* define themselves by their jobs, young people don't.

Harry Stallings, 27, is a spot welder on the assembly line at an auto plant. "They'll give better care to that machine than they will to you. You somehow get the feeling that that machine is better than you. You really begin to wonder. Look at the price they put on that machine. If it breaks down, there's somebody out there to fix it right away. If I break down, I'm just pushed over to the other side till another man takes my place. The only thing the company has in mind is to keep that line running. A man would be more eager to do a better job if he were given proper respect and the time to do it."

A farm equipment worker in Moline complains that the careless worker who turns out more that is bad is better regarded than the careful craftsman who turns out less that is good. The first is an ally of the Gross National Product. The other is a threat to the GNP, a kook—and the sooner he is penalized, the better.

Stallings keeps his own counsel. "I've been working three years for the company and have only 27 years to go until my pension." His laughter is without mirth. "I could maybe find a better place to work, but let's face it, where could I make the money I'm making? And this recession . . . Many young guys won't accept the stuff the old guys take. I can't blame the old guys. How would you feel if you had only two years to go till your pension?"

You would think that Ralph Grayson, a 25-year-old black, has it made. He supervises 20 people in the audit department of a large bank. Yet he is singularly discontented. He describes his job as watching other people. "You're like a foreman on an assembly line. Or like a technician sitting in a computer room watching the machinery. It's good for a person who enjoys that kind of job, who can dominate somebody else's life. I'm not too wrapped up in seeing a woman, 50 years old—white, incidentally—get thrown off her job because she can't cut it like the younger ones.

"I told my management she was a kind and gentle person. They said, 'We're not interested in your personal feelings. Document it up.' They look over my appraisal and say, 'We'll give her about five months to shape up or ship out.' People aren't treated as good as an IBM machine around here. I promised I'd never get myself an ulcer, so I'm looking around for something else."

It's too late for Geraldine Merton to look around for something else. Middle-aged, ailing, she works in a luggage factory. Though she is the union steward and quite militant in the matter of women's rights, she has been grievously hurt by members of her own sex.

"I attended a Governors' Conference on the status of women. Most of the others were teachers, social workers and nurses. When they found out what my job was, they were ice cold. I felt like I was a little piece of scum."

A bitter laugh erupts suddenly. "Don't they know how important I am? How could we employ teachers if it wasn't for the factory workers who manufacture the books they use—or the briefcases I make?"

The hunger persists, obstinately, for pride in a man's work. Conditions may be horrendous, tensions high and humiliations frequent, yet Paul Dietch finds his small triumphs. He drives his own truck, interstate, as a steel hauler. "Every load is a challenge. When I'm going to Hotpoint in Milwaukee, and I off-load, I have a feeling of having done a vital piece of work. It's not like putting a rivet in some machine, the end of which I'll never see. They're going to turn my steel into 10,000 washing machines, a hundred farm implements. I have problems in the morning with heartburn. I can't eat. Once I off-load, the pressure is gone. Then I can eat anything. I accomplished something."

Al Preston, a veteran car hiker, chuckles quietly. "The Cadillac owner will go around the car and I go around with him, lookin' for that scratch. It hurts my pride but I won't give him the satisfaction of showing it.

"I can drive any car like a baby, like a woman changes her baby's diapers. I could handle a car with one hand. Lot of customers would say: 'How you do this?' I'd say: 'Just the way you bake a cake, miss.' Oh, I'll admit it, the thrill is gone now. When I was younger, I could swing with that car. With one hand, I could back it all the way and whip it into that hole, with two inches to spare. They call me Lovin' Al, the Wizard. Now I'm older and tired and drive normal like everybody else."

Yolanda Leif graphically describes the trials of a waitress in a quality restaurant. They are compounded by her refusal to be demeaned. Yet pride in her skills helps her through the night.

"When I put the plate down, you don't hear a sound. When I pick up a glass, I want it to be just right. When someone says, 'How come you're just a waitress?' I say, 'Don't you think you deserve being served by me?' I feel like a ballerina when I move between the tables. I do it with an air. If I drop a fork, there's a certain way I pick it up, my way. I do it delicately. I spilled my tray once, with steaks for seven on it, a gigantic T-bone. When the tray fell, I moved with it, never made a sound. I like to have my station looking nice. I believe in pride and beauty."

Peggy Terry has her own sense of pride and beauty. Her jobs have varied with geography, climate and the ever-felt pinch of circumstance. "What I hated worst was being a waitress, the way you're treated. One guy said, 'You don't have to smile. I'm gonna give you a tip anyway.' I said, 'Keep it, I wasn't smiling for a tip.' Tipping should be done away with. It's like throwing a dog a bone. It makes you feel small."

Ballplayer. Laborer. Receptionist. Assembly line worker. Truck driver. Bank official. Car hiker. Waitress. What with the computer and all manner of automation, add scores of hundreds of new occupations and, thus, new heroes and anti-heroes to Walt Whitman's old anthem. The sound, though, is no longer melodious. The desperation is unquiet.

Perhaps Nora Watson has put her finger on it. She reflects on her father's work. He was a fundamentalist preacher, with whom she had been profoundly at odds.

"Whatever he was, he was. It was his calling, his vocation. He saw himself as a core resource of the community. He liked his work even though his family barely survived, because that was what he was supposed to be doing. His work was his life. He himself was not separate and apart from his calling. I think this is what all of us are looking for, a calling, not just a job. Most of us, like the assembly line worker, have jobs that are too small for our spirit. Jobs are just not big enough for people."

The most impertinent of all questions is asked *sotto voce*. More and more it surfaces in indiviudal lives, as an acquaintance suffers a breakdown, as another quits his "career" in middle age, as most quietly dissolve and are suddenly old. There is the fixed smile of the "retired" as against the fixed scowl of the man at work.

The common end appears to be a question mark.

What is there to show?

Does my job have any real meaning?

With technology, whether it be a wild horse or tamed, the questions transcend youth and age.

How to counter alienation in the plant*

Richard E. Walton

A plant where work teams perform without supervisors, where many decisions are based on employee consensus, and where most of the staff functions are assigned to line operators—in what future organization would such a phenomenon exist? Probably in most, because such radical innovations are part of the emerging answer to alienation in the workplace. Total, "systemic" restructuring of the way work is done is required to both meet the changing expectations of employees and increase productivity. Some companies, in fact, have already used this approach with considerable success—and they have the productivity and high morale to prove it. After analyzing the employee dissatisfaction that dictates the innovations recommended, lessons are drawn from a redesign effort implemented in a pet-food plant by a particularly forward-looking organization.

Managers don't need anyone to tell them that employee alienation exists. Terms such as "blue-collar blues" and "salaried drop-outs" are all too familiar. But are they willing to undertake the major innovations necessary for redesigning work organizations to deal effectively with the root causes of alienation? My purpose in this article is to urge them to do so, for two reasons:

1. The current alienation is not merely a phase that will pass in due time.

2. The innovations needed to correct the problem can simultaneously enhance the quality of work life (thereby lessening alienation) and improve productivity.

In the first part of the article, I shall risk covering terrain already familiar to some readers in order to establish that alienation is a basic, long-term, and mounting problem. Then I shall present some examples of the comprehensive redesign that I believe is required.

I also hope to provide today's managers with a glimpse at what may be the

* Harvard Business Review, Vol. 50. no. 6, November–December 1972. Copyright 1972 by the President and Fellows of Harvard College; all rights reserved.

Author's note: An earlier version of this article was prepared for the Work in America Project, sponsored by the Secretary of the Department of Health, Education and Welfare, as a basis for assessing the nature of problems and potential crises associated with work in the United States.

industrial work environment of the future, as illustrated by a pet-food plant which opened in January 1971.

In this facility, management set out to incorporate features that would provide a high quality of work life, enlist unusual human involvement, and result in high productivity. The positive results of the experiment to date are impressive, and the difficulties encountered in implementing it are instructive. Moreover, similar possibilities for *comprehensive* innovations exist in a wide variety of settings and industries.

The word "comprehensive" is important because my argument is that each technique in the standard fare of personnel and organization development programs (e.g., job enrichment, management by objectives, sensitivity training, confrontation and team-building sessions, participative decision making) has grasped only a limited truth and has fallen far short of producing meaningful change. In short, more radical, comprehensive, and systemic redesign of organizations is necessary.

ANATOMY OF ALIENATION

There are two parts to the problem of employee alienation: (1) the productivity output of work systems, and (2) the social costs associated with employee inputs. Regarding the first, U.S. productivity is not adequate to the challenges posed by international competition and inflation; it cannot sustain impressive economic growth. (I do not refer here to economic growth as something to be valued merely for its own sake—it is politically a precondition for the income redistribution that will make equality of opportunity possible in the United States.) Regarding the second, the social and psychological costs of work systems are excessive, as evidenced by their effects on the mental and physical health of employees and on the social health of families and communities.

Employee alienation *affects* productivity and *reflects* social costs incurred in the workplace. Increasingly, blue- and white-collar employees and, to some extent, middle managers tend to dislike their jobs and resent their bosses. Workers tend to rebel against their union leaders. They are becoming less concerned about the quality of the product of their labor and more angered about the quality of the context in which they labor.

In some cases, alienation is expressed by passive withdrawal—tardiness, absenteeism and turnover, and inattention on the job. In other cases, it is expressed by active attacks—pilferage, sabotage, deliberate waste, assaults, bomb threats, and other disruptions of work routines. Demonstrations have taken place and underground newspapers have appeared in large organizations in recent years to protest company policies. Even more recently, employees have cooperated with newsmen, Congressional committees, regulatory agencies, and protest groups in exposing objectionable practices.

These trends all have been mentioned in the media, but one expression of alienation has been underreported: pilferage and violence against property and persons. Such acts are less likely to be revealed to the police and the media when they occur in a private company than when they occur in a high school, a ghetto business district, or a suburban town. Moreover, dramatic increases in these forms of violence are taking place at the plant level. This trend is not reported in local newspapers and there is little or no appreciation of it at corporate headquarters. Local management keeps quiet because violence is felt to reflect unfavorably both on its effectiveness and on its plant as a place to work.

Roots of conflict

The acts of sabotage and other forms of protest are overt manifestations of a conflict between changing employee attitudes and organizational inertia. Increasingly, what employees expect from their jobs is different from what organizations are prepared to offer them. These evolving expectations of workers conflict with the demands, conditions, and rewards of employing organizations in at least six important ways:

1. Employees want challenge and personal growth, but work tends to be simplified and specialties tend to be used repeatedly in work assignments. This pattern exploits the narrow skills of a worker, while limiting his or her opportunities to broaden or develop.

2. Employees want to be included in patterns of mutual influence; they want egalitarian treatment. But organizations are characterized by tall hierarchies, status differentials, and chains of command.

3. Employee commitment to an organization is increasingly influenced by the intrinsic interest of the work itself, the human dignity afforded by management, and the social responsibility reflected in the organization's products. Yet organization practices still emphasize material rewards and employment security and neglect other employee concerns.

4. What employees want from careers, they are apt to want *right now*. But when organizations design job hierarchies and career paths, they continue to assume that today's workers are as willing to postpone gratifications as were yesterday's workers.

5. Employees want more attention to the emotional aspects of organization life, such as individual self-esteem, openness between people, and expressions of warmth. Yet organizations emphasize rationality and seldom legitimize the emotional part of the organizational experience.

6. Employees are becoming less driven by competitive urges, less likely to identify competition as the "American way." Nevertheless, managers continue to plan career patterns, organize work, and design reward systems as if employees valued competition as highly as they used to.

Pervasive social forces: The foregoing needs and desires that employees bring to their work are but a local reflection of more basic, and not readily reversible, trends in U.S. society. These trends are fueled by family and social experience

EXHIBIT 1
Diagnosis of alienation

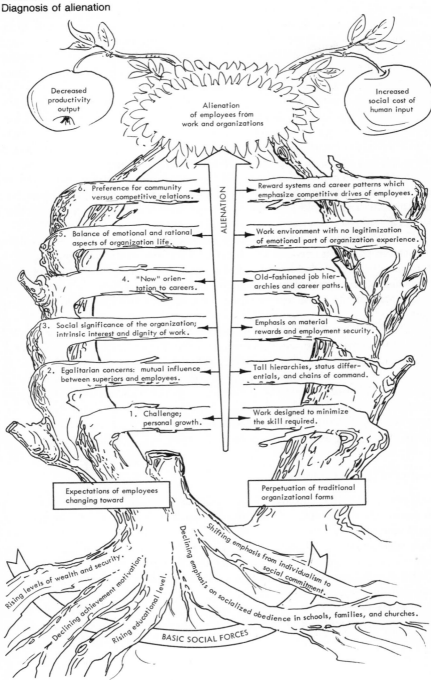

Decreased productivity output

Alienation of employees from work and organizations

Increased social cost of human input

ALIENATION

6. Preference for community versus competitive relations.
→ Reward systems and career patterns which emphasize competitive drives of employees.

5. Balance of emotional and rational aspects of organization life.
→ Work environment with no legitimization of emotional part of organization experience.

4. "Now" orientation to careers.
→ Old-fashioned job hierarchies and career paths.

3. Social significance of the organization; intrinsic interest and dignity of work.
→ Emphasis on material rewards and employment security.

2. Egalitarian concerns: mutual influence between superiors and employees.
→ Tall hierarchies, status differentials, and chains of command.

1. Challenge; personal growth.
→ Work designed to minimize the skill required.

Expectations of employees changing toward

Perpetuation of traditional organizational forms

Shifting emphasis from individualism to social commitment.

Declining emphasis on socialized obedience in schools, families, and churches.

Rising levels of wealth and security.

Declining achievement motivation.

Rising educational level.

BASIC SOCIAL FORCES

as well as by social institutions, especially schools. Among the most significant are:

The rising level of education—Employees bring to the workplace more abilities and, correspondingly, higher expectations than in the past.

The rising level of wealth and security—Vast segments of today's society never have wanted for the tangible essentials of life; thus they are decreasingly motivated by pay and security, which are taken for granted.

The decreased emphasis given by churches, schools, and families to obedience to authority—These socialization agencies have promoted indiviudal initiative, self-responsibility and self-control, the relativity of values, and other social patterns that make subordinacy in traditional organizations an increasingly bitter pill to swallow for each successive wave of entrants to the U.S. work force.

The decline in achievement motivation—For example, whereas the books my parents read in primary school taught them the virtues of hard work and competition, my children's books emphasize self-expression and actualizing one's potential. The workplace has not yet fully recognized this change in employee values.

The shifting emphasis from individualism to social commitment—This shift is driven in part by a need for the direct gratifications of human connectedness (for example, as provided by commune living experiments). It also results from a growing appreciation of our interdependence, and it renders obsolete many traditional workplace concepts regarding the division of labor and work incentives.

Exhibit 1 shows how these basic societal forces underlie, and contribute to, the problem of alienation and also sums up the discussion thus far. Actually, I believe that protests in the workplace will mount even more rapidly than is indicated by the contributing trends postulated here. The latent dissatisfaction of workers will be activated as (a) the issues receive public attention and (b) some examples of attempted solutions serve to raise expectations (just as the blacks' expressions of dissatisfaction with social and economic inequities were triggered in the 1950's, and women's discontent expanded late in the 1960's).

Revitalization and reform

It seems clear that employee expectations are not likely to revert to those of an earlier day. As Exhibit 1 shows, the conflicts between these expectations and traditional organizations result in alienation. This alienation, in turn, exacts a deplorable psychological and social cost as well as causing worker behavior that depresses productivity and constrains growth. In short, we need major innovative efforts to redesign work organizations, efforts that take employee expectations into account.

Over the past two decades we have witnessed a parade of organization development, personnel, and labor relations programs that promised to revitalize organizations:

Job enrichment would provide more varied and challenging content in the work.

Participative decision making would enable the information, judgments, and concerns of subordinates to influence the decisions that affect them.

Management by objectives would enable subordinates to understand and shape the objectives toward which they strive and against which they are evaluated.

Sensitivity training or *encounter groups* would enable people to relate to each other as human beings with feelings and psychological needs.

Productivity bargaining would revise work rules and increase management's flexibility with a quid pro quo whereby the union ensures that workers share in the fruits of the resulting productivity increases.

Each of the preceding programs *by itself* is an inadequate reform of the workplace and has typically failed in its more limited objectives. While application is often based on a correct diagnosis, each approach is only a partial remedy; therefore, the organizational system soon returns to an earlier equilibrium.

The lesson we must learn in the area of work reform is similar to one we have learned in another area of national concern. It is now recognized that a health program, a welfare program, a housing program, or an employment program alone is unable to make a lasting impact on the urban-poor syndrome. Poor health, unemployment, and other interdependent aspects of poverty must be attacked in a coordinated or systemic way.

So it is with meaningful reform of the workplace: we must think "systemically" when approaching the problem. We must coordinate the redesign of the way tasks are packaged into jobs, the way workers are required to relate to each other, the way performance is measured and rewards are made available, the way positions of authority and status symbols are structured, and the way career paths are conceived. Moreover, because these types of changes in work organizations imply new employee skills and different organizational cultures, transitional programs must be established.

A PROTOTYPE OF CHANGE

A number of major organization design efforts meet the requirements of being systemic and comprehensive. One experience in which I have been deeply involved is particularly instructive. As a recent and radical effort, it generally encompasses and goes beyond what has been done elsewhere.

During 1968, a large pet-food manufacturer was planning an additional plant at a new location. The existing manufacturing facility was then experiencing many of the symptoms of alienation that I have already outlined. There were frequent instances of employee indifference and inattention that, because of the continuous-process technology, led to plant shutdowns, product waste, and costly recycling. Employees effectively worked only a modest number of hours per day, and they resisted changes toward fuller utilization of manpower. A series of acts of sabotage and violence occurred.

Because of these pressures and the fact that it was not difficult to link substantial manufacturing costs to worker alienation, management was receptive to basic innovations in the new plant. It decided to design the plant to both accommodate changes in the expectations of employees and utilize knowledge developed by the behavioral sciences.

Key design features

The early development of the plant took more than two years. This involved planning, education, skill training, and building the nucleus of the new organization into a team.

During this early period, four newly selected managers and their superior met with behavioral science experts and visited other industrial plants that were experimenting with innovative organizational methods. Thus they were stimulated to think about departures from traditional work organizations and given reassurance that other organizational modes were not only possible but also more viable in the current social context. While the consultations and plant visits provided some raw material for designing the new organization, the theretofore latent knowledge of the five managers played the largest role. Their insights into the aspirations of people and basically optimistic assumptions about the capacities of human beings were particularly instrumental in the design of the innovative plant. In the remainder of this section, I shall present the nine key features of this design.

1. *Autonomous work groups.* Self-managed work teams are given collective responsibility for large segments of the production process. The total work force of approximately 70 employees is organized into six teams. A processing team and a packaging team operate during each shift. The processing team's jurisdiction includes unloading, storage of materials, drawing ingredients from storage, mixing, and then performing the series of steps that transform ingredients into a pet-food product. The packaging team's responsibilities include the finishing stages of product manufacturing—packaging operations, warehousing, and shipping.

A team is comprised of from 7 to 14 members (called "operators") and a team leader. Its size is large enough to include a natural set of highly interdependent tasks, yet small enough to allow effective face-to-face meetings for decision making and coordination. Assignments of individuals to sets of tasks are subject to team consensus. Although at any given time one operator has primary responsibility for a set of tasks within the team's jurisdiction, some tasks can be shared by several operators. Moreover, tasks can be redefined by the team in light of individual capabilities and interests. In contrast, individuals in the old plant were permanently assigned to specific jobs.

Other matters that fall within the scope of team deliberation, recommendation, or decision making include:

Coping with manufacturing problems that occur within or between the teams' areas of responsibilities.

Temporarily redistributing tasks to cover for absent employees.

Selecting team operators to serve on plantwide committees or task forces.

Screening and selecting employees to replace departing operators.

Counseling those who do not meet team standards (e.g., regarding absences or giving assistance to others).

2. *Integrated support functions.* Staff units and job specialties are avoided. Activities typically performed by maintenance, quality control, custodial, industrial engineering, and personnel units are built into an operating team's responsibilities. For example, each team member maintains the equipment he operates (except for complicated electrical maintenance) and housekeeps the area in which he works. Each team has responsibility for performing quality tests and ensuring quality standards. In addition, team members perform what is normally a personnel function when they screen job applicants.

3. *Challenging job assignments.* While the designers understood that job assignments would undergo redefinition in light of experience and the varying interests and abilities on the work teams, the initial job assignments established an important design principle. Every set of tasks is designed to include functions requiring higher-order human abilities and responsibilities, such as planning, diagnosing mechanical or process problems, and liaison work.

The integrated support functions just discussed provide one important source of tasks to enrich jobs. In addition, the basic technology employed in the plant is designed to eliminate dull or routine jobs as much as possible. But some nonchallenging, yet basic, tasks still have to be compensated for. The forklift truck operation, for example, is not technically challenging. Therefore, the team member responsible for it is assigned other, more mentally demanding tasks (e.g., planning warehouse space utilization and shipping activities).

Housekeeping duties are also included in every assignment, despite the fact that they contribute nothing to enriching the work, in order to avoid having members of the plant community who do nothing but menial cleaning.

4. *Job mobility and rewards for learning.* Because all sets of tasks (jobs) are designed to be equally challenging (although each set comprises unique skill demands), it is possible to have a single job classification for all operators. Pay increases are geared to an employee mastering an increasing proportion of jobs first in the team and then in the total plant. In effect, team members are payed for learning more and more aspects of the total manufacturing system. Because there are no limits on the number of operators that can qualify for higher pay brackets, employees are also encouraged to teach each other. The old plant, in contrast, featured large numbers of differentiated jobs and numerous job classifications, with pay increases based on progress up the job hierarchy.

5. *Facilitative leadership.* Team leaders are chosen from foreman-level talent and are largely responsible for team development and group decision making.

This contrasts with the old plant's use of supervisors to plan, direct, and control the work of subordinates. Management feels that in time the teams will be self-directed and so the formal team leader position might not be required.

6. *"Managerial" decision information for operators.* The design of the new plant provides operators with economic information and managerial decision rules. Thus production decisions ordinarily made by supervisors can now be made at the operator level.

7. *Self-government for the plant community.* The management group that developed the basic organization plan before the plant was manned refrained from specifying in advance any plant rules. Rather, it is committed to letting these rules evolve from collective experience.

8. *Congruent physical and social context.* The differential status symbols that characterize traditional work organizations are minimized in the new plant. There is an open parking lot, a single entrance for both the office and plant, and a common decor throughout the reception area, offices, locker rooms, and cafeteria.

The architecture facilitates the congregating of team members during working hours. For example, rather than following the plan that made the air conditioned control room in the process tower so small that employees could not congregate there, management decided to enlarge it so that process team operators could use it when not on duty elsewhere. The assumption here is that rooms which encourage ad hoc gatherings provide opportunities not only for enjoyable human exchanges but also for work coordination and learning about others' jobs.

9. *Learning and evolution.* The most basic feature of the new plant system is management's commitment to continually assess both the plant's productivity and its relevance to employee concerns in light of experience.

I believe pressures will mount in this system with two apparently opposite implications for automation:

On the one hand, people will consider ways of automating the highly repetitive tasks. (There are still back-breaking routine tasks in this plant; for example, a 50-pound bags pile up at the end of the production line, someone must grab them and throw them on a pallet.)

On the other hand, some processes may be slightly de-automated. The original design featured fully automated or "goof-proof" systems to monitor and adjust several segments of the manufacturing process; yet some employees have become confident that they can improve on the systems if they are allowed to intervene with their own judgments. These employees suggest that organizations may benefit more from operators who are alert and who care than from goof-proof systems.

Implementation difficulties

Since the plant start-up in January 1971, a number of difficulties have created at least temporary, and in some cases enduring, gaps between ideal expectations and reality.

The matter of compensation, for example, has been an important source of tension within this work community. There are four basic pay rates: starting rate, single job rate (for mastering the first job assignment), team rate (for mastering all jobs within the team's jurisdiction), and plant rate. In addition, an employee can qualify for a "specialty" add-on if he has particular strengths—e.g., in electrical maintenance.

Employees who comprised the initial work force were all hired at the same time, a circumstance that enabled them to directly compare their experiences. With one or two exceptions on each team, operators all received their single job rates at the same time, about six weeks after the plant started. Five months later, however, about one third of the members of each team had been awarded the team rate.

The evaluative implications of awarding different rates of pay have stirred strong emotions in people who work so closely with each other. The individual pay decisions had been largely those of the team leaders who, however, were also aware of operators' assessments of each other. In fact, pay rates and member contributions were discussed openly between team leaders and their operators as well as among operators themselves. Questions naturally arose:

Were the judgments about job mastery appropriate?
Did everyone have an equal opportunity to learn other jobs?
Did team leaders depart from job mastery criteria and include additional considerations in their promotions to team rate?

Thus the basic concepts of pay progression are not easy to treat operationally. Moreover, two underlying orientations compete with each other and create ambivalences for team leaders and operators alike:

A desire for more equality, which tends to enhance cohesiveness.
A desire for more differential rewards for individual merit, which may be more equitable but can be divisive.

Similar team and operator problems have also occurred in other areas. Four of these are particularly instructive and are listed in the ruled insert on the facing page.

Management, too, has been a source of difficulty. For example, acceptance and support from superiors and influential staff groups at corporate headquarters did not always come easily, thus creating anxiety and uncertainty within the new plant community.

Management resistance to innovative efforts of this type has a variety of explanations apart from natural and healthy skepticism. Some staff departments feel threatened by an experiment in which their functions no longer require separate units at the plant level. Other headquarters staff who are not basically threatened may nevertheless resist an innovation that deviates from otherwise uniform practices in quality control, accounting, engineering, or personnel. Moreover, many managers resent radical change, presuming that it implies they have been doing their jobs poorly.

Evidence of success

While the productivity and the human benefits of this innovative organization cannot be calculated precisely, there have nevertheless been some impressive results:

Using standard principles, industrial engineers originally estimated that 110 employees should man the plant. Yet the team concept, coupled with the integration of support activities into team responsibilities, has resulted in a manpower level of slightly less than 70 people.

After 18 months, the new plant's fixed overhead rate was 33 percent lower than in the old plant. Reductions in variable manufacturing costs (e.g., 92 percent fewer quality rejects and an absenteeism rate 9 percent below the industry norm) resulted in annual savings of $600,000. The safety record was one of the best in the company and the turnover was far below average. New equipment is responsible for some of these results, but I believe that more than one half of them derive from the innovative human organization.

Operators, team leaders, and managers alike have become more involved in their work and also have derived high satisfaction from it. For example, when asked what work is like in the plant and how it differs from other places they have worked, employees typically replied: "I never get bored." "I can make my own decisions." "People will help you; even the operations manager will pitch in to help you clean up a mess—he doesn't act like he is better than you are." I was especially impressed with the diversity of employees who made such responses. Different operators emphasized different aspects of the work culture, indicating that the new system had unique meaning for each member. This fact confirms the importance of systemwide innovation. A program of job enrichment, for example, will meet the priority psychological needs of one worker, but not another. Other single efforts are similarly limited.

Positive assessments of team members and team leaders in the new plant are typically reciprocal. Operators report favorably on the greater influence that they enjoy and the open relations which they experience between superiors and themselves; superiors report favorably on the capacities and sense of responsibility that operators have developed.

While the plant is not without the occasional rumor that reflects some distrust and cynicism, such symptomatic occurrences are both shorter-lived and less frequent than are those that characterize other work organizations with which I am familiar. Similarly, although the plant work force is not without evidence of individual prejudice toward racial groups and women, I believe that the manifestations of these social ills can be handled more effectively in the innovative environment.

Team leaders and other plant managers have been unusually active in civic affairs (more active than employees of other plants in the same community). This fact lends support to the theory that participatory democracy introduced in the plant will spread to other institutional settings. Some social scientist, notably Carole Pateman, argue that this will indeed be the case.[1]

The apparent effectiveness of the new plant organization has caught the attention of top management and encouraged it to create a new corporate-level unit to transfer the organizational and managerial innovations to other work environments. The line manager responsible for manufacturing, who initiated the design of the innovative system, was

---

[1] *Participation and Democratic Theory* (Cambridge, England: Cambridge University Press, 1970).

chosen to head this corporate diffusion effort. He can now report significant successes in the organizational experiments under way in several units of the old pet-food plant.

What it cost

I have already suggested what the pet-food manufacturer expected to gain from the new plant system: a more reliable, more flexible, and lower-cost manufacturing plant; a healthier work climate; and learning that could be transferred to other corporate units.

What did it invest? To my knowledge, no one has calculated the extra costs incurred prior to and during start-up that were specifically related to the innovative character of the organization. (This is probably because such costs were relatively minor compared with the amounts involved in other decisions made during the same time period.) However, some areas of extra cost can be cited:

Four managers and six team leaders were brought on board several months earlier than they otherwise would have been. The cost of outside plant visits, training, and consulting was directly related to the innovative effort. And a few plant layout and equipment design changes, which slightly increased the initial cost of the new plant, were justified primarily in terms of the organizational requirements.

During the start-up of the new plant, there was a greater than usual commitment to learning from doing. Operators were allowed to make more decisions on their own and to learn from their own experience, including mistakes. From my knowledge of the situation, I infer that there was a short-term—first quarter— sacrifice of volume, but that it was recouped during the third quarter when the more indelible experiences began to pay off. In fact, I would be surprised if the pay-back period for the company's entire extra investment was greater than the first year of operation.

Why it works

Listed below are eight factors which facilitated the success of the new plant.

1. The particular technology and manufacturing processes in this business provided significant room for human attitudes and motivation to affect cost; therefore, by more fully utilizing the human potential of employees, the organization was able to both enhance the quality of work life and reduce costs.

2. It was technically and economically feasible to eliminate some (but not all) of the routinized, inherently boring work and some (but not all) of the physically disagreeable tasks.

3. The system was introduced in a new plant. It is easier to change employees' deeply ingrained expectations about work and management in a new plant culture. Also, when the initial work force is hired at one time, teams can be formed without having to worry about cliques.

4. The physical isolation of the pet-food plant from other parts of the company facilitated the development of unique organizational patterns.

5. The small size of the work force made individual recognition and identification easy.

6. The absence of a labor union at the outset gave plant management greater freedom to experiment.

7. The technology called for and permitted communication among and between members of the work teams.

8. Pet foods are socially positive products, and the company has a good image; therefore, employees were able to form a positive attitude toward the product and the company.

I want to stress, however, that these are merely facilitating factors and are *not* preconditions for success.

For example, while a new plant clearly facilitates the planning for comprehensive plantwide change (Factor 3), such change is also possible in ongoing plants. In the latter case, the change effort must focus on a limited part of the plant—say, one department or section at a time. Thus in the ongoing facility, one must be satisfied with a longer time horizon for plantwide innovation.

Similarly, the presence of a labor union (Factor 6) does not preclude innovation, although it can complicate the process of introducing change. To avoid this, management can enter into a dialogue with the union about the changing expectations of workers, the need for change, and the nature and intent of the changes contemplated. Out of such dialogue can come an agreement between management and union representatives on principles for sharing the fruits of any productivity increases.

One factor I do regard as essential, however, is that the management group immediately involved must be committed to innovation and able to reach consensus about the guiding philosophy for the organization. A higher-level executive who has sufficient confidence in the innovative effort is another essential. He or she will act to protect the experiment from premature evaluations and from the inevitable, reactive pressures to bring it into line with existing corporate policies and practices.

Management and supervisors must work hard to make such a system succeed—harder, I believe, than in a more traditional system. In the case of the pet-food group, more work was required than in the traditional plant, but the human satisfactions were also much greater.

THE OTHER INNOVATORS

While the pet-food plant has a unique character and identity, it also has much in common with innovative plants of such U.S. corporations as Procter & Gamble and TRW Systems. Moreover, innovative efforts have been mounted by many foreign-based companies—e.g., Shell Refining Co., Ltd. (England), Northern Electric Co., Ltd. (Canada), Alcan Aluminium (smelting plants in Quebec Province, Canada), and Norsk-Hydro (a Norwegian manufacturer of fertilizers and chemicals). Related experiments have been made in the shipping industry in Scandinavia and the textile industry in Ahmedabad, India. Productivity increases or benefits for these organizations are reported in the range of 20 to 40 percent and higher, although I should caution that all evidence on this score involves judgment and interpretation.

All of these experiments have been influenced by the pioneering effort made in 1950 in the British coal mining industry by Eric Trist and his Tavistock Institute colleagues.[2]

Procter & Gamble has been a particularly noteworthy innovator. One of its newer plants includes many design features also employed in the pet-food plant. High emphasis has been placed on the development of "business teams" in which organization and employee identification coincides with a particular product family. Moreover, the designers were perhaps even more ambitious than their pet-food predecessors in eliminating first-line supervision. In terms of performance, results are reportedly extraordinary, although they have not been publicized. In addition, employees have been unusually active in working for social change in the outside community.[3]

Progressive assembly lines

Critics often argue that experiments like those I have discussed are not transferable to other work settings, especially ones that debase human dignity. The automobile assembly line is usually cited as a case in point.

I agree that different work technologies create different opportunities and different levels of constraint. I also agree that the automotive assembly plant represents a difficult challenge to those who wish to redesign work to decrease human and social costs and increase productivity. Yet serious experimental efforts to meet these challenges are now under way both in the United States and overseas.

To my knowledge, the most advanced projects are taking place in the Saab-Scandia automotive plants in Södertälje, Sweden. Consider, for example, these major design features of a truck assembly plant:

Production workers have been included as members of development groups that discuss such matters as new tool and machine designs before they are approved for construction.

Workers leave their stations on the assembly line for temporary assignments (e.g., to work with a team of production engineers "rebalancing" jobs on the line).

Responsibility for in-process inspection has been shifted from a separate quality-inspection unit to individual production workers. The separate quality section instead devotes all its efforts to checking and testing completed trucks.

---

[2] See E. L. Trist, G. W. Higgin, H. Murray, and A. B. Pollock, *Organizational Choice* (London: Tavistock Publications, 1963).

[3] Personal correspondence with Charles Krone, Internal Consultant, Procter & Gamble.

Work tasks have been expanded to include maintenance care of equipment, which was previously the responsibility of special mechanics.

Individuals have been encouraged to learn several jobs. In some cases, a worker has proved capable of assembling a complete engine.

Encouraged by the results of these limited inovations, the company is applying them in a new factory for the manufacture and assembly of car engines, which was opened in January 1972. In the new plant, seven assembly groups have replaced the continuous production line; assembly work within each group is not controlled mechanically; and eventually the degree of specialization, methods of instruction, and work supervision will vary widely among the assembly groups.

In effect, the seven groups fall along a spectrum of decreasing specialization. At one end is a group of workers with little or no experience in engine assembly; at the other end is a group of workers with extensive experience in total engine assembly. It is hoped that, ultimately, each group member will have the opportunity to assemble an entire engine.[4]

In addition to the improvements that have made jobs more interesting and challenging for workers, management anticipates business gains that include: (a) a work system less sensitive to disruption than is the production line (a factor of considerable significance in the company's recent experience); and (b) the twofold ability to recruit workers and reduce absenteeism and turnover. (The company has encountered difficulty in recruiting labor and has experienced high turnover and absenteeism.)

Another Swedish company, Volvo, also has ambitious programs for new forms of work systems and organization. Especially interesting is a new type of car assembly plant being built at Kalmar. Here are its major features:

Instead of the traditional assembly line, work teams of 15–25 men will be assigned responsibility for particular sections of a car (e.g., the electrical system, brakes and wheels, steering and controls).

Within teams, members will decide how work should be divided and distributed.

Car bodies will be carried on self-propelled carriages controlled by the teams.

Buffer stocks between work regions will allow variations in the rate of work and "stock piling" for short pauses in the work flow.

The unique design of the building will provide more outside windows, many small workshops to reinforce the team atmosphere, and individual team entrances, changing rooms, and relaxation areas.

The plant, scheduled to open in 1974, will cost 10 percent more than a comparable conventional car plant, or an estimated premium of $2 million. It will employ 600 people and have a capacity to produce 30,000 cars each year. Acknowledging the additional capital investment per employee, with its implica-

---

[4] For a more complete description of this plant, see Jan-Peter Norstedt, *Work Organization and Job Design at Saab-Scandia in Södertälje* (Stockholm, Technical Department, Swedish Employers' Confederation, December 1970).

tion for fixed costs, Volvo nevertheless justifies this experiment as "another stage in the company's general attempt to create greater satisfaction at work."[5]

Question of values

The designers of the Procter & Gamble and pet-food plants were able to create organizational systems that both improved productivity and enhanced the quality of work life for employees. It is hard to say, however, whether the new Saab-Scandia and Volvo plants will result in comparable improvements in both areas. (As I mentioned earlier, the assembly line presents a particularly difficult challenge.)

In any event, I am certain that managers who concern themselves with these two values will find points at which they must make trade-offs—i.e., that they can only enhance the quality of work life at the expense of productivity or vice versa. What concerns me is that it is easier to measure productivity than to measure the quality of work life, and that this fact will bias how trade-off situations are resolved.

Productivity may not be susceptible to a single definition or to precise measurement, but business managers do have ways of gauging changes in it over time and comparing it from one plant to the next. They certainly can tell whether their productivity is adequate for their competitive situation.

But we do not have equally effective means for assessing the quality of work life or measuring the associated psychological and social costs of gains for workers.[6] We need such measurements if this value is to take its appropriate place in work organizations.

CONCLUSION

The emerging obligation of employers in our society is a twin one: (1) to use effectively the capacities of a major natural resource—namely, the manpower they employ; and (2) to take steps to both minimize the social costs associated with utilizing that manpower and enhance the work environment for those they employ.

Fulfillment of this obligation requires major reform and innovation in work organizations. The initiative will eventually come from many quarters, but I urge professional managers and professional schools to take leadership roles. There are ample behavioral science findings and a number of specific experiences from which to learn and on which to build.

Furthermore, the nature of the problem and the accumulating knowledge about solutions indicate that organizational redesign should be systemic; it should

---

[5] Press release from Volvo offices, Gothenburg, Sweden, June 29, 1972.

[6] For the beginning of a remedy to this operational deficiency, see Louis E. Davis and Eric L. Trist, *Improving the Quality of Work Life: Experience of the Socio-Technical Approach* (Washington, D.C., Upjohn Institute, scheduled for publication in 1973).

embrace the division of labor, authority and status structures, control procedures, career paths, allocation of the economic fruits of work, and the nature of social contacts among workers. Obviously, the revisions in these many elements must be coordinated and must result in a new, internally consistent whole.

This call for widespread innovation does *not* mean general application of a particular work system, such as the one devised for the pet-food plant. There are important differences within work forces and between organizations. Regional variances, education, age, sex, ethnic background, attitudes developed from earlier work experiences, and the urban-rural nature of the population all will influence the salient expectations in the workplace. Moreover, there are inherent differences in the nature of primary task technologies, differences that create opportunities for and impose constraints on the way work can be redesigned.

DATE DUE

MR 07 '86	MAR 17 '86		
GAYLORD			PRINTED IN U.S.A.